FOUNDATIONS OF PHYSICAL EDUCATION

Courtesy D. M. Massé, Waddell Elementary School, Manchester, Conn.

Courtesy The Forbes Magazine Fitness Center, New York, N.Y.

FOUNDATIONS OF PHYSICAL EDUCATION

CHARLES A. BUCHER, A.B., M.A., Ed.D.

Professor of Education and Director,
Physical Education and Sport, School of Education,
Health, Nursing, and Arts Professions, New York University,
New York, New York

EIGHTH EDITION

with 290 *illustrations*

THE C. V. MOSBY COMPANY

ST. LOUIS • TORONTO • LONDON   1979

EIGHTH EDITION

Copyright © 1979 by The C. V. Mosby Company

Previous editions copyrighted 1952, 1956, 1960, 1964, 1968, 1972, 1975

Printed in the United States of America

The C. V. Mosby Company
11830 Westline Industrial Drive, St. Louis, Missouri 63141

Library of Congress Cataloging in Publication Data

Bucher, Charles Augustus, 1912-
    Foundations of physical education.

    Includes bibliographies and index.
    1. Physical education and training. I. Title.
GV341.B86 1979   613.7   78-17035
ISBN 0-8016-0867-8

GW/MO/B 9 8 7 6 5 4 3 2 1

Preface

The eighth edition of *Foundations of Physical Education* represents the most extensive revision in the more than 25-year history of this text. The many changes that have taken place in the world, in the United States, and in education and physical education have necessitated a thorough updating of the entire book, plus the addition of several new chapters.

The tone for the text is set in the first chapter on physical education looks to the future, which discusses several ways in which physical education has changed and is changing. Three new chapters have been added to keep abreast of new national developments that have had and are having a dramatic impact on physical education programs from coast to coast: Chapter 6 on the growth of sports in the American culture, Chapter 9 on the end of sex discrimination in sport and physical education, and Chapter 10 on physical education for handicapped and exceptional persons, including mainstreaming.

Other developments affecting physical education and physical educators that are discussed in this revision include the back-to-basics movement (Chapter 4), movement—the keystone of physical education and biomechanics (Chapter 8), perceptual-motor learning (Chapter 13), exercise physiology (Chapter 12), values and valuing (Chapter 14), developing settings for physical education programs in industry, health spas, and centers for the elderly (Chapter 15), specialization and employment opportunities within physical education, such as athletic training, athletic administration, elementary school physical education, dance, physical education for the handicapped, exercise physiology, ergonomics and biome-

chanics, and the behavioral foundations of sport (Chapters 18 and 21), and the many challenges facing physical education, such as the tightening job market, the need for young scholarly leaders in physical education at a time when faculties are becoming more stable, and the fragmentation of physical education (Chapter 20).

Only a sampling of the new developments and changes that have been made in this text have been outlined. Each chapter has been carefully reviewed to present a current and up-to-date picture of what is happening in the field of physical education. To accomplish this task, material was deleted, chapters were combined, the format was changed, and many new illustrations were included.

One other new feature should be mentioned in connection with the eighth edition of this text that will be of help to both the instructor and the students. *Instructional objectives and competencies are listed at the beginning of each chapter* to indicate the important points that the student should study carefully. Then, at the *end of each chapter are listed self-assessment tests* to assist the student in determining whether the material and competencies that were presented have been mastered.

The eighth edition of this text includes information that prospective physical educators as well as practitioners in the field want and need to know so that they can render the greatest service to their consumers and help their field of endeavor gain respect which will ensure a strong professional status in a changing world.

Charles A. Bucher

Contents

NATURE AND SCOPE OF PHYSICAL EDUCATION

Courtesy Public School No. 15, Brooklyn, N.Y.

Physical education looks to the future

INSTRUCTIONAL OBJECTIVES AND COMPETENCIES TO BE ACHIEVED

After reading this chapter the student should be able to—

1. Identify important changes that have taken place in the world during the last few years and that have a bearing on career decisions.
2. Discuss the growth of sports in the American culture and the public's interest in health and physical fitness.
3. Understand the ways in which physical education has changed in recent years.
4. Answer questions regarding the advantages and disadvantages of a career in physical education and sport.
5. State how physical education is becoming more scholarly and scientific.
6. Give examples of how physical education is becoming more specialized.
7. Show how physical education is becoming more applicable to all human segments of society.
8. List some of the qualifications for entering the field of physical education.

The young person trying to decide on a career in today's world finds that he or she is faced with making a critical decision. Many changes have occurred in the last few years that make such a choice extremely difficult. The nation's economy has been thrown into a state of upheaval, resulting in problems such as budget cutbacks, inflated prices, inner-city difficulties, unemployment, and mounting government deficits. Inadequate sources of energy have re-

sulted in curbs on transportation and on the manufacturing of oil-based products and have affected the way people spend their leisure hours. Concern for the environment has led to the implementation of protective measures against noise, radiation, and the pollution or destruction of land, forests, and streams. The stress on accountability has resulted in taxpayers wanting to know what they receive for each dollar they spend. The emphasis on equal opportunity has resulted in girls and women playing a more assertive role in society. The recognition that the nation needs to be undergirded by a sound value system has led to government investigations into corruption, the popularity of some religious cults, and the concern of educators for the affective domain.

The nation is going through a significant period of change. A different way of life, equal opportunity for minorities, and technological advances mean challenging decisions as well as opportunities for young people in today's world. These changes also influence a young person's decision about what career to enter.

In contrast to the 1960s, when activists were drawing large numbers of students to antiwar demonstrations and leading takeovers of campus buildings, students today seem to be less interested in playing active political and social roles. Although outwardly inactive, students who grew up watching a war on their living-room television sets seem to be far better informed about current issues and injustices in the world than their predecessors of two decades ago. In addition, they are more curious and academic minded, particularly about the knowledge and skills that will influence the particular career they choose. They want to enter a vocation that will guarantee them satisfaction as well as security. Above all, they are very much concerned with the tightening job market.

Although young people are academic minded, at the same time they are interested in participant sports, in activities such as jogging, and in spectator sports that are making a big comeback on some campuses.

A major change that has taken place in recent years and that directly affects physical education is the growth of sports in the American culture and the public's interest in health and physical fitness. For example, in sports the growth of soccer and tennis, and in the area of physical fitness the great number of persons jogging illustrate the growth in these areas.

More people are engaging in games of all types, the number of spectators at sport events is growing, and the sale of sports equipment is booming. There is worldwide coverage of sports events. More young people are aware of more and different sports. They are also more sophisticated with high self-expectation and a desire for instruction in skills to play these sports. New interest has also been generated in health and fitness. More persons than ever before in history are concerned with their body image, the food they eat, the calories they ingest, and their physical fitness status.

Most young people like sports and other forms of physical activity. They are also concerned with the nation's health and fitness. As a result, many young persons are exploring the field of physical education and sport as a possible career. As part of this exploration process, they want to know if there are employment opportunities in this field of endeavor and what they can contribute to the profession. They also want to know the developing trends in the field, what the future holds for the profession, and the personal and other qualities that will help guarantee them success if they choose physical education and sport as a career.

Young people want information that will give them new insights into the true meaning of physical education, a sound philosophy that will guide them in their future endeavors, and the scientific biological, psychological, and so-

Courtesy The Athletic Institute, North Palm Beach, Fla.

There has been a major expansion of sport programs in general and particularly in the area of girls' and women's sports.

ciological foundations on which this profession rests.

This text is designed to supply young people with the answers to these and other pertinent and thought-provoking questions. It will also provide insights into the meaning, objectives, and philosophy of physical education. It traces the history of physical education and the changes that have taken place since the beginning of time, including the stress on movement as the keystone of physical education, the growth of girls' and women's sports, and the importance of physical education for the handicapped. The text investigates the scientific foundations of physical activity as they relate to the biological, psychological, and sociological development of human beings. It describes the settings where physical education programs are conducted and the relation of physical education to the allied fields of health education and recreation. It looks at the role of the physical educator, including qualifications and duties performed. Finally, it provides a coverage of professional concerns such as the organizations to which members belong, the certification requirements and employment opportunities for those persons entering the pro-

Boys' and men's sports continue to grow in popularity.

fession, and some of the challenges that face those individuals who select physical education and sport as a career.

PHYSICAL EDUCATION HAS CHANGED

The young person who is selecting a career today wants to make sure that physical education is in tune with the times and represents a more challenging and significant field of endeavor than he or she experienced as a student during the elementary and high school years. Many of these young people were disenchanted by what they experienced during their precollege days and do not want to pursue such a career if it is merely concerned with meaningless exercise and senseless activity. Instead, they want to become practitioners in a dynamic, challenging profession that is selective, renders a service to society, and has the respect of the public at large as well as the academic community.

The fact that physical education is not the same as it was 10 and 20 years ago will come as good news to these young people who are ex-

ploring this field as a possible career. It is gaining maturity. It is becoming more professional. It is achieving its destiny. Young people can be assured that in selecting physical education and sport as a career they are entering an area of endeavor which is rapidly gaining professional stature and is being recognized by society as rendering a necessary and important service to human welfare.

PHYSICAL EDUCATION IS BECOMING MORE SCHOLARLY AND SCIENTIFIC

The emphasis today in physical education is on research and the development of a discipline that has a solid scientific foundation. Physical educators are stressing scholarship, with the result that they are beginning to find some of the answers to problems such as how motor skills can be most effectively taught, the key concepts that should be imparted to young people to change their behavior so that they include physical activity as part of their life-style, the best means to achieve and maintain a high state of physical fitness, ways to enhance physical performance, how to predict and prevent athlet-

Physical education has changed in recent years. Young woman jogs, knowing that it contributes to physical fitness.

ic injuries, and the manner in which sports can be utilized to contribute to a sound value system in young people.

Physical educators understand the scientific foundations for what they do much better than they did years ago. They no longer conduct exercise and physical activities simply for the purpose of entertainment or to stimulate muscular activity for its own sake. Today, they are interested in providing exercise and physical activities that will accomplish specific objectives for the participant, such as helping a handicapped person to have a sense of accomplishment in physical activity to enhance his or her self-concept, or assisting an industrial executive in determining his or her state of fitness through sophisticated measurement techniques

and then using the findings to plan a program that will develop and maintain an optimum level of fitness. Today, physical educators are also utilizing computer technology to store information that is ready for instant retrieval and application to their field, whether in analyzing budget allocations or predicting the possibility of injury to a person because he is loose jointed or tight jointed. The science of sports medicine is expanding, with physical educators and physicians working together as a team to accomplish goals such as preventing injuries and improving physical performance. Furthermore, years ago physical activity was largely conducted in a vacuum without a sound scientific explanation of why it was important, whereas today physical educators, as a result of their

Coeducational water polo, grades 6 to 8, Cumberland Valley School District, Mechanicsburg, Pa. Physical educators no longer conduct exercise and physical activities simply for the purpose of entertainment or to stimulate muscular activity for its own sake. Today they have specific objectives in mind.

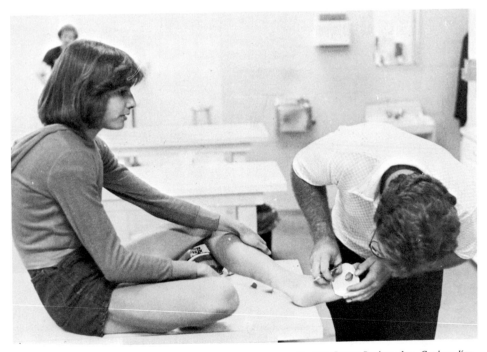

Courtesy Cramer Products, Inc., Gardner, Kan.

Today the science of sports medicine is growing. An athletic trainer helps to prevent injury.

Courtesy The Forbes Magazine Fitness Center, New York City.

Physical education is becoming more applicable to all human segments of society. Top, a businessman works out at the Aerobics Activity Center, Dallas, Texas. Bottom, employees engage in physical activity at the Forbes Magazine Fitness Center in New York City.

investigations, can scientifically support their claims that physical activity is a medium of improving human existence.

PHYSICAL EDUCATION IS BECOMING MORE SPECIALIZED

Physical education, like medicine, is moving away from the concept of the general practitioner and moving in the direction of the specialist. Just as there are ophthalmologists, obstetricians, gerontologists, and ear, nose, and throat specialists in the field of medicine, so today the physical educator who is bent on getting a position after graduation from college specializes in areas such as exercise physiology, motor learning, athletic training, behavioral aspects of sport, athletic administration, or biomechanics. Furthermore, the employment opportunities that are available to the prospective physical educator today are not solely centered in schools and colleges as they were years ago. They also exist in settings such as industry, health clubs, youth-serving centers, centers for the elderly, and professional and amateur sport organizations. These organizations are looking for physical educators who have specialized in that phase of physical education which is utilized and important to their particular settings and the people with whom they work. For example, executive fitness programs in industry are looking primarily for exercise physiologists who can research, plan, prescribe, and supervise exercise programs for their executives. Many health clubs not only are interested in physical educators who can prescribe and supervise exercise programs for their clientele but also want these individuals to have a background in various business skills essential to running such a commercial enterprise.

PHYSICAL EDUCATION IS BECOMING MORE APPLICABLE TO ALL HUMAN SEGMENTS OF SOCIETY

Physical education is no longer focused solely on the student who goes to school or college. Instead, it applies to all segments of the population, regardless of age, physical ability, and physical status. Physical education programs for the handicapped, girls and women, and the elderly are examples to support this development.

Physical education is rendering a service to handicapped persons. Programs for the mentally retarded, physically handicapped, emotionally disturbed, and culturally disadvantaged are receiving much attention because of developments such as laws that guarantee their rights and the injection of federal and state funds to support such programs.

Physical education for girls and women has expanded greatly with the equal opportunity movement and the passage of Title IX legislation. Girls and women today have greater access to physical education facilities, budgetary allocations that are approaching those of boys and men, and opportunities to engage in more highly organized sports competition of their own choosing.

Physical education for the elderly is becoming a reality. Studies have shown that older persons have been neglected in respect to programs of physical education. As a result of the current emphasis on providing programs for all segments of the population as well as the increasing political clout of older people, who represent one out of every ten Americans, there is more and more emphasis on providing recreational opportunities for them so that they may utilize their many leisure hours in a more enjoyable and profitable manner and thereby enhance their health and well-being.

By observing physical education programs in various settings, the young person will see that this is a profession which no longer is mainly interested in the highly skilled athlete or boys and men. Instead, it is expanding its programs and services to meet the needs and interests of the entire population.

THE PHYSICAL EDUCATOR IS CHANGING

The young person exploring physical education as a career should note that the type of person who is going into this field today has qualifications that are different from those required of the physical educator in the past.

Today's physical educators are well grounded in psychology, sociology, kinesiology, physiology, and the philosophical aspects of physical education and sport. They are more sensitive to research findings and understand the scientific foundations underlying the need for

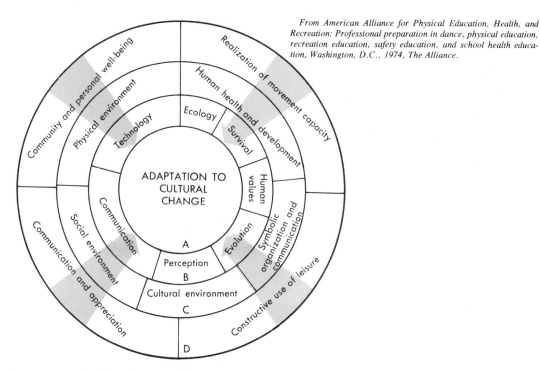

From American Alliance for Physical Education, Health, and Recreation: Professional preparation in dance, physical education, recreation education, safety education, and school health education, Washington, D.C., 1974, The Alliance.

A = Central core of adaption to cultural change
B = Categories effecting cultural change
C = Categories of general education
D = Areas of emphasis for Association disciplines

The physical educator is changing. A physical educator at Hudson Falls Central School in Hudson Falls, New York, helps a second-grade boy to do a back bend in the school's flexibility program.

physical activity as it relates to human development. The curriculum they follow takes into account the needs and interests of the participant. They guide their students in the learning process rather than acting as the final authority for what should be known and accomplished. They motivate participants to evaluate their own progress. They are democratic and humanistic in their actions. They do not consider themselves to be models; rather, they stress problem solving and self-evaluation, with participants arriving independently at solutions to their problems.

The young person who selects physical education as a career today can feel confident of entering an area of endeavor that is on the move and gaining respect in the public's eye. Physical educators have shed such labels as "jocks," "supine Charlies," and "muscle men and women." They are no longer concerned merely with muscles and perspiration and conducting physical activity as an end in itself. Today, physical educators view their profession as a means to an end — the end being a fuller, richer, and more productive existence for humankind. They are gaining respect for their expertise and scientific knowledge, ability, and skill in being able to meet certain basic biological, psychological, and sociological needs of human beings.

SELF-ASSESSMENT TESTS

These tests are to assist students in determining if material and competencies presented in this chapter have been mastered.

1. Describe five important changes that have taken place in the world in the last 10 years and how each of these changes might affect career choices of today's college graduates.

2. Your professor has requested that you supply evidence to show there is substantial interest today in sports, health, and physical fitness. Cite evidence of this interest and the implications of such evidence for a career in physical education and sport.

3. Prepare a chart on the subject, "How Physical Education Has Changed." Divide the chart into two columns. In one column list the key characteristics of the physical education program in the junior high school that you attended. In the other column, list the key characteristics of today's physical education as a result of reading this chapter and an actual visitation by you to a junior high school physical education program. Compare the two columns and identify the changes that have taken place.

4. List the advantages and disadvantages of pursuing a career in physical education and sport.

5. Prepare a 2-minute presentation to be given to your class showing how physical education is becoming more scholarly and scientific.

6. Identify three areas of specialization within the field of physical education and sport. Then, explore the professional literature to determine the nature and scope of each area of specialization that you have selected, the duties performed by such a specialist, and the job opportunities for this person.

7. Without consulting your text, state how physical education is rendering services to different segments of the population in the United States.

8. Prepare a list of qualifications that are needed to be successful in physical education today and then conduct a self-evaluation to determine how your qualifications rate.

READING ASSIGNMENT

Bucher, Charles A.: Dimensions of physical education, ed. 2, St. Louis, 1974, The C. V. Mosby Co., Reading selections 2, 4, and 6.

SELECTED REFERENCES

American Academy of Physical Education: The academy papers: focus on action alternatives, no. 7. Minneapolis, April, 1973, Meeting of The American Academy of Physical Education.

American Academy of Physical Education: The academy papers: realms of meaning, no. 9, Atlantic City, March, 1975, Meeting of The American Academy of Physical Education.

Bucher, Charles A.: National adult physical fitness survey: some implications, Journal of Health, Physical Education and Recreation **45:**25, Jan., 1974.

Bucher, Charles A.: Administration of health and physical education programs including athletics, ed. 7, St. Louis, 1979, The C. V. Mosby Co.

Bucher, Charles A., and Koenig, Constance: Methods and materials for secondary school physical education, ed. 5, St. Louis, 1978, The C. V. Mosby Co.

Clayton, Robert D., and Clayton, Joyce A., et al.: Concepts and careers in physical education, ed. 2, Minneapolis, 1977, Burgess Publishing Co.

Leonard, George: The ultimate athlete, New York, 1975, The Viking Press, Inc.

The National Association for Physical Education for College Women and The National College Physical Education Association for Men: Directions, Quest summer issue, 1977.

Talamini, John T., and Page, Charles: Sport and society — an anthology, Boston, 1973, Little, Brown & Co., Inc.

Welsh, Raymond: Physical education — a view toward the future, St. Louis, 1977, The C. V. Mosby Co.

2

Physical education—its meaning and philosophy

INSTRUCTIONAL OBJECTIVES AND COMPETENCIES TO BE ACHIEVED

After reading this chapter the student should be able to—

1. Define the following terms: hypokinetics, ergonomics, biomechanics, exercise physiology, hygiene, physical culture, gymnastics, physical training, physical fitness, health, recreation, sports medicine, movement education, and physical education.
2. State why physical education is an important part of the educational process.
3. Identify and discuss the major components of which the discipline of philosophy is composed.
4. Illustrate and distinguish among each of the following levels of discussion: emotional, factual, explanatory, and philosophical.
5. Justify the need for every physical educator to develop a well-thought-through philosophy of physical education.
6. Discuss the key concepts of each of the following general philosophies: idealism, realism, pragmatism, naturalism, and existentialism.
7. Compare the characteristics of educational programs that are guided by traditional and modern educational philosophies.

The word *physical* refers to the body. It is often used in reference to various bodily characteristics such as physical strength, physical development, physical prowess, physical health, and physical appearance. It refers to the body as contrasted to the mind. Therefore, when the word *education* is added to the word *physical*, thus forming the phrase *physical education*, it refers to the process of education that concerns activities which develop and maintain the human body. When an individual is playing a game, swimming, marching, working out on the parallel bars, skating, or performing in any one of the gamut of physical education activities, education is taking place at the same time. This education may be conducive to the enrichment of the individual's life, or it may be detrimental. It may be a satisfying experience, or it may be an unhappy one. It may help in the building of a strong and cohesive society, or it may have antisocial results for the participant. Whether physical education helps or inhibits the attainment of educational objectives will depend to a great extent on the leadership responsible for its direction.

Physical education is an important part of the educational process. It is not a "frill" or an "ornament" tacked on to the school program as a means of keeping students busy. It is, instead, a vital part of education. Through a well-directed physical education program, young people develop skills for the worthy use of leisure time, engage in activities conducive to healthful living, develop socially, and contribute to their physical and mental health.

A study of history reveals that other civilizations have recognized the important place of physical education in the training of their youth. In ancient Athens, for example, three main subjects were studied by every Athenian: gymnastics, grammar, and music. Here in the United

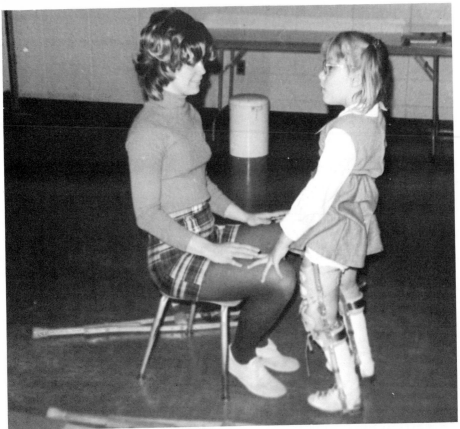

Physical education is an important part of the educational process, serving the needs of all students. A handicapped child and a physical educator work together in the Township of Ocean School District, Oakhurst, New Jersey.

States the contributions of physical education to the educational program have been recognized for many years. In 1918 the National Educational Association set forth its well-known *Cardinal Principles of Secondary Education*, which listed seven objectives of education: health, command of fundamental processes, worthy home membership, vocation, citizenship, worthy use of leisure time, and ethical character. Physical education is playing an important part in achieving these objectives. As a result of such contributions as the benefits of exercise to physical health, the fundamental physical skills that make for a more interesting, efficient, and vigorous life, and the social education that contributes to the development of character and good human relations, these cardinal principles are brought nearer to realization.

TERMINOLOGY

The multiplicity of terms that are sometimes used synonymously for physical education makes it imperative that the meaning of these various terms be clarified.

Hypokinetics. Hypokinetics refers to that phase of physical education where an insufficient amount of muscular activity exists. In other words, it applies to those persons who are sedentary and do not engage in sufficient physical activity to enhance their health status.

Ergonomics. Ergonomics is the study of the relationship of human beings to their working environment. Environment in this sense refers not only to the physical environment in which they work but also to their methods of work, organization of work, people with whom they work, and other aspects of their working conditions. It also relates to the health conditions under which humans work. Contributing to ergonomics are disciplines such as anatomy and physiology, physiological psychology, experimental psychology, industrial medicine, physics, and engineering.

Biomechanics. Biomechanics is the study of the various forces that act on the human body and the effects such forces produce. It is concerned with both the internal and external forces and their participation in performance. In sports it helps to determine the techniques that will enhance or limit performance.

Exercise physiology. Exercise physiology is applied physiology, or the study of the impact that exercise and work conditions have on the human body. It is concerned with things such as aerobic capacity, fatigue, and the manner in which the nerve impulse originates and is transmitted, together with the nature of the resulting action.

Hygiene. Hygiene comes from the Greek word *hygieinos,* meaning healthful. It refers to the science of preserving one's health. Hygiene often refers to rules or principles prescribed for the purpose of developing and maintaining health. In past years many school physical education departments were known as departments of hygiene; a few still use this term. It appears that the term became popular as a result of legislation in various states that sought to have the effects of tobacco and alcohol brought to the attention of all students through a course often known by the name of hygiene. There are still many laws on the statute books prescribing such instruction. Since World War I the term *hygiene* has become more or less obsolete. Newer terminology is being used such as health education and personal and community health.

Physical culture. The term *physical culture* is obsolete in education. It was used in the late nineteenth century to parallel names of other courses, such as religious culture, social culture, and intellectual culture. This term is still used by some faddists in commercial ventures to popularize the beneficial effects of exercise. Physical culture has been used synonymously for physical training. It implies that health may be promoted through various physical activities.

Gymnastics. The word *gymnastics* refers to exercises that are adaptable to or are performed in a gymnasium. It is the art of performing various types of physical exercises and feats of skill. The term has been and still is used extensively in the various physical education programs in Europe. Anyone trained in physical education has heard mention of programs such as the German and Swedish systems of gymnastics. Formal drills such as calisthenics were utilized extensively in many physical education programs in the United States until recently. Today, when one thinks of gymnastics, what comes to mind is formal drills conducted either with or without the use of apparatus. Americans do not use the term synonymously with physical education but, instead, with just that phase of the physical education program concerned with formal drills. Physical education programs today are more concerned with allowing individuals to express themselves in various types of games rather than just in formal drill.

Physical training. To many individuals, the term *physical training* has a military tinge. It is a term that has been used in school programs of physical activity and also in the armed forces. Clark Hetherington used the term to connote big-muscle activity in the school program of physical education. On the other hand, during World War II and at the present time, this term refers to the entire program of physical conditioning that the armed forces require recruits to go through as preparation for their rigorous duties. Most individuals agree that because of the military connection, the term is used to imply training. This term has become rather outmoded for the present physical education programs found in the public schools. Today, physical education programs realize outcomes other than just those concerned with the physical aspects. For example, there are sociological outcomes that result in an individual's better adaptation to group living. The term *physical education* also implies that physical activity serves the field of education in a much broader sense than physical training does.

Fitness and physical fitness. A group of members of the American Association for Health, Physical Education, and Recreation approved the following definition of fitness: ''That state which characterizes the degree to which the person is able to function.'' In other words, fitness represents the capacity to live most vigorously and effectively with one's own resources. Physical fitness refers primarily to bodily aspects of fitness. It implies abilities such as that of resisting fatigue, performing with an acceptable degree of motor ability, and being able to adapt to muscular stress.

Health. Health, according to the World Health Organization, refers to such qualities as physical, mental, emotional, and social health; it is not limited to the mere absence of disease and infirmity. It means total fitness.

Recreation. Recreation is concerned with those activities performed by an individual during hours not at work. It is frequently referred to as leisure-time activity. Recreation education is aimed at teaching people to utilize their leisure hours in a constructive manner. This implies a careful selection of activities.

Physical fitness refers to the bodily aspects of fitness. Boys work out on an exercise machine at Regis High School in New York City to improve their degree of physical fitness.

Athletics. The term *athletics* refers to the games or sports that are usually engaged in by robust and skilled individuals. The interest in athletics in the United States has been largely inherited from Great Britain. With the introduction of athletics into colleges and universities, there has been a rapid growth in all sports engaged in on an intercollegiate basis.

Many lay persons frequently think of athletics and physical education as being similar in meaning. However, most physical education personnel think of athletics as one phase of a broad physical education program—that division of the program concerned with interscholastic or intercollegiate sports competition. The primary responsibility of a director of athletics in a school is the direction of this competitive program.

Sports medicine. Dr. Neal Tremble,* a Fellow in the American College of Sports Medicine, points out that the meaning of sports medicine involves the interprofessional and interdisciplinary implications of the following components:

Athletic medicine
  Accident prevention
  Athletic training
  Evaluation and management of injuries
  Traumatology

Biomechanics
  Anatomic analysis of movement
  Kinetic analysis of movement

Clinical medicine
  Clinical consequences of physical activity
  Health appraisal of physical activity
  Pharmacology
  Physical activity and health
  Prescriptions of activity for patients
  Therapy and rehabilitation

Growth and development
  Maturation and aging
  Physical anthropology
  Tissue changes

Physiology
  Biochemistry of exercise
  Environmental influences

---

*Tremble, Neal: What is sports medicine? Iowa Journal of Health, Physical Education, and Recreation **40:**11, 1969.

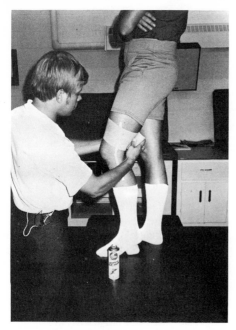

Courtesy Cramer Products, Inc., Gardner, Kan.

Athletic training is an aspect of sports medicine according to Tremble's definition. An athletic trainer is shown at work.

Human performance
Nutritional considerations
Pathophysiological conditions and exercise

Psychology and sociology
Behavior
Cybernetics
Group dynamics
Motor learning
Perception

Movement education. The concept of movement education in physical education stresses body awareness or an understanding of how the body moves to develop efficient and effective motor development. Children are taught, using the problem-solving method and other techniques, how to control the ways in which their bodies are able to move. This topic will be discussed in great detail in Chapter 8.

Human movement phenomena. The term *human movement phenomena* was proposed by a national research project that endeavored to describe a theoretical structure of physical education as an area of scholarly study and re-

search. The term *human movement phenomena* may be defined as the broad category under which the body of knowledge labeled as *physical education* can best be subsumed.* The areas that comprise the human movement phenomena each have an individual focus for human movement, but they share a meaningful relationship with the other areas. A depiction of the discipline–body of knowledge relationship is shown by the model in the accompanying figure. Of course, many other disciplines could be added to form a multifaceted star.

Physical education. The term *physical education* is much broader and much more meaningful for day-to-day living than many of those term discussed previously. It is more closely allied to the larger area of education, of which it is a vital part. It implies that its program consists of something other than mere exercises done at command. A physical education program under qualified leadership aids in the enrichment of an individual's life.

Following is my suggested definition of physical education: *Physical education, an integral part of the total education process, is a field of endeavor that has as its aim the improvement of human performance through the medium of physical activities that have been selected with a view to realizing this outcome.*

In a larger sense, this definition of physical education means that leaders in this field must develop a program of activities in which participants will develop body awareness and realize results beneficial to their growth and development; that they will develop through participation such physical characteristics as endurance, strength, and the ability to resist and recover from fatigue; that neuromuscular skill will become a part of their motor mechanism so that they may have proficiency in performing physical acts; that socially they will become educated to play an effective part in democratic group living; and that they will be better able to interpret new situations in a more meaningful and purposeful manner as a result of these physical education experiences.

---

*American Association for Health, Physical Education, and Recreation: Tones of theory, Washington, D.C., 1972, The Association.

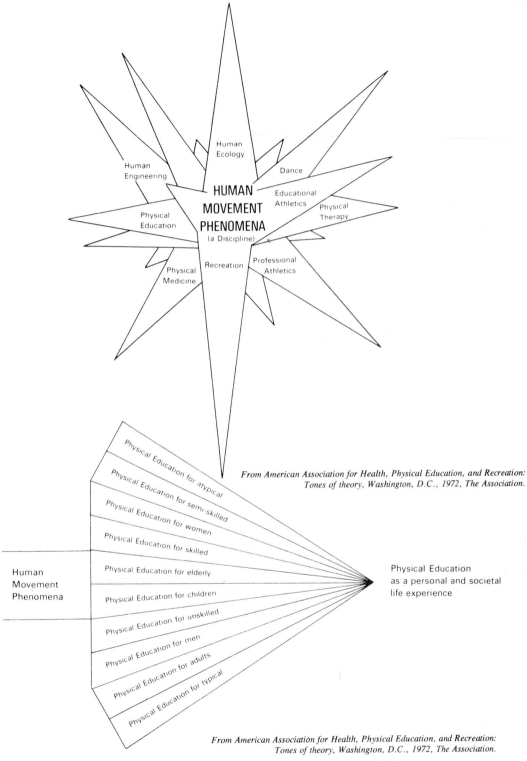

Human Ecology

Human Engineering

Dance

HUMAN MOVEMENT PHENOMENA
(a Discipline)

Educational Athletics

Physical Education

Physical Therapy

Physical Medicine

Recreation

Professional Athletics

From American Association for Health, Physical Education, and Recreation: Tones of theory, Washington, D.C., 1972, The Association.

Physical Education for atypical

Physical Education for semi-skilled

Physical Education for women

Physical Education for skilled

Human Movement Phenomena

Physical Education for elderly

Physical Education for children

Physical Education for unskilled

Physical Education for men

Physical Education for adults

Physical Education for typical

Physical Education as a personal and societal life experience

From American Association for Health, Physical Education, and Recreation: Tones of theory, Washington, D.C., 1972, The Association.

Physical education thrusts—human movement phenomena and physical education as a personal and societal life experience.

A NEW NAME FOR PHYSICAL EDUCATION?

In recent years there has been considerable discussion regarding whether physical education is the best name for this field of endeavor. Other names that have been suggested include movement education, kinesiology, sports education, physical fitness, sport, applied physical sciences, and motor education. The term that is used widely at the present time is *physical education and sport,* which incorporates the traditional emphasis on physical education and at the same time stresses the area of sport with which physical education is vitally concerned and involved. Several departments, such as the one at New York University, have changed their names to physical education and sport. Also, NASPE in the American Alliance for Health, Physical Education, and Recreation (AAHPER) represents the abbreviations for National Association for Sport and Physical Education.

WHAT IS PHILOSOPHY?

Just as terminology is essential to the understanding of physical education, so is philoso-phy. The essence of any discipline can only be appreciated by a thorough consideration of philosophy in general and the philosophies of the particular field being investigated.

Philosophy is a field of inquiry that attempts to help individuals evaluate, in a satisfying and meaningful manner, their relationships to the universe. Philosophy seeks to help people evaluate themselves and their world by giving them a basis with which to deal with the problems of life and death, good and evil, freedom and restraint, beauty and ugliness.

Aristotle said that philosophy is the grouping of the knowledge of the universals. A dictionary definition reports that it is the love of wisdom, the science that investigates the facts and principles of reality and of human nature and conduct. Copleston* writes: ''Philosophy . . . is rooted in the desire to understand the world, in the desire to find an intelligible pattern in events and to answer problems which occur to the mind in connection with the world.'' In defining the word *philosophy* Web-

---

*Copleston, Frederick, S. J.: Contemporary philosophy, Westminster, Md., 1966, The Newman Press.

Physical education is concerned with improving human performance. Children at Oak View Elementary School in Fairfax, Virginia, crawl through geometric forms to develop space awareness.

ster* says: "Love of wisdom means the desire to search for the real facts and values in life and in the universe, and to evaluate and interpret these with an unbiased and unprejudiced mind." As can be seen from these definitions, philosophy offers an explanation of life and the principles that guide human lives.

Some questions that reflect the concern of philosophers include the following:

What is the role of human beings on this earth?
What is the origin and nature of the universe?
What constitutes good and evil, right and wrong?
What constitutes truth?
Is there a God?
Do human beings have souls, that is, something which exists but cannot be seen?
What is the function of education in society?
What relationship exists between mind and matter?

To comprehend more clearly the meaning of philosophy, it is important to examine the major components of which philosophy is composed.

Metaphysics

Metaphysics is associated with the principles of being. This component attempts to answer a series of related questions: What is the meaning of existence? What is real? How are human actions governed? How and why did the universe evolve? What is the nature of God? The question: What experiences in the physical education program will better enable students to meet the challenges of the real world? is metaphysical in nature. Will Durant, a contemporary philosopher, says that metaphysics investigates the reality of everything concerned with human beings and the universe.

Epistemology

Epistemology is concerned with methods of obtaining knowledge and the kinds of knowledge that can be gained. It is a comprehensive study of knowledge that attempts to define the sources, authority, principles, limitations, and validity of knowledge. In physical education one is concerned with knowledge regarding

the role of physical activity and its impact on the physical, mental, emotional, and social development of individuals. Students are seeking the truth about physical education, and epistemology seeks to answer the question: What is true?

Axiology

Axiology helps to determine to what use truth is to be put. It asks: How do we determine what has value, and on what criteria is this judgment based? Axiology is concerned with the aims and values of society and is extremely important in physical education because the aims and values set by society become the basis of the curriculum used in schools and colleges. In physical education the following question must be answered: How can the values that society holds so dearly be embraced in the physical education program? American society holds dearly the value of "equality for all," which is exemplified by having students from all walks of life playing together and developing tolerance for one another. Students who learn to respect one another on the playing fields, it is hoped, will be more likely to carry those feelings off the field.

Ethics

Ethics is a more individualized and personalized subdivision of axiology. It helps to define moral character and serves as a basis for an individual code of conduct. Ethics attempts to answer the question: What is the highest standard of behavior each person should strive to attain? The strengthening of moral conduct is an important function of physical education. In physical education the following questions must be answered: How can games and sports be utilized to help the individual learn right conduct? Is character education through physical education possible? Physical education places individuals in situations that reveal their true nature and character. One who plays on a team may soon realize that using "four-letter words" is not acceptable. The student who plays by the "rules" and acts like a "sportsman" or "sportswoman" at all times will win the respect of teammates. It is hoped that the relationships formed in physical education and

---

*Webster, Randolph W.: Philosophy of physical education, Dubuque, Iowa, 1965, William C. Brown Co.

the character that is developed will carry over to behavioral situations occurring out of school.

Logic

Logic seeks to provide human beings with a sound and intelligent method of living. Logic describes the steps that should be taken in thinking and puts ideas into an orderly, structured sequence that leads to accurate thinking. It helps to set up standards by which the accuracy of ideas may be measured. Logic concerns itself with the orderly connection of one fact or idea with another. It asks the question: What method of reasoning will lead to the truth? Physical educators must use logical thought processes in arriving at the truth. When students ask questions such as: "Why should I play football?" the physical education teacher must not answer by saying: "Because it's in the program." The teacher should explain in clear reasoning the benefits and risks associated with playing football, since only then will the student really understand its true value.

Esthetics

Esthetics is the study and determination of criteria for beauty in nature and the arts, including dance, drama, sculpture, painting, music, and writing. Esthetics, which is a less scientific branch of axiology, is concerned not only with art but also with the artist and the appreciation of what he or she has created. In an attempt to determine the close relationship of art to nature, esthetics asks the question: What is beauty? There is esthetic appreciation involved in watching a gymnast perform on the trampoline, a football player leap high to catch a pass, or a baseball player dive to catch a line drive, just as there is an esthetic appreciation gained from viewing great works of art or listening to a symphony orchestra. The physical movements that one can view in athletics are often a source of great pleasure.

• • •

The components known as metaphysics, epistemology, axiology, ethics, logic, and esthetics represent aspects of philosophy. In developing a philosophy for any particular field, one would turn for information to each of these

Courtesy The Athletic Institute, North Palm Beach, Fla.

Physical education is concerned with esthetics. This picture illustrates the beauty of movement in a dance.

areas. These components would be applied in formulating a philosophy for any particular field within the educational endeavor, such as in health, physical education, or recreation. Philosophy yields a comprehensive understanding of reality, which, when applied to education or any other field of interest, gives direction that would likely be lacking otherwise.

PHILOSOPHY AND LEVELS OF DISCUSSION

Broudy* lists four levels of discussion applicable to a progressive step-by-step exploration of education problems. These levels of discussion help to clarify the implications of philosophy for the physical educator.

Emotional or uncritical level

On the emotional level individuals discuss the advantages or disadvantages of an issue mainly in terms of their own limited experience. The arguments presented are not based

*Broudy, Harry S.: Building a philosophy of education, New York, 1954, Prentice-Hall, Inc., pp. 20-24.

Greek physical education was developed on classical philosophical grounds, which embraced it as an essential to the education of youth.

on reflective thinking but, instead, on impulse and emotional feeling. A statement by a high school basketball coach that: "All boys who play high school basketball perform better in the classroom than those who do not play" may be an emotional or uncritical statement. The coach may only have had experience with his own team and cannot know for sure whether all boys who play high school basketball perform better in the classroom than those who do not play. It is generally agreed that the emotional level of thinking is the most unreliable and few differences of opinion can be settled by using the emotional level of thought and action.

Factual or informational level

The factual level of discussion involves the gathering of evidence to support one's arguments. By mobilizing statistics and other types of factual evidence, tangible support is often given to a particular argument. However, this level of discussion can be unreliable and misleading, since it depends on the facts used, whether they are valid and applicable and whether they are significant, and other conditions that exist in the particular situation in question. A statement by a physical education teacher that: "In an experiment, students who participated in the physical education program showed greater improvement in strength than those who did not participate" is a factual statement. The teacher can introduce all kinds of impressive statistics to prove his point. However, one cannot be sure whether the experiment was properly conducted. Nevertheless, the mobilizing of accurate facts in a discussion can frequently result in the solution of a problem and the satisfactory finalizing of a discussion on an argumentative topic.

Explanatory or theoretical level

Facts offer solid support, but they are most effective when they are associated with theories that make them dynamic and applicable. A statement by a physical educator that: "The jump shot in basketball should be taught as a whole and not broken down into its component parts," is theoretically valid. The teacher's statement can be supported by reference to the "Gestalt theory" and such thinkers as Kurt Koffka and Wolfgang Kohler, whose theories stress the idea that learning takes place as a whole because of the essential unity that exists in nature. At this level of discussion the introduction of a reliable scientific explanation provides strong evidence for rational individuals.

Philosophical level

The highest level of discussion involves asking questions relative to what is really true, valuable, right, or real. The application of such values is universal and eternal. This is the ultimate to which any discussion can go. A statement by the physical education teacher asking: "Do students participating in team sports develop strong human relationships?" is characteristic of the philosophical level. At this level there is self-criticism of programs, and physical educators try to decide what they want to have happen to their students in the gymnasium. This level of discussion finds the greatest use when problems fail to yield a clear solution and when facts and science are limited and inconclusive. (There are many such problems in education and in physical education that merit a philosophical discussion.)

PHILOSOPHY OF EDUCATION AND THE GOOD LIFE

Dewey* has stated: "The problem of restoring integration and cooperation between man's beliefs about the world in which he lives and his beliefs about the values and purposes that should direct his conduct is the deepest problem of modern life." Dewey has further stated that it is through one's philosophy that this problem can be solved. A philosophy is extremely valuable because it determines one's thinking and leads one to ultimate goals.

Philosophy has both a "synthetic" and "analytical" function. The synthetic function of philosophy is mainly concerned with formulating hypotheses, which serve as the tools for interpreting questions concerned with the nature and experiences of human beings. The analytical function of philosophy attempts to determine what the key concepts are in any field and as its name suggests, studies the methods of inquiry used in the various fields.

In education, as in any other field, important questions will be answered by one's philosophy. A philosophy of education is extremely important to all those who intend entering the teaching profession. One cannot be an effective teacher in today's changing society if he or she does not have a well-thought-through philosophy. A philosophy of education attempts to determine what kind of life one should lead.

*Dewey, John: The quest for certainty, London, 1930, George Allen Junior, Ltd., p. 243.

Viewing people in a systematic fashion, a philosophy of education is instrumental in giving purpose and direction to one's actions.

Before a personal philosophy of education can be formulated, the future teacher must have a clear concept of the person he or she wants to produce. Therefore it becomes necessary to define that type of life which reflects the most satisfying and worthwhile type of existence. This is the type of life on which educational aims, methods, facilities, staff, and other essentials should be focused. For purposes of discussion this may be called the "good life."

Philosophers have used the term *good life* to indicate the happiest and most successful type of existence. For example, in his book *Education and the Good Life,* Bertrand Russell lists vitality, sensitiveness, courage, intelligence, and love as his characteristics of the "good life." Others have said that it is characterized by pleasure. These thinkers differ, however, as to the meaning of the word *pleasure.* John Stuart Mill and Epicurus were two such philosophers. Still others have varied in saying the "good life" is the simple life, or the one characterized by vast possessions and great power, or the one devoted to worthy causes and religious fervor. Broudy in his book *Building a Philosophy of Education* points out that, although philosophers have not agreed entirely in their thinking, most have said that the "good life" consists of the following characteristics. First, it is a life that is pleasurable with excessive pain eliminated and in which disease, poverty, and hardship are kept to a minimum. Second, the "good life" emphasizes love, emotional security, and understanding. There is freedom from fears, anxiety, frustration, despair, and loneliness. Third, the "good life" means that the individual accomplishes, achieves, renders a service, is respected, and is allowed to exercise individual potentialities. There is respect for the dignity and worth of the human being. Fourth, the "good life" is interesting and exciting. If the interest and excitement are permanent and of the highest type, they are tied in closely with other people and future events. They are not solely self-centered and concerned with what is going on at present.

Amount of Emphasis

Principle

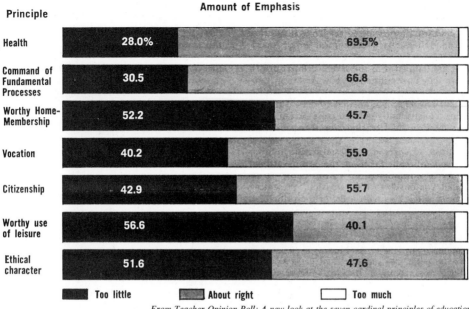

Principle	Too little	About right
Health	28.0%	69.5%
Command of Fundamental Processes	30.5	66.8
Worthy Home-Membership	52.2	45.7
Vocation	40.2	55.9
Citizenship	42.9	55.7
Worthy use of leisure	56.6	40.1
Ethical character	51.6	47.6

■ Too little   ▨ About right   □ Too much

From Teacher-Opinion Poll: A new look at the seven cardinal principles of education,
NEA Journal 56:54, Jan., 1967.

A national survey of teachers to determine where they thought the emphasis is placed in education.

Any analysis or definition of the "good life" must include the viewpoints of both the individual and society. Both play an important part in determining the true ingredients.

PHILOSOPHY AND PHYSICAL EDUCATION—WHY HAVE A PHILOSOPHY?

In today's changing society, there must be a sound philosophy of physical education for the profession to survive. Physical educators must ask themselves such important questions as: What has value in today's society? What is relevant to the needs of today's youth and adults? A philosophy of physical education will serve the following functions.

A philosophy of physical education is essential to professonal education. Persons who claim to be physical educators should have developed carefully thought-through philosophies. In so doing, it will help them to have a common basis for thinking about their profession, properly articulate the meaning and worth of their field of endeavor to the public at large, become motivated to achieve greater

professional accomplishments, and better evaluate physical education programs and practices.

A philosophy of physical education guides one's actions. To function as an intelligent being, one needs a philosophy of life that will guide one's actions. One needs knowledge about what is right before any program can be created. A philosophy will help the teacher to decide what he or she wants to have happen to students in the gymnasium.

A philosophy of physical education provides the direction for the profession. Today in physical education many of the curriculums lack order and direction. A philosophy of physical education will help to give direction to programs. When assumptions are made by the physical education teacher, for example, that physical education strengthens human relationships because children play together, they should be based on a system of reflective educational thinking that embraces logic and other philosophical components. A philosophy of physical education will help to provide this system.

A philosophy of physical education makes

society aware that physical education contributes to its values. Physical education in the coming decades is going to have to face the fact that people are not going to be satisfied with only such facts as students who participate in physical education show improvement in endurance. This is important, but it does not go far enough. In today's changing society, people want to know how physical education can contribute to human performance, quality of life, and productivity. A well-thought-through philosophy of physical education will assist in interpreting those values important in society so that programs can be established to help meet these needs.

A philosophy of physical education aids in bringing the members of the profession closer together. Many members of the physical education profession are dissatisfied with what they see happening in their field today. A philosophy of physical education will enable physical educators to determine how they can best contribute to mankind and to society and thus provide members of the profession the op-

portunity to work together in making such a contribution.

A philosophy of physical education explains the relationship between physical education and general education. A philosophy of physical education will help in the development of a rationale showing that the field has objectives that are closely related to the objectives of general education. In the definition of physical education the importance of education "of and through the physical" is stressed. The goal, as in general education, is to develop the "whole" student. A philosophy of physical education that enunciates basic goals will give evidence that the profession has objectives related to those of general education.

Physical educators must strive to develop their educational philosophies in a rational, logical, and systematic manner and to represent the best interests of all humans. This means that scientific facts must be assembled and workable theories applied which support the worth of physical education as an important and necessary service to humanity.

Physical education should contribute to society's values. First-grade class in physical education at Cumberland Valley School District, Mechanicsburg, Pennsylvania. From such an experience certain values should be realized.

A PHILOSOPHY OF PHYSICAL EDUCATION FOR PROGRAMS OUTSIDE THE SCHOOL

Although this chapter places considerable emphasis on philosophy as it applies to physical education programs in schools and colleges, the implications are clear for programs outside the school. A philosophy of physical education must also be applicable to these programs. For example, today there is considerable emphasis on physical education for all segments of the population, including industrial employees, the elderly, youth, and the public in general. Physical educators who serve as leaders, administrators, and instructors in these settings should also be concerned with developing a sound philosophy of physical education. Most of the concepts of a philosophy for schools and colleges that are discussed are also applicable to programs that exist outside the educational domain. For example, a philosophy for physical education other than schools should also be humanistic in its approach, meet the needs of the participant, have a sound scientific basis, be concerned with an understanding of the role of physical activity in human performance, and enhance the quality of life for participants. Therefore the physical educator who plans to seek employment or has a position in a setting other than the schools will benefit from reading this chapter.

SOME GENERAL PHILOSOPHIES

Five philosophies have prevailed down through the years and have influenced educational thinking. They are idealism, realism, pragmatism, naturalism, and existentialism.

Idealism

The philosophy of idealism has come down through the ages as a heritage from the earliest Greek philosophers and thinkers. The key concepts of idealism follow.

1. *The mind is the focus of a person's being.* The idealist believes that the mind is more real than anything else which exists. Anything that is real is essentially a product of the mind and is equated by thoughts and ideas.

2. *In the scheme of the universe, people are more important than nature.* Because to the idealist the mind and spirit are the keys to life, the physical world plays a subordinate role to human beings. People interpret nature in terms of mind, spirit, and being.

3. *Values exist independently of individuals and are permanent.* People are capable of exercising free will. Through the use of this power, they recognize the existence in the world of good and evil, beauty and ugliness, freedom and restraint and interpret these in relation to themselves. The idealist acknowledges that although these values may be interpreted differently, they are permanent and do not change in the light of varying interpretations.

4. *Reasoning and intuition help individuals to arrive at the truth.* Mind is considered to be the basic creative force that helps people learn more about their world. But the idealist also believes that scientific methods of investigation and research are valuable *aids* in seeking the truth.

The Greek philosopher Plato is often referred to as the father of idealism. He believed that ideas had an enduring quality and that physical objects were ideas expressed in a less-than-perfect fashion. Plato said that there were, in fact, two classes of ideas: those which exist in the minds of people and those which exist outside of their minds. Aristotle expanded on Plato's philosophy and was responsible for the earliest origins of the scientific method. Aristotle stressed arriving at the truth through reasoning and observation. René Descartes is one of the most famous of the idealist philosophers. His often-cited quotation: "I think, therefore I am" is the essential element in the philosophy of the idealist. Both Baruch Spinoza and Gottfried W. Leibniz expressed the view that something enduring and unchanging exists beyond the universe. Whereas Spinoza referred to this phenomenon as a "substance," Leibniz termed it a "God." George Berkeley, Immanuel Kant, and George Hegel all espoused the belief that the mind is the key to all things. Some of the more modern idealists, whose views encompassed many of the same elements as the men who preceded them, were Louis Agassiz, Henry Barnard, Carl Follen, Francis Lieber, Henry Wadsworth Longfellow, and Horace Mann.

IDEALISM AND EDUCATION

1. *Education develops the personality of the individual.* Idealists show great concern for the moral and spiritual values in society. For idealists to fulfill their moral and spiritual destiny, it becomes necessary for education to help in the development of the individual personality of each student. Education must provide opportunities for all individuals to develop to their full worth.

2. *Knowledge and the development of the mind are important.* Idealism emphasizes the importance of rationality and the need for the cultivation of reason. Each person's mind must strive to realize itself. Education is seen by the idealists as the means to this end.

3. *Education is a process that originates within the self.* Idealists view students as creative beings. The individual self contains within it the properties for its own growth. The learning process must be self-initiated to warrant the label *idealist*. The idealistic educator stresses the importance of self-activity because it gives students the impetus for learning and development.

4. *The curriculum is centered around ideals.* Because of their emphasis on the development of the personality, idealists place great stress on programs that provide students with the opportunity to develop the essential qualities of self-reliance, self-responsibility, and self-direction. The idealistic curriculum stresses those areas of study which help the student build an ideal intellectual, spiritual, and moral character. Art, literature, and history in their classical forms are the foundation of the curriculum in the idealist school.

5. *The student is a creative being who is guided by the teacher.* The student in the idealistic school formulates ideas and learns in an environment created by the teacher. The idealistic teacher conceives the objectives and organizes the subject matter. The learning environment of the idealistic teacher would include the formulation of ideas through the project method, the lecture method, and/or the question and answer method. The idealistic teacher might tell students what the "possible" answers are, and then the students must discover their own conclusions. In this manner the ideal-

istic teacher guides students through a thought process that will lead to the truth.

IDEALISM AND PHYSICAL EDUCATION

1. *Physical education involves more than the "physical."* Idealists believe that the body should be developed simultaneously with the mind. Physical education should contribute to the development of the individual's intellect. For example, the physical education teacher, after describing a difficult skill such as the "kip" on the low bar, can ask students questions such as: "What angle should the hands be in when they are grasping the bar?" According to idealists, physical education activities can and must help students think for themselves.

2. *Strength and fitness activities contribute to the development of one's personality.* The idealistic physical educator must make sure that the selected activities are related to important aspects of life. The idealist will accept vigorous exercise activities that emphasize development of strength and fitness because of the self-discipline and effort required and will select such activities because they contribute to the development of one's personality; however, activities will not be selected if their sole aim is developing strength or fitness.

3. *Physical education is centered around ideals.* Idealists believe that activities must be offered which aid the student in developing the qualities of honesty, courage, creativity, and sportsmanship. The idealistic physical educator aims for perfection. The idealist envisions the students becoming aware of what is true and genuine and wants the students to develop strong moral character. The idealist will encourage student-created gymnastic routines because of the emphasis on creativity and will want "team sports" dominated by students and thus will reject a basketball game dominated by the coach because the students will not get the opportunity to think for themselves. Idealistic physical educators stress the fact that students can only develop when they are playing an important part in the activity.

4. *The teacher must be a model for students.* The idealistic physical education teacher must set a good example for all students—must be

the type of person whom students want to imitate. Through personal example of vigorous health and personality, the idealistic physical educator will lead students toward greater accomplishments.

5. *The teacher is responsible for the effectiveness of the program*. Idealism believes that the firm and rather paternalistic guidance of the teacher is more important in carrying out the program than are equipment and facilities available. The idealistic physical educator, feeling responsible for the effectiveness of the program, will not be confined to any one way of teaching and uses the question and answer, the lecture, the project, and other methods of teaching.

6. *Education is for life*. The idealistic physical education teacher believes that equally important to developing physical skills or having knowledge of a sport is thinking reflectively and that the ability to analyze problems is as important as knowing the rules of a game. Idealism emphasizes a well-organized, well-guided program that contributes to the full mental and physical development of the individual for life.

Realism

Realism asserted itself as a distinct and separate philosophy during the late nineteenth and early twentieth centuries. For many centuries preceding that time, realism was greatly overshadowed by idealism. The roots of realism date back as far as the origins of idealism, and it was, in fact, a philosophical revolt against idealism. The growth of scientific methods and the philosophy of modern realism emerged at about the same time. Realism has many subdivisions. Its adherents do not always agree on particular interpretations, but the key concepts of realism may be defined in general terms.

1. *The physical world is a real world*. The realist accepts the physical world, or world of nature, as it is. This person does not contend that the world is made by humans but says that it is made up of matter. The physical world is in no way dependent on the human mind. The realist says that people come to an understand-

The teacher is responsible for the effectiveness of the program. Students perform Filipino stick dance in the Oak View Elementary School in Fairfax, Virginia.

ing of the physical world through their senses and through experience.

2. *All physical events that occur in the universe are the result of the laws of nature.* The realist contends that forces within the universe, which are physical laws, control the physical world. This belief has given rise to the physical sciences. The realist says that the environment is a result of cause and effect and that good, morality, and beauty conform to the laws of nature. Those things that do not conform to the laws of nature are wrong, immoral, and ugly. People perceive the physical world through observation.

3. *The truth may be best determined through the scientific method.* The realist does not hope for or anticipate full control or complete comprehension of everything in the physical world. The realist does expect to modify and understand it as well as possible through the tools of science. The realist believes that science and philosophy form the best method of arriving at the truth.

4. *The mind and the body have a close and harmonious relationship.* The realists have two views on the origin of human behavior. One school of thought says that human behavior may be a result of natural laws. A second opinion is that all behavior may be a result of learning. Both sides agree, however, that the mind and the body are inseparable and that neither takes precedence over the other.

5. *Religion and philosophy can coexist.* The realist can hold religious beliefs without compromising either religion or philosophy. This individual may be a staunch atheist or a pantheist or hold beliefs anywhere between the two extremes. The philosophy of realism does not insist on any one position as being the correct one. The individual realist is free to coordinate religious beliefs with philosophical viewpoints.

Philosophers often lend their thinking to the shaping of more than one philosophy. Thus many of the persons who helped to define idealism also adhered to elements of realistic thinking. The early realists ascribed much to a belief in the powers of a supreme being, or God. Aristotle said that truth and reality were one and the same and that the power of reasoning made human beings unique. Because of this

viewpoint, Aristotle is often referred to as the father of realism. St. Thomas Aquinas and René Descartes both said that matter was real and created by a God. Descartes' writing is believed to be the basis for the field of mathematical physics. Comenius, Spinoza, Kant, John Locke, and William James all contributed clarifications of this philosophy.

REALISM AND EDUCATION

1. *Education develops one's reasoning power.* To the realist, education is a process of learning how to acquire knowledge, acquiring knowledge, and putting that knowledge to practical use. The realistic educator stresses the fact that individuals must become the rational masters of themselves, since only then will they be able to control the environment.

2. *Education is for life.* The realistic educator believes that education is basic to life and that all education should have a useful purpose. The realistic educator attempts to develop students in such a manner that they can understand and make adjustments to the "real world." The realistic educator wants students to view the "real world" in an orderly and systematic fashion. Learning experiences are presented in an orderly fashion and relate to the problems of the outside world. The realistic educator believes that such experiences will aid students in their adjustment to the "real world," the world that will enfold them when they leave the school environment.

3. *Education is objective.* The realistic educator attempts to be objective, like the scientist, and employs objective methods of teaching, testing, and evaluation. Because the realist wants students to be exact, the facts are presented clearly in an objective and logical sequence. The realistic educator urges students to master the facts that are presented to them. Because the realist wants to bring the "real world" into the school environment, such techniques as audiovisual aids may be employed.

4. *The educational process proceeds in an orderly fashion.* The realistic educator wants teaching to be dependable and presents as facts only those things which have been proved by objective means. The realistic educator proceeds in a step-by-step fashion, always follow-

ing scientific rules, believing this to be the only way that teaching can be dependable. Students are guided through a process of inductive reasoning, eventually leading to a unified concept of the physical world.

5. *The curriculum is scientifically oriented.* The realistic curriculum stresses the sciences. Although mastery of fundamental facts is accomplished by means of drill and memorization, mastery of a body of knowledge is implemented by experimentation, demonstration, and observation. The realistic educator places great emphasis on research and the scientific method and stresses the importance of learning as large a number of scientific facts and principles as possible.

6. *There should be standardization of measurement techniques in education.* The realist educator favors the devising of standards of performance for students in various activities. The progress of students is evaluated by objective standardized tests. The realist gathers all the possible reliable data and measures students according to standards created. Realism has often been credited with being a major influence on the development and use of standardized tests.

REALISM AND PHYSICAL EDUCATION

1. *Education is for life.* The realist views physical education as a valuable part of the school curriculum. It is considered a unit of study that helps prepare students to adjust to the world in which they live. Participation in physical activities is viewed as a means of learning to adjust, and the emphasis is placed on the outcome of the activity in terms of adjustment. For example, the emphasis in teaching basketball is to develop such qualities as fair play and sportsmanship, as well as in teaching a student how to shoot a basket.

2. *Physical fitness results in greater productivity.* The realist physical educator emphasizes the values related to the human body—for example, "physical fitness" because of its intrinsic value. The realist physical educator stresses the point that one who possesses a physically fit body is one who may be most productive in society.

3. *Programs are based on scientific knowl-*

edge. The realist physical education teacher accomplishes the objectives by means of a scientifically formulated curriculum. Activities are selected on the basis of scientific evidence of their worth from a study of anatomy, physiology, or kinesiology. For example, in training a young man to be a "lineman" in football, it is necessary to be aware of the proper form that provides optimum stability. Anatomical knowledge dealing with the question of "base of support" will yield this information. A physical educator cannot be an effective teacher unless he or she possesses knowledge of scientific movement principles.

4. *Drills play an important part in the learning process.* The realist physical educator uses drills extensively and breaks units of work down into orderly progressions. The teaching emphasis is placed on fundamentals of games and activities, with each skill broken down into its component parts. In this manner the realist hopes to develop habits in student responses. The realist believes that breaking down the elements of a sport like soccer into all its component parts will lead to correct responses in game situations.

5. *Interscholastic athletic programs can lead to desirable social behavior.* The realist approves of interscholastic athletic programs insofar as they teach desirable social behavior. The realist approves of a team sport like baseball particularly because it develops such qualities as sportsmanship, fair play, and tolerance. The realist physical educator will not be interested in having a baseball program that only emphasizes "winning."

6. *Play and recreation aid in life adjustment.* The physical educator who is a realist believes that students who participate in play and recreational activities are better able to function in society. Through such activities, students are brought into contact with aspects of the "real world" of which they will become a part when they leave the school setting.

Pragmatism

Pragmatism emphasizes experience as a key to life. Rather than being concerned with reality, this philosophy is concerned with knowledge. Because of this view, in its early stages, pragmatism was often called *experimentalism*. The term *pragmatism* was not coined until the late 1800s. In its modern concept, this philosophy is considered an American one.

1. *Human experience causes changes in the concept of reality*. The pragmatist believes in change. This person does not hold that ideas, values, or realities are inflexible but contends, instead, that human experiences cause ideas, values, and realities to be dynamic. The pragmatist says that experience is the only possible way to seek the truth and that which is not experienced cannot be known or proved.

2. *Success is the only criterion of the value and truth of a theory*. Knowledge and experience help the individual to discover what is true. But truth is considered flexible, and today's truth may be tomorrow's falsehood. The pragmatist strongly believes in the scientific method of problem solving and considers it the best way to gain knowledge. Knowledge itself is thought to be only a stepping-stone on the path to further knowledge and experimentation. The pragmatist believes that a workable theory is a true theory and that the unworkable theory has been proved false.

3. *Individuals are an integral part of a larger society, and their actions reflect on that society*. The pragmatist contends that people and society must live harmoniously and that the actions of one directly affect the other. The pragmatist believes in democracy; that is, the needs of a group must always incorporate the needs of each individual in the group. To the pragmatist, values are an individual matter. What is right or wrong depends on the judgment of the individual, the environment, and the circumstances. However, the result of any action by an individual is to be measured in terms of its worth to society as a whole.

Heraclitus was an early Greek exponent of pragmatism. He stated the belief, still held today, that the world and its values and ideas are in a constant state of flux. Quintilian said that learning was a product of experience. Francis Bacon, an Englishman, put forth the theory that society and science must work together to achieve knowledge and that one cannot function effectively without the other. The first outstanding American pragmatist was Charles S. Pierce. He wrote that the practicality of a truth was the only criterion on which that truth could be measured. William James said that a theory was good if it worked and wrong if it was not practical. The most famous of the American pragmatists was John Dewey. Occasionally pragmatism is referred to as "Deweyism" because of the influence of Dewey's thinking on the philosophy. Dewey brought forth the theory that everything human beings know is subject to change and can in no way be considered static. Dewey viewed life as a continuing, never-ending experiment. He believed that learning how to think was one of the most important goals in life. Dewey's philosophy had a most profound influence on the field of education.

PRAGMATISM AND EDUCATION

1. *The individual learns through experience*. Experience is the key word in the educational process of the pragmatist. The individual learns through experience, which involves inquiring, observing, and participating in various activities. Experience is viewed as the key to all learning, and the application of intelligence to new experiences is that which makes the educational process effective. Pragmatists believe that children learn what they live, and consequently great importance is placed on student interests, devoting much time and energy in motivating those things which interest students.

2. *Education is for social efficiency*. The pragmatist believes that the major aim of the educational process is to teach students the knowledge and skills which will enable them to take their place in society. Education provides students with the necessary tools to enable them to adjust to their environment and solve the many problems that may arise. Pragmatists maintain that schools must provide experiences which aid the student in becoming an active member of society. The school must be involved in community affairs and give students the opportunity to participate in discussions. Students are given the opportunity to work together as members of social groups so that they can get the valuable experience which will prove beneficial when they become functioning members of society.

3. *Education is child centered.* The pragmatist emphasizes the study of the child. Pragmatists recognize the importance of individual differences; therefore each child is treated differently, thus permitting each to progress at his or her own speed. The pragmatic teacher serves as an inspiration, guide, and leader. The child is viewed as the most important thing in the school and as a whole being, rather than an intellect without a body. The child's needs, interests, and prior experiences guide the teacher toward better helping each child adjust to society.

4. *Problem solving is necessary in a world of change.* Since the pragmatist emphasizes the fact that there is constant change, education must prepare students to face situations which are still unknown. Pragmatic educators stress the point that when they leave school, students face a world which is considerably different from the one which they face when they first begin their educational career. For this reason, pragmatists emphasize the importance of having the knowledge to solve problems that may arise in an ever-changing world. Students are taught to define problems. They learn how to collect data, formulate and test hypotheses, and arrive at conclusions that will enable them to find the solution to those problems. This is the "problem-solving" method made famous by John Dewey. Pragmatic educators do not believe that it is necessary for their students to learn great numbers of facts; rather, it is more important that they learn those concepts which may be useful in solving a particular problem on which they are working.

PRAGMATISM AND PHYSICAL EDUCATION

1. *More meaningful experiences are presented when there is a variety of activity.* The pragmatic physical educator likes a varied program of physical education. Participants are provided with intriguing problems to solve and challenges to face in preparation for effective functioning in society. Creative activities such as dance and experiences in boating, camping, and outdoor living, as well as all types of sports, are highly valued. Through these activities the person not only learns by doing but also gains a measure of self-control and discipline and learns to cooperate with others.

2. *Activities are socializing in nature.* The pragmatic approach to physical education is one of integrating the person and society. Any activity that has social value is acceptable. Team sports and group recreational activities are found satisfying to the pragmatist. Calisthenic drills and exercises are largely discarded from the pragmatic physical education program. The pragmatic sees education as life. Sports, by providing emotional involvement, competition, and interaction, contribute to the socialization of the individual.

3. *The program is determined by the needs*

Attention in education should be focused on the child.

and interests of the learner. Learning is accomplished in the pragmatic program by experiencing those things which have proved beneficial to the learner and which result from the learner's own interests. Activities that are challenging and creative are the major ones selected. Thus activities such as team sports, dance, and recreational activities are included in the pragmatist program because they satisfy the needs and interests of the participant.

4. *Learning is accomplished through the problem-solving method.* The pragmatic physical education teacher believes that problem solving helps to make learning more purposeful. The ability of participants to recognize and solve problems encourages thinking. Dance activities are satisfying to the pragmatic physical educator because of the elements of creativity involved. Movement education, which emphasizes the problem-solving method, also is extremely valuable to the pragmatist because of the emphasis on self-discovery.

5. *The teacher is a motivator.* The pragmatic physical educator is a leader and motivator of the students. Students are encouraged to participate in activities that the teacher believes are most beneficial to them. The pragmatic teacher guides students in making the correct choices but does not direct them or tell them that they must do things his or her way. The pragmatic teacher employs the use of student leaders and tries to give as many students as possible a leadership experience.

6. *Standardization is not a part of the program.* The pragmatic physical education teacher dislikes standardization because of the belief that such a practice makes all programs alike. Pragmatists place a higher value on evaluation than measurement. They are not as interested in measuring muscle strength as in determining whether students will be able to face the challenges that life will present to them. To the pragmatist, evaluating whether a student who participates in a baseball game learns the elements of fair play is equally as important as learning to hit a ball.

Naturalism

Naturalism, pragmatism, and realism share many key concepts, although naturalism as a philosophy is the oldest one known to the Western world. Naturalism is often referred to as a materialistic philosophy, since it says that those things which actually and physically exist are the only things which have value.

1. *Any reality that exists exists only within the physical realm of nature.* To the naturalist, the physical world is the key to life. It contains all we see, observe, and think about, including the beauty or ugliness of a tree and the complexities of nuclear physics. The physical world is viewed as being in a constant state of growth and change, but it is considered to be a predictable and reliable force. Since the physical world is the key to life, the naturalist does not accept the existence of a God or any other supreme being. The philosophy of naturalism says that scientific methods are the best ways to gain knowledge about the world of nature.

2. *Nature is the source of value.* Because nature is omnipotent, anything that is of value exists only within nature and is predicated by nature; no values can exist separately from nature in any form. Like pragmatism, a thing is of value if it is workable.

3. *The individual is more important than society.* Naturalism does agree, however, that democracy comes from a group process, but it contends that each individual is more important than the group as a whole. Society reaps the benefits of the interaction of individuals and nature. Conversely, it is the individual who advances nature.

The men who first defined the philosophy of naturalism were in strong agreement that all things are derived from nature, including learning. This view was especially put forth by Democritus, Leucippus, Epicurus, and Comenius. In the eighteenth century, Rousseau, Basedow, and Pestalozzi set the foundations for the naturalistic process in education. Rousseau is more of a prime source for theses educational objectives, but Basedow put them into actual use. Herbert Spencer further defined education under naturalism and is mainly responsible for modern educational thought among the naturalists.

NATURALISM AND EDUCATION

1. *Education must satisfy the inborn needs of the individual.* Naturalists declare that when a child is born, he or she already possesses cer-

tain capacities and inborn powers that determine individual needs. There are fundamental forces within the individual that seek satisfaction, such as the need for social affiliation and achievement. Naturalists state that it is the role of education to satisfy these basic needs.

2. *Education is geared to the individual growth rate of each child.* Education is focused on the student. Naturalist educators believe that each child follows a logical pattern of growth and development and that education must be attuned to these natural patterns. Activities are selected according to the developing maturity level of the individual. Furthermore, according to the naturalists, the laws of growth and development are investigated when programs are developed.

3. *Education is not simply mental in nature.* Naturalists emphasize the point that education is not only mental but that it is also physical and moral. Naturalists advocate the education of both mind and body, with neither taking precedence. Education encourages the development of moral character, self-discipline, and physical well-being.

4. *Students educate themselves.* Naturalists emphasize the point that education involves self-activity. Students take an active part in their own educational development. When students learn with their whole body, they establish relationships and thus educate themselves to a certain degree. According to the naturalist educators, activities are offered for exploratory purposes and for the development of natural abilities and self-expression.

5. *The teacher has an understanding of the laws of nature.* It is the role of the teacher to learn how each student learns and to act as a guide through the educational process. The teacher has knowledge of the laws of nature and helps the child develop according to these laws. The teacher is aware that nature has made all people different, and therefore each child has distinct learning needs that require individual types of learning activities.

6. *The teacher is a guide in the educational process.* The teacher, by example and demonstration, guides students through an investigative procedure that helps them to draw their own conclusions. The method of instruction

The teacher is a guide in the euucational process. A teacher in the Oak View Elementary School in Fairfax, Virginia, guides children in a physical education class with pegboards to develop small muscle coordination.

used is mainly inductive. The method of teaching is informal and permits students to develop naturally at their own speed and according to their own needs and interests.

NATURALISM AND PHYSICAL EDUCATION

1. *Physical activities are more than just "physical" in nature.* Naturalists agree that physical activities do more than just develop strength and fitness. The naturalist believes that activity is the main source of development of the individual. By means of physical activity, children learn to become contributing members of a group, develop high moral standards, learn to express themselves in an acceptable manner, and become individuals who have more nearly reached their full potential.

2. *Learning is accomplished through self-activity.* Naturalists state that activity is the main source of the development of certain capabilities which have been embedded in the individual by heredity. Security and recognition are capabilities that are developed by self-activity. The naturalist offers a wide variety of activities so that the participant will be able to adjust to the environment. The naturalist approves of all physical activity, including team and individual sports and outdoor education. This physical educator introduces new activities only when students are ready for them and have a need for and interest in them. Naturalists stress the point that students can only learn when they are "ready" physiologically, psychologically, and sociologically.

3. *Play is an important part of the educational process.* Naturalist physical educators believe that play, resulting directly from the interests of the child, provides the starting point for teaching desirable social behaviors. Through play, children become aware of the world of which they are a part, permitting the teacher to introduce many of the essential features of social relationships. In the naturalist physical educator's program, students interact with one another in playful activities and develop social habits that will prove beneficial to them when they leave the school environment.

4. *Highly competitive performance between individuals is discouraged.* Self-improvement is encouraged in the naturalist physical educa-

tion program, and evaluation goes on continuously. The emphasis in evaluation is placed on the individual's own performance. The naturalist does not approve of intense competition between groups. Participants must be in competition against themselves to better their performance and to improve in light of what they have done in past performances.

5. *Physical education is concerned with the whole individual.* According to naturalist physical educators, physical education has a mental aspect. In every physical activity one's volitional processes are at work. In a complex sport such as football, to be successful one constantly thinks and develops the correct responses. However, naturalists do not believe in making students mentally fit and disregarding their physical fitness. Education is for the body as well as the mind. Physical education activities result in physical and mental development that prepares students to function well in society.

Existentialism

The chief concern of existentialism is individuality. The existentialist fears that people are being forced to conform to society and are thus forfeiting their individuality. Existentialism, which received its impetus immediately after World War II, is entirely a modern philosophy in that it did not arise from any of the ancient philosophies. As a way of philosophical thought, it had its earliest beginnings in the midnineteenth century.

1. *Human existence is the only true reality.* People are what they cause themselves to become and no more and no less. Each person has the ultimate responsibility for the past, present, and future. Each person has the choice of accepting those things which exist outside human experience, but an individual who does accept them forfeits a part of himself or herself. The existentialist does not contend that God does or does not exist but only that each person must decide the answer to this question individually in the light of an objective analysis of his or her own being.

2. *Individuals must determine their own systems of values.* Any value that an individual has not fully decided on cannot be a real value.

Any value that is dictated is a meaningless value. Accepting a value that is not self-determined leads away from individuality. Self-respect is attainable only if ideals and values are of one's own choosing and, once decided on, one is willing to accept the responsibility for them.

3. *Individuals are more important than society.* The existentialist believes that society as a whole is indifferent to the individuals who compose it. Individuals can make their mark and keep contact with reality only if they continually search for their own place as individuals. Once a man or woman subjugates personal values, personality, and ideals to those of society, he or she ceases to function as an individual.

Sören Kierkegaard, a nineteenth century theologian and philosopher, is considered to be the father of existentialist thought. He was concerned with seeking the meaning of each person's individuality. Most of the modern existentialist philosophers do not necessarily follow the guides set down by Kierkegaard, although they all place the major emphasis on the individual and his or her behavior. Jean-Paul Sartre is the outstanding atheistic existentialist. He denies that human beings will make any progress, and he sees the ultimate failure of both humankind and society. Karl Jaspers, Paul Tillich, and Reinhold Niebuhr are theistic existentialists and offer viewpoints that are far more optimistic than Sartre's. They say that to reach their ultimate reality, individuals must participate in life rather than be mere spectators. Martin Heidegger has remained fairly clear of the atheist-theist controversy and instead writes that people cannot stop searching for the meaning in life, no matter what that meaning may be.

EXISTENTIALISM AND EDUCATION

1. *Individuals discover their "inner selves."* Existentialist educators believe that individuals discover their inner selves and have an understanding of themselves. Existentialist students decide those values and goals which are important and discover their own truths. The school supplies the environment, the tools, and the opportunity for this discovery.

2. *Education is an individual process.* General education is viewed by the existentialist as an individual rather than a group process. The purpose of the school is to set an environment that allows the student to learn what he or she is interested in learning. The existentialist educational system permits great variety in its methods. Because students are different, they are not educated at the same rate or in the same way.

3. *The curriculum is centered on the individual.* The existentialist student rather than the teacher selects the subject matter and the learning method. Students base these decisions on their views of themselves in the present and projected into the future. The subject matter aids individuals is discovering their inner selves. Since the meaning of existence is embedded in human life, the program is based on the individual so a person can discover the true meaning of existence. The Socratic method of learning is used because it forces individual students to probe into their minds. The existentialist program offers many courses in the arts, humanities, and social sciences because these subjects reveal the nature of humankind.

4. *The teacher acts as a stimulator.* The existentialist teacher serves as a stimulus for students. This individual encourages students to discover their own truths by prodding their moral and intellectual curiosity. Existentialists encourage their students to be creative, critical, and original thinkers. The existentialist teacher enters into relationships with students that will result in the development of their curiosity. This is essential if the student is to discover the truth. The existentialist teacher, in stimulating students, assists them in their goal toward self-realization.

5. *Education is to teach responsibility.* The existentialist educator aids the individual in responsible decision making. Students are presented with experiences in the school environment that enable them to be more responsible citizens. They are made aware of the fact that they must take full responsibility for their decisions. Education develops the inner self of the student, according to the existentialist, since it is only after the discovery of the inner self that the individual is able to accept the

responsibility for the consequences of personal actions.

1. *There is freedom of choice.* Physical education programs should provide some freedom of choice on the part of the student. This, however, presents some difficulties when programs are exposed to the problem of implementation. For example, if the teacher practices complete freedom in determining the program, how can the student exercise the freedom of choice that is so vital to existentialism? And if the student is totally free to choose activities, does he or she have the ability to do so? Given absolute freedom of choice and decision making, it is conceivable that among a class of thirty students up to thirty different activities are selected for pursuit during a single class period. However, when a wide variety of individual and dual activities is offered, the existentialist aim can be carried out at least in part.

2. *There should be a variety of activity.* The existentialist physical educator provides a balanced and varied program that satisfies individual needs and interests. Within the activity selected, students are expected to evaluate themselves and, on this judgment, make a selection of the skills and activities to be pursued. It is the role of the teacher to provide the activities and to create an atmosphere in which students learn to take the responsibility for themselves, but only after showing the maturity to earn this privilege.

3. *Play results in the development of creativity.* Existentialist physical educators emphasize that when students are playing, they are involved in creativity. Existentialists emphasize individual and team sports; however, team sports whose only goal is winning are viewed as having little value. Dance and gymnastics fit into the existentialist program because of the element of creativity involved.

4. *Students "know themselves."* The existentialist physical educator's student has self-knowledge, since such an understanding is necessary to make choices that better the student and the rest of society. By participating in individual and dual activities, students gain knowledge about themselves. Competition is acceptable; however, it is the effect of competition on the individual that is important. Existentialist physical educators also place emphasis on self-testing activities because they aid in the development of self-responsibility and require students to "know themselves."

5. *The teacher is a counselor.* Existentialist physical educators are personally concerned about their students. Students are made to feel more responsible in the existentialist physical education program than in other programs discussed. The teacher believes that it is most important to give students the opportunity to try out their judgments in activities presented to them. In such a manner the existentialist physical educator's students develop the quality of self-responsibility. In the learning process the teacher acts in the role of a counselor and guide, explaining the various alternatives and giving direction so that the student does not flounder.

TRADITIONAL AND MODERN EDUCATIONAL PHILOSOPHIES

From your readings it may be apparent that some philosophies tend to be more traditional than others. In other words, many philosophical thoughts are no longer adapted to general or physical education programs. Most schools today follow a modern educational philosophy that is based on much of what John Dewey advocated.

Education today stresses the individual by recognizing that people have differing needs. Individualized learning is learning for all, including programs for the retarded, emotionally disturbed, and handicapped. Students are often free to choose the subjects they want to study and to receive training in various vocational areas.

It may be said that education today teaches the whole person. Educators are not only concerned about academic excellence but also about improving speech, coordination, and social effectiveness. Teachers with this philosophy of education try to help a person overcome emotional and physical problems and have rapport with other human beings.

A MODERN VIEW OF
PHYSICAL EDUCATION

Much of what is true for education in general comprises a modern philosophy of physical education. Physical education must also treat students as individuals with different needs, ambitions, and problems. One type of physical education program is not suited to all individuals. Students, especially those in the higher grades, need a wide choice of activities that includes individual and team sports. Many schools conduct surveys to elicit from the students the types of activities they desire to engage in.

In addition, physical education programs have an important responsibility to those students who are handicapped. Special teachers, facilities, and programs are essential for these students.

An important aspect of a modern philosophy of physical education is communication. Communication between physical education departments, home, and the community is essential. In times of rising costs and shrinking school budgets, physical educators must educate the public about the benefits of its programming. Without proper communication of this type, many citizens may not object to cutting the budget by curtailing or dropping physical education programs.

A HUMANISTIC PHILOSOPHY

Humanism may be defined as a revolt against depersonalization and as the emergence of the belief that every human being is an individual and should be treated as an individual rather than as part of a larger group. The humanist

Courtesy American Blind Bowling Association

A humanistic philosophy is concerned as much with the handicapped as with normal children and adults. Elmer Carey, Cincinnati, is a bowler who is totally blind.

Comparison of school programs guided by traditional and modern educational philosophies

Modern	*Traditional*
Child centered	Teacher centered
Permissive classroom atmosphere	Rigid classroom atmosphere
Based on pupil's interests and needs and relating to needs of society	Based on fact, knowledge, and subject matter, irrespective of societal changes or needs
Teacher a guide—plans along with child	Teacher a taskmaster
Focus on total development of child—physical, emotional, and social needs complement and supplement the mental needs	Focus on intellectual development
Self-directed study; opportunities for creative expression, socialization, problem solving, and experimentation	Formal drills, memorization, lectures, questions-answers, and examinations
Close school-community relationship and parental cooperation	School isolated from home and community
Self-discipline	Discipline by external authority
Broad curriculum	Limited curriculum
Healthful school environment	Austere environment
Geared to individual student	Geared to mass of students
Classroom a laboratory for testing new ideas	Classroom impervious to change

---

philosophy allows for individual development of talents and total fulfillment. Humanism encourages total involvement and participation in all that is going on around us.

The humanist teacher must encourage students toward self-actualization and fulfillment. Following are some of the ways in which this philosophy can be imparted:

1. Expressing open, genuine feelings
2. Placing a value on humanity and the individual
3. Accepting oneself and others for what they are
4. Adapting readily to innovative teaching methods
5. Being creative and independent and encouraging the same in students
6. Working effectively with others and increasing experiences and person-to-person interaction

• • •

What is your philosophy of physical education? Have you been able to formulate a philosophy of physical education as you have read this chapter? This is a difficult task but one that should be done for you to proceed in a fairly straight line toward the goal of becoming a physical educator. The information in this chapter and the references at the end of the chapter will help you to determine an individual philosophy. Of course, philosophies will and do change as one learns more and comes in contact with different people. In addition, philosophies of education often change after one has had actual teaching experience. Therefore it is important to be somewhat flexible about your philosophical outlook as you continue with your education and as different experiences play a part in your life.

SELF-ASSESSMENT TESTS

These tests are to assist students in determining if the material and competencies presented in this chapter have been mastered.

1. Without consulting your test, write a brief definition of each of the following terms: hypokinetics, ergonomics, biomechanics, exercise physiology, physical fitness, health, recreation, sports medicine, movement education, and physical education.

2. Prepare a position paper on the topic: "Physical education is as important a subject in schools and colleges as English or Science." Read the paper to your class and have them critically evaluate the evidence that you have presented to support your position.

3. Imagine that you are majoring in philosophy. Indicate the names of some of the subjects you would take, the purpose they serve, and why they are included in the program of studies for a major in philosophy.

4. Assume that you are a debater and have been requested to debate for the affirmative side, the topic: "Resolved: that only persons trained in the field of physical education should be permitted to coach athletic teams." Present a series of arguments that you would set forth on each of the following levels of discussion: emotional, factual, explanatory, and philosophical. Ask the class to determine which set of arguments were most convincing and why.

5. You are an employer and are interviewing candidates for a physical education position. Given two physical educators, one who has a well-thought-through philosophy and one who cannot articulate any philosophy of physical education whatsoever, which physical educator would you hire? Defend your decision.

6. All philosophers want to know the truth. What means would each of the following utilize in attempting to find the truth: idealist, realist, pragmatist, naturalist, and existentialist?

7. Write an essay describing the changes that have taken place in schools in the last 50 years, that is, the difference in characteristics of those schools guided by a traditional and those guided by a modern philosophy of education.

READING ASSIGNMENT

Bucher, Charles A.: Dimensions of physical education, ed. 2, St. Louis, 1974, The C. V. Mosby Co., Reading selections 11 to 17.

SELECTED REFERENCES

American Alliance for Health, Physical Education, and Recreation: HPER omnibus—comments and concepts by Gulick Award recipients of AAHPER, Washington, D.C., 1976, The Alliance.

American Association for Health, Physical Education, and Recreation: Tones of theory, Washington, D.C., 1972, The Association.

Brameld, Theodore: Philosophies of education in cultural perspective, New York, 1955, The Dryden Press.

Broudy, Harry S.: Building a philosophy of education, Englewood Cliffs, N.J., 1954, Prentice-Hall, Inc.

Brubacher, John S.: Eclectic philosophy of education, Englewood Cliffs, N.J., 1951, Prentice-Hall, Inc.

Caldwell, S. F.: Toward a humanistic physical education, Journal of Health, Physical Education, and Recreation **43**:31, May, 1972.

Davis, Elwood Craig: The philosophic process in physical education, Philadelphia, 1967, Lea & Febiger.

Dewey, John: The quest for certainty, London, 1930, George Allen Junior, Ltd.

Durant, Will: The story of philosophy, New York, 1953, Simon & Schuster, Inc., Publishers.

Frankel, Charles: A review for the teacher—philosophy, National Education Association Journal **51**:50, Dec., 1962.

Gulick, Luther Halsey: A philosophy of play, New York, Charles Scribner's Sons.

Horne, Herman Harrell: The philosophy of education, New York, 1908, The Macmillan Co.

Lockhart, Aileene, and Spears, Betty: Chronicle of American physical education, Dubuque, Iowa, 1972, William C. Brown Co.

McCloy, Charles Harold: Philosophical bases for physical education, New York, 1940, F. S. Crofts & Co.

Morris, Van Cleve: Physical education and the philosophy of education, Journal of Health, Physical Education, and Recreation **27**:21, March, 1956.

Park, Roberta J.: The philosophy of John Dewey and physical education, The Physical Educator **26**:55, 1969.

Postma, J. W.: Introduction to the theory of physical education, New York, 1970, International Publications Service.

Runes, Dagobert D.: Dictionary of philosophy, New York, 1942, Philosophical Library.

Russell, Bertrand: Philosophy, New York, 1927, W. W. Norton Co.

Russell, Bertrand: Education and the good life, New York, 1962, Liveright Publishing Corp.

Slusher, Howard S.: Existentialism and physical education, The Physical Educator **20**:4, Dec., 1963.

Ulrich, Celeste: To seek and find, Washington, D.C., 1976. American Alliance for Health, Physical Education, and Recreation.

Van Dalen, Deobold B.: Philosophical profiles for physical educators, The Physical Educator **21**:3, Oct., 1964.

Ziegler, Earle F.: Philosophical foundations for physical, health, and recreation education, Englewood Cliffs, N.J., 1964, Prentice-Hall, Inc.

Ziegler, Earle F.: Research in the history, philosophy and comparative aspects of physical education and sport, Champaign, Ill., 1971, Stipes Publishing Co.

3

Objectives of physical education

INSTRUCTIONAL OBJECTIVES AND COMPETENCIES TO BE ACHIEVED

After reading this chapter the student should be able to—

1. Justify why physical educators should have clearly stated professional objectives for what they do.
2. Identify and trace the objectives of physical education from early times until the present.
3. Discuss the principles that give support and a scientific foundation to objectives.
4. Clearly show why physical development, motor and movement development, cognitive development, and social development are important objectives of physical education.
5. Give examples of behavioral objectives and identify their purpose in physical education programs.
6. Determine what constitutes a priority for the objectives of physical education.
7. Describe what is meant by the conceptual approach to physical education and its relationship to objectives.
8. Identify the characteristics of a physically educated person.

Professional objectives are essential in physical education so that this field of endeavor may know the goals toward which it is striving. In recent years there has also been stress on instructional objectives, behavioral objectives, and performance or competency objectives as a means of better achieving professional objectives.

WHAT DO WE MEAN BY THE TERM "OBJECTIVES"?

In this chapter the term *objectives* is used in a general sense to include aims, purposes, and outcomes derived from participating in the physical education program. In other words, participation in physical activities under skilled leadership should result in certain constructive outcomes for the participant. These outcomes are the objectives of physical education.

Children, youth, and adults are involved with *movement*—getting their bodies into action. Movement is the medium through which physical education achieves its objectives. Movement offers people an avenue for fun, recreation, physical fitness, sociability, emotional release, communication, exploration, and healthful growth. Movement is a medium for educating people in regard to their physical, mental, emotional, and social development.

WHY ARE OBJECTIVES NEEDED IN PHYSICAL EDUCATION?

Physical educators must have clearly stated objectives. Some of the reasons for objectives are as follows:

1. *An understanding of objectives will help physical educators to understand better what they are trying to achieve.* There is purpose in physical education. This purpose must be clearly imprinted on the teacher's mind when instructing students in physical skills and on the leader's thinking when instructing an activity

class in a YMCA. If the objectives are clearly understood, this will have an impact on what activities are taught and how they are taught. The objectives will serve as guidelines for the physical educator in steering a course that is meaningful, worth while, and in the interest of human welfare.

2. *An understanding of objectives will help physical educators to understand better the worth of their field in education.* Physical education objectives must be compatible with general education objectives. Objectives of physical education that are identified and delineated represent goals compatible with and essential to the total educational effort in society.

3. *An understanding of objectives will help physical educators to make more meaningful decisions when issues and problems arise.* Physical educators will face problems daily as they carry out their responsibilities and administer their various programs. Parents, civic clubs, booster clubs, general administrators, professional sports promoters, big league players, and others who do not understand the objectives of physical education may try to influence programs in the direction they think important. An understanding of the objectives of physical education will help leaders in the field to make wise decisions when such pressures and issues arise.

4. *An understanding of objectives will help physical educators to interpret better their field of endeavor to general educators and lay persons.* Physical education is often misunderstood. One reason for this misunderstanding is that professional objectives are not known. Therefore, if physical educators know the objectives of their field and are imbued with their worth, they will be better able to correct the misunderstandings that exist and interpret their programs accurately.

WHAT ARE THE OBJECTIVES OF PHYSICAL EDUCATION?

The objectives of physical education have been stated many times by current and past leaders in the field. It is interesting to look first at what was conceived as the objectives of physical education in the past.

Historical analysis of the objectives of physical education

The physical education of primitive people was informal and unstructured, with the main purpose being survival. They needed physical strength and prowess to fight their enemies, build shelters, obtain food, and resist some of the forces of nature.

The Greeks probably represented the first people to give some structure to physical education. Some of the thinking about physical education during this time was reflected in the writings of Plato, the Greek philosopher. Plato stressed that there were objectives to physical education other than organic development when he pointed out the relation of mental development to physical development.

They are not intended, one to train body, the other mind, except incidentally, but to insure a proper harmony between energy and initiative on the one hand and reason on the other, by tuning each to the right pitch. And so we may venture to assert that anyone who can produce the best blend of the physical and intellectual sides of education and apply them to the training of character, is producing harmony in a far more important sense than any musician.

Much of Plato's thinking has influenced philosophers and physical educators down through history to accept the premise that close mind-body relationships do exist. Although this thinking did not have much impact on the early settlers in colonial America because of the doctrine of puritanism, the concept of the *unity of the human being* became increasingly recognized.

The early history of the United States saw systems of gymnastics, philosophies, and objectives imported from Europe. The programs to a great extent were formal in nature and gave precedence to the development *of* the physical rather than outcomes that could be accomplished *through* the physical.

At the turn of the century, however, a "new physical education" was developing, which resulted in a broadening of objectives and a recognition of the contributions that physical education could make to the "whole" individual. For example, in the 1880s, Dudley A. Sargent, the Director of Physical Education of the Hemenway Gymnasium at Harvard University, cited hygienic, educative, recreative, and remedial objectives in his program. During this same period, Thomas D. Wood, of Stanford University and later of Columbia University, another leading physical educator of the time, stressed that physical education should contribute to the complete education of the individual. Clark Hetherington, a colleague of Dr. Wood's and one of the greatest thinkers ever produced by the field of physical education, also stressed along with Dr. Wood that physical education was concerned with mental, moral, and social contributions to the student. Jesse Feiring Williams of Columbia University, also during the early 1900s, stressed the need for a physical education program that was concerned with education *through* the physical as well as an education *of* the physical.

The thinking of these early leaders influenced the objectives of the "new physical education" that are largely embraced by physical educators today.

Objectives of physical education as indicated by research studies and professional associations

Several studies aimed at determining the objectives toward which physical educators are striving have been conducted. In 1934 the Committee on Objectives of the American Physical Education Association listed the following five objectives of physical education: (1) physical fitness, (2) mental health and efficiency, (3) social-moral character, (4) emotional expression and control, and (5) appreciations. The committee listed knowledge, skills, and attitudes for each of these key objectives.

The Committee on Curriculum Research of the College Physical Education Association, under the direction of LaPorte, published in 1936 a review of objectives after a perusal of the literature. The committee indicated that they found 174 objectives in the literature that could be classified into ten categories.

In a doctoral dissertation at Stanford University in 1947, Agnes Stoodley analyzed physical education objectives as they were stated by twenty-two different authors in the professional literature. These objectives were classified under five headings: (1) health, physical, or organic development, (2) mental-emotional development, (3) neuromuscular development, (4) social development, and (5) intellectual development.

A joint committee of the American Association for Health, Physical Education, and Recre-

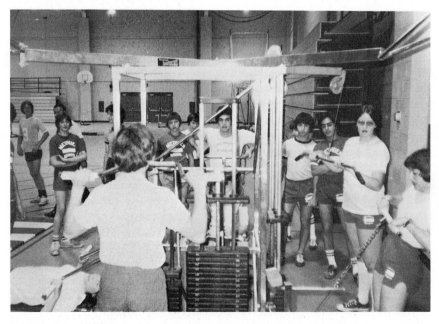

Physical fitness is one objective of physical education. Students work out on exercise apparatus to improve their physical fitness in the Methuen Public Schools, Methuen, Massachusetts.

ation (AAHPER) and the Society of State Directors of Health, Physical Education, and Recreation developed a platform for physical education in 1950 that included a statement of the objectives of physical education as follows: (1) to develop and maintain maximum physical efficiency, (2) to develop useful skills, (3) to conduct oneself in socially useful ways, and (4) to enjoy wholesome recreation.

The AAHPER publication entitled *This is Physical Education* incorporates a statement prepared by professional leaders of the physical education division of the AAHPER. This publication lists five major educational purposes for physical education:

1. To help children move in a skillful and effective manner in all the selected activities in which they engage in the physical education program, and also in those situations which they will experience during their lifetime.
2. To develop an understanding and appreciation of movement in children and youth so that their lives will become more meaningful, purposive, and productive.
3. To develop an understanding and appreciation of certain scientific principles concerned with movement that relate to such factors as time, space, force, and mass-energy relationships.
4. To develop through the medium of games and sports better interpersonal relationships.
5. To develop the various organic systems of the body so they will respond in a healthful way to the increased demands placed on them.

Rosentswieg of Texas Woman's University identified the following ten objectives of physical education from a study of the literature: (1) organic vigor, (2) democratic values, (3) social competency, (4) cultural appreciation, (5) leisure-time activities, (6) self-realization, (7) mental development, (8) emotional stability, (9) neuromuscular skills, and (10) spiritual and moral strength.

Foundations from which today's objectives of physical education are derived

In a strict sense of the term, *physical education* is not a discipline in itself but derives its objectives and scientific foundations from the disciplines of philosophy, biology, psychology, and sociology. Each of these areas is treated in detail in this text. The scientific foundations derived from the discipline of philosophy have already been discussed in Chapter 2. The scientific foundations derived from the discipline of biology are discussed in Chapters 11 and 12. The scientific foundations derived from the discipline of psychology are discussed in Chapter 13. The scientific foundations derived from the discipline of sociology are discussed in Chapter 14.

OBJECTIVES OF STUDENTS IN PHYSICAL EDUCATION PROGRAMS

A survey of approximately 2,500 students at various educational levels was conducted in my classes to determine what students' objectives were in taking physical education. Students were surveyed concerning who represented various kinds of individual differences and constituted the following categories: normal, academically gifted, culturally disadvantaged, poorly coordinated, emotionally disturbed, mentally retarded, and physically handicapped. Each student was asked the following two questions: "What do you want to get out of your physical education class?" and "What should the physical education program do for you as a student?" The following represents a summary of the findings of this survey.

1. *At the primary grade level* (kindergarten to third grade), students viewed the physical education program as a place to run, have fun, and learn games. These youngsters also desired exercise so that they could grow to be big and strong. Some students at this early age indicated that they wanted to learn how to become an athlete and wanted to play on a team. Poorly coordinated children hoped that they could improve their fitness so that they could rejoin their regular class. Mentally retarded youngsters indicated that they hoped physical education would make them "smarter."

2. *At the intermediate grade level* (fourth to sixth grades), students indicated that the physical education program should provide an opportunity to have fun and to learn skills and various sports. They also indicated the need for exercise to improve their fitness. At this age level it was almost unanimous that physical education

At the primary grade level the survey showed that students viewed the physical education program as a place to run, have fun, and learn games. A second-grade class is engaged in ball throwing and activities using fleece balls at Hudson Falls Central School, Hudson Falls, New York.

was viewed as a place where new friendships could be made. Students also emphasized the point that the physical education program gave them the opportunity to "show off" and that they were also able to relieve their tensions.

3. *At the junior high level* (seventh to ninth grades), students again stated that physical education should be concerned with improving one's fitness and health. Students indicated that they wanted to learn new skills and many sports. They also indicated that physical education should do more than just develop the body; it should also develop the mind and prepare students for their future work. Junior high level students viewed physical education as a place to learn fair play and good sportsmanship. They also emphasized the point that they wanted to learn activities which would prove useful in their leisure hours. The majority of students at this age also indicated the desire to play on a team.

4. *At the high school level* (tenth to twelfth grades), students stressed the point that exercise was important because it improved one's health and fitness. Students indicated that they wanted to learn many skills and sports. They also

wanted to participate in activities that will benefit them in their leisure time. At this level, students desired to play harmoniously with others and to participate in team play. Students at the high school level viewed the physical education class as a place where they could learn to respect their fellow students. Students also indicated that the physical education program provided them with a change of pace from their academic subjects.

5. *At the college level,* students emphasized the importance that physical education plays in neuromuscular development and cardiovascular efficiency. Students indicated that physical education provided them with mental stimulation and gave them the opportunity to socialize with others. College students also stated that physical education provided them with mental relaxation from their academic studies and introduced them to activities which would prove useful in their leisure time. College students viewed physical education as a contribution to one's mental, physical, psychological, and social development.

Most of the students surveyed, regardless of how they differed from the other students, had

DEVELOPMENTAL OBJECTIVES OF PHYSICAL EDUCATION

ORGANIC

Proper functioning of the body systems so that the individual may adequately meet the demands placed upon him by his environment. A foundation for skill development.

Muscle Strength

The maximum amount of force exerted by a muscle or muscle group.

Muscle Endurance

The ability of a muscle or muscle group to sustain effort for a prolonged period of time.

Cardiovascular Endurance

The capacity of an individual to persist in strenuous activity for periods of some duration. This is dependent upon the combined efficiency of the blood vessels, heart, and lungs.

Flexibility

The range of motion in joints needed to produce efficient movement and minimize injury.

NEUROMUSCULAR

A harmonious functioning of the nervous and muscular systems to produce desired movements.

Locomotor Skills

Walking   Skipping   Sliding   Leaping   Pushing
Running   Galloping   Hopping   Rolling   Pulling

Nonlocomotor Skills

Swaying   Twisting   Shaking   Stretching
Bending   Handing   Stooping

Game Type Fundamental Skills

Striking   Catching   Kicking   Stopping
Throwing   Batting   Starting   Changing direction

Motor Factors

Accuracy   Rhythm   Kinesthetic awareness
Power   Balance   Reaction time   Agility

Sport Skills

Soccer   Softball   Volleyball   Wrestling
Track & Field   Football   Baseball
Basketball   Archery   Speedball   Hockey
Fencing   Golf   Bowling   Tennis

Recreational Skills

Shuffleboard   Croquet   Deck tennis   Hiking
Table tennis   Swimming   Horseshoes   Boating

INTERPRETIVE

The ability to explore, to discover, to understand, to acquire knowledge, and to make value judgments.

A knowledge of game rules, safety measures, and etiquette.

The use of strategies and techniques involved in organized activities.

A knowledge of how the body functions and its relationship to physical activity.

A development of appreciation for personal performance. The use of judgment related to distance, time, space, force, speed, and direction in the use of activity implements, balls, and self.

An understanding of growth and developmental factors affected by movement.

The ability to solve developmental problems through movement.

SOCIAL

An adjustment to both self and others by an integration of the individual to society and his environment.

The ability to make judgments in a group situation.

Learning to communicate with others.

The ability to exchange and evaluate ideas within a group.

The development of the social phases of personality, attitudes, and values in order to become a functioning member of society.

The development of a sense of belonging and acceptance by society.

The development of positive personality traits.

Learnings for constructive use of leisure time.

A development of attitude that reflects good moral character.

EMOTIONAL

A healthy response to physical activity through a fulfillment of basic needs.

The development of positive reactions in spectatorship and participation through either success or failure.

The release of tension through suitable physical activities.

An outlet for self-expression and creativity.

An appreciation of the aesthetic experiences derived from correlated activities.

The ability to have fun.

From Annarino, Anthony A.: The five traditional objectives of physical education, Journal of Health, Physical Education, and Recreation **41:**24, *June, 1970.*

similar ideas as to the contribution physical education could make to their lives.

OBJECTIVES IN TERMS OF SCIENTIFIC PRINCIPLES

The professional literature has several books that discuss the principles of physical education. According to Williams,* principles are concepts that have a scientific foundation and are based on facts or on philosophical inquiry. The source of principles therefore can come from philosophy through insight, experience, or understanding, such as the principle that the democratic concept helps to assure the dignity of human beings. In the field of physical education a principle of this type might be that the welfare of the participant rather than the welfare of the school should dominate athletic programs.

Principles also are derived from scientific facts from sources such as anatomy, physiology, psychology, and other sciences. Darwin, for example, found that the principle of natural selection was valid from his study of animal life, and Cannon found that the principle of homeostasis was valid from his studies. In the field of physical education the sciences of anatomy, physiology, and psychology, for example, provide principles regarding the developmental stages of the vital organs and the laws of learning.

Principles that give support and a scientific foundation to objectives have been set forth by Adams† based on his research into the writings of many outstanding leaders in the field.

1. *Education involves the whole organism.* Oneness of mind and body or the unity of human beings is a recognized basic tenet of education.

2. *Physical education is a phase of general education.* The objectives toward which physical education is striving are compatible and contribute to the objectives of general education.

3. *Physical education activity is conducive to*

---

*Williams, Jesse Feiring: The principles of physical education, Philadelphia, 1964, W. B. Saunders Co., Chapter 1.
†Adams, Miller K.: Principles for determining high school grading procedures in physical education for boys, Doctoral thesis, New York University, 1959.

growth and development. The optimum development of the organic systems of the human body depend on physical activity.

4. *Physical education contributes to the constructive use of leisure time.* Many skills and activities learned in physical education have implications for free hours during all of a person's life.

5. *Physical education provides for leadership training.* There is great potential and opportunity within physical education to involve students in the planning and operation of the program.

6. *Physical education provides opportunity for expression and creativity.* There are many opportunities in physical education to utilize the body as a means of expressing one's feelings and creating new patterns of movement and ideas.

7. *Physical education provides for cultural development.* Sports and physical activities play an important role in the cultures of all peoples. These activities are a positive source of both esthetic appreciations and artistic production for the participant.

8. *Physical education provides opportunities to control emotions.* The give and take of games and sports offers opportunities for both emotional release and the controlling of the emotions.

9. *Physical education provides for personality and character development.* Group effort, loyalty to the team, and strong ties are much in evidence on play and sports fields. As such, they provide a valuable contribution to the development of character and personality. The daily adjustments to teammates and opponents become a laboratory in personal social adjustment.

10. *Physical education provides for organic development—physical fitness.* Exercise and knowledge about one's body and its requirements contribute immeasurably to physical fitness.

11. *Physical education develops neuromuscular skills.* Skills in a variety of sports and activities present many opportunities for instructing pupils in this phase of their development.

12. *Physical education develops habits of health and safety.* The teacher of physical edu-

cation instructs the pupils in habits of health and safety, and games and contests are played under conditions conducive to learning safety and health practices.

13. *Physical education provides for mental development.* The learning of game rules, techniques, and strategies, as well as the judgments necessary to good play in competitive games, requires interpretive development. Other avenues for mental development are inculcating understanding about one's body and how it functions, the history of sports, the place of athletic activities in the cultures of the world, and other knowledge closely allied to physical education.

14. *Physical education contributes to democratic processes.* The physical education class is conducted in a manner that provides pupils with the opportunity to participate in planning and carrying out class activities.

15. *Physical education has biological, psychological, and sociological foundations.* Physical education has its bases in the sciences of biology, psychology, and sociology. The program is planned by teachers and administrators who draw on these sciences for realistic and effective programs.

16. *Physical education is based on human needs.* Movement is recognized as an important human need. The need for physical activity is essential to life itself. Modern living with its sedentary aspects presents a challenge to physical education.

17. *Play is an instinctive drive that has educational potential.* The dynamic quality of play can be utilized to instill in participants proper forms of conduct and behavior.

FULLER DISCUSSION OF OBJECTIVES OF PHYSICAL EDUCATION

A study of the objectives as stated by leaders in physical education reveals a great deal of similarity. This is as it should be in that the physical education profession should be united and directing itself toward common goals. Only through a uniformity of purpose will it be possible for the thousands of professional leaders in this field to be continually conscious of what they are trying to accomplish when they meet their class, organize a game, supervise a program of activities, and evaluate their work. In unity there is strength.

The aim of all education is to enable one to live an enriched and abundant life. This is the ultimate goal on which all who are concerned with education have trained their sights. The objectives of physical education are more definite and specific than this aim, and with these objectives the ultimate goal is brought nearer to realization.

A study of human beings reveals four general directions or phases in which growth and development take place: physical development, motor and movement development, mental development, and social development. Each of these phases contributes to the well-rounded individual who will become a worthy member of society. Physical education can contribute importantly to each of these phases of growth and development. The objectives listed by current leaders of physical education in the majority of cases may be incorporated under these groupings. It is believed that physical education will justify its existence if it can accomplish the objectives that are set forth under these four headings.

Physical development objective*

The objective of physical development deals with the program of activities that build physical power in an individual by developing the various organic systems of the body. It results in the ability to sustain adaptive effort, the ability to recover, and the ability to resist fatigue. The value of this objective is based on the fact that an individual will be more active, have better performance, and be healthier if the organic systems of the body are adequately developed and functioning properly.

Muscular activity plays a major role in the development of the organic systems of the body. The term *organic* refers to the digestive, circulatory, excretory, heat regulatory, respiratory, and other systems of the human body. These systems are stimulated and trained through activities such as hanging, climbing, running, throwing, leaping, carrying, and

---

*See also Chapters 11 and 12.

jumping. Health is also related to muscular activity; therefore activities that bring into play all the fundamental "big-muscle" groups in the body should be engaged in regularly. Furthermore, the activity should be of a vigorous nature so that the various organic systems are sufficiently stimulated.

With vigorous muscular activity, several beneficial results take place. The trained heart provides better nourishment to the entire body. The trained heart beats slower than the untrained heart and pumps more blood per stroke, with the result that more food is delivered to the cells and there is better removal of waste products. During exercise the trained heart's speed increases less and has a longer rest period between beats, and after exercise it returns to normal much more rapidly. The end result of this state is that the trained individual can perform work for a longer period of time, with less expenditure of energy, and much more efficiently than the untrained individual. This trained condition is necessary to a vigorous and abundant life. From the time of arising in the morning to retiring at night, an individual is continually in need of vitality, strength, endurance, and stamina to perform routine tasks and to be prepared for emergencies and lead a vigorous life. Therefore physical education should aid in the development of the trained individual so that he or she will be better able to perform routine tasks and live a healthful and happy existence.

Hetherington* points out that physical activity is the only source of development of the latent powers of the organism that are inherited. Although sleep, nutrition, and rest, for example, contribute to the proper functioning of the organism, they have no power to develop latent resources, which physical activity does accomplish. Hetherington also points out that a healthy nervous system depends on vigorous physical activity during the early years of childhood and youth. He explains that the only way in which nerve centers can be reached and developed is through physical activity involving exercising the muscles which the nervous system controls.

Hein and Ryan* did an extensive research study, collecting and analyzing clinical observations and scientific findings on the contributions of physical activity to physical health. They believe the following conclusions can be justified as a result of their work:

1. Regular exercise can assist in the prevention of obesity with the result that the shortened life span and degenerative conditions caused by such a condition can be influenced.
2. Regular physical activity throughout life appears to inhibit coronary heart disease.
3. Regular physical activity assists in delaying the aging process and probably favorably influences longevity.
4. Regular physical activity contributes to a body condition that enables the individual to better meet emergencies and thus, in turn, enhance health and avoid disability.

Motor and movement development objective

The motor and movement development objective is concerned with developing body awareness and making physical movement useful, with as little expenditure of energy as possible, and with being proficient, graceful, and esthetic in this movement. This has implications for one's work, play, and other activities that require physical movement. The name *motor* is derived from the relationship to a nerve or nerve fiber that connects the central nervous system or a ganglion with a muscle. As a consequence of the impulse it transmits, movement results. The impulse it delivers is known as the motor impulse.

Effective movement and motor behavior results in esthetic qualities of movement and in the development of a movement sense, which in essence is the development of motor skill together with appropriate knowledge about the skill and an appropriate attitude toward its development and use. In other words, proper control of skill in movement during all life's pat-

---

*Hetherington, Clark W.: School program in physical education, New York, 1922, Harcourt, Brace & World, Inc.

*Hein, Fred V., and Ryan, Allan J.: The contributions of physical activity to physical health, Research Quarterly **31:**263, 1960.

From Michaelson, Mike: Judo: now it's a safe family sport, Today's Health, Feb., 1969.

Judo contributes to physical development objective.

A basketball becomes a piece of physical education equipment for an elementary school student in a movement exploration program at Public School No. 15, Brooklyn, New York.

terns and routines takes place in the movement-educated person.

Effective motor movement depends on a harmonious working together of the muscular and nervous systems. It results in greater distance between fatigue and peak performance; it is found in activities such as running, hanging, jumping, dodging, leaping, kicking, bending, twisting, carrying, and throwing; and it will enable a person to perform his daily work much more efficiently and without reaching the point of being "worn out" so quickly.

In physical education activities the function of efficient body movement, or *neuromuscular skill* as it is often called, is to provide the individual with the ability to perform with a degree of perfection. This will result in an enjoyment of participation. Most individuals enjoy doing those particular things in which they have acquired some degree of mastery or skill. For example, if a child has mastered the ability to throw a ball consistently at a designated spot and has developed batting and fielding power, he or she will like to play baseball or softball. If the child can kick and throw a ball with some degree of accuracy, then it will be soccer or football. Few individuals enjoy participating in activities in which they have little skill. Therefore it is the objective of physical education to develop in all individuals as many skills as possible so that their interests will be wide and varied. This will not only result in more enjoyment for the participant, but at the same time it will allow for a better adjustment to the group situation.

Other values of skill are that it cuts down on expenditure of energy, contributes to confidence, brings recognition, enhances physical and mental health, makes participation safer, and contributes to the esthetic sense.

The motor objective also has important implications for the health and recreational outcomes of the program. The skills that persons acquire will determine to a great extent how their leisure time will be spent. If a person excels in swimming, much leisure time is going to be spent in a pool, lake, or other body of water. If the person excels in tennis, he or she will be found frequently on the courts. Physical educators should develop in all individuals an understanding and appreciation of human movement and their unique movement potentialities.

When considering the value to young people who are in school of having in their possession fundamental skills that will afford them much satisfaction and happiness throughout life, it is important to consider the balance that should exist in any physical education program between team sports and dual and individual sports. Team sports such as football, basketball, and baseball perform a great service in providing an opportunity for students to devel-

op physical power and enjoy exhilarating competition. However, in many school programs of physical education they dominate the curriculum at the expense of various individual and dual sports, such as tennis, swimming, badminton, handball, and golf. In such cases the students are being deprived of the opportunity for developing skills in activities that they can participate in throughout their adult life. It has been estimated that only one out of every 1,000 students who play football, for example, ever play the game again after they leave school. On the other hand, if they have the skill, many students will swim or play tennis, badminton, handball, or golf. Only through a well-balanced program of team, dual, and individual sports will it be possible to develop the well-rounded individual.

Physical educators can and should be proud of the contribution they make to humanity. It is

Courtesy American Broadcasting Co.

Skill in bowling.

within their power to help many persons learn physical skills and thus help them to lead healthier, happier, and more worthwhile and productive lives. The world is a better place in which to live as a result of their work because *physical skill has value*.

Cognitive development objective

The cognitive development objective deals with the accumulation of a body of knowledge and the ability to think and to interpret this knowledge.

Physical education has a subject matter that is concerned with movement. There is a body of knowledge that comes from the sciences, humanities, and other sources, which interprets the nature of human movement and the impact of movement on the growth and development of the individual and on his culture. Scientific principles regarding movement, including those which relate to such factors as time, space, and flow, should be considered. This subject matter should be part of the education of each person who comes in contact with a physical education program.

Physical activities must be learned; hence there is a need for thinking on the part of the intellectual mechanism, with a resulting acquisition of knowledge. The coordinations involved in various movements must be mastered and adapted to the environment in which the individual lives, whether it be in walking, running, or wielding a tennis racquet. In all these movements the participant must think and coordinate the muscular and nervous systems. Furthermore, this type of knowledge is acquired through trial and error, and then, as a result of this experience, there is a changed meaning in the situation. Coordinations are learned, with the result that an act which once was difficult and awkward to perform becomes easy.

The individual not only should learn coordination but also should acquire a knowledge of rules, techniques, and strategies involved in physical activities. Basketball can be used as an example. In this sport a person should know the rules, the strategy in offense and defense, the various types of passes, the difference between screening and blocking, and finally, the values that are derived from playing this sport. Tech-

niques learned through experience result in knowledge that should also be acquired. For example, a ball travels faster and more accurately if one steps with a pass, and time is saved when the pass is made from the same position in which it is received. Furthermore, a knowledge of followership, leadership, courage, self-reliance, assistance to others, safety, and adaptation to group patterns is important.

Knowledge concerning health should play an important part in the program. All individuals should know about their bodies, the importance of cleanliness, factors in disease prevention, importance of exercise, need for a well-balanced diet, values of good health attitudes and habits, and the community and school agencies that provide health services. With the accumulation of a knowledge of these facts, activities will take on a new meaning, and health practices will be associated with definite purposes. This will help each individual live a healthier and more purposeful life.

Physical educators can intellectualize their activities more. Physical activities are not performed in a vacuum. Physical educators should continually provide appropriate knowledge and information for participants and encourage them to ask the question, "Why?" *Why* is it important to play this activity? *Why* should an hour a day be devoted to physical education? *Why* is exercise important? *Why* is it important to play according to the rules? Physical educators should also give participants more opportunities to think, that is, allow them to make choices, plan strategies, and call plays and not usurp all of this responsibility themselves. *The more thinking that takes place on the part of the participant the more educational the activity becomes.*

Social development objective

The social development objective is concerned with helping an individual in making personal adjustments, group adjustments, and adjustments as a member of society. Activities in the physical education program offer one of the best opportunities for making these adjustments, provided there is proper leadership.

Physical educators should find as many ways as possible to influence human behavior for the good. The rules of the game are the rules of the democratic way of life. In games, one sees democracy in action and appreciates an individual on the basis of ability and performance. Economic status, background, race, or other discriminatory characteristics do not play a role. Performance is the sole criterion of success.

Another aspect of the social objective of physical education that is being recognized is the need for each person to develop an appropriate self-concept. Participants need to develop wholesome attitudes toward themselves as maturing persons. During the various stages of physical growth through which young people go, they are often accepted or rejected by their classmates because of their physical characteristics. It is therefore important for individuals to develop themselves physically, not only for reasons of their own self-awareness but also because of the implications that their physique and physical skills have for their social image.

Each individual has certain basic social needs that must be met. These include a feeling of belonging, recognition, self-respect, and love. When these needs are met, the individual becomes well adjusted socially. When they are not met, antisocial characteristics develop. For example, the aggressive bully may be seeking recognition, and the member of the gang may be seeking a feeling of belonging. The "needs" theory has implications for the manner in which physical education programs are conducted. The desire to win, for example, should be subordinated to meeting the needs of the participants.

All human beings should experience success. This factor can be realized in play. Through successful experience in play activities, persons develop self-confidence and find happiness in their achievements. Physical education can provide for this successful experience by offering a variety of activities and developing the necessary skills for success in these activities.

In the democratic society it is necessary to have all individuals develop a sense of group consciousness and cooperative living. This should be one of the most important objectives of the program. Whether children will grow up to be good citizens and contribute to the welfare of all will depend to a great extent on the training they receive during their youth. Therefore in various play activities the following factors should be stressed: aid for the less skilled and weaker players, respect for the rights of others,

All human beings should experience success. These students are experiencing success as they go over homemade hurdles of conduit tubing at Oak View Elementary School in Fairfax, Virginia.

subordination of one's desires to the will of the group, and realization of cooperative living as being essential to the success of society. Individuals should be made to feel that they belong to the group and have the responsibility of directing their actions in its behalf. The rules of sportsmanship should be developed and practiced in all activities offered in the program. Qualities such as courtesy, sympathy, truthfulness, fairness, honesty, respect for authority, and abiding by the rules will help considerably in the promotion of social efficiency. The necessity of good leadership and followership should also be stressed as important to the interests of society.

"Plus factor"—affective development objective

Another factor that should not be overlooked is the "plus factor," or affective development.

Physical educators cannot be content once they have developed the physical body, laid down the skills in the nervous system, and developed the amenities of social behavior. There is still something else, affective development, and this represents one of the greatest challenges to the field in which so many young people have a drive to engage.

Members of the physical education profession should be concerned with helping young people to clarify and think through their value judgments, appreciations, and attitudes. Although physical educators should not indoctrinate the student with their individual value system, much can be done to motivate boys and girls to analyze and assess their own values and attitudes. If physical educators achieve these things, their profession will grow and prosper because it has been built on strong foundations; it will be used in the interest of helping people to live more abundant lives and to achieve excellence in their endeavors.

Adults are also interested in achieving the objectives of physical education. Two adults play racquetball at the Fitness and Recreation Center, Xerox Corporation, Leesburg, Virginia.

A NEW LOOK AT OBJECTIVES

The most systematic approach in developing a system of objectives has been worked out by Bloom* and Krathwohl and associates† in their "taxonomic system." The purpose of this system is to enable teachers and other educators to effectively communicate the nature and scope of instructional objectives.

In developing this system, they divided instructional objectives into the following three domains:

1. *Cognitive.* The recognition of knowledge in the development of intellectual ability and skill
2. *Affective.* An expression of an individual's attitudes, values, and appreciation
3. *Psychomotor.* Development of manipulative skills

---

*Bloom, Benjamin S., editor: Taxonomy of educational objectives. Handbook I. Cognitive domain, New York, 1956, David McKay Co., Inc.
†Krathwohl, David R., and others: Taxonomy of educational objectives. Handbook II. Affective domain, New York, 1956, David McKay Co., Inc.

These three objective domains are interdependent and continuous, and all the domains are responsive to the individual needs and developmental tasks of the learner. The accompanying illustration represents the interdependence of the three domains.

BEHAVIORAL OBJECTIVES

Behavioral objective is a term frequently used in recent years and is a method of specifically stating educational goals by observing and measuring student behavior.

It is generally agreed that students exhibit behavior in the three domains previously discussed: the cognitive, affective, and psychomotor domains. Behavioral objectives may be developed for each of these domains, and they should contain two essential parts: (1) the observable behavior and (2) the criteria of acceptable performance. It is extremely important that behavioral objectives be specific. For example, a behavioral objective might be as follows: The

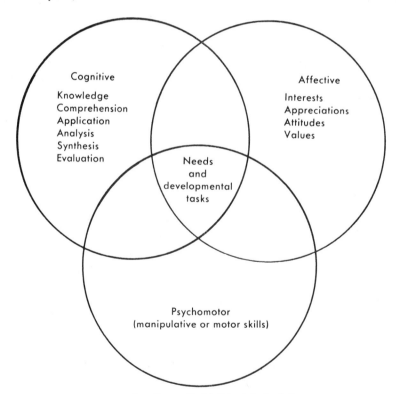

From Tanner, Daniel: Using behavioral objectives in the classroom, New York, 1972. The Macmillan Co.

Interdependence of cognitive, affective, and psychomotor domains and their relationship to needs and developmental tasks.

student will return the tennis ball in a forehand position over the net. This objective in the psychomotor domain specifically states that the observable behavior is returning the ball in a forehand position, and the criteria of acceptability is that ball be returned over the net. The important point to remember is that the physical educator must be specific in the behavior he wants to elicit from the student.

PERFORMANCE AND COMPETENCY OBJECTIVES

Competency may be defined as a demonstrated ability that can be required for performance in a specific occupational or professional role. The major purposes of competency or performance-based programs are as follows:

1. To identify and state educational goals in terms of the competencies (that is, skills, knowledge, abilities) learners should acquire
2. To develop procedures whereby individuals may be assessed and awarded credentials when these competencies are mastered
3. To develop educational experiences that will result in the attainment of competencies

Traditionally, the assessment of learning has been based on how persons compare with others in the comprehension of subject matter. Competency-based learning, however, stresses the results of the learning rather than the process. It is the competency of each individual that matters, not his or her competency when compared with that of others.

IS THERE A PRIORITY FOR OBJECTIVES OF PHYSICAL EDUCATION?

Leaders of physical education are beginning to ask questions such as: Is one objective of physical education more important than the others? Where should the emphasis in physical education programs be placed? Physical educators cannot do everything, but what comes first? Does physical education have a master purpose? Is there a hierarchy of objectives?

Historically, as previously discussed, physical education in its early days was primarily concerned with organic development. However, at the turn of the century with the introduction of the "new physical education," other objectives more closely identified with general education, such as social development, were included. Today, there are varying viewpoints in regard to the question of priority of objectives.

A survey of selected leaders in the field of physical education asking for their views about a priority of objectives resulted in some interesting information. Most professionals contacted believed that organic development and neuromuscular and movement development are the objectives which should get highest priority. These leaders listed reasons such as the following: These objectives are uniquely tied in with physical education, they are essential for fitness throughout life, they provide the impetus for the program, and they represent the objectives that can more readily be achieved. After organic and neuromuscular development, the leaders surveyed indicated that the most widely accepted objective in terms of importance is mental or interpretive development. The reasons listed for the importance of this objective included the fact that it is important to develop a favorable attitude toward physical education if any objective is to be achieved at all. Also included was the fact that education is primarily involved with developing a thinking, rational human being in respect to all matters, whether it be concerned with one's physical development or other aspects of living. Social development ranked lowest in the survey. Reasons given to support this place on the priority listing were that all areas of education are interested in the social objectives and that it was not the unique responsibility of one field, such as physical education. Therefore the other objectives should receive a higher priority rating.

The survey of national leaders in physical education brought out another important consideration. Many professional leaders stressed the point that, with the national curriculum reform movement taking place today and with increased emphasis on educational priorities, physical educators should rethink their positions in regard to their place in the educational system. They should reexamine how they can contribute their best effort and make their greatest contribution in today's changing world.

Rosentswieg* conducted a study in which he

---

*Rosentswieg, Joel: A ranking of the objectives of physical education, Research Quarterly **40:**783, 1969.

had 100 college physical educators in Texas rank ten objectives of physical education. Rosentwieg's findings showed that these 100 physical educators ranked the organic and neuromuscular objectives higher than all the rest. When the male physical educators were compared with the female physical educators, there was disagreement on the primary objective of physical education. The statistical results of the study are illustrated in Tables 3-1 and 3-2.

Perhaps it will help the reader to clarify his or her own priority system by answering the following questions.

1. *Does the nature of education give us a clue to a priority arrangement of physical education objectives?* According to many educational leaders today, the business of education is concerned primarily with the development of the intellect, the power of good reasoning, and the application of logic. The "life adjustment" type of education is being sidetracked, and more and more emphasis is being given to the development of mental skills, the acquisition of knowledge, and cognitive development. Does this mean that physical education, since it is a part of education and since we use the term *physical education*, should also give more emphasis in this direction? Such emphasis would not be for the purpose of being labeled *academic* but instead to help human beings become more fully aware of the values of physical activity in their physical, social and mental development.

2. *Does history give us a clue?* A historical analysis of objectives of physical education indicates that in addition to organic development and the teaching of physical skills, it is also important to consider the interpretive-mental and social development objectives. History seems to have recorded that physical educators should not limit themselves merely to muscular grace but should also be concerned with these objectives, which can be accomplished through the physical. The emphasis on human relations—for example, the fact that this nation is a democracy and the belief that the individual has worth—should permeate programs of physical education.

3. *Do the outcomes that we more readily achieve give us a clue?* Physical educators proudly demonstrate with measurement and evaluation instruments the amount of strength and other qualities of physical fitness they develop in their students. The headlines of newspapers and other communication media proclaim the success that is theirs in developing skills. However, data are not readily available to show the degree to which physical educators develop mental skills and qualities such as sportsmanship, respect for opponents, and courage. It is not difficult for physical education to show its accomplishments in the physical and skill objectives, but there is less evidence for the other objectives. Part of the reason for this lies in the lack of objective instruments for measurement purposes, such as being able to mea-

Table 3-1. Comparison ranking of objectives of physical education*

Objective	Ranking
Organic vigor	1
Neuromuscular skills	2
Leisure-time activities	3
Self-realization	4
Emotional stability	5
Democratic values	6
Mental development	7
Social competency	8
Spiritual and moral strength	9
Cultural appreciation	10

*From Rosentswieg, Joel: A ranking of the objectives of physical education, Research Quarterly **40:**783, 1969.

Table 3-2. Ranking of objectives by sex*

Objective	Ranking	
	Males	Females
Organic vigor	1	2
Neuromuscular skills	2	1
Leisure-time activities	3	3
Self-realization	4	4
Emotional stability	5	5
Social competency	6	8
Democratic values	7	7
Mental development	8	6
Spiritual and moral strength	9	9
Cultural appreciation	10	10

*From Rosentswieg, Joel: A ranking of the objectives of physical education, Research Quarterly **40:**783, 1969.

sure qualities of sportsmanship. However, at the same time it may also indicate the lack of interest on the part of many physical educators to gear their programs in these directions, their failure to recognize the importance of these objectives, the difficulties encountered in trying to achieve these goals, or a belief that such responsibilities should be accomplished by the academic subjects or the home.

4. *Do the nature and needs of society and the individual give us a clue?* Will the study of society's social problems, including poverty, juvenile delinquency, crime, and health, provide a clue as to what we should be concerned with in physical education? If so, does this mean that objectives become more important in some segments of society than in others? Also, what about the needs of the individual? What represents the needs of human beings for the "good life"? Are they physical, mental, neuromuscular, or social? What needs are the most important for physical education to consider? What needs should be met by the home, church, and school? Which ones should be met by academic subjects — by physical education — and by agencies outside the school? If a boy or girl is subpar physically, does this mean that the organic development objective should get priority? If he or she is a delinquent, should the social objective get priority? What does it mean?

5. *Does the term "physical education" give us a clue?* If physical education is concerned with education of and through the physical, does this indicate a priority? All the objectives of physical education are implied in the term as defined. Physical educators are concerned with the *physical* and also with *education*. This means that all objectives should be involved. But does it provide a priority rating?

6. *Does the "fitness" movement give us a clue?* As a result of the concern of the government for the physical fitness of the nation's children and youth and as a result of the establishment of the President's Council for Physical Fitness and Sports, with its wide exposure by communication media, there has been much emphasis on physical fitness — one objective of physical education. In some institutions of learning and in other agencies, priority has been

given to the organic development or the physical fitness development objective. Has this been good or harmful?

Should all objectives receive equal emphasis? Is this the answer? How do physical educators resolve this important problem? Professional associations should give considerable thought and effort to finding the answer. Leadership must be given because many practitioners are seeking the answer.

Regardless of what the outcome is, in the last analysis the individual physical educator will be the person to make the decision. What is emphasized within the program from day to day will be the answer. This will depend on the instructor's philosophy and understanding of the worth of physical education and what physical education can and should be trying to contribute to human beings and to society.

CONCEPT APPROACH AND SCHOOL PROGRAMS OF PHYSICAL EDUCATION

Jerome Bruner, in his book *The Process of Education,* discusses the structure of subject matter and states: "The more fundamental or basic the idea learned, the greater will be its breadth of applicability." A concept is an idea and is derived from the Latin word meaning "to conceive." Webster defines a concept as "a mental image of a thing formed by generalizations from particulars." In other words, it means abstracting and generalizing. Concepts are derived from facts and are expressed in understandable form. They evolve gradually.

According to Bruner, any educational discipline includes basic concepts, principles, generalizations, and insights. The curriculum should have a structure that contains subdivisions of knowledge pertinent to the field of specialization. The problem is then one of developing a structure that embraces the basic concepts around which basic principles, theories, and knowledge can be organized and discussed in meaningful terms. The real purpose of education is to teach concepts. If students understand a concept, it will free them from remembering many isolated facts.

Physical education should consider the use of established concepts as a means of structuring its field so that physical education can be taught in a more meaningful manner. The basic concepts of physical education are to be found within the stated objectives of the field.

Physical education, as a part of education, should provide each person with carefully planned experiences that result in knowledge about the value of physical activity, essential motor skills, strength, stamina, and other essential physical characteristics and the social qualities that make for effective citizenship.

Each subject-matter field has objectives toward which it teaches and that represent the worth of the field. Physical education has traditionally advocated the four objectives of organic development, neuromuscular development, cognitive development, and social development. These goals have proved valuable as targets toward which both the teacher and student strive. At the same time, they are rather general in nature and it seems do not provide the best basis for the most effective structural organization of physical education.

In creating this structure of physical educa-

tion, an analogy can be drawn between this field and the construction of a house. Just as there are key pillars and beams that give the house form and support, so are there key unifying elements within physical education that give it a strong foundational framework and hold it together as a valuable educational experience for every boy and girl. These key elements would be identified and would tie together the various parts of the discipline into a meaningful and cohesive learning package. These elements would be the *concepts* of physical education and, as such, would represent the basic structure of physical education in the school program. They would be the key ideas, principles, skills, values, or attitudes that represent points on which physical educators should focus their attention. They would be part of both the teacher's and the student's thinking and would range from simple ideas to high-level abstractions. They would start with simple, elementary, fundamental experiences and in a sequential, progressive, and developmental pattern gain depth and comprehensiveness over the years as schooling pro-

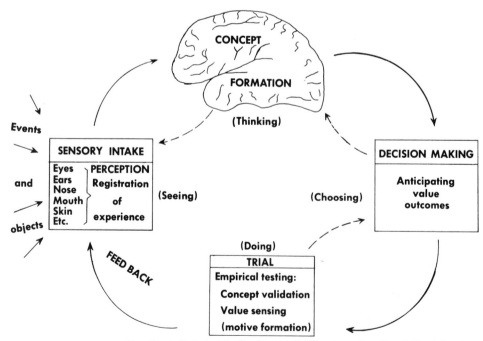

From Woodruff, Asahael D.: Cognitive models of learning and teaching. In Siegel, L., editor:
Contemporary theories of instruction, San Francisco, Chandler Publishing Co.

Cognitive cycle in behavior and learning.

Preamble*

1. Physical education activities should be progressively administered from simple to complex levels throughout the period of the secondary school.
2. Appropriate records on all students should be maintained.
3. Appropriate provisions should be made for the handicapped and low-fitness students.
4. Comprehensive and effective intramural and interschool programs supplement the instructional program.
5. Participation in musical organizations, driver education, or military training should not be permitted to serve as a substitute for instruction in physical education since the specific objectives and the means of attaining the objectives of each differ widely.

The physically educated boy and girl

Attitudes	*Knowledge and appreciations*	*Skills*	*Social attributes*
1. Interest in health and being healthy	1. Understanding and appreciation of his or her body, and a feeling of responsibility for personal maintenance	1. The body in proper balance while standing, sitting, and walking	1. Secure in social situations, i.e., acts with confidence, is courteous, etc.
2. Desire to participate in physical education activities and enjoy play with group	2. Basic understanding of physical movement and relaxation	2. Ability to relax	2. Respects his opponent
3. Desire to become physically educated	3. Knowledge of interrelationship of physical, mental, emotional and social aspects of the human being	3. Proper rhythmic response to music including basic skills in square, folk, social and modern dance	3. Respects and cooperates with authority
	4. An understanding of the rules, strategies, techniques, and history of games, sports, and other physical activities important in our culture	4. Application of fundamental skills such as running, jumping, skipping, and throwing to actual game situations	4. Plays within the letter as well as the spirit of the rules
	5. An understanding of the importance of exercise to health	5. Swim one-quarter mile and be secure in deep water	5. Uses acceptable language in all situations
	6. An insight into individual capacities and limitations in regard to physical activity	6. Skill and proficiency in a minimum of one different team sport each season of the year	6. Maintains self-control at all times
	7. An understanding of the signs and symptoms of fitness and unfitness	7. Skill and proficiency in a minimum of one different individual sport each year	
		8. An annual experience during the secondary school period in self-testing activities such as apparatus, tumbling, track and field, marching, calisthenics, etc.	

*National Conference on Fitness for Secondary School Youth, Washington, D.C., Dec., 1958 (mimeographed).

gresses and the student matures. These concepts would thus define the domain of physical education.

Concepts in physical education would not be memorized by the students. Rather, they would be ideas, analytical generalizations that would emerge and be understood by the student as a result of school experiences in physical education. They would also provide the student with a reservoir of information, skills, and understandings that would be of help in meeting new problems and situations.

The concepts, of course, would have to be carefully selected according to acceptable criteria and be scientifically sound. Furthermore, after the concepts have been identified, there would be a need for extensive testing of their validity by many experts, including teachers in the field and specialists in curriculum development.

To implement the concepts within the physical education structure, the identified concepts would need to be delineated into meaningful units and topics that would be progressive in nature and reinforce the concepts that had been identified. The subdivisions of concepts in the structure would represent basic elements needed to develop a meaningful course of study and bring about desirable behavior. Furthermore, they would emanate and flow from the key concepts and would help to give greater meaning and understanding to them. As the conceptual unifying threads were developed at each ascending grade and educational level, the student would be provided with new challenges to which the information, skills, and understanding that has been acquired could be applied. The result would be that finally the student would reach a point where he or she could arrive at valid answers and make wise decisions in the area of physical education.

As a result of the conceptual approach, students would have a greater mastery of the field of physical education, increased understanding and power in dealing with new and unfamiliar problems related to their physical selves, and be better motivated to want to become physically educated in the true sense of the term. The approach would provide a stable system of knowledge and provide guideposts for thinking intelligently about physical education.

PHYSICALLY EDUCATED BOYS AND GIRLS: THE ULTIMATE OBJECTIVE FOR SCHOOL PROGRAMS OF PHYSICAL EDUCATION

When a boy or girl becomes mathematically educated, he or she has taken fundamental courses in arithmetic, algebra, geometry, trigonometry, and calculus. When he or she becomes science educated, experiences have been provided in general science, biology, physics, chemistry, and the other sciences.

What does it mean to be *physically educated?* An important challenge facing the profession of physical education is to establish standards in regard to skills, knowledge, attitudes, and social attributes for the various educational levels, the mastery of which will result in a student being physically educated. When this job has been accomplished, the profession will have taken a forward step in establishing itself as a more important part of the educational program.

In 1958 a subcommittee of the National Conference for Fitness of Secondary School Youth prepared the material on p. 59 as their attempt to formulate some standards for the physically educated boy and girl. It represents an effort to establish standards for the profession of physical education.

Wireman* lists the qualities he believes constitute a physically educated person. They are presented here in adapted form.

1. *The physically educated person understands the history of physical education.* No person can become physically educated unless he or she understands and has historical perspective concerning the events that have affected the historical growth of the beliefs about physical education and what is possible in the years to come.

2. *The physically educated person is proficient in leisure-time skill and utilizes this skill for relaxation and recreation.* Some skill is necessary for enjoyment of the physical activity. Furthermore, leisure hours are utilized to some degree in putting the skill to use.

3. *The physically educated person is cognizant of the relationship of exercise, diet, and weight control.* An understanding of what con-

*Wireman, Billy O.: What are the underlying values in physical education? The Physical Educator **22:**53, May, 1965.

stitutes a desirable weight control program and the role of exercise and diet in such a program is desirable.

4. *The physically educated person is knowledgeable about the role of sports in the nation's culture.* Sports play a significant role in the American culture, and therefore it is important to be informed as to their influence on culture. Also, within reasonable limits, a person should be an intelligent spectator, as well as a skilled participant.

5. *The physically educated person has a body capable of meeting the demands of day-to-day living.* It is important to have an understanding of such factors as physical fitness, the ingredients that make it up, and how it is maintained.

6. *The physically educated person understands the concept of total health.* An understanding and appreciation of what constitutes total fitness, including the mental, physical, and psychological aspects and the interrelationship of each, are important.

SELF-ASSESSMENT TESTS

These tests are to assist students in determining if material and competencies presented in this chapter have been mastered.

1. Describe what would happen to a physical education program with no objectives that it desired to achieve.

2. Prepare a graph showing the various periods in history and the objectives of physical education that were stressed during each of these periods.

3. List six scientific principles that support the professional objectives of physical education.

4. You are in attendance at a PTA meeting. One of the parents asks you to tell why physical development, motor development, cognitive development, and social development are important objectives of physical education. Answer the parent's question.

5. Assume that you are a physical education instructor and utilize behavioral objectives. What are some behavioral objectives that you would use in teaching the game of soccer to tenth-grade students?

6. Survey the physical education faculty at your institution to determine what priority they would give to physical education objectives. Give a report to your class summarizing the results of your survey.

7. Prepare a list of concepts that would be important to keep in mind in teaching physical education activities.

8. Summarize what you consider to be the characteristics of a physically educated boy and a physically educated girl.

READING ASSIGNMENT

Bucher, Charles A.: Dimensions of physical education, ed. 2, St. Louis, 1974, The C. V. Mosby Co., Reading selections 16, 34, 41, and 56.

SELECTED REFERENCES

Annarino, Anthony A.: The five traditional objectives of physical education, Journal of Health, Physical Education, and Recreation **41:**24, June, 1970.

Annarino, Anthony A.: Physical education objectives: traditional vs developmental, Journal of Physical Education and Recreation **48:**22, Oct., 1977.

Bloom, Benjamin S., editor: Taxonomy of education objectives. Handbook I: Cognitive domain, New York, 1956, David McKay Co., Inc.

Bucher, Charles A.: Administrative dimensions of health and physical education programs, including athletics, St. Louis, 1971, The C. V. Mosby Co.

Bucher, Charles A.: Administration of health and physical education programs, including athletics, ed. 7, St. Louis, 1979, The C. V. Mosby Co.

Bucher, Charles A., and Koenig, Constance: Methods and materials for secondary school physical education, ed. 5, St. Louis, 1978, The C. V. Mosby Co.

Burton, Elsie Carter: The new physical education for elementary school children, Boston, 1977, Houghton Mifflin Co.

Gallup, George H.: Seventh annual Gallup Poll of public attitudes toward education, Phi Delta Kappan **57:**227, Dec., 1975.

Hellison, Donald R.: Humanistic physical education, Englewood Cliffs, N.J., 1973, Prentice-Hall, Inc.

Hess, Ford A.: American objectives of physical education from 1900-1957 assessed in the light of certain historical events, Doctoral dissertation, New York University, 1959 (microcarded).

Hetherington, Clark W.: School program in physical education, New York, 1922, World Book Co.

Krathwohl, David R., and others: Taxonomy of educational objectives. Handbook II. Affective domain, New York, 1956, David McKay Co., Inc.

Lawson, Barbara: An alternative program model for secondary school physical education, Journal of Physical Education and Recreation **48:**38, Feb., 1977.

Martens, Rainer: Social psychology and physical activity, New York, 1975, Harper & Row, Publishers.

Newport, John F.: What do you really know about behavioral objectives? Phi Delta Kappan **57:**241, 1975.

Physical Education Association of Great Britain: The concept of physical education, British Journal of Physical Education **1:**81, 1970.

Price, Hartley D.: The establishment of the principles which are essential for the realization of the objectives of physical education, Doctoral dissertation, New York University, 1946 (microcarded).

Rosentswieg, Joel: A ranking of the objectives of physical education, Research Quarterly **40:**783, 1969.

Sherman, W.: Performance objectives, Journal of Health, Physical Education, and Recreation **42:**37, Sept., 1971.

Shockley, J. M.: Needed: behavioral objectives in physical

education, Journal of Health, Physical Education, and Recreation **44:**44, April, 1973.

Stoodley, Agnes L.: The stated objectives of physical education for college women, Doctoral dissertation, Stanford University, 1947 (microcarded).

Tanner, David: Using behavioral objectives in the classroom, New York, 1972, The Macmillan Co.

Tyler, Ralph: The father of behavioral objectives criticizes them, Phi Delta Kappan **55:**55, 1973.

Welsh, Raymond, editor: Physical education — a view toward the future, St. Louis, 1977, The C. V. Mosby Co.

Weston, Arthur: The making of American physical education, New York, 1962, Appleton-Century-Crofts.

Wood, Thomas Denison, and Cassidy, Rosalind Frances: The new physical education, New York, 1931, The Macmillan Co.

4

Back-to-basics trend and role of physical education in general education

INSTRUCTIONAL OBJECTIVES AND COMPETENCIES TO BE ACHIEVED

After reading this chapter the student should be able to—

1. Relate what constitutes the "back-to-basics" movement in education, together with the implications it has for physical education.
2. Define education and general education and the role of physical education within each.
3. Explain what is meant by the cognitive, psychomotor, and affective domains of education and how physical education contributes to each.
4. Interpret the role of physical education in general education to colleagues and the lay public.

The latest Gallup Poll regarding the public's attitude toward the schools shows a strong emphasis on educating the nation's children and youth in the basic skills of learning. The public wants its young people to achieve higher standards in subjects such as reading, writing, and arithmetic. The quality of education in the basic intellectual disciplines, they say, has deteriorated and must be improved.

More specifically, some of the reforms the back-to-basics proponents want, according to Brodinsky,* are as follows:

*Brodinsky, Ben: Back-to-basics: the movement and its meaning, Phi Delta Kappan **58:**522, 1977.

1. The major part of school time in the elementary grades to be spent on reading, writing, and arithmetic.
2. Most of the time in secondary schools to be devoted to English, science, mathematics, and history.
3. Teaching methodology to emphasize teacher-directed activities, frequent testing, and homework.
4. The nation's classrooms should stress strict discipline, required courses, and few if any electives.
5. Promotion from grade to grade to be based on skill mastery and demonstrated achievement as indicated by passing marks on tests.
6. The elimination of such frills as sex education, volleyball, weaving, and flute practice.
7. The elimination of such social services as driver education, guidance, and physical education.
8. More emphasis on patriotism.

What has created the back-to-basics movement? Some of the reasons are associated with the public's current stress on accountability, the conservative trend that is taking place in society and in education, the disintegration of the family, the poor writing and reading ability of students throughout the nation, and the troubled economy with less money for education and the feeling that a program which stresses only the basics will be more economical.

The back-to-basics movement has made

Some advocates of the back-to-basics movement would eliminate physical education from the educational curriculum. Boys play paddle ball in the physical education class at Plymouth Community School District, Plymouth Canton High School, Plymouth, Michigan.

considerable progress in recent years as evidenced by the following facts:

A greater emphasis should be placed on the basic subjects in the curriculum, according to four fifths of the nation's school boards.

The popularity of the competency-based learning approach.

The great number of competency-based teacher education programs in existence.

The Council for Basic Education's statement that many, many school systems throughout the United States have adopted the fundamental or traditional concepts that they endorse, including such states as Florida, which has passed legislation requiring pupil performance as the basis of promotion rather than social promotion.

The prediction of several educators that by 1984 nearly all states will require minimal competency testing for promotion and graduation requirements.

The reduction of personnel and the deemphasis of physical education in some schools and colleges.

IMPLICATIONS OF THE BACK-TO-BASICS MOVEMENT FOR PHYSICAL EDUCATION

The back-to-basics movement has important implications for physical education. Since some of the advocates of this movement look on physical education as a frill and as a social service that cannot be justified in today's educational programs, it may mean survival or nonsurvival for some programs as they are known today.

The best strategy, it seems, for physical educators to follow in counteracting the back-to-basics movement is to show how physical education is one of the "basics" and why it

Physical education as a phase of the total educational process. Parachute activity at Hudson Falls Central School, Hudson Falls, New York.

should be viewed as such in today's educational curriculum. To do this, physical education needs to set forth clearly and articulately how and why it is part of the general education program of every educational institution.

THE ROLE OF EDUCATION IN TODAY'S SOCIETY

The role of education in general and physical education in particular is constantly undergoing change. At one time, education was left to the educators, but this is no longer the case, as characterized by parent committees, student curriculum groups, widespread teacher evaluation procedures, and constant reappraisal of education policies.

Education contributes to the development, advancement, and perpetuation of the nation's culture. Educational institutions play a primary role in the development of the human resources of society. Schools, colleges, and universities are clearly the most powerful and effective institutions that this society has for the achievement of intellectual skill, knowledge, understanding, and appreciation necessary to make wise decisions, good judgments, and logical analysis of problems. Directly or indirectly,

these educational institutions are the chief agents of society's progress, whether it is progress concerned with knowledge, arts, technology, social conscience, or other areas essential to a nation's growth. Education must meet the challenges presented in society. In the present decade this means that the nation's schools and colleges should be concerned with the well-being of students in their preparation for a productive and happy life in which their potentialities as individuals are enlarged and fulfilled and in which freedom will be assured.

Physical education, as a phase of the total educational process, helps in realizing these purposes. It is one link in a chain of many influences that help to realize the country's ideals and contribute to the proper functioning of American society. It is continually striving for excellence so that it can become an increasingly dynamic force in education.

MEANING OF THE TERM "EDUCATION"

Before one can evaluate the role of education, one must understand the meaning of the word. The term *education* means different things to different individuals. One individual will define it as a training process that comes about through study and instruction; another person will say it is a series of experiences that enable a person to better understand new experiences; and to others it means growth and adjustment. John Dewey, an educator who has most profoundly influenced education, defines education as the reconstruction of events which compose the lives of individuals so that new happenings and new events become more purposeful and more meaningful. Furthermore, as a result of education, individuals will be better able to regulate the direction of ensuing experience. Dewey's interpretation, it seems, sums up in a few words what is meant by education. It means that a person thinks in terms of previous experiences. It further means that the individual's education consists of everything he or she does from birth until death. Education is a "doing" phenomenon. One learns through doing. Education takes place in the classroom, in the library, on the playground, in the gymnasium, on trips, and at home. It is not confined to a school or a church but takes place wherever individuals congregate.

The problem now arises as to what experiences will best result in a happy and rich life. The solution seems to be in the provision of experiences that will have a practical value in the lives of individuals as they live from day to day. Worthwhile experiences will enable a person to live a more purposeful, a more interesting, and a more vigorous life. The aim or goals of education therefore should receive consideration if a person is to know in what direction educational experiences are to be guided. The Educational Policies Commission, in discussing policies for education in American democracy, stated the following as the purpose of education:

. . . The primary business of education in effecting the promises of American democracy, is to guard, cherish, advance, and make available in the life of coming generations the funded and growing wisdom, knowledge, and aspirations of the race. This involves the dissemination of knowledge, the liberation of minds, the development of skills, the promotion of free inquiries, the encouragement of the creative or inventive spirit, and the establishment

of wholesome attitudes toward order and change—all useful in the good life for each person, in the practical arts, and in the maintenance and improvement of American society, as our society, in the world of nations. So conceived, education seems to transcend our poor powers of accomplishment. It does in fact, if perfection be expected; but such is the primary business of public education in the United States; theory supports it; practice inadequately illustrates and confirms it.*

It is of interest to note while reflecting on this statement of the purpose of education that knowledge in itself is not enough. In addition, such a thing as ethics is also indispensable. As this report points out: "The nature of the knowledge to be disseminated is qualified by the condition, 'useful in the good life and in the maintenance and improvement of American society.' Both ethics and the nature of American civilization are drawn into immediate and inescapable consideration."†

The commission further pointed out that education is as much concerned with the training of the body and spirit as with the transmission of knowledge.

It is not merely with the transmission of knowledge that education is deeply concerned. The functions of the schools are not fully described by a summary of programs, curriculum, and methods. No written or spoken words do, or can, completely convey the meaning of education as the day-to-day living force that it is in fact and may be—in the transactions of the classroom, in the relations of teacher and pupil, in the associations of pupil and pupil, and in the experiences of the library and athletic field. Here are exchanges, bearings, and influences too subtle for logical expression and exact measurement. Yet we cannot doubt their existence, at least those of us who recall our own educational experiences and see teachers at work. Here, in the classroom, the auditorium, laboratory, and gymnasium, are in constant operation moral and cultural forces just as indispensable to civilization as knowledge or any material elements—indeed primordial

---

*Educational Policies Commission: Policies for education in American democracy, Washington, D.C., 1946, National Education Association and American Association of School Administrators, p. 60.
†Educational Policies Commission: Policies for education in American democracy, Washington, D.C., 1946, National Education Association and American Association of School Administrators, p. 62.

in nature and the pre-conditions for the civilized uses of material things.*

Physical education plays an important role in the educational process. The mind and body represent a unity in human beings. One gives strength to the other, one supports the other, and both function harmoniously in the educated person. When physical education is applied to education, it can readily be seen that it plays an instrumental role in the educational process.

MEANING OF THE TERM "GENERAL EDUCATION"

The term *general education* is often confused with the term *liberal education,* and it is

---

*Educational Policies Commission: Policies for education in American democracy, Washington, D.C., 1946, National Education Association and American Association of School Administrators, p. 64.

Courtesy Regis High School, Regis, N.Y.

"Here, in the . . . gymnasium are in constant operation moral and cultural forces just as indispensable to civilization as knowledge or any material elements—indeed primordial in nature and the pre-conditions for the civilized uses of material things." Basketball game at Regis High School in New York.

necessary to differentiate between the two to understand fully the meaning of the term *general education.* Morse* has stated that liberal education is subject centered, with content material which is logically organized. Its goal is the stimulation of reflective thinking, with little emphasis on behavior, and is primarily concerned with the intellectual person. General education, on the other hand, is more concerned with the learner than content, which may be organized with little regard for traditional fields of knowledge. Its goals are individual development, with emphasis on behavior and social usefulness together with intellectual development as an outcome of learning.

General education is concerned with developing a good life for all people. It seeks to prepare students for full and meaningful lives as members of families and organizations and as future citizens. Viewing socialization as an important educational goal, general education emphasizes the point that all citizens are members of one system, be it economic or political, and, unless they can function cooperatively with one another, there is going to be chaos. Wynne† has stated that one of the functions of general education is to widen the area of common interests and concerns. Civic responsibility is viewed as an important educational goal, and students are encouraged to communicate with one another. The learning of respect, tolerance, and self-responsibility are viewed in general education as being extremely valuable to future citizens. General education emphasizes the point that students must be given the opportunity to participate in experiences which develop intelligence and effective thinking. The Harvard Committee,‡ in their report entitled *General Education in a Free Society,* emphasized this need for effective thinking. Intellectual development is not the only goal of

---

* Morse, Horace T.: Liberal and general education: a problem of differentiation. Quoted by Rice, James G., editor: General education, Washington, D.C., 1964, National Education Association.

† Wynne, J. P.: General education in theory and practice, New York, 1952, Bookman Associates, p. 37.

‡ General education in a free society, report of the Harvard Committee, Cambridge, Mass., 1945, Harvard University Press.

general education. Knowledge of the body is also viewed as an important objective. Seeking to make possible the maximum development of the individual, general education enunciates the importance of health and well-being.

The Educational Policies Commission has pointed out that the function of education cannot be confined to facts but also includes training of the body and spirit. Knowledge in itself is not sufficient in the achievement of excellence.

Today, general education is looked on as preparing the individual for a meaningful, self-directed existence. For students to be prepared to accomplish this goal means that they must have an understanding of (1) the nature of self and others and growth in capacity for continuing self-development and for relating to others, (2) the contemporary social scene and the values and skills necessary for effective participation, (3) their cultural heritage and the ability to evaluate it, (4) the role of communication and skill in communicating, (5) the world of nature and the ability to adapt to it, and (6) the role of esthetic forms in human living and the capacity for self-expression through them.

PHYSICAL EDUCATION AS APPLIED TO GENERAL EDUCATION

Physical education, with its emphasis on building a physically, emotionally, mentally, and socially fit society, plays an important role in general education. A heavy responsibility rests on the shoulders of those who spend a large share of their time with the youth of today. If experiences are provided that are satisfying, successful, and directed toward enriching an individual's life, these purposes of education will be accomplished.

A fuller description of the role of physical education in the educational process based on these concepts is needed at this point. The role of physical education will be discussed in relation to the three domains, namely, cognitive, affective, and psychomotor.

Cognitive domain

The objective of cognitive development is concerned with knowledge and understanding. Physical education contributes to cognitive development in the following ways:

1. *Physical education contributes to academic achievement.* Research findings indicate that physical education programs contribute to academic achievement by providing daily movement experiences and instruction in selected basic motor activities consistent with the developmental level of the students; by promoting physical fitness; by providing knowledge and modifying behavior in regard to good health practices; and by aiding in the process of social and emotional development, which leads to a more positive self-concept. Research findings also indicate that intellectual, physical, and emotional developments are closely associated. Endocrinology has shown that mentality changes as body chemistry changes. Biology has linked the cell to the learning experience. Psychology points to the fact that the child's earliest learnings are factual and kinesthetic. Just as it is important to teach English so that students can communicate effectively with one another, history so that they have an understanding of their cultural heritage, and mathematics so they can understand the technology of society, it is also important to educate students regarding their physical selves so they can function most efficiently as human beings.

2. *Motor activity is related to higher thought processes.* Psychologist Newell C. Kephart, former Executive Director of the Achievement Center for Children at Purdue University, points out that motor activity is related to higher thought processes. He also indicates that a child's behavior cannot function better than the motor abilities on which it is based.

Authorities such as Swiss psychologist Jean Piaget have found that a child's earliest learnings are motor (involving neuromuscular systems and resulting in movement such as running, reaching, etc.) in nature and form the foundation of subsequent learnings.

Various research studies indicate that the child's earliest and first learnings accrue from an interaction with the physical and social environment. Physical movement provides the experience to clarify and make meaningful concepts of size, shape, direction, and other characteristics. In addition, through physical activities the child has new feelings and develops new interests as well as satisfies old curiosities.

3. *Physical education contributes to knowledge of exercise, health, and disease.* The educated person has an understanding of the facts pertinent to exercise, health, and disease. To a great degree, an individual's success depends on personal health. One's state of health and physical fitness will determine in large measure whether one succeeds in realizing self-potentialities.

Physical education contributes to this knowledge by instructing individuals about the importance of nutrition, physical activity, rest, and sleep; by informing them of the dangers of drugs; by exploring the preventive and control measures that exist to guard against diseases; by providing opportunities for vigorous out-of-doors activity; by motivating the formation of wholesome health attitudes and habits; by stressing safety factors for the prevention of accidents; and by establishing various health services.

The educated person has a knowledge of sound health practices and gets adequate amounts of exercise, rest, and sleep; eats the right kind of food; engages in activity conducive to mental as well as physical health; and sees that others also have the same opportunities to maintain and improve their health. The educated person realizes that health is a product which increases in proportion as it is shared with other individuals, and this individual knows that health is everybody's business.

4. *Physical education contributes to an understanding of the human body.* Individuals should know something about their physical bodies and their biological makeup. Physical education provides knowledge and understanding relating to the various organic systems and how these systems function and can be best maintained. Such knowledge and understanding can result in greater intellectual productivity and is an important part of the general education of each individual.

5. *Physical education contributes to an understanding of the role of physical activity and sports in the American and other cultures of the world.* Sports and physical activity constitute a very important part of the American culture as well as the other cultures of the world. They affect the country's politics, government, economy, and educational systems. Sport and physical activity dominate the newspapers, magazines, radio, and television. There are 1,300 books in print alone on the subject of physical fitness, together with many thousand more books devoted to various sports, thus giving

Motor activity is related to higher thought processes, according to Kephart. Movement education class at Public School No. 38 in Brooklyn, New York, where students are using their bodies to construct words—this formation spells the word LOVE.

this part of Americana an important place in the literature. Outstanding scholars such as Paul Weiss, former Yale professor of philosophy, and James Michener, outstanding novelist, have contributed books to this field of endeavor. Therefore, since sports and physical activity represent an important part of American culture, they should be known and understood not only from a biological but also from a sociological and psychological point of view.

6. *Physical education contributes to the wise consumption of goods and services*. The educated person buys goods and services with wisdom, is well informed as to their worth and utility, utilizes standards for guiding expenditures, and follows appropriate procedures to safeguard personal interests.

Physical education helps to inform children and adults about the relative values of goods and services that influence their health and physical fitness. The field of health is an area in which goods and services of doubtful value find a ready public market. If a person selects many of the more popular magazines and reads the advertisements with care, it would seem that one would need to eat certain types of cereal to be an outstanding athlete, to visit certain salons and slenderizing parlors to have a well-developed body, and to use special types of toothpaste to keep teeth shiny. Literature that offers advice on health matters occupies a prominent place on newsstands, drugstore counters, and various shops throughout the country. Advice is also seen and heard through billboards, posters, press, radio, and films. Much of the material is specially prepared and disseminated as a money-making scheme to exploit the public. Human welfare is not considered in much of the advice being given.

By nature of their position and background in health matters, physical educators help the student and the adult to take a critical view of such literature and pronouncements.

Affective domain

The affective domain is primarily concerned with interests, appreciations, attitudes, and values. It stresses the individual's value system and philosophy that are basic to maturity. Following are some of the contributions of physical education to this domain:

1. *Physical education contributes to an appreciation of beauty*. The educated person has developed an appreciation of the beautiful. From the time of early childhood the foundation of an appreciation of beautiful things can be developed. Architecture, landscapes, paintings, music, furnishings, trees, rivers, and animals should ring a note of beauty in the mind of the growing child and in the adult.

Physical education has much to offer in the way of beauty. The human body is a thing of beauty if it has been properly developed. The Greeks stressed the "body beautiful" and performed their exercises and athletic events in the nude to display the fine contours of their bodies. Nothing is more beautiful than a perfectly proportioned and developed human body. Physical activity is one of the keys to a beautiful body. Also, there is a beauty of movement that is developed through physical activity. When a person picks up an object from the floor, it can be done with great skill and grace, or it can be done crudely and awkwardly. When a football pass is caught, a basketball goal made, a high jump executed, a two and one-half somersault dive performed, or a difficult dance displayed, included in the performance of these acts can be rhythm, grace, poise, and ease of movement that is beauty in action. Anyone who has seen Sandra Palmer drive a golf ball, Chris Evert stroke a tennis ball, Dave Cowens hook a shot through the net, or Johnny Bench hit a home run knows what beauty of performance means. Such beauty comes only with practice and perfection.

2. *Physical education contributes to directing one's life toward worthwhile goals*. The educated person conscientiously attempts to guide his or her life in the proper direction. On the shoulders of each individual rests the responsibility of determining how one will live, what religion one will choose, the moral code one will accept, the standard of values one will follow, and the code of ethics one will believe. This is characteristic of the democratic way of life.

A person must develop a philosophy of life. The way one treats fellow human beings, the manner in which one assumes responsibility, the objectives one sets to attain, and the type of government in which one believes will all be affected by this philosophy. As a result of the philosophy that is established, individuals form their own destiny.

Physical education helps in the formulation of an individual's philosophy of life. Through the medium of physical education activities, guidance is given as to what is right and proper, goals that are worth competing for, intrinsic and extrinsic values, autocratic and democratic procedures, and standards of conduct. Children and youth are great imitators, and the beliefs, actions, and conduct of the coach and the teacher are frequently reflected in the beliefs, actions, and conduct of the student.

3. *The physical education program stresses good human relations.* The human being is the most valuable and important consideration in this life. Therefore human welfare should receive careful consideration in all walks of life. When a new law is passed by Congress, there should be due consideration for its effect on human welfare; when a machine is invented, whether it will affect people beneficially or adversely should be taken into consideration; and when an accusation is made, the effect on human welfare should be considered.

The physical education program stresses human welfare. When an activity is planned, it takes into consideration the needs and welfare of the participants; when a rule or regulation is made, the player's welfare is considered; when a student is reprimanded, the welfare of the student and that of others are considered. The physical education program takes into consideration the weak, the less skilled, and the handicapped and makes sure that adequate arrangements have been made for such individuals. It is a student-centered program, with the attention focused on the individuals for whom the program exists. Throughout the entire procedure the thought that the human aspects are the most important consideration is prevalent among students, teachers, and administrators.

4. *The physical education program enables each individual to enjoy a rich social experience through play.* Play experiences offer an opportunity for a rich social experience, which

Courtesy D. M. Massé, Waddell Elementary School, Manchester, Conn.

The physical education program enables each individual to enjoy a rich social experience through play. Each of these children at Waddell Elementary School in Manchester, Connecticut, is having a rich social experience as they participate in a wand relay.

can help greatly in rounding out a child's or youth's personality, in helping the child to adapt to the group situation, in developing proper standards of conduct, in creating a feeling of "belonging," and in developing a sound code of ethics.

Children and youths need the social experience that can be gained by associating with other persons in a play atmosphere. Many children and youths live in cities, in slum areas, and in communities where delinquency runs rampant, where their parents do not know the next-door neighbor, and where the environment is not conducive to a rich social experience. In such neighborhoods the school is one place where children and youths have an opportunity to mingle, and physical education offers an opportunity for them to play together. The potentialities are limitless in planning social experiences through "tag" and "it" games, rhythms, games of low organization, and the more highly organized games. Here the child or youth learns behavior traits characteristic of a democratic society. Because of the drive for play, a child will be more willing to abide by the rules, accept responsibility, contribute to the welfare of the group, and respect the rights of others.

5. *The physical education program helps individuals to play cooperatively with others.* The physical education program stresses cooperation as the basis for achieving the goals an individual or group desires. Each member of the group works as though he or she were a part of a machine. The machine runs smoothly, and every part does its share of the work. Pulling and working together bring results that never are obtained if everyone goes in different directions.

Physical education stresses leadership and followership traits. Everyone cannot be a captain on a basketball, relay, or soccer team. Everyone does not have leadership ability. Both leaders and followers are needed for the accomplishment of any enterprise.

6. *The physical education program teaches courtesy, fair play, and good sportsmanship.* The amenities of social behavior are a part of the repertoire of every educated person. Courtesy and politeness are characteristic of good

family training, just as fair play and sportsmanship are characteristic of good training in physical education activities. On the one hand, it reflects the character of the parent or guardian and, on the other, the teacher or coach. When a player kicks an opponent in the groin, trips him or her up, or does not play according to the rules, this behavior may reflect the spirit of the leader. The main objective is to provide an experience that will help the members of a group realize values that will help them live an enriched life.

7. *Physical education contributes to humanitarianism.* Physical education can, within reason, emotionalize democratic play experiences to the point at which young people see the importance and the value of cooperative living and contributing to the welfare of all. Here is an ideal setting for developing humanitarian values. Children and youth from all walks of life, all creeds, colors, and races are brought together for a social experience. Interest and a natural drive for activity provide a laboratory for actual practice in developing these values.

Psychomotor domain

In physical education the psychomotor domain is largely concerned with manipulative or motor skills. In the schools a planned program of physical activity is offered as an essential to optimum body functioning of young people during this developmental period of their lives.

1. *Physical education contributes to skill as a participant and spectator in sports.* The development of physical skills in all persons rather than in just a few select individuals is an educationally sound objective and is encouraged more and more by educators. The so-called recreational sports receive greater emphasis so that activities may be engaged in during an entire lifetime. Swimming, golf, tennis, camping, and similar activities occupy a prominent place in many physical education programs.

Physical education not only develops skill in the participant but at the same time develops an interest and knowledge of other activities that at times may be engaged in by individuals from the standpoint of a spectator. Although the benefits from participation outweigh the benefits of being a spectator with regard to physical activity, nevertheless, many leisure hours may be spent in a wholesome manner, observing a ball game or some other sports activity. Physical education helps by supplying a knowledge of various sports so that the role of the spectator may be more meaningful and interesting.

2. *Physical education contributes skills to utilize leisure hours in mental and cultural pursuits.* There is a whole gamut of activities that offer entertainment and relaxation after working hours for a great many people. A sport such as fishing motivates the development of a skill and a hobby such as tying flies. Many other examples could be listed.

3. *Physical education contributes skills essential to the preservation of the natural environment.* Part of the great wealth that belongs to the United States is represented in terms of wildlife, fish, forests, water, soil, and scenic beauty. These resources contribute to the living standard, appreciation of beauty, recreation, and pride that characterize this country. Physical education is concerned with ecology and especially with preserving national resources such as wildlife, fish, water, and forests. These represent the media through which many enjoyable moments are spent by sportsmen, campers, and seekers of recreation and relaxation. Many physical educators teach skills such as the right method and procedure for making a campfire, the right way to preserve wildlife and fish, and how to prevent forest fires.

SELF-ASSESSMENT TESTS

These tests are to assist students in determining if material and competencies presented in this chapter have been mastered.

1. Prepare a plan that the profession of physical education could successfully use to counteract those advocates of the "back-to-basics" movement who would eliminate physical education from school programs.

2. You are attending a school faculty meeting and one of the members of the faculty states that he does not consider physical education to be a phase of

Courtesy Milwaukee Public Schools, Division of Municipal Recreation and Community Education.

Physical education contributes to the utilization of leisure hours. City children learn something about fishing.

general education. You disagree and make a presentation that indicates you believe that physical education is an important part of general education. What did you say?

3. Summarize what is meant by the cognitive, psychomotor, and affective domains of education. Identify the main elements of each. Show how physical education contributes to each domain.

4. You have been invited to speak to a group of high school seniors on the role of physical education in schools and colleges. Prepare a speech indicating the contributions that physical education makes to students and why it should be a required subject in all schools and colleges in the nation.

READING ASSIGNMENT

Bucher, Charles A.: Dimensions of physical education, ed. 2, St. Louis, 1974, The C. V. Mosby Co., Reading selections 11 to 16.

SELECTED REFERENCES

American Alliance for Health, Physical Education, and Recreation: HPER omnibus—comments and concepts by Gulick Award recipients of AAHPER, Washington, D.C., 1976, The Alliance.

Brameld, Theodore: Philosophies of education in cultural perspective, New York, 1955, The Dryden Press.

Briggs, Paul W.: The opportunity to be relevant, Journal of Health, Physical Education, and Recreation **41:**41, May, 1970.

Brodinsky, Ben: Back to the basics: the movement and its meaning, Phi Delta Kappan **58:**522, 1977.

Bucher, Charles A.: Health, physical education, and academic achievement, National Education Association Journal **54:**38, May, 1965.

Bucher, Charles A.: Administration of health and physical education programs, including athletics, ed. 7, St. Louis, 1979, The C. V. Mosby Co.

Bucher, Charles A., and Koenig, Constance: Methods and materials for secondary school physical education, ed. 5, St. Louis, 1978, The C. V. Mosby Co.

Bucher, Charles A., Olsen, Einar A., and Willgoose, Carl E.: The foundations of health, New York, 1976, Appleton-Century-Crofts.

Cratty, Bryant J.: Teaching motor skills, Englewood Cliffs, N.J., 1973, Prentice-Hall, Inc.

Educational Policies Commission, National Education Association and American Association of School Administrators, Washington, D.C.:
The unique function of education in American democracy, 1937.
The purpose of education in American democracy, 1938.
Education and the defense of American democracy, 1940.
Education of free men in American democracy, 1941.
Education for all American youth, 1944.
Policies for education in American democracy, 1946.
Education for all American children, 1948.

Gardner, John W.: Excellence, New York, 1961, Harper & Row, Publishers.

General Education in a Free Society: Report of the Harvard Committee, Cambridge, Mass., 1945, Harvard University Press.

Hellison, Donald R.: Humanistic physical education, Englewood Cliffs, N.J., 1973, Prentice-Hall, Inc.

Morse, Harace T.: Liberal and general education: a problem of differentiation. Quoted by Rice, James G., editor: General education, Washington, D.C., 1964, National Education Association.

Oberteuffer, D.: Some contributions of physical education to an educated life, Journal of Health, Recreation, and Physical Education **16:**3, Jan., 1945.

Radler, D. H., and Kephart, Newell C.: Success through play, New York, 1960, Harper & Row, Publishers.

Singer, Robert N., and others: Physical education: an interdisciplinary approach, New York, 1972, The Macmillan Co.

Spears, Harold: Kappans ponder the goals of education, Phi Delta Kappan **55:**29, Sept., 1973.

Talamini, John T., and Page, Charles H.: Sport and society—an anthology, Boston, 1973, Little, Brown & Co., Inc.

The National Association for Physical Education of College Women and The National College Physical Education Association for Men: The scholarly enterprise, Quest, Monograph 20, summer issue, June, 1973.

Ulrich, Celeste: To seek and find, Washington, D.C., 1976, American Alliance for Health, Physical Education and Recreation.

Wellington, James K.: American education: its failure and its future, Phi Delta Kappan **58:**527, 1977.

Whitehead, Alfred North: The aims of education, New York, 1929, The Macmillan Co.

PART TWO

CHANGING CONCEPTS
IN PHYSICAL EDUCATION

Courtesy Project Active.

Physical educators teach handicapped students at Monmouth College in New Jersey.

5

Historical foundations of physical education

INSTRUCTIONAL OBJECTIVES AND COMPETENCIES TO BE ACHIEVED

After reading this chapter the student should be able to—

1. Trace the history of physical education from earliest times to the present.
2. Explain the contributions of the Athenian Greeks to physical education.
3. Explain why asceticism, scholasticism, and puritanism were deterrents to physical education's progress.
4. Identify some of the outstanding leaders in physical education over the course of history and the contributions each made to this field of endeavor.
5. Draw implications from the study of history that will assist in guiding the professional future of physical education.
6. Project future developments for physical education based on current trends.

The beliefs and experience of physical education today rest on the history of this field of endeavor. It is the source of physical education's identity. In a sense there is little basis for this professional field except its past. There is little to guide the field except that provided by the experience of yesteryear. There is no professional maturity except that which is built on the events of days and years gone by. By knowing what the accomplishments of leaders in the past were, today's physical educators attempt to build on their achievements. There is one qualification—physical educators must use only that from the past which is true, significant, and applicable to the present and the future.

What can one learn about physical education from studying its history? Many of today's activities have their forerunners in history. For example, the first Olympics date back to 776 B.C. in ancient Greece. Yoga and karate, activities with much recent interest, date back to ancient Oriental societies. Many more facts that will help the physical educator to understand the present better can be gained by studying the past.

It is interesting to note the various purposes for which physical education has existed in the lives of people of various countries and cultures. From the earliest times to the present, either directly or indirectly, physical activity has played a part in the lives of all people. Sometimes this activity has been motivated by a factor such as the necessity for earning a livelihood, whereas in other instances it has resulted from a desire to live a fuller life. Furthermore, it is clear that the objectives of physical education have changed over the course of history so that at the present time they are directed at the better development of human beings, not only physically but also emotionally, socially, and intellectually. These changing concepts of physical education have come about as a result of many years of experience and study in regard to the values inherent in participating in physical activity under qualified leadership.

PHYSICAL EDUCATION IN ANCIENT ORIENTAL NATIONS

Primitive society did not think of physical education as people do today. There was no organized physical education program in primitive society or in the cultures of the ancient Oriental nations. From the physical point of view, primitive people did not need to set aside a period during the day when they could participate in various forms of activity—activity was a part of their daily regimen. Well-developed bodies and sound organic systems were commonplace among primitive people. Their physical activity was obtained in the search for food, in erecting shelters, and in protecting themselves from a hostile environment.

History has shown that certain tendencies in human beings have been responsible for their formal and informal participation in physical activity. Some of the more important of these throughout history have been the search for food to satisfy hunger, the desire for protection against enemies, innate drives for mating and propagation, the urge to manipulate brain and brawn, fear of the strange and unknown, and the need to associate with others. Hunting, fishing, warfare, dancing, and play evolved as a result of these general tendencies, explaining to some extent why primitive people and all persons in general have been likely to engage in motor activities whether they wanted to or not. Whether these activities should be characterized as "work" or as "play" depends on the motive behind the participation in the activity. "Work" is characterized by need and necessity and is more or less compulsory. On the other hand, "play" is spontaneous, internally driven, and utilized for fun and relaxation.

Civilization has brought the need for an organized physical education program. As a result of labor-saving devices, sedentary pursuits, and security, the need has arisen for some type of planned program whereby individuals may realize the physical benefits that were once a part of a person's daily routine, as well as many emotional, sociological, psychological, and intellectual benefits. Therefore it is interesting to examine certain of these ancient cultures to determine the part that physical education played in the lives of their people. Through an understanding of the past or history of physical education, a person is better able to understand and interpret the field today.

China

Ancient China followed a policy of isolation. This country did not care to associate with the rest of the world but, instead, desired to live unto itself. At first, the topography of the land provided China with the necessary protection against invaders. When the Himalaya Mountains no longer served this purpose, the Great Wall was built; and when the wall became obsolete, laws were passed to keep invaders out of the country.

The fact that ancient China lived an isolated existence was detrimental in many ways to a belief in physical education. Since China did not fear aggression, it lacked the military motivating factor of being physically strong. Furthermore, the teachings of the people of ancient China were mainly concerned with memorizing the works of Confucius. Ancestor worship was also an important part of their religious life. Individuality was suppressed, and all persons were destined to live a rigid and stereotyped existence. In a country where such beliefs held sway, there was little room for organized physical education. Physical activity meant stress on the importance of the body and individual freedom of expression, which were contrary to the teachings in this ancient culture.

There were certain evidences of participation in physical education activities in China, however, despite the emphasis on intellectual excellence and the influences of Taoism, Confucianism, and Buddhism, which emphasized the studious, quiet, and contemplative life. In many Chinese classics, discussions abound of how sons of rich families engaged in music, dancing, and archery. Wrestling, jujitsu, boxing, football (ts' u chu), polo, tug-of-war, water games, ch' ui wan (in many respects similar to golf), shuttlecock, and flying kites were also popular.

It is interesting to note that the Chinese thought that certain diseases were caused from inactivity. As a result, history discloses that the Cong Fu gymnastics were developed in 2698 B.C. These were medical gymnastics intended to keep the body in good organic condition. It was believed that illnesses were caused by internal stoppages and by malfunctioning of organs. Therefore, if certain kneeling, bending, lying, and standing exercises could be performed, together with certain types of respiratory training, the illness could be alleviated.

Although there does not seem to have been much participation in formal physical activities by the masses in early China, play was engaged in by the more favored classes.

India

Ancient India in many ways was similar to ancient China. People in this country lived an existence that was very religious in nature. Hinduism stressed that the human soul passed through several reincarnations before being united with Brahma, the supreme goal. The quickest and most certain way to attain this goal was to refrain from catering to the body and enjoying worldly things. The person who desired to be holy ignored the physical needs of the body and concentrated solely on spiritual needs. It can readily be seen that physical activity had little place in the culture of this religious people.

Buddha's prohibitions of games, amusements, and exercises in ancient India did not totally prevent participation in such activities. Evidence is available about pastimes such as dice, throwing balls, plowing contests, tumbling, chariot races, marbles, riding elephants and horses, swordsmanship, races, wrestling, boxing, and dancing. Yoga, an activity common in India and involving exercises in posture and regulated breathing, was popular. This disciplining of mind and body required the instruction of experts, and a person fully trained in this activity followed a routine involving eighty-four different postures.

Ancient Near East

The civilizations of ancient Egypt, Assyria, Babylonia, Syria, Palestine, and Persia mark a turning point in the history of physical education. Whereas the objectives in China and India had stressed religious and intellectual matters, these countries were not restricted by a static society and religious ritual. On the contrary, they believed in living a full life, and therefore all types of physical activity contributed to this objective. It is in these countries that physical education also received an

impetus from the military, who saw in it an opportunity to build stronger and more powerful armies.

Egyptian youths were reared in a manner involving much physical activity. When young boys, they were instructed in the use of various weapons of war, such as bow and arrow, battle-axe, mace, lance, and shield. They were required to participate in exercises and activities designed to make the body supple, strong, and capable of great endurance and stamina. These activities included marching, running, jumping, wrestling, pirouetting, and leaping. Before their military training started, they had numerous opportunities to engage in many sports and gymnastic exercises. They also found great enjoyment in hunting and fishing expeditions.

In the countries between the Tigris and Euphrates rivers, great stress was placed on physical education activities, especially among the upper classes. Whereas the lower social strata of the population found few opportunities for recreation and play, the upper classes indulged themselves in these pastimes at regular intervals. Horsemanship, use of bow and arrow, water activities, and training in physical exercises were considered on a par with instruction that was more intellectual in character.

Persia is a good example of a state that had as its main objective the building of an empire through military aggression. A strong Persian army meant a healthy and physically fit army. Under King Cyrus the Great, the imperialistic dreams of Persia were realized. At the end of his rule in 529 B.C., the Persian Empire encompassed the area that is referred to today as the Near East. The success of King Cyrus' campaigns was largely the result of the moral and physical conditioning of his soldiers. At the age of 6 years, the state took all boys away from their homes for training, which consisted of such events as running, slinging, shooting with a bow, throwing the javelin, riding, hunting, and marching. The soldier had to be able to travel without much food and clothing and was compelled to endure all sorts of hardship.

Where the military emphasis existed, physical education was aimed at imperialistic ends. Strength, endurance, stamina, agility, and other physical characteristics were not developed so that the individual could live a full, vigorous, and more interesting life but, instead, so that the state could utilize these physical attributes in achieving its own selfish militaristic aims.

PHYSICAL EDUCATION IN GREECE

Physical education experienced a "golden age" in ancient Greece. The Greeks strove for physical perfection, and this objective affected all phases of their life. It had its influence on the political and educational systems, on sculpturing and painting, and in the thinking and writings of that day. It was a unifying force in Greek life, played a major part in the national festivals, and helped in building strong military establishments. No country in history has held physical education in such high respect as did ancient Greece.

As early as 2500 B.C., there were evidences of physical education activities being popular in Cretan culture. Archeological investigations at Mycenae and other centers of Aegean civilization have unearthed buildings, pottery, and other materials that point to the important place of physical education in this ancient culture. Literature such as Homer's *Iliad* and *Odyssey* also is a source of this information. Lion hunting, deer hunting, bull grappling, boxing, wrestling, dancing, and swimming are commonly referred to by historians who have written about these ancient civilizations.

Physical education was a vital part of the education of every boy in Greece. Gymnastics and music were considered the two most important subjects—music for the spirit, and gymnastics for the body. "Exercise for the body and music for the soul" was a common pronouncement. Gymnastics, it was believed, contributed to courage, discipline, and physical well-being. Furthermore, gymnastics stressed a sense of fair play, development of the individual's esthetic values, amateurism, and the utilitarian values inherent in the activity. Professionalism was frowned on. Individuals ran, wrestled, jumped, danced, or threw the javelin not for reward but for what it would do for their bodies. Beauty of physique was stressed, and everyone participated in the nude, which motivated development of the "body beautiful."

Because of the topography of the land and for various political reasons, Greece was composed of several city-states, each exercising its own sovereignty and existing as a separate entity. It waged war and conducted all its affairs separately from the other city-states. This situation had an influence not only on the political aspects of each city-state but also on the objectives of physical education within each state. Sparta and Athens exemplify two such city-states.

In Sparta, a city-state in the Peloponnesus district of Greece, the main objective of physical education was to contribute to a strong and powerful army. The individual in Sparta existed for the state. Each person was subservient to the state and was required to help defend it against all enemies. Women, as well as men, were required to be in good physical condition. It was believed that healthy and strong mothers would bear healthy and strong sons. Spartan women may have begun their physical conditioning as early as 7 years of age and continued gymnastics in public until they were married.

Courtesy British Museum, London, and Dr. Anne Gayle Ingram, University of Maryland.

East Greek amphora 550-525 B.C. Found at Fikellura, Rhodes. A running man.

Newborn infants, if found to be defective or weak, were left on Mount Taygetus to die. Woody points out that mothers bathed babies in wine to test their bodies and to temper them for future ordeals. A boy was allowed to stay at home only for the first 6 years of his life. After this he was required to stay in the public barracks and entered the agoge, a system of public, compulsory training, in which he underwent an extremely vigorous and rigid training schedule. If he failed in this ordeal, he was deprived of all future honors. A major part of this training consisted of such physical activities as wrestling, jumping, running, throwing the javelin and discus, marching, horseback riding, and hunting. This conditioning program secured for Sparta a strong army that was second to none.

Athens, a city-state in eastern Greece, was the antithesis of Sparta. Here the democratic way of life flourished, and consequently it had a great bearing on the objectives of physical education. Athens did not control and regulate the individual's life as rigidly as Sparta. In Athens the people enjoyed the freedom that is characteristic of a truly democratic government. Although the military emphasis was not as strong in Athens as in Sparta, the emphasis on physical education was just as great or greater. Athenians engaged in physical activity to develop their bodies, for esthetic values, and to live a fuller and more vigorous life. An ideal of Athenian education was to achieve a proper balance in moral, mental, physical, and esthetic development. To the Hellenes, each person was a whole and was as strong as his or her weakest part.

Gymnastics for the youth were practiced in the palaestra, a building that provided rooms for various physical activities, for oiling and sanding their bodies, and an open space for activities such as jumping and wrestling.

Some of the more noted palaestras were those of Taureas, Timeas, and Siburtios. The paidotribe, or proprietor of the palaestra, was similar to a present-day physical educator. He taught many activities, understood how certain exercises should be adapted to various physical conditions, knew how to develop strength and endurance, and was an individual who could be trusted with children in the important task of making youthful bodies serve their minds. As a boy approached manhood, he left the palaestra and attended the gymnasium.

Gymnasiums became the physical, social, and intellectual centers of Greece. Although the first use was for physical activity, men such as Plato, Aristotle, and Antisthenes were responsible for making such gymnasiums as the Academy, Lyceum, and Kynosarges outstanding intellectual centers as well. Youth usually entered the gymnasium at about 14 to 16 years of age. Here special sports and exercises received the main attention under expert instruction. Although activities that had been engaged in at the palaestra were continued, other sports such as riding, driving, racing, and hunting were added. Instruction in the gymnasium was given by a paidotribe and also a gymnast. The paidotribe had charge of the general physical training program, whereas the gymnast was a specialist responsible for training youth in gymnastic contests. The chief official at the gymnasium, in overall charge of the entire program, was called a gymnasiarch. In keeping with the close association between physical education and religion, each gymnasium recognized a particular deity. For example, the Academy recognized Athena; the Lyceum, Apollo; and Kynosarges, Hercules.

The national festivals were events that were most important in the lives of the Greeks and were also important in laying the foundation for the modern Olympic games. These national festivals were in honor of some hero or divinity and consisted of feasting, dancing, singing, and events involving physical prowess. Although many of these national festivals were conducted in all parts of Greece, four of them were of special importance and attracted national attention. The first and most famous of the four was the Olympia festival in honor of Zeus, the supreme god, which was held in the western Peloponnesus district. Another was the Pythia festival in honor of Apollo, the god of light and truth, held at Delphi, which was located north of the Corinthian Gulf. A third was the Nemea festival held in honor of Zeus at Argolis near Cleonae. The fourth was the Isthmia festival in honor of Poseidon, the god of the sea; it was held on the isthmus of Corinth. Athletic events were the main attraction and

Greek physical education. The Greeks have a rich tradition in physical education as a part of general education.

drawing force in each. People came from all over Greece to see the games. At Olympia the stadium provided standing space for approximately 40,000 spectators.

During the time the games were held, a truce was declared by all the city-states in Greece, and it was believed that if this truce were broken, the wrath of the gods would be visited on the guilty. By the middle of the fifth century this truce probably lasted for 3 months.

A rigid set of requirements had to be met before anyone could participate as a contestant in the games. For example, the contestant had to be in training for 10 months; he had to be a free man; he had to be of perfect physique and of good character; he could not have any

criminal record; and he had to compete in accordance with the rules. An oath also had to be taken that he would not use illegal tactics to win, to which fathers, brothers, and trainers also had to swear. Once enrolled for a contest, the athlete had to compete. Physical unfitness was not a good excuse. Events included foot racing, throwing the javelin, throwing the discus, wrestling, high jumping, broad jumping, weight throwing, boxing, and horse racing. The victor in these events did not receive any material reward for his victory. Instead, a wreath of olive branches was presented. However, he was a hero in everyone's eyes and had many receptions given in his honor. Furthermore, he had many privileges bestowed on

Greeks marching.

him by his home city-state. To be crowned a victor in an Olympic event was to receive the highest honor that could be bestowed in Greece. The Olympic games were first held in 776 B.C. and continued every fourth year thereafter until abolished by the Romans in A.D. 394. However, they have since been resumed and today are held every fourth year in a different country.*

Physical education in ancient Greece will always be viewed with pride by members of this profession. The high ideals that motivated the various gymnastic events are objectives that all should try to emulate.

PHYSICAL EDUCATION IN ROME

While the Hellenes were settling in the Grecian peninsula about 200 B.C., another Indo-European people was migrating to Italy and settling in the central and southern parts of this country. One of these wandering tribes, known in history as Latins, settled near the Tiber River, a settlement that later became known as Rome. The Romans were to have a decided

effect not only on the objectives of physical education in their own state but also on that of the Greek world, which they conquered.

The Romans, through their great leaders and well-disciplined army, extended their influence throughout most of the Mediterranean area and the whole of Europe. This success on the battlefield brought influences into Roman life that affected Roman ideals. They were not truly interested in the cultural aspects of life, although sometimes some of the finer aspects of Hellenic culture were taken on as a means of show. Particularly during the later days of the Roman Empire, wealth became the objective of most citizens, and vulgar display became the essence of wealth. Luxury, corruption, extravagance, and vice became commonplace.

In respect to physical education, the average Roman believed that exercise was for health and military purposes. He did not see the value of play as an enjoyable pastime. During the period of conquest, when Rome was following its strong imperialistic policy and before the time of professional troops, citizens were liable for military service from 17 to 60 years of age. Consequently, during this period of Roman history, army life was considered important, and physical activity was considered essential to be in good physical shape and ready to serve

---

*For an evaluation of Olympic games, see Bucher, Charles A.: Sports Illustrated, Aug. 8, 1955; Reader's Digest, Sept., 1955.

the state at a moment's notice. Soldiers followed a rigid training schedule that consisted of activities such as marching, running, jumping, swimming, and throwing the javelin and discus. However, during the last century of the Republic, mercenary troops were used, with the result that the objectives of physical training were not considered as important for the average Roman.

After the conquest of Greece, Greek gymnastics were introduced to the Romans, but they were never well received. The Romans lacked the drive for clean competition. They did not believe in developing the "body beautiful." They did not like nakedness of performers. They preferred to be spectators rather than participants. They preferred professionalism to amateurism.

Athletic sports were not conducted on the same high level as in ancient Athenian Greece. The Roman wanted something exciting, bloody, ghastly, and sensational. At the chariot races and gladiatorial combats, excitement ran high. Men were pitted against wild animals or against one another and fought to the death to satisfy the craving of the spectator for excitement and brutality. Frequently, large groups of men fought each other in mortal battle before thousands of pleased spectators.

The rewards and incomes of some individuals who engaged in the chariot races were enormous. Diocles of Spain retired at 42 years of age, having won 1,462 of 4,257 races and rewards totaling approximately $2 million. Other famous contestants were Thallus, Crescens, and Scorpus.*

The thermae and the Campus Martius in

---

*At the site where once the inhabitants of Rome yelled with delight at the skill and daring of their favorite charioteers and gladiators, Romans of today are applauding the exploits of soccer players, who have replaced the chariot drivers and slaves in the public estimation.

The Circus Maximus, the oldest and greatest of the Roman circuses, was situated at the foot of the Palatine Hill and dated back to the last king of Rome, Tarquinius the Younger (534-510 B.C.). It reached its greatest splendor in imperial times and seated as many as 200,000 persons. It reached its final form under Trajan (A.D. 53-117). The Rome Municipal Council decided that this unusual site, formerly occupied by the Circus Maximus, should be transformed into a sports center.

Rome took the place of the gymnasium in Greece. The thermae were the public baths, where provision was also made for exercise, and the Campus Martius was an exercise ground on the outskirts of the city. Most of the exercise was recreational in nature.

PHYSICAL EDUCATION DURING THE DARK AGES

The fall of the Roman Empire in the west about A.D. 476 resulted in a period of history that is frequently referred to as the Dark Ages. This period, however, was anything but dark in respect to the physical rejuvenation brought about by the overrunning of the Roman Empire by the Teutonic barbarians.

Before considering the Dark Ages, it is interesting for the student of physical education to note a cause of the fall of Rome that brought on this new period in history. Historians list many causes for the breakdown of the Roman Empire, but the most outstanding was the physical and moral decay of the Roman people. The type of life the Romans led, characterized by divorce, games, and suicide, caused a decrease in population. Extravagance, doles, slave labor, and misuse of public funds caused moral depravity and economic ruin; luxurious living, vice, and excesses caused poor health and physical deterioration. The lesson is borne out in Rome, as it has been in many civilizations which have fallen along the way, that for a nation to remain strong and endure, it must be physically as well as morally fit.

As a morally and physically weak Roman Empire crumbled, morally and physically strong Teutonic barbarians overran the lands that once were the pride of the Latins. The Visigoths overran Spain, the Vandals overran North Africa, the Franks and Burgundians overran Gaul, the Angles and Saxons overran Britain, and the Ostrogoths overran Italy. These invasions brought about the lowest ebb in literature and learning known to history. The so-called cultural aspects of living were disregarded.

Despite all the backwardness that accompanied the invasions with respect to learning, public works, and government and that resulted in the name "Dark Ages" being attached to this period of history, the entire world still received physical benefits. The Teutonic barbarians were a nomadic people who lived out of doors on simple fare. They were mainly concerned with a life characterized by hunting, caring for their cattle and sheep, and participating in vigorous outdoor sports and warfare. A regimen such as this built strong and physically fit bodies and well-ordered nervous systems. The Teutonic barbarians helped to guarantee a stronger, healthier, and more robust stock of future generations of people.

Asceticism and scholasticism

Although the Teutonic invasions of the Dark Ages supported the value of physical activity, two other movements during approximately this same period in history worked to its disadvantage—asceticism and scholasticism.

Out of pagan and immoral Rome, Christianity and asceticism grew and thrived. Certain individuals in ancient Rome became incensed with the immorality and worldliness that existed in Roman society. They believed in "rendering unto Caesar the things that are Caesar's and unto God the things that are God's." They would not worship the Roman gods, attend the baths, or visit the games. They did not believe in worldly pleasures and catered to the spirit and not to the body. They believed that this life should be used as a means of preparing for the next world. They thought that all sorts of physical activity were foolish pursuits in that they were designed to improve the body. The body was evil and should be tortured rather than improved. They preached that the mind and body were distinct and separate entities in man and that one had no bearing on the other. The Christian emperor Theodosius abolished the Olympic games in A.D. 394 as being pagan.

The spread of Christianity resulted in the rise of asceticism. This was the belief that evil exists in the body, and therefore it should be subordinated to the spirit, which is pure. Worldly pursuits are evil, and individuals should spend their time by being alone and meditating. The body is possessed of the devil and should be tortured. Individuals wore hair shirts, walked on hot coals, sat on thorns, carried chains around their legs, and exposed themselves to the elements so that they might bring their worldly body under better control. Such practices led to poor health and shattered nervous systems on the part of many.

As Christianity spread, monasteries were built where Christians could isolate themselves from the world and its evils. Later, schools were attached to these monasteries, but early Christianity would not allow physical education to become a part of the curriculum. The medieval university also frowned on physical education.

Another influence that has had a major impact on the history of physical education is scholasticism—the belief that facts are the most essential items in one's education. The key to a successful life is knowing the facts and developing one's mental and intellectual powers. Scholasticism deemphasized the physical as being unimportant and unnecessary. This movement developed among the scholars and universities of the Middle Ages.

PHYSICAL EDUCATION DURING THE AGE OF FEUDALISM

As a result of the decentralization of government during the period of the Dark Ages, the period of feudalism came into being between the ninth and fourteenth centuries.

The feudalistic period appeared because people needed protection, and since there was a shortage of strong monarchs and governments that could supply this protection, the people turned to noblemen and others who built castles, had large land holdings, and made themselves strong. Feudalism was a system of land tenure based on allegiance and service to the nobleman or lord. The lord who owned the land, called a *fief*, let it out to a subordinate who was called his *vassal*. In return for the use of this land, the vassal owed his allegiance and certain obligations to his lord. The large part of the population, however, was made up of serfs, who worked the land and shared little in the profits. They were attached to the land, and as it was transferred from vassal to vassal, they were also transferred.

Two careers were open to sons of noblemen during feudalistic times. They might enter training for the church and become members of the clergy, or they might enter chivalry and become knights. If they decided in favor of the church, they pursued an education that was religious and academic in nature, and if they decided in favor of chivalry, they pursued an education that was physical, social, and military in nature. To the average boy, chivalry had much more appeal than the church.

The training that a boy experienced in becoming a knight was long and thorough. Physical training played a major role during this period. At the age of 7 years a boy was usually sent to the castle of some nobleman for training and as preparation for knighthood. First, he was known as a page, and his instructor and teacher was usually one of the women in the lord's castle. During his tenure as a page, a boy learned court etiquette, waited on tables, ran errands, and helped with household tasks. During the rest of the time he participated in various forms of physical activity that would serve him well as a knight and harden and strengthen him for the arduous years ahead. He practiced for events such as boxing, running, fencing, jumping, and swimming.

At the age of 14 years the boy became a squire and was attached to some knight. His duties included keeping the knight's weapons in good condition, caring for his horses, helping him with his armor, attending to his injuries, and guarding his prisoners. During the time the boy was a squire, more and more emphasis was placed on physical training. He was continually required to engage in vigorous sports and exercises, such as hunting, scaling walls, shooting with the bow, running, swordsmanship, horsemanship, and climbing.

If the squire proved his fitness, he became a knight at 21 years of age. The ceremony through which he passed to become a knight was solemn and memorable. The prospective knight took a bath of purification, dressed in white, and spent an entire night in meditation and prayer. In the morning the lord placed his sword on the knight's shoulder, a ceremony known as the accolade; this marked the conferring of knighthood.

Jousts and tournaments were two special events in which all knights engaged several times during their lifetime and that were tests of their fitness. These special events served both as amusement and as training for battle. In the jousts, two knights attempted to unseat one another from their horses with blows from lances and by skill in horsemanship. In tournaments many knights were utilized in a program designed to exhibit the skill and showmanship gained during their long period of training. They were lined up as two teams at each end of the *lists*, as the grounds were called, and on a signal they attempted to unseat the members of the opposing team. This meleé kept on until one team was declared the victor. Many knights wore their lady's colors on their armor and attempted with all their strength and skill to uphold her honor. During these tournaments, death often resulted for many participants. It was during these exhibitions that a knight had the opportunity to display his personal bravery, skill, prowess, strength, and courage.

PHYSICAL EDUCATION DURING THE RENAISSANCE

The transitional period in history between the dark years of the medieval period and the beginning of modern times, the fourteenth to sixteenth centuries, was known as the period of the Renaissance and was an age of great progress for humankind.

During the medieval period, people lacked originality. Individuality was a lost concept, and interest in the hereafter was so prevalent that people did not enjoy the present. The Renaissance caused a change in this way of life. There was a revival or rebirth of learning, a belief in the dignity of human beings, a renewed spirit of nationalism, an increase of trade among countries, and a period of exploration. Scientific research was used to solve problems; books were printed and thereby made available to more people; and there was a renewed interest in the classics. This period is associated with names such as Petrarch, Boccaccio, Michelangelo, Erasmus, da Vinci, da Gama, Columbus, Galileo, and Harvey.

The Renaissance period also had an impact on physical education. With more attention being placed on enjoyment of the present and the development of the body, asceticism lost its hold on the masses. During the Renaissance the theory that the body and the soul were inseparable, that they were indivisible, and that one was necessary for the optimum functioning of the other became more popular. It was believed that learning could be promoted through good physical health. A person needed rest and recreation from study and work. The body needed to be developed for purposes of health and for preparation for warfare.

Some outstanding leaders in the Renaissance period who were responsible for spreading these beliefs concerning physical education are mentioned briefly.

Vittorino da Feltra (1378-1446) taught in the court schools of northern Italy and was believed to be one of the first teachers to combine physical and mental training in a school situation. He incorporated daily exercises in the curriculum, which included dancing, riding, fencing, swimming, wrestling, running, jumping, archery, hunting, and fishing. His objectives of physical education emphasized that it was good for disciplining the body, for preparation for war, and for rest and recreation and that good physical condition helped children learn other subject matter much better.

Pietro Vergerio (1349-1428) of Padua and Florence wrote a treatise entitled *De Ingenius Moribus*, in which the following objectives were emphasized: physical education is necessary for the total education of the individual, as preparation for warfare, to better undergo strain and hardship, as a means of fortifying the mind and body, as an essential for good health, and as a means of recreation to give a lift to the spirit and the body.

Pope Pius II's (1405-1464) objectives of physical education were good posture, body health, and aid to learning.

Sir Thomas Elyot (1490-1546) of England wrote the treatise on education entitled *The Governor*, which elaborated on such objectives of physical education as recreation and physical benefits to the body.

Martin Luther (1483-1546), the leader of the Protestant Reformation, did not preach asceticism as a means of salvation. He saw in physical education a substitute for vice and evil pursuits during leisure hours such as gambling and drinking, a means of obtaining elasticity of the body, and a medium of promoting one's health.

François Rabelais (1490-1553), a French educational theorist, emphasized the objectives of physical welfare and the fact that physical education is an important part of education, aids in mental training, and is good preparation for warfare.

Roger Asham (1515-1568), professor at Cambridge in England, proclaimed the value of physical education as a preparation for war and as a means of resting the mind.

John Milton (1608-1674), the English poet, expressed his views on physical education in his *Tractate on Education*. In this treatise he discussed how physical education helps in body development, is a means of recreation, and is good preparation for warfare.

John Locke (1632-1704), famous English philosopher and a student of medicine, supported physical education in a work entitled *Some Thoughts Concerning Education*. His objectives could be summed up under health as a means of meeting emergencies involving hardships and fatigue and as a means of having a vigorous body at one's command.

Michel de Montaigne (1533-1592), a French essayist, stressed that physical education was necessary for both body and soul and that it was impossible to divide an individual into two such components, since they are indivisible and together comprise the individual being trained.

John Comenius (1592-1671), a Bohemian educational reformer, and *Richard Mulcaster* (1530-1611), an English schoolmaster, had as their objectives of physical education a means of maintaining health and physical fitness and of obtaining rest from study.

Jean Jacques Rousseau (1712-1778), a French writer, in his book *Emile* points out that in an ideal education, physical education would contribute to the objectives of health and a vigorous body. He stressed that an individual's mind and body are an indivisible entity and that both are bound together.

The Renaissance period helped to interpret the worth of physical education to the public in general. It also demonstrated how a society that promotes the dignity and freedom of the individual and recognizes the value of human life will also place in high respect the development and maintenance of the human body. The belief became prevalent that physical education is necessary for health, as a preparation for warfare, and as a means of developing the body.

PHYSICAL EDUCATION IN EUROPE

A study of the various men and countries that influenced physical education during the modern European period shows what each contributed to the growth and advancement of this field.

Germany

Physical education in Germany during the modern European period is associated with names such as Basedow, Guts Muths, Jahn, and Spiess.

Johann Bernhard Basedow (1723-1790) was born in Hamburg and early in life went to Denmark as a teacher. Here he witnessed physical education in practice as part of a combined physical and mental training program. After gaining a wealth of experience in Denmark, he went back to Germany and decided to spend all his time in the reform of educational methods. In 1774 he was able to realize his objective of establishing at Dessau a school that he called the Philanthropinum. In this model school, physical education played an important part in the daily program of all students. The activities included dancing, fencing, riding, running, jumping, wrestling, swimming, skating, and marching. This was the first school in modern Europe that admitted children from every class in society and that offered a program in which physical education was a part of the curriculum. Such an innovation by Basedow did much to influence the growth of physical education in Germany as well as in the rest of the world.

Johann Christoph Friedrich Guts Muths (1759-1839) brought his influence to bear on the field of physical education through his association with the Schnepfenthal Educational Institute, which had been founded by Christian Gotthilf Salzmann (1744-1811). Guts Muths succeeded Christian Carl Andre as the instructor of physical education at this institution and remained on the staff for 50 years. His beliefs and practices in physical education were recorded for history in various books, two of which are of special importance, *Gymnastics for the Young* and *Games*. These books provide illustrations of various exercises and pieces of apparatus, arguments in favor of physical education, and discussion of the relation of physical education to educational institutions. Because of his outstanding contributions, Guts Muths is often referred to as one of the founders of modern physical education in Germany.

Friedrich Ludwig Jahn (1778-1852) is a name associated with the Turnverein, an association of gymnasts that has been in evidence ever since its innovation by Jahn. Jahn's incentive for inaugurating the Turnverein movement was love of his country. It was during his lifetime that Napoleon overran Germany and caused it to be divided into several independent German states. Jahn made it his life's work and ambition to help in bringing about an independent Germany free from foreign control. He believed that he could best help in this movement by molding German youth into strong and hardy citizens who would be capable of throwing off this foreign yoke.

To help in the achievement of his objective, Jahn accepted a teaching position in Plamann's Boys School. In this position he worked regularly with the boys in various outdoor activities. He set up an exercise ground outside the city called the Hasenheide. Before long Jahn had erected various pieces of apparatus, including equipment for jumping, vaulting, balancing, climbing, and running. The program grew in popularity; soon hundreds of boys were visiting the exercise ground or turnplatz regularly, and more apparatus was added.

Jahn's system of gymnastics was recognized throughout Germany, and in many cities Turnvereins were formed, using as a guide the instructions that Jahn incorporated in his book *Die Deutsche Turnkunst*. When Jahn died, his work carried on, and turner societies became more numerous. In 1870 there were 1,500 turner societies, in 1880 there were 2,200, in 1890 there were 4,000, in 1900 there were 7,200, and 1920 there were 10,000. Turnvereins are still in existence in many parts of the world.

Adolph Spiess (1810-1858) was the founder of school gymnastics in Germany, and more than any other individual in German history, he helped to make physical education a part of school life. Spiess was proficient in physical education activities himself and was well informed as to the theories of such men as Guts Muths and Jahn. His own theory was that the school should be interested in the total growth of the child—mental, emotional, physical, and social. Physical education should receive the same consideration as the important academic subjects such as mathematics and language. It should be required of all students, with the possible exception of those whom a physician would excuse. There should be provisions for an indoor as well as an outdoor program. Elementary schoolchildren should have a minimum of 1 hour of the school day devoted to physical education activities, which should be taught by the regular classroom teacher. The upper grades should have a progressively smaller amount, which should be conducted by specialists who were educators first but who were also experts in the field of physical education. The physical education program should be progressive, starting with simple exercises and proceeding to the more difficult. Girls as well as boys need an adapted program of physical activity. Exercises combined with music offer an opportunity for freer individual expression. Marching exercises aid in class organization, discipline, and posture development. Formalism should not be practiced to the exclusion of games, dancing, and sports.

There are other outstanding individuals in modern German history who have influenced physical education, including Eiselen, Koch, Hermann, and Von Schenckendorff. However, the names of Basedow, Guts Muths, Jahn, and Spiess stand out as the ones who, in large part, have influenced physical education the most.

Sweden

The name of *Per Henrik Ling* (1776-1839) is symbolic of the rise of physical education to a place of importance in Sweden. The "Lingaid," held at Stockholm, in which representatives of many nations of the world participate, is a tribute to this great man.

Ling's greatest contribution is that he strove to make physical education a science. Formerly physical education had been conducted mainly on the premise that people believed it was good for the human body because it increased the size of one's musculature; contributed to strength, stamina, endurance, and agility; and left one exhilarated. However, many claims for physical education had never been proved scientifically. Ling approached the field with the mind of a scientist. Applying the sciences of anatomy and physiology, he examined the body to determine what was inherent in physical activity to enable the body to function in a more nearly optimum capacity. His aims were directed at determining such things as the effect of exercise on the heart, the musculature, and the various organic systems of the body. He believed that through such a scientific approach, he would be better able to understand the hu-

The turnplatz.

man body and its needs and to select and apply physical activity intelligently.

Ling is noted for establishing the Royal Central Institute of Gymnastics at Stockholm, where teachers of physical education received their preparation in one of three categories — educational gymnastics, military gymnastics, or medical gymnastics.

Ling believed that physical education was necessary for the weak as well as the strong, that exercise must be prescribed on the basis of individual differences, that the mind and body must function harmoniously together, and that teachers of physical education must have a foundational knowledge of the effects of exercise on the human body.

In 1839 *Lars Gabriel Branting* (1799-1881) became the director of the Royal Central Institute of Gymnastics on the death of Ling. Branting spent the major part of his time in the area of medical gymnastics. His teachings were based on the premise that activity causes changes not only in the muscular system of the body but in the nervous and circulatory systems as well. Branting's successor was *Gustaf Nyblaeus* (1816-1902), who specialized in military gymnastics. An innovation during his tenure was the inclusion of women in the school.

The incorporation of physical education programs in the schools of Sweden did not materialize as rapidly as many leaders in the field had hoped. As a result of the teachings of Ling and other leaders, a law was passed in 1820 requiring a course of physical education on the secondary level. More progress was made in education when the values of physical education to the growth and development of children became apparent in Sweden. To *Hjalmar Fredrik Ling* (1820-1886), most of the credit is due for the organization of educational gymnastics in Sweden. He was largely responsible for physical education becoming an essential subject in all schools for both boys and girls and on all institutional levels.

Denmark

Denmark has been one of the leading European countries in the promotion of physical education. *Franz Nachtegall* (1777-1847) was largely responsible for the early interest in this field. He had a direct influence in introducing physical education into the public schools of Denmark and in preparing teachers of this subject.

Franz Nachtegall had been interested in various forms of physical activity since childhood

The Idla Girls, the famous Swedish group of amateur women gymnasts, displaying their graceful program in front of the seventeenth-century Royal Palace of Drottningholm.

and had achieved some degree of skill in vaulting and fencing. He began early in life to teach gymnastics, first to students who visited his home and then in 1799 in a private outdoor gymnasium, the first to be devoted entirely to physical training. In 1804 Nachtegall became the first director of a Training School for Teachers of Gymnastics in the Army. The need was great for instructors in public schools and in teachers' colleges so that graduates readily found employment. In 1809 the secondary schools and in 1814 the elementary schools

Danish gymnastic team performing at New York University.

Acme Photo.

Courtesy Harold L. Ray, Western Michigan University, Kalamazoo, Mich.

Wand drills were an important part of program activities in the 1890s.

were requested to provide a program of physical education with qualified instructors. It was shortly after this that Nachtegall received the appointment of Director of Gymnastics for all Denmark.

The death of Nachtegall in 1847 did not stop the expansion of physical education throughout Denmark. Some of the important advances since his death have been the organization of Danish Rifle Clubs or gymnastic societies, the introduction of the Ling system of gymnastics, complete civilian supervision and control of programs of physical education as opposed to military supervision and control, greater provision for teacher education, government aid, the incorporation of sports and games into the program, and the work of *Niels Bukh* (1880-1950).

One of the innovations in the field of physical education has been the contribution of Niels Bukh with his "Primitive Gymnastics." Patterned to some extent after the work of Ling, they attempted to build the perfect physique through a series of exercises performed without cessation of movement. His routine included exercises for arms, legs, abdomen, neck, back, and the various joints. In 1925 he toured the United States with some of his students, demonstrating his "Primitive Gymnastics."

Great Britain

Great Britain is known as the home of outdoor sports, and her contribution to this field has influenced physical education the world over. When other European countries were utilizing the Ling, Jahn, and Guts Muths systems of gymnastics, England was utilizing a program of organized games and sports.

Athletic sports are a feature of English life. As early as the time of Henry II, English youth were wrestling, throwing, riding, fishing, hunting, swimming, rowing, skating, shooting the bow, and participating in various other sports. The games of hockey and quoits, for example, were played in England as early as the fifteenth century, tennis as early as 1300, golf as early as 1600, and cricket as early as 1700. Football is one of the oldest of English national sports.

In addition to outdoor sports, England's chief contribution to physical education has been through the work of *Archibald Maclaren* (1820-1884). Maclaren at an early age enjoyed participating in many sports, especially fencing and gymnastics. He also studied medicine and was eager to make a science of physical training. In 1858 he opened a private gymnasium where he was able to experiment. In 1860 Maclaren was designated to devise a system of physical education for the British Army. As a result of this appointment, he incorporated his recommendations in a treatise entitled *A Military System of Gymnastic Exercises for the Use of Instructors*. This system was adopted by the military.

Maclaren contributed several other books to the field of physical education, including *National Systems of Bodily Exercise, A System of Fencing, Training in Theory and Practice,* and *A System of Physical Education*. In his works he points out that the objectives of physical education should take into consideration that health is more important than strength; that the antidote for tension, weariness, nervousness, and hard work is physical action; that recreative exercise as found in games and sports is not enough in itself for growing boys and girls; that physical exercise is essential to optimum growth and development; that physical training and mental training are inseparable; that mind and body represent a "oneness" in human beings and sustain and support each other; that exercises must be progressive in nature; that exercises should be adapted to an individual's fitness; and that physical education should be an essential part of any school curriculum.

Since the time of Maclaren the Swedish system of gymnastics has been introduced into England and has been well received. Many ideas were also imported from Denmark and other countries.

One of the major contributions of England to physical education has been movement education, which is discussed at length in Chapter 8.

•   •   •

Germany, Sweden, Denmark, and England led Europe in the promotion of physical education. Other countries of Europe as a rule imported the various systems of Jahn, Guts Muths, and Ling. There are persons from other countries who have also contributed much to the field of physical education and who should be mentioned. From Switzerland, Pestalozzi with his educational theories, Dalcroze and his system of eurythmics, and Clias did a great deal to advance the field of physical education. Colonel Amoros from France inaugurated a system of gymnastics, and Baron Pierre de Coubertin was instrumental in reviving the Olympic games in 1896 at Athens. Johann Happel from Belgium was outstanding in physical education and was director of a normal school of gymnastics. Dr. Tyrs from Czechoslovakia organized the first gymnastic society in his country.

PHYSICAL EDUCATION IN THE UNITED STATES

Physical education in the United States has experienced a period of great expansion from the colonial period. At that time there was little regard for any planned program of activity as contrasted with today, when programs are required in the public schools of most of the states and when physical education is becoming a respected profession.

Colonial period

During the colonial period, conditions were not conducive to organized physical education programs. The majority of the population lived an agrarian existence and thought that they received enough physical exercise working on the farms. Also, there were few leisure hours during this period that could be devoted to various forms of recreational activities. In certain sections of the country such as New England, religious beliefs were contrary to participation in play. The Puritans, especially, denounced play as the work of the devil. Participation in games was believed to be just cause for eternal damnation. Pleasures and recreation were banned. Stern discipline, austerity, and frugality were thought to be the secrets to eternal life and blessedness.

People of some sections of the nation, however, brought with them from their mother countries the knowledge and desire for various sports. The Dutch in New York liked to engage in sports such as skating, coasting, hunting, and fishing. However, the outstanding favorite was bowling. In Virginia many sports were popular, such as running, boxing, wrestling, horse racing, cockfights, fox hunts, and, later, cricket and football.

During the colonial period little emphasis was given to any form of physical activity in the schools. The emphasis was on the three R's at the elementary level and the classics at the secondary level. The teachers were ill prepared in the methodology of teaching. Furthermore, at the secondary level, students were prepared mainly for college, and it was thought that physical activity was a waste of time in such preparation.

National period*

During the national period of the history of the United States, physical education began to assume an important place in society.

The academies, as many of the secondary schools were called, provided terminal education for students; instead of preparing for college, they prepared for living. These educational institutions utilized games and sports as after-school activity. They had not reached the point, however, at which they thought its value was such that it should occupy a place in the daily school schedule. They encouraged participation during after-school hours on the premise that it promotes a healthy change from the mental phases of school life.

The U.S. Military Academy was founded in 1802 and gave physical training an important place in its program of activities. Throughout history this training school has maintained such a program.

It was during the national period that German gymnastics were introduced to the United States. Charles Beck introduced Jahn's ideas at the Round Hill School at Northampton, Massachusetts, in 1823; and Charles Follen introduced them at Harvard University and in Boston. Both Beck and Follen were turners and proficient in the execution of German gymnastics. Their attempt to introduce German gymnastics into the United States, however, was not successful at this time. A few years later

---

*The period from the American Revolution to the Civil War.

they were introduced with more success in German settlements located in cities such as Kansas City, Cincinnati, St. Louis, and Davenport. Turnverein associations were organized, and gymnastics were accepted with considerable enthusiasm by the residents of German extraction. As for native Americans, the majority thought that a formal type of gymnastic program was not suitable for their purposes.

The Turnverein organizations spread, and by 1852 there were twenty-two societies in the North. The oldest Turnverein in the United States, which flourishes to the present day, is the Cincinnati Turnverein, founded November 21, 1848. The Philadelphia Turnverein, one of the strongest societies today, was founded on May 15, 1849. A national organization of Turnvereins, now known as the American Turnerbund, was established in 1850 and held its first national turnfest in Philadelphia in 1851. Societies from New York, Boston, Cincinnati, Brooklyn, Utica, Philadelphia, and Newark were represented. There were 1,672 turners in the United States in 1851. At the outbreak of the Civil War there were approximately 150 Turnverein societies and 10,000 turners in the United States. After the Civil War these organizations continued to grow and exercised considerable influence on the expanding physical education profession. The Turnverein organizations were responsible for the establishment of the Normal College of the American Gymnastic Union. Many outstanding physical education leaders graduated from this school.

There were notable advances in physical education prior to the Civil War. In 1828 a planned program of physical education, composed mainly of calisthenics performed to music, was incorporated by Catherine E. Beecher in the Hartford Female Seminary in Connecticut, a famous institution of higher learning for women and girls. The introduction of the Swedish Movement Cure in America, the building of gymnasiums in many large cities, the formation of gymnastic and athletic clubs by many leading institutions of higher learning, and the invention of baseball were all events of importance in the progress of physical education in America during this period.

Physical education from the Civil War until 1900

Many outstanding leaders and new ideas influenced physical education in the United States in the period from the Civil War to 1900.

After the Civil War the Turnverein societies were established for both boys and girls. The members of these associations gave support to various phases of physical education and especially encouraged the program in the public schools. The objectives of the turners were notable. They disapproved of too much stress being placed on winning games and professionalism. They believed that the main objectives should be to promote physical welfare and to provide social and moral training. They opposed military training in the schools as a substitute for physical education and supported the playground movement.

In 1852 Catherine Beecher founded the American Women's Educational Association.

From 1859 to the early 1870s, Dr. George Barker Winship gained considerable publicity by emphasizing gymnastics as a means of building strength and large muscles.

In 1860 Dr. Dio Lewis devised a new system of gymnastics and introduced it in Boston. As opposed to Winship, Lewis was not concerned with building muscles and strength. He was more interested in the weak and feeble persons in society. Instead of large muscles, he aimed at developing agility, grace of movement, flexibility, and improving one's general health and posture. He also stressed that teachers should be well prepared, and in 1861 he established a normal school of physical education in Boston for training teachers. Lewis opposed military training in schools. He thought that sports in themselves would not provide an adequate program but that gymnastics should also be included. Through lectures and written articles, Lewis became a leading authority on gymnastics used in the schools and the public in general. He is noted for advancing physical education to a respected position in United States society. Several leading educators, after hearing Lewis, set up planned physical education programs in their school systems.

In the 1880s the Swedish Movement Cure was made popular by Hartvig Nissen, head of the Swedish Health Institute in Washington. This system was based on the Ling or Swedish gymnastics, so well known in Europe and recognized in the United States for inherent medical values. Also in the 1880s Mrs. Hemenway and Amy Morris Homans added their contributions to physical education. They stimulated the growth of Swedish gymnastics; founded a normal school for teachers at Framingham, Massachusetts; contributed to the schoolchildren of Boston, Massachusetts, by offering courses of instruction in Swedish gymnastics to schoolteachers; and influenced the establishment of the Boston Normal School of Gymnastics.

In the 1890s the Delsarte System of Physical Culture was introduced by Francois Delsarte. It was based on the belief that by contributing to poise, grace, beauty, and health certain physical exercises were conducive to better dramatics and better singing.

During this period, American sports began to achieve some degree of popularity. Tennis was introduced in 1874, and in 1880 The United States Lawn Tennis Association was organized. Golf came to the United States in the late 1880s,

and in 1894 the United States Golfing Association was formed. Bowling had been popular since the time of the early Dutch in New York, but it was not until 1895 that the American Bowling Congress was organized. Basketball, one of the few sports originating in the United States, was invented by James Naismith in 1891. Some other sports that became popular during this period were wrestling, boxing, volleyball, skating, skiing, lacrosse, handball, archery, track, soccer, squash, football, and swimming. In 1879 the National Association of Amateur Athletics of America was developed, from which the American Athletic Union was formed.

Physical education has played a large part in the Young Men's Christian Association, an organization that is worldwide in scope and that is devoted to developing Christian character and better living standards. Robert J. Roberts was an outstanding authority in physical education for the YMCA in the late 1800s. In 1885, an International Training School of the YMCA was founded at Springfield, Massachusetts. Roberts became an instructor there, as did Luther Gulick, who later became Director of Phys-

Courtesy Harold L. Ray, Western Michigan University, Kalamazoo, Mich.

Exhibition on the parallel bars by men's physical education class.

ical Training for the New York City Public Schools. After Gulick left Springfield, Dr. Mc-Curdy became head of the physical education department.

The first Young Women's Christian Association was founded in Boston in 1866 by Mrs. Henry Durant. This organization is similar to the Young Men's Christian Association and has a broad physical education program for its members.

Physical education made major advances in colleges and universities with the construction of gymnasiums and the development of departments in this area. Two of the leaders in physical education during the last half of the nineteenth century were Dr. Dudley Allen Sargent, who was in charge of physical education at Harvard University, and Dr. Edward Hitchcock, who was head of the physical education department at Amherst College. Sargent is known for his work in teacher preparation, remedial equipment, exercise devices, college organization and administration, anthropometric measurement, experimentation, physical diagnosis as a basis for activity, and scientific

research. Some of the schools that constructed gymnasiums were Harvard, Yale, Princeton, Bowdoin, Oberlin, Wesleyan, Williams, Dartmouth, Mt. Holyoke, Vassar, Beloit, Wisconsin, California, Smith, and Vanderbilt. Intercollegiate sports also began to play a prominent part, with the first intercollegiate meet in the form of a crew race between Harvard and Yale in 1852. Williams and Amherst played the first intercollegiate baseball game in 1859, and Rutgers and Princeton, the first football game in 1869. Other intercollegiate contests in tennis, swimming, basketball, squash, and soccer were soon to follow.

Organized physical education programs as part of the curriculum began to appear early in the 1850s in elementary and secondary schools. Boston was one of the first communities to take the step under the direction of Superintendent of Schools, Nathan Bishop. The cities of St. Louis and Cincinnati followed soon afterward. During the next two decades, physical education was made part of the school program in only a few instances. However, in the 1880s there was a renewed drive in this

Courtesy Harold L. Ray, Western Michigan University, Kalamazoo, Mich.

Staff and first normal class in physical education of the Chautauqua school, dated 1886. Pioneers in the field who taught this first operational summer school of physical education are identified by numbers as follows: *1,* Dr. Eliza M. Mosher, Brooklyn; *2,* Dr. Jay W. Seaver, Yale; *3,* Hope Narey, Holyoke; *4,* Dr. Julius King, Cleveland; *5,* Dr. Claes Enebuske, Boston; *6,* Dr. Henry Boice, Trenton; *7,* Henry S. Anderson, Yale and Brooklyn; *8,* Emily M. Bishop, Jamestown and New York City; *9,* Dr. William G. Anderson; *10,* Lee Pennock, Jamestown and New York City; *11,* Dr. Louis Collin, Boston; *12,* Gertrude Jeffords, Jamestown, accompanist. Those persons not identified by numbers were students.

direction, with the result that physical directors were appointed in many of the larger cities, and many more communities recognized the need for planned programs in their educational systems.

In 1885 in Brooklyn the American Association for the Advancement of Physical Education was organized with Edward Hitchcock as the first president and Dudley Sargent, Edward Thwing, and Miss H. C. Putnam as vice-presidents. William G. Anderson was elected secretary and J. D. Andrews, treasurer. This association later became the American Physical Education Association and until recently was known as the American Association for Health, Physical Education, and Recreation. It is now known as the American Alliance for Health, Physical Education, and Recreation.

A struggle between the Swedish, German, and other systems of gymnastics developed in the 1890s. Advocates of each system did their best to spread the merits of their particular program and attempted to have them incorporated as part of school systems. In 1890 Baron Nils Posse introduced the Swedish system in the Boston schools, where it proved popular, and it was later adopted throughout the schools of Massachusetts. The Swedish system had more popularity in the East, and the German system was more prevalent in the Middle West. A survey in the 1890s points out not only the prevalence of the various systems of gymnastics but also the prevalence of physical education programs in general throughout the country. It was reported after a study of 272 cities that eighty-three had a director of physical education for their school systems; eighty-one had no director, but teachers were responsible for giving exercises to the students; and in 108 cities the teachers could decide for themselves whether exercises should be a part of their daily school programs. A report on the dates the physical education programs were established in the schools surveyed show that 10% were established before 1887, 7% from 1887 to 1888, 29% from 1889 to 1890, and 54% from 1891 to

From the J. Clarence Davies Collection, Museum of the City of New York.

Dr. Rich's Institute for Physical Education.

1892. In respect to the system of gymnastics used, the report showed 41% used the German type of gymnastics, 29% Swedish, 12% Delsartian, and 18% eclectic.* Only eleven cities had equipped gymnasiums. It was not long, however, before there was greater expansion in gymnasiums, equipment, trained teachers, and interest in physical education. Ohio in 1892 was the first state to pass a law requiring physical education in the public schools. Other states followed, and there were thirty-three in 1925. Today there are only a few that have not provided such legislation.

Developments affecting physical education at the turn of the century

Many new developments were taking place at the turn of the century in the area of general education that were to leave their impact on physical education.

Professional education was given increased attention. Teachers College, Columbia University, was organized. A School of Education was established at the University of Chicago, and a Graduate School of Education came into being at Harvard. The first junior college was founded in Joliet, Illinois, in 1902.

---

*A combination of the various systems of gymnastics.

Psychology was influencing educational thinking. In 1878 *Wilhelm Max Wundt* (1832-1920), a German physiologist, founded a psychological laboratory in Leipzig that many American students attended. Wundt's studies in the area of the play interest of animals and humans stimulated much interest at home and abroad. *William James* (1842-1910), a follower of Wundt, was known particularly for his research into habit formation, mental discipline, transfer of training, and instincts. *E. L. Thorndike* (1874-1949), who studied under William James, made contributions in such areas as the learning process, mental testing, and child psychology. He was particularly well known for his introduction of the stimulus–response (S–R) theory of learning.

Sociology was influencing educational thinking. *George H. Mead* (1863-1931) expounded on the theory that man is the product of his social interaction with other men. *John Dewey* (1859-1952) interpreted the impact of industrial and social changes on education.

The importance of child study gained great emphasis. *G. Stanley Hall* (1845-1924) was the leader of the Child-Study Movement and advocated the "Recapitulation" theory of play. Hall was particularly interested in play and games as a means of fulfilling the health needs

From Library of Congress photographic collection.

An early physical education program.

of children and youth. Much of the emphasis on rhythms and dancing, he believed, should take place during the adolescent period. He stressed that informal play and games were superior to the formal calisthenic type of exercise. *John Mason Tyler* (1851-1929), a biologist, stressed the need to know the biological characteristics of children to prescribe the physical activities best suited to their needs. He stressed gymnastics as well as play and games.

Physical education programs in schools and colleges gained momentum. As a result of these and other developments, a survey by the North American Gymnastic Union of physical education programs in fifty-two cities showed that gymnastic programs averaged 15 minutes in the elementary schools and two periods weekly in the secondary schools. Cities that were surveyed showed 323 gymnasiums in existence and many more under construction. Extensive interscholastic programs also existed, as a survey of 290 high schools in 1907 showed that 28% of the students engaged in one or more sports. The controversy over interscholastic athletics for girls was pronounced, with people such as *Jessie Bancroft* and *Elizabeth Burchenal* stressing the importance of intramural games for girls rather than interscholastic competition. A majority of colleges and uni-

versities had departments of physical education, and most institutions of higher learning provided some program of gymnastics for their students. A survey by *Thomas D. Storey* in 1908 gave information concerning leadership in physical education. It showed that of the institutions surveyed, 41% of the directors of physical education possessed medical degrees, 3% of the directors held doctor of philosophy degrees, and the remaining possessed a bachelor's degree. Intercollegiate athletics were brought under more rigid academic control as the abuses mounted. Intramural athletics gained in prominence as the emphasis on athletics for all gained momentum.

Physical education in the early twentieth century

Some of the names that should be mentioned in any discussion of the history of physical education during the early part of the twentieth century include the following:

Thomas Dennison Wood made an outstanding contribution to the field of physical education. He attended Oberlin College, was the first director of the physical education department at Stanford University, and later became associated with Teachers College, Columbia University. He believed there should be more em-

From J. Clarence Davies Collection, Museum of the City of New York.

Skating in Central Park, New York, 1885.

RECREATION AND STUDY

Chautauqua Affords Opportunity for Instruction Under the Best Instructors, Together with Abundant Outdoor Recreation and an Attractive Program of Concerts, Popular Lectures and the Best Entertainments.

THE CHAUTAUQUA CREW

Courtesy Harold L. Ray, Western Michigan University, Kalamazoo, Mich.

Boating on Lake Chautauqua. The Chautauqua institution, located on Lake Chautauqua in southwestern New York State, was an early showcase for physical education in the late 1800s and early 1900s. William G. Anderson, founder of the American Association for Health, Physical Education, and Recreation, was active at this institution.

phasis on games and game skills and introduced his new program under the name "Natural Gymnastics."

Clark Hetherington was influenced by his close association with Thomas D. Wood, who chose Hetherington as his assistant when he was at Stanford. Hetherington's contributions resulted in a clearer understanding of children's play activities in terms of survival and continued participation. This was also true of athletics and athletic skills. Hetherington became head of the physical education department at New York University and, along with his successor, *Jay B. Nash,* was responsible for its

becoming one of the leading teacher training schools in the nation.

Robert Tait McKenzie, a physical educator, surgeon-scientist, and artist-sculptor, served distinguished periods at McGill University and the University of Pennsylvania. He was known for his contribution to sculpture, for his dedication to helping physically underdeveloped and atypical individuals overcome their deficiencies, and for his writing of books such as *Exercise in Education and Medicine,* published in 1910.

Jessie H. Bancroft, a woman pioneer in the field of physical education, taught at Davenport, Iowa, Hunter College, and Brooklyn and New York City Public Schools. She greatly influenced the development of physical education as a responsibility of homeroom teachers in elementary schools. She also contributed much to the field of posture and body mechanics, was the first living member of the AAHPER to receive the Gulick Award, and was well known for her book *Games for the Playground, Home, School, and Gymnasium.*

Delphine Hanna, an outstanding woman leader of physical education, developed a department of physical education at Oberlin College, which sent outstanding graduates all over the country. She was instrumental in motivating not only many leaders in the female ranks but also encouraged men such as Thomas Wood, Luther Gulick, and Fred Leonard to follow illustrious careers in physical education.

James H. McCurdy studied at the Training School of Christian Workers at Springfield Medical School of New York University, Harvard Medical School, Springfield College, and Clark University. He was closely association with Springfield College, where he provided leadership in the field of physical education. He published *The Physiology of Exercise* and was editor of the *American Physical Education Review.*

Luther Gulick, born in Honolulu, was director of physical education at Springfield College, principal of Pratt High School in Brooklyn, Director of Physical Education for Greater New York City Public Schools, and president of the American Physical Education Association. He taught philosophy of play at New York University, helped to found and was the first president of the Playground Association of America (later to become the National Recreation Association), was associated with the Russell Sage Foundation as director of recreation, and was president of Camp Fire Girls, Inc.

The playground movement had a rapid period of growth after the first sand garden was set up in 1885 in Boston. In 1888 New York passed a law that provided for a study of places where children might play out of doors. In New York the name of *Jacob A. Riis* was symbolic of the playground movement in that city. In Chicago a playground was managed by Hull House. In 1906 the Playground and Recreation Association of America was established to promote the development of rural and urban playgrounds, with Dr. Gulick as president.

In the field of teacher education in physical education, higher standards were established and better trained leaders were produced. The 2-year normal school became a thing of the past, with 4 years of preparation being required. The trend in professional preparation required of students a broad general education, a knowledge of child growth and development and the psychology of learning, and specialized training in physical education.

Sports, athletics, and team games became more important in the early twentieth century, with broad and extensive programs being established in schools, recreational organizations, and other agencies. The National Collegiate Athletic Association, National Association of Intercollegiate Athletics, and other leagues, organizations, and associations were formed to keep a watchful eye on competitive sports.

During the early twentieth century a new physical education started to evolve. By means of a scientific basis, it attempted to discover the physical needs of individuals and the part that a planned physical education program can play in meeting these needs. This new physical education recognized that education is a "doing" process and that the individual learns by doing. It stressed leadership, in which exercises and activities are not a matter of mere physical routine but, instead, are meaningful and significant to the participant. A varied program of activities was stressed that included the fundamental skills of running, jumping, climbing, carrying, throwing, and leaping; camping activities; self-testing activities; "tag" and "it" games; dancing and rhythmical activities; dual and individual sports; and team games. It stressed the need for more research and investigation into what type of physical education program best serves the needs of children and adults. It stressed the need for a wider use of measurement and evaluation techniques to determine how well objectives are being achieved. Finally, it provided a program that better served to adapt individuals to the democratic way of life.

World War I (1916-1919)

World War I started in 1914, and the United States' entry in 1918 had a critical impact on the nation and education. The Selective Service Act of 1917 called to service all men between the ages of 18 and 25 years. Health statistics gleaned from Selective Service examinations aroused considerable interest in the nation's health.

Social forces were also at work during this period. The emancipation of women was furthered by passage of the Nineteenth Amendment. Women also began to show interest in sports and physical education, as well as in other fields formerly considered to be "off limits."

During World War I many physical educators provided leadership for physical conditioning programs for the armed forces and also for the people on the home front. Persons such as Dudley Sargent, Luther Gulick, Thomas Storey, and R. Tait McKenzie contributed their services to the armed forces. The Commission on Training Camp Activities of the War Department was created, and Raymond Fosdick was named as the head of this program. Joseph E. Raycroft of Princeton University and Walter Camp, the creator of "All-Americans," were named to head the athletic divisions of the Army and the Navy, respectively. Women physical educators were also active in conditioning programs in communities and in industry at home.

After the war was over, the public had an

Courtesy Aldrich & Aldrich.

Physical education costumes for American women in early years.

opportunity to study the medical examiner's report for the men who had been called to military duty. One third of the men were found physically unfit for armed service and many more were physically inept. Also, a survey by the National Council on Education in 1918 showed that children in the elementary and secondary schools of the nation were woefully subpar physically. The result was the passing of much legislation in the various states to upgrade physical education programs in the schools. The following states listed laws enacted between 1917 and 1919: Alabama, California, Delaware, Indiana, Maine, Maryland, Michigan, Nevada, New Jersey, Oregon, Pennsylvania, Rhode Island, Utah, and Washington. To provide supervision and leadership for the expanded programs of physical education, state departments of public instruction established administrative heads for their states in many sections of the country.

Golden 20s (1920-1929)

The period between 1920 and 1929 showed the way for a "new physical education" advocated by such leaders as Hetherington, Wood, Nash, and Williams. The move away from the formal gymnastic systems of Europe was well received. The temperament of the times seemed to emphasize a less formal type of program. More games, sports, and free play were the order of the day.

The belief that physical education had greater worth than building strength and other physical qualities, as incorporated in the thinking of the "new physical education," aroused much discussion. Franklin Bobbit, a University of Chicago educator, commented: "There appears to be a feeling among physical educationists that the physical side of man's nature is lower than the social or mental, and that . . . they, too, must aim primarily at those more exalted nonphysical things of mental and social type." William Burnham, of Clark University, thought that physical education could contribute to the whole individual. Clark Hetherington believed that physical education had different functions in a democratic society than in Europe where some of the gymnastic systems prevailed. Jesse Feiring Williams stressed the importance of physical education in general education.

Thomas D. Wood, Rosalind Cassidy, and Jesse Feiring Williams published their book *The New Physical Education* in 1927; it stressed the biological, psychological, and sociological foundations of physical education.

Another development during this period included the stress on measurement in physical education by such persons as David K. Brace and Frederick Rand Rogers, as a means of grouping students, measuring achievement, and motivating performance.

Programs of physical education continued to expand in schools and colleges. The elementary school program of physical education stressed mainly formal activities. The secondary school program also felt the influence of the formalists. In addition, there were periodic lectures on hygiene. Interscholastic athletics continued to grow in popularity, with the need being felt to institute controls. The National Federation of High School Athletic Associations was established in 1923. At the college and university level a study by George L. Meylan reported in 1921 that of 230 institutions surveyed, 199 had departments of physical education presided over by administrative heads and an average of four staff members per institution. Many of the staff members had professorial rank. More than three fourths of the institutions required physical education for their students, with the most general requirement being for 2 years in length. The 1920s also saw a boom in the area of stadium construction.

Many problems arose in respect to college athletics. As a result, the Carnegie Foundation provided a grant in 1923 for a study of intercollegiate athletics in certain institutions in the South by a Committee of the Association of Colleges and Secondary Schools. Later, a study was conducted of athletic practices in American colleges and universities. The report of this study was published in 1929 under the title *American College Athletics*. The report denounced athletics as being professional rather than amateur in nature and as a means of public entertainment and commercialization. Problems such as recruiting and subsidizing athletics also were exposed.

During this period there was an increase in the intramural athletic programs in colleges and universities. Women's programs experienced an increase in the number of staff, hours required for student participation, activities offered, and physical education buildings in use.

Depression years (1930-1939)

The 1929 stock market crash ushered in the Great Depression, which affected education. Unemployment and poverty reigned. Health and physical education had a difficult time surviving in many communities.

Fifty Years Ago in the Journal

The currently controversial issue of sex instruction in the schools was a topic of concern to members of the American Physical Education Association in March 1919. "Sex Instruction in Connection with Physical Training in High Schools" was the subject of a meeting in Connecticut, at which statements of policy were agreed to by participants, who represented both college and high school physical education programs. The document was published in full in the Journal of fifty years ago, and the quotations below show that while some of the arguments are still pertinent, the developing role of the school health educator has brought about a new perspective on sex education in today's schools.

"The necessity for sex education in high schools is plain and apparent. Since, however, investigations show that knowledge of sexual matters comes to children before high school age the desirability of sex education in grammar and primary grades is established. At the present time, however, it may be more practical to confine sex education to high school pupils. . . .

"Physical training holds a unique position in this respect [as an agency to communicate the facts to all high school students] for all high school pupils no matter what courses they might elect come for physical training. This is the first advantage of the physical training teacher. All teaching is so much more effective if it can be linked up with life itself and if it can be made practicable. In this respect physical training has once more unusual opportunities.

"The practice of physical education in a high school makes necessary certain precautionary measures in regard to both sexes so that no harm may come to the sexual apparatus by exercise. This means for the female be made acquainted with the facts underlying menstruation and the effect of exercise thereon. This matter must be broached to every female student in a high school and might as well be made then the basis of further sex instruction which will come in as a matter of course. In dealing with the males, advice as to the wearing of protective appliances so as to prevent harm to the testes in physical training practice is likewise necessary and opens the way for general sex instruction. . . .

"Physical work in itself is an antidote against undue manifestations of sexual life in the young. . . . The selection of individuals for games gives occasion to point out that sexual development is closely allied with the development of not only physical properties but also mental and moral ones as evidenced especially in the different physiques and mentalities in domestic animals where unsexing is practiced. The advantage of continence to preserve fitness for certain games, the unfitting influence of premature sexual indulgence, can be readily brought to the attention of especially the male in the high school.

"With all this advantage of physical education one thing must be insisted upon that such knowledge gained by formal and informal instruction will be no help unless character building is coupled with it. The demand then for character building through physical education must be reiterated in this connection."

From Journal of Health, Physical Education, and Recreation **40**:42, March, 1969.

50 Years Ago in the Journal

The February 1919 issue of the *American Physical Education Review* was the "Western District Convention Number." It contained the two-day program details on one and a half pages of its 6" x 9" format. In contrast with one of today's district meetings, the program consisted of general sessions only, seven in number, plus three demonstrations (swimming, dance, and calisthenics). Both morning and afternoon schedules had "community singing" breaks, evidently a welcome moment of relaxation since the second day's program began with a display of calisthenics by the cadets of the School of Military Aeronautics (University of California, Berkeley) at 6:20 a.m.

The impact of World War I on the theory, philosophy, and curriculum of physical education is evident in the titles of the main articles for the issue—"Physical Education in the Light of the Present National Situation," "American Athletics Versus German Militarism," and "The Influence of the War Upon Physical Education"—and the notes, which included a synopsis of the practical guide used by the French centers of military and physical re-education.

Of special interest is the description of a new game invented by James Naismith. Called Vrille (or Vree) Ball, its underlying principle was "to be simple enough so that it could be played by the novice and yet require such skill as to interest the expert," but it never gained the popularity of the other game Naismith created. Played on a rectangle 24' x 24' by two teams of three men each, the game involved batting a ball back and forth so that on each exchange it bounced off a rectangular wood or cement target on the ground in the middle of the field. The regulation ball was a leather covered rubber bladder 12" in circumference and it was hit with the hands. Like basketball, it was invented by Naismith to fit certain requirements demanded by the physical education instructional program. It was designed to give many of the benefits of handball or tennis, providing exercise, developing skills, and combining recreation with competition. It was economical of expense and space; elastic enough to be played on almost any kind of grounds; and capable of being played when only two could get together but flexible enough to accommodate several. Perhaps in attempting to meet too many special requirements, it failed to meet a basic need of maintaining enthusiasm. We would be interested in knowing if any teacher is still using Vrille Ball in his physical education classes.

From Journal of Health, Physical Education, and Recreation **40**:42, Feb., 1969.

During the period of the economic depression in the United States, many gains achieved by physical education in the schools of the nation were lost. Budgets were cut back, and programs in many cases were either dropped or downgraded. In the 1932-1934 period an estimated 40% of the physical education programs were dropped completely. There were legislative moves in several of the states, such as Illinois and California, to do away with the physical education requirement.

Another development during the depression years was that the physical educator became more involved in recreation programs in the agencies and projects concerned with unemployed persons. These later programs were being subsidized with special governmental assistance. The national association, recognizing the increased interest in recreation, voted to change its title to include the word *recreation*—the American Association for Health, Physical Education, and Recreation.

A new interest captivated many physical educators—that of facilities concerned with programs of physical education, athletics, and recreation. Several publications appeared before the end of the 1920s on this subject.

The trend in physical education programs was away from the formal type to an informal games and sports approach. Also, what constitutes an acceptable program of physical education at various school and college levels was outlined by William R. LaPorte of the University of Southern California in his publication *The Physical Education Curriculum—A National Program,* published in 1937.

Interscholastic athletic programs continued to grow and in some situations dominated physical education programs and created many educational problems. The collegiate athletic program received a temporary setback from the Carnegie Report but then started to grow again. The National Association of Intercollegiate Basketball was established in 1940 for the purpose of providing an association for the smaller colleges. It later changed its name to National Association of Intercollegiate Athletics in 1952. In 1937 representatives of the Junior Colleges of California met for the purpose of forming the National Junior College Athletic Association.

Intramural athletics continued to grow in colleges and universities. Women's athletic associations also increased in number. The principles that guided such programs were established largely during the early years by the National Section on Women's Athletics.

Physical education in the midtwentieth century

Physical education made progress in the middle of the twentieth century.

IMPACT OF WORLD WAR II

The country was jolted from depression by World War II. Physical education received an impetus as physical training programs were established under Gene Tunney in the Navy, Hank Greenburg in the Air Force, and sports leaders in other branches of the armed forces. Schools and colleges were urged to help develop physical fitness in the youth of the nation. A return to more formalized conditioning programs resulted.

The need for a national program of physical fitness was evident as a result of Selective Service examinations and other indications that young people were not in sound physical shape. Several steps were taken in this direction. President Roosevelt appointed John B. Kelly of Philadelphia National Director of Physical Training. In 1941 Mayor Fiorello LaGuardia of New York City was appointed by President Roosevelt as Director of Civilian Defense in Charge of Physical Fitness, and a National Advisory Board was established. William L. Hughes of the national association was appointed chairman. In 1942 a Division of Physical Fitness was established in the Office of Defense, Health, and Welfare Services. In 1943 John B. Kelly was appointed chairman of a Committee of Physical Fitness within the Office of the Administrator, Federal Security Agency.

The war years had their impact on programs of physical education in schools and colleges of the nation. In many instances, elementary school physical education classes met daily, and secondary and college classes also increased in number. The program of activities took on a more formal nature with the purpose of physically conditioning the children and youth of the United States for the national emergency that existed. Girls and women, as well as boys and men, were exposed to these programs.

THE PHYSICAL FITNESS MOVEMENT

In December, 1953, an article was published in the *Journal of the American Association for Health, Physical Education, and Recreation* entitled "Muscular Fitness and Health." The article discussed the physical deficiencies of American children in contrast with European children and brought to the attention of the American people the deplorable physical condition of the nation's youth. As a result, a series of events followed that may be called the physical fitness movement.

James B. Kelly of Philadelphia and Senator James Duff of Pennsylvania called the information discussed in this article to the attention of the President of the United States. In July, 1955, President Eisenhower convened a group of prominent sports figures in Washington, D.C., to explore the fitness problem. Later, he called a Youth Fitness Conference at the Naval Academy in Annapolis. At the conclusion of the conference President Eisenhower issued an executive order establishing a President's Council on Youth Fitness and appointed Dr. Shane MacCarthy as executive director. After this a President's Citizens Advisory Committee on Fitness of American Youth was appointed.

As a result of President Eisenhower's decrees, fitness became a national topic for consideration. Several states established their own committees on physical fitness. Cities such as Flint and Detroit developed special projects. The YMCA, Amateur Athletic Union, and other organizations put forth special efforts to promote fitness. Several business concerns became involved. The magazine *Sports Illustrated* devoted regular features to fitness. The National Research Council on the AAHPER authorized the testing of American children in regard to their physical fitness. The College Physical Education Association for Men published a special report entitled "Fit for College." Operation Fitness USA was inaugurated by the AAHPER to promote fitness, leadership, public relations, and research. The project

established motivational devices such as certificates of recognition, achievement awards, and emblems for students at various levels of achievement.

When John F. Kennedy became President of the United States, he appointed Charles "Bud" Wilkinson of Oklahoma to head his council on youth fitness. The name was changed to the President's Council on Physical Fitness. The council introduced its "Blue Book" with suggestions for school-centered programs.

When Lyndon Johnson became President, he appointed Stan Musial to head his Council on Physical Fitness. Later, when Stan Musial resigned this position, the President appointed Captain James A. Lovell, Jr., U.S.N. (now retired), to replace him. The council's name was again changed to the President's Council on Physical Fitness and Sports.

PROFESSIONAL PREPARATION

The war and postwar teacher shortage represented a critical problem for the nation. During the war 200,000 teachers left jobs, and 100,000 emergency certificates were issued. Many of those who left did not return, and inadequately trained replacements were hired. The critical shortage forced administrators to discard their standards in selecting teachers.

Professional preparation programs increased in number during this period, with over 600 colleges and universities participating in such programs. Some of the larger institutions developed separate professional programs for health, physical education, and recreation personnel, whereas many smaller institutions concerned themselves with only physical education.

ATHLETICS

There were four significant developments in respect to the development of athletics during the midtwentieth century. There was a renewed interest in girls' and women's sports, intramurals, lifetime sports, and sport programs for boys and girls below the high school age.

Girls' and women's sports. In 1962 the Division for Girl's and Women's Sports (DGWS) and the Division of Men's Athletics of the AAHPER held their first joint conference so that the views of both men and women in the profession could be expressed. Two years later the first National Institute on Girls' Sports was held for the purpose of promoting sports for girls and women. In 1965 a study conference met to discuss and develop guidelines needed in the area of competition for girls and women. In addition to these steps that were taken to promote girls' and women's sports, other moves included the development of a liaison with Olympic Games officials as a part of the Olympic development movement, the publication of guidelines for girls and women in competitive sports by the DGWS, and the exploration of the social changes in society that had implications for sport programs for women. All these steps represented a new departure toward providing greater opportunities for girls and women to engage in competitive sports at both the high school and college levels. (For more information on sports for women see Chapters 6 and 9.)

Intramurals. As sports became more and more popular at various educational levels, there was a renewed interest in providing sports competition for all students, not just the skilled elite. A meeting that helped to spur this movement was held in 1956, when the National Conference on Intramural Sports for College Men and Women met in Washington, D.C. Its purpose was to consider intramural programs for college men and women, to formulate principles, to recommend administrative procedures relating to current and future programs, and to provide greater opportunity for more young men and women to participate in healthful recreational activities. The intramural movement continued to grow, with leadership being provided by the National Intramural Association.

Lifetime sports. This period saw a stress on sports that can be played during a person's entire lifetime. Giving leadership to this movement was the establishment of the Lifetime Sports Foundation in 1965. Its purpose was to promote fitness and lifetime sports and to give assistance to groups engaged in these areas. This same year the AAHPER approved the Lifetime Sports Education Project, an adjunct of the Lifetime Sports Foundation. School and college physical education programs reflected the influence of such projects, with greater emphasis being given to the teaching of activities such as bowling, tennis, golf, and badminton.

Sport programs for boys and girls below the high school level. Considerable controversy was generated during this period concerning sports for children below the high school level. In 1953 a National Conference on Program Planning in Games and Sports for Boys and Girls of Elementary School Age was held in Washington, D.C. It was the first time that organizations representing medicine, education, recreation, and other organizations serving the child had ever met with leaders of organizations who promote highly organized competitive activities for children. Two recommendations to come out of this conference were (1) that programs of games and sports should be based on the developmental level of children and that there should be no contact sports for children under 12 years of age and (2) that competition is inherent in the growth and development of the child and will be harmful or beneficial depending on a variety of factors. (For more information on sports see Chapter 6.)

INTERNATIONAL DEVELOPMENTS

International meetings of leaders of health, physical education, and recreation from various parts of the world were initiated in the mid-twentieth century. Furthermore, the Peace Corps recruited many physical educators to work in selected countries of the world.

World seminars in physical education were held, such as the one in Helsinki in 1952. The first International Congress in Physical Education was held in the United States in 1953 and considered such topics as recreation, sports, correctives, dance, and tests and measurements.

In 1958 at the annual meeting of the World Confederation of Organizations of the Teaching Profession (WCOTP), a committee was appointed to make plans for a World Federation of National and International Associations of Health Education, Physical Education, and Recreation. The purpose was to provide a way in which to unite representatives from all associations of these fields in a worldwide organization. The following year the WCOTP established the International Council of Health, Physical Education, and Recreation (ICHPER). (For more information on international developments see Chapter 7.)

THE HANDICAPPED

In the midtwentieth century physical educators realized that their field of specialization could make a contribution to the handicapped student, including the mentally retarded, the physically handicapped, the poorly coordinated, and the culturally disadvantaged. One event that accented this movement was a grant from the Joseph P. Kennedy, Jr., Foundation in 1965, which enabled the AAHPER to establish the Project on Recreation and Fitness for the Mentally Retarded for the purposes of research, program development, and leadership training.

Adapted physical education programs received increasing attention, with special programs being included in professional preparation institutions to provide leadership for this area. Furthermore, governmental grants of funds enabled greater stress to be placed on this particular phase of the physical education program. (For more recent developments on the handicapped see Chapter 10.)

RESEARCH

The need for research in physical education grew to much greater importance in the eyes of physical educators than it had heretofore. The Research Council of the AAHPER was established in 1952 as a section under the General Division. Its functions and purposes included those of promoting research along strategic lines, developing long-range plans, preparing and disseminating materials to aid research workers in the field, and synthesizing research materials in areas related to the professional fields.

As a result of the increased recognition of the importance of research, studies were conducted in areas such as exercise physiology, motor learning, sociology of sport, and teaching methods.

FACILITIES AND EQUIPMENT

With the growth of physical education programs and the construction of new facilities to accommodate these programs, meetings, re-

Courtesy Julian Stein, AAHPER.

A physical education program for the handicapped in action.

search, and interest were generated regarding facilities and equipment for physical education.

In 1947 a grant was made by the Athletic Institute to help sponsor a National Facilities Conference at Jackson's Mill, West Virginia. Fifty-four outstanding education, park, and recreation leaders met with architects, engineers, and city planners to prepare a guide for planning facilities for health, physical education, and recreation programs. Facilities conferences have been held periodically in various parts of the United States since 1947.

The Council on Equipment and Supplies of the AAHPER was formed in 1954. Its purpose was to allow manufacturers, distributors, buyers, and consumers of materials used in the areas of health education, physical education,

and recreation to work together on problems of mutual concern.

The great amount of monies expended for facilities and equipment in physical education, including sports programs, has been responsible for continued interest in this area so that these monies may be expended in the most profitable manner possible.

SIGNIFICANT CURRENT DEVELOPMENTS HAVING IMPLICATIONS FOR PHYSICAL EDUCATION

Education is undergoing a period of change, and physical education, as a part of education, is also undergoing change. The teacher's and coach's roles are changing as the needs of society change, student involvement raises many

Courtesy American Blind Bowling Association.

Physical education makes a contribution to handicapped persons. Joseph Luckett, Cincinnati, Ohio, is a bowler who is partially blind.

questions as to the administration and conduct of programs, curriculum reform is widespread as the old way of doing things is found to be outmoded, the stress on sports continues to increase but is associated with many problems, Title IX is affecting physical education, and new types of facilities are being utilized. There is a new look in elementary school physical education, and mainstreaming is being stressed for the handicapped. Performance- or competency-based teacher education is taking hold. These and other significant current developments are discussed in the various chapters throughout this text with particular emphasis being given to selected new trends in physical education and sport in Chapters 6 to 10.

PROJECTING PHYSICAL EDUCATION INTO THE FUTURE

What will the twenty-first century be like? It will probably be an age where what is accomplished today may be obsolete tomorrow. Happenings that were once just dreamed about may suddenly be in existence. It will be an age in which knowledge will be essential and change must be coped with daily. The following conditions can also be expected in the twenty-first century.

Three hundred fifty million people will inhabit the United States. Three out of four persons will reside in cities—elongated strips of land dotted with thousands of homes and other buildings. College will be a reality for four out of five high school graduates, most of whom will later go into the ranks of the professional and white-collar workers.

High income and more leisure will change the lives of most people. The total population will spend $10 billion a year on sporting goods alone to play all types of games, many of which will be imported from abroad by millions of Americans who go overseas annually.

The future will find that the health of people can be vitally improved for the better. Life expectancy will be increased as a result of a better understanding of medical science. Interchangeable human parts will help to ensure longer life. Other conditions and new techniques that are predicted for the years ahead include transistorized gadgets to stimulate dam-aged muscles; pocket radars to help the blind to see and the deaf to hear; and drug control of personality.

Computer centers will be established on a regional basis throughout the United States. Each will link many colleges and research institutions together in a high-speed computer network.

Forecast for the future—general education

Education will undergo many changes in the future that will have implications for students who attend schools and colleges, the teachers who make up the faculties of these institutions, the administration responsible for the vast educational undertaking, and the educational programs offered.

STUDENTS

Students will begin their education much earlier, in most cases at 3 and 4 years of age. More of the educational budget will be spent in the earlier years of education, which will be designed to increase the sensory input from which young children develop their intelligence.

Education will become more individualized, with greater stress on the needs of each student, including the handicapped, mentally retarded, emotionally disturbed, gifted, and others. These atypical conditions will be identified earlier in the educational process, provided for from the earliest educational levels, and continued as long as necessary throughout the school years. More effective diagnostic tools will be used to indicate what students can benefit most from what types of educational programs.

There will be more emphasis placed on student involvement in the learning process. Students will play an active part in determining at what rate they will proceed and in what projects and experiences they will participate.

The growth in the number of college-age men and women will begin to decline. With nearly three fourths of the high school graduates now going on to higher education, it is unlikely that there will be any further increase in the percentage of high school graduates con-

Division of Birdair Structures, Inc., Buffalo, N.Y.

Airshelters. The city of the future.

tinuing their education. Even a major influx of nonwhites, who have been underrepresented in college in the past, will not affect the total numbers significantly. The major influx of students will be into graduate schools, where they will work on advanced degrees.

EDUCATORS

Educators will prepare for specialized roles in which they can make the greatest contribution to education. They will develop competencies in teaching and their special areas, since performance- or competency-based teaching will be utilized.

The role of the teacher will be more of a "learning clinician," whose responsibility is to provide meaningful psychosocial treatment for students. The teacher will be especially concerned with factors such as the environment, learning styles of students, and interpersonal relations. Teachers will also play a more important role in the administration and decision-making process of schools and colleges. The beginning teacher will be given more time to orient to the task of a full-time teacher. Furthermore, the relationship with professional preparation institutions will be extended, with follow-up to help and advise the beginning teacher regarding problems encountered during the first years on the job.

There will be many more paraprofessionals —teacher aides who will assist regular teachers. These assistants will assume clerical work, noon-hour supervision, and other details that do not require the attention of trained teachers. Consequently, teachers will be free to spend more time on teaching, helping students, and doing those things for which their training indicates the greatest service can be rendered. The teacher will also have more time for planning and thinking about the tasks to be performed.

Professional associations of teachers will play a more important role in seeing that proper ethical standards are maintained by the teaching profession and also will participate more in the certification and standard establishment processes for determining who is or is not eligible to teach in schools.

Teachers will become more militant. Labor

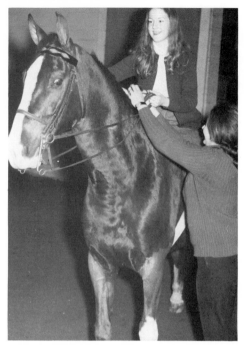

Photo by Rollie Baird, Dellarson Studios.

Paraprofessional teaching an off-campus course in riding at Regina High School, Minneapolis, Minnesota.

unions will infiltrate into the schools and colleges on a wide scale. The unions, utilizing strikes and other labor union techniques, will be effective in securing teacher demands.

Teachers of the future will not have to repeat themselves, since taped classroom discussions will be kept on file to facilitate makeup work for students who have missed class for some reason or who failed to get material that has already been presented. Videotapes will also assist teachers in critically evaluating their presentations, and, in this way, teaching will become more of an art.

Salaries for teachers will continue to increase, particularly for those persons who become master teachers and research scholars. The single-salary schedule will eventually give way to a merit plan that pays salaries to outstanding teachers on a scale comparable to the business and industrial executive class.

Teachers in schools will be given more released time from teaching duties to pursue research studies and conduct experiments in their local research and development centers.

Changes at the college level will find the retirement age of faculty members being extended, an increase in the sense of faculty stability and institutional identification, more selective tenure decisions, and a greater faculty involvement in the decision-making process.

ADMINISTRATION

Those individuals desiring to be administrators will be required to serve internships after graduating from college (much like physicians do today) and pursue graduate study that will include an extensive study of administrative theory, particularly as it relates to the behavioral sciences.

School administration will be much more democratic, with faculties and students working with administrators in shaping policies and making decisions.

Administrators and boards of education will be required to justify the amount of money that they spend on education in terms of more tangible results. For example, how effectively does the physical education program teach skills to all its students?

Federal and state involvement in the educational process will increase. Many new demands will be made on educational programs by federal and state authorities to ensure that all children receive an acceptable standard of education.

In addition to the local contributions, more and more money invested in education will come from federal and state levels as well as business sources.

Forecast for the future—physical education

There will be many changes in physical education in the years ahead. During the 1980s most of the programs that exist will be different from those which prevailed in the schools and colleges during the 1960s and 1970s. Changes will take place in areas such as the teaching staff, physical education programs, and facilities.

PHYSICAL EDUCATORS

The teacher of physical education in the future will have a specialized role to play. All teachers will not perform the same duties. For

One type of teacher for the future will be primarily interested in teaching handicapped persons, demonstrated by this teacher at South Carolina School for the Deaf and Blind, Spartansburg, South Carolina.

the elementary and secondary school levels three types of teachers will be trained. First, there will be the teacher who is primarily interested in teaching movement education and physical education skills. This teacher will be a specialist in these areas and utilize an analytical method, breaking down the various skills into their most minute subdivisions and then teaching from a movement exploration and kinesiological approach so that the student learns the basic scientific principles underlying good movement.

The second type of physical education instructor will be an expert in research techniques and will understand thoroughly the scientific basis underlying physical activity as it relates to human development. Furthermore, as a result of the knowledge of teaching techniques, this teacher will be able to apply this information to program development, as well as communicate this knowledge to the student in an interesting, clear, and accurate manner.

A third type of instructor will work with handicapped persons, specializing in various aspects of special education as well as physical education for the handicapped.

These three types of physical education in-

structors will make up one part of a team that conducts the program in the gymnasium, playground, and swimming pool, as well as in the classroom. Other members of the team will include clerical help, student teachers, and consultants from the disciplines of biology, psychology, and sociology.

At the college and university level, the three types of instructors will also be present in the basic instruction and in the professional preparation programs. As in the case of the precollege level, many members of the staff will have released time to do research. In some cases, teachers and professors will have joint appointments in the biology, psychology, sociology, or special education departments.

In addition to these basic types of roles that physical educators will play, there will also be specialists in coaching, athletic training, and audiovisual media.

Many physical educators, in addition to teaching in schools and colleges, will be prepared for careers in industry, centers for the elderly, health spas, correctional institutions, youth-serving agencies, and other settings where these physical education programs will exist.

PROGRAM

Students will play an increasingly active role in determining the type of physical education program that will best meet their needs and interests. This will be reflected by innovations such as more elective programs, in which students select from groups of activities those in which they want to specialize. In addition, there will be independent study, in which a student may spend an entire semester on some particular sport project or activity, and also provisions for students to take tests, which, if passed, will provide exemption from the physical education requirement.

The physical education program will become more instructional and sequential in nature as it proceeds through the primary, middle, secondary, and college levels of education. Some national standards will be established whereby individual schools, students, and administrators may compare themselves at any particular age or educational level with national norms. In many schools, programs will be placed on a voluntary basis rather than being required. Alternate programs will also be utilized to meet educational requirements.

The future will see a greater emphasis on research, with physical education programs reflecting new knowledge in areas such as motor learning, biomechanics, sociology of sport, working with the handicapped, and programs that are best for the inner city.

Physical education will grow in importance at the elementary and middle school levels as there is increased recognition among educators regarding the contribution that perceptual-motor training, interdisciplinary emphasis, and movement education can make to children, such as improving their self-concept and contributing to scholastic skills.

The future will see the extensive utilization of computers and measurement instruments to group students accurately into physical education teaching units according to abilities, traits, skills, physical fitness, and previous experiences in physical education.

A system of records will be kept for each student from kindergarten until graduation from college. These records will ensure a better organized program related to each individual's needs and a more progressive program through the grades and college. These records will follow students everywhere they go in school or college and will contain information such as physical fitness ratings, skills mastered, and knowledge accumulated. At the college level these records will have particular value in determining those students who will pursue the voluntary program in physical education and those who will have to take the required program because they have entered college with below-standard development in physical skills, knowledge, or some other aspect of fitness. Physical education will not be required of every student, only those who fall below acceptable university standards.

The program of physical education will be aimed at developing physically educated students, with a trend away from teacher-induced learnings toward student-motivated learnings.

Textbooks will be used in physical education classes and homework assigned as in other subject-matter fields. The aim will be to get at the *why* of the activity as well as the activity itself, with physical education meeting in the classroom as well as in the gymnasium. Although physical education will remain activity oriented, the goal will be to physically educate students so that they understand and identify closely with the importance of physical activity in their lives and its relationship to their physical, psychological, and sociological development. Specialists in physical education will be in charge of programs starting early in the elementary school years and continuing through college. At the nursery school and primary grade levels the classroom teacher will work closely with the specialist in the conduct of the physical education program.

The movement emphasis will permeate the program throughout the school and college life of students, showing them how to use the body most efficiently. Physical movement will be analyzed in relation to the basic motion factors of weight, space, time, and flow. Many activities will be provided that give rise to the exploration and analysis of free and spontaneous movements of the whole body.

There will be many other program developments in physical education to provide for all

The movement emphasis will permeate future programs in physical education. These students are playing homemade board games, emphasizing hand-eye coordination at Oak View Elementary School, Fairfax, Virginia.

types of atypical students. Students who fall into these classifications will be identified early in their school years, and educational programs will be adapted throughout their school life to meet their needs in the best way possible. Specialized programs and teachers trained for working with the handicapped will find prominent places in programs of physical education at both precollege and college educational levels.

The "club" movement will grow as a means of providing students and persons with special activity interests the opportunities to engage in their favorite activities. There will be all kinds of clubs, including bicycling, surfing, skydiving, hiking, and skish. Faculty, school, and college sponsorship will give support to this development. The only criterion for membership will be interest in the activity. The only eligibility rule will be that the participant be a bona fide student.

The simple pleasures will continue to attract most participants, such as swimming, bicycling, fishing, hunting, camping, ice skating, hiking, walking, and sledding. But because of increased income, more activities usually associated with people in upper income brackets will be popular, such as boating, horseback riding, tennis, skiing, squash, sailing, water skiing, and golfing. Furthermore, school programs will place more emphasis on activities that can be enjoyed throughout a lifetime.

The speed and increased frequency of travel, in spite of the energy crisis, will find many sports played on an international basis. Teams will be scheduled in Europe, South America, and Asia. There will be international sports leagues at the college level: Yale and Oxford may be battling it out for the rugby title and Reed and Nihon for the tennis championship. High schools will have television meets with their counterparts in other lands—Shaker Heights High School in Cleveland may schedule King George V High School in Hong Kong for archery.

There will be more interschool and intercollegiate athletic competition for women. Teams and leagues in many sports will become much more popular. In addition, many schools and colleges will have varsity and intramural teams made up of both boys and girls and men and women in noncontact sports such as golf, tennis, and swimming. As a result of this emphasis, there will be increased involvement on the part of educators in Olympic development so that the best girl and women athletes can participate in this international festival. (For other changes in sports programs see Chapters 6 and 9).

FACILITIES

Increased population, rising school enrollments, city life, limited space, and skyrocketing labor and material costs will alter physical education and sports facilities. Outdoor swimming pools will be used year-round, with plastic bubbles covering them when the snow comes. Playgrounds and athletic fields will also be used continuously and, in addition, will have convertible features; baseball fields and football gridirons will become hockey areas and basketball courts within an hour's time. Neighborhood playing fields on the roofs of apartment houses and civic buildings will serve inhabitants of housing developments in congested areas.

New ideas and new materials will be used in all construction. Artificial turf will make outdoor facilities similar to grass-covered areas. New methods of supporting roof structures will produce large areas where activities can be en-

Photo by Frank Lotz Miller.

Louisiana's Superdome, constructed on the fringe of the New Orleans Central Business District, is a spectacular sight on the city skyline. The mammoth, multipurpose structure seats more than 80,000 people and is the world's first complete stadium-auditorium-convention-entertainment complex. Some of the uses for which the Superdome has been designed are football stadium, baseball stadium, Madison Square Garden–type arena, auditorium, convention-trade show complex and exhibit hall, giant screen television theater, and downtown parking complex.

gaged in free from poles, columns, and other obstructions. The "floating roof" will become common in all amphitheaters. The size of rooms and play areas will be flexible with increasing use of electrically powered equipment to change partitions, fold bleachers, and remove apparatus from play areas.

Weather will not prove a deterrent to the holding of athletic contests. Seasonal activities will operate year-round, if desired. Huge arenas with roofs that roll back and form an outdoor amphitheater or, when closed, protect against rain, wind, or snow will exist in every section of the country.

Nighttime will not prove a handicap to participation, since golf courses, tennis courts, and playfields will be illuminated so as to give daylight effect and serve the greater number of people who desire to participate.

Gymnasiums will become larger, more adaptable, more all-purpose, and more mechanical. Teachers will operate a control board, and at the push of the right buttons, the necessary equipment for each class will, in the span of a few seconds, either come out of the wall, lower from the ceiling, or come up out of special floor compartments. There will be plastic gym flooring, requiring little maintenance, guaranteed not to warp, and with all the necessary marking and lines impregnated and wear-proof. There will be wall and ceiling panels sensitive to electrical impulse instead of light bulbs.

Audiovisual centers will be readily available for individual student study on various sport skills or other aspects of physical education. Centers will contain television, movies, Super-8 cassettes, tapes, and teaching machines. Materials such as rules, strategies, facts of anatomy, and first aid will be programmed so that more time will be free for skill development.

At the college level, athletic and recreation facilities, such as tennis and handball courts, and swimming facilities will be strategically located throughout the entire campus, using the open green space around dormitories and other campus structures. Furthermore, to cut costs, there will be interinstitutional cooperation among colleges and universities close to one another. Colleges will share gymnasiums, libraries, cafeterias, and other facilities.

Manufacturers will continue to discover new ways to improve equipment. New and better materials for shoes and clothing will make them lighter and provide for easier movement. Uniforms for physical education classes will be made of throwaway material and will be disposed of after wearing. It will be cheaper to do this and be more energy efficient than laundering them even once.

Shaver and Co., Architects, Salina, Kan.

Exterior of Sherwood Elementary School, Greeley, Colorado.

SELF-ASSESSMENT TESTS

These tests are to assist students in determining if material and competencies presented in this chapter have been mastered.

1. Reflect on the history of physical education and then prepare a graph that traces its history from ancient times until the present. Identify the high and low points of physical education in the graph, supplying the rationale for your analysis.

2. Conduct an evaluation of Athenian Greek physical education. As a result of this evaluation, identify the contributions that can be traced directly to the Athenian Greeks. Be specific in your answer.

3. Prepare a bulletin board display that depicts some of the milestones in the history of physical education. Include in this historical display some facts and/or illustrations to show why the doctrines of asceticism, scholasticism, and puritanism did not support the importance of physical education as making a contribution to human existence.

4. After each of the following names, write a sentence that will identify the person and his or her historical contribution to physical education:

Rousseau	Sargent	McKenzie
Jahn	Hitchcock	Hanna
Ling	Wood	Gulick
Maclaren	Hetherington	Anderson

5. Prepare a plan for guiding the professional destiny of physical education in the future based on what you have learned from a study of its history.

6. Prepare an essay on the topic, "Projecting Physical Education Into The Future." In this essay describe what education and physical education programs will be like in the year 2000 A.D. Support your projections by utilizing developing trends in education and physical education.

READING ASSIGNMENT

Bucher, Charles A.: Dimensions of physical education, ed. 2, St. Louis, 1974, The C. V. Mosby Co., Reading selections 2, 4, 23 to 30, and 62.

SELECTED REFERENCES

Abbott, E. A.: Society and politics in ancient Rome, New York, 1909, Charles Scribner's Sons.
Barnes, H. E.: The history of western civilization, New York, 1935, Harcourt, Brace & Co., Inc.
Bell, J. A.: Plato, the ghetto and physical education, The Physical Educator **29:**87, May, 1972.
Bucher, Charles A.: Scorekeepers vs. first principles, Journal of Health, Physical Education, and Recreation **35:**26, Sept., 1964.
Butler, A. J.: Sport in classic times, London, 1930, Ernest Benn, Ltd.
Buttree, J. M.: The rhythm of the redman, New York, 1930, A. S. Barnes & Co.
Caillois, Roger: Man, play, and games, New York, 1961, The Free Press of Glencoe, Inc. (translated from the French).
Carcopino, J.: Daily life in ancient Rome, New Haven, Conn., 1940, Yale University Press (translated by E. O. Lorimer).
Clark, Ellery H.: The Olympic games and their influence upon physical education, The American Physical Education Review.
Dulles, Foster Rhea: America learns to play, New York, 1966, Appleton-Century-Crofts.
Falkener, E.: Games ancient and oriental and how to play them, London, 1892, Longmans.
Fuld, L. F.: Physical education in Greece and Rome, American Physical Education Review **12:**1, March, 1907.
Genasci, James E., and Klissouras, Vasillis: The delphic spirit in sports, Journal of Health, Physical Education, and Recreation **37:**43, Feb., 1966.
Hackensmith, C. W.: History of physical education, New York, 1966, Harper & Row, Publishers.
Lucas, John A.: Coubertin's philosophy of pedagogical sport, Journal of Health, Physical Education, and Recreation **35:**26, Sept., 1964.
Schleppi, J. R.: Architecture and sports, The Physical Educator **23:**123, Oct. 1966.
Seventh-fifth Anniversary of the AAHPER, Journal of Health, Physical Education, and Recreation **31:**April, 1960.
Shane, Harold G., and Shane, June Grant: Forecast for the 70s, Today's Education **58:**29, Jan., 1969.
The New Physical Education, Journal of Health, Physical Education, and Recreation, p. 24, Sept., 1971.
Thompson, S. G.: Sport, athletics, and gymnastics in ancient Greece, National College Physical Education Association for Men **75:**87, 1972.
Trekell, Marianna: Speaking to the future, Journal of Health, Physical Education, and Recreation **37:**29, Feb., 1966.
Twenter, C. J.: History speaks but who listens? The Physical Educator **29:**89, May, 1972.
Van Dalen, Deobold B., and Bennett, B. L.: A world history of physical education, Englewood Cliffs, N.J., 1971, Prentice-Hall, Inc.
Wagman, E.: Physical education and the disadvantaged, Journal of Health, Physical Education, and Recreation **44:**29, March, 1973.
Wells, H. G.: The outline of history, New York, 1931, Garden City Publishing Co., Inc.
Welsh, Raymond, editor: Physical education—a view toward the future, St. Louis, 1977, The C. V. Mosby Co.
Weston, Arthur: The making of American physical education, New York, 1962, Appleton-Century-Crofts.

6

Growth of sports in the American culture

INSTRUCTIONAL OBJECTIVES AND COMPETENCIES TO BE ACHIEVED

After reading this chapter the student should be able to—

1. Relate important aspects of the history of sport and the impact that cultures such as China, Greece, Rome, and the United States have had on the growth of sports.
2. Trace the growth of sports in educational institutions in the United States and the attitude of educators toward this growth.
3. Identify and evaluate the values that are claimed for sports.
4. Describe standards that professional associations and leaders in sport and physical education recommend to ensure that school and college athletic programs contribute to educational goals and are in the best interest of participants.
5. Know the dimensions of selected problems with which sport is confronted today, such as those concerned with girls and women, children, the Olympics, violence, the black athlete, amateurism, antiathletic mood, and coaching.
6. Formulate a philosophy of sport.

Sports have captured the thinking of Americans.* Weekend television programs monopolize the coaxial cable. Educational programs such as "Sixty Minutes" are preempted by all kinds of games and sports. Millions of Americans are glued to their chairs when featured football, baseball, basketball, and golf contests are scheduled. Millions of dollars are spent each year by product manufacturers to advertise their wares during the commercial breaks on the tube. In addition to the impact of television on sports, astronomical sums of money are spent by professional organizations to obtain the best college talent for their teams. Newspaper space devoted to sports consumes more space than all the arts combined, and sport symbols infiltrate American language, art, and politics.

Sport has been defined in many ways. Francis Logan Paxson, a historian, called it a safety valve for society. Lewis Mumford labeled it "one of the mass-duties of the machine age." Webster's dictionary defines sport as a pastime, a diversion, and says it is synonymous with fun.

ROOTS OF AMERICAN SPORT

The roots of sport go back into primitive days when the meaning of the term meant more than fun or diversion. Sport during early times meant survival, since human beings found it necessary to hunt, fish, and hurl missiles, not for pleasure but to survive the elements and the enemies that surrounded them.

As civilization developed, the Egyptians and other people who lived in the Middle East and other parts of the world participated in various sports. However, it was the privileged and wealthy class that did the playing and not the laborers and general population.

Football goes back nearly 2,000 years in China, according to some historians. It was first played in China with a leather ball filled with hair, but by the fifth century the ball was being

---

*For information on sport as a sociological phenomenon see Chapter 14.

inflated with air. In one version of the game, six holes were dug along ends of a field and each team tried to score using set formations for attack and defense. During the T'ang Dynasty (A.D. 618-907), another type of football used bamboo poles bent to form an arch, from which were hung strips of colored cloth. A small opening provided a goal through which players attempted to kick the ball. Winners of football contests were feted with fruit, wine, flowers, and silver, whereas the losers were flogged and suffered other indignities.

The Greeks are well known in history for their love of sports and particularly for their creation of the Olympic Games. The Olympics began in ancient Greece in 776 B.C. and were held every 4 years until they were abolished in A.D. 294 by the Roman Emperor Theodosius. They originated as festivals of various kinds in which athletics played a major part. The Olympic Games included foot races over various distances, armored races, boxing, chariot races, and a pentathlon. The individual winners were crowned with laurel wreaths and became public heroes in the eyes of the Greeks. The Olympic Games were also a great unifying force in Greece, since the country was divided into city-states that were constantly at war with each oth-

Courtesy British Museum, London, and
Dr. Anne Gayle Ingram, University of Maryland.

Girl running, probably Spartan, about 500 B.C. Found in Albania.

Greek physical education subscribes to the individual of wisdom and the individual of action.

Table 6-1. Chronological distribution of established dates of origins*

Sport	Date of origin†	Sport	Date of origin†
Wrestling	(2160) 1788 B.C.	Soccer	1859
Boxing	(2160?) 850 B.C.	Squash racquets	1859
Field events	(900 B.C.?) 776 B.C.	Swimming	(1530) 1859
Track events	(900 B.C.?) 776 B.C.	Roller skating	1863
Hunting	(2357) 400 B.C.	Trap shooting	1866
Kite flying	(1121) 221 B.C.	Field trials	1866
Coursing	7 A.D.	Bicycle racing	1868
Cock fighting	77	Badminton	1870
Angling	200	Skiing	(1750) 1870
Falconry	350	Target pistol shooting	1871
Horse racing	(648 B.C.) 1174	Model sailboat racing	1872
Tennis	1230	Lawn tennis	1873
Lawn bowls	1366	Football (American)	1874
Quoits	(450 B.C.) 1409	Dog racing	(1810?) 1876
Golf	(1380?) 1457	Roque	1879
Target rifle shooting	1498	Ice hockey	(1810) 1880
Fencing	1517	Rodeo	(1830) 1880
Hurling	1527	Judo	1882
Shuffleboard	1532	Tobogganing	(1837?) 1883
Archery (target)	(1530) 1585	Water polo	1885
Billiards	(1520?) 1590	Field hockey	(B.C.?) 1886
Fowling	(2475 B.C.) 1596	Birling	1888
Polo	(475?) 1596	Table tennis	1889
Curling	1607	Darts	(1850?) 1890
Ice skating	(500) 1659	Rope spinning	(1850?) 1890
Cricket	(1600) 1744	Squash tennis	1890
Fives	1746	Basketball	1891
Yacht racing	(1675) 1775	Automobile racing	1895
Pedestrianism	(1610) 1792	Volleyball	1895
Racquets	(1555) 1799	Jai alai	1896
Horseshoes	(1750?) 1801	Paddle tennis	1898
Coaching	(1590) 1807	Motorcycle racing	1902
Steeplechasing	(1740) 1810	Corkball	1904
Mountaineering	(1780?) 1811	Motorboat racing	1904
Gymnastics	(1790) 1816	Model airplane flying	1905
Pigeon racing	(1800) 1818	Airplane flying	1907
Harness racing	1825	Soaring	1909
Sculling	(1715) 1839	Speedball	1920
Lacrosse	(1400) 1839	Softball	(1890) 1923
Rowing	1839	Miniature golf	(1860) 1927
Bowling (ten pins)	(1600) 1840	Soapbox racing	1927
Croquet	1840	Six man football	1933
Handball	(1500?) 1840	Skin diving	1934
Baseball	(1750) 1846	Miniature auto racing	1936
Rugby	1846	Water skiing	1939
Iceboating	(1720) 1850	Skish	(1880?) 1939
Weight lifting	(1720) 1854	Flickerball	1948
Canoe racing	(1790?) 1859		

*Eyler, Marvin H.: Research Quarterly **32**:484, 1961.

†The date given after each sport is that of the earliest documented evidence of its origin in organized form. Dates shown in parentheses are those of documented evidence of previous existence as unorganized or noncompetitive activity. A date in parentheses with a question mark indicates that reputed evidence previous to this date may not actually refer to this specific sport.

er. However, during the time that the Games were in progress, a truce was declared and no fighting was permitted. In time, the Olympic Games deteriorated as contestant victories led to gifts, tax exemptions, and other favors, as well as unsportsmanlike conduct. (For more information on the Olympics see Chapter 5.)

The modern Olympic Games were revived by Baron Pierre de Coubertin in 1896. While studying the mushrooming sports movements in the United States, Canada, and England, de Coubertin recognized the potential value of international competition. He organized an international Olympic Committee in 1894, which approved Athens as the site of the first modern Olympic Games in 1896. Since then, the Olympics have been held every 4 years, except during the period of World War II. Women entered competition in 1912, and the winter sports were added in 1934. The Olympics were conceived to honor individual winners rather than countries. No nation is officially declared the winner although the newspapers have devised a point system by which unofficial standings of the various countries are maintained.

After the Greeks, the Romans brought professionalism to sports on a major scale. The cry of the populace for bread and games led to gory spectacles to please the multitudes. Furthermore, the Romans as a nation, seemed to be more interested in being spectators than participants in sports.

Sport during the Middle Ages was largely a carryover of the activities of prior years. Sport particularly became associated with military motives, since many of the activities were designed to harden and strengthen men for combat. For example, during the feudalistic period the training for knighthood involved many strenuous sporting activities, including horsemanship while the knight was encased in heavy armor. On festival occasions the knights would engage in jousts to try to see if they could unseat their opponents and thus win the favor of the onlookers as well as their ladies. Indeed, they carried their ladies' colors with them in jousts as well as in combat.

The Renaissance, with its emphasis on enjoyment of the present rather than a concern for the hereafter, created a more favorable outlook toward sport as a leisure-time activity. As a result

sports became more popular among the masses.

The modern European period saw a continued growth in sports, together with the revival of the Olympic Games and an emphasis on outdoor sports in England. However, it was to remain for the United States gradually to initiate the movement toward sports on a major scale.

SPORT IN THE AMERICAN CULTURE

Sport has had an interesting history in the United States. From the time of colonial days, when sport for sports' sake was frowned on, until today, when sports have become big business, there has been a steady growth of this phase of the American culture.

Colonial America was concerned with survival. The life-style of the early American settlers was concerned with work, not play. Play, in fact, was looked on as a sinful pursuit for adults, particularly in the New England colonies. Only on special occasions did the colonists permit themselves the luxury of engaging in hunts and contests of strength and competition in wrestling, running and jumping. However, as years went by and more settlers came to the United States, those activities which were popular in seventeenth-century England were introduced. These sports included horseracing, ninepins, hunting, fishing, marksmanship, and dice and card games. Also, the Dutch colonists introduced activities such as bowling, skating, and various types of ball games. With this influx of activities the opposition to sports as voiced by the Puritans gradually gave way to a more liberal and favorable attitude toward participation in games and related activities.

In the postrevolutionary period in the United States there was an increased interest in sports, which continued through the remainder of the eighteenth century and into the nineteenth century. Activities such as rowing and sailing regattas, wrestling and shooting matches, and foot races became popular. In addition, this period saw the introduction of sports into some schools that were modeled after the English educational institutions. The first school to integrate games and sports into the curriculum was the Dummer Grammar School in Byfield, Massachusetts, in 1782. Soccer and batball were played at Exeter early in the nineteenth century. In college, sports started to be introduced in the

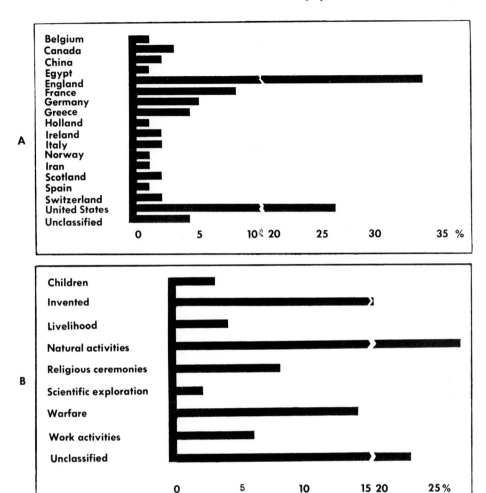

From Eyler, Marvin H.: Research Quarterly 32:483, 1961.

Origins of contemporary sports. **A,** Percentage distribution of place of origin for ninety-five sports. **B,** Percentage distribution of activities from which the ninety-five sports evolved.

middle 1800s, with tennis, baseball, football, rowing, handball, golf, roller skating, ice hockey, and lacrosse becoming popular.

During the last half of the nineteenth century the expansion of sport programs in colleges was slowed to some extent but still steadily increased in popularity. A significant development during this period was the formation of associations of various colleges and universities to have better control of their athletic programs.

In the early 1900s there was a renewed interest in sports throughout the nation as well as in educational institutions. For example, during the last quarter of the eighteenth century, for the first time in the United States there was a Ken-

tucky Derby, lawn tennis game, National League baseball, Amateur Athletic Union, sports page in a newspaper, and a Madison Square Garden.

The 1920s saw one of the greatest explosions in sports in the United States. This period produced such outstanding sports figures as Babe Ruth, Bill Tilden, Jack Dempsey, and Ken Strong. The 1920s also saw the beginning of large crowds to witness sport spectaculars. For example, previous to this time boxing had only four $100,000 gates. However, in the 1920s it was common to exceed gates of $1 million and even $2 million.

Since the 1920s there has been a continual

expansion of sport enterprises in all major sports such as baseball, basketball, tennis, football, soccer, and golf. Sport has become big business with billions of dollars being spent on equipment, salaries, stadia, and supporting supplies. The day of the million-dollar athlete also has arrived. Whereas superstars formerly signed for hundreds and thousands of dollars, now they sign contracts for millions of dollars. Indeed, the New York Yankees have so many high-salaried players that they have been referred to as the team of millionaires.

GROWTH OF SPORTS IN EDUCATIONAL INSTITUTIONS

The growth of sports in schools and colleges has been comparatively recent in the United States society. The period from 1875 to 1900 saw for the first time a Harvard-Yale football game, a Big Ten Conference, and an All-American team. The advent of the radio and ''lunar craters'', as football coach Alonzo Stagg called the athletic arenas, resulted in an increase in ''spectatoritis'' and the exploitation of sport for its commercial value.

As sport programs grew, they were extended downward into the lower educational levels. Athletics started at the college level with a crew race between Harvard and Yale in 1852, followed by the introduction of other sports to the college campus. As higher education athletic programs gained recognition and popularity, the high schools thought that sports should also be a part of their educational offerings. Next, the junior high schools initiated inter-school athletic programs, many of which were carbon copies of those in the senior high schools, which previously had copied the colleges. Today, some elementary schools are scheduling games as competitive sports are pushed further down the educational ladder.

From the beginning, sports were of concern to educators because of their questionable educational worth and the way they can distort a school's or nation's sense of values. For example, as reported in *Sports Illustrated,* in honor of Walter Camp, Yale alumni helped raise $180,000 for the memorial gateway to the Yale Bowl, but other Yale admirers of Josiah Willard Gibbs, one of the greatest physicists the coun-

Sports have made large gains in educational institutions. Branch Rickey Gymnasium at Ohio Wesleyan University, Delaware, Ohio.

try had produced, were unable to muster $12,000 for a more modest tribute.

Despite some educator's objections, athletics and sports in the nation's schools and colleges have continued to grow until in a single recent year nearly 4 million boys alone participated in athletic programs in some 18,000 high schools. Member colleges of the National Collegiate Athletic Association indicate that each year in their institutions more than 154,000 students participate in as many as twenty-four sports. Title IX and the women's liberation movement have become factors in the participation of an increasing number of girls and women in sports in educational institutions. The number of girls and women participating, it is estimated, will gradually approach a figure equal to that of boys and men.

Today, school and college athletics are experiencing difficulties beyond those provided by their educational critics. The economy, austerity school budgets, student criticism, and racial problems, such as the concern for the black athlete, have caused educational institutions to curtail, abolish, or reevaluate their sport programs.

EDUCATIONAL VALUES CLAIMED FOR SPORTS

The educational values of sports are many. A few of the benefits are discussed here.

Physical fitness

Sports contribute to physical fitness. Through the intensive training provided for competition, various components of physical fitness such as strength, speed, endurance, agility, and coordination are developed. The participant submits to an arduous training program, essential to excellence in competitive athletics. Many students willingly and voluntarily participate in these vigorous conditioning programs to prove their worth and ability in sports competition, thus enhancing their peer status.

Skill

Sports contribute to the development of physical skills. The acquisition of skill through sports leads to a high level of proficiency, and skill is essential to achievement in the sports arena. The development of skill, furt results in recognition, a feeling of bei achievement, and other psychological benefits for the participant. In addition, skill has proved to be a medium of upward social mobility for many minority groups.

Individual development

Self-discipline, self-realization, and a desire to achieve are individual qualities that many sports leaders say can be developed through sports. An individual's self-image is gained through an assessment of how one believes one appears to others as well as what one thinks of oneself. To realize and assume their roles, participants must be cognizant of the roles of others. Only by differentiating themselves from others, and by perceiving the attitudes of others toward them, may players perceive their own self-image. Furthermore, self-evaluation is based on a continuing perception of the attitudes of others toward themselves. Therefore an individual's self-conception depends, in part, on having opportunities to observe others. The highly dynamic and competitive nature of athletics provides many such opportunities for comparison.

Self-control, many sports leaders also claim, may be enhanced through athletics. The ability to withstand or adjust to emotional stress is believed to be a result of the stress adaptation mechanism that is conditioned by exercise. Athletics provide the exercise leading to stress adaptation and, in addition, provide a highly charged atmosphere in which the individual may test and develop his or her ability to exercise self-control.

Self-discipline may also be developed, since sports require a great deal of self-sacrifice. The player is called on to subordinate personal desires and wishes to those of the group, to accept the consequences of personal decisions, and to submit to strenuous training programs and training rules.

Social development

The playing field provides a laboratory for the individual to compete as well as to cooperate. An individual must first compete with other members of the team for a position, then must cooperate with teammates when they compete with other teams. Under wise and effective leadership, sports leaders maintain, the playing field will provide a place for fairness, adherence to the rules, understanding and respect for others, and the ability to accept decisions and defeat.

Other values

The benefits of sports have been extolled by many research studies and references in the professional literature. For example, they have indicated that sports are a source of fun and enjoyment and an acceptable outlet for excess energy. They provide a common bond for unifying a school and student body, keep students from dropping out of school, provide an opportunity to learn worthwhile skills, develop physical abilities and fitness, and test a broad range of physical, interpersonal, leadership, and intellectual skills. Furthermore, these references suggest that sports build confidence and improve self-concept. In a practical sense, it is pointed out, they provide opportunities for scholarships and success that lie outside the formal academic structure. A study in Philadelphia, for example, showed that of 1,129 college-bound seniors participating in the athletic program, nearly 50% received scholarships.

In regard to sports motivating students to stay in school, a 3-year study in Cleveland, Ohio, showed only two dropouts among 391 athletes in a school within a setting where, at the time the study was undertaken, more than 40% of the general student body dropped out.

SOME EDUCATIONAL BENEFITS CLAIMED FOR SPORTS ARE QUESTIONED

Research evidence has questioned the claims of coaches and sports enthusiasts that certain behavioral changes take place in those persons who participate in sport. Some studies suggest that athletes may possess many personality traits and characteristics that are more socially desirable than those possessed by persons who do not participate in athletics. However, evidence of researchers such as McAfee, Olgivie, Tutko, Seymour, and Whittle, suggests that persons who participate in sports probably al-

ready possess these personality traits and do not develop such qualities as a result of their athletic participation. For example, Bruce C. Ogilvie and Thomas A. Tutko, professors of psychology at San Jose State College in California, raise a question as to whether athletics build character. Their study, based on a survey of 15,000 athletes, contends that the personality of the ideal athlete is not the result of any molding process but, instead, can be explained by the careful selection process which takes place at all levels of sport. They further maintain their study suggests that athletic competition has no more beneficial effect for the participant than intense personal endeavor in any other field.

SOME SUGGESTED GENERAL STANDARDS FOR EDUCATIONAL SPORTS*

To obtain the greatest values and benefits from sport participation, standards have been designed by professional associations and sport and physical education leaders. A summary of general standards that have been recommended include the following in respect to factors such as organization, staff, finances, health and safety, eligibility, recruiting, and awards.

Organization

1. The sports program is the ultimate responsibility of the school or college administration.
2. The formulation and supervision of sport policy should involve a committee of the faculty.
3. Sport policy should be implemented by both the director of physical education and the director of athletics.
4. Wherever feasible, sports should be organized as an integral part of the department of physical education.

Staff

1. Members of the coaching staff should also be members of the faculty.
2. Coaches should be hired in respect to

---

*Modified from Bucher, Charles A., and Dupee, Ralph: Athletics in schools and colleges, New York, 1965, The Center for Applied Research in Education, Inc.

their educational qualifications and not simply their won-lost records.

3. Coaches should enjoy the privileges of tenure, rank, and salary that are provided other members of the educational faculty.
4. Coaches who are hired for precollege educational positions should have preparation in the field of physical education.

Finances

1. Sport financing should be conducted in the same manner in which other educational activities are conducted.
2. Gate receipts should be considered an incidental source of revenue and go into the general fund.

Health and safety

1. Physical examinations should be required for all participants prior to engaging in a sports program.
2. Each institution should have a written policy concerning an injury-care program.
3. Each institution should make athletic insurance available to all participants.
4. Coaches should be well qualified in the prevention and care of athletic injuries.
5. A physician should be in attendance at all contests where injuries are possible.
6. Care should be taken to provide for the best equipment and supplies, that is, equipment and supplies that offer safety and the best protection, including proper size and fitting.
7. Competition among educational institutions should be scheduled only where teams of comparable ability are involved.
8. Preconditioning should be provided for prior to any sport season.
9. Playing fields and sport facilities should meet adequate standards of size and safety.

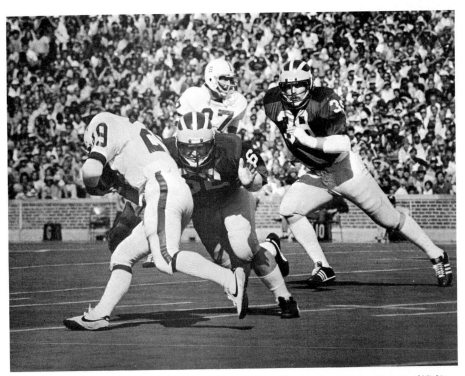

Courtesy Don Canham, University of Michigan.

Big-time college football at the University of Michigan.

Eligibility

1. All institutions should abide by rules and regulations of all sport and athletic associations under whose jurisdiction they operate and/or of which they are members.
2. Only bona fide students should be permitted to participate in the sports program.

Recruiting

1. All students should be admitted to a school or college according to the same admission standards.
2. Financial aid should be administered according to the same standards for all students in a school or college, and the recipient of financial aid should be given a statement of the amount, duration and conditions of the award.

Awards

1. The value of athletic awards should be minimal.
2. Awards for different varsity sports should be the same.
3. Awards for all-star, most-valuable player, etc., should be discouraged.

SELECTED PROBLEMS IN SPORTS TODAY

Although sports are highly popular, have benefits for the participants and for the nation, they also are affected by many problems. James A. Michener, the novelist, points out in his book entitled, *Sports in America,** some of the problems:

Girls and women are discriminated against.
Adults who are in charge of children's programs place too much stress on winning.
Children engage in highly competitive sports at too early an age.
Too much money is spent by universities to maintain big-time sport teams.
The way in which high school athletes are recruited is scandalous.
Television threatens to destroy many of the values that can accrue from sports.
There is too much violence in sports.

---

*Michener, James A.: Sports in America, New York, 1976, Random House, Inc.

Political units use public monies to build large stadia and then provide them to professional teams at minimal rental rates.

A few of the major problems facing sports today, as I view them, are discussed in this section.

Girls and women in sports

The popular magazines devote much space to the liberation of American women. Best-selling books, television talk shows, and lecturers from coast to coast stress the new female freedom and power. The Harris poll, realizing the growing influence of women, has sampled their political views and found them to be a potent force. Women are playing a more prominent role in American life, not only in politics, business, and government, but also in the field of sport.

Times have changed. When the first Olympic Games were held in 776 B.C. in ancient Greece, women were not even permitted to be spectators on Mount Olympus. Those who had the audacity to peek and then were caught lost their lives. They were thrown to their death from the highest peak of a giant rock. Years later, when the modern Olympics were started by Pierre de Coubertin, women were still not permitted to compete in any event.

Today, a different picture appears, not only in the Olympics, where many events are open to women, but also throughout the sports world — professional, amateur, and in schools and colleges. More sport opportunities are being provided girls and women, making it possible for them to participate in many different sports as well as on a higher competitive plane. This increased participation of girls and women in sports has resulted in many favorable reactions as well as some criticisms and problems.

Title IX (discussed in Chapter 9) enhances the number of opportunities for girls and women to participate in sports. The National Federation of State High School Associations has indicated that female sports are increasing. Over a recent 4-year period, they point out, male sports participation rose by 11%. However, female sports participation rose by 342% over the same period of time. One problem raised by such increased participation is whether or not men and women should have their own programs in sports, that is, whether or not the interests of both sexes can best be served by separate teams or by integrated teams.

Title IX is not the only factor that has resulted in a giant increase in female sports. Sports leaders among the women have also indicated that they perceive an increased interest in sports because of the Olympics and outstanding sports figures who have participated in this festival such as Dorothy Hamill and Nadia Comenici. Then, in the professional field, stars such as Chrissie Evert and Sandra Palmer have also left their impact on the sports-minded woman.

The increased interest and participation among women is especially noticeable at the college and university level. In higher education, athletic scholarships are being given, female high school athletes are being recruited, and more spectators are in attendance at women's events.

The economic aspects of the increase in girls' and women's participation have not been overlooked. Sporting goods manufacturers have increased their efforts to design equipment and uniforms for the female athlete. For example, there is now a softball glove called the "Debutante" and a bat called "Lady Luck."

The Association for Intercollegiate Athletics for Women, the women's equivalent of the National Collegiate Athletic Association, has grown by leaps and bounds. It was organized in 1971 and 1972 with 260 educational institutions that averaged about four sports each. Today, there are nearly 900 members, averaging about ten sports each. At last count there were over 350 colleges that were providing scholarships. It is estimated that there will be well over 100,000 women participating in intercollegiate athletics by the 1980s.

There are problems resulting from the rapid growth in girl's and women's sports in schools and colleges, in addition to the one previously mentioned, that is, the disagreement among some educators about whether separate or integrated teams are better. In many colleges and high schools there is still considerable discrimination against women. In these institutions male student participation in sports far exceeds female participation. The budgets for boys' and girls' sports are not equitable. Coaches for boys' and men's athletics are often paid more than the coaches for girls' and women's teams. Newspapers devote more space to the men than to the women. There is frequently an elaborate network of tournaments sets up for high school

Shaker Heights High School, Cleveland, Ohio

Title IX has resulted in a great growth in girls' and women's sports.

and college men but not for high school and college women.

These are only a few of the problems. Perhaps it should be recognized that problems are bound to occur with such a rapid change in the world of sport. Perhaps not. Regardless, these problems must and will be solved in the future. In the meantime, girls and women now have the opportunity to engage competitively in the sport or sports of their choosing. Years ago this was not so.

Children and youth sports

The drive to win is traditional in the United States and must be preserved, but a child will absorb that lesson soon enough in high school. During grammar school years it is more important that the child's activity be guided toward other objectives — the fun of playing rather than the winning, the child rather than the game, the many rather than the few, informal rather than formal activity, and the development of skills in many activities rather than specialization. This statement describes a concern of many people today with the tremendous growth of children and youth sports in the United States.

Presently, there are more than 3 million 7 to 12-year-old boys playing organized baseball and more than 1 million playing organized football. In addition, there are organized sport ventures in basketball, ice hockey, tennis, golf, gymnastics, and swimming. The desire to provide sports participation for youngsters is being projected more and more down into the tender years of childhood. Then, to compound the problem, many well-intentioned but uninformed adults are sponsoring these activities to further their own or their child's sports image.

The arguments for children and youth sports are that they promote physical fitness, emotional development, social adjustment, a competitive attitude, and an insulation against delinquency. In addition, it is maintained, there is no evidence to show that harm is done, they provide additional play opportunities, more highly skilled athletes result from such an experience, and organized sports are safer and healthier than the sandlot variety.

Those persons who oppose youth sports say

Youth sports have grown in recent years. Olympic Swim Meet at Cumberland Valley School District, Mechanicsburg, Pennsylvania.

that there is an overemphasis on winning, children's physical bodies are underdeveloped for such activities, sports result in a highly emotional strain on youth, the players are psychologically immature, sports at such an early age represent too much specialization, activities are run by overenthusiastic adults, and the teams are too selective.

Finally, there is a middle position taken by some of the leaders in the field of physical education who maintain that competitive sports for youth are not inherently bad or good. Instead, they point out, they are what one makes them. Under sound leadership, where the welfare of the young person is the primary consideration, where the environment is warm and friendly, and where the sports are administered in light of the needs and characteristics of the players, much good can be accomplished. However, where the opposite is true, that is, where poor leadership is provided, harm will accrue. Other recommendations set forth by these physical education leaders include the provision for participation of all children and youth and of both sexes; the necessity to offer a wide variety of sports; the availability in every sports league of a physician who makes policy concerning the health of the players; the need for coaches to understand child growth and development; and the institution of specific regulations for various sports, for example, pitching the curve ball in baseball should *not* be permitted, and children and youth should be involved in the decision-making process.

The Olympics

The Olympics are embroiled in many problems. In recent years there have been many political disputes, including the North Korean pullout in 1964, the terrorist attack of 1972, and the China-Taiwan dispute and African boycott of 1976. There are also controversies regarding the amateur and professional status of athletes, and nationalism flares anew each 4 years. Furthermore, the structure and scope of amateur athletics is under attack.

As a result of the many problems associated with the Olympic Games, some persons have asked whether they are worth retaining as pres-

ently organized. If they are to be retained, say most observers, they must be reformed.

Bill Bradley, former Rhodes Scholar and professional basketball star, suggests five ways by which the Olympics can be reformed. First, he says, open the Olympics to everyone who has the physical skill regardless of whether the player is labeled amateur or professional. Second, eliminate all team sports that have the tendency to whip up national passions. Third, award every participant in the Olympics a medal—silver and bronze medals should be eliminated and a gold medal should go only to those persons who break Olympic records— in this way the participant competes against a standard and not against an athlete from another country. Fourth, locate the Olympic competition in Greece, where a permanent facility should be constructed and financed by all participating nations. Fifth, make the Olympics more participant oriented. This can be partly accomplished by expanding the time in which the Olympics are held, possibly for a 2-month period so that contestants may get to know each other better as they live together in Olympic Village. Also, expand the cultural and artistic offerings so that aspects other than athletics of the world cultures can be emphasized.

Bill Bradley's suggestions do not stand alone. Other keen observers of the international scene have stressed the need to emphasize individual achievement to a great extent and to abolish each country's flags, anthems, and nationalistic trappings, which now distract from the individual participant.

A recent development is the report of the President's Commission on Olympic Sports, which recommended sweeping changes in the structure and scope of amateur athletics in the United States. Some of the recommendations of the twenty-four–member panel who compiled the report include the creation of a central sports organization, a bill of rights for athletes, national fund-raising programs, expanded criteria for national governing bodies, and a legal means for settling franchise disputes. This report resulted after many hearings and investigations into the problems confronting United States amateur athletes.

The Olympic Games represent an adhesive

thread that, despite many differences and problems, pulls people together all over the earth.
The athletes from many nations, who live hap-
pily and cooperatively in Olympic Village,
throw their arms around each other after hard-
fought contests, and socialize together in the
evenings, offer support to this thesis.

Each person at an Olympic dinner I attended
a short time ago was given a medallion—a rep-
lica of the belt buckle from the official parade
uniform of the United States summer Olympic
team. On the back of the memento were these
words, reflecting the purpose of sports and the
Olympics:

The rings which form the Olympic symbol originally represented the five major continents, namely,
Europe, Asia, Africa, Australia and America (both
North and South). The true concept, however, is
that the rings are linked together to denote the sporting friendship of the peoples of the earth, whatever
their creed or color. The colors were chosen because
at least one of them (blue, yellow, black, green and
red) appears in the flag of every nation in the world.

Violence

Violence is one of the major problems facing
sport today. The newspapers give glowing ac-
counts, and movie and television shows depict
it in vivid color. There are increasing incidents
of violence among players, spectators, and
both. Violence is particularly noticeable in contact sports, such as football and ice hockey.
Fist fights occur periodically, whisky bottles
are thrown on the field, fans are ejected from
the stands, and criminal charges have been
brought against players. As Thomas Tutko, a
psychologist at San Jose State College, has
said, "Too often athletics have become a direct
substitute for war." A Harvard psychiatrist
points out that in football "the coach must
have his players feeling they not only can kill
but they should kill."

Some experts suggest that the professionals
in sport have become the model for such behavior and amateur athletes have followed their
example. Then, high school athletes, in turn,
adopt similar attitudes. Other persons say that

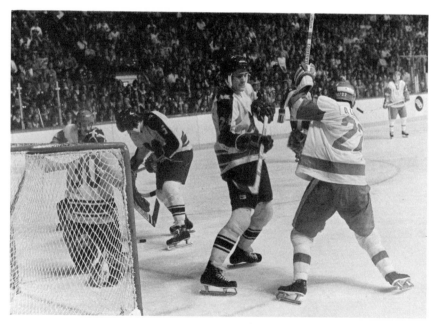

Courtesy Don Canham, University of Michigan.

Violence is a problem in sports today. Michigan goaltender Rick Palmer (no. 30) eyes the puck
along with the Wolverine's John McCahill (no. 5) and Wisconsin's Dave Herbst while Michigan's
Russ Blanzy (no. 24) defends the net against the Badger's Dave Lundeen (no. 22) in the NCAA
finals, won by Wisconsin 6-5 in overtime (March 26, 1977, at Detroit Olympia).

fighting and other examples of violence occur during the heat of the game and are a natural outlet when a player's adrenaline is flowing.

There are no simple solutions to violence. There is general agreement, however, that some type of control must be instituted and much of this control must start with persons who love sport and want to protect it from intrusions which will deter its value. They point out that violence is to be abhorred, particularly because it interferes with proper play, detracts from excellent player performance, and is barbaric in nature. Most spectators, it is suggested, do not want to see players hurt or crippled. They want to see clean, hard tackles and hard body checks. This is the essence of the game and of sport itself.

Tutko suggests that to reduce violence the entire penalty structure of sport should be restructured. For example, if a quarterback in football is knocked out, the team responsible should also be forced to complete the game using a second string quarterback. Or, in baseball, if a bean ball is thrown by a pitcher, the player should be given as many as three bases as a penalty.

The real and best solution, however, to the problem of violence is a change in attitude on the part of all persons concerned. The ideals of playing within the spirit as well as the letter of the rules, defeating one's opponent when at one's best, and having respect for the other player will, if subscribed to by professional and amateur players, coaches, spectators, sport entrepreneurs, and the public in general, eradicate violence from the playing fields and sports arenas of the United States.

The black athlete

Over the course of history in sports, it has been commonly regarded that athletics represent a setting where prejudice and discrimination have been effectively solved. It has been said, for example, that "sports are color blind" and that on the playing field the person is recognized for ability alone; reward is given without regard to race or class. Yet many black athletes claim that much racial discrimination exists today. They claim that quota systems exist for black players in some professional leagues and that coaches, managers, and front office personnel are seldom blacks.

Sports have produced a major arena for the world to see the plight of oppressed people. For example, a few years ago the Olympic boycott by black athletes and their refusal to compete with citizens of the Republic of South Africa helped to publicize the struggle blacks are waging against whites and to bring about improved conditions.

In school and college circles black athletes have brought attention to the authoritarianism on the part of coaches and to discriminatory conditions that athletes face as part of a school or college team. The point is made that too often the black athlete's job in college is to compete in sports, not to get an education.

In a symposium on problems of black athletes, conditions such as the following were listed: (1) Problems of poor facilities are far greater in black schools, (2) family problems frequently affect the play of the black athlete, (3) incidents that occur in sports when blacks are playing often get a bad press, (4) black

Courtesy The Athletic Institute, Chicago, Ill.

The black athlete.

athletes on athletic scholarships are pressured at times to sacrifice their educational goals, (5) black athletes may suffer from isolation and be made to feel intellectually and socially inferior to whites, and (6) prejudice sometimes exists among white coaches and administrators.

Efforts are being made by educators and coaches to resolve the problems of the black athlete. To do this all players must be treated equally, and there must be open avenues of communication for all to voice their complaints and feelings. The blacks must be recruited not only because they are good athletes but also because they are good scholars. Every attempt must be made to encourage them to fulfill all of their educational goals. The role that the black athlete has played in American sports has been an inspiration to all, black and white alike.

Amateurism

The growth of sports in the United States and other cultures of the world and the acclaim given those nations and athletes who excel have contributed to a significant change in the concept of the amateur in sports. Although traditionally amateurs did not receive money or have active government support for demonstrating their athletic prowess, today they are frequently given financial remuneration in terms of expenses and in other forms, and they receive government support in some nations of the world. The "open" tournament has become commonplace.

Many reasons have been suggested for the changing concept of what constitutes an amateur in sports. One important consideration is that times have changed. When the ancient Olympic games were staged, the concept of national sports programs did not exist. When the Olympics were revived in 1896 by de Coubertin, there were few professionals. The stress was on individual performance.

As has been mentioned, probably one of the most significant reasons for the changing concept of amateurism is that it affects a nation's image. Historically, we know this to be true. An example is the feats of Jesse Owens in the 1936 Olympics in Berlin and his snub by Hitler. Many people believed that American prestige was enhanced as a result of Owens' winning the gold medals. A nation's image is af-

fected by how well its athletes perform in the Olympics and other international contests. Consequently, the eligibility of athletes to represent a nation has implications for how effective the performance of that nation will be in the athletic contests in which they participate.

The eligibility of athletes is determined to a great extent in the way the word *amateur* is interpreted. The definition of amateurism adhered to in the United States, according to many public figures, works against the best interests of this country and its prestige in world affairs. Therefore, these persons argue, it is important to review the whole matter of international athletics carefully in light of the concept of amateurism that exists in the countries of the world. The fact that some social systems do not distinguish, as in the United States, between the professional and the amateur places some countries at a disadvantage when they hold to traditional concepts that have become outdated.

Antiathletics mood

Throughout the United States many high school and college students are demanding a stronger voice in the educational process. Many students at present are complaining that the money spent on big-time college athletic programs and high school sports cannot be justified. Newspaper reports indicate that some California college students have urged that the money given annually to athletic departments be spent in a manner more broadly representative of all students. In addition, these students criticized the construction of an expensive press box on the football stadium. In Texas, students protested the spending of several millions of dollars on an addition to the football stadium, whereas much less money was being spent on a new humanities research center.

Some students and faculty complain that athletics are too authoritarian and militaristic. Others say they cannot be justified because too few students benefit from the program. Surveys taken across the United States find that students in the East, Far West, and South were less interested in sports. The students thought that they should devote more of their time to the social causes of the day rather than to sports.

Another nationwide study found that students

thought they were being cheated in physical education because of the emphasis on the skilled athlete. Furthermore, reports indicate that the voting down of school budgets has resulted in curtailment of programs, facilities, and personnel.

Coaching

Coaching represents a highly insecure profession in many organizations. Pressure from alumni, sports writers, students, and the public can cause loss of the job when the number of games in the "won" column does not meet with their approval. Many coaches have done commendable work and yet have been forced to leave their jobs because the individuals with whom they had to work were not of championship caliber. William Hughes and Jesse Feiring Williams of Columbia University many years ago pointed out some significant facts in respect to the problems associated with coaching when they said:

Whereas no Professor of English is judged by the number of Miltons, Stevensons, Shakespeares or Howells he graduates from his courses, the coach is judged by his team's scores. Regardless of whether or not his team plays well, knows the game, conducts itself as gentlemen, is alert, reliable, and resourceful, the measure of winning still remains the sole criterion of success.*

Coaches may be tempted, because of the insecurity of the position, to place considerable emphasis on achieving a winning season. In so doing, at times coaches seek outcomes not educational in nature and procedures not permitted by athletic associations. Periodically, colleges and schools are placed on probation because of such conduct.

Coaches must be of strong character and be willing to follow an unswerving course in the direction of what they know to be right. This makes coaching a challenging field of work.

TOWARD A PHILOSOPHY OF SPORT

It is interesting to note that the Greeks provided civilization with two disciplines. The first described how sport could be most helpful in the training of a strong and graceful performance and body. The second provided civilization with the basics of philosophical thinking. As the historian Isocrates said:

. . . Certain of our ancestors, long before our time, invented and bequeathed to us two disciplines: physical training for the body, of which gymnastics is a part, and for the mind, philosophy. These twin arts are parallel and complementary, by which their masters prepare the mind to become more intelligent and the body to become more serviceable, nor separating sharply the two kinds of education, but using similar methods of instruction, exercise and discipline.

Every student of physical education and sport should develop a philosophy of that discipline. A philosophy will represent a guide to decision making, since it will clarify the worth of this field of endeavor in the human experience. Such a philosophy might include how sport should be conducted to make the greatest contribution to humankind. It should help to determine the parameters of educational sport as well as sport outside the formal domains of schools, colleges, and other educational institutions. It should provide an understanding of the history of sport and the contributions it has made over the years, as well as show how it has been misused and has been detrimental to humankind. A philosophy will also help point the way to achieving excellence of performance on the athletic field.

Sports are extremely popular and have a firm foothold in United States educational institutions. Therefore it is imperative to give direction to athletic programs in a way that will better contribute to the achievement of educational goals. I would like to suggest four guidelines for the conduct of sport programs that will help in making them more worthwhile.*

Guideline 1—Restructure athletics to achieve cognitive, psychomotor, and affective learnings

Bloom's† cognitive, psychomotor, and affective learning system represents a worthy goal for athletics in education. It has been demon-

---

*Hughes, William Leonard, and Williams, Jesse Feiring: Sports, their organization and administration, New York, 1944, A. S. Barnes & Co.

*Modified from Bucher, Charles A.: After the game is over, Physical Educator **30:**171, Dec., 1973.
†Bloom, Benjamin S., editor: Taxonomy of educational objectives, New York, 1956, David McKay Co.

strated that cognitive learnings, such as knowledge of rules, player assignments, and the game strategies associated with playing a sport, as well as the phenomena associated with the economic, political, and other interrelationships that exist between sport and society, can be accomplished. It has also been demonstrated that psychomotor learnings in the form of physical skills which are acquired by the participant as a result of engaging in athletics can be achieved. However, affective learnings may not be accomplished in light of the research that questions the role of sports in bringing about behavioral changes. Therefore some restructuring may need to take place as a means of using sport as a medium for learning social behavior.

Sheehan and Alsop,* drawing on social psychological research findings in respect to how attitudes and values (behavioral prerequisites) are influenced and also on valid principles of transfer, have shown experimentally that it is possible to modify attitudes of individuals who engage in sport in respect to social situations regarding cooperation, competition, and social conflict. The sport playlike environment, according to the researchers, reflects and replicates the society to which it is indigenous. To paraphrase the researchers, within this sport environment are involved elements such as cooperation and competition, together with players, coaches, and teachers who are in authority, all of whom are involved in a situation that is task oriented and conditioned by boundaries, norms, and sanctions. Therefore athletics, if properly structured, provide the social environment whereby societal norms can be internalized by the participant and their social attitudes shaped in a positive manner through social stimulus situations. Furthermore, the sport experiences can be so structured that the participant assimilates attitudinal learnings and with purposeful teaching for transfer taking place as principles are identified regarding the behavior, it is possible to transfer the attitude to other situations.

The researchers, using an instructional teaching model specifically designed to modify attitudes toward specific learning targets, conducted a study aimed at the social attitude of cooperation. Through the medium of the sport of soccer and utilizing pretests and posttests with the use of an operationally defined concept of cooperation and the semantic differential, which can be used as an attitudinal measuring instrument, the findings showed that the experimental group's attitudes toward cooperation were changed significantly. The researchers also indicate there have been five other studies, including those of Blatnik* and Alsop,† where attitudes have also been changed using the same structured teaching model that was developed by Sheehan in his doctoral dissertation at Ohio State University in 1965.

Although more research in this area is needed, Sheehan's and Alsop's work needs to be investigated further, since it may have promise as a desirable future direction for athletic programs. Sport and athletics are the heart of physical education programs in schools and colleges in the United States and have great appeal to young people of all ages, races, colors, and creeds. At the same time society is faced with many social problems, including relations between blacks and whites, the need for cooperative endeavor in achieving goals in a democratic society, and the necessity for constructive rather than destructive competition as people attempt to achieve their personal goals. Therefore, if athletics through a restructuring process can help in bringing about more desirable social attitudes among the many young people who participate in them, in addition to achieving cognitive and psychomotor goals, they would obviously play a much more valuable role in educational programs.

---

*Sheehan, Thomas J., and Alsop, William L.: Educational sport, Journal of Health, Physical Education and Recreation **43**:41, May, 1972.

*Blatnik, A. M.: An experimental study in selected required college physical education courses to determine the effect of a teaching model structured to produce positive attitudes toward participation in lifetime sports and conditioning activities for physiological and psychological well-being throughout life, unpublished doctoral dissertation, Morgantown, W. Va., 1968, West Virginia University.

†Alsop, William L.: Doctoral dissertation in progress.

Guideline 2—Provide an athletic program where the intensity of the competition is developmental in nature

The views of psychologist Jersild* are similar to those of other experts well versed in human growth and development when he discusses how physical and motor growth follow a progressive sequence from the time of early childhood to maturity. In other words, they follow a developmental pattern (the large muscles develop before the fine muscles, etc.)

What is true of the physical is also true of the mental and emotional aspects—they are also developmental in nature. Therefore, since the intensity of athletic competition is related to a person's growth and development, it should also reflect a progressive sequence. It would then follow that athletic competition should be

---

*Jersild, Arthur T.: Child psychology, Englewood Cliffs, N.J., 1968, Prentice-Hall, Inc.

of a very low intensity during the early years of childhood and then gradually be increased as the child grows older and becomes more mature.

The intensity of athletic competition is increased when elements are introduced into the athletic experience that provide added motivation for and additional pressure on the participant to excel, and where there is more at stake in the competition. For example, when spectators are in the stands, games are scheduled with schools in other communities, awards are offered, admission is charged, sports writers are in attendance, or playoff games for championships are sponsored, the intensity of the competition is increased.

Relating the elements which increase the intensity of the competition to the developmental levels of the student, it is proposed that four levels of intensity of competition for a developmental athletic program exist. These four levels

Intramural athletics at the University of Colorado at Boulder.

of competition should be progressively scheduled during the school years in a way that best fits the student and also the administrative grade pattern in the school. The four levels of intensity of athletic competition are as follows:

First developmental level — absence of any structured athletic competition.

Second developmental level — intramurals with their low-key competitive involvement of classmates provide the first structured step-up in the intensity of competition.

Third developmental level — extramurals, such as occasional play days, sports days, and invitational meets with schools in other communities, where the stress is on the social and fun aspects of the event rather than the winning, represent an intermediate athletic developmental competitive experience between intramurals and varsity interschool athletics.

Fourth developmental level — varsity athletic competition with elements such as spectators, publicity, leagues, and awards, represents a major step-up in the intensity of competition. This type of experience may be provided after each of the previous developmental levels of competition have been utilized for a significant period of time and where the player can successfully cope physically, mentally, emotionally, and socially with such an experience.

Guideline 3—Provide more athletic opportunities for girls and women

Dr. Vera Skubic, Department of Ergonomics and Physical Education, University of California at Santa Barbara, has given the subject of participation by girls and women on varsity school teams much thought and study. She points out the following:

Athletics are a part of the total school program, and, in a democratically oriented institution, all members of the student body (males and females) should have the opportunity to compete for a place on the team. Any rule which excludes girls and women from participating in a regular school program is unfair and discriminates against them on the basis of sex . . . In this day and age, females should have equal rights and opportunities to reach their potential in whatever programs a school has to offer. Surely the social, health and fitness benefits of athletic competition should be made available to *all* students . . . The trend toward providing more and better interscholastic and intercollegiate

sports opportunities for girls and women is a good one and deserves strong support in terms of funds, facilities and encouragement. If all students are going to have a chance to reach their potential in sports, then the schools must provide many types and levels of competition, plus the freedom to choose.*

Guideline 4—Institute changes in the organization and administration of athletic programs

School administrators play a key role in the development of a sound educational athletic program. They are the persons who are responsible for such programs and should provide the leadership necessary to bring about desirable change. Areas in which change is needed include the following:

1. Schedule and limit in length practice sessions and number of games played so as not to disrupt the educational process or take a disproportionate amount of the student's time.
2. Conduct sport contests only on school premises — the public arena, where educators are not in control and where gamblers and rabid spectators are present, is not the place to conduct athletic contests.
3. Appoint coaches on the basis of their educational qualifications. A knowledge of and an interest in participants, including their physical, mental, emotional and social makeup, is one of the most important qualifications.
4. Administer athletics as an integral part of the total physical education program.
5. Permit hair length and other personal preferences of players to be a matter of individual decision as long as they do not interfere with the safety, health, and performance of participants.

Sport reflects what the United States is — its people, its character, its values, its philosophy of life. This country needs more sports, not less, and greater participation of more people, not fewer people. Furthermore, Americans

---

*Bucher, Charles A.: Girls and women in sports: pros and cons, Syndicated Newspaper column for August 5-6, 1972, Washington, D.C., President's Council on Physical Fitness and Sports.

need to recognize that, regardless of individual ability, sport is within everyone's grasp. Any person can go up to the plate and swing. Anyone can throw a ball, get into the water, pedal a bicycle, and go out on the road and run. And to do so will help in the development of those qualities that have traditionally made this country great and thus provide some of the glue that is necessary to hold it together as a strong nation.

SELF-ASSESSMENT TESTS

These tests are to assist students in determining if material and competencies presented in this chapter have been mastered.

1. Prepare a 5-minute presentation to be given to your class on the subject, "The History of Sport." In your presentation credit various countries of the world that have contributed to the growth of sports. Indicate the contribution each made.

2. Interpret the following statement, giving your own reaction as to the direction in which the growth has taken place: "Sports in educational institutions were initiated at the college level and then expanded downward into the high school, junior high school, and elementary school levels.'"

3. Survey two coaches and two professors of academic subjects to determine what they believe constitutes the values that can be derived from participating in sports. Compare the values they state with those which have been listed in this chapter. What is your reaction?

4. Without consulting your text, prepare a list of standards for educational athletics under each of the following headings: organization, staff, finances, health and safety, player eligibility, recruiting, and awards.

5. Evaluate each of the following statements:
   a. Title IX has resulted in an expansion in girls' and women's sports but this expansion has created many problems.
   b. Elementary schoolchildren should not engage in highly competitive sports.
   c. The Olympic Games should be abolished.
   d. Increasing violence is becoming a part of competition in sports.
   e. The concept of amateurism should be abolished.
   f. More and more studies raise the question about whether or not intercollegiate athletics are worth while.
   g. A coach's tenure should not be affected by losing games.

6. Formulate a philosophy of sport that will clarify the worth of athletics and give direction for conducting them so that they will make the greatest contribution to humankind.

SELECTED REFERENCES

The Athletic Institute, Chicago, Illinois, Sportscope **15:**1, June, 1970.

Barnes, Mildred: An invitation to the state high school athletic associations, Journal of Physical Education and Recreation **46:**53, March, 1975.

Briggs, Paul W., Superintendent of Schools, Cleveland, Ohio: Presentation to the Third National Conference for State High School Coaches Association, April 19, 1970.

Lumpkin, Angela: Let's set the record straight, Journal of Physical Education and Recreation **48:**40, March, 1977.

McAffe, R.: Sportsmanship attitudes of sixth, seventh, and eighth grade boys, Research Quarterly **26:**120, March, 1955.

Ogilvie, Bruce C., and Tutko, Thomas A.: Sport: if YOU want to build character, try something else, Psychology Today **5:**60, Oct., 1971.

Seymour, E. W.: Comparative study of certain behavior characteristics of participant and non-participant boys in Little League baseball, Research Quarterly **27:**338, Oct., 1956.

Talamini, John T., and Page, Charles: Sport and society—an anthology, Boston, 1973, Little, Brown & Co., Inc.

American Association for Health, Physical Education and Recreation: Update, p. 7, Dec., 1971.

The National Association for Physical Education of College Women and The National College Physical Education Association for Men: Sport in America, Quest, Monograph 27, winter issue, 1977 (entire issue devoted to sport).

Whittle, H. D.: Effects of elementary school physical education upon aspects of physical, motor, and personality development, Research Quarterly **32:**249, 1961.

7

International foundations of physical education

During an age when international strife is prevalent in many parts of the globe, when peace is a constant goal of humanity, when better understanding among the peoples of the world is a desperate need, when international education is an urgent necessity, and when emerging nations need assistance, physical educators can render a valuable service in utilizing their skills to help those in need. This service can be rendered here, in the United States, as well as abroad.

WHAT IS INTERNATIONAL EDUCATION?

International education is a term used to describe the many types of educational relations among countries of the world. It applies to the ways various governments and people of the world communicate with each other through such means as individuals and materials. It is also the study that goes on to achieve a better understanding of the many peoples of the world. The aim of international education is to promote better cooperation and harmony among nations.

International education is a term that contributes to the goal of humans living peacefully with their counterparts in all sections of the world. It involves knowledge and human behavior that transcends cultures, boundaries, and nationalism and recognizes the dignity of people and their interdependent relationship with other people wherever they live.

International education is a term that recognizes the uniqueness of individuals and cultures. International education recognizes that various peoples have customs, traditions, and beliefs which differ from other countries and cultures. These ways of thinking and behaving are a part of a way of life that should be recognized and accepted for their own worth without any attempt from the outside to change them. Each culture has a right to live according to its own belief and standard of values.

International education tries to correct international misunderstanding and ill will. International education is aimed at the study of nations, the forces that cause misunderstandings, and the control of these forces by peaceful educational means. It attempts to present true and accurate facts as a means of countering propaganda and information that distort and erroneously describe a culture, country, or its people.

Somsak Tongaram, former great Thai athlete.

PHYSICAL EDUCATION AROUND THE WORLD

Fitness and physical well-being are important objectives that concern all peoples. Individuals the world over are interested in sports, games, and other physical education activities. A tennis match at Forest Hills or Wimbledon often includes players from Australia, Brazil, Spain, and France. The British Open Golf Tournament attracts enthusiasts from all over the world. Specialists in winter sports from many countries display their prowess at Saint Moritz. The Olympic festival is, of course, the greatest and most famous sports gathering, bringing together athletes from many nations. Because of these international events, physical education has potentialities as one medium by which international understanding may be reached and by which people of various countries may be brought closer together.

Through activities such as Olympic festivals; competition in sports such as tennis, golf, crew, polo, soccer, and hockey; seminars on physical education; international conferences; and relations between educational institutions, other agencies, and individuals of various lands, good will can be promoted, and the people of many cultures can come to understand each other better.

Leadership

There are many dedicated leaders in the professional fields of physical education, health, and recreation in other countries. These outstanding leaders, whether in Europe, Canada, Africa, Australia, Asia, or elsewhere, render a service to students and citizens of their country and place their profession on a respected level in schools and colleges.

Students majoring in physical education in professional preparation institutions in many countries stimulate a traveler's interest. Their eagerness to know about world developments in their professional fields, the enthusiasm they display for the games and sports in which they engage, and the keen sense of humor they possess make it a joy to be with them. One realizes that there is a rich reservoir of leader-

Peace Corps volunteer teaches a new game to her physical education class at Petchburi Vittayalong-korn Teacher Training School in Bangkok, Thailand. This Peace Corps volunteer has a degree in physical education from the University of Akron in Ohio.

ship in their respective nations for the years ahead.

Facilities

In some foreign schools and colleges and in some sections of a country, province, or city, there are beautiful and modern facilities that compare favorably with those in the United States. However, assessing facilities in the world as a whole, the United States is much more richly blessed with good facilities on a broad scale than are other nations. The eyes of many foreign physical education teachers would open wide if they could see some of the indoor swimming pools, spacious gymnasiums, health suites, and playground facilities. Japanese teachers, for example, would notice the green grass on playfields compared with the dirt with which they have to contend and the showers our athletes take after a workout compared with the cold sponge baths some of their sports participants must endure.

Activities

The activities that constitute the physical education programs in other countries are varied and interesting. In the Far East, for example, one is impressed to see more basketball being played in the Philippines than in the United States, the dexterity with which young and older persons alike kick the rattan ball in the game of sipa, and the beautiful folk dances that play such an important part in the Philippine culture.

The many sports and game activities in Hong Kong are a carryover from England because of the British influence. More high school boys play field hockey than do girls. Cricket is engaged in by various clubs but not to any degree in the schools. Track and field events are popular.

In Japan, judo, kindo (fencing), Japanese tennis, as well as many of the typical activities offered in the United States, are popular. In traveling throughout Japan it is interesting to also note the great amount of formal activity, such as calisthenics, apparatus activity, and stunts.

The use of textbooks and discussion groups in physical education in some schools shows the importance placed on getting at the "why"

of physical activity, as well as the activity itself.

Athletic clubs in many different activities exist in some foreign schools, colleges, and communities. These clubs sponsor and provide for instruction and participation in many sports and other activities. Students and adults engage in apparatus, riding, dance, tennis, soccer, basketball, or other activities on a voluntary basis.

GUIDELINES FOR INTERNATIONAL RELATIONS IN PHYSICAL EDUCATION

The United States is deeply involved in international affairs. If it is to occupy a position of leadership in the world it must promote many facets of relationships to establish common bonds among peoples everywhere. One of these common bonds is physical education. Through sports and physical activities a medium is offered to further international relationships.

Many organizations are making outstanding contributions. The American Alliance for Health, Physical Education, and Recreation, through its International Relations Council is an example. Some of these contributions include the following:

1. *Consultant services*—To domestic groups within the profession, professional groups in other countries, and in other ways
2. *Program services*—Developing and presenting programs at national and international meetings
3. *Book project*—Books and professional publications collected within the United States and sent to other countries
4. *Hospitality*—Orienting, socializing with, and in general making guests from other countries feel at home and benefiting from their visit to the United States

International cooperation, however, must not stop at the national level but must extend into the schools and other organizations located in villages and cities from coast to coast.

OPPORTUNITIES FOR SERVICE AT HOME

The physical educator does not need to travel to other countries to further good international relations. There is much work to be done in the

Courtesy Dr. Gunsun Hoh, Republic of China.

Physical education programs in the Republic of China.

The author lecturing at Cheng Kung University, Taiwan.

United States—at home. Some opportunities that are open to each physical educator on the home front are as follows:

1. *Teach national and cultural backgrounds of dances and games in physical education classes.* Sports, dances, and games should not be conducted in a vacuum. Boys and girls should understand the origin of these activities and the role they play in the various cultures of the world. Physical education classes can play a dynamic part in furthering international understanding by orienting students about other countries through the medium of physical activities.

2. *Welcome foreigners.* Many physical educators, sports enthusiasts, and athletes visit and travel throughout the world. Each physical educator should be hospitable, make the person or persons welcome, and act as a guide to show and tell them about our programs. These courtesies will help to cultivate new friends for the profession and countries.

3. *Send books, CARE playground kits, and sports equipment to other countries.* People in other countries want information about our physical education programs. They welcome books, periodicals, and other literature that describe our programs, methods, and teaching techniques. An important service can be rendered by contributing literature to this worthy cause. Other countries are also interested in receiving sports equipment.

4. *Join international associations.* Physical educators should become involved in professional association work in international relations. The AAHPER and many state associations have active sections or divisions in this area. In addition, organizations such as the International Association of Physical Education and Sports for Girls and Women are seeking members to help to carry out their objectives.

5. *Be knowledgeable about international affairs.* The physical educator should become acquainted with happenings on the international scene, world events that are taking place, and the work of organizations such as the United Nations. The physical educator who becomes better informed about international happenings will be more qualified to give students such information.

OPPORTUNITIES FOR SERVICE ABROAD

For the physical educator who is interested in serving abroad, there are many opportunities. A selected few are as follows:

1. *Student and teacher exchange programs.* Each year more than 7,000 persons representing over 100 countries are exchanged to teach, study, lecture, and engage in research or in other educational or cultural activities through programs sponsored by the Department of State. For more information write Teacher Exchange Section, Bureau of International Education, U.S. Office of Education, Washington, D.C. 20201.

2. *Peace Corps.* On September 21, 1961, the Peace Corps Act was passed by the United States Congress. Today there are thousands of Peace Corps volunteers serving in foreign assignments. Many physical educators are a part of the Peace Corps, and the AAHPER is working closely with this organization. Applicants may obtain Peace Corps questionnaires from the AAHPER, post offices, or Action/Peace Corps, Washington, D.C. 20525.

The Peace Corps and VISTA have merged into a new agency called ACTION, the citizens' service corps. Under the new arrangement, volunteers can be assigned either to developing countries or to cities and other locations in this country.

A few foreign countries and areas where physical education specialists have been used are the Ivory Coast, Tunisia, Ceylon, Iran, Thailand, Colombia, and Indonesia. According to the AAHPER, the criteria used in respect to physical education and athletic programs include obtaining volunteers who are graduates from accredited institutions with a physical education major or minor with a recommendation from the college, athletes who have graduated from college and are recommended by the physical education department, and individuals trained in physical education or outstanding athletes strongly recommended by professional people in the field.

3. *Teach Corps.* The National Education Association has established a Teach Corps, which utilizes the services of experienced American teachers in providing summer in-

service training for teachers in foreign lands. For further information write Committee on International Relations, National Education Association, 1201 16th St., N.W., Washington, D.C. 20036.

4. *United Nations Educational, Scientific, and Cultural Organization.* UNESCO seeks teachers to serve in developing countries around the world. It has an international fellowship and travel study program in war-devastated or underdeveloped countries. Write to UNESCO, Place de Fontenoy, Paris 75700, France, *or* U.N. Liason office 2201 U.N. Bldg. N.Y., N.Y. 10017.

5. *Armed forces.* Bases operated overseas by the armed forces have teaching positions available for elementary and secondary school teachers. For details write to the chief of personnel of the particular branch of service in which you are interested.

6. *World Health Organization.* For physical educators with competencies in the area of health, opportunities exist in various parts of the world. Write to Personnel Office, World Health Organization, Avenue Appia, Geneva, Switzerland, *or* Pan American Sanitary Bureau, 23rd St., and Virginia Ave., N.W., Washington, D.C. 20037.

7. *Fulbright grants.* An avenue for foreign service for those with advanced education and degrees may be available through the Fulbright program. This program has been in operation for several years and has been popular for those interested in lecturing or teaching abroad for a year. If you are interested, write Conference Board of Associated Research Councils, Committee on International Exchange of Persons, Washington, D.C.

8. *United States Agency for International Development (AID).* The AID program exists in areas of the world such as Asia, Africa, Far East, Near East, Greece, and Turkey. Most positions are at the teacher training level, with 2 years considered to be the minimum length of assignment. For more information write to AID, U.S. Department of State, Washington, D.C. 20520.

9. *The Association of Commonwealth Universities.* This association has vacancies for recently graduated students from colleges and universities. The address is 36 Gordon Square, London W.C. 1, England.

10. *Central Bureau for Educational Visits and Exchanges.* This bureau serves as an office and clearinghouse for information on educational travel and official exchanges. Write to Bureau of Educational and Cultural Affairs, U.S. Department of State, 2201 "C" St., N.W., Washington, D.C. 20520.

11. *Council on International Exchange.* This council, which serves as a clearinghouse for information on exchange programs and travel throughout the world, has its offices at 777 United Nations Plaza, New York, N.Y. 10017.

12. *Institute of International Education.* The institute conducts educational exchange programs for colleges, universities, foundations, corporations, foreign governments, and other organizations. Write to the Institute, 809 United Nations Plaza, New York, N.Y. 10017.

13. *Pan American Health Organization.* This organization considers applications in fields such as nursing, public health, and medicine. It has its office at Pan American Sanitary Bureau, 525 23rd St., N.W., Washington, D.C. 20037.

14. *Schools in outlying areas.* The Panama Canal Zone, Territory of Guam, American Samoa, Trust Territory of the Pacific Islands, and the Virgin Islands offer teaching opportunities in elementary and secondary schools and in colleges. For more information write to the area of interest.

15. *Binational centers.* Private organizations have established binational centers in many countries to bring about better understanding between the United States and these countries. Binational centers are presently located in the Near East, Europe, and the Far East. Classes are offered at all educational levels. For more information write to the U.S. Department of State, Washington, D.C. 20520.

16. *Schools in the Middle East, Far East, Africa, and Europe sponsored by the International Schools Service.* A wide range of educational services are offered through this independent, nonprofit organization concerned with international programs of technical aid, diplomacy and industrial efficiency. For more information write International School Services, 126 Alexander St., Princeton, N.J. 08540.

17. *Schools in Latin American republics*

through the Inter-American School Service.
American-sponsored administrative and teaching positions exist in Latin America through the Inter-American Schools Service. For more information write to the U.S. Department of State, Washington, D.C. 20520.

18. *Church-sponsored schools.* Protestant-, Catholic-, and Jewish-sponsored schools and colleges in many countries of the world offer teaching opportunities for those interested.

19. *Schools operated by American firms overseas.* Some American business and industrial concerns operate elementary and secondary schools in several countries for the children of American employees. Teaching opportunities exist in these schools.

SELECTED INTERNATIONAL COMPETITIONS
Olympic games

The First Olympiad was held in 776 B.C. at Olympia, Greece. It was originally a 5-day event held every 4 years during the month of August. The facilities for these contests were open fields, and spectators lined the sides or sat on convenient slopes. The United States participated in 1896, the Asian nations joined in 1932, and Russia entered for the first time in 1952. The first modern Olympics included competition in track and field, weight lifting, wrestling, swimming, cycling, tennis, gymnastics, fencing, and shooting. In addition to these the scope of competition now includes boxing, rowing, yachting, water polo, canoeing, field hockey, basketball, the modern pentathlon, riding, soccer, handball, and judo. Tennis is no longer part of the Olympics.

The winter Olympic games were initiated in 1924 in Chamonix, France. They are now held in the same year as the summer Olympics, but they need not be held in the same country. Events in the winter Olympics include the luge, ice hockey, speed and figure skating, skiing, and bobsledding. (For more information on the Olympics see Chapter 6.)

The International Olympic Committee is responsible for the conduct of the games.

Asian Games

The Asian Games were first held in Manila in 1913. The participating countries of China,

Japan, and the Philippines held what they called the First Oriental Olympic Games in that year. After 1921 the competition was renamed the Far Eastern Championships. Ceylon, India, Indonesia, Malaya, and Thailand were invited to join but were prevented from doing so by financial difficulties. A political dispute ended the competition between the three original nations in 1934. At that time, India invited Ceylon, Afghanistan, and Palestine to compete in the West Asiatic Games. War ended the competition after the first year. The First Asian Games were held in New Delhi, India, in 1951 under the sponsorship of the Asian Games Federation. Initially, competition was to be held every 3 years, but it is presently held every 4 years. In 1954 eighteen countries participated, and nineteen competed in 1958. By 1962 twenty-two nations were involved. Competition for men includes boxing, cycling, field hockey, soccer, basketball, riflery, water polo, weight lifting, and wrestling. Men and women compete in their own divisions in badminton, swimming and diving, table tennis, track and field, volleyball, and tennis.

Pan-American Games

The Pan-American Games, initiated in 1951, are limited to nations of the western hemisphere, including, among others, the United States, Canada, Argentina, Mexico, Bolivia, and Brazil. Presently about twenty-four nations compete in these games, which are held every 4 years, between Olympics. The Pan-American Sports Organization administers the same guidelines set down for Olympic competition.

Men compete in many of the same activities that are included in the Olympics, with the addition of tennis and baseball. Women compete in Olympic events and also include basketball, tennis, and synchronized swimming in their schedule of events.

British Empire and Commonwealth Games

This competition is limited to member nations of the British Empire. The games began in 1930 and are held every 4 years in a non-Olympic year. The British Empire and Commonwealth Games Federation administers the competition in which approximately forty na-

From Klafs, C. E., and Lyon, M. J.: The female athlete, ed. 2, St. Louis, 1978, The C. V. Mosby Co.

An Olympic gymnast shows excellent shoulder and arm strength in executing a one-handed walk over.

tions join. The events are of an individual rather than a team nature and include badminton, boxing, cycling, fencing, shooting, swimming and diving, track and field, weight lifting, and wrestling.

World Maccabiah Games

These games were initiated in 1931 and are held in Israel every 4 years. They are limited to Jewish athletes. The International Maccabiah Games Committee administers the games on the Olympic pattern. Presently twen-

ty-five or more nations participate. Men compete in many Olympic events plus golf, bowling, and table tennis. Women also compete in Olympic-type events and in such activities as golf and table tennis.

World University Games

The International Federation of University Sports has conducted this competition since 1947. It is held every 2 years during an odd-numbered year. Approximately thirty-five countries send university students to participate

Courtesy Public Relations Department, Thailand.

Calisthenics demonstration by cadet academy students at Asian games.

Maccabiah Games.

in the games. Events included are track and field, basketball, soccer, gymnastics, tennis, fencing, and swimming and diving.

SELECTED MAJOR INTERNATIONAL COMPETITIONS IN SELECTED AMATEUR SPORTS

Badminton. The International Badminton Federation sponsors international competition in this sport. The Thomas Cup for men was initiated in 1940 and the Uber Cup for women in 1956. Competition is held every 3 years.

Chess. The first World Chess Championships were held in 1851 under the sponsorship of the International Chess Federation, which continues to host this competition on a yearly basis.

Cycling. The Tour de France, sponsored by the International Cycling Union, is a yearly event.

Golf. The Americas Cup Golf Match, between the United States, Mexico, and Canada, has been held every 2 years since 1952. The Ryder Cup Match first held in 1922 matches the United States against Great Britain every 2 years. The World Cup golf matches involve players from around the globe.

Ice skating. The World Figure Skating Championships have been held yearly since the late 1870s. The World Speed Skating Championships have been a yearly event since 1893. Both are under the sponsorship of the International Skating Union.

Riding. The International Horse Show is held on a yearly basis.

Rowing. The Royal Yacht Club has sponsored the Henley-on-Thames Royal Regatta yearly since 1839.

Shooting. The National Rifle Association each year sponsors several international postal matches under the rules set down by the International Shooting Union: the International Free-Pistol Postal Match, the Mayleigh Cup International Smallbore Rifle Postal Match for Women, and the International Smallbore Rifle Three-Position Postal Match.

Skiing. The International Federation of Skiing sponsors the World Ski Championships every 3 years.

Soccer. Every 4 years the International Federation of Soccer sponsors the World Cup Matches.

Swimming. The International Amateur Swimming Federation sponsors the World Swimming Championships every year.

Tennis. The United States Outdoor Tennis Championships have been sponsored yearly since 1881 by the U.S. Lawn Tennis Association. Under the guidance of the International Lawn Tennis Association, committees of nations involved have sponsored the Wimbledon Championships since 1877; the Davis Cup for men since 1900; and the Wightman Cup for women of the United States and England since 1923.

Yachting. About every 3 years since 1851

Table 7-1. Spectator sports and popular dances of other countries*

Country	Sport	Dance
Australia	Soccer, cricket, boxing, swimming, tennis, rugby	Modern, ballet
Belgium	Soccer, cycling, tennis	Ballet, folk
Canada	Hockey, football, baseball, basketball, skiing	Modern, ballet
Denmark	Soccer, gymnastics, handball, swimming, track and field	Modern, ballet
Dominican Republic	Baseball, tennis	Folk
England	Football (soccer), boxing, cricket, tennis, rugby	Modern, ballet
France	Soccer, tennis, cycling, boxing	Ballet
India	Soccer, cricket, field hockey, tennis, badminton	Folk
Mexico	Bullfighting, soccer, baseball, jai alai	Modern, folk
Norway	Skiing, soccer, skating, track and field, swimming	Modern, folk
Peru	Soccer, bullfighting, boxing, track and field	Folk
Russia	Soccer, track and field, gymnastics, hockey, basketball	Ballet

*From Wessel, Janet: Movement fundamentals, Englewood Cliffs, N.J., 1961, Prentice-Hall, Inc., p. 271. Updated by author.

the New York Yacht Club has sponsored the America's Cup in cooperation with the yachting body of the challenging nation.

SELECTED INTERNATIONAL ORGANIZATIONS

There are many organizations concerned with physical education in international affairs that render an invaluable service to humanity. A few of the outstanding international professional organizations with which the physical educator should be familiar are as follows.

The Bi-National Commission for Exchange in Physical Education

The International Relations Council (IRC) established the Bi-National Commission for Exchange in Physical Education in the summer of 1972. The objectives of the commission are as follows:

1. Study and integrate projects and cooperative programs between the United States and Mexico, based on individual strengths and interests
2. Establish bases of mutual understanding between people with different cultural and language patterns
3. Seek to define a model that could serve as a pattern of exchange in the field

The commission uses scholarships, clinics, workshops, exchange of written and audiovisual material, and experts in the field to fulfill their objectives.

Council for Cultural Co-operation of the Council of Europe

The Council of Europe, of which the Council for Cultural Co-operation is a subgroup, was created in 1949 as an outgrowth of the post–World War II movement for economic cooperation among Western European nations. The organization has its headquarters in Strasbourg, France.

World Confederation of Organizations of the Teaching Profession

The World Confederation of Organizations of the Teaching Profession (WCOTP) was founded at Copenhagen, Denmark, in 1952. It is composed of 140 national members and sixty-five associate members, who represent 5 million teachers in ninety countries.

The purposes of the WCOTP include providing an organization in which professional teachers at all educational levels can utilize education for furthering international understanding and world peace, teachers can unite their efforts to upgrade their educational policies and practices throughout the world, and international educational policies can be molded by the associated effort of teachers from all the countries represented in the organization.

WCOTP has three international members concerned with specialized phases of education: the International Council on Health, Physical Education, and Recreation (ICHPER), the International Council on Education for Teaching (ICET), and the International Reading Association (IRA).

The WCOTP works closely with the United Nations, especially with the World Health Organization, Economic and Social Council, and the Food and Agriculture Organization.

International Council on Health, Physical Education, and Recreation

At the annual meeting of the WCOTP in Rome in 1958, a special committee discussed and formulated a statement of the purposes and functions of organizations of health, physical education, and recreation. In 1959 at the annual meeting of the WCOTP in Washington, D.C., an official decision was made to form an International Council on Health, Physical Education, and Recreation (ICHPER). WCOTP approved this organization in August, 1959.

The purposes of ICHPER include helping WCOTP to accomplish its objectives; encouraging, developing, and upgrading programs of health, physical education, and recreation throughout the world; working closely with other international organizations concerned with these special fields; improving the professional status of teachers; supporting, encouraging, and sponsoring the exchange of research findings and information for the profession; and promoting the exchange of teachers and students among different countries.

The groups throughout the world who are eligible to join ICHPER are international organizations in health, physical education, and recreation, national organizations, and regional or geographical area organizations. The aim of the council is to bring representatives from countries into this one organization so that it can be the official world spokesman for the professions. With such representation it hopes to promote better school programs in health, physical education, and recreation. More specifically, it will do this by attempting to improve teaching methods, training teachers, providing materials for teaching, and doing research. It is anticipated that ICHPER will plan and conduct conferences, seminars, courses, world congresses, lectures, demonstrations, exhibits, and many other experiences to carry out its objectives.

Materials and information on ICHPER can be secured by writing to this organization at 1201 16th St., N.W., Washington, D.C. 20036.

ICHPER conference in Seoul, Korea. Members of the Kyung-Hee University gymnastic team performing before the delegates of the congress.

International Association of Physical Education and Sports for Girls and Women (APESYW)

Women in physical education, feeling the need to know about and participate in sports in other countries and to solve common problems, prompted the foundation of the International Association of Physical Education and Sports for Girls and Women. Membership is open to women who engage in physical education work at any educational level, elementary through college, as well as leaders in adult programs. Members can participate in the congresses that are held, usually every fourth or fifth year, in one of the fifty-one countries that participate in the association. Meetings have been held in Stockholm, Paris, London, Washington, D.C., Cologne, and Tokyo. Aims of the association are as follows:

1. To promote closer working relationships among women physical educators in various countries of the world
2. To work closely with various organizations that render services to women
3. To afford opportunities through congresses and meetings to discuss and help in the solving of mutual problems
4. To encourage research and exchange of persons and ideas and to promote other activities related to physical education and sports for women

For more information write to the association, c/o Dr. Gladys Bean, 555 Sherbrooke St. W., Montreal, PQ H3A 1E3, Canada.

International Amateur Athletic Federation

On July 17, 1912, representatives from the athletic associations of sixteen countries met in Stockholm, Sweden, with the aim of establishing an international organization devoted to amateur athletics. The first official meeting of the International Amateur Athletic Federation (IAAF) took place in Berlin in 1913.

Some of the objectives of the IAAF are as follows:

1. To attempt to eliminate racial, political, and religious discrimination from athletics
2. To foster friendship and cooperation between members of the federation
3. To prevent any country or individual being

denied the right to participate in international athletics on racial, religious, or political grounds

4. To establish rules and regulations governing international competition in amateur athletics
5. To help in the organization of the Olympic Games
6. To establish standards for the establishment of World and Olympic records

The organization is governed by a president, an honorary secretary, and a fifteen-member council, which is composed of representatives from each of the following area groups: Africa, Asia, Australia, Europe, North America, and South America.

The address of the IAAF is 162-164 Upper Richmond Rd., London, S.W. 15, England.

International Federation of Physical Education

The International Federation of Physical Education (FIEP) was founded in 1923 in Brussels. The home office is now located in Lisbon, Portugal. The aims of this organization are to promote health, wholesome recreation, and the social adaptation of the individual. The federation is concerned with the scientific, technical, pedagogical, and social aspects of physical education and sport.

Its bulletin is printed quarterly in five languages and carries articles related to research in the areas of science and exercise, book reviews, and international views of physical education.

International Council of Sport and Physical Education

The International Council of Sport and Physical Education (ICSPE) was founded in 1956 in Melbourne, Australia. The General Assemblies have been held in such countries as Iran and Mexico.

The aims of this organization include acting as a clearinghouse for international cooperation in sports and physical education, promoting the social good of sports and physical education, and promoting research and the exchange of ideas and assistance between countries. The ICSPE cooperates closely with the UNESCO, ICHPER, and other related organiza-

tions such as the International Olympic Committee.

International Bureau of Education

The International Bureau of Education (Bureau International d'Education—BIE) was founded in 1925 in Geneva and serves as an international educational information center for all countries. In 1946, after the founding of UNESCO, that organization joined the BIE in setting up a common program. Subsequently an agreement was reached by the two organizations whereby the BIE transferred its resources and functions to UNESCO. In November, 1968, the General Conference of UNESCO adopted statutes establishing the BIE as an integral part of the organization.

This organization publishes research studies on educational organizations and an international bulletin printed in English and French. The Ministries of Education in member countries send an educational progress report each year that is incorporated into an educational yearbook. An Intergovernmental Conference on Public Education is sponsored each year. The bureau also maintains an extensive library of education textbooks, journals, and legislative documents pertaining to education. The address of the Bureau is Palais Wilson, 1211 Geneva 14, Geneva, Switzerland.

International University Sports Federation

The International University Sports Federation (Fédération Internationale de Sport Universitaire—FISU) was established in 1948 in Luxembourg. The United States has been affiliated with this organization since 1957, but it began to participate actively through the United States National Student Association in 1964. Following are the purposes of the federation:

1. To encourage the development of physical education among students of all countries by exchanging information on university sports
2. To sponsor international sports meetings
3. To promote the moral value of sports on an amateur basis

The FISU is composed of national organizations, National University of Sports Organizations, or National Union of Students, in more than sixty countries. FISU has sponsored biennial World Student Games in summer and winter sports (Universiades) in places such as Sofia, Porto Alegre, Budapest, Tokyo, Chamonix, Villars, Sestriere, and Innsbruck.

All correspondence to FISU should be directed to FISU Secretariat, BP 75, Leuven 1, Belgium.

International Sports Organization for the Disabled

The International Sports Organization for the Disabled was established March 26, 1961, in Paris under the auspices of the World Veterans Federation. Some activities of the organization include sports meetings, training courses for coaches, seminars, and exhibitions. The aims of the organization are as follows:

1. To promote sports for the handicapped or disabled on an international level
2. To coordinate all international functions of member organizations

The membership of the International Sports Organization for the Disabled is composed of national associations for the disabled in seventeen countries. The address of the organization is Stokes Mandiville Sports Stadium, Harvy Road, Aylesbury, Buckshire, England.

International Federation of Sportive Medicine

The International Federation of Sportive Medicine (Fédération Internationale de Medicine Sportive—FIMS) was founded in St. Moritz in 1928. Following are the aims of the Federation:

1. To improve physical and moral health by sporting activities, particularly physical education, gymnastics, games, and other sports
2. To make scientific studies of the effect of participating in sporting activities

The FIMS membership includes national federations in thirty-eight countries. Its members are persons interested in research, teaching, coaching, and medical aspects of sports. They concern themselves with the physiological aspects of sports, as well as the prevention and care of injuries incurred in sports. Further information may be obtained by writing Farnham Park Rehabilitation Center, Farnham Royale, Slough SL2 3LR, Bucks, England.

People-to-People Sports Committee

The People-to-People Sports Committee is one of the forty-one people-to-people programs established in 1956. It has as its main purpose the involvement of Americans in the conduct of international affairs through sports. The membership consists of individuals in the United States who are prominent in the field of sports or its promotion. Its headquarters is at 98 Cutter Mill Rd., Great Neck, N.Y. 11021.

It is nongovernmental, nonprofit, membership corporation that has engaged in projects such as tours of the United States by basketball teams from other countries and sending boys' basketball teams from California to Japan and Korea. Its key to success has been its ability and willingness to get individual and business help in defraying expenses for foreign visitors and in helping American athletes go overseas.

World Leisure and Recreation Association

The World Leisure and Recreation Association (WLRA), formerly the International Recreation Association, was founded in 1956 in Philadelphia. This organization seeks to advance recreation on an international basis by aiding various countries in need of assistance, by answering inquiries, by placing qualified teachers and leaders in youth agencies, and by distributing information.

The World Leisure and Recreation Association has made significant contributions in the following areas:

1. Organizing and conducting exchange programs for governments, foundations, and recreation agencies and enabling more than 300 leaders from fifty countries to observe and study recreation in the United States
2. Recruiting and training volunteers who have served in more than eighty countries
3. Arranging for an exchange of recreation leaders from various countries

The association distributes helpful information about recreation to affiliated agencies and informs leaders of government, business, and professions of the importance of planning for leisure. The address of the WLRA is 345 East 46th St., New York, N.Y. 10017.

PHYSICAL EDUCATION IN SELECTED COUNTRIES AROUND THE WORLD

Australia

The island continent of Australia, composed of six states, is approximately the same size as the mainland United States.

Educational structure. Education is compulsory between the ages of 6 and 15 years, except in Tasmania, where the upper age is 16. The six state governments are responsible for the progress of education in their own states. A director of education heads the state education department in each capital city, under whom are the directors of the specific educational areas. Each state has a state director of physical education.

Philosophy of physical education. Physical education is required in all elementary and secondary schools and in all teacher-training curriculums in colleges and universities. It seeks to develop physical fitness in students by promoting proper growth and by building adequate amounts of strength, endurance, and coordination. Social and emotional development and the learning of recreational skills are also primary aims.

Physical education in infants' schools. These schools are attached to the primary schools, and children may enter when they are 5 years of age. Physical education is the responsibility of the classroom teacher and is a phase of the total program. The emphasis is on creativity, self-expression, and the acquisition of skills needed in later school years. Dancing and rhythmics make up the bulk of the physical education activities.

Physical education in elementary schools. Physical education is the responsibility of the classroom teacher, who may call on physical education resource people attached to the state education department. In grades one through four, approximately 1 hour a week is devoted to physical education, whereas grades five through seven have approximately 2 hours of physical education a week. The activities included in the program are games, marching, stunts and tumbling, gymnastics, track and field, and lead-up games for such sports as tennis, softball, and basketball. Where a pool is available, swimming is taught.

Physical education in secondary schools. All secondary schools have physical education specialists, although two schools may share the services of a single specialist. Up to 3 hours a week, including participation in the intramural program, are devoted to physical education. Dancing, rhythmics, the skills of various sports, gymnastics, games, track and field, and swimming are all parts of the program.

Physical education in higher education. Physical education is required only for those planning to enter the teaching profession.

Physical education facilities. Indoor facilities, especially gymnasiums, are generally poor, but many indoor facilities are currently under construction. Equipment is generally inadequate. Outdoor facilities are more than ample.

Teacher training. A diploma course lasts 3 years and a degree course from 4 to 5 years, depending on the amount of part-time study the prospective teacher engages in.

Canada

Canada is the second largest nation in square miles in the world.

Educational structure. Each of the ten Canadian provinces controls and administers its own schools. Thus, although the compulsory entry age for school is 5 years nationwide, the age that youth may leave the schools may be from 14 to 16 years, depending on the particular province. Likewise, some elementary schools include only the first six grades, whereas in other provinces the first seven or eight grades are part of the elementary school. Canada has many church-supported schools that set individual policies free of any provincial controls.

Philosophy of physical education. The attainment of physical fitness, basic skills needed for life and leisure, and social and emotional fitness are major objectives. The development of recreational skills has always been of major importance. Canada also places great emphasis on educating for movement and is considered to be a leader in the area of movement education.

Physical education in elementary schools. A general shortage of trained elementary school physical educators has placed the classroom teacher in the role of responsibility for physical education on this level. In general, three 15-minute periods of physical education a week are given. The activities included are movement skills, sport skills, and activities designed to increase physical fitness.

Physical education in secondary schools. In general, two 35-minute periods a week are conducted by a trained physical educator. The activities of the elementary school are continued, and dance, gymnastics, tumbling, basketball, volleyball, and other team and individual sports are added. Where a pool is available, swimming instruction is included in the program. In some schools the program is much like that found in high schools in the United States, but sports particularly enjoyed by Canadians, such as rugby, curling, and ice hockey, are parts of the program.

Physical education in higher education. Physical education on the college and university levels is limited. Where programs and requirements are in effect, football, hockey, basketball, swimming, tennis, and badminton are among the activities offered.

Physical education facilities. Although most elementary schools have playrooms rather than gymnasiums, facilities in general are good and improving. There is much continuing construction of gymnasiums. The appointment of qualified staff for all school programs is a goal of professional associations in Canada.

Teacher training. Common courses required of all teachers are methods, history, and philosophy of physical education, educational psychology, and student teaching. Because of particular provincial standards, a teacher certified in one province may not be eligible for certification in another.

England

Most of the people of England are urbanized and engage mainly in the manufacture of steel and other commodities.

Educational structure. England has a dualistic educational structure, made up of state-supported and independent schools. Although there is a ministry of education, all state schools are autonomous. They form their own educational syllabuses and establish their own curriculums.

Philosophy of physical education. Although there is no common syllabus for physical education, both the state and the independent schools attempt to help the child gain a joy and appreciation of bodily movement, to develop and maintain fitness, and to gain the skills, attitudes, and appreciations one needs to enjoy one's leisure and to work productively.

Physical education in elementary schools. Education in England is compulsory from the age of 5 years. At that time the children begin an almost daily program of physical education under the guidance of classroom teachers. Four times a week, for about 40 minutes each time, children engage in vigorous outdoor sports and games. They run, climb, jump, throw, and explore all the varieties of movement. As they progress through elementary school, children begin to learn some of the skills of gymnastics, apparatus, and dance and fundamentals of dual sports such as boxing and tennis, and they engage in track and field events. They are introduced to basketball, soccer, rugby, cricket, lacrosse, and hockey.

Physical education in secondary schools. The secondary schools have a specialist in physical education on the staff, although the classroom teacher may often supplement and help the work of the specialist. The program for boys and girls is separate and is heavily weighted with gymnastics. The skills of the elementary grades are improved on, and swimming is often added to the curriculum. Physical education is offered four periods a week. Two periods are instructional, and the other is a double period once a week during which a single game or sport is played, often competitively.

Physical education in higher education. There is no required program in physical education except for those preparing to teach in the elementary schools. Facilities, equipment, and personnel are available if the student wishes to participate in physical activities.

Physical education facilities. The quality and quantity of facilities vary widely. Playing fields are abundant at all schools, but few elementary schools have gymnasiums. School camp facilities are often provided, and athletic clubs often make their facilities available to the schools.

Teacher training. Elementary classroom teachers must take courses in physical education to prepare them to teach this part of the program. Teacher training for grades above the elementary level is accomplished through programs ranging from 1 to 3 years in length. College graduates who wish to teach physical education must take a 1-year specialized course.

Israel

Only a third of the population of Israel is native born. Immigrants from Asia, Africa, and Europe make up most of the population. Hebrew is the official language of the country, but English is frequently spoken.

Educational structure. Education is free and compulsory between the ages of 5 and 14 years. Beyond the age of 14, tuition is charged in the public schools. The Ministry of Education and Culture is responsible for all phases of primary and secondary education.

Physical education in India.

Students engaging in physical education activity at Wingate Institute for Physical Education, Israel.

Philosophy of physical education. Physical education is conducted under the guidance of an Authority for Sports and Physical Education, a state arm that is responsible for the coordination of all physical education. Physical education is primarily devoted to increasing and maintaining physical fitness and to providing instruction in leisure-time pursuits.

Physical education in kindergartens. Although school need not be started by children until the age of 5 years, these schools are provided for students from the ages of 3 through 5 years. Physical education is required for a period of 2 hours each week. The program includes dances, rhythmics, games, and native activities.

Physical education in elementary schools. This school terminates with the eighth grade. Physical education is required 2 hours each week, and the program of the kindergarten is continued through third grade. Beginning with the fourth grade, the skills of sports such as soccer and basketball are added, and specialists are in charge of the program.

Physical education in secondary schools. In addition to the 2-hour physical education requirement, there is a 2-hour premilitary training period weekly, based on physical education activities. The programs, taught by specialist, include rhythmics, wrestling, handball, table tennis, swimming, track, soccer, gymnastics, apparatus, volleyball, and basketball.

Physical education in higher education. Except in programs of teacher training, physical education is not offered or required.

Physical education facilities. Facilities are extremely poor according to standards in the United States, both indoors and out-of-doors. In many areas the school building itself is inadequate, even for the process of general education.

Teacher training. The Physical Education

Courtesy S. Ebashi, University of Tokyo, Tokyo, Japan.

Japanese physical education programs.

Teachers College at Wingate Institute and the related Institute of Education for Movement offer a 2-year professional program in physical education.

Japan

Japan has a large population and shows one of the highest rates of population increase in the world.

Educational structure. The ministry of education and local school boards help to advance the progress of Japanese education. The ministry of education, however, is a liaison agency rather than a controlling one. Its functions are to give guidance to educational and research institutions, aid with procurement and disbursing of educational funds and materials, and co-ordinate many of the educational services. The school boards serve the same function as do those in the United States.

Philosophy of physical education. Physical education is compulsory from elementary school through college. The aim is to develop sound and fit minds and bodies, to imbue a spirit of democracy in sports and life, and to develop a healthy and health-knowledgeable individual.

Physical education in elementary schools. The ministry of education publishes a course of study that is followed in the elementary schools.

All children have three 45-minute periods of physical education each week, and, in addition, they may participate in intramurals. The activities covered are rhythmics, apparatus, gymnastics, calisthenics, track and field, and various ball games. The skills of swimming, skiing, and skating are often included, and physical performance tests are administered periodically.

Physical education in upper elementary schools. This level covers grades seven through nine. In the seventh grade, physical education classes are held three times each week. In grades eight and nine, one period of health and two of physical education are offered. The activities of the lower elementary school are continued, but boys also receive instruction in judo, kindo, and sumo, whereas girls have additional instruction in dance and rhythmical exercise. Performance tests are also given at this school level.

Physical education in secondary schools. The basic elementary program is continued for all students, with the addition of team sports such as basketball, softball, and volleyball. Individual and dual activities include tennis, badminton, and advanced instruction in swimming and diving.

Physical education in higher education. The activity program of the secondary schools

The author meets with Japanese students. Professor Ebashi of the University of Tokyo is the interpreter.

is carried over to the colleges and universities. All students are required to take two university credits in activity courses and two additional credits in physical education theory courses. Electives among the latter include kinesiology, physiology, the history of physical education, and the administration of physical education.

Physical education facilities. Japan has inadequate facilities in many of its elementary schools and few parks for recreation. It lacks research facilities and adequate laboratories for major students in colleges and universities. Some public schools do have adequate gymnasiums, and many have substantial outdoor play areas.

Teacher training. The private schools and universities prepare teachers for the secondary schools in a 4-year program. The junior colleges offer a 2-year program geared toward those students who are preparing to teach in the elementary schools.

Mexico

The climate of Mexico varies according to altitude and rainfall.

Educational structure. Each of the twenty-nine states in Mexico controls and administers its own schools. Education in the territories and the federal district is administered by the federal government.

Philosophy of physical education. The major objectives of physical education include the development of the human body; the development of physical, intellectual, and moral qualities; and the training of individuals so that they can be most productive.

Physical education in elementary schools. Elementary school physical education is similar to that of the United States, with emphasis on rhythmical activities, games of low organization, gymnastics, and various traditional Mexican games (rondas).

Physical education in secondary schools. Physical education in the secondary schools is mainly concerned with the six "basic" sports —track, basketball, soccer, swimming, volleyball, and gymnastics—with the choice of these activities left to the student.

Physical education facilities. Because of the limited space around the schools in urban areas, both physical education and recreational programs suffer. However, these limited areas are supplemented with indoor facilities, where possible, by the Social Security Institute and other agencies.

Teacher training. On graduating from the secundaria (grade nine), those students who wish to become physical education teachers enter one of the four schools of physical education for a period of 3 years.

New Zealand

In general, the climate of New Zealand is temperate. The Maoris, a Polynesian people, make up a very small segment of the population of 3 million. Most New Zealanders are of British birth or descent. The terrain of the nation is irregular and mountainous to the extent that some children cannot travel to school and must study at home by radio or through correspondence courses.

Educational structure. Education is compulsory from the age of 6 through 14 years, although almost all children attend from age 5 to 15 years. The state education department controls all education, including syllabuses, but delegates much of its authority to local education boards. The secondary schools are run by boards of governors. Parent committees help to run the primary schools. The education department has a division of physical education.

New Zealand has its own Ministry of Recreation and Sport.

Philosophy of physical education. The schools of New Zealand believe strongly in physical fitness and its maintenance, in the development of lifetime sports skills, and in striving to help the individual become a thinking, mature, and responsible adult.

Physical education in elementary schools. In grades one through six, the classroom teacher, at times aided by a physical education specialist, is responsible for instruction. Three 30-minute instructional periods a week are supplemented by a single 30-minute game period each week. This latter period is highly organized. Basic movement skills, dances, games, and the sport skills of tennis, netball, cricket, gymnastics, apparatus, rugby, and swimming are included in the program. All children can swim by the time they enter high school.

Physical education in secondary schools. A physical education specialist is available in the secondary schools. Two 40-minute instructional periods and a 30-minute game period are standard in most schools. The elementary school skills are continued, and winter and summer sports, leisure-time activities, field hockey, basketball, soccer, life-saving, rowing, hiking, and track and field are added to the program. Physical education is not compulsory after the tenth grade. Sports competition and tournaments among secondary schools are keenly contested.

Physical education in higher education. Physical education is not required in the colleges and universities of New Zealand. However, many university students participate in a wide variety of sports. The seven universities hold a winter and summer sports tournament annually.

Physical education facilities. The elementary schools have good outdoor facilities but have limited or no indoor facilities. However, swimming pools are available on a wide scale. The secondary schools usually have an indoor, gymnasium-type room and adequate equipment for the program.

The climate and country favor year-round outdoor activity, including all water and mountain sports, and even the smallest communities have well-organized sports programs and clubs and outdoor facilities.

Teacher training. The courses vary in length from 2 to 3 years, depending on whether the preparation is for the elementary or secondary school level.

Philippines

The Republic of the Philippines consists of an archipelago of approximately 7,100 islands.

Educational structure. The law requires all children between the ages of 7 and 10 years to attend elementary school through fourth grade. Many children complete the full 6-year elementary school and then go on to the 4-year high school.

New Zealand physical education.

Philosophy of physical education. The Philippine society stresses physical activity, with the aim of developing motor fitness. There is a growing emphasis in physical education on human development, with the ultimate goal of enhancing the individual's self-concept.

Physical education in the elementary schools. At the nursery and kindergarten levels, no definite time allotment is given to physical education. However, in grades one through four, physical education, together with art and music, is allotted 40 minutes a day, and in grades five and six, 50 minutes a day. Calisthenics, simple stunts and tumbling, rhythmics, games, and dance are a part of the program.

Physical education in secondary schools. The 4-year secondary school is designed for both college- and vocation-bound students. One period of 40 minutes a day is allotted for physical education. During the first and second years of high school, physical education is allotted a double period (80 minutes) a day. High school physical education stresses competitive athletics, big-muscle activity, and sports skill development. There is also much stress on Philippine folk dances.

Physical education in higher education. On the college level, physical education is prescribed as a requirement for graduation. At least four semester units of physical education are required in courses such as natural movement, gymnastics, rhythmical activities, and fundamental skills and athletics.

Physical education facilities. Since most of the Philippines' physical education is conducted outdoors, these facilities are adequate. However, indoor facilities are often poor or entirely lacking.

Teacher training. Credits are needed to satisfy general education requirements, and an additional eighteen units are needed to fulfill the requirements for a concentration in physical education.

Sweden

The people of Sweden populate most heavily the large cities and towns of the south.

Educational structure. The Royal Board of Education oversees and administers the schools of Sweden but delegates much of its authority to the provincial school boards. Education is compulsory through the ninth grade.

Philosophy of physical education. Physical education in Sweden has as its major objective the all-around development of each individual, both physiologically and psychologically.

Physical education in elementary schools. In grades one through five, boys and girls are taught together by the classroom teacher. They have two or three physical education classes a week for a total of 1½ hours. Folk dance, rhythmics, games, and winter sports make up the program.

Physical education in intermediate schools. The intermediate school encompasses grades four through six. The physical education classes are still taught by the classroom teacher, and the program is the same as that of the elementary school.

Physical education in senior schools. In grades seven through nine, physical education is taught by a specialist. The program includes folk dance, gymnastics, games, track and field, swimming, winter sports, and orienteering. The

University of the East, Manila, Philippines.
Philippine folk dances.

classes are held three times a week for a total of about an hour and are conducted out-of-doors whenever possible.

Physical education in secondary schools. The secondary school is a 3-year school designed for the college- or university-bound student. Physical education is conducted from 1 to 4 hours a week, depending on the individual school. The program parallels that of the senior school.

Physical education in higher education. Physical education is not required in the colleges and universities of Sweden, but ample facilities and equipment are available for those who wish to participate in activity.

Physical education facilities. All Swedish schools have a gymnasium, a playroom, and an outdoor play area. There are also many parks, swimming pools, and private and public athletic clubs with ample facilities.

Teacher training. The Royal Central Gymnastic Institute and twenty teacher-training schools offer 2-year teacher preparation courses.

Union of Soviet Socialist Republics

Much of the population of the Soviet Union is urban. There are more than 200 ethnic groups who speak at least 150 languages. The Russian-speaking people make up half the population. This diversity of culture and language affects the schools: Over the country as a whole, forty languages are used in the instructional programs, with the Russian language itself a common elective subject.

Educational structure. The process and progress of education in Russia are directly controlled by the state through its Ministry of Higher Education and the Ministry of Culture, a subordinate body. Within each of the fifteen Soviet republics, there is also a Ministry of Education that is responsible to the state.

Physical education in Russia is also under state control. Subordinate to the Presidium of the Central Committee is the Republic Sports Committee and, under it, the fifteen regional sports committees. Most aspects of physical education, from teacher placement to sports clubs, to curriculum and the publishing of journals, are controlled, organized, and scrutinized by the Central Committee.

Philosophy of physical education. The purpose of physical education in the Soviet Union is to build a nation of superbly physically fit individuals. The Soviets regard physical fitness as the key to the survival and progress of their nation. Physical education is compulsory for all students until the completion of their second year in a university, vocational, or technical school. Great emphasis is placed on physical activity as a recreational pursuit for all citizens, and many mass activities are provided for

Toledo Public Schools, Toledo, Ohio.

Toledo schools teach Philippine dances.

Courtesy Embassy of the USSR, Washington, D.C.
Tamara Lazakovich on the high-and-low bars in the USSR Gymnastics Cup tournament.

everyone, regardless of age. The spectator is not regarded as a productive citizen.

Physical education in preschools. The Ministries of Health and Education provide and supervise preschool institutions. A child may be accepted into one of these schools beginning at 2 months of age. For those old enough to participate, the physical education program is essentially one of basic movement. Children are taught and encouraged to run, climb, jump, throw, and play games of low organization.

Physical education in elementary schools. At the age of 7 years, Soviet children begin their years of compulsory schooling. In the first and second grades the emphasis in physical education is on rhythmical activities, gymnastics, and active games. At the third-grade level, skiing and track and field are added to the program. Through the fourth grade, the child is taught by his classroom teacher. During the elementary school years, the child receives 45 minutes of physical education instruction at least twice a week, along with supplementary activity periods at the discretion of the teacher.

Physical education in secondary schools. Secondary education includes grades five through eleven, and physical education is taught by a specialist. Although the major emphasis is still on gymnastics, activities such as basketball, soccer, volleyball, and water sports are also stressed. The skills of skiing and track and field continue as part of the program. Unless the weather interferes, the program is an outdoor one and coeducational. The classroom teacher continues to provide periods of vigorous activity over and above the biweekly 45-minute instructional periods. It is at this level that the lifelong concept of intense competition is introduced.

Physical education in higher education. Physical education is required in the first 2 years of university-level education. Students are given a variety of activities to choose from, but all must learn to swim, and all are required to pass physical fitness tests.

Physical education facilities. The facilities provided for physical education are excellent. Parks are set aside specifically for recreational and cultural pursuits. There are many camps, sports clubs, and youth groups, all with their own facilities. Beyond this, there are special sports schools devoted to giving intensive instruction to children. Between the ages of 12 and 18 years, a child with a high degree of facility in a sport is recommended for acceptance at one of these schools. Here, outside of school hours, the child receives concentrated coaching twice a week for 2 hours each time. This system has helped to develop many of the Russian champion athletes.

Teacher training. The Soviet Union prepares its physical educators to be either teachers or coaches. The coaches concentrate on one particular sport and work in the sports clubs. The teachers who go into the schools are trained intensively in gymnastics.

Graduates of 11-year secondary schools may enter one of the sixteen training institutions for physical educators or go to one of the fifty colleges or universities or one of the more than twenty other specialized schools of physical education.

West Germany

The population of the German Federal Republic, which is almost entirely urban, includes many refugees from East Germany.

Educational structure. Each of the ten states of West Germany has its own Ministry of Education, which is directed by a Minister of Education.

Philosophy of physical education. The aim of the program is to contribute to the total development of the individual with activity and participation. Sought-after goals are the development of physical fitness, a love of movement, creativity, and a sense of fair play.

Physical education in elementary schools. During the first 4 years of schooling, classes in physical education are held two or three times a week for a total of 1 hour. Activities include basic movement skills, such as running, jumping, throwing, and climbing; gymnastics; tumbling and apparatus; games of low organization; and swimming.

Physical education in intermediate schools. This school includes grades five through ten. Physical education is offered two or three times a week for a total of about an hour. The program of the elementary school is continued in

German physical education.

the intermediate school with the addition of track and field, soccer, volleyball, and basketball.

Physical education in secondary schools. This school division encompasses grades five through thirteen. Physical education is taught three times a week for a total of 1 hour. The program is essentially the same as that of the intermediate school, but in some schools rowing, skiing, ice skating, and hiking are added to the curriculum.

Physical education in higher education. West German universities have departments of physical education, and some training is compulsory for all students. However, the program is limited at the university level, both by equipment and facilities and the lack of sufficient status of these departments in the educational structure.

Physical education facilities. West Germany has a shortage of facilities.

Teacher training. Germany has colleges and universities that offer degree courses in physical education. Students elect to teach on the elementary level or the intermediate or secondary level.

SELF-ASSESSMENT TESTS

These tests are to assist students in determining if material and competencies presented in this chapter have been mastered.

1. Without consulting your text, write a definition of international education in your own words and list the purposes for which a physical educator should be interested in the subject of international education.

2. Assume that you are in charge of the placement office in your college or university. A student informs you that she would like to obtain a position in another country. Advise her in regard to the opportunities for such service. Also, tell her what opportunities exist at home to serve the cause of international education.

3. Prepare a table according to the following format, identifying five important international sports competitions:

Name of international sports competition	Countries involved	Sports engaged in	How often competitions are conducted

4. Prepare a chart identifying five international organizations according to the following format:

International organization	Purpose	People involved

5. Tabulate the following information for each of five countries of the world other than the United States: (a) location of country, (b) educational structure, (c) philosophy of education, (d) type of physical education program in elementary and secondary schools, (e) facilities available, and (f) how physical education teachers are trained.

READING ASSIGNMENT

Past issues of *The Physical Educator,* section on "Elsewhere in the World."

SELECTED REFERENCES

American Alliance for Health, Physical Education and Recreation: A credo for international professional relations, Journal of Physical Education and Recreation **46:**6, March, 1975, International Relations Committee, The Alliance.

American Council on Education: Universities of the world outside the U.S.A., 1875 Massachusetts Ave., N.W., Washington, D.C. 20036.

Bi-National Commission for Exchange in Physical Education, Journal of Health, Physical Education, and Recreation **44:**6, April, 1973.

Ebbeck, F. N.: Learning from play in other cultures, Childhood Education **48:**68, Nov., 1971.

Institute of International Education: Handbook on international study, 1 East 67th St., New York, N.Y.

International Council of Health, Physical Education, and Recreation (assorted publications), 1201 16th St., N.W., Washington, D.C. 20036.

Jackson, C. O.: Physical education in British primary schools, The Physical Educator **28:**49, March, 1971.

Jackson, C. O.: Physical education in the Philippines, The Physical Educator **28:**209, Dec., 1971.

Jernigan, Sara Stafford, and Vendein, C. Lynn: Playtime—a world recreation handbook, New York, 1972, McGraw-Hill Book Co.

Johnson, William, editor: Physical education around the world, Monographs nos. 1, 2, and 3, Indianapolis, 1966, 1968-1969, Phi Epsilon Kappa Fraternity.

Parker, Franklin: International organizations promoting sports and physical education, The Physical Educator **28:**65, May, 1971.

Publications of the World Confederation of Organizations of the Teaching Profession: Panorama: teaching throughout the world and Echo. (Also assorted publications, 1201 16th St., N.W., Washington, D.C. 20036.)

United States Olympic Committee Newsletter no. 7, Oct., 1972.

Van Dalen, Deobold, and Bennett, Bruce: A world history of physical education, Englewood Cliffs, N.J., 1971, Prentice-Hall, Inc.

World University Games, Journal of Health, Physical Education, and Recreation **43:**22, May, 1972.

8

Movement—the keystone of physical education

INSTRUCTIONAL OBJECTIVES AND COMPETENCIES TO BE ACHIEVED

After reading this chapter the student should be able to—

1. Explain why movement is the keystone of physical education.
2. Identify some of the various biomechanical factors that affect movement.
3. Demonstrate how movement education programs are conducted.
4. Trace the development and history of movement education in Europe and the United States.
5. Compare the traditional approach to teaching physical education with the movement education approach.
6. Identify the key concepts of movement education.

Movement represents the key concern of physical educators. The central focus of their field of endeavor is the task of helping human beings to move efficiently to increase the quality of their performance, to enhance their ability to learn, and to promote health status. Since movement represents the keystone of physical education, it is important for professionals in the field to understand some of its dimensions. The emphasis on the scientific aspects of movement represents a comparatively new major emphasis in physical education. As such, it is included in Part Two of this text.

Human movement pertains to many aspects of physical education, including various locomotor movement skills such as running, jumping, and leaping and nonlocomotor movement

skills such as bending, twisting, turning, pushing, and swinging. These skills form the basis for more complex and involved specialized skills that are utilized in sports and other physical education activities, work, and life situations where human beings are involved in movement.

GENERAL FACTORS THAT AFFECT MOVEMENT

Human movement involves many of the organic systems of the body. For example, it involves the skeletal system (e.g., skeletal levers), the nervous system (e.g., impulses send messages to the muscle to contract), and the muscular system (e.g., muscle contraction results in the release of force). It also is concerned with mechanical principles, or the forces that act on the human body and the effects that these forces produce (e.g., gravity).

Physiological factors affect movement. Physical fitness and body build are two factors among many that affect the way humans move. Poor muscular development is a deterring factor in generating force, and the mechanical advantage of levers might be reduced in a person who is small in stature. Furthermore, physical fitness qualities like flexibility, endurance, and strength are basic to and will greatly influence motor performance.

Psychological factors affect movement. Phenomena such as fear, anxiety, and self-concept might affect human movement in a positive or negative way. Fear or anxiety, for example, might prevent a relaxed state in the performer, thus impeding effective performance.

Sociological factors affect movement. The persons with whom one is competing or performing, the relationship of the performer to the group, and the desire for social mobility are examples of sociological factors that might leave their impact on the quality of movement.

The physiological, psychological, and sociological factors that affect human movement are discussed in other chapters in this text, particularly in Part Three.

BIOMECHANICAL FACTORS THAT AFFECT MOVEMENT

The term *biomechanics* is generally accepted in physical education at the present time as the science that studies the effects of internal and external forces on human performance. In the past, terms such as *homokinetics, biokinetics, kinanthropology,* and *mechanical kinesiology* have been given to this area of study. Biomechanics, a field of study that is growing rapidly, stresses in particular the mechanical analysis of human motion. It also stresses the biological aspect, for example, examining func-

tional anatomy. Electromyography constitutes an important research tool.

Principles of biomechanics in sport and physical education are concerned with factors such as velocity, acceleration, force, torque, energy, power, momentum, stability, motion, aerodynamics, and hydrodynamics. Entire books are devoted to these principles. This discussion limits itself to a brief consideration of the principles of stability, motion, force, and leverage to provide physical educators with some insight into the importance of the study of biomechanics to their field of endeavor.

Stability

Stability is an important factor in movement that is related to equilibrium, or a state of rest of the body. Stability enables the body to return to a position of equilibrium after it has been displaced. In some cases stability is referred to as balance. Maintenance of body stability, or balance, is closely associated with gravity, or the natural force that pulls all objects toward the center of the earth. An important feature of gravitational pull is that it occurs through the center of weight or mass of an

Ability of the body to maintain stability or balance is closely associated with gravity. The weight lifter seeks a low center of gravity to gain stability.

object. In the human body the center of weight is known as the center of gravity—the point from which the body can be suspended in perfect balance and a point that constantly changes during movement and shifts in the direction of the movement or additional weight. When human beings stand erect with their hands at their sides, the center of gravity is located in the center of the body at the level of the hips.

Some primary principles relating to stability are as follows:

The closer the center of gravity is to the base of support the greater will be the stability. This principle explains why, in activities that require stability, the performers lower the body and bend at the knees, thus lowering the center of gravity, for example, the football lineman who assumes a three-point stance.

The nearer to the center of the base of support the center of gravity is the more stable the body will be. In activities where the purpose is to move quickly in one direction, the weight should be shifted in the direction of the movement, for example, where the sprinter leans forward at the start of a race.

The larger or wider the base of support the more stable the body will be. The feet are spread to increase the base and thus increase stability; for example, the football player who is on the line in football widens his stance to prevent the offensive player from knocking him off his feet.

Motion

Motion implies movement, and movement upsets the equilibrium of the human body. A force is required to start a body in motion, to slow it down, to stop it, to change the direction of its motion, or to make it move faster. Newton's laws of motion are examples of ways to describe movement and predict the motion of an object.

Newton's First Law, the law of inertia, states that a body at rest will remain at rest and a body in motion will remain in motion at the same speed and in the same direction unless acted on by some outside force. This means that for movement to occur a force must act on a body sufficiently to overcome that object's inertia. If the applied force is less than the re-sistance offered by the object, motion will not occur.

Newton's Second Law, the law of acceleration, states that a change in velocity (acceleration) of an object is directly proportional to the force producing it and inversely proportional to its mass. This can be demonstrated by three applications of the law, as follows: The heavier the object the more force needed to speed it up or slow it down; an increase in speed is proportional to the amount of force that is applied; and the greater the amount of force that is imparted to an object the greater the object's speed. Also, if the same amount of force is exerted on two bodies of different mass, greater acceleration will be produced by the lighter or the less massive object. With all the balls, bats, and other equipment that are used in physical education activities, one can readily see the importance of understanding Newton's Second Law.

Newton's Third Law, the law of action and reaction, states that for every action there is an equal and opposite reaction. Bouncing on a trampoline or springing on a diving board are examples. The more force one exerts on the downward bounce the higher will be the spring in the air.

Force

Force is the effect that one body has on another and is always present when motion occurs. There can be force without movement, such as when a person pushes against a nonmovable wall. Body force is produced by the muscles of the body, and the stronger the muscles the more force the body can generate. However, the force of the muscle(s) must be applied in the same direction and in the proper sequence to realize the greatest force. For example, in the high jump the body is lowered to enable the jumper to contract the muscles of the thigh. The upward movement of the arms give added force to the jump when coordinated with the upward push of the legs.

Force must also be generated to propel objects, whether a football, baseball, or other object. The application of force is greatest when it is applied in the direction in which the object is to travel.

Absorption of force is also an important consideration, whether catching a football, landing after a jump in pole vaulting, or performing some other activity where force must be absorbed. The impact of the force should be gradually reduced and spread over as large an area as possible.

Leverage, levers, and movement

Leverage and levers impinge on many other factors relating to efficient body movement. However, since levers are so important for efficient body movement, they receive a separate discussion.

The bones of the body act as levers, the joints act as fulcrums, and the force to move the bone (lever) about the joint (fulcrum) is produced by the contraction of the muscles. Levers are of three types and are determined by the relationship of the fulcrum (axis), the weight, and the point of application of force. There are first,

second, and third class levers. In the first class lever the fulcrum is located between the weight and the point of application of force. In the second class lever the weight is between the fulcrum and the force. In a third class lever the force is between the fulcrum and the weight.

Levers enable a person to gain a mechanical advantage by producing either strength or speed. First class levers may produce both strength and speed unless the fulcrum is in the middle of the force and weight, which then produces a balanced condition. Second class levers favor force, and third class levers favor speed.

• • •

It can be seen from a brief discussion of biomechanics why it is growing rapidly as an important field for specialization in physical education. It is particularly important to sport and performance in physical education activities, since it provides a sound, logical, and scientific way to evaluate techniques that contribute to championship and most productive performance.

NATURE OF MOVEMENT EDUCATION

Movement education is an important aspect of physical education programs, particularly at the elementary school level. Movement education exploits the science of movement and consists of an educational program designed to help young people become more aware of their bodies and how to have better and more effective movement.

Physical education in the elementary school is emerging as the art and science of human movement. It instills in the child the "why" of movement, and "how" of movement, and the physiological, sociological, and psychological results of movement. In addition, there is concern for movement skills and motor patterns that comprise the movement repertoire of human beings.

Through movement children express themselves, are creative, develop a positive self-image, and gain a better understanding of their physical selves. It is through movement experiences that young children explore, develop, and grow in a meaningful manner.

Force is the effect that one body has on another and is always present when motion occurs. This girl at Northland College, Ashland, Wisconsin, applies force to a volleyball.

Movement is integral to the human being. Everything that people do, whether they are reacting to the environment or simply expressing themselves, involves movement of some sort. Movement in itself is thus a tool of life; the more efficiently a person moves the more meaningful life is.

Movement is a means of communication, oftentimes called *preverbal language*. It is with movement that one can express feelings without using spoken language. Dance educators have long advocated that it is almost impossible to communicate the emotions of a dance by using language, but with the body the imagery of a dance can be conveyed.

Movement experiences can be extremely beautiful, and a knowledge of movement will contribute to a richer appreciation of such experiences. Being aware of the gracefulness of a skier gliding down the slopes or the well-controlled movements of the gymnast performing on the parallel bars can make these events more worth while for the viewer. Of course, the experience derived by the individual performer yields the greatest rewards of all.

Movement educators seek not only to have the individual understand and appreciate the movement of which he or she is capable but also to appreciate the varieties of movement of which others are capable.

Programs of movement education are not conducted haphazardly. Rather, they are structured on a problem-solving basis, leaving individuals free to relate to force, time, and space through their particular use of balance, leverage, and technique. Movement educators hold that numerous activities have common elements, all of which are based on a comprehensive knowledge of movement fundamentals. The better the individual is able to perceive movement patterns, they believe, the more ease there will be in developing skills, since these skills will tend to develop as a concomitant of learning to move.

Movement education strives to make the individual aware of the movement of the entire body and to become intellectually as well as physically involved. The challenge set by a problem in movement is first perceived by the intellect and then solved by the body moving

Movement exploration with balls at Oak View Elementary School in Fairfax, Virginia.

through space, reacting to any obstacles within that space and to the limitations and existing restrictions. Learning accrues as the individual accepts and attempts to solve increasingly difficult problems. Inherent in this is the concept of individual differences. There may be numerous ways to solve a stated problem, and one chooses the method that best suits one's abilities and capacities. Individual rather than group development is the basic premise of movement education.

Thus movement education may be defined as individual exploration of the ability of the body to relate and react to the physical concepts of the environment and to factors in the environment, be they material or human.

Both the terms *movement education* and *movement exploration* are used in educational circles—sometimes synonymously. However, those who have studied this subject intensively generally think that the term *movement education* refers to the system, the sum of the educational experiences, or programs which are

Movement education in a dance class at Hampton Institute, Hampton, Virginia.

utilized in teaching children about their body and movement and which help them to develop desirable movement responses. On the other hand, *movement exploration* refers more to the methodology, or the process, that is used, such as the problem-solving approach, which helps children to develop body awareness and utilize their bodies in an effective manner unique to their own physical resources.

ORIGINS OF MOVEMENT EDUCATION

The roots of movement education may be traced back to the theories of Rudolf Laban, a dancer, and to the effect his theories had on physical education in England. Laban fled Germany during World War II and eventually settled in England, where he established the Laban Art of Movement Center, an institution that has trained many movement educators.

Laban stressed that the body is the instrument through and by which people move and that each individual is endowed with certain natural kinds of movement. Laban believed strongly in exploratory movement and in a spontaneous quality in movement. He was op-

posed to the rigidity of set series of exercises that left no room for creativity or self-expression. Laban was a movement analyst, and as such be believed that people could not only learn to move efficiently and effectively but could also develop a strong kinesthetic awareness of movement.

During World War II, England revised its entire educational structure and restated its philosophy of education. Whereas physical education had once been little more than formal gymnastics, now the freedom of bodily movement, creativity, and expression were stressed. Laban's principles were freely employed. Over the years they have been expanded and broadened into the concept of movement education as it is carried on in England today.

In England the classroom teacher is in charge of physical education in the elementary schools, and both boys and girls, beginning in the first grade, are educated in movement. In the secondary schools the movement education program is continued for girls under the guidance of a trained physical educator. The program is based on problem solving. The teacher sets the problem, then guides, assists, and suggests,

Movement education at Oak View Elementary School in Fairfax, Virginia. Children hurdling over homemade hurdles of conduit tubing.

but in no way dictates a solution. There is no teacher demonstration and thus no imitation, leaving children to establish their own patterns of movement, set their own tempo, and make wise use of space.

Within the last 20 to 25 years a trend toward concentrated movement education has developed in the United States, based on the English programs. Unlike England, however, where movement education is concentrated in the early school years, in the United States movement education first received its impetus in the college and university physical education programs for women. These programs have attempted to develop movement patterns as the dancer's vehicle of expression. A working definition of movement education terms was introduced in 1956 by the National Association for Physical Education of College Women so that educators could communicate with each other more effectively.

In recent years, movement education has become incorporated into elementary school programs in the United States. The leaders in the field of movement education are in agree-

Movement education in New Zealand.

ment that this concept should play a vital role in determining the future direction of physical education, particularly in the lower grades.

SCHOOLS OF THOUGHT

Despite varied viewpoints concerning movement education, it is generally agreed that it is activity centered rather than verbally centered, and thus the movement itself, the awareness of the body, and its range of abilities are important. Rather than a force to be overcome, the body becomes the prime tool through which all movement takes place.

It is necessary at this point to take a look at the various schools of thought in movement education to gain greater insight as to why leaders in the field believe it will play an important role in the future of physical education.

Dance educators have long used the philosophy of educating for movement. As early as 1914 a dancer named Diana Watts published a book entitled *The Renaissance of the Greek Ideal* in the United States. The book was her philosophy of movement, drawn from her research into early Greek statues and paintings of athletes in motion. Dance educators often describe dance as nonverbal communication. Dance is viewed as creative and expressive movement in time and space through the instrument of the body. Dance educators have also expressed the belief that movement by the body has important academic implications. They believe that through movement the child is given the opportunity to develop judgment and curiosity and thus become more resourceful and creative.

Kinesiologists are students of human movement and view it as an academic discipline. They look at physical education as a process whereby human movement is studied and refined as an educational procedure. Kinesiologists contend that students who have a knowledge of how their bodies move not only will learn skills more readily but also will perform more effectively and efficiently. They agree with movement educators that movement education utilizes physical activity predominantly and that activity is also the end result of the process of movement education.

Physical educators have used many of the concepts of movement education, often without cognition. In physical education the student can be guided toward development only if the body is put to use, since movement of the body is the basic tool of physical education. However, in many physical education programs, intellectual awareness of the body is not developed, and thus there is no understanding of how the body moves through time and space. As physical educators are becoming more aware of the applications and implications of movement education, many are beginning to provide experiences in movement for their students and are guiding them into an understanding of and an appreciation for these experiences.

On the college level, particularly in programs for women, courses called by titles such as movement education, foundations of movement, or body mechanics are now being offered. These courses allow for exploration of the capacities of the human body and for the discovery and increased understanding of its movement abilities.

Physical educators are becoming increasingly concerned with the development of the individual and are making more allowances for individual differences in rate of skill learning. The intellect and body are increasingly viewed as interactive and interdependent. Those who have made a study of motor learning state that movement problems must be meaningful; that is, the student must understand the fundamentals of movement before he or she can successfully attempt the learning of a complex skill. It is up to the instructor to set the problem, ascertain whether the student understands it, and then observe and guide the learning in relation to the abilities, capacities, and needs of that student.

TRADITIONAL APPROACH VERSUS MOVEMENT EDUCATION

The traditional approach to physical education needs little explanation. Syllabuses, or course outlines, specify several weeks of one activity followed by several weeks of another, often unrelated. In the elementary schools in the United States, games of low organization, folk and square dances, tumbling and gymnastics, and lead-up games often comprise the major part of the program. Later school years, for both boys and girls, are devoted to the learn-

Movement education class with children shaping their bodies into various patterns at Public School No. 38 in Brooklyn, New York.

ing of specific sport skills. Rhythmics, or fundamental movement, is sometimes included, but as a minor phase of the program.

The movement education approach to physical education is founded on an entirely different premise. Movement education is not a gap filler of several lessons but an ongoing method of teaching physical education, beginning with the earliest school years. Movement education does not abandon or fully supplant the traditional approach as we know it. Rather, it forms a firmer foundation for more meaningful skill learning, for increased pleasure in the skillful use of the body, and for the development of lifelong physical effectiveness and efficiency.

To understand the full meaning of movement education, it is necessary to identify and compare its various key concepts. In so doing it will be possible to see it as a part of the whole that is physical education. Table 8-1 gives a comparison of movement education concepts and traditional physical education concepts that will prove useful in differentiating between these two approaches to the teaching of physical education.

KEY CONCEPTS OF MOVEMENT EDUCATION

Movement education has been widely accepted by physical educators because of certain basic concepts that emphasize its importance in educational programs.

Movement education is individual exploration

Through individual exploration each student is encouraged to find his or her own solution to a problem involving physical movement. Although there may be various ways to solve the problem, children choose the method that best suits their abilities. Furthermore, this individual exploration is concerned with the natural movements of childhood. Children enjoy running, jumping, climbing, leaping, and other physical movements, and they tend to perform these movements of their own volition. Movement educators seek to capitalize on these natural movements of childhood as they guide the child through an individual exploration of the many varieties of these movements.

Formalized physical education programs tend to stress conformity to stylized patterns of

Table 8-1. A comparison of movement education and traditional physical education concepts

Movement education	*Traditional physical education*
A. The program	
1. The program is activity centered.	1. The program is verbally centered.
2. The program is student centered.	2. The program is teacher centered.
3. The program attempts to develop an intellectual awareness of the body.	3. The program attempts to develop skills oftentimes lacking in intellectual comprehension.
4. The program places an emphasis on the problem-solving method, which includes exploration and discovery, based on the individual needs of the student.	4. The teacher serves as a model to be imitated by the students, and the method includes lecture and demonstration based on the needs of the group.
5. Repetition of problems leads to a greater variety of solutions.	5. Repetition of drills leads to an improved performance in motor skills.
6. Syllabus develops as each class period uncovers the needs of the individual that must be explored.	6. Syllabus, often unrelated to previous learning experiences, is presented to the students.
B. Role of the teacher	
1. In the learning process the teacher educates students.	1. In the learning process the teacher trains students.
2. The teacher is imaginative and creative in the methods used.	2. The teacher utilizes the traditional methods of teaching.
3. The teacher guides students in their activities.	3. The teacher leads students in their activities.
C. Role of students	
1. Motivation for learning comes from inner self.	1. Motivation for learning comes from the teacher.
2. Students experience the joy of their own natural movements and unique style.	2. Individual body types are not considered.
3. Students demonstrate their ability to reason logically and intelligently.	3. Students demonstrate their ability to take orders and follow directions.
4. Students demonstrate independence.	4. Students often lack independence.
5. Students face each new situation in an enthusiastic and intelligent manner.	5. Students oftentimes exhibit difficulty when confronted with new situations.
6. Students evaluate their own progress.	6. The teacher evaluates each student's progress.
7. Students develop at their own rate of progress.	7. Rate of progress depends on the norm of the student development within the class.
8. Success is based on each student's goals.	8. Success is based on the teacher's goals.
9. Students compete with themselves.	9. Students compete with classmates.
D. Class atmosphere	
1. There is an informal class atmosphere.	1. There is a formal class atmosphere.
2. Varied formations are used.	2. Set formations are used.
3. The teacher exhibits permissive behavior.	3. The teacher exhibits strict behavior.
4. Individual needs of the students are the determining factor in the allotment of time for any activity.	4. The completion of the subject matter is the determining factor in the allotment of time for any activity.
E. Facilities and equipment	
1. The facilities are considered secondary to the need for a resourceful and creative teacher.	1. Facilities are of prime importance, although the need for a resourceful and creative teacher is recognized.
2. The equipment is created to meet the needs of the individual.	2. The individual must adjust to the equipment used.
3. The equipment is used in many different situations.	3. The equipment is limited in its use.

movement. With movement education it is believed the child's individualized patterns of movement can be reinforced and retained. Movement education classes provide an unlimited opportunity for children to explore the uses of their bodies for movement in ways that are creative and self-expressive.

There are many patterns used for the exploration process, two of which are the locomotion and balance patterns. In the locomotion pattern the child moves about from one area to another. For example, a child may be asked to walk around a room without colliding with other children or with walls or apparatus. This is the beginning of learning to use space wisely and controlling the body within the confines of an area. With the various locomotor patterns such as running, jumping, and hopping the child is encouraged to analyze the differences between these movements and the concept known was walking. The child who is given the opportunity to participate in such experiences will soon become aware of how the movements of one part of the body influence the other parts. For example, the child who runs around in a circle will become aware of how the body leans toward the center as this movement pattern is performed. By individual exploration the child is encouraged to discover what the body can and cannot do when walking, running, or jumping.

Through individual exploration the child is also given the opportunity to participate in experiences that will help in understanding the concept known as balance. The child will become more fully aware of the mechanisms involved in maintaining the same position in space by participating in the various balance patterns. One of the basic balance patterns is the standing position. Through individual exploration the child, by changing the position of the feet or by moving the head, will become aware of the position that must be maintained if proper balance is to result. For example, the child who places all body weight on the toes will soon realize that he or she also is not standing in the proper position, and by exploring other foot positions, the child will become aware that weight must be concentrated on the whole foot if one is to experience proper balance.

With individual exploration the child is given the opportunity to be creative. As one participates in various movement patterns, one discovers what movements the body can make, in what directions the body can move, and what parts of the body are involved in executing a specific movement. Individual exploration is an extremely important concept of movement education. Physical education teachers should motivate their students and encourage them to participate in experiences that will aid them in creating various movement patterns. Hopefully, through individual exploration students will discover their unique abilities and solutions to their particular problems.

Movement education is student centered

Whereas traditional physical education has been concerned with the role of the teacher in the learning process and has focused much attention on the teacher, movement education looks to the student as the center of the learning process. In movement education the individual needs of each student have priority, and the motivation for learning comes from the student's inner self rather than from the teacher. The teacher is not a model to be imitated by the students. It is the task of the teacher to guide, observe, and set the tone of each class. In movement education, students are given the opportunity to experience the joy of their own natural movements and unique style. The student who participates in movement programs does not merely take orders and follow the teacher's directions but, instead, demonstrates independence and ability to reason logically and intelligently. Students are challenged to discover their own unique methods and techniques for solving problems in movement or in a skill performance. No one method is assumed to be the only acceptable answer, leaving students free to use their own bodies in an individually suitable manner.

The teacher should be creative and imaginative, guiding students to success by helping them to evaluate and refine their movements and by providing encouragement. For example, if a child is experiencing difficulty in attempting to jump onto a platform, the teacher might ask: "Can you use your arms in any way to help you jump higher?'' After receiving this information from the teacher, the student will still be encouraged to perform the movement and discover by individual exploration whether the arms help in jumping higher. Thus students become resourceful and are better able to face new problems with the confidence that they can solve them.

Any student can participate meaningfully in the movement education program regardless of size or athletic abilities. Individual students can work on their own needs and progress at their own pace, compete with themselves rather than with the group as a whole, and look to personal abilities to provide solutions to problems.

In movement education programs it is frequently apparent that while some children are working on a simple movement, others in the class are working on a more complex movement. The answers that the children find to their own problems will be different, but all are acceptable because success is measured with respect to the particular movement and abilities of the participants in performing that movement.

Movement education involves problem solving

Movement education begins with simple problems. Learning accrues as the student solves these problems and then seeks to solve increasingly more complex ones. Repetition of various problems is aimed at obtaining a greater variety of solutions. If children are first asked to walk around a room without colliding with each other and perform successfully, building on this the movement educator may then ask the children to run or hop or jump around the room again without colliding. By beginning with the simple, natural skills of childhood, the movement educator is adhering closely to the known facts of child growth and development; that is, the large muscles and gross motor skills develop first. The movement educator seeks to enhance this development to pave the way for the later development of the finer motor skills and coordinations.

A child who is becoming educated in movement begins with the walking, running, twisting, and falling problems. As the child solves the initial problem of walking without colliding, he or she may then be asked to express a mood or feeling, to change direction at will, to change direction at a signal from the teacher, or to walk while using the hands and arms in different ways. Music may be added to lessons. As a specific lesson progresses, games may be played encompassing the problem that has been set. A lesson in hopping or leaping may include a game of modified tag. At the conclusion of a lesson, there may be a period of demonstration by the children so that the movements they have created may be evaluated and discussed by the entire class. In this way a depth of understanding is reached concerning the movements.

As apparatus is added, the problem facing the child may be to move along a horizontal ladder in any way desired. As facility is gained, the problem may be made more complex by

From American Association for Health, Physical Education, and Recreation: Tones of theory, Washington, D.C., 1972, The Association.

Discipline of human movement phenomena.

specifying that the child move along using hands only or using the outside rails only. With other equipment the same procedure is used. General movement precedes more advanced problems such as mounting, vaulting, and dismounting. This approach allows each child to succeed, since no patterns of movement are required or specified. As children experience success, they are motivated to improve on their performance.

The problem-solving method allows students to be less dependent on the teacher, thus forcing them to use their own thought processes. In such a manner, children will be developing independence. Students who merely imitate the actions of the teacher will not benefit as much as those who attempt to discover various solutions to problems by themselves. The educated student is one who has developed the ability to analyze critically each new situation with which he or she is faced in an intelligent and logical manner. Teachers should not be models for students, since the best education will only result when students discover the meaning to questions by utilizing their own thought processes and resources.

Children learn to perceive the position of each segment of their bodies intellectually before attempting any physical skill performance. By utilizing the problem-solving approach, children begin to think about what their bodies can do and how they can be best utilized. The understandings that result help to give children insight into individual differences in skill performance as well as help them to develop confidence in the capabilities and capacities of their own bodies for movement. Time, space, force, and flow of movement are key words. Children learn to consider these factors intellectually as the core of the movements they execute.

Movement education is less formal than traditional physical education

In movement education, class organization does not follow the formalized patterns of traditional physical education. Lines, circles, and set formations are avoided. For the sake of safety, penalties may be imposed for collisions or needless use of space or equipment. Interaction is encouraged, and frequently the individual may work with a partner or in small groups, depending on the nature of the problem. Since the determining factor in deciding what problems are to be presented to the class is based on the needs of individuals within the group rather than the group as an entity, most instructions by the teacher are given on an individual basis rather than to the class as a whole. For example, the teacher will instruct a student who is working on the balance beam to discover "what he or she can do," "where he or she can move," etc. Furthermore, in movement education there are no formal drills or highly organized classes of activities. The learning climate is intentionally informal so that children will be free to express themselves

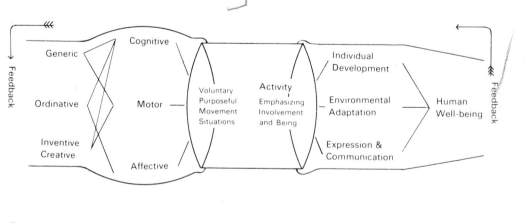

Process _____ Media _____ Result _____

From American Association for Health, Physical Education, and Recreation: Tones of theory, Washington, D.C., 1972, The Association.

Physical education's cable of concern.

as individuals rather than as instruments who move to the command of the teacher.

At the same time, movement education is highly organized and structured in the sense that it has definite objectives that must be met, classes follow a logical sequence, and progression exists that leads to the realization of program objectives and goals. In addition, these programs are not lacking in discipline. Much of the discipline in movement education classes comes from the activity and from the inner direction of the children themselves. Movement education classes demand much of the teacher in regard to a concrete philosophy, sound objectives, logical progressions, the understanding of proper techniques and methodology, and liberal amounts of imagination and creativity.

Movement education facilitates the learning of motor skills

The natural movements of childhood form the basis for future motor skill development. These movements will tend to develop haphazardly, and future skill performances will be inefficient unless the body is effectively educated in movement.

The ability of the child to perceive the body as an entity helps to promote physical skill development. Children who are retarded in physical skill development often do not have the insight to consider their bodies as wholes. They tend to be concerned first with the individual segments, and thus they attempt to correct performance errors by altering the position or action of a single arm or leg and fail to measurably improve their performance. Movement educators believe that the experience will be most meaningful if the child learns to consider the interaction of all parts of the body before skill performance is significantly improved. Movement educators recognize the need to learn specific sports skills, such as strokes of swimming, methods of pitching or batting a softball, thrusts and parries of fencing, or ways to trap and kick a soccer ball. The English have found that many of these specific skills must be taught by traditional methods, and they allot time in their physical education programs to accomplish these tasks. However, they have found that prior experience in the solving of problems in movement gives the child a vast store of knowledge on which to build so that specific skill learnings in the context of their application to a game are made easier. For example, a problem-solving experience in using the feet or legs to stop a rolling ball will help the child in learning the fundamentals of a soccer trap. Solving a problem in propelling the body across a shallow pool will help the child discover how the body reacts in water and give the child confidence in learning some strokes in swimming.

Movement education seeks to produce a feeling of satisfaction in movement

Movement educators seek to produce a feeling of satisfaction in the movement experiences engaged in by students. By emphasizing individual explorations, it is hoped that students will participate in meaningful and pertinent activities. By making the student the explorer in the educational process, it is hoped that this child will be encouraged to try new activities and to discover new insights in relationships to other persons. By utilizing the problem-solving method, it is hoped that the child will select a solution to the problem based on personal abilities and therefore personally meaningful. By emphasizing an informal class atmosphere, where students are given instructions based on their individual needs, it is hoped that students will better understand their own physical movements. By not emphasizing competition, movement educators believe that children will be free from the tensions that can be aroused by participating in highly competitive activities. Movement educators believe that when such a learning environment is established, students will derive meaning from the activities in which they are participating, and a feeling of satisfaction will result.

Movement education encourages an analysis of movement

Traditional physical education gives little instruction to students in the analysis of movement. Movement education provides an opportunity for students to observe and analyze themselves and others in the process of movement. At the conclusion of a lesson, there may be a period of student demonstration so that the movements in which students have been involved can be evaluated and discussed by the entire class. Greater understanding of movement is an outcome of this process. For example, demonstrations at the end of the lesson may show that one child vaults higher than another because he or she has learned that the use of the arms will aid the jump. Discussion of this point by the class will give helpful information to those children who find their own vaults inadequate but have not been able to discover why. Through an analysis of their own movements and those of other children, they will better understand what needs to be done to achieve the best performance.

Movement education involves equipment

Many pieces of apparatus and equipment found in a regular physical education class can be used in movement education classes. At times the teacher will have to devise various pieces of equipment to fit the needs of a particular lesson. When apparatus or equipment is used, rules of safety, space, and appropriateness of use need to be stressed. Equipment and apparatus must conform to the age and size of the child. Balls should be easy to grasp, and paddles should fit the hand of the child. Heavy apparatus such as vaulting boxes and climbing ladders must be scaled to the size most appropriate to the children using them.

Movement education programs must be constantly evaluated

The need for program modifications and adaptations are frequent in movement education. The need for revision will be noted only if programs are objectively evaluated periodically to see whether the goals that have been set are being achieved.

DEVELOPING A MOVEMENT EDUCATION PROGRAM
Elementary school*

The elementary school child requires a wide variety of experiences in basic movement and

*Parts of this section have been taken from Bucher, Charles A., and Reade, Evelyn: Physical education and health in the elementary school, New York, 1971, The Macmillan Co.

movement patterns. Common movement elements help the educator to devise a movement education program that moves toward its objectives in a logical progression.

In the early elementary school grades, kindergarten to grade three, the major emphasis should be on the natural movements of childhood. The locomotor movements—including running, walking, jumping, skipping, hopping, and sliding—and the nonlocomotor movements—including pulling, pushing, lifting, twisting, and stretching—should be emphasized.

Beginning with grade four, the techniques of handling implements may be a part of the program. In grades four to eight, locomotor and nonlocomotor movements should continue to receive stress but in a more sophisticated form. The child may also be introduced to the handling of implements such as softball bats and field hockey sticks and to skills such as soccer-type kicks and traps that can be used in lead-up game situations.

The movement educator must have a thorough understanding of each skill before presenting it to the children in a problem-solving situation. The teacher must understand the mechanics involved in a skill before a child's performance of this skill can be evaluated. Furthermore, the teacher must know the end result desired from the performance of this or another skill or combination of skills.

Problems must be properly devised and set by the teacher so that the desired end result can be achieved. If, for example, the teacher has planned a first-grade lesson in walking, certain specifications must be made so that the children will achieve the desired response. Proper use of space, force, timing, and flow of the movement should be considered and presented to the children as parts of the problem before beginning any physical movements.

Variety must be planned into each movement education class. On any given day a movement education class should include a review of problems solved previously, and new challenges should be presented in a progressive order. After new problems have been explored, the class may conclude with a noncompetitive game that incorporates many of the skills the children have already learned or are currently practicing.

Skills must be progressively taught from grade to grade. Whereas a class of first-grade children may concentrate their efforts on a unit of running involving the correct performance in the execution of the skill, a second-grade class might progress to running with a partner or running through obstacle courses that require starting, stopping, and changes of direction.

Standards of skill performance must relate to the individual child. Each child in a movement education class must be evaluated on the basis of individual performance. The exploratory nature of movement education demands that individual rather than group standards be set. A single common standard of performance cannot be demanded or expected.

The program must help children to gain confidence in their own performance. Satis-faction in meeting basic and simple challenges will help the child to gain confidence. More difficult problems in tumbling, for example, such as cooperating with a partner in Eskimo rolls and pyramid building, should be introduced only after the children have gained control of their own bodies and have confidence in the use of their bodily skills.

A sound foundation of basic movement skills should precede the introduction of games of low organization. Many games of low organization can be adapted to use for any age and grade level. For example, games of the tag type can be introduced as soon as children have learned the skills essential for that activity. Low organization games that contain elements unfamiliar to children in a particular class should not be incorporated into the program for that class until the children are thoroughly ready for them.

Flint Public Schools, Flint, Mich.

The balance beam provides a medium for movement experiences.

A sound foundation of basic movement skills should precede the introduction of specific sport skills. In traditional physical education programs on the elementary school level, such games as kickball and softball are often mainstays of the program. Frequently, children play these games without having had adequate instruction and practice in the highly specific skills involved. Introduction of these activities as a concomitant of a sound movement education experience helps place them in their proper perspective in the elementary school physical education program.

Secondary school*

Secondary school students can appreciate the values of movement education, whether or not they were involved in an elementary school movement program. Although it would be difficult, if not impossible, to rely on the use of the natural movement of early childhood in the secondary school situation, one can use movement to enhance skills and further develop a youth's self-concept.

Problem-solving techniques can be readily used to develop and improve skills. For example, if a soccer unit is introduced, students may be asked how many different ways they can think of to use their feet to propel the ball. After an exploratory period, questions are elicited from the class, and different questions are posed by the instructor. Throughout this movement experience the instructor observes and guides the students and does not assume an authoritarian role. This is essential to the problem-solving concept of movement education.

In addition, movement education lends itself to dance. Dance is a creative area and is attractive to secondary students, especially girls. At the same time, young boys who have taken part in movement education in elementary school programs have shown great skill and derived much enjoyment from this activity. Older boys can also be taught to experience a sense of joy through dance. Trampolines and other gymnastic equipment open up a variety of problem-solving experiences. However, it is essential that safety procedures be stressed prior to any use of such equipment.

Problem-solving situations are basic to all movement education. Secondary school students relate well to this concept in that it allows a certain amount of freedom and individuality and students have responsibility to develop their own skills.

Inner-city school

An interesting program of movement education was conducted at Public School No. 134, Queens, New York City, a heavily populated inner-city school. The program conducted by York College hoped to generate a developmental series of lessons in movement education for highly active first-grade students. In addition, the York College staff and students hoped to demonstrate to classroom teachers the uses of movement education in their curriculum.

Such concepts as spatial awareness, safety, the individual's self-concept, awareness of body shapes and parts, and development of manipulative skills were stressed. The program proved successful, and the children were eager participants. The program stressed the individual child, utilizing no norm or standard with which to keep pace. Children in inner cities frequently have poor images of themselves, and this concentration on the individual was most valuable in improving their self-concept. In addition, many children who were considered disruptive channeled their energy productively in the movement education program.

Children who have difficulty expressing themselves

At the Early Childhood Unit of the University Elementary School, University of California at Los Angeles, a movement behavior program was introduced to help young children who had difficulty expressing themselves.* A variety of opportunities were offered to the children, including some of the following.

---

*Parts of this section have been taken from Bucher, Charles A., and Koenig, C.: Methods and materials for secondary school physical education, ed. 5, St. Louis, 1978, The C. V. Mosby Co.

*Buchanan, E. A., and Hanson, D. S.: Free expression through movement, National Elementary School Principal **52:**46, Oct., 1972.

Movement education in one inner-city school. Public School No. 15 in Brooklyn, New York.

1. Touching and being touched by self and others and also touching objects and telling about the experiences
2. Exploring and discussing joint movements
3. Exploring the space around self in different positions—up, down, backward, forward, and sideways
4. Experiencing confinement to a particular space alone or with others
5. Experiencing change of orientation by an adult or mechanized device
6. Exploring weights of objects through push-pull activities and variety of movements
7. Using rhythmic floor patterns to explore movement
8. Challenging different obstacles by moving in new ways
9. Discussing environmental changes, especially those in texture, space, and temperature

This program was successful because the children began to respond. It was found that children who were free to move their bodies in different ways became more responsive and were also able to socialize and be more at ease with other children and adults.

The study found that the following implications for education emerged from the movement program:

1. There is a definite need to formulate objectives related to a child's expression of feelings.
2. Instructional techniques that employ touching, moving, and feeling can change inappropriate behavior.
3. Multisensory learning is more effective than traditional learning techniques for most learners.

SELF-ASSESSMENT TESTS

These tests are to assist students in determining if material and competencies presented in this chapter have been mastered.

1. You have been asked by the President of a PTA to give a presentation on the subject, "Movement—The Keystone of Physical Education." Prepare in writing your presentation.

2. Analyze biomechanical principles that would be associated with executing the following physical acts:

> Hitting a baseball
> Playing tackle in a football game
> Running 100 meters
> Bouncing on a trampoline

3. Imagine that you are in charge of a seventh-grade physical education class. Using your classmates as subjects, conduct a 10-minute class session utilizing a basic movement education approach.

4. Prepare in your own words a 250-word essay on the subject, "The History of Movement Education."

5. You are in charge of arranging a debate in your class on the following subject: Resolved that: "Movement education is better than the traditional approach in teaching physical education." Meet with both the affirmative and negative teams and outline some arguments that would be pertinent for each side in this debate.

6. Develop a table that sets forth the key concepts that support the use of movement education in a physical education program. Develop the rationale to support the worth of each concept.

READING ASSIGNMENT

Bucher, Charles A.: Dimensions of physical education, ed. 2, St. Louis, 1974, The C. V. Mosby Co., Reading selections 31 to 33.

SELECTED REFERENCES

Allenbaugh, Naomi: Learning about movement, National Education Association Journal **56:**48, March, 1967.

Barham, Jerry N.: Toward a science and discipline of human movement, Journal of Health, Physical Education, and Recreation **37:**65, Oct., 1966.

Braley, William T.: The Dayton program for developing sensory and motor skills in three, four, and five-year-old children; perceptual-motor foundations: a multidisciplinary concern, Washington, D.C., American Association for Health, Physical Education, and Recreation, pp. 109-111.

Brown, Margaret C.: The English method of education in movement gymnastics, The Reporter, p. 9, Jan., 1966.

Buchanan, E. A., and Hanson, D. S.: Free expression through movement, National Elementary School Principal **52:**46, Oct., 1972.

Bucher, Charles A., and Koenig, C.: Methods and materials for secondary school physical education, ed. 5, St. Louis, 1978, The C. V. Mosby Co.

Burton, Elsie C.: The new physical education for elementary school children, Boston, 1977, Houghton Mifflin Co.

De Maria, C. R.: Movement education: an overview, The Physical Educator **29:**73, May, 1972.

Godfrey, Barbara B., and Kephart, Newell C.: Movement patterns and motor education, New York, 1969, Appleton-Century-Crofts.

Hackett, Layne C., and Jenson, Robert G.: A guide to movement exploration, Palo Alto, Calif., 1966, Peek Publication.

Herkowitz, Jacqueline: Movement experiences for preschool children, Journal of Physical Education and Recreation **48:**15, March, 1977.

Howard, Shirley: The movement education approach to teaching in English elementary schools, Journal of Health, Physical Education, and Recreation **38:**31, Jan., 1967.

Kleinman, Seymour: The significance of human movement: a phenomenological approach, National Association of Physical Education for College Women Report, 1962, p. 123.

Locke, Lawrence F.: Movement education—a description and critique. In Brown, Roscoe C., Jr., and Cratty, Bryant J., editors: New perspectives of man in action, Englewood Cliffs, N.J., 1969, Prentice-Hall, Inc.

Ludwig, Elizabeth A.: Basic movement education in England, Journal of Health, Physical Education, and Recreation **32:**18, Dec., 1961.

Ludwig, Elizabeth A.: Toward an understanding of basic movement education in the elementary schools, Journal of Health, Physical Education, and Recreation **39:**26, March, 1968.

Metheny, Eleanor: Movement and meaning, New York, 1968, McGraw-Hill Book Co.

Miller, Arthur G., and others: Physical education—teaching human movement in the elementary schools, Englewood Cliffs, N.J., 1974, Prentice-Hall, Inc.

National Association of Physical Education for College Women and National College Physical Education Association for Men: Quest, Monograph 2, Tucson, 1964.

Porter, Lorena.: Movement education for children, Washington, D.C., 1969, American Association of Elementary-Kindergarten Nursery Educators.

Porter, Lorena: The movement movement, Today's Education **61:**42, May, 1972.

Rizzitiello, T.: Movement education challenges an inner-city school, Journal of Health, Physical Education, and Recreation **43:**35, Jan., 1972.

Schurr, Evelyn L.: Movement experiences for children, Englewood Cliffs, N.J., 1975, Prentice-Hall, Inc.

Smith, Hope M.: Introduction to human movement, Reading, Mass., 1968, Addison-Wesley Publishing Co.

Smith, Hope M.: Implications for movement education experience drawn from perceptual motor research, Journal of Health, Physical Education, and Recreation **41:**30, April, 1970.

Sweigard, Lula E.: Human movement: its idiokinetic facilitation, New York, 1974, Dodd, Mead & Co., Inc.

Tillotson, Joan: A brief theory of movement education, mimeographed.

9

End of sex discrimination in sport and physical education*

INSTRUCTIONAL OBJECTIVES AND COMPETENCIES TO BE ACHIEVED

After reading this chapter the student should be able to—

1. Interpret the various provisions of Title IX and why it came into being.
2. Document the dramatic change that has taken place in recent years in girls' and women's sports competition.
3. Assess the problems created by the rapid growth of girls' and women's sports.
4. Describe the procedure for implementing compliance with Title IX.
5. Project a plan for ending complete sex discrimination in sport and physical education.

"No person in the United States shall on the basis of sex be excluded from participation in, be denied the benefits of, or be subjected to discrimination under any education program or activity receiving Federal financial assis-

---

*Parts of this chapter have been taken directly from government documents relating to Title IX, particularly the following documents:

U.S. Department of Health, Education, and Welfare, Office for Civil Rights: Final Title IX regulation implementing education amendments of 1972—prohibiting sex discrimination in education, Washington, D.C., July 21, 1975, Government Printing Office.

U.S. Department of Health, Education, and Welfare, Office for Civil Rights: Memorandum to chief state school officers, superintendents of local educational agencies and college and university presidents. Subject: Elimination of sex discrimination in athletic programs, Washington, D.C., Sept., 1975, Government Printing Office.

tance . . ." This, in essence, is the theme of the legislation that Congress passed in June, 1972, and that affects nearly all educational institutions in the United States. The law was initiated in 1971 as an amendment to the Civil Rights Act of 1964. After some changes the bill emerged as what is known as Title IX of the Education Amendments of 1972. This legislation is having wide-reaching effects on physical education and athletic programs in the United States.

One of the major reasons why Title IX came into being was to ensure that girls and women received the same rights as boys and men. Testimony before congressional committees prior to enactment of this legislation indicated that girls and women were being discriminated against in many education programs, including physical education and athletics. A survey conducted by the National Education Association showed that although women constituted 67% of all public school teachers nationally, at the time the survey was conducted, they held only 15% of the principalships in the schools and 0.6% of the superintendencies. Another survey conducted by the National Center for Educational Statistics showed that salaries for women faculty members in colleges and universities were considerably lower than for their male counterparts. Furthermore, it was well established that for many years girls and women were discriminated against in many educational institutions in respect to physical education and athletics facilities, budgets, salaries, and scholarships.

While the proposed legislation was under

187

Courtesy Don Canham, University of Michigan.

Men's sports have dominated the college scene until recent years. Michigan rightwinger Doug Todd (15) guides the puck into the net on a pass from leftwinger Mark Miller (14) as Michigan State goaltender Dave Versical and defenseman Ted Huesing (3) watch in vain. The Spartans, however, managed a 7-5 victory. (December 10, 1977, at Munn Ice Arnea in East Lansing, Michigan.)

consideration in the Congress of the United States, voluminous amounts of mail and public comments showed that there was great public concern in six areas:

Sex discrimination in sports and athletic programs

Coeducational physical education classes

Sex stereotyping of textbooks

Impact of the legislation on fraternities and sororities

Scholarships

Employment

Although Title IX applies to all types of educational programs, probably the most dramatically affected have been sport and physical education programs. Girls' and women's athletic programs, in particular, have grown rapidly in only a few years. In the early 1970s there were comparatively few varsity interscholastic and intercollegiate teams for girls and women. Today, however, as a result of the federal regulation banning sex discrimination, it is a different story. Girls' and women's sport teams have come into their own and are in evidence throughout the nation.

DRAMATIC CHANGE IN GIRLS' AND WOMEN'S SPORTS COMPETITION

During the year prior to the birth of Title IX, 3,366,000 boys and 294,000 girls competed in interscholastic sports in the United States. Seven years later the figures showed 4,109,000 boys and 1,645,000 girls in the same activities. The participation by girls in interscholastic sports increased 460% during the interim. Furthermore, the participation of girls increased from 7% of the total number of students involved to 29%. In addition, approximately 500 colleges now offer athletic scholarships to women athletes. The Association for Intercollegiate Athletics for Women, the organization that governs women's intercollegiate athletics, now has nearly 900 member schools—the largest collegiate athletic association in the United States.

PROBLEMS CREATED BY THE RAPID GROWTH OF GIRLS' AND WOMEN'S SPORTS

The number of girls and women participating in sports has grown by leaps and bounds but so have their problems, most of which are the result of this growth.

One problem relates to the need to achieve and maintain high-quality athletic programs. The budget crunch and distressed economy have not provided for needed additional facilities such as locker rooms, gymnasia, athletic fields, and equipment. Although girls and women are entitled to an equitable share of these necessities, these items exist in insufficient number to accommodate the expanded girls' and women's sport programs.

Girls' and women's athletic programs are beginning to be faced with the same pressures that boys' and men's programs have faced over the years: emphasis on winning, recruiting, unethical means of obtaining star players, and the demand for scholarships. Some women physical educators, as a result, are being exposed to the same temptations to produce winning teams.

Girls' and women's programs are also finding it difficult in some instances to be adequately prepared for coaching responsibilities. Title IX has brought about so many changes in such a short period that many women are assigned to coaching responsibilities, and they are finding that coaching is different from teaching. During many years of teaching and little varsity team coaching they have developed philosophies that at times are in conflict with the demands on them to coach highly skilled varsity teams who are supposed to win games.

Girls' and women's programs are also being engulfed in publicity and promotion of a magnitude they never experienced prior to the present emphasis on highly organized competition for women. Girls' and women's sports are featured in the newspaper headlines, television coverage, and radio news. They have become "big time." As a result of such exposure, girls and women are having difficulty keeping their sport programs in proper perspective and observing sound ethical practices.

PROVISIONS OF TITLE IX AFFECTING PHYSICAL EDUCATION AND ATHLETIC PROGRAMS

Some of the provisions of Title IX affecting physical education and athletic programs include the following:

General provisions

Military and religious schools are exempted from the law where the provisions of the legislation are inconsistent with the basic religious tenets of the institution.

Membership requirements for social fraternities and sororities at the postsecondary level who receive federal funds, including the Boy Scouts, Camp Fire Girls, YWCA, and YMCA, are exempted from the regulation with the provision that where their educational programs are conducted for nonmembers, these programs must not discriminate on the basis of sex.

Scholarships may be restricted in nature if created by means such as a will, trust, or similar legal instrument or act of a foreign government.

Discrimination in housing is forbidden, with the exception that single-sex housing is permissible.

Comparable facilities for each sex are mandated, including locker rooms, shower facilities, and toilets.

Enrollment in course offerings and extracurricular activities should be open and not involve discrimination except that classes in health education may hold separate sessions in elementary and secondary schools when the subject matter concerns human sexuality exclusively.

Provision for physical education classes

Physical education classes must be organized on a coeducational basis.

Classes may be separated by sex for contact sports such as wrestling, boxing, basketball, and football. Also, within classes students may be grouped on ability or other basis, except that of sex, even though such grouping results in single-sex or predominately single-sex grouping.

Provision for athletics

Separate teams for boys and girls, or a coeducational team, must be provided in schools and colleges. For example, if there is only one team in a particular school, such as swimming, then students of both sexes must be permitted to try out for this team.

Equal opportunities must be provided for both sexes in educational institutions in equipment and supplies, use of facilities for practice and games, medical and training services, coaching and academic tutoring, travel allowances, housing and dining facilities, compensation of coaches, and publicity.

Equal aggregate expenditures are not required;

Under Title IX regulations physical education provides for coeducational classes. A coeducational dance class at Florida A. & M. University, Tallahassee, Florida.

Physical education is a campus-wide concern at Hampton Institute, Hampton, Virginia.

however, equal opportunity for men and women is mandated.

Where men are given the opportunity for athletic scholarships, women must also be given the same opportunity.

Contact sports such as football, basketball, boxing, wrestling, rugby, and ice hockey may be offered either separately or on a unitary basis.

The emphasis of Title IX is that of providing equal opportunity for both sexes. In determining whether equal opportunity is provided, it is important to know whether the interests and abilities of students of both sexes have been met and whether such things as adequate facilities and equipment are available to both sexes in each sport.

PROCEDURES FOR ASSURING COMPLIANCE WITH TITLE IX

To make sure that the provisions of Title IX have been complied with by an educational institution, certain procedures are followed. Each educational institution usually has some member of the faculty or staff coordinate a self-evaluation and assure compliance.

The steps that have been followed in some physical education and athletic programs is first to develop a statement of physical education philosophy that provides a guide for equality of opportunity for both sexes. Then, student interest is determined in regard to the activities they desire in the physical education and athletic program. Furthermore, all written materials concerned with items such as curriculum, employment, administration, and course content are reviewed to see that needed changes are made to ensure that physical education activities are being taught coeducationally. Also, such things as practice times for all teams, provision for supplies and equipment, travel expenses, number of coaches assigned to teams, and salaries of coaches are examined to see if there are any discrepancies between the sexes. The membership requirements to clubs and other student organizations associated with physical education and athletics are reviewed. The amount of publicity and information services provided for physical education and athletic programs are checked. Eligibility requirements for scholarships and financial aid, medi-

cal and accident policies, award systems, and employment procedures are examined. Teaching loads, coaching assignments, and facility assignments are also included in such an appraisal.

The procedure followed by the Oklahoma City Public Schools illustrates what one school system has done in implementing the regulations advocated by Title IX.* The school system followed this procedure:

It appointed an assistant superintendent as Title IX coordinator.

It committed itself to the implementation of Title IX according to the letter and intent of the law.

Tasks involved in implementing Title IX were assigned to the following committees: athletics, curriculum and physical education, employment/affirmative action, extracurricular activities, and guidance. These committees were composed of teachers, students, principals, and concerned patrons.

It obtained in-service training assistance from the University of Oklahoma.

It clearly defined the information needed in regard to possible discrimination in each of the committee areas.

It enlisted more than 200 people in collecting and assessing data following the in-service training program provided by the University of Oklahoma.

It prepared a report recommending remedial actions and began implementing changes.

The Oklahoma City Schools, in implementing this plan, stressed the need to recognize that affirmative actions are necessary, remedial actions are necessary, and clear affirmative policies are needed. When in doubt, decisions should be made in favor of equalized opportunity, and every effort should be made to follow the full intent of the law.

INTERPRETATIONS OF REGULATIONS CONCERNING TITLE IX

Although the Title IX regulations have been effective since July 21, 1975, there are few fixed guidelines emanating from the Department of Health, Education, and Welfare to assist in the implementation of this legislation.

---

*Schnee, Ronald G.: Frying pan to fire: school advocacy of Title IX, Phi Delta Kappan **58**:423, Jan., 1977.

In fact, persons who have written to the department for interpretations have found that it takes several months to get a reply. Therefore it is helpful to know the interpretation of certain provisions of Title IX that affect physical education and athletic programs and that have caused confusion among physical educators throughout the nation. These interpretations have been made only after careful study and/or communication with officers of the Office of Civil Rights of the Department of Health, Education, and Welfare. Some of these interpretations* are provided in question-and-answer format.

---

*These interpretations come from the following sources:

Arnold, Don E.: Compliance with Title IX in secondary school physical education, Journal of Physical Education and Recreation **48**:19, Jan., 1977.

New York State Public High School Athletic Association: Spot News, Feb., 16, 1976.

U.S. Department of Health, Education, and Welfare: Final Title IX regulation implementing education amendments of 1972—prohibiting sex discrimination in education, Washington, D.C., July 25, 1975, Government Printing Office.

U.S. Department of Health, Education, and Welfare: Memorandum to chief state school officers, superintendents of local education agencies and college and university presidents, Washington, D.C., Sept., 1975, Government Printing Office.

Physical education

Sex designations associated with class schedules, activities, and budgets are not permitted.

The term *girls' gymnasium* can be used; however, the scheduling of this facility must be nondiscriminatory in respect to each sex.

Policies and procedures in regard to items such as uniforms and attendance must apply to both sexes.

Sex-segregated administrative units, such as departments, do not necessarily have to be merged, although having faculty of men and women in integrated offices in newly combined administrative units is encouraged.

If a significantly greater number of one sex is enrolled in a particular physical education class, the administration, if called on, should be prepared to provide the rationale for such organization.

Supervision of locker rooms may be assigned to teacher aides, paraprofessionals, or teachers in other departments.

Marks or grades that are given in physical education classes should reflect individual growth and performance and not compare sexes with one another.

Standards of performance that provide an unfair comparison for one sex should not be utilized. In some cases separate standards might be used for each sex; for example, on a physical fitness rating, where boys may be taller and

Coeducational water volleyball at the State University of New York at Stony Brook, New York.

stronger than girls, separate standards might be used.

By writing to the regional Office for Civil Rights and providing the necessary rationale, it may be possible to get a sport, other than those listed by the Title IX regulation, classified as a contact sport.

Athletics

The term *athletics* encompasses sports that are a part of interscholastic, intercollegiate, club, or intramural programs.

Separate teams for men and women are allowed when selection is based on competitive skill or the activity concerned is a contact sport. Separate teams may be provided for men and women, or a single team may be provided that is open to both sexes. If separate teams are offered, a recipient institution may not discriminate on the basis of sex in providing equipment or supplies or in any other manner.

Schools should have separate teams for each sex when this is the only way to provide for the interests and abilities of both sexes.

If a school provides for only one team in a sport, objective measures must be used in selecting those students who will compete.

Teams that are composed of one sex should not be denied an athletic trainer of the opposite sex.

The length of seasons and number of athletic contests must be comparable for both sexes when separate teams are provided.

Certain circumstances must exist to permit one sex to try out for other sex-based teams. According to the New York State Public High School Athletic Association in their *Spot News* of February 16, 1976, the National Federation of High School Athletic Associations lists three criteria that must be met before the Department of Health, Education, and Welfare can require schools to do this:

1. The sport must be noncontact.
2. Separate teams for boys and girls in a sport do not exist. If there are separate teams for boys and girls in a sport, schools cannot be required by Title IX to permit a boy or girl to try out for teams of the opposite sex. However, schools *may* permit boys and girls to do this.
3. Athletic opportunities must have been previously limited. Limited opportunity is determined by a comparison of the boys' program with the girls' program, together with a consideration of student interests and abilities.

QUESTIONS AND ANSWERS ON ATHLETICS UNDER TITLE IX PROVISION

Question: If a school operates a baseball team for boys and a softball team for girls in the spring,

Courtesy D. M. Massé.

Coeducational physical education at the Waddell Elementary School in Manchester, Connecticut.

must the school permit a girl to try out for the baseball team?

Answer: No, assuming that the interests and abilities of most of the female students are satisfied by the softball team and other teams offered for them.

Question: If a school has a boys' soccer team and a girls' field hockey team in the fall, must it permit girls to try out for the soccer team?

Answer: No.

Question: If a school has a team for girls in a non-contact sport such as badminton, but not for boys, must it permit boys to try out for the team?

Answer: No, unless—and this would be rare—boys' athletic opportunities at the school have been limited.

Question: A school has sponsored separate teams for boys and girls in golf, tennis, track and field, swimming, and diving. For some reason the school terminates the dual program and starts single programs in these sports. All but a few girls are eliminated from these programs. Assuming that the rest of the boys' and girls' sports programs are equal, has the school violated any provision of Title IX?

Answer: Assuming there are still a sufficient number of girls to field teams in these sports and the inter-

ests and abilities are not accommodated by the remaining sports, it would appear that the school has violated Title IX.

Question: If there are sufficient women interested in basketball to form a viable women's basketball team, is an institution that fields a men's basketball team required to provide such a team for women?

Answer: One of the factors to be considered in determining whether equal opportunities are provided is whether the selection of sports and levels of competition effectively accommodate the interests and abilities of members of both sexes. Therefore, if a school provides basketball for men and the only way in which the school can accommodate the interests and abilities of women is to offer a separate basketball team for women, such a team must be provided.

Question: If there are insufficient women interested in participating on a women's track team, must the institution allow an interested woman to compete for a position on a men's track team?

Answer: If athletic opportunities have previously been limited for women at that school, it must allow women to compete for the men's team if the sport is of the noncontact variety such as track. The school may preclude women from partic-

Coeducational volleyball at Methuen Public Schools, Methuen, Massachusetts.

ipating on a men's team in a contact sport. A school may preclude men or women from participating on teams for the other sex if athletic opportunities have not been limited in the past for them, regardless of whether the sport is contact or noncontact.

Question: Can a school be exempt from Title IX if its athletic conference forbids men and women on the same noncontact team?

Answer: No. Title IX preempts all state or local laws or other requirements that conflict with Title IX.

PROSPECTS FOR THE FUTURE

Title IX is now the law of the land. All institutions, and this includes most schools and colleges, who receive federal financial assistance must comply. Furthermore, since it is

Courtesy Recreation Department.

Coeducational softball at Intramurals at the University of Colorado at Boulder, Colorado.

difficult for the federal government to supervise and make decisions for the 16,000 schools and 2,700 postsecondary educational institutions, a major share of the responsibility rests with each individual institution. Each school district and each college or university or other institution is unique and as a result must develop its own plan for compliance. Noncompliance can present many problems and difficulties. The government will no longer tolerate and this nation can no longer justify inequities in the manner in which both sexes are treated.

Each institution and each educational program will face many problems in complying with Title IX. This is true particularly in light of the budget crises that many schools and colleges face at the present time. For example, it will be difficult for many institutions to increase items such as the course offerings, budgets, and facilities for an expanded athletic program for girls without curtailing some other parts of the educational program at the same time, possibly that of the boys. It will be difficult to bear the increased costs of adding faculty, facilities, supplies and equipment, and scholarships to provide girls and women with a physical education and athletics program comparable with that which boys and men now possess. There will be many problems concerned with implementing coeducational class activities.

All of these problems can be solved, however, as they are being solved in thousands of educational institutions from coast to coast. For example, there are many schools and colleges where athletic and physical education activities are being modified so that students may engage in them on a coeducational basis. Basketball is being played with modifications such as three women and two men on a team, with field goals scored by women counting four points and those by men two points, and with men not being permitted to enter the free-throw lane at any time at either end of the court. Volleyball is being played with four men and four women; men are not permitted to spike and must serve underhand. Furthermore, at least one woman must touch the ball before it is volleyed back over the net by her team. Adaptations and modifications can be devel-

Coeducational water polo in grades 6 to 8 at the Cumberland Valley School District at Mechanicsburg, Pennsylvania.

oped in most activities to make them suitable for coeducational use.

Instructors of physical education classes and coaches of athletic teams, when assigned to teams of the opposite sex or on a coeducational basis, have proved successful. Budgets have been increased for girls' and women's programs in many cases without harming the overall physical education and athletic program. Schedules have been revised so that both males and females have access to facilities on an equitable basis. Many other changes have also taken place to comply with Title IX.

Compliance may be achieved according to the letter and the spirit of the federal mandate providing there is a willingness to comply and a desire to cooperate with other members of an educational institution. The first and foremost way to achieve desirable results is to work through the system in one's local situation. It should be recognized that resistance in some cases will be encountered, since change seldom comes easily. However, the law demands equity for both sexes, and as a result such changes will eventually take place. The Office for Civil Rights is willing to assist school officials in meeting their Title IX responsibili-

ties. Regional offices exist in ten different locations throughout the nation where help may be secured.

Physical education and athletics occupy a very important place in the American culture. The turmoil and reorganization implicit in the federal requirement for equity offer an opportunity to let this field of endeavor contribute to the health and welfare of all human beings rather than to only a few.

SELF-ASSESSMENT TESTS

These tests are to assist students in determining if material and competencies presented in this chapter have been mastered.

1. Without consulting your text, see how many provisions of Title IX you can list on a sheet of paper.

2. Prepare a research paper on the subject, "The Growth of Girls' and Women's Sports." Document your statements from as many authoritative, valid, and up-to-date sources as possible.

3. Prepare a chart identifying four major problems that have resulted from the expanded growth of girls' and women's sports competition, utilizing the following format:

Problem	Cause of problem	Proposed solution

4. Develop a modus operandi for a physical education program that will assure complete compliance with Title IX regulations.

5. Formulate a plan that will end sex discrimination in sport and physical education in the true sense of the regulation. As part of your research in the development of this plan, consult with several women professors and coaches to obtain their views and ideas for such a plan.

READING ASSIGNMENT

Obtain and read the documents relating to Title IX listed on the first page of this chapter.

SELECTED REFERENCES

American Alliance for Health, Physical Education, and Recreation: Title IX, Education amendments of 1972—details of regulations affecting HPER, Update, Oct., 1975.

American Alliance for Health, Physical Education, and Recreation: Some often-asked questions about Title IX, Update, Nov., 1975.

American Alliance for Health, Physical Education, and Recreation: More often-asked questions about Title IX, Update, Dec., 1975.

American Alliance for Health, Physical Education, and Recreation: Questions about implementation of Title IX, Update, Jan., 1976.

American Alliance for Health, Physical Education, and Recreation: Questions about implementation of Title IX, Update, Feb., 1976.

American Alliance for Health, Physical Education, and Recreation: Management strategies for implementation of Title IX, Update, Feb., 1977.

American Alliance for Health, Physical Education, and Recreation: Sex integrated high school programs that work, Update, April, 1977.

Dodson, Claudia: Title IX, Woman Coach **1:**8, April, 1975.

Oglesby, Carole A.: Title IX—how to realize its potential, Woman Coach **1:**8, Jan.-Feb., 1975.

U.S. Department of Health, Education, and Welfare, Office for Civil Rights: Final Title IX regulations implementing education amendments of 1972—prohibiting sex discrimination in education, Washington, D.C., 1975, Government Printing Office.

Wedemeyer, Dee: Women score in college sports, New York Times, May 25, 1977.

10

Physical education for handicapped and exceptional persons, including mainstreaming

INSTRUCTIONAL OBJECTIVES AND COMPETENCIES TO BE ACHIEVED

After reading this chapter the student should be able to—

1. Describe what constitutes "handicapped" and "exceptional" persons and the various types in each category.
2. Show the extent to which handicapped persons exist in the United States and their rights under the law.
3. Explain what the term *mainstreaming* means, its advantages and disadvantages, and some alternatives to mainstreaming.
4. Describe the implications that mainstreaming has for physical education.
5. Outline the competencies that a physical educator should have to work effectively with handicapped persons.
6. Identify the characteristics of specific types of handicapped and exceptional students and the contributions that physical education can make to each type.

Physical education for handicapped and exceptional students has become a priority in programs throughout the nation. Many students have some atypical physical condition, and physical educators should try to alleviate or eliminate them. Physical educators sometimes do an excellent job in helping healthy and gifted students to become healthier and more skilled but do a poor job in helping unhealthy, handicapped, or exceptional students develop to their optimum capacity. A valuable service can and should be performed by physical educators in the adapted physical education program. Since there is considerable emphasis on educating the handicapped student, this subject is treated at length in this chapter.

DEFINING THE HANDICAPPED AND EXCEPTIONAL PERSON

The handicapped or exceptional person is so classified because of many factors—physical, mental, emotional, or social in nature. Included under the heading of physical deviations are postural problems, heart malfunction, nutritional deficiencies, locomotive problems, speech impediments, and vision and hearing defects. Also, there is the problem of the physically gifted and creative student.

Emotional deviations include many maladjustments, such as aggressiveness, antisocial behavior, withdrawal, or depression. These maladjustments will not be helped by programs that are not adapted to the physical and mental abilities of the child and that fail to ensure satisfactory emotional and social development.

The mentally handicapped or exceptional student may be either gifted, possibly to the point of genius, or retarded.

Socially handicapped or exceptional students include those who have specific deviations in their human relations, who are culturally disadvantaged, or who exhibit disruptive behavior.

College student at Florida A. & M. University, Tallahassee, working with the handicapped.

THE NATION'S HANDICAPPED PERSONS AND THEIR RIGHTS

The nation's estimated 50 million handicapped persons are engaged in an aggressive civil rights movement. Suits have been filed, demonstrations held, and picketing and lobbying have been a common occurrence in recent years. These actions are aimed at obtaining the equal protection that is promised under the Fourteenth Amendment to the Constitution of the United States.

As a result of the actions on the part of handicapped persons, the nation is finally awakening to their needs. Until recently in the nation's history, handicapped persons were viewed as nonproductive. As a result, it has been common for handicapped persons to be discouraged and not even attempt to accomplish anything in life. Today, however, the picture has changed. The handicapped are demanding and are achieving their rights under the Constitution of the United States and are being employed in gainful jobs and taking their rightful place in society.

According to figures provided by agencies such as the National Arts and the Handicapped Information Service, The National Center for Health Statistics, and other sources, the following represent an estimate of the number of persons with various types of handicaps in the United States (some persons fall into more than one category)*:

11.7 million physically disabled persons
12.5 million temporarily injured persons (broken limb, etc.)
2.4 million deaf persons
11 million hearing impaired persons
1.3 million blind persons
8.2 million visually impaired persons
6.8 million mentally disabled persons (retarded, etc.)
1.7 million homebound persons (chronic health disorders, etc.)
2.1 million institutionalized persons

A milestone in legislative proposals providing for the handicapped was the passage of the Education of All Handicapped Children Act of 1975, which was signed into law by the Presi-

---

*New York Times, p. 8E, Feb. 13, 1977.

Courtesy Project Active.

Active training program for persons working with the handicapped. Monmouth College, West Long Branch, New Jersey.

Courtesy Project Active.

Active training program for persons working with the handicapped. Monmouth College, West Long Branch, New Jersey.

dent of the United States as Public Law 94-142. This legislation spells out the federal government's commitment to educating handicapped children and provides for annual funding on a sliding scale for this purpose. It provides educational services to handicapped children who are not receiving a free and appropriate public education and assistance for severely handicapped children who are receiving inadequate help. Section 504 of P.L. 93-112 bans any discrimination against handicapped persons.

There are specific implications in Public Law 94-142 for physical education. Special education has been defined within this legislation as ". . . specially designed instruction, at no cost to parents or guardians, to meet the unique needs of a handicapped child including classroom instruction, instruction in *physical education* [my italics], home instruction, and instruction in hospitals and institutions." In addition, ". . . related services means transportation, and such developmental, corrective, and other supportive services (including occupational therapy, recreation, and medical and counseling services . . .)." Other specific provisions of this legislation include the following:

The right of all handicapped children to a free and appropriate public education

Individualized planning of educational programs, with conferences between parents, children, and teachers

Procedural safeguards including due process for parents and children so that they may secure their rights under the law

The responsibility of the state educational agency for carrying out the program

The development of a system of personnel training, including pre-service and in-service training for teachers

A per pupil expenditure for handicapped children at least as great as that of other children in the state or school district

Proof that free appropriate public education is available to all handicapped children*

MAINSTREAMING

The Education for All Handicapped Children Act (Public Law 94-142) provides for mainstreaming some handicapped children in the public schools. Mainstreaming is a relatively new concept in education. It is a means of helping handicapped children participate as much as possible in society, especially in the public schools. It is a commitment to integrating persons who are exceptional into society rather than excluding them. It is the movement of handicapped children from a segregated status in special education classes to an integrating status with normal children in regular classes. It is a trend in education that is designed to increase the contact that handicapped children have with nonhandicapped children in a normal everyday environment. It can mean an opportunity for children who are severely handicapped to play with normal children. For the less severely handicapped children it can mean an opportunity to participate more and more in regular public school classes.

Each handicapped child does not necessarily have to be mainstreamed. Deno† identifies and

Working with a handicapped person in archery, South Carolina School for the Deaf and the Blind, Spartanburg, South Carolina.

views mainstreaming as a continuum ranging from nonparticipation to full participation in the regular classroom. At the nonparticipation level there are a few children in residential facilities. They are severely handicapped, with the result that they are isolated. At the full participation level the largest number of handicapped children participate in the regular classroom.

In recent years court decisions and an increasing number of state laws and regulations have legislated that handicapped children should have the same educational rights as other children. They are entitled to an education at the public's expense. In some states this principle is in the form of state law and in other states it is covered by regulations of the State Board of Education. The courts have ruled in favor of the handicapped in many states. For example, in Utah the courts ruled that the state was required to provide free public education

---

*Education of All Handicapped Children Act: Implications for physical education and recreation, IRUC Briefings 1:Jan./Feb., 1976.

†Deno, Evelyn: Strategies for improvement of educational opportunities for handicapped children, Exceptional Children in the Regular Classroom, Minneapolis, 1971, University of Minnesota.

for trainable retarded children, and in the District of Columbia the courts affirmed the right of all children to public education. Such legislation, however, does not mean that all handicapped children will be placed in classes with regular students. It does mean that those handicapped students, who after careful screening are considered able to profit from learning with regular students without detriment to either group, would be assigned to regular classes.

Some of the reasons why mainstreaming has gained acceptance in this country are that schools are better able to provide special education today, some psychological testing that resulted in students being labeled as retarded has proved to be unreliable, segregating handicapped students can cause harm, and some special education classes have shown a disproportionate number of minority students enrolled. Furthermore, the research is not conclusive that handicapped children advance scholastically faster when segregated than when grouped with children in a regular classroom, fiscal considerations encourage integrated rather than special classes, and pressures from parents who do not want their children segregated have used administrative and legal means to achieve their goals.

Advantages and disadvantages of mainstreaming

Mainstreaming can have many advantages. It can have a positive effect upon handicapped children. It does away with isolation and segregation. It can help a child learn to cope better with the outside world. Some researchers have shown that low achievers perform better in school when grouped with high achievers. It can remove some of the stigma of special class placement, and the handicapped child can begin to feel better about himself or herself. It provides a normal learning and social environment. Mainstreaming is an effective means to get away from labeling and overprotective parents. It is economically feasible, since it costs less than special schools. It provides realistic situations in school to prepare the handicapped for experiences they will eventually face when they are no longer students. It is a way to eliminate prejudices and enhance understanding.

Some disadvantages of mainstreaming, as pointed out by those persons who oppose the movement, are that it represents a major danger in regard to class size, since classes in many cases are already too large and with mainstreaming the size will be further increased. It is thought that when middle and high achievers among students are placed with low achievers, it has a negative effect on the middle and high achievers. Furthermore, it is stated that there is a lack of understanding of the handicapped by peers, teachers, and parents of the nonhandicapped students. The attitude of normal children to handicapped children can be frustrating to the latter group. It also makes the regular teacher's job much harder, and the regular classroom teacher is not as well equipped or prepared to handle the handicapped as is the special teacher.

One school in Vermont has developed and implemented a mainstreaming system whereby teaching plans are formulated according to the specific needs of each child. The classrooms are large, open-space environments, and teachers work in teams with the assistance of a paraprofessional. All the teachers receive training in assessing the instruction that is needed, in developing objectives and teaching-learning procedures, and in evaluating the effectiveness of the program. The aim is to develop an individualized program for each child while still helping each student in the mainstream. Frequent meetings are scheduled for the teachers (both tutor and classroom teachers) to ensure that the skills taught during the tutor sessions are maintained in the regular classroom.

Alternatives to mainstreaming

It has been suggested that possible alternatives to total mainstreaming might be in the form of selective integration. For example, some handicapped children might be placed in a regular program and the others in the special program. Another alternative would be for part-time placement of the handicapped child in the regular class and the rest of the time in a special class. Instead of attending the regular physical education class 5 days a week, the student could participate possibly twice a week in a regular class and three times a week in a special class. Another alternative might be to have handicapped students assigned to nonacademic activities with normal students (lunch, clubs, etc.) but be segregated in academic classes.

IMPLICATIONS FOR PHYSICAL EDUCATION

Physical education can render a valuable contribution to handicapped students. To do so means that the curriculum must be designed to meet the individual needs of students. The physical educator needs to be informed concerning specific medical problems that apply to each student. Program goals must be specific, and skills must be taught in a developmental pattern starting with the most simple and progressing to complex and complicated skills. Physical educators need to recognize that the psychological aspects of the class situation are equally or more important than the substantive physical education objectives. Also, keeping students motivated requires creative teaching.

The physical educator should have goals in mind such as helping students to develop a positive self-image, to develop effective interpersonal relations, to understand and appreciate their physical capacities and limitations, to correct atypical physical conditions that are capable of being alleviated, to develop a safety consciousness, and to become as physically fit as possible within their capabilities.

The potential value of mainstreaming is illustrated by what happened to one youth in a Massachusetts school. He was severely visually handicapped at 14 years of age. He had been enrolled in a special school for the blind but was transferred to another institution and enrolled in regular classes. He is now taking all subjects, including physical education, in a regular high school. He wears strong glasses to help him with his vision. Physical education activities are modified. One of his favorite activities is playing with an electronic "beep" ball. He also participates in bicycle riding on a tandem bike with classmates. Faculty members, although experiencing some frustration at first and having feelings of inadequacy about how to help this student, later gained an understanding of the boy and his handicap. As a result, their anxieties and fears were dissipated, and they developed a highly satisfying feeling when they saw the achievement and progress made by this student.

Working with a handicapped person on the trampoline, South Carolina School for the Deaf and the Blind, Spartanburg, South Carolina.

COMPETENCIES OF A PHYSICAL EDUCATOR IN A MAINSTREAMED SETTING

To be effective in a mainstreamed setting, the physical educator should be able to work effectively with the various types of handicapped children. A physical examination should be required of all children, and a list of activities in which the student can engage should be prescribed. A set of objectives for each student should be established rather than a blanket set of objectives for an entire class. Facilities and supplies should be such as to accommodate the handicapped child. Activities should be adapted so that each child may accomplish as much as possible. It would also be helpful to have a resource room where students might go for extra help and also receive greater individualized attention. Records should be kept and periodical evaluations conducted. Finally, the physical education program should be flexible, allowing for change where necessary.

Some specific competencies that the physical educator should have to contribute most to handicapped students in a mainstreamed setting include an understanding of the philosophy of special education, physical education, and mainstreaming; a knowledge of human growth and development, both normal and abnormal; an acquaintance with specific types of handicapping conditions that affect motor performance; a realization of the contribution that physical activity can make to the total growth and development of handicapped students; the ability to modify physical education activities to meet the needs of each student; the ability to administer and interpret physical fitness and other tests that are utilized in the program; and an understanding of current trends and developments regarding physical education for the handicapped.

Many materials have been developed to aid impaired, disabled, and handicapped persons. An excellent source of such materials is AAHPER's Unit on Programs for the Handicapped under the direction of Dr. Julian U. Stein. An Information and Research Utilization Center for Physical Education and Recreation for the Handicapped (IRUC), has been developed, which disseminates information on ma-

Courtesy Julian Stein, AAHPER.

The physical educator who works in a mainstreamed setting needs special qualifications. Teaching physical education to the handicapped represents one of the most promising areas of employment for physical educators.

terials for handicapped persons, stimulates research, encourages curriculum development, and coordinates leadership among those persons who are engaged in programs for the handicapped.

SPECIFIC TYPES OF HANDICAPPED AND EXCEPTIONAL PERSONS

A discussion of various kinds of handicapping and exceptional conditions together with guidelines for a physical education program for each will enable the physical educator to make a greater contribution to handicapped and exceptional students.

Mentally retarded students

Mentally retarded children need physical education, and a valuable service can be rendered by providing programs for these students. Yet in many schools throughout the United States, there is no provision made for meeting this need. It has been estimated that there are now about 7 million mentally retarded chil-

dren and adults in the United States. Between 100,000 and 200,000 mentally retarded babies are born in this country each year. An estimated 800,000 to 1 million mentally retarded children are attending elementary and secondary schools in the United States.

Mental retardation is a major problem and one to which the field of physical education needs to give more attention. Little research has been conducted in the area of mental retardation by physical educators. At present, there are only a few professional preparation programs in physical education that train teachers of the mentally retarded, although there is a great need for physical educators trained in this area. The Joseph P. Kennedy, Jr. Foundation is an organization concerned with all phases of research on and education for the mentally retarded.

The mentally retarded boys and girls who attend public school benefit from a program of physical activity carefully tailored to their needs. These children show a wide range of

Courtesy Julian Stein, AAHPER.

Physical education activity for the handicapped.

intellectual ability and, in general, are below average in physical performance and capacity. Although some mentally retarded boys and girls are sufficiently skilled to participate in a regular program of physical education, the vast majority are physically 2 to 4 years behind normal youngsters of the same age. The mentally retarded are not as physically strong, lack endurance, and tend to be overweight. Although their physical development is slower, they seem to mature physically at an earlier age than do most boys and girls. In general, the retarded have poor motor coordination, lack physical and organic fitness, and have poor posture. Some mentally retarded children have physical handicaps, and some also have personality disturbances.

Research reports published in England and the United States have drawn similar conclusions concerning the effect of a well-balanced program of physical education. The researchers have pointed out that although normal boys and girls attain high scores on physical performance tests, the mentally retarded received scores almost as high after exposure to a physical education program designed to meet their specific needs. Other researchers have said that the difference in motor performance between the mentally retarded and the normal individual is based on the differences in mental ability rather than on any significant difference in natural motor ability.

Still other researchers have pointed out that mentally retarded children have been denied planned programs in physical education. Often, they are placed in regular physical education classes without regard to their unique needs. Surveys have indicated that most mentally retarded individuals spend their leisure time in sedentary pursuits, have little interest in hobbies, and have not been encouraged to be active. Also, they are given little opportunity to participate in organized, leisure-time physical education or recreation programs. Because they have not had a strong background of play experience, the mentally retarded must be taught how to play.

Physical education teachers who are responsible for teaching a group of mentally retarded children cannot proceed as they would with a

group of normal children. Mentally retarded children need to be successful; they need to achieve. Thus any goals that are set must be reachable ones. The mentally retarded often lack confidence and pride. They need a patient teacher who will praise the smallest effort or improvement. Continued frustration at failure to reach a skill level that is too high and lack of recognition often lead to aggressive or asocial behavior. The mentally retarded make slow progress in skill development and have great difficulty in abstract thinking. Their program of physical education must be a varied and interesting one. Skills must be taught by demonstration. Because the attention span of mentally retarded children is short and because they tire easily, the program must be designed to maintain interest and involve them personally.

Those who have extensively taught the mentally retarded find that they enjoy swimming, tumbling, rhythmics, climbing over obstacles, lead-up games, and trampolining. They point out that the concept of team play is too abstract and that the retarded at times have difficulty in following directions. Thus lead-up games present the needed challenge and competition and prevent the frustration encountered in the more highly organized team sports. Movement education seems almost ideally suited to programs for the mentally retarded.

Physical education is essential to the mental and physical development of the retarded. A well-planned program will help these youngsters to develop the fitness and endurance they need. Physical education adds to their physical and mental well-being and gives them an opportunity to experience success and achievement.

Physically handicapped students

Physical handicaps may stem from congenital or hereditary causes or may develop later in life from environmental factors such as malnutrition or from disease or accident. Sometimes negative psychological and social traits develop because of the limitations imposed on the individual by a severe physical handicap.

The physically handicapped student may have a temporary disability, such as a broken arm, or he may be in a postoperative stage of recovery. Other physically handicapped students suffer from more permanent disabilities such as blindness, deafness, or irremediable orthopedic conditions. The range of physical handicaps extends from minor to major in severity and directly affects the kinds and amounts of participation in physical activity.

There are about 3 million children and youth between the ages of 4 and 19 years in the United States who are physically handicapped in varying degrees, according to estimates made by the Bureau of Census through its ongoing National Health Survey. Many of the more severely handicapped schoolchildren attend special schools where their unique needs can be met by highly trained staff members. The remainder are enrolled in the public schools. It is this latter group with whom the physical educator must be especially concerned.

Whatever the disability, a physical education program should be provided. Some handicapped students will be able to participate in a regular program of physical education with certain minor modifications. A separate, adapted program should be provided for those students who cannot participate in the basic instructional program of the school. Physically handicapped students cannot be permitted to sit on the sidelines and become only spectators. They need to have the opportunity to develop and maintain adequate skill abilities and fitness levels.

The blind or deaf student or the student with a severe speech impairment has different problems from the orthopedically handicapped student because they cannot communicate with great facility. The orthopedically handicapped student is limited in the physical education class but not necessarily in the academic classroom. The student with vision, hearing, or speech problems may be limited in both the physical education classroom and the academic classroom.

There is a lack of physical educators specifically trained to teach the physically handicapped. Many school systems find that the cost of providing special classes taught by specially trained physical educators is prohibitive. Where there are no special classes, the physical educator must provide, within the regular instructional program, those activities that will meet the needs of handicapped students. In addition, placing them in a regular physical education class will help to give them a feeling of belonging.

To be able to provide an adequate program for physically handicapped students, the physical educator needs special training. Advanced courses in anatomy, physiology, physiology of activity, and kinesiology are essential, along with work in special education, psychology, and adapted physical education.

The physical educator must have an understanding of the physical disability of each handicapped student and must be aware of any psychological, social, or behavioral problems that may accompany the disability. The physical educator must know the capacities of each handicapped student so that the teacher can provide the student with an individualized program. Some handicapped students will be able to participate in almost all the activities that nonhandicapped students enjoy. Blind students, for example, have successfully engaged in team sports in which they can receive oral cues from their sighted classmates. Some athletic equipment manufacturers have placed bells inside game balls, and the blind student is then able to rely on this sound as well as on the supplementary oral cues. Ropes or covered wires acting as hand guides also enable the blind student to participate in track and field events. Still other activities, such as swimming, dance, calisthenics, and tumbling, require little adaptation or none at all, except in regard to heightened safety precautions.

In general, deaf students will not be restricted in any way from participating in a full physical education program. Some deaf students experience difficulty in activities requiring precise balance, such as balance-beam walking, and may require some remedial work in this area. The physical educator should be prepared to offer any extra help that is needed.

Other physically handicapped students will have a variety of limitations and a variety of skill abilities. Appropriate program adaptations and modifications must be made to meet this range of individual needs.

Emotionally disturbed students

Emotionally disturbed students have difficulty in maintaining good relationships with their classmates and teachers. Some of their abnormal behavior patterns stem from a need and craving for attention. Sometimes the disruptive student exhibits gross patterns of aggressiveness and destructiveness. Other emotionally unstable students may be so withdrawn from the group that they refuse to participate in the activities of the class, even to the extent of refusing to report for class. In the physical education class the disruptive student may refuse to dress for the activity. These measures draw both student and teacher reaction, focusing the desired attention on the nonconforming student.

Emotionally disturbed students are often restless and unable to pay attention. In a physical education class they may poke and prod other students, refuse to line up with the rest of the class, or insist on bouncing a game ball while a lesson is in progress. These are also ploys to gain attention; the student behaves similarly in the academic classroom for the same reason.

Some disruptive students may have physical or mental handicaps that contribute to their behavior. Others may be concerned about what they consider to be poor personal appearance, such as extremes of height or weight or physical maturity not in keeping with their chronological age. Still other disruptive students may simply be in the process of growing up and are finding it difficult to handle their adolescence.

Emotionally disturbed students are in need of guidance and counseling. The school cannot impose discipline on disruptive students before the causes for their behavior have been ascertained. The school has many services available to it through which it can help emotionally disturbed students. School psychologists can test students, and social welfare agencies can assist by working with both students and their families. Case studies of students and conferences with their teachers can be invaluable in determining their needs. Teachers can more effectively help such students if they are aware at the beginning of the school year that a problem exists. The school health team will also

have pertinent information to contribute, as will these student's guidance counselors. Conferences with these students also help to open the doors to understanding.

If physical educators are faced with many disruptive students in a single class, they must first examine their relationship to that class. A physical educator's rapport with the entire class, relationships with individual students, disciplinary standards, and program will all affect student behavior to some degree.

If negative student behavior stems from some aspect of a student's personality, then the physical educator must take positive steps to resolve the problem so that teaching can take place. The physical educator must deal with each behavioral problem on an individual basis and seek help from the school personnel best equipped to give aid. The student's guidance counselor will have information that will be of help to the physical educator. A conference with the counselor may reveal methods that have proved effective with the student in the past. Furthermore, the observations made by the physical educator will be of value to the guidance counselor's continuing study of the student.

Much of the physical educator's task is student guidance. In individual cases of disruptive behavior, physical educators should exhaust all their personal resources to alleviate the problem. Sometimes the solution may be in a deviation from normal—being more strict or more lenient with these students than with other students. More praise, lower achievement standards, and assigning them special jobs (coaching, scorekeeping, setting up equipment) whereby they obtain personal recognition may also help the disruptive student. Any case of disruptive behavior demands immediate action on the part of the physical educator to prevent minor problems from becoming major ones.

A majority of pupils enjoy physical activity and physical education. They look forward to the physical education class as one part of the school day in which they can express themselves and gain a release of tension in an atmosphere that encourages it. For this reason the student who is emotionally disturbed is often one of the best citizens in the physical education class.

Culturally disadvantaged students

Culturally disadvantaged individuals are of many races and colors. Physical educators can render a valuable service by organizing programs adapted to their needs and interests. The culturally disadvantaged live in the slums of the large cities or in rural poverty pockets in all areas of the country. Their numbers are constantly increasing particularly in the large cities. Estimates made by the Ford Foundation classify 50% of children who live in large cities as culturally disadvantaged.

The culturally disadvantaged child does not resemble middle- or upper-class peers in home and neighborhood environment, economic level, scholastic achievement, motivation, or aspiration level. These differences set the culturally disadvantaged child apart and are, in fact, the causes of many scholastic and personal adjustment problems.

Culturally disadvantaged children often reflect the negative influences of their homes and neighborhood environment in a school situation. The cultural standards of these environments are frequently inconsistent. Because the home is often a place where neither conversation is stimulated nor reading encouraged, the child enters school ill equipped to communicate easily or to adapt to the learning environment as readily as the more advantaged child.

The culturally disadvantaged often resent the school, the teachers, and its administrators because each represents the unattainable middle-class image of society at large. Education is viewed as valuable, but the values are different in context from those sought or defined by the advantaged segment of society.

Culturally disadvantaged children do not feel a part of the society in which they live. In a classroom situation the child is unable to compete. This child is unstable emotionally, and excitability and restlessness may contribute to a short attention span. The child cannot think in the abstract, form concepts, use logic, or communicate well verbally. Thus he or she falls behind grade level in achievement and attains low scores on intelligence and standardized tests. These failures contribute to a lack of motivation, a low level of aspiration, and of ambition. The final result of years of failure is a negative self-image expressed by hostile, aggressive, and nonconforming behavior.

Education must be adapted to the specific needs of the culturally disadvantaged child. What motivation, creativity, and abilities these children do possess should be fostered and encouraged rather than suppressed. Understanding teachers and a classroom climate geared to the specific needs of these children are of the utmost importance. They need an opportunity to change the negative image of themselves to a positive one. A chance to succeed on their own level rather than on imposed levels will aid not only in building a more positive image but also in increasing self-respect, poise, and confidence.

Physical education can contribute to the culturally disadvantaged student in a positive manner. Frequently, the disadvantaged child has no recreational facility available. Streets or littered lots must be used, and games and sports are unsupervised. Within the environment of the school, the disadvantaged child can be given a worthwhile physical education experience geared to individual needs. A small class size will allow the instructor to give each student the attention, help, encouragement, and praise he or she needs. Within a relaxed, low-pressure, and informal environment, discipline will be easier to learn and maintain. Skill learnings will accrue more readily. Careful progressions in the skills that are offered will increase the opportunities to achieve success and give a measure of personal satisfaction. The instructor must strive to develop rapport with these students and must be able to understand and respect them.

Team, dual, and individual sports all have their place in a physical education program for the culturally disadvantaged. On the elementary school level, movement education and its jumping, running, throwing, and other activities natural to childhood will help encourage creativity and provide the child with needed self-expression and activity. For older children bowling, skating, swimming, archery, rhythmics, and self-testing activities not only provide

Culturally disadvantaged children use jump ropes creatively to construct different shapes, at Public School No. 15 in Brooklyn, New York.

constant activity but also offer a broad exposure to those skills from which children can gain confidence as they achieve higher skill levels. Team sports provide an invaluable opportunity to compete, to let off steam in an acceptable manner, and to learn the give-and-take that these sports help to teach. After school hours the physical education program can do invaluable service to the culturally disadvantaged by organizing intramurals and providing supervision for leagues in various sports.

Poorly coordinated students

Students with low motor ability are often ignored by the physical educator. They may be unpopular with classmates because they are poor in team sports. They may be undesirable as partners in dual sports and therefore are paired with equally uncoordinated and awkward partners. Students with low motor ability need special attention so that they can improve physical skill performances, derive pleasure from success in physical activity, and gain a background in lifetime sports.

Physical education makes special arrangements for the physically handicapped, the men-

tally retarded, and the athlete. Too little is done for the poorly coordinated student. This is where physical educators can render a valuable service.

The poorly coordinated student exhibits a measurable lack of physical ability. Less often considered is the psychological effect of the student's physical inabilities. The poorly coordinated student who is not given special help in the school often becomes the adult who abhors any physical activity and who is reluctant to participate in adult recreational activities.

The poorly coordinated student may resist learning new activities because the challenge this presents offers little chance for success and may create such tension within the student that he or she becomes physically ill. In other instances this tension may result in negative behavior.

Poor coordination may be the result of several factors. The student may not be physically fit, may have poor reflexes, or may not have the ability to use mental imagery. For some reason, such as a lengthy childhood illness, the poorly coordinated student may not have been normally physically active. Other poorly coordinated students, for example, will enter a secondary school physical education program from an elementary school that lacked a trained physical educator, had no facilities for physical education, or had a poor program of physical education. A single factor or a combination of any of them will help to retard motor skill development.

In working with poorly coordinated students, physical educators must exercise the utmost patience. They must know why the student is poorly coordinated and be able to devise an individual program that will help the student to move and perform more effectively. Physical educators must be sure that the student understands the need for special help and should try to motivate the individual to succeed. When a skill is performed with even a modicum of improvement, the effort must be praised and the achievement reinforced.

With a large class and only one instructor, relatively little time can be spent with each individual. The buddy system, in which a poorly coordinated student is paired with a well-coordinated partner, if properly done, may enable both students to progress faster. Immediate success will not be forthcoming for the poorly coordinated student, and the physical educator must be careful not to push the student beyond individual limits. An overly difficult challenge, coupled with the fatigue that results from trying too hard, may result in retarding rather than accelerating improvement. Any goal set for the poorly coordinated student must be a reachable goal.

The physical educator has a definite responsibility to the poorly coordinated student. Poor attitudes concerning physical activity can too easily be carried over into adult life. If these negative attitudes can be reversed by the physical educator early in the student's school career, the student may be motivated to develop abilities in several of the lifetime sports.

Physically gifted or creative students

Gifted and creative students in physical education are atypical because they also need a specially tailored physical education experience. We are concerned here with the student who is exceptional in motor skill abilities in many activities and maintains a high level of physical fitness. He or she may be a star athlete, but in general this student is simply a good all-around performer. In a game situation this person always seems to be in the right place at the right time.

Physically gifted students learn quickly and require a minimum of individual instruction. They are usually enthusiastic about physical activity and practice skills without being told to do so. Any individual instruction they do require is in the form of coaching rather than remedial correction. The physically gifted student has a strong sense of kinesthetic awareness and understands the principles of human movement. The student may not be able to articulate these two qualities, but observation by the physical educator will reveal that the student has discovered how to exploit the body as a tool for movement.

The physically gifted student may also have special problems. He or she may be impatient, even to the point of causing class disturbance, during instructional periods. This student already knows how to perform the skill or play the game and does not enjoy standing and listening but instead wants action and participation. Gifted students may become bored and lose interest in physical education if the program does not constantly stimulate them.

Physically creative students also have a well-developed sense of kinesthetic awareness and know how to use their bodies properly, dancing with ease and grace or showing a high degree of skill in free exercise, tumbling, or gymnastics. These students develop their own sophisticated routines in dance, tumbling, gymnastics, apparatus, and synchronized swimming. They may or may not be extraordinarily adept in other physical education activities but are as highly teachable as are the physically gifted.

The physically gifted or the physically creative student may not have attempted a wide range of activities but have experienced only those activities offered in the school physical education program. Both the physically gifted and the physically creative student, as well as the average student, will be stimulated and challenged by the introduction of new activities.

Physically gifted persons also need special attention and activities. Game of soccer at Regis High School in New York City.

The creative student in dance may be introduced to a new kind of music, or the boy or girl who is skilled on apparatus may enjoy adding new moves to routines. The athlete may be a good performer but may need to become a better team player. He or she may rely on superior skills rather than on a complete knowledge of the rules and strategies of sports and games.

The physical educator has a contribution to make to each student in the physical education program. The challenges presented by students of exceptional ability will help to keep the physical educator alert, stimulated, and enthusiastic about teaching. Some ways in which the physically gifted and creative student may be helped in physical education include using them in the leaders' program, providing special challenges in the form of research and reading on various aspects of physical education, using them in the buddy system (working with and helping a poorly coordinated student), requesting them to design a new dance or game strategy, assigning students to coaching responsibilities, and using them to demonstrate skills during instructional periods.

SELF-ASSESSMENT TESTS

These tests are to assist students in determining if material and competencies presented in this chapter have been mastered.

1. Compare the characteristics of a ''normal'' person with those of a ''handicapped'' and ''exceptional'' person.

2. Engage in a role-playing exercise with a friend. Imagine that you are a parent who has a handicapped child. Set forth your feelings about the handicapped, including the percentage of the population of the United States that is handicapped and what legal rights you have under Public Law 94-142.

3. Prepare two charts, one for a so-called normal child and one for a handicapped child. Discuss the concept of mainstreaming and list the advantages and disadvantages of such a procedure for the normal child and also the handicapped child.

4. You are in charge of a physical education class. Five mentally retarded students have been assigned to your class. What are the implications for physical education and how will you conduct the class? Describe in detail what you will do.

5. You are a father of a handicapped child. Describe the characteristics of the physical education teacher you would like to teach your child.

6. Prepare a table according to the prescribed format that will include information for various types of handicapping or exceptional conditions. The format would include the following:

Type of handicapped or exceptional condition	Characteristics	Needs	Implications for physical education
Mentally retarded			
Emotionally disturbed			
Physically handicapped			
Culturally disadvantaged			
Poorly coordinated			
Physically gifted			
Creative			

READING ASSIGNMENT

Bucher, Charles A.: Dimensions of physical education, ed. 2, St. Louis, 1974, The C. V. Mosby Co., reading selections 55 and 57.

SELECTED REFERENCES

Adams, Ronald, and others: Games, sports and exercises for the physically handicapped, Philadelphia, 1975, Lea & Febiger.

American Association for Health, Physical Education, and Recreation: Annotated bibliography in physical education, recreation, and psychomotor function of mentally retarded persons, Washington, D.C., 1975, The Association.

Arnheim, Daniel D., Auxter, David, and Crowe, Walter C.: Principles and methods of adapted physical education and recreation, ed. 3, St. Louis, 1977, The C. V. Mosby Co.

Arnheim, Daniel D., and Sinclair, William A.: The clumsy child, St. Louis, 1975, The C. V. Mosby Co.

Buell, Charles: Physical education and recreation for the visually handicapped, Washington, D.C., 1973, American Association for Health, Physical Education, and Recreation.

Cratty, Bryant: Perceptual and motor development in infants and children, New York, 1970, The Macmillan Co.

Cratty, Bryant: Learning about human behavior through active games, Englewood Cliffs, N.J., 1975, Prentice-Hall, Inc.

Cratty, Bryant: Remedial motor activity for children, Philadelphia, 1975, Lea & Febiger.

Fait, Hollis: Special physical education, Philadelphia, 1978, W. B. Saunders Co.

Vodola, Tom: Low physical vitality: an individualized program, Township of Ocean School Districts, Oakhurst, N.J., 1975.

Vodola, Tom: Individualized physical education program for the handicapped child, Englewood Cliffs, N.J., 1975, Prentice-Hall, Inc.

PART THREE

SCIENTIFIC FOUNDATIONS OF PHYSICAL EDUCATION

Courtesy Nautilus Sports/Medical Industries,
DeLand, Fla.

Scientific foundations of physical education.

11

Biological foundations of the human body

INSTRUCTIONAL OBJECTIVES AND COMPETENCIES TO BE ACHIEVED

After reading this chapter the student should be able to—

1. Understand the makeup of the human body, including its various organic systems.
2. Appreciate the biological defects of humans in light of their body structure.
3. Determine the role that heredity plays in the physical differentiation among humans.
4. Identify the various physical and motor growth and development characteristics of human beings at various age levels and the implication each has for the type of physical education experiences that should be provided.
5. Identify the various body types and the implications of each for physical education and sport.
6. Explain the implications that the biological nature of humans has for a physically active existence.

Physical education is a body-oriented discipline, as well as a mental and social discipline. Physical educators must have a strong grasp of the physical functioning of the body to best understand its utilization in athletic activity. Especially today, when movement education is so important, knowledge of how human bodies function is crucial to excellence in teaching.

Today, physical education is based on scientific facts and principles. As such, its program is developed as a result of systematized knowledge based on verifiable general laws. This knowledge covers many areas of learning. The physical education program is established with respect to the biological, psychological, and sociological aspects of growth and development. It aims to develop youth into citizens who have the capacity to enjoy a happy, vigorous, and interesting life. To accomplish this task, it is necessary to know the individual, how the physical body functions, and how the individual learns, and each person's relation to the group, society, and world of which he or she is a part. Furthermore, the human being represents a unified whole, each part being necessary to the successful functioning of every other part. The individual reacts as a "whole" organism and not just in parts. Therefore education should be concerned with activities that benefit the "whole" individual and not just one part. When a child swims, there should be concern not only for the physical development that ensues from this experience but for the social, mental, and emotional aspects as well.

Chapters 11 through 14 discuss some of the scientific knowledge that has a bearing on physical education and the "whole" individual from the standpoint of biology, psychology, and sociology. Such knowledge will help to clarify the role of physical education in society.

BIOLOGICAL HISTORY

This chapter is devoted to the fundamental scientific interpretations of physical education that are biological in nature.

Human potential—and performance

Joseph W. Still spent many years studying human physical and intellectual behavior. The accompanying illustration depicts his research into the physical growth and ages and the psychic growth and ages of the human race. Although Still's research was conducted several years ago, it is still applicable today.

A study of these charts will show that not more than 5% of the population follow the upper success curves (dotted line). The failure curve in regard to physical growth shows that the physical development of people today is lacking. They are exposed to little physical exercise; they eat, drink, and smoke too much; and they decline rapidly after 30 years of age. It will also be noted that four periods are identified during which peak performance in various sports occurs. The psychological growth chart also emphasizes the failure type of performance. Mental traits excel at different stages of development. Memorizing ability is great in

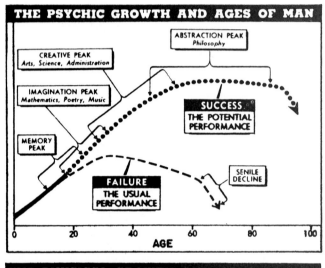

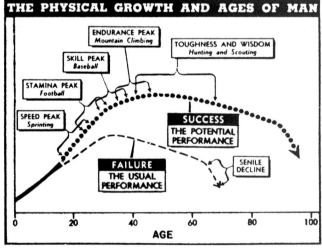

From Still, Joseph W.: The New York Times Magazine,
Nov. 24, 1957.

Physical and psychic growths and ages of human beings—possibility and performance. The upper lines indicate the physical and psychological potentials of normal people, with peak periods for various activities. The lower lines indicate how most people fail to measure up.

youth, creative imagination reaches its height in the twenties and thirties, skill in analysis and synthesis of subject matter reigns in the middle years, and the age of philosophy characterizes the later years. Still raises the question: "How can we prevent these failures?" He goes on to point out: "As a starter, everyone should say: If I want respect as a human being I have the obligation to respect and care for and develop my body and mind."* I am sure we would all agree that this is a sound philosophy for successful living.

Biologically, human beings are designed to be active creatures. Although changes in civilization have resulted in a decrease in the amount of activity needed in accomplishing the basic tasks associated with living, the human body has not changed. Therefore people must become well informed as to the health requirements that their biological base demands and recognize the importance of vigorous physical activity in their lives. If they do not, health, productivity, and effectiveness in life will suffer. Being physically educated is essential to proper functioning in life. Furthermore, it is closely tied with human mental, emotional, social, and spiritual powers.

Evolution

A study of human evolution points to the necessity for physical activity. Evolution refers to the period of development of a race or of a species, during which a series of changes take place and morphological and physiological characteristics are acquired that distinguish a particular species or group.

The evolution of humans shows that they have made great progress in developing from a lower form of life. A study of the history of humankind reveals that humans have evolved gradually. Evidence shows that there have been many eras of growth. During the first era only one-celled plants and animals existed. Next came the era of the invertebrates, when forms of life without a spinal column such as sponges and starfish existed. Then followed the age of fishes, amphibians, reptiles, dinosaurs, mam-

mals, birds, *Homo sapiens,* and, finally, historical man and woman. Thus humankind has evolved.

Physical education must help to develop a higher and better plane of living as its part in this "evolving" process if it is to justify its worth. A study of evolution shows that people should not follow a sedentary existence but, instead, should be active, should exercise the various parts of their bodies, and should spend more time in the out-of-doors. Therefore physical education has many potentialities. To train youth successfully, nature's methods should be followed. This holds true also in regard to the activities in which humans engage. Primitive people obtained food, provided shelter, and protected themselves against a hostile environment through activities that involved walking, running, hopping, climbing, throwing, carrying, leaping, and hanging. These are consistent with the evolutionary process and have formed the basic movements for humans throughout their long history. They are a part of our inheritance. The games, dances, and other physical education activities that are utilized today have as a basis these racially old activities. For example, basketball is running and throwing, and dancing is walking, leaping, stretching, and hopping. Human beings, in their attempt to evolve into a higher and higher plane of living, should follow a physical education program based on these fundamental activities rather than on one that does not conform to such standards. These activities will best serve the purposes of developing a body with a strong framework and adequate motor mechanism. They will aid people to move with freedom, with rhythm and grace, and with less utilization of energy.

Biological defects of human beings in light of their structure

Biologically the "evolving" process in humans has resulted in many advantages and also many disadvantages. People have a high standard of living in the United States. There are automobiles, trains, and jet planes to take people wherever they want to go, television and radio sets to see and hear world events, highly mechanized machinery to manufacture

---

*Still, Joseph W.: New York Times Magazine, Nov. 24, 1957.

Biologically, human beings are designed to be active creatures. Businessman working out at the Aerobics Activity Center in Dallas, Texas.

goods for every need and desire, beautiful houses and buildings in which to live and congregate, and other conveniences and luxuries to please and entertain. However, there is another side to the picture. Are all these devices, inventions, and luxuries that are characteristic of this mode of life helping humans biologically? Hickman,* an expert on physiology, points out some interesting facts in respect to the highly specialized and artificial life that people lead. These are summarized in the following paragraphs.

In this "evolving" process, human beings have changed their means of locomotion from a quadruped to a biped position. This has had implications for human health. It is believed that humans originally walked on all fours.† An upright position has influenced adversely the human digestive and circulatory systems. It has compressed the large intestine, with result-

ing conditions of constipation and colitis. This position has caused an irregular distribution of blood as a result of the heart's being below several parts of the body. It is a contributing cause of fainting. Hemorrhoids and varicose veins are caused to some degree by the increased blood pressure in lower regions of the body. An upright posture has increased the difficulty of balance, and consequently many postural problems have developed. In a report to the National Academy of Sciences, S. W. Briton, University of Virginia scientist, pointed out that the upright position was the result of the development of a superior brain but that at the same time such a position resulted in fallen arches, varicose veins, and possibly sinus and heart trouble. He also reported that such a position resulted in major adjustments by the circulatory and nervous systems.

The problems that arise as a result of the biped position can be alleviated through physical education activities that stress standing, walking, jumping, leaping, and other fundamental movements. It is important to compensate for this position by developing in each child a strong trunk musculature to house the vital organs and nerve centers. It is important

---

*Hickman, C.: Physiological hygiene, New York, 1950, Prentice-Hall, Inc.
†According to the April 3, 1950, issue of *Life Magazine*, there is now evidence to show that primitive prehumans stood erect. Raymond Dart, famed anthropologist from South Africa, discovered the pelvis of an early ape man that indicated an erect posture.

to strengthen the abdominal muscles so that the viscera are in proper position. Furthermore, the elements of body mechanics must be recognized so that there is proper body balance as human beings carry themselves on their legs.

The human being has a complex nervous system that has difficulty adapting to present-day living. Evidence of this is the high rate of mental disorders that prevails. University psychiatrists have reported an increase in students utilizing their services. Approximately 700,000 people die each year of heart disease, which many individuals think is at least partially related to the nervous tension involved in living.

Human beings are placing more and more reliance on drugs and narcotics as a means of enjoyment, stimulation, and escape. Tobacco, coffee, tea, Valium, alcohol, LSD, and marijuana are examples. Many other drugs and narcotics are used as sedatives and to eliminate pain. Such indulgence and self-medication has resulted in mental and physical deterioration in many users. Instead of aiding and helping to cure maladjustments, these drugs and narcotics have frequently tended to aggravate the situation.

Tobacco, drugs, colds, and respiratory diseases, according to some medical experts, are blunting the human senses of taste and smell to the point that they are now greatly inferior to those of other animals. Also, close work, writing, and the like have been detrimental to human eyesight. The noise from jet planes, the screeching of subway trains, loud music, and the blare of automobile horns have affected hearing. Some of the senses that have been of great assistance over the years in interpreting the environment are being damaged.

It has been stated that individuals in the United States are the best fed of those anywhere in the world but at the same time are the most undernourished. Steaks, chops, and other choice cuts of meat taste good but are lower in nutritional content than many of the lower-priced cuts, such as liver and kidneys. Many people also eat an overabundance of fast foods and rich sweets and pastries, to the neglect of selecting their diet from the four basic groups

of food. Such practices have led to dental caries and possibly to disorders of the stomach, such as ulcers, tumors, and cancer. Furthermore, much of the food lacks bulk, and consequently the alimentary tract may not function satisfactorily.

Venereal disease has become an increasing problem in recent years, especially in people between the ages of 13 and 24 years. Reported cases are in the hundreds of thousands, and yet they are few compared with the number of cases that go unreported. Some of the reasons for the alarming increases in venereal diseases include (1) lack of public attention and education, (2) a moral code that has resulted in sexual relationships at an earlier age, (3) greater promiscuity, (4) the development of new strains resistant to antibodies, and (5) the birth control pill. In addition, many people do not know the disease symptoms and therefore go untreated while still spreading the disease.

Along with less outdoor life, people are congregating in cities where hundreds of people live in one block and breathe germs into each other's faces. Early existence was in the wide open spaces where human beings developed strong and sturdy bodies and nervous systems that were adapted to their needs. The changeover to an urban, indoor existence has been so rapid in history that adaptation is far from being realized at the present time.

A perusal of the facts would tend to encourage one to believe that people are living a decrepit, weak, and unhealthy existence and are degenerating to the point where humankind may become extinct. Whether the human species can adapt itself to a highly industrialized, urban, inactive existence remains to be seen. At the present time, the facts in regard to the mental and physical deterioration sound a warning. The great advances made by the medical profession in combating infectious diseases have been outstanding. These diseases are rapidly being brought under control. But what about such maladies as nervous disorders, heart disease, and cancer? What are the solutions to these scourges of humankind? Is the human species attempting to change too rapidly from an existence characterized by out-of-door living, simple diet, active pursuits, and quiet living to one characterized by an indoor existence, poor nutrition, and inaction? Is the human nervous system adequate to meet such a rapid change? The answers lie in the future.

HEALTH OF THE NATION

The United States ranks high in regard to the health of its people when compared with the other nations of the world. However, in analyzing the health statistics of this country, it can readily be seen that disease and ill health are highly prevalent, much of which is preventable. Although this country has the best facilities and personnel in the world for combating disease, there is still room for improvement. The high cost of medical and hospital care, the inequitable distribution of medical personnel throughout the nation, and the unavailability of health services to serve people present problems.

In respect to young people, health statistics show that, as a result of better nutrition, boys and girls in the United States are taller and heavier than their parents. At the turn of the century fewer than four out of 100 men attained a height of 6 feet or more. Today more than twenty-five out of 100 men are this tall. Women are also increasing in height, with many now reaching 5 feet 7 inches. College statistics of young people tell a similar story. In 1885 the average Yale freshman was 5 feet 7½ inches tall and weighed 136 pounds. Only about 5% of the class stood more than 6 feet tall. Today the average freshman is more than 3 inches taller and 20 pounds heavier, and better than 30% of the class is over 6 feet tall. Young women at Vassar and Smith colleges are about 2 inches taller and 10 pounds heavier than at the turn of the century. Girls are also maturing earlier, as indicated by the onset of menstruation, which has dropped from the age of 14 years of age in 1900 to approximately 12.8 years today. However, an estimated 10% to 15% of American teenagers are obese and have poor eating habits. Many of them are physically inactive. The statistics indicate, however, that the stamina and skill of teenagers in the United States is improving.

In spite of some encouraging signs, people continue to be victims of many preventable defects and diseases. Industrial life, with its concentration of people in urban areas, air pol-

Kindergarten class using barrels with bottoms cut out at Oak View Elementary School in Fairfax, Virginia.

lution, sedentary pursuits, routine work, unemployment, and other problems, may be listed as a contributing factor. Despite the fact that the United States has a high standard of living, many of its citizens are still living a second-class existence. In the inner-city areas, poverty and disease are widespread. A child who is born of poor parents has a much greater risk of dying earlier in life than the child of a wealthy family. Research has indicated that the poor suffer from more chronic conditions than other citizens. The diseases that take the lives of many inner-city residents are tuberculosis, pneumonia, and influenza. In many of our poverty-stricken areas, venereal disease and drug abuse are also widespread. There is a need for a greater number of physicians, nurses, and psychiatrists and for more facilities to aid in the prevention and cure of disease. More important, it is a matter of priorities and putting primary health care services where they are needed. Furthermore, there should be more measures established to cross the chasm between medical services and low incomes.

ORGANIC FOUNDATIONS OF THE HUMAN BODY
Biological basis of life

The cell of the human body is the biological basis of life. The human body starts from one cell and, as a result of many divisions and redivisions, many thousands of cells are formed. Many of the cells are formed into units that function as the organic systems of the body. Every part of the body has cells—the brain, liver, stomach, and arms and legs included. One estimate has been made that there are 400 billion cells in the body and approximately 5 million cells in a small drop of blood.

The cells of the body are alive. They take in food and oxygen and give off waste material. To survive, the organism must have food and oxygen and must eliminate wastes. The cells perform this function. They are bathed in a liquid called lymph that carried food and oxygen to the cells and takes away wastes.

The muscles of the body are made up of cells. In the evolutionary process these muscle cells developed from rather simple to complex structures. The muscular system developed before many other systems of the body. As the muscle cells became more specialized, other units of cells were needed to carry food and oxygen to the various parts of the body and to carry away wastes. Thus began the excretory, digestive, respiratory, and circulatory systems. These systems developed in response to a need that was stimulated and initiated by the muscular system. They develop in a human body and grow strong in response to the work placed on

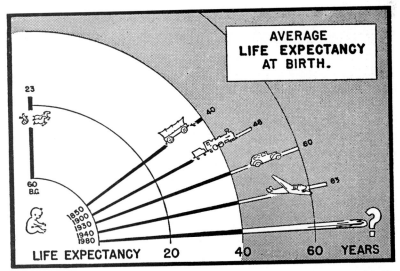

From Adult Hygiene and Geriatrics, Indiana State Board of Health.

them by the muscular system. Therefore muscular work increases the capacity of the individual for performance.

Makeup of the human body

The human body is an intricate mechanism, the makeup of which should be familiar to every physical educator. Students of physical education will study the human body in detail during their training. The following discussion will be concerned with only a brief review of some of the aspects of the human nechanism

that have special implications for the biological interpretations of physical education.

The skeleton. The skeleton of the human body in many ways can be compared with the framework of a building under construction. The framework represents the foundation or outline on which the building will be constructed—the building's size, shape, and contour. The skeleton also performs this function for the human body because it is a framework that protects the various bodily systems.

The bones that make up the skeleton in older

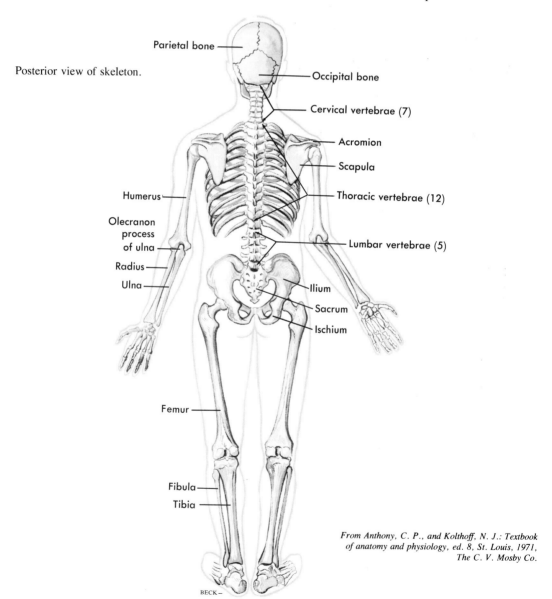

Posterior view of skeleton.

Parietal bone

Occipital bone

Cervical vertebrae (7)

Acromion

Scapula

Humerus

Thoracic vertebrae (12)

Olecranon process of ulna

Radius

Lumbar vertebrae (5)

Ulna

Ilium

Sacrum

Ischium

Femur

Fibula

Tibia

BECK—

From Anthony, C. P., and Kolthoff, N. J.: Textbook of anatomy and physiology, ed. 8, St. Louis, 1971, The C. V. Mosby Co.

persons have less animal matter than do the bones of children. Therefore an elderly individual's bones are brittle, break easily, and heal slowly. In children, small amounts of mineral matter make bones more flexible, and consequently they can be bent in various shapes. This has implications for a child's posture. The child's skeleton is extremely flexible; therefore such practices as habitual standing and sitting in a stooped position for long periods of time may result in abnormal posture.

The skeleton is made up of joints that make movement possible. There are three main kinds of joints: the *synarthroses,* or immovable joints; the *amphidiarthroses,* or slightly movable joints; and the *diarthroses,* or freely movable joints. Diarthrotic joints are the ones with which physical educators should be most concerned, especially the ball and socket and the hinge. Examples of the ball-and-socket joint are the shoulder and hip, and examples of the hinge joint are the elbow, knee, or fingers. The joints of the body are essential to movement. Some of the more important movements

Anterior view of skeleton.

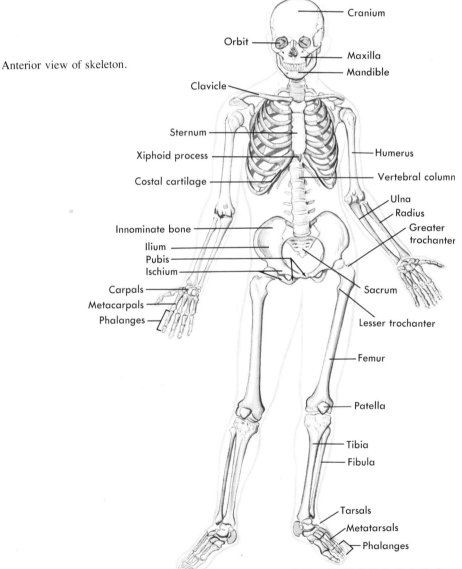

From Anthony, C. P., and Kolthoff, N. J.: Textbook of anatomy and physiology, ed. 8, St. Louis, 1971, The C. V. Mosby Co.

BECK –

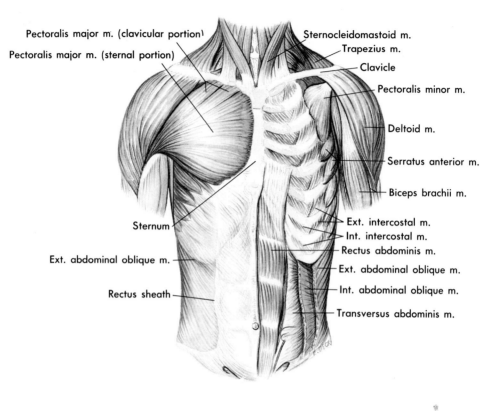

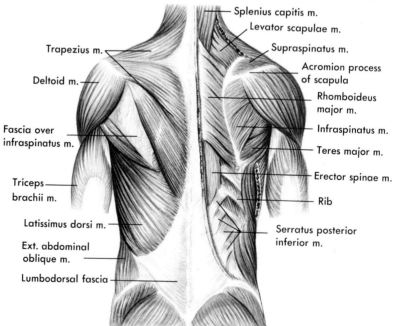

From Anthony, C. P., and Kolthoff, N. J.: Textbook of anatomy and physiology,
ed. 8, St. Louis, 1971, The C. V. Mosby Co.

Superficial muscles of the anterior and posterior surfaces of the trunk.

of which the physical educator should be aware are the following: *flexion* (movement that reduces the angle between the bones, as in bending fingers to close the hand); *extension* (movement that increases the angle between bones, as in straightening the fingers to open the hand); *abduction* (movement away from the midline of the body, as in moving the arm straight out to the side); and *adduction* (movement toward the midline of the body, as in returning the arm back to the side of the body).

Physical educators should be well informed as to the action of the joints in various activities, the care and training needed to develop and strengthen these areas and the common disorders of the skeletal system. One disorder is *rickets,* a disease of the bone resulting from a deficiency of vitamin D and of sunlight. Physical educators must become familiar with some of the common signs of this disease if they are to recognize it in their students. Children with rickets are usually irritable, weak, and restless and appear to have deformities such as knock-knees and bowlegs. Physical educators can play an important part in recognizing such deformities and can thus inform the individual's family of their findings, which will hopefully lead to the necessary medical treatment.

Musculature. The musculature of the human body is an essential to movement; consequently, physical educators should be familiar with its composition and action. In studying anatomy and kinesiology physical educators will discover in detail the various muscles and how they function in body movement; how important muscles are to the human body; how they provide for locomotion, give form to the body, produce body heat, and make breathing, circulation, and other vital movements possible.

There are three types of muscles in the human body: *skeletal* muscle, *smooth* muscle, and *cardiac* muscle. Skeletal muscles are voluntary and under the control of an individual's conscious will. They are attached to the bones and make it possible to move about during daily activities. It is skeletal muscles with which the physical educator should be most concerned.

Two principles with which every physical educator should be familiar are *muscle tonus* and *reciprocal innervation. Muscle tonus* means the constant, partial contraction of the muscles of the body resulting from the elasticity of muscle. This is essential to good posture and to the efficient functioning of some of the organic systems. This slight muscle contraction enables muscles to react to stimuli within the space of a very short time and with a minimum expenditure of energy. A state of muscle tonus is essential to good body health.

Reciprocal innervation refers to the part that antagonistic muscles play in performing coordinated movements. This principle works on the theory that whenever a group of muscles contracts to perform a movement, the antagonistic muscles relax, so that a coordinated, smooth, rhythmical movement results. A good example of this principle is the movement of flexing the arm. The biceps contracts and the antagonistic muscle, or triceps, relaxes, resulting in free and easy action. When a person is a novice in a game, he or she often performs in an awkward and uncoordinated manner because the antagonistic muscles do not relax and allow for free and easy movement. The proper coordinations between the muscle groups have not been established.

Circulatory system. The circulatory system of the body carries food and oxygen to and brings wastes from the multitude of cells that make up the organism. These elements are transported by means of blood through a system of tubes called blood vessels. The blood is kept flowing as a result of heart action.

There are two sets of blood vessels—the *arteries* that carry the blood from the heart and the *veins* that carry the blood to the heart. Arteries divide into smaller and smaller branches called capillaries, which connect with the cells. The capillaries unite with veins and then the veins, with various small tributaries, unite into larger veins going to the heart.

The heart has four chambers, the two upper chambers being the atria and the two lower chambers the ventricles. The veins send blood to the atria, the walls of which contract, and the blood then goes to the ventricles. The ventricles contract, sending blood to the various parts of the body. After forcing the blood into the arteries, the heart relaxes for a moment and rests. Then the process is repeated. There are two valves between the atria and the ventricles and two at the mouths of the arteries. The valves prevent the blood from flowing backward.

The blood follows a definite route through the heart. The right side of the heart sends blood to the lungs, where the blood picks up oxygen and then goes back to the left side of the heart. On the left side of the heart, the blood is forced into the arteries and to the entire body. After nourishing the cells and picking up the wastes, it goes back to the right side of the heart. The entire process consumes less than a minute.

The composition of the blood is interesting to examine. The liquid part is known as plasma. Within the plasma float millions of minute red and white corpuscles. The red corpuscles carry oxygen from the lungs to the various cells throughout the body, and the white corpuscles kill disease germs that enter the body. About nine tenths of the blood is plasma; the rest is dissolved food and other materials such as wastes. The capillary walls are thin, and as the blood goes through them, the plasma escapes and becomes lymph surrounding the cells. Oxygen breaks loose from the red corpuscles and passes into the lymph and to the cells. Waste materials pass through the lymph into the blood. The lymph acts as a middleman between the cells and the blood as it passes oxygen and food to the cells and wastes to the blood. In addition to the blood capillaries, lymphatic capillaries take the impure lymph from among the cells and carry it to the blood.

The organ that is the center of the circulatory system is the heart. Its action results in nourishment being sent to the millions of cells throughout the body. It beats continuously day and night. It is essential to life. Nothing should be done to harm this delicate piece of machinery. The body should be protected against disease that might impair its use. Exercise should be adapted to an individual's needs so as not to place too much of a strain on the heart. This is especially true of adults who have passed middle life. However, it should be remembered that the heart is a muscle, and, like all muscles, it becomes stronger with use. This has

implications for the physical educator in providing activities for children of school age. If a child's heart is normal and healthy, it cannot be injured by exercise. There is considerable evidence to support this tenet. This should not preclude, however, a physical educator determining through an examination of health records and consultations with physicians whether a child has a rheumatic fever history or some other cardiac disturbance that might make strenuous exercise questionable. Furthermore, the physical educator should know that even though the normal heart tissue of children cannot be damaged by exercise, very strenuous exercise can do damage to other parts of the body beside the heart. For example, overfatigue has implications for a child's emotional health.

Respiratory system. The respiratory system consists of air tubes leading into billions of microscopic permeable air sacs in the lungs. It has two main functions—taking oxygen into the body and giving off carbon dioxide.

In respect to oxygen, the body leads a hand-to-mouth existence. Oxygen cannot be stored; it must be taken in as needed. The body takes in oxygen every minute of the day and night. If the organism stops breathing, it will die within a short time. Carbon dioxide is given off through the respiratory system. It is formed in the cells and carried by the blood to the lungs and then escapes into the air.

The chest cavity, where the lungs and also the heart are located, is protected by the sternum, or breast bone, and the ribs. In breathing the ribs lift upward and outward, and the diaphragm is pulled downward. Air passes to the lungs through the trachea, which is kept open by rings of cartilage. The trachea divides, with a branch going to each lung. Within the lungs these branches divide again and again and end in little air sacs. The branches of the trachea are called *bronchial tubes*. The walls of the air sacs are thin, and the blood flows in them through capillaries. Oxygen passes into the blood through the walls of the air sacs. Carbon dioxide passes into the sacs and out of the lungs. The air in the lungs gives off oxygen and takes on carbon dioxide.

One important point should be clear to physical educators in interpreting the respiratory system for their work. So-called "breathing exercises" are not beneficial to the human mechanism. They should be discounted because it is a physiological fact that oxygen cannot be stored up for future use but is taken in as needed. The respiratory system supplies enough oxygen in normal activity for body needs. The amount of oxygen used by cells is determined by the needs of tissues and not by the oxygen that is available. Except for corrective therapy, breathing exercises have no value for the human body.

Nervous system. The nervous system is the "control center" of the human body. It issues the orders and controls and regulates everything the organism does. It controls the organs and other parts of the body; acts as an organ of the mind; regulates body heat, secretion of digestive juices, and excretion of wastes; and controls every movement that is made. The nervous system primarily comprises the brain, spinal cord, nerves that go out from the brain and spinal cord to various parts of the body, and ganglia, or masses of gray tissue found in inner organs of the body.

The fundamental unit of the nervous system, the nerve cell or neuron, is found in all parts of the nervous system and especially in the brain and spinal cord. It is of gray color. Through the neuron, messages are carried between the receptors, or cells that receive the impulses, to the effectors, or cells that react to the impulses, such as found in a muscle or gland. The nerve fibers that connect nerve cells with various parts of the body are white in color (gray in the center) and form the machinery that carries the messages, or impulses. The gray core of the fiber is a branch of a nerve cell.

Three kinds of neurons are found in the nervous system: (1) the *sensory* neuron, (2) the *motor* neuron, and (3) the *intermediate* neuron.

The sensory, or afferent, neuron carries impulses into the central nervous system. These impulses may be carried from the skin, eye, ear, and various other parts of the body to the brain. These impulses are responsible for feeling, seeing, hearing, and understanding the condition of the body at all times. The motor, or efferent, neuron sends messages from the spinal cord to the muscles and results in muscular action. The intermediate neuron lies entirely within the central nervous system itself and has no contact with the outside.

The brain, a vital part of the nervous system, is located within the cranial cavity and weighs approximately 50 ounces. It has three principal divisions. The first division is the *cerebrum,* or major part of the brain. The gray outer layer of the cerebrum, or *cortex,* is the seat of intelligence. It thinks and feels, decides what individuals will do, and governs the whole body. The second section, the *cerebellum,* is located under the back lobes of the cerebrum. It assists in controlling muscles of locomotion, balance, and equilibrium. The third division, the *medulla oblongata,* is the enlarged upper end of the spinal cord and is largely composed of fibers that connect various parts of the body and brain, some of which are sensory and some motor fibers. The medulla also has centers that control the heart and lungs. When the medulla is injured, death results. The heart stops beating and breathing stops.

The nervous system controls the body to a great degree unconsciously or involuntarily. This is called *reflex action.* An example of this can be seen after striking an individual just below the kneecap. Involuntarily the leg will move upward. Practically all control of the internal organs is carried on by reflexes. These are natural reflexes, with which the organism is born.

Another set of reflexes, different from the natural ones, consists of those which can be developed as a result of practice. Swimmers do not think of how they are going to swim, how they are going to move their arms or their legs in the crawl stroke. Instead, it becomes automatic as a result of practice. An important part of education is concerned with developing the right kind of reflexes. In physical education social reflexes such as fair play, respect for the individual, and courtesy are important. As a result of practice, these attributes become a reality without thought to one's actions. In a sense these habits can be viewed as reflexes formed by repetition of acts. Physical educators should remember that this type of reaction is most readily formed in youth and that many situations exist in the playground, gymnasium, and swimming pool where they can be most readily practiced.

The nervous system needs good care if it is to serve the individual. Adequate sleep is an essential for a well-ordered nervous system. Continual loss of sleep will make one irritable, cross, and upset. Fresh air and exercise are an antidote for people who find themselves getting a "case of nerves." Finally, a peaceful mind free from worry, fear, and hate is conducive to an existence free from emotional strife and an upset nervous system.

Digestive system. The digestive system is responsible for preparing foods for absorption so that they may be transported to cells throughout the body. The absorption of food is important because foods supply the energy that the body needs while it builds and repairs tissue and controls the various metabolic processes essential to a healthy life. The organs of the *alimentary canal* are the prime components of the digestive system. They include the *mouth, tongue, teeth, pharynx, esophagus, stomach, small intestine,* and *large intestine.* The accessory glands that also play an important part in digestion are the *liver* and *pancreas.*

In the digestive process the first step takes place in the mouth, where *mastication* reduces the food to small particles and mixes it with saliva. *Deglutition* follows mastication. There is now a formation of a *bolus* of food and a subsequent propelling of the bolus from the mouth through the pharynx and the esophagus to the stomach. In the stomach the food is churned, mixed with gastric juices, and converted to a substance known as *chyme.* In the small intestine, bile from the liver and pancreatic juices combine with the chyme. Foods are then broken down into amino acids, simple sugar, and fatty acids, which are used by the cells for energy. Waste materials that are not absorbed by the cells for energy are carried into the large instestine to be excreted.

Basically, the digestive system has little, if any, function during actual exercising. However, it is important to follow a proper diet to have the necessary energy that most activities require. Irregular meals can interfere with the orderly propulsion of food through the digestive

system, and too many carbohydrates can result in an overweight condition that can lead to obesity. These deficiencies can interfere with the normal functioning of the digestive system and can limit the amount of energy needed for normal functioning. Physical educators should educate their students regarding foods that are the best energy producers. Physical education teachers, including coaches, should also provide their students with information about weight control. Proper exercise programs together with knowledge of proper nutrition can help students achieve a higher level of fitness.

Excretory system. Wastes produced by the cells and picked up by the bloodstream must be eliminated from the body. This is accomplished by four widely separated organs. The *lungs* eliminate the carobon dioxide as previously explained. Water, salts, and small amounts of other wastes are eliminated by the *perspiration glands* in the skin. The *kidneys* extract water, salts, and urea, which is the waste produced from the use of certain foods by the cells. The *liver* helps in the process of removing wastes from the bloodstream.

The large intestine is often classified as an organ of excretion, although it has little to do with getting rid of the wastes produced by the body cells. The large intestine eliminates undigested food.

Endocrine system. There are two general classes of glands in the body that manufacture substances or secretions used by the body. The glands with ducts or passageways pour their secretions into another organ like the salivary glands and the liver. There is a second type of gland called an *endocrine,* or *ductless, gland,* which produces substances that are absorbed directly into the bloodstream and carried throughout the entire body. These substances contain important chemicals known as hormones, which have far-reaching effects on body growth, development, and function.

Examples of endocrine glands are the *thyroid,* which produces a hormone that regulates the rate of metabolism or the chemical changes that take place in cells to produce energy; the *pituitary,* the so-called "master gland" that manufactures several hormones of great importance in physical growth and development; and the *gonads,* which are responsible for the bodily changes in boys and girls at adolescence.

The work of the endocrine glands is so interrelated that it is hard to assign a specific function to a specific gland. The hormones work together to stimulate and regulate many body characteristics such as size, shape, and appearance and many body functions such as metabolic rate.

Integumentary system. The skin and membranes of the body are grouped together to form the integumentary system. Their major task is protection of underlying tissues.

The skin covers the surface of the body and provides a tough layer of protection from bacteria, dirt, mechanical injury, and temperature. It also contains glands that produce oil to keep the skin pliable and perspiration, which is of importance in regulating body temperature.

The internal organs of the body are lined with membranes that also serve as protection to underlying tissues. Many of these membranes secrete lubricating substances, such as mucus, which among other things keeps tissues moist.

Reproductive system. The continuation of the race is accomplished through the reproductive systems of men and women. The sex organs of male and female unite to produce gametes that form the zygote and eventually a new human being. The reproductive glands are known as *gonads.* In the male they are called testes and produce sperm. In the female they are called ovaries and produce eggs, or ova. In addition to the ovaries, the female reproductive system includes the uterus and a passageway, the vagina, from the uterus to the outside of the body. In the male, tubes lead from the testes to the outside of the body by way of the penis.

The impact of heredity

The difference in growth rates, as well as the differences in the physical makeup of human beings, is the result of heredity, the process by which certain physical and mental characteristics are transmitted from parents to their children. Not all personal characteristics are inherited. Other factors, such as education and environment, influence one's characteristics.

Heredity does give the color of one color and texture of one's hair, the shape of one's facial features, the col one's skin, and one's basic body build.

Some physical defects may be inherited from parents, for example, color blindness, deafness, and extra fingers and toes. Scientists are still uncertain about the role heredity plays in intelligence, but reliable evidence suggests that both high and low levels of intelligence run in families.

A person is the result of a complex biological process in which each parent contributed certain characteristics to his or her makeup, as they in turn, and all others in their family back through time, were produced by the same random selection of characteristics from their parents. Those individuals who produce children will similarly pass on certain characteristics, but neither they nor their parents nor their parents before them have any control over the characteristics transmitted to the next generation. So it is that the body build, hair color, skin color, and so on that make up a person are individual in nature. Unless a person is an identical twin, this individual will find that the other members of his or her family may differ greatly in size and appearance.

Chromosomes and genes. One's existence as a human being is the result of the union of a male germ cell (sperm) with a female germ cell (ovum) to form a single cell or fertilized egg. Over approximately a 9-month period, the fertilized egg divides and subdivides and grows in size until a human being is formed.

Within each of the male and female germ cells are tiny structures called *chromosomes.* There are forty-six such chromosomes in the nucleus of each human cell. Each of these chromosomes, in turn, carries thousands of additional structures called *genes,* which determine the characteristics that are inherited by human beings.

Genes are arranged in rows of fine fibers within the chromosome, looking much like a string of beads when examined under a microscope. (Genes, by the way, are so small—some scientists believe them to be the size of viruses —that until the development of the electron microscope in recent years, study of them was

airs within the cells
ing the union of the
male germ cell, each
of genes to the other,
r of genes. The sep-
That is, if your father
carry a pair of genes
have a pair of mixed
air producing brown
eyes (which, for him, are dominant) and one
half of the pair capable of producing blue eyes.
Your mother, on the other hand, may have
blue eyes, in which case she carries only blue-
eyed genes. In the union of germ cells that produced you, if the male cell carried your father's
gene for brown eyes to your mother's gene for
blue eyes, you will have brown eyes. But you
will be a mixed brown, having a pair of genes,
one of which produces brown eyes, and the
other of which produce blue. Thus you might
produce a blue-eyed baby.

If, on the other hand, your father were mixed
brown and passed the blue-eyed gene to your
mother, you would be blue-eyed, meaning that
the pair of genes you possess for eye color
carry only blue-eyedness. If you, in turn, married a blue-eyed person, your children would
probably have blue eyes. If you married a person with brown eyes, you might have either
blue-eyed or brown-eyed children.

The chance nature of genetic selection is
best seen perhaps in the determination of sex.
Each human being possesses what is called
the *sex chromosome*. The woman produces X
chromosomes (two in number), but the man
produces both an X chromosome and a Y chromosome. The male germ cell, then, carries
either an X or a Y chromosome, but not both,
when it unites with the female germ cell. If the
male X is carried to the female (X), a female
child (XX) results. If the male germ cell carries a Y chromosome to the female, a male
child (XY) is formed. Since thousands of male
germ cells are present each time sexual inter-
course occurs but only one female egg (and
then only at certain times), the random or
chance nature of fertilization and heredity is
obvious, since only one of the germ cells from
the man can unite with the germ cell of the
woman. Also, each germ cell (whether male or

female) carries one half of a pair of characteristics that unite to form one complete pair of
characteristics in the new cell.

PHYSICAL AND MOTOR GROWTH AND DEVELOPMENT

Physical educators should be familiar with
the various physical characteristics, in addition to those already presented, that are present
in human beings from infancy to adulthood. A
thorough knowledge of these factors will enable
physical educators to plan a program of activity that will meet the needs and interests of each
individual with whom they work. Such a knowledge would include the following:

1. Various ages by which individuals are classified
2. Various aspects of physical and motor growth
   during infancy, preschool years, the elementary school period, and adolescence
3. Physiological differences between males and
   females
4. General rules that should be followed in respect
   to physical and motor growth and development

Ages of development. Individuals are classified in various ways according to age. The most
common are estimations of chronological,
anatomical, physiological, and mental age.
These may all be helpful to the teacher of physical education.

Chronological age represents the age of an
individual in calendar years and months. *Anatomical* age is usually related to the ossification
of bones. Frequently, the small bones in the
wrist are used for this purpose. An x-ray examination is needed to determine anatomical age.
Sometimes the stage of dentition is also used to
determine this type of age. *Physiological* age
is related to puberty. It may be determined in
some cases by the quality and texture of the
pubic hair in boys and by menstruation in girls.
The last classification is *mental* age, which is
determined through tests that measure the degree to which an individual has adjusted to the
environment and is able to solve certain problems.

Although physical educators will be interested in all the age classifications of the individuals with whom they work, they should

have special interest in the physiological age. It seems that this, more than any other age classification, is a determining factor in arranging a program of activities adapted to the needs and interests of any one person.

Physical and motor growth at various levels. The characteristics of physical and motor growth in the child during infancy, the preschool, elementary school years, and adolescence are interesting for the physical educator. From a study of these characteristics, one can see that the child, a dynamic individual, craves activity. The type of program provided should depend to a great degree on child growth and development characteristics, such as the maturation level of the child.

Infancy. During prenatal life the fetus grows rapidly. For example, there is an increase in height to an average of 20½ inches. After birth, growth continues to be rapid for a period of 2 years and then begins to slow down. At birth and for about 18 months thereafter, the head is big in proportion to the rest of the body.

Development occurs from the head downward, or in the *cephalocaudal* direction. The fact that the arms develop faster than the legs is an indication of this. During prenatal life the arm buds develop before the leg buds. Development also is from the axes of the body to the extremities, or in the *proximodistal* direction. For example, the ability to use the hand develops in the palm of the hand before the fingers. This may be seen by watching a baby manipulate a block, The baby pushes it around with the palm of the hand for some time before being able to pick it up with the fingers.

In discussing the cephalocaudal and proximodistal directions of development, it seems wise to examine whether educational programs for young children should be concerned mainly with big-muscle activity or with fine-muscle activity that is associated with the use of the fingers, eyes, and the like. Many educators claim that the child's main concern during the growing years should be big-muscle activity. This is based on the premise that fine-muscle coordinations develop after the large-muscle coordinations in the child. Fine-muscle skills such as reading and writing, according to some educators, are frequently utilized in the educational

process too early in life. Some psychologists, on the other hand, point out that there is some basis for this argument but that it is not entirely true. They point out that a child can pick up objects with the thumb and forefinger and perform many manual manipulations, thus utilizing the fine muscles before being able to walk and run—activities that use the large muscles. According to these psychologists, the choice of play materials should not be based only on whether they involve large-muscle or small-muscle activity but should provide for both types of activity. On the basis of physiological facts it would seem that big-muscle activity plays an important role in normal growth and development and that during the growing years the child should have ample opportunity for such activity to become a well-developed, healthy human being.

Other implications for physical educators include a knowledge of the infant's skeleton. The skeleton is largely made up of cartilage and fibrous tissues, and as a result the bones are soft. Proper care must be given to avoid deformities and postural difficulties. The spine of a child is flexible, and for proper development it should receive proper physical activity. This will minimize the possibility of increased lumbar curve.

Preschool years. During the preschool years the child develops many physical skills, including running, climbing, and skipping. These not only aid in physical development but also provide a basis for social relationships. The child associates with other children and finds out how they react to their environment. During this period the child gains great pleasure from physical activity. This affects the child's emotional life, since gaining ability in certain physical acts stimulates self-confidence. The child has better use of the arms and legs and utilizes more and more skills. This motor development makes possible more avenues of learning as he or she begins to explore the environment.

Certain maturation levels should be recognized in children. If allowed to develop independently to a certain point, a child will do things as a part of the natural course of growth. Psychologists list several examples of this. They explain how 2-year-old children are sometimes prompted to button their own clothes. However, at the end of several weeks of practice they do not do any better than another group of children of the same age who had not practiced. They show how this also applies in the learning of skills such as skipping and tricycling. The motor skills that are provided for children should definitely be related to their readiness to utilize and perform them. More research is needed into the skills that children should have at various ages. More should be known about skills that are of value in themselves, as distinguished from skills that develop a child socially and intellectually, and skills useful for a limited period of time, as contrasted with skills that are developed for future use.

Motor learning has been recognized as an essential for all children and important to their social and emotional life. It helps the individual to become independent. It plays a part in one's intellectual development. Through motor skills the child acquires concepts of size and weight and finds out about such things as gravity and balance. From an emotional standpoint motor skills help children to solve problems that would otherwise enrage and stump them. Newell Kephart, former head of the Achievement Center at Purdue University, has conducted much research that supports the relation of motor skills to the child's mental and physical development.

Elementary school years. During the elementary school years, children acquire fundamental skills that they will use throughout life. According to a study of men 20 years old and older, it was found that many of their hobbies and adult leisure-time interests were based on their childhood experiences. Physical educators should recognize this as having implications for their work. If adults are to have physical skill in various activities, their foundation should be laid during the early years.

During the elementary school years the child develops socially, making contacts through motor activities. Children are accepted by the group if they can participate with some degree of skill. They gain independence by learning to do things by themselves. They increase their knowledge in respect to the environment. In all this development, motor skills play an important part.

Preschool years.

Physical educators need to know what skills children possess at certain age levels, those skills possessed by most children and those possessed by just a few, the importance of skills in the lives of children, and the environmental factors contributing to or thwarting skill development. These are essential facts if physical education is to contribute further in the development of the child.

Adolescence. During adolescent years the body reaches maximum powers in the use of its musculature. This also applies to its capacity to learn motor skills.

During the elementary years, boys are superior to girls in activities such as running, jumping, and throwing. This is even more pronounced in the adolescent years. This can be explained by the fact that boys have more opportunities than girls to participate in these activities and also because of certain anatomical differences. A girl has a wider pelvis, and the angle of attachment of the femur to the thigh is different from that in boys. Boys are also stronger than girls. Girls are generally larger than boys from about 10 to 14 years of age,

Elementary schoolchildren at Waddell Elementary School, Manchester, Connecticut, are given instruction in track.

but after the age of 14 or 15 years, boys become larger and much stronger.

In the middle and later adolescent years, activity decreases in most individuals. In a large part, this decrease results from interest in an occupation, reduction in the number of different activities in which one can engage, and social and other interests that appear to be stronger. Available evidence shows that there are more excuses from physical education classes in high school than elementary and junior high school. This falling off of activity continues into adult life and produces a problem with which physical educators should be concerned. The public should be better informed as to the value of activity throughout life.

Postadolescent years. Physiological maturity has been reached in the postadolescent years. Boys are still developing muscularly. Improved motor coordination becomes evident in those youths who are active in many different types of physical activity. These are years when endurance increases, emotional balance is better, interest in physical attractiveness increases, and recreational activities become popular. It is a time when people are more interested in their body conformation and sometimes use techniques such as exercises and diet pills in an attempt to change their body size. It is also a time when strong convictions and ideals are being developed, prejudices and antagonisms become intensified, there is a desire for deeper friendships, and much thought is given to the future. There is a need during these postadolescent years for periodic health examinations, for information about proper weight control, for opportunities to participate in coeducational and recreational activities, for experiences in helping others in the development of skills and playing of games, for practice in planning for many social activities, for opportunities to gain increased skill and competence in chosen activity areas, and for practice in critical thinking and problem solving.

Differences in boys and girls. The physical educator should be cognizant of certain differences in the physical makeup of boys and girls. The pelvic girdle of the female is much broader than that of the male and does not completely develop until in the twenties. Boys are often stronger than girls, especially in the shoulder girdle region. The thigh bones of girls join the

Photo by Rollie Baird, Dellarson Studios.

Cooperative school physical education program at Regina High School, Minneapolis, Minnesota.

pelvis at a more oblique angle than in boys. The center of gravity is lower in girls. In respect to body weight the muscular strength of girls usually is lower than in boys.

In respect to strength, some research has indicated that the female may be less responsive to training than the male. It has been found that female body temperature rises 2° to 3° C. higher than in males before the sweating and cooling-off process begins. Such a factor may be a consideration in dealing with vigorous physical activities, such as swimming in hot weather. Other differences include a more stable knee joint in girls than in boys, greater length of bones in boys than girls, and, on the average, greater height and weight in boys than girls. Some medical experts believe that the skeletal structure of the female makes her more susceptible to athletic injuries than the male. Injuries involving overstraining, such as in foot deficiencies and tendon inflammations, have been found to be more common in the female.

The new emphasis on girls and women in sports has clearly demonstrated that women can participate in all sports and can compete with men in many activities.

Implications for junior high school athletics

One of the most controversial areas in athletic programs is the one concerned with junior high school students.

Biologically, students in grades seven to nine are preadolescents and young adolescents. In grade seven, among 11-, 12-, and 13-year-old students, preadolescents predominate—approximately two thirds are boys, and one third are girls. In grade 8, among 12-, 13-, and 14-year-olds, young adolescents increase in number. In grade 9, among 13-, 14-, and 15-year-olds, young adolescents predominate.

Preadolescents are children who belong to later childhood. They have not yet experienced the growth spurt. Instead, growth is usually slow. Young adolescents are characterized by fast-growing arms and legs, changing facial

Courtesy The Athletic Institute.

Girls and women have become more active in sports. In this photograph, two women show their prowess in field hockey.

features, broadening hips and shoulders, and changing voices. They resemble men and women more than they do children.

The growth spurt, experienced by junior high school students, is a rapid and spectacular one both from its outward expression in the form of height, weight, and size and also in respect to sensitive biochemical activity resulting in internal physical changes.

Girls normally have their growth spurt between the ages of 8½ and 11½ years, reaching a peak at about 12½ years and leveling off at 15 to 16 years of age. Boys begin later than girls, with their growth spurt normally occurring between the ages of 10½ and 14½ years and peaking at about 14½. After this there is a gradual decline, the rate of growth usually being complete between the ages of 17 and 20 years.

Biologically, an adapted program of activities is needed to meet the changing physical makeup of the junior high school student. The period of growth and development through which the student is passing requires a program adapted to individual needs. There is a special need for team-type activities that will satisfy the group urge. There is a need for competition. There is a need for a wide variety of activities that will help in the development of body control, enable each student to experience success, provide consideration for energy output and fatigue, and protect the sensitive individual. There is a need for activities that will offer a channel of release for tensions rather than increase the amount of tension. Furthermore, in selecting activities the danger of injury to the skeletal framework, as well as dangers of students overextending themselves to the point of exhaustion through competitive activity, must be kept in mind. There is a need to keep accurate records of growth and achievement, to have a program of health supervision and medical services, and to make provision for work in body mechanics.

Because of the uneven way in which growth takes place, it is difficult to know how old a student is during the early adolescent period. "Old" in this frame of reference does not refer to years but to other kinds of age—age of the skeleton, mental age, physiological maturity, and emotional maturity. This raises the question of how students can be properly grouped for forms of athletic activity that in many instances should be limited rightfully to the "older" youngsters.

Implications for girls' and women's athletics

The question of athletics for girls is a controversial matter. The questions of how much, how little, and what is a happy medium are frequently raised with enthusiastic supporters on all sides of the issue. There is a consensus that athletics can render a valuable service to girls. The question arises as to what type of program can best render this service. Girls can develop a better state of total fitness, skills for worthy use of leisure time, and other desirable qualities and attributes just as boys and men can. However, it must be recognized that girls and women are not boys and men. There are many biological, sociological, and other differences that must be taken into consideration. It is impossible to take the boys' program and duplicate it for the girls without any changes or modifications.

Critics of athletic competition for girls have frequently declared that such competition can interfere with the female menstrual cycle and cause problems associated with the reproductive system. Much of this criticism, however, has not been fully substantiated. On the other hand, physical activity for girls has been found to improve the development of abdominal and spinal muscles, which in turn may prove beneficial in the progress of pregnancy. Gendel* has stated that those girls who have had little physical activity may have increased postpartum problems of back pain. Physical activities that strengthen the abdominal muscles can alleviate this discomfort.

It is important that the men and women in charge of physical education programs and those who do the officiating be qualified. Training programs are needed for the preparation of teachers, coaches, and officials. There is need for the nation's sports leaders to unite their efforts and organize the type of program that will most benefit the girl athlete. The Association for Girls' and Women's Sports of the American Alliance for Health, Physical Education, and Recreation has established guidelines for female athletes. These guidelines should be reviewed and followed wherever such programs exist.

In the future there will be an increasing demand for more athletic competition for girls. The current women's liberation movement and Title IX have been instrumental in emphasizing the point that women should be emancipated politically, socially, economically, and sexually. Women now wish to be emancipated athletically. For example, the woman jockey is becoming a more frequent sight at many race tracks, and girls are playing on Little League baseball teams with boys. Girls and women are playing varsity sports in school and colleges. Athletic competition for girls is a common occurrence.

General principles pertinent to physical and motor growth and development

Certain general principles may be stated in respect to physical and motor growth and de-

velopment. The physical educator should continually be conscious of the following principles in planning and directing a physical education program for children:

1. Normal children need from 2 to 6 hours of activity a day. Since all their activity cannot take place during school hours, the time spent in activity in school should be devoted to providing instruction that may be utilized in after-school hours.
2. Aside from heredity and the nutritive environment, the organic systems of the body can be developed only through muscular activity.
3. Because of the softness of a young child's bones, particular attention should be given to the prevention of postural abnormalities.
4. A child's physiological age is an important consideration in determining the type of phys-

A normal child needs 2 to 6 hours of activity a day.

---

*Gendel, Evelyn S.: Women and the medical aspects of sports, Journal of School Health **37:**427, 1967.

ical education program best fitted to individual growth and development.

5. Large-muscle activity is an essential for the proper growth and development of normal children.
6. The various parts of a child's body grow at different rates of speed.
7. A child's intellectual, social, and emotional growth and development are increased through motor activity.
8. A "skills" program should take into consideration the maturation levels of children.
9. Disease, malnutrition, and insufficient exercise are causes of growth disturbances in children.
10. Skills utilized in adult leisure hours are frequently acquired during childhood.
11. The acquisition of skills aids the awkward adolescent child to obtain satisfaction and enjoyment through participation.
12. Adolescent boys and girls should participate in physical education programs that are adapted to their needs and physiological makeup.
13. The values of physical activity to everyone, regardless of age and sex, should be brought to the attention of all.

BODY TYPES

Psychologists often classify individuals on the basis of "body types," or physique. With such a classification it has been thought possible to distinguish certain physiological and personality traits that might be associated with each type.

One method of classification is that promulgated by Kretschmer, who classified the human body into four groupings based on physical features. Types distinguished are the *asthenic,* from the Greek meaning "without strength," referring to those individuals who are lean, slim, shallow chested, and tall in proportion to their weight; the *athletic,* from the Greek meaning "a contender for a prize"—the muscular individual, with broad shoulders and well-developed chest, robust and strong; the *pyknic,* from the Greek meaning "thick," referring to the individual who has a broad, rounded figure, large head, heavy neck, and ruddy face; and the *dysplastic,* from the Greek meaning "badly formed," designating individuals who have abnormal body builds not found in the asthenic, athletic, and pyknic types.

Within certain limits, body types may be used as an indication of athletic ability. For example, the pyknic type usually will be interested in a sport such as football, soccer, or hockey, whereas the asthenic type will choose running or tennis. Classifications based on body types, however, are not always reliable, and physical educators should be careful as to how much they rely on them as a basis for classifying groups for physical education activities. Age, physiological maturity, interests, skill, size, strength, physical fitness, and other similar criteria should be used with the various body-type classifications in making such judgments.

Another classification that has been used divides body types into *endomorph,* which is similar to Kretschmer's pyknic type; *mesomorph,* similar to the athletic type, and *ectomorph,* similar to the asthenic type. Sheldon uses these classifications and has developed a system of somatotyping, whereby an individual's body classification can be more accurately analyzed by giving it a number classification showing relationship to endomorph, mesomorph, or ectomorph. This is based on the premise that there are no clear-cut or absolute "endomorphs," "mesomorphs," or "ectomorphs." Instead, body build represents a variation of all three. Sheldon then goes on to give a detailed description of the various somatotypes that he has found in his research.

Willgoose relates body types and physical fitness. Table 11-1 shows that within certain groups of somatotypes there are different interests and abilities in athletics. Willgoose points out there is some overlapping in this structure but that it might be useful in considering athletic performance.

BODY MECHANICS

The attitudes about good posture have changed from that favoring a rigid, static, upright, unnatural position to one of efficient, graceful, yet somewhat relaxed body movement. Physical educators are concerned with dynamic posture in sitting, standing, walking, running, and other body positions. The aim is to have individuals develop a body carriage suited to their own body build. The best posture will be characterized by balance and proper

Table 11-1. Body types and physical fitness*

Mesomorphic endomorphs	Endomorphic mesomorphs	Extreme mesomorphs	Ectomorphic mesomorphs	Mesomorphic ectomorphs
(S-types: 631, 532, 541, 542, 543)†	(S-types: 452, 361, 462, 451, 453)	(S-types: 171, 162, 262, 172, 252)	(S-types: 253, 254, 163, 164, 265)	(S-types: 235, 126, 136, 145, 146)
Table tennis	Baseball	Sprints	Lightweight wrestling	Bicycling
Floating (swimming)	Football (lineman)	Basketball	Long-distance running	Cross-country
Croquet	Heavyweight boxing	Middleweight boxing	Tennis	Table tennis
Fly and bait casting	Heavyweight wrestling	Middleweight wrestling	Gymnastics	Basketball center (short periods)
Bowling	Swimming	Quarterbacks	Weight lifting	Archery
	Soccer (backs)	Football (backs)	Javelin	(Also many athletic games, except those requiring weight and sheer strength)
	Ice hockey (backs)	Divers	Pole vault	
	Weight tossing	Tumbling	High jump	
		Lacrosse	Fencing	
		Soccer (forwards)	Badminton	
		Ice hockey (forwards)	Skiing	
		Handball	Jockey	

*Willgoose, Carl E.: Journal of Health, Physical Education, and Recreation 27:26, Sept., 1956.
†S-types in the table refer to those body types given in Sheldon, William H.: Atlas of men, New York, 1954, Harper & Row, Publishers.

alignment of body segments to give one maximum support and movement with the least strain.

Good posture is valuable for appearance, since it influences the concept others have of the individual. One's posture may even influence self-concepts and attitude of mind. Good posture makes for efficiency of movement, since poor posture causes additional muscular effort, fatigue, and undue strain. In some cases the strain may be enough to alter structure, resulting in limited use of body parts. In extreme cases, chronic strain may lead to arthritic conditions.

Poor posture may have several causes, including weak musculature, faulty diet, fatigue, disease, arthritis, vision and hearing defects, overweight condition and obesity, skeletal defects, faulty postural habits, and injuries such as back strain. Even negative attitudes toward exercise and desirable posture can be basic causes of poor body carriage.

Physical educators must be aware of the various deviations in body mechanics. They can be either *functional* or *structural*. Functional deviations can be corrected. They are primarily associated with muscles and liga-

ments, and exercises can help alleviate the problem. Structural deviations are those which have not been corrected in time and have become permanent. Physical educators must be especially concerned with functional deviations, since in many cases students can be aided by proper exercise programs.

SELF-ASSESSMENT TESTS

These tests are to assist students in determining if material and competencies presented in this chapter have been mastered.

1. Justify in your own words why it is important for you as a physical educator to understand the makeup of each of the following parts of the human body: skeleton, musculature, circulatory system, respiratory system, nervous system, digestive system, integumentary system, and reproductive system.

2. Show how the evolution of humans, from the time when it was believed they walked on all fours to today where they assume an upright position, has resulted in many advantages but at the same time has caused many health problems.

3. Select two of your classmates. Describe the physical characteristics of each in respect to factors such as height, body build, and skin color. Show how each of these characteristics is associated with their heredity.

4. Construct a chart depicting the physical and motor growth of a person during infancy, preschool years, elementary school years, adolescence, and postadolescence.

5. Select one of your classes and categorize members into endomorphs, mesomorphs, or ectomorphs.

6. Write a short essay on the topic "A Close Relationship Exists Between the Biological Nature of Human Beings and Their Need for a Physically Active Existence."

READING ASSIGNMENT

Bucher, Charles A.: Dimensions of physical education, ed. 2, St. Louis, 1974, The C. V. Mosby Co., Reading selections 34 to 40.

SELECTED REFERENCES

American Association for Health, Physical Education, and Recreation: Children and fitness, 1964; The growing years—adolescence, 1962; Washington, D.C., The Association.

The Athletic Institute in cooperation with the American College of Sports Medicine: Health and fitness in the modern world, a collection of papers presented at the Institute of Normal Human Anatomy, Viala Regina Elena, 289, and the Ministry of Foreign Affairs, Rome, Italy, 1961, The Athletic Institute.

Bartley, F. H., and Chute, E.: Fatigue and impairment in man, New York, 1947, McGraw-Hill Book Co.

Bucher, Charles A.: Interscholastic athletics at the junior high school level, Albany, 1965, New York State Department of Education.

Bucher, Charles A., Olsen, Einar A., and Willgoose, Carl E.: The foundations of health, New York, 1976, Prentice-Hall, Inc.

Competitive athletics for children of elementary school age, Pediatrics **42:**703, 1968.

deVries, Herbert A.: Physiology of exercise, Dubuque, 1974, William C. Brown Co., Publishers.

Dowell, Linus J.: Environmental factors of childhood competitive athletics, The Physical Educator **28:**17, March, 1971.

Essentials of life and health, New York, 1977, Random House, Inc.

Gendel, Evelyn S.: Women and the medical aspects of sports, Journal of School Health **37:**427, 1967.

Getchell, Bud: Physical fitness—a way of life, New York, 1976, John Wiley & Sons, Inc.

Johnson, Warren R., editor: Science and medicine of exercise and sports, 1974, New York, Harper & Row, Publishers.

Johnson, Warren R.: Health in action, New York, 1977, Holt, Rinehart & Winston, Inc.

Kretschmer, E.: Physique and character, translated by W. J. H. Sprott, London, 1925, Kegan Paul, Trench, Trubner.

Mathews, Donald K., and Fox, Edward L.: The physiological basis of physical education and athletics, Philadelphia, 1971, W. B. Saunders Co.

Selye, Hans: The stress of life, New York, 1956, McGraw-Hill Book Co.

Sheldon, W. H.: The varieties of human physique, New York, 1940, Harper & Row, Publishers.

Singer, Robert N., and others: Physical education, an interdisciplinary approach, New York, 1972, The Macmillan Co.

Still, Joseph W.: Man's potential—and his performance, New York Times Magazine, Nov. 24, 1957.

Time, Inc.: The healthy life, Time-Life Books Special Report, New York, 1966, Time, Inc.

12

Exercise physiology and biological fitness

INSTRUCTIONAL OBJECTIVES AND COMPETENCIES TO BE ACHIEVED

After reading this chapter the student should be able to—

1. Describe what is meant by fitness and physical fitness and the extent of interest among the general public in this subject today.
2. Understand and appreciate the role of exercise in achieving physical fitness.
3. Explain the impact of training programs on the various organic systems of the human body and the procedures and considerations necessary to initiate these programs.
4. Show how certain life-styles, tobacco, alcohol, and drugs are deterrents to fitness.
5. Determine the impact of physical activity on weight control, stress, and fatigue.
6. Assess the physical fitness of the nation's children, youth, industrial executives, adults, and handicapped.

A fitness explosion is occurring in the United States. According to Sindlinger's Economic Service, a record 87.5 million adults in the United States who are 18 years of age and older are now actively engaging in some type of physical activity to improve their fitness. Enrollment in health spas is increasing about 25% each year, according to some estimates. Fifty thousand industrial firms in the United States spend an estimated $2 billion each year on fitness and recreational programs for their employees. Millions of dollars are being spent on fitness supplies, equipment, facilities, and programs. YMCAS and YWCAS that formerly sought men and women to fill their fitness classes are now finding they have long waiting lists. An estimated 1,300 books on fitness are currently in print, some of which have sold millions of copies in a year.

The American public is fitness minded, more so than ever before in history, and this movement represents an opportunity for physical educators to see how well their professional resources can be utilized in improving the nation's fitness. Furthermore, it represents a challenge to see whether physical educators will be recognized by the public at large as the specialists who possess expertise in this area.

EDUCATION FOR FITNESS

Since many youths and adults do not fully understand and appreciate the importance of health and fitness, a heavy responsibility rests on the shoulders of educators. If a nation is to remain strong physically, mentally, spiritually, and socially, there must be *education* for *fitness*. Furthermore, this education must take place largely through the formal processes of physical education, health education, and recreation programs in schools and colleges. Knowledge about the human body must be imparted, desirable health attitudes inculcated, and proper health practices instilled. The responsibility for accomplishing this herculean task must be assumed mainly by physical educators, health educators, and recreation educators. They must continually strive for sound school and community programs in their special fields.

Children in the Hudson Falls Central Schools at Hudson Falls, New York, are fitness conscious. Here a youngster does chin-ups, which is part of the daily exercise program in this school.

MEANING OF PHYSICAL FITNESS TO CHILDREN AND YOUNG PEOPLE

To discover what the term *physical fitness* means to elementary, high school, and college students, I surveyed 10,000 children and young people throughout the United States. The answers given were then analyzed to determine the most common concepts held by students in regard to their understanding of the term *physical fitness*.

The implications of this survey as to what children and young people regard as the meaning of the term *physical fitness* include the following:

1. As an objective of physical education, students do not clearly understand the meaning of physical fitness and its place in educational programs.
2. There is a need for communicating the meaning of the term *physical fitness* to students at all educational levels and to the public in general.

3. Physical educators should assume the responsibility for communicating key concepts to students in regard to terms such as *physical fitness*. This responsibility should be part of the subject matter and the theory underlying their field of endeavor.
4. There should be better communication between professional leaders in physical education and those practitioners functioning in schools, colleges, and various agencies at the "grass roots" level.
5. Physical education cannot be limited to activity alone. There must also be provision for getting at basic concepts underlying the field of physical education and making sure these basic concepts are understood by all persons concerned.

This chapter is designed to define and analyze the terms *fitness* and *physical fitness* and to discuss their implications for the profession of physical education.

FITNESS AND HEALTH

According to many health experts, the way each human being lives will be a major determining factor for the health and fitness of that individual. Although heredity plays a part, to a large degree health and fitness are acquired characteristics. The food that is eaten, amount of rest obtained, physical activity engaged in, and other health practices that are followed play important roles in determining human welfare. In other words, it is important to follow a good health regimen if one is to be healthy and fit.

Education is essential to help people follow a healthful regimen. It is important to educate students about English so that they can communicate articulately with their fellow human beings, about mathematics so that they can add their grocery bills accurately, and about the fine arts so that they can appreciate and enjoy Chagal and Beethoven. It is also important to educate people about their physical selves so that they can function most efficiently as human beings and accomplish all they are capable of achieving. And to attain this objective they need to know scientific facts essential to good health, possess desirable health attitudes, develop skills to make activity exciting and enjoyable, and be physically active. The end result will be productive, vigorous, and rewarding lives. And as the philosopher Will Durant advises, health is mostly within each person's will. "In many cases, sickness is a crime," this philosopher states. "We have done something physiologically foolish, and nature is being hard put to it to repair our mistakes. The pain we endure is the tuition we pay for our instruction in living."

Much of this education should take place early in life when the organic foundations are being laid, skills are more easily learned, and attitudes are formed. Unfortunately, too many people do not recognize the need for this education until cholesterol deposits have closed their arteries, ulcers have penetrated their duodenum, or cancer has started its insidious attack on their lungs. As one wise man has said, "We never appreciate health so much as when we lose it." Although it may be difficult to change the health habits of adults, schools and colleges *can* and *should* educate young people about their health and fitness. This is not only essential from the individual's point of view but also in view of this country's national posture. Former President Kennedy stated: "The strength of our democracy is no greater than the collective well-being of our people. The vigor of our country is no stronger than the vitality and will of our countrymen. The level of physical, mental, moral, and spiritual fitness of every American citizen must be our constant concern."

The fact that thousands of schoolchildren cannot pass a screening test of minimum physical fitness and that many more have undesirable health practices offers some evidence that educational programs are inadequate in this regard.

Sound school physical education programs are needed. To have outstanding programs, educators must have a clear understanding of the philosophy of physical education and its worth in education. The following definition of terms and concepts will be of help in setting the stage for education for fitness of young and old people alike.

1. *Fitness implies more than physical fitness.* Fitness is the ability of a person to live a full and balanced existence. The totally fit person possesses physical well-being but also qualities such as good human relations, maturity, and high ethical standards. He or she also satisfies

such basic needs as love, affection, security, and self-respect. School physical education programs are vitally concerned with physical fitness but also strive to contribute to total health and fitness.

2. *Physical fitness includes more than muscular strength.* The term *physical fitness* implies soundness of body organs such as the heart and lungs, a human mechanism that performs efficiently under exercise or work conditions (such as having sufficient stamina and strength to engage in vigorous physical activity), and a reasonable measure of skill in the performance of selected physical activities. Physical fitness is related to the tasks the person must perform, the potential for physical effort, and the relationship of physical fitness to total self. The same degree of physical fitness is not necessary for everyone. It should be sufficient to meet the requirements of the job plus a little extra as a reserve for emergencies. The student who plays football needs a different type of physical fitness from the student who plays in the school orchestra. The question "fitness for what?" must always be asked. Furthermore, determining the physical fitness of a person must be done in relation to that person's own human resources and not those of others. It depends on one's potentialities in the light of individual physical makeup. Finally, physical fitness cannot be considered by itself but, instead, as it is affected by mental, emotional, and social factors as well. Human beings function as a whole and not as segmented parts.

3. *Physical education is not the same as health education.* Although closely allied, health and physical education are separate fields of specialization. Whereas physical education is concerned primarily with education of and through the physical, the school health program is concerned with teaching for health (e.g., imparting facts about good nutrition), living healthfully at school (e.g., providing a healthful physical and emotional environment), and providing services for health improvement (e.g., instituting measures for communicable disease control).

4. *Physical education contributes to physical fitness.* The student needs to engage in regular physical activity but, in addition, needs to un-

From Michelson, Mike: Judo: Now it's a safe family sport,
Today's Health, Feb., 1969.

These young persons are physically fit, meaning they have more than muscular strength.

derstand the impact this activity has on the body and mind. The student needs to have activities fitted to individual requirements but also to have these activities conducted in a safe and healthful environment. The student should develop skill in various sports but also should develop skill in first aid and home nursing. These are only a few examples of how the physical education program helps to achieve the objective of physical fitness.

5. *Physical education must be an integral part of the educational program to achieve the goal of physical fitness most effectively.* This subject is not a frill or appendage of the school's curriculum or a means for entertaining students. It should be a vital part of every educational program in this country. Furthermore, such a concept must be repeatedly injected into programming, scheduling, and other practices that reflect the true educational philosophy of each school.

6. *Good leadership is the key to effective physical education.* The excellent physical education teacher is not someone who merely looks healthy, can produce a string of sports victories,

or give a good speech before the Rotary Club. Leadership is basic to the physical education profession, and this means men and women who know their subject, the boys and girls they are teaching, and the best methods and techniques for teaching.

7. *Physical fitness is not synonymous with physical education.* Physical fitness is *one* objective of physical education. It is important to have physically fit boys and girls. However, as long as the word *education* is a part of the term *physical education,* there are other responsibilities. Developing physical skills, imparting knowledge about the human organism, and using the body as a vehicle for achieving desirable social traits also represent desirable goals. Any program or curriculum aimed merely at building strength and muscle is failing in its educational mission.

8. *Interschool athletics represent only one part of the total physical education program that contributes to physical fitness.* The school physical education program includes the class program for all students, the adapted program that fits the activities to handicapped or atypical

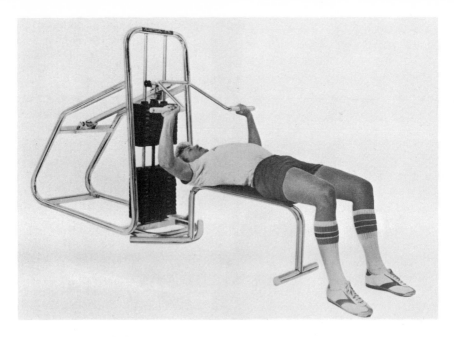

Special equipment has been devised to help those persons who desire to be physically fit. Universal's Centurion II Chest Press provides up to 390 pounds of lifting resistance. It includes Dynamic Variable Resistance (DVR), which provides for maximum development of muscular strength throughout the movement cycle.

individuals, the intramural and extramural program that provides a laboratory experience for skills and knowledge imparted in the class program, and the interscholastic athletic program for those students with exceptional physical skill. All four of these aspects of the physical education program must function in a manner that affords balance and harmony and allows for the achievement of physical fitness and other objectives for *all* students.

9. *The development of physical skills is a major contribution to long-term physical fitness of students.* Obstacle courses and calisthenics represent forms of "canned" activities that yield organic benefits to the student, but a major contribution of any physical education program is to teach boys and girls a wide variety of physical skills. Skills are the motivating agents that will accelerate a student to engage in activities and promote physical fitness, not only in the present but throughout a lifetime.

10. *Administrative support and understanding are needed to achieve physical fitness.* The quality of school physical education programs will be largely determined by the administrative leadership of the school and community. Boards of education, superintendents of schools, principals, and other administrative officials will decide the prestige these programs have in the eyes of the students, whether credit is given to the subjects when calculating the requirements for graduation, how much money is provided in the budget for their development, the attention given to girls as well as to boys, the degree of emphasis on physically underdeveloped students compared with gifted athletes, and the answers to other administrative matters that affect the physical fitness of students.

PATHS TO PHYSICAL FITNESS

The American Medical Association has outlined seven paths that lead to physical fitness. The physical educator should recognize the many-faceted approach to physical fitness and thereby understand that this quality cannot be achieved solely through physical activity.

1. *Proper medical care* — To be physically fit requires regular medical examinations, immunizations against communicable diseases, emergency care, and prompt treatment by qualified medical personnel when such care is warranted.

2. *Nutrition* — "You are what you eat" has much meaning in regard to physical fitness. The right kind of food should be eaten in the right amounts.

3. *Dental services* — Good oral hygiene is essential to physical fitness. This means regular visits to the dentist, treatment of dental caries, and proper mastication.

4. *Exercise* — Exercise is important, but to have a salutary effect there must be a proper selection of activities adapted to the age, condition, and other needs of the individual, together with proper exposure to these activities in terms of time and intensity of workout.

5. *Satisfying work* — Work that is adapted to one's interests and abilities and performed in a satisfying working climate is essential to physical fitness. There should be good mental attitude, recognition, and a sense of achievement and belonging.

6. *Healthy play and recreation* — To achieve physical fitness requires play and recreation in an atmosphere that has as its by-products fun, enjoyable companionship, and happy thoughts.

7. *Rest and relaxation* — Adequate sleep, rest, and relaxation are essential to good health and physical fitness.

COMPONENTS OF PHYSICAL FITNESS

Larson and Yocom* surveyed physiological research and listed the following ten factors as the components of physical fitness. These have implications for the physical education profession. They are presented here in modified form.

1. *Resistance to disease.* Heredity and environment both help to determine the ability of the individual to resist disease. Among the important environmental factors are diet, exercise and recreation, rest habits, and proper personal hygiene.

2. *Muscular strength and muscular endurance.* A person who has sufficient strength and endurance can sustain vigorous activity and perform strenuous work over an extended period. A physically fit individual must have strong and efficient muscles, a balanced proportion of good muscle fibers, the ability to bring the needed number of muscle fibers into play when there is work to be done by the muscles, efficient body levers, a working rhythm, and good coordination.

3. *Cardiovascular-respiratory endurance.* When a

---

*Larson, Leonard A., and Yocom, Rachael Dunaven: Measurement and evaluation in physical health, recreation, and education, St. Louis, 1951, The C. V. Mosby Co., pp. 158-162.

Courtesy Nautilus Sports/Medical Industries, DeLand, Fla.

Special equipment for persons who desire to be physically fit.

person contracts a series of muscle groups over a period of time long enough to put a strain on the circulatory and respiratory systems, but without causing a stoppage of the work, that individual has cardiovascular-respiratory endurance. These two systems are important to fitness because they work together to supply the muscles with fuel and oxygen, both of which are needed for muscular contractions. The more efficient the cardiovascular and respiratory systems the longer the individual will be able to sustain work, since the muscles will be well supplied with their fuel and oxygen. The individual who has a high degree of this kind of endurance has improved physical fitness, since the muscles receive large supplies of fuel and oxygen; pulse rate is slower and blood pressure is lower; the lungs have a larger surface area, allowing for the absorption of more oxygen by the blood; the supply of red corpuscles is larger, which also aids in increasing the oxygen supply; and susceptibility to fatigue is decreased.

4. *Muscular power.* Muscular power is explosive power such as that needed for putting the shot, high

jumping, and sprinting. A person who has muscular power also has two of the components of muscular power: strength and speed. The powerful individual can use speed and strength in an efficient, coordinated, and skillful manner.

5. *Flexibility*. Total body flexibility depends on the flexibility of the individual body joints and their supporting structures. Flexibility infers that the body is capable of making a wide range of movements, such as those needed for swimming, diving, and tumbling. The more flexible a person is the less energy is spent in accomplishing a skill.

6. *Speed*. A person who possesses speed is able to make a series of similar movements in a short span of time. Speed in swimming relates to the number of arm and leg strokes a swimmer takes in a given period of time. Muscular strength and the aspect of speed are highly related.

7. *Agility*. The agile individual can change body position in space efficiently and easily. Agility, strength, and endurance are important factors in agility. Agility is particularly important to the hurdler, lacrosse player, and diver.

8. *Coordination*. The coordinated individual is able to put together a series of movements into a flowing and rhythmical pattern. Different kinds of activities and bodily movements require different kinds of coordination. Agility, balance, and speed are important components of coordination.

9. *Balance*. Balance is the maintenance of equilibrium through neuromuscular control. Many physical education skills, such as tumbling, trampolining, and skiing, require good balance. Coordination is a factor in balance and, for some skills, agility also plays a part.

10. *Accuracy*. The accurate individual can control the movement of one object toward another, such as pitching in baseball, throwing for a goal in lacrosse, or casting a fishing fly. Although there is some relationship between accuracy and balance, they are not related closely enough to have a strong dependency on each other.

EXERCISE AND PHYSICAL FITNESS

Surveys have shown that coronary heart disease occurs twice as frequently in the sedentary as in active individuals. Diseases such as diabetes, duodenal ulcer, low back pain, and certain emotional problems have also been found to have a higher incidence among more sedentary individuals.

Coronary heart disease is the United States' greatest killer and claims more than 700,000

persons annually. It causes death in 40% of men in the age group of 40 to 59 years.* Autopsies have discovered early development of heart disease in soldiers killed in action and young people killed in automobile accidents. There are numerous coronary risk factors; however, considerable evidence does exist to indicate that physical inactivity plays an important role in coronary disease.

Dr. Menard Gertler, of New York University, has demonstrated that the physical activity of the U.S. Marines' basic training keeps the fat content of the blood down, even though the men were eating large amounts of calories each day consisting of animal fats — just the type that is supposed to increase fat and cholesterol in the blood.

A group of researchers from Harvard University investigated the farmers of a 2-mile-high

---

*Physical activity and coronary heart disease, Physical Fitness Research Digest, Series 2, No. 2, April, 1972.

Skiing represents an excellent sport for contributing to physical fitness (Northland College, Ashland, Wisconsin).

	EIGHTEEN TESTS OF FITNESS	NORMAL MEN (% PASSED)	NORMAL WOMEN (% PASSED)	YOU
1	Assume a diver's stance, arms outstretched, standing on your toes with your eyes closed. Hold this stance—and your balance—for 20 seconds.	95%	56%	
2	Squat with your palms on the floor. Tip forward, resting your legs on your elbows, toes off the ground in a squat handstand, and hold for 10 seconds.	25%	14%	
3	With your finger touching the floor, walk in a circle around it 10 times in 30 seconds. Then walk a straight 10-foot line within five seconds.	1%	36%	
4	Keeping your legs together and knees straight, bend at the waist and touch the floor with your finger tips. Women should touch palms of their hands.	75%	86%	
5	Slowly bend from a sitting position, knees flat, until your forehead is eight inches, or two fists, one atop the other, from the floor.	67%	73%	
6	Lying on your stomach with your feet pinned to the floor and your fingers laced behind your neck, raise your chin until it is 18 inches from the floor.	35%	25%	
7	Kneel with your insteps flat on the floor. Using just your back and arms, spring erect, both feet together, and hold your balance for three seconds.	65%	25%	
8	From a standing position, jack-spring from the floor, touching your toes at waist height without bending your legs. Repeat five times quickly.	38%	13%	
9	Repeat six times: (1) squat; (2) kick legs backward; (3) kick legs forward between arms; (4) turn over; (5) squat; (6) stand.	10%	14%	
10	With a partner who is lying down (and who is within 10 pounds of your weight), lift and carry him fireman-style—all in 10 seconds from floor to carry.	94%	54%	
11	With your hands on your hips and the back of your head on a partner's knee or the edge of a chair or sofa, hold your body rigid for 30 seconds.	78%	66%	
12	Lying prone, with arms outstretched, lift your midsection four inches in an extended press-up using just hands and toes. Women may use forearms.	1%	60%	
13	Do a standing broad jump the length of your height. If you are under 25, the distance should be the same as your height plus one foot.	71%	8%	
14	Do 15 full-length push-ups with your hands positioned beneath your shoulders. Women should do 30 push-ups, keeping their knees on the floor.	65%	34%	
15	Chin yourself, or, on your back, straddled by a partner, grasp his hands and pull up until your chest strikes his legs. Men repeat 20 times, women 10.	79%	73%	
16	Sit on the floor with your knees stiff. With hands on hips, lean back so your legs come off the floor in a V-sit, and hold 60 seconds.	68%	40%	
17	Run in place for two minutes at double time, or 180 steps per minute. Then take three breaths and hold your breath for 30 seconds.	15%	12%	
18	Do 200 two-foot hops, 200 straddle hops, 200 scissor, or alternate stride, hops, 50 hops on each foot and 50 squat jumps.	9%	6%	
	TOTAL PASSING SCORES	10	7	

Categories (left margin): BALANCE (1-3), AGILITY (4-6), POWER (7-9), FLEXIBILITY (10-12), STRENGTH (13-15), ENDURANCE (16-18)

A stiff but reliable test of fitness.

Swiss village in the Alps. Each day the men climbed 3,000 feet to farm a plateau. Although they ate a high–animal fat diet, the blood cholesterol levels were down.

Other experiments have shown that exercise decreases the tendency of the blood to clot and increases the capacity of the blood to dissolve clots already formed.

In general, exercise lowers blood pressure and slows heart rate — two important considerations in heart conditions.

Being active is a continuing essential for good health. Exercise is needed all year long. The benefits of physical activity cannot be "canned up" when the temperature is hovering in the 80s and "dished out" as it drops into the 20s any more than the body can be put in cold storage on Labor Day and thawed on the Fourth of July. For proper functioning the human organism needs this essential ingredient on a regular basis, just as it demands nutritious food every day.

Many busy men and women limit their sports and activity to the summer months. There are others who even deplore the thought of getting into action at any time of the year.

Dr. Edward C. Schneider, a famous physiologist, after a lifetime study of the effects of exercise, came to the conclusion that: "Frequently repeated exercise, extending over months and years . . . is necessary for healthy existence; it is a physiologic need of a primitive kind which cannot safely be eliminated by civilization. It is difficult to find men who have been injured by muscular exercise but easy to find many who have failed of normal development and been ruined by the lack of it."

The "don'ts" of exercise are well known. Don't exercise after 40 years of age. Don't exercise when you're tired, when it's cold, or after eating. Don't exercise — it will injure your heart and you will die sooner. More should be said about the "dos." You do need exercise to get the most out of life. You do need exercise to keep in the best of health. Exercise is good for the normal heart. Exercise contributes to good mental health.

Dr. George W. Calver, former physician for the Supreme Court and Congress, outlined ten commandments for keeping government officials fit. Two of these were "exercise rational-

ly" and "play enthusiastically." As Dr. Calver counseled: "Give 5% of your time to keeping well and you won't have to give 100% getting over being sick."

The worth of exercise rests on a basic principle, the law of use. Hippocrates called attention to this many hundreds of years ago, when he said: "That which is used develops and that which is not used wastes away." Modern medical practice recognizes the law of use.

Although there are many claims for exercise that are false, many accusations against it are also false. Two of these are that exercise will shorten life and that it is harmful to the heart. Sir Alan Rook, former Senior Health Officer of Cambridge University, compared the longevity of 834 sportsmen from his university with a group of "intellectuals" and men chosen at random. Sir Alan concluded: "No evidence could be adduced from the information available that cardiovascular causes of death were more prominent in the sportsmen or occurred at an earlier age." Other research studies have come to the same conclusion.

Medical authorities state that proper exercise cannot harm the heart. Dr. E. Cowles Andrus, former president of the American Heart Association, advised: ". . . it is clear that strenuous exercise, properly supervised, does not cause disease in the normal heart." Dr. Paul Dudley White, the late world-renowned authority on heart disease, reasoned this way: Men who slow down at 40 years of age may have a heart attack sooner. For some reason that cannot be explained at the present time, such a slowdown seems to increase the possibility of hardening of the arteries. He capped his reasoning with this remark: "The general warning to stop vigorous exercise at 40 seems to me ridiculous." Dr. White cited the following five benefits from exercise:

1. Maintains muscle tone.
2. Relieves nervous tensions and provides relaxation.
3. Aids digestion.
4. Helps to control obesity.
5. Improves functioning of the lungs by deepening of respiration.

In addition to Dr. White's benefits, other advantages of exercise cited by experts include the following:

1. Added strength and endurance help in performing daily tasks with less fatigue.
2. Better movement accrues for the human body.
3. Exercise helps to maintain health of the heart and blood vessels.
4. Exercise helps in the building of a desirable self-concept.
5. Exercise helps in the prevention of accidents.

Other fitness myths that have been cited include the following: middle age begins at 40 years of age—chronologically it starts at about 26 years of age; hardening of the arteries is a natural part of getting old—not necessarily, blood vessels are partially dependent on regular exercise to keep in shape; rest or sleep is the best way to eliminate fatigue—not always, physical activity can act as an antidote to some kinds of fatigue; youngsters will be harmed through sustained exercise—it depends, if they are fit, their physical endurance is great and the exercise will be conducive to good health; and there are shortcuts to fitness—no, the truth rests in a continuing program of activity, good nutrition, rest, sleep, relaxation, and adequate health care.

The values of exercise are not limited to the body; they also contribute to sound mental health. Exercise makes a person feel better. I spoke with at least 1,000 people on this subject. In addition, my students have surveyed at least 10,000 more. Comments follow a pattern: ''I feel more alive when I exercise''; ''I have more energy''; ''I don't feel as tired in the evening''; ''I can do a lot more work.'' Those who exercise regularly never fail to mention that exercise makes them feel better. If people feel better, their attitude toward others will probably be friendlier. They are happier and make wiser decisions, and the world in general looks better.

The benefits to sound mental health are especially great when a person engages in games and sports. One finds release from tensions, relaxes, forgets troubles, and loses oneself in the game. Dr. William Menninger, the famous psychiatrist, pointed out that physical activity provides an outlet for instinctive aggressive drives by enabling an individual to ''blow off steam,'' provides relaxation and is a supplement for daily work. He stressed the fact that ''recreation, which is literally re-creating relaxation from regular activity, is a morale builder. It is not a luxury, a waste of time or a sin.''

Socialization is also provided in many games and sports. Psychologists say every human being has the desire to belong to a club, gang, or association. This is an essential human need. Games and sports offer opportunity for recognition and a feeling that one belongs to a group. Like the ex-convict said who was caught in an Eastern city: ''I'm glad to go back to jail. Here I'm nothing, but up there I'm first baseman on the baseball team.''

Although exercise has many physical, mental, and social benefits, this does not mean a person should rush out and buy a tennis racket and schedule three sets of tennis for Saturday afternoon. To secure these benefits, one must exercise with discretion. Following are some suggestions that reflect the opinion of medical experts and provide good advice for physical educators:

1. Encourage a thorough medical examination at regular intervals to determine the type of exercise most beneficial to the individual.
2. Encourage people to select, if possible, a sport or an activity around the house, such as gardening, in preference to calisthenics. The mental and social values are greater.
3. After 40 years of age, encourage people to cut down on the ''explosive'' sports requiring fast starts, quick stops, and prolonged activity without rest. Examples are badminton, tennis, handball singles, basketball, and squash.
4. If a person is out of training in a sport, advise him or her to return to action gradually. A little today and a little more tomorrow is a good prescription.
5. Encourage persons to exercise out-of-doors if possible.
6. Encourage persons to select activities that are adapted to them.
7. Encourage people to give their full attention to the activity and leave their worries at the office.
8. Encourage individuals engaging in sports that involve body contact or other hazards to use essential protective equipment, especially for head, neck, eyes, and teeth.
9. Encourage individuals to play in areas where safety precautions have been taken to avoid the danger of injuries.
10. Encourage individuals to participate with others of the approximate same degree of

skill, training, and size when these factors are pertinent to the competition.

11. The way a person recuperates after exercise should be a guide in its wise use. Breathing and heart rate should not be excessively fast 10 minutes after stopping exercise. Extreme fatigue should not persist 2 hours after stopping. The activity should not cause broken sleep at night or a tired feeling the next day. If any of these symptoms occur, the activity should be cut down. If they continue, the person should see a physician. Exercise is good, but it must be adapted to the individual's needs.

Exercise and general health

Exercise and training have important implications for the general health of a person. Studies of 5,000 patients at the Columbia Presbyterian Medical Center in New York City and the Institute of Physical Medicine and Rehabilitation, New York University, indicated that approximately 80% of patients with low back pain experienced this difficulty because of muscle weakness or stiffness. Follow-up studies showed that pain symptoms decreased as muscle strength and flexibility increased. If exercise was stopped, the ailments returned. Other

Table 12-1. Physical fitness ratings of popular sports in the United States*

Sport	Endurance	Agility	Strength			Age range recommended
			Leg	Abdomen	Arm and shoulders	
Archery	L	L	L	M	H	All ages
Badminton	H-M	H	H	M	M	Singles to 50
Basketball	H	H	H	L	L	Under 30
Baseball	M	H	H	M	M	Under 45
Bicycling	M	L	H	L	L	All ages
Bowling	L	L	M	L	M	All ages
Boating	M	L	M	M	H	All ages
Field hockey	H	H	H	M	M	Under 30
Football	H	H	H	H	H	Under 30
Golf	L	L	M	L	L	All ages
Handball	H-M	H	H	M	H	Singles to 45
Heavy apparatus Tumbling	L	H	H-M	H	H	Under 45
Hiking	M	L	H	L	L	All ages
Horseshoes	L	L	L	L	M	All ages
Judo	H	H	H	H	H	Under 30
Lifesaving	H	M	H	H	H	Under 45
Skating Speed	H	M	H	M	L	Under 45
Figure	M	H	H	L	L	All ages
Skiing	H	H	H	M	M	Under 45
Soccer	H	H	H	M	L	Under 45
Swimming Recreational	M	L	M	L	M	All ages
Competitive	H	M	H	M	H	Under 30
Table tennis	L	M	M	L	L	All ages
Tennis	H-M	H	H	M	M	Singles to 45
Track Distance	H	L	H	M	M	Under 45
Sprints	M	M	H	M	M	Under 45
Volleyball	L	M	M	L	M	All ages
Wrestling	H	H	H	H	H	Under 30

Key: H, high; M, medium; L, low (fitness values).
*Steinhaus, Arthur H.: How to keep fit and like it, Chicago, 1957, The Dartnell Corp., p. 70; copyrighted by George Williams College.

studies in recent years have added to a gradually accumulating volume of evidence that exercise has a salutary impact on degenerative diseases, on slowing the aging process, on the ability of an individual to meet emergencies, and on the prevention of vascular degeneration.

Steinhaus took twenty-five popular sports and rated each in respect to various components of physical fitness. The participant can use Table 12-1 as a checklist to determine what activities will best meet one's fitness needs.

Aerobic exercise

More and more people are accepting the fact that aerobic exercise is essential to a healthy cardiovascular system. In brief, aerobic exercise is activity that can be sustained for an extended period of time without building an oxygen debt in the muscles. It is a type of exercise that overloads the heart and lungs and causes them to work harder than they do when a person is at rest. Aerobic exercise is being engaged in by many Americans in forms such as jogging, skipping rope, bicycling, swimming, and walking.

Some of the benefits of aerobic exercise include the ability to utilize more oxygen during strenuous exercise, a lower heart rate at rest, the production of less lactic acid, and greater endurance. Also, many exercise physiologists have found that it reduces blood pressure and changes blood chemistry. It also improves the efficiency of the heart. More evidence is needed to substantiate the belief by some persons that aerobic exercise is responsible for the development of supplemental blood vessels to the heart, which would be helpful in the event of a heart attack, and also that such exercise results in increasing the size of coronary arteries and thus assisting the flow of blood to the heart when the artery is narrowed by a clot or atherosclerosis.

Before a person engages in strenuous exercise, it is recommended that a physician's approval and/or in many instances a stress test be taken. Those persons who are approved for activity should plan a progressive program, start-

Physical fitness testing in a high school in Tainan, Taiwan. This was part of the test program carried out in Southeast Asia to compare results with those of the performance of American children.

Courtesy Dr. Gunsun Hoh, Republic of China.

ing slowly and gradually increasing the intensity of the exercise until they reach an exercise level that conditions their heart. It is suggested that this level represent 70% to 85% of a person's maximal heart or pulse rate. To roughly calculate one's maximum heart rate, subtract the person's age from the number 220 and then take 70% to 85% of this figure. Thus, if a person is 45 years old, the maximal heart rate would be 175 beats per minute, and therefore the pulse rate to use as a target would be about 122 to 145 beats per minute. Taking one's pulse rate at the carotid artery in the neck represents an accurate way to obtain this figure. It is further recommended that a person should aim at reaching his or her target zone a minimum of three times a week, not on consecutive days, and sustaining the target pulse rate for about 20 minutes each time. Prior to the strenuous exercise there should be a warming-up period and after the exercise a cool-down period.

Isotonic and isometric exercises*

Muscles function by contracting in such a manner that the muscle shortens and the ends are brought together (concentric), or the muscle lengthens and the ends go away from the center as in the beginning of a pull-up when one lowers oneself into a hanging position (eccentric) (isotonic). Or, a muscle contracts when the muscle builds up tension and holds without any shortening or lengthening (static or isometric is derived from the words *iso,* meaning same, and *metric,* meaning length).

If claims of isometrics are true, the value of this system of physical activity is not limited in use to star high school, college, and professional athletes. It can be used by anyone who has the desire to improve strength. Isometrics may be better suited to a slightly weak person than to the superhealthy, physically fit person because improvement will be more rapid and pronounced. This fact was demonstrated as far back as 1958, when isometrics proved their value to some average high school boys. In a study conducted by Rarick and Larsen, the students

performed a daily, single, 6-second workout. After only 6 weeks the boys, regardless of whether they were tall, short, or thin, improved their strength. This experiment, together with other studies, impressed many professional physical educators with the worth of isometrics for students.

What are the differences between isometric exercise and isotonic exercise? Since physical educators are interested in building strength, a first concern is to know what strength is. A professor at the University of California defines it as the ability to work against resistance. In everyday terms it is known as possessing that physical quality which enables a person to lift a 50-pound bag of cement, climb a rope in the gymnasium, or lift a girl in his arms.

Strength, when combined with other physical elements, yields additional qualities important to any person who wants to get the most out of his or her body. For example, strength combined with speed gives power. Power is that quality that permits Julius Erving to jump high and snare rebounds off the board, Nancy Lopez to hit the ball 200 yards down the fairway, Reggie Jackson to throw a baseball with rifle-shot precision to home plate from center field, and Jim Ryun to sprint like a deer down the cinder path.

The traditional way of building strength is to get muscles into action by increasing the resistance offered them. Terms commonly used for this form of exercise are *isotonic* and *dynamic.* The classical story is of the man who started lifting a small animal weighing about 25 pounds and continued to lift the animal each day until it became full grown, weighing over 200 pounds. The man's muscles gained strength as the workload was progressively increased from day to day. The people who lift weights in the school gymnasium or YMCA are trying to do the same thing—build strength by following what is called the principle of overload. They gradually increase the amount of weight they lift.

In isotonic or dynamic contraction the muscle shortens, and the resistance, such as that offered when a stack of books is lifted from a school desk, is overcome. Physical work is accomplished by utilizing movement and resis-

---

*This discussion is based on Bucher, Charles A., and Nagel, John: Isometrics: new method for new muscles, unpublished.

tance in the exercise. Isometric contractions, on the other hand, are static types of contractions, since there is no joint or muscle movement. Instead, the muscle is put in a state of tension. All the energy that is expended in contracting the muscle isometrically is converted into heat. The resistance, whether it be a radiator, desk, office file, wall, or anything immovable, cannot be overcome. In other words, a force is exerted against an immovable object in which neither muscle nor object moves but in which the pressure or exertion is applied to create a tension within the contracting muscle.

Here is a simple example. Place yourself between two walls. Put your back against one wall and your hands against the other wall. Now push with all your strength against the wall. Even though you grunt and groan and give it all you have as you contract your muscles maximally, it is impossible to move the resistance, in this case the wall. This is the way strength is developed in isometric exercise. As you can see, it is a simple procedure. There are still several points that need to be known before starting to exercise, such as how much force to apply, how long to apply it, and what to do after a desirable level of strength has been achieved.

Where did it all start? When did isometric exercise start? What is its history? Briefly, the principles underlying isometric contractions have been public domain for years. One physiologist relates how scientists shortly after World War I used frogs in their experiments. In 1953 two German physiologists, Dr. T. Hettinger and Dr. E. A. Muller, did considerable research and published their findings in a German magazine. This article attracted attention and created an interest in isometric exercises. In the United States such men as Steinhaus, Karpovich, Drury, McCloy, Rasch, Morehouse, and Bender, realizing the significance of the Germans' study, started conducting their own experiments. Many of their findings confirmed the work done in Europe—isometric exercises are of real value in building strength in human beings.

In the last 20 to 25 years an increased interest in applying this method of exercise to patients and in the treatment of injuries was developed.

Probably the greatest boost was given when it was found that isometric contractions had value for athletic performance, which greatly interested school and college personnel and the coaches, trainers, and owners of professional teams. Today, although some physiologists have reservations about all the claims made for isometrics, it is generally agreed that they can play an important role in developing body strength.

Some research findings on isometric and isotonic exercises. Physical educators should be acquainted with the research in respect to isometric and isotonic exercises and use these studies as a guide to their utilization of these techniques. Selected research studies* indicate the following:

1. Both forms of exercise, isotonic and isometric, build muscular strength. However, the result of over a dozen studies show little if any difference in the effectiveness of the two forms of achieving strength increase.
2. Isometrics can be carried on in many different locations, including one's office or when waiting for a train.
3. The motivation factor is seldom as great in the case of isometrics as with isotonics.
4. Studies have now shown a strength gain of 5% per week (claimed by some persons) for 10 weeks (50% for the entire period) when a single 6-second contraction was used against resistance equal to two thirds of the muscle's strength. Most studies support a strength gain, but it has not been as great. Many of them show only 2% or 3% a week.
5. Rarick and Larsen found that strength that was retained after the exercise programs were followed over a period of time was greater in the case of isotonic than isometric exercises.
6. Bender, Kaplan, and Johnson found that isometric contractions were often harmful when exercises of a gross nature, such as pressing the whole body upward against a bar, were used. Many times the wrong muscles are developed.
7. Bender and Kaplan found that isometric contractions must be executed at various angles throughout the range of motion if benefits are

---

*Clarke, H. Harrison: Physical fitness newsletter, Research Review, No. 3, May, 1965. For other references, see end of chapter.

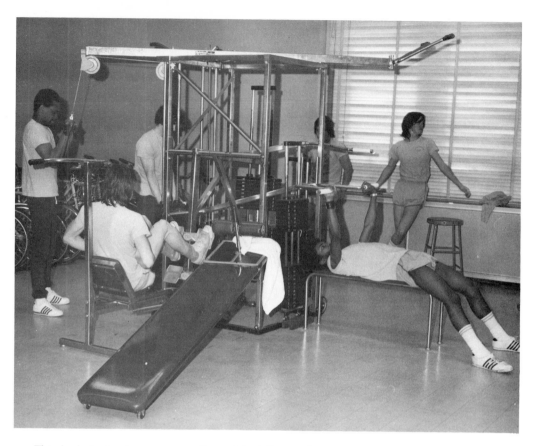

The physical education program at Staten Island Community College in New York has equipment that makes it possible to participate in both isotonic and isometric exercise.

to accrue, rather than at one point in the range of motion of a joint.

8. Royce found that there is a greater interference in circulation to an exercising muscle in isometric than in isotonic contractions.

9. Clarke found that oxygen debt is 40% greater in isometric exercises.

10. Thompson found that the effects of isometric and isotonic work have different effects on blood pressure.

11. Berger found that isotonic exercises will improve jumping ability better than will isometrics.

12. The evidence from existing research seems to favor isotonic exercise rather than isometric exercise as a means of conditioning a muscle.

TRAINING AND PHYSICAL FITNESS

There are many aspects of training that are pertinent to a high state of physical fitness.

Principles of training

Some principles of training have been compiled by Forbes Carlile.* These will be helpful to the physical educator who is interested in helping students achieve peak performance in sports or other forms of physical activity. They are presented in adapted form.

1. The training load should follow the principles of frequency and intensity. The load must be severe and frequently applied so that the body can adapt maximally to a particular activity.

2. Training is an individual problem. As such, factors like age, work and study load, physical makeup, time available for sleep and rest, and training facilities available are important considerations in arranging a training schedule for any person.

---

*Carlile, Forbes: Ten principles of training, Track Techniques **1**:23, Sept., 1960.

3. Physical and emotional stresses, in addition to the training exercise routine, must be taken into consideration for each individual. For example, conditions such as manual labor performed, daily traveling, and emotional pressures from home, school, and other sources are important considerations.
4. Excessive stress on the individual will lower the performance level, and therefore attention should be constantly given for manifestations of stress.
5. Periods of rest and physical and mental relaxation must be interwoven with doses of exercise to get the best results. This is true during a single training session as well as week by week.
6. Training for a particular sport and many times for different events within a sport (such as sprinters and distance runners in track) is specific and geared to the particular sport or event. Therefore training procedures for one sport or activity are not necessarily helpful for other sports or activities.
7. Flexibility and strength are two components that are essential to free-flowing movements and efficiency in sports performance. There should be provision for exercises that develop these qualities especially during the off-season. Such exercises should be carefully designed and directed at specific groups of muscles and joints. Scientifically designed weight-training exercises plus stretching exercises are especially good.
8. Interval training has been found to be one of the best procedures for a modern training schedule. This consists of rhythmically carrying out an activity from 30 to 60 seconds at fairly intense effort (but not all out). Each period of exercise is followed by 10 seconds to 2 minutes of slow recuperative activity.
9. Nutrition is an important consideration in any training schedule. Therefore the person in training should adhere to a good diet that contains the essential food groups.
10. Three popular conditioning and training techniques are as follows:
    a. *Circuit training*—this represents a series of exercises, usually ten, that are performed in a circuit and in a progressive manner, doing a prescribed allocation of work at each station, and then checking the progress against the clock. As the performer becomes stronger, the number of repetitions and the quality of the exercise

are increased. Activities should be selected with care.
    b. *Fartlek* (Swedish for speed play)—this is free-relaxed running. The course usually consists of a soft surface and considerable uphill and downhill running. The following schedule is recommended: (a) easy running for 5 to 10 minutes, (b) steady, fast running, (c) easy running with wind sprints for 50 to 60 yards, (d) rapid walking for 5 minutes, (e) uphill running, and (f) maintaining a fast pace for about 1 minute.
    c. *Interval training*—this has been briefly mentioned above. Four factors that are important in using this technique are as follows: (a) distance (to build endurance)—should be long enough to create a stress in the performer, (b) speed—runner increases speed over a designated distance that is possible to repeat allowing rest between each run, (c) number of repetitions—depends on its value or purpose, and (d) rest or recovery period—the recovery interval is gradually reduced as training progresses.
11. The most important fact in a program of training is to achieve the goals of physical readiness and psychological readiness when your schedule indicates it is important.

Effects of training

The results derived from regular period of muscular work or exercise are many and varied. Individuals who participate regularly in exercise adapted to their needs and thereby attain a state of physical fitness may be called "trained." Individuals who allow their muscles to get soft and flabby and are in a poor physical condition may be referred to as "untrained."

Space does not permit listing all the advantages of the "trained" state. Therefore certain advantages that seem to stand out as being important to the body's vital organs will be mentioned here.

Effects of training on general health of heart muscle. Evidence is available to show that the heart muscle increases in size through use. With greater demands placed on the heart as a result of physical activity, a hypertrophic condition exists. This is a healthy condition. The term *athletic heart* has often been used to

Training for athletic competition has many desirable effects.

connote a heart that has pathological or diseased indications because of participation in physical activity. Physiologists maintain this in incorrect. Instead, they indicate that an ''athletic heart'' is a normal condition which follows the law of use. The law of use may be stated in these terms: ''That which is used develops and that which is not used atrophies.'' This applies to all the muscles of the body. Since the heart is a muscle, this condition indicates a stronger and better developed heart.

There is considerable controversy concerning whether a heart may be impaired by extreme muscular effort. It is generally agreed that a child with a normal heart cannot damage this vital organ by exercise. The controversy concerns individuals of 35 or 40 years of age. The proponents of the theory that a sound and normal heart cannot be impaired by activity are many, Others believe that sudden, explosive exertions may cause heart strain. A report published by the American Association for Health, Physical Education, and Recreation, prepared after considerable research by physicians, physiologists, and health and physical educators, points out that the normal heart and circulatory system become stronger through use. However, the report continues, strenuous competitive physical activity should not be engaged in by older persons *unless* they have done this regularly and have kept themselves physically fit.

Effects of training on stroke volume of heart. As a result of research on such men as DeMar, the great marathon runner, Olympic athletes, and others, it is generally agreed that there is a greater volume of blood per heartbeat pumped through the body of the trained person than the untrained person. The research on DeMar showed that his heart pumped 22 liters of blood as contrasted with 10.2 liters in an untrained individual.

Effects of training on pulse rate. As a result of evidence gathered from tests performed on Olympic athletes and others, there appears to be evidence that the trained individual has a lower pulse rate than the untrained person. One estimate has been made that the human heart beats from six to eight beats slower when the person is in training compared with out of training. In many athletes, pulse rates are ten, twenty, and as much as thirty beats lower than in

those individuals who follow sedentary pursuits.

Before exercise the trained individual's heart has a lower rate than an untrained person's heart, but under exercise both increase about the same proportion.

Individuals convalescing from an illness show by their pulse rates the effects of training. As their condition improves and they become more physically fit, their pulse rate decreases. If the pulse rate does not go down, it is interpreted as a lack of improvement in their physical fitness.

The pulse rate of the trained individual returns to normal much more quickly after exercise than does the pulse rate of the untrained individual. Many cardiovascular tests have been patterned on this premise.

Effects of training on blood makeup. The rate of lactic acid formation is lower in the trained individual, resulting in a lower blood lactate concentration. This allows for greater work output on the part of the trained individual. Lactic acid is the substance that is transferred from glucose when a muscle contracts. The more lactic acid, the more fatigued an individual will become. Lactic acid begins to appear in the blood when the oxygen supply gets low and is inadequate. It escapes from the muscles and goes into the blood. Some of it is buffered. The liver transforms some into glycogen, and then it is sent back to the muscles as needed in the form of blood glucose. Some is eliminated through the kidneys.

In addition to the lower rate of lactic acid formation, another effect of training on the blood is the reduction in the osmotic resistance of red corpuscles. It is thought that this may result from the rise in body temperature during muscular work.

Effects of training on arterial blood pressures. Schneider and Karpovich point out that experiments on DeMar showed that the increase in blood pressure is less in the trained individual than in the untrained individual. They further point out that under exercise DeMar's systolic blood pressure increase was 50 mm. Hg, whereas the increase in an untrained man, who was used as a means of comparison, was 125 mm. Hg.

Karpovich, in a later work, refers to addition-

Table 12-2. Average pulse rates in physical fitness test (male employees of Metropolitan Life Insurance Company)*

Characteristics	Number of employees	Before test	Pulse rate per minute		
			Upon completion of exercise	One minute after exercise	Two minutes after exercise
Age					
Under 30	412	71.7	125.5	109.6	98.4
30 and over	369	72.0	128.2	112.1	101.3
Smoking habits					
Nonsmoker	587	71.4	126.7	110.4	99.2
Smoker	194	72.9	127.0	112.0	101.3
Physical activity					
Active	209	71.9	123.7	108.4	97.1
Inactive	572	71.7	127.9	111.7	100.7
Weight					
Normal	660	71.5	125.9	109.9	98.7
Overweight	121	73.7	131.5	115.9	105.3
Total	781	71.8	126.8	110.8	99.7

*Average pulse rates in physical fitness test of male employees of Metropolitan Life Insurance Company, Statistical Bulletin. **58:**2, April, 1977. Courtesy Metropolitan Life Insurance Company.

al studies in which this condition has also held true.

The relation of blood pressure to muscular work depends on duration of the exercise, intensity, and rate of performance.

Effects of training on red corpuscles. There is considerable disagreement as to the effect of training on the red corpuscle count. However, there appears to be agreement that, as a result of training, the bone marrow becomes redder, indicating an increased rate of blood manufacture. As a result of this agreement, it seems reasonable to conclude that there is an increase in the number of red corpuscles in the trained individual.

The person who follows a sedentary or inactive existence and then pursues strenuous work destroys a considerable number of red corpuscles, which it takes several days to restore. A period of anemia results, and the individual is not fit to follow strenuous muscular effort for a period of several days. However, the trained individual has developed the red marrow in the bones. Any ordinary destruction of red corpuscles, for any given time, does not affect the individual because the loss is quickly made up. In the trained individual there is a better balance between the destruction and manufacture of red corpuscles.

Effects of training on white blood cells. More knowledge is needed concerning the effects of training on the white blood cells. However, it seems clear that white blood cells, or leukocytes, increase in number in the blood after a period of muscular work, whether it be mild or severe. The increase in white blood cells seems to vary in proportion to the degree of intensity of muscular work. It is thought by many that the increase can be credited to a redistribution of the cells in the vascular system.

Effects of training on respiration. Evidence is available to show that there are several effects of training on the respiratory system. Some of these are as follows:

1. There is greater expansion of the chest. This is true during the early years but not especially during adulthood.
2. There is a slower rate of breathing. Some evidence shows that the trained person takes as little as six to eight breaths a minute compared with eighteen to twenty by the untrained person.
3. The depth of the chest is increased.
4. The blood is exposed to oxygen over a greater area. This is not true of sedentary or inactive individuals because a greater portion of their lungs becomes closed off to air that is inhaled.

5. There is deep diaphragmatic breathing. In the untrained person the diaphragm moves little.
6. In performing similar work, a trained individual takes in smaller amounts of air and absorbs oxygen from the air in greater amounts than does an individual not in training. It is believed that the increased number of capillaries in the lungs, caused by greater amounts of blood being exposed to the air at any given time, is responsible for this economy in respiration.

Effects of training on the muscular system. Evidence is available to show that there are several beneficial effects of training on the muscular system. Some of these are as follows:

1. The sarcolemma of the muscle fibers (the part that surrounds each fiber by a connective tissue sheath) becomes thicker and stronger.
2. The amount of connective tissue within the muscle thickens.
3. The size of the muscle increases. It is believed that the muscle fibers increase in size but not in number.
4. The muscle has greater strength. It is necessary to exercise a muscle to increase its strength.
5. The muscle gains in endurance. An experiment is reported on an ergograph being attached to the flexor muscles of a finger and the number of contractions recorded. The increase was from 273 contractions to 918.
6. There is a chemical change in the muscle—an increase in phosphocreatine content, glycogen, nonnitrogenous substances, and hemoglobin. All these aid the muscles in working more efficiently.
7. The nerve impulse travels more readily across the motor end plate in the muscle fiber.
8. There is a greater number of capillaries. This results in better circulation of blood to muscles.

Effects of training on the digestive and excretory systems. Exercise helps to keep the digestive and excretory organs in good condition. The nerves and muscles of the stomach and intestines become well toned and better able to function in an efficient manner. Also, exercise usually makes a person hungry, and, in general, hunger can improve digestion.

Effects of training on the nervous system. Nerves and muscles work together because the muscles are controlled by the nerves. Messages are relayed by the nerves to the muscles, which react in the way the individual wishes, whether by running, playing a musical instrument, or hitting a tennis ball. Consequently, any kind of muscular exercise enhances nerve-muscle coordination. Furthermore, nervous fatigue may be lessened by pleasant physical activity because the nervous fatigue that has accumulated as a result of anxiety or mental work is offset through muscular activity.

Effects of training on the endocrine system. There is some evidence that the hormones produced by the adrenal medulla (adrenaline and noradrenaline) are affected by training. The plasma level of noradrenaline has been found to increase considerably during exercise, whereas that of adrenaline is only slightly increased. Increased amounts of noradrenaline are responsible for vasoconstriction of the heart, whereas increased amounts of adrenaline are responsible for the increased metabolic rate of the body. Adrenaline and noradrenaline prepare the organism for action by increasing the blood pressure and heart rate of the individual. These hormones are also responsible for the release of more energy by the organism, thus aiding the individual in strenuous activities.

Effects of training on body temperature. Increased muscular activity generates more body heat. In demanding activities, such as long-distance running, the deep muscle temperature of the body has been known to rise to over 100° F. Such increases in muscle temperature also produce a rise in body temperature. The heat that has been generated by such an activity must be dissipated. Sweating is the prime body mechanism for the dissipation of heat. Research has shown that during training, the composition of sweat differs from one person to another. The larger, heavier person is likely to produce more sweat than the smaller person. The skin temperature of the organism is related to the environment more so than the body temperature is. Exercising in a cold environment may result in the skin temperature dropping down to 80° F., although the body temperature, because of the muscular activity that is taking place, still remains over 100° F.

Effects of training on women. There has been concern in recent years that training can interfere with female sexual and reproductive functions. Research by Klaus* has indicated that women are more susceptible to athletic injuries than men. There is considerable evidence to support the claim that women should not engage in training during the later stages of pregnancy because of the greater demands placed on the heart. However, observation of female athletes has shown that there is no disturbance on the onset of menarche. It had been thought that athletic women would have difficulty in childbirth because of the development of the abdominal walls. Research by Gendel† has indicated that athletic women have quick and easy births. Gendel points out that women should participate in training programs that increase their abdominal strength and circulation because of the beneficial effects this can have on their reproductive ability.

Differences between trained and untrained individuals. A trained individual is in a better state of physical fitness than the individual who follows a sedentary, inactive life. When two individuals, one trained and one untrained, of approximately the same build are performing the

*Klaus, E. J.: The athletic status of woman. In Jokl, E., and Simon, E., editors: International research in sport and physical education, Springfield, Ill., 1964, Charles C Thomas, Publisher.
†Gendel, Evelyn S.: Women and the medical aspects of sports, Journal of School Health **37:**427, 1967.

same amount of moderate muscular work, there is evidence to indicate that the trained individual has a lower oxygen consumption, lower pulse rate, larger stroke volume per heartbeat, less rise in blood pressure, greater red and white corpuscle counts, slower rate of breathing, lower rate of lactic acid formation, and a faster return to normal of blood pressure and heart rate. The heart becomes more efficient and is able to circulate more blood while beating less frequently. Furthermore, in work of a strenuous nature that cannot be performed for any great period of time, the trained individual has greater endurance, a capacity for higher oxygen consumption, and a faster return to normal of heart rate and blood pressure. Training results in a more efficient organism. Since a greater efficiency of heart action enables a larger flow of blood to reach the muscles and thus ensure an increased supply of fuel and oxygen, more work is performed at less cost; improvements in strength, power, neuromuscular coordination, and endurance occur; there is a better coordination and timing of movements; and an improved state of physical fitness results.

Oxygen and training and fitness

One of the most controversial questions in athletics concerns the use of oxygen as an aid to performance. It might seem logical to some per-

Courtesy National Collegiate Athletic Association.
NCAA championship competition in water polo requires high standards of training.

sons that oxygen would increase fitness by producing a greater capacity for exertion and recovery. However, because oxygen cannot be stored, this is not the case. Research by Miller* has shown that inhalation of oxygen before an event does not affect performance or rate of recovery. Miller, in a study of performers using the treadmill, indicated that the greatest benefit to the performer that oxygen may have is psychological. Most coaches agree that athletes should not be conditioned to the use of oxygen because of the psychological effect it may have if the athlete is deprived of its use at an important event.

Environment and training and fitness

It is important to have an understanding of the effects of the environment on physiological state. The environment characterized by pollution will definitely decrease participation in activities. Smog has been known to lower the motivation of runners because of chest discomforts and increasing eye irritations. An understanding of the influence of the environment on activities is important. This discussion is concerned with activities that take place in a cold environment, a hot environment, and high altitudes.

In a cold environment, such as on the ski slopes, athletes must realize the importance of proper dress. The greatest danger to an athlete exercising in a cold environment is the sudden changes in temperature. Temperatures may drop 30° to 40° during a day of skiing. The participant's dress should be comfortable and protective at any time during the changes in temperatures. Many athletes perspire a great deal even in a cold environment. It is not rare to see a football player walking off the field in Green Bay, Wisconsin, in the middle of winter with sweat running down his face. Metabolic rates increase when engaging in vigorous activities, regardless of cold or warm weather environments, and the body must dissipate the heat that accumulates by sweating.

Research has indicated that athletes who compete in cold weather environments and perform vigorous activities should wear light clothing that allows sweating. Not all people react to a cold environment in the same manner. Physique is an important factor in determining who can exercise in a cold environment with the least body discomfort. Research has indicated that the heavier person, because of greater fat tissue, will be better able to withstand exercising in a cold environment. Fat tissue is an insulator and preserves heat.

An individual who exercises in a hot environment usually faces more problems than one who exercises in a cold environment. For example, in Nevada, where the air is both hot and extremely humid, sweating will be difficult because of the deficiency in the volume of air available. The human body is limited as to the amount of heat it can tolerate. Too much exposure can lead to heat cramps, heat exhaustion, and heat stroke.

Heat cramps are caused primarily by a deficiency in salt. During strenuous exercising in a hot environment there is a great deal of salt loss. Heat exhaustion occurs when there is too great a stress on the circulatory system of the body and the body's heat controlling system fails. The individual will normally feel cold and dizzy, there is an immediate increase in body temperature, and medical treatment is necessary. Heat stroke, a state of exhaustion usually accompanied by fever caused by exposure to extensive heat over an extended period of time, has been a leading cause of death for many young football players who engage in this vigorous activity during the summer. Coaches must take adequate precautions with their players to avoid overexertion under such climatic conditions. The National Federation of State High School Athletic Associations and the Committee on the Medical Aspects of Sports of the American Medical Association* have indicated that frequent rest breaks, ample supplies of drinking water, and increased salt intake will help to decrease the possibilities of heat disorders during vigorous workouts in extremely high temperatures.

The 1968 Olympic Games held in Mexico

---

*Miller, A. T., Jr.: Influence of oxygen administration on cardiovascular function during exercise and recovery, Journal of Applied Physiology **5:**165, 1952.

*Tips on Athletic Training XII, American Medical Association, Committee on the Medical Aspects of Sports, 1970, p. 8.

City raised questions as to the ability of athletes to participate in activities at high altitudes. Could athletes who set records at sea level retain their titles at an altitude 7,349 feet above sea level or lose them to athletes who participated in activities at high altitudes for many years? For the most part, the majority of champion athletes left Mexico City with their titles. However, others succumbed to the altitude and lost their competitive edge. What effect does the altitude have on the body when exercising? High altitudes decrease the availability of oxygen to the tissues because the partial pressure of oxygen is lower at high altitudes than at sea level. Events most affected by high altitudes are running and swimming that last longer than 2 minutes because performance in prolonged events depends largely on inspired air. Before engaging in exercises at high altitudes, it is important to acclimate to this environment. Dr. Merrit H. Stiles,* former Chairman of the Medical and Training Services Committee of the United States Olympic Committee, stated that vigorous workouts speed up acclimatization and improve performance at high altitudes. Dr. Stiles indicated that 2 to 3 weeks of training at high altitudes will adapt a person to this environment. Other persons indicate that it takes a much longer period of time. The adaptive changes the organism undergoes increase the cardiac output and maximum oxygen uptake of the performer.

Warm-up and training and fitness

A major discussion concerns the use of some type of warm-up procedure before engaging in physical activity. The physical educator and coach should be familiar with the available evidence before determining whether or not to use the warm-up or how to use it most effectively.

Neuberger,† in an analysis of the research on warm-up appearing in the *Research Quarterly* of the AAHPER over a 13-year period, indicated that 95% of the studies demonstrated that to achieve peak physical performance the individ-

ual should warm up. Warm-ups have been found to increase speed, strength, muscular endurance, and power. The research indicates that vigorous, long warm-ups are better than less moderate ones. Related warm-ups (those similar to the activity to be engaged in) are preferable to unrelated ones because of the practice effect that also results. Attitudes toward warm-up are also related to efficiency in performance. An individual with a positive attitude toward warm-up appears to benefit more from such an experience than one who has a negative attitude. It has been determined that combinations of intensity and duration contribute to the desired effects of a warm-up. Insufficient warm-up does not achieve the high level of muscle strength and temperature desired, and excessive warm-up can lead to fatigue and thus decrease the performance level.

Warm-ups have been found to be important in preventing injury and muscle soreness. It appears that muscle injury can result when vigorous exercises are not preceded by a related warm-up. An effective quick warm-up can also be an effective motivator. Students who get satisfaction from an effective warm-up usually have a stronger desire to participate in the activity. By contrast, a poor warm-up can lead to fatigue and boredom, limiting the students' attention and ultimately resulting in a poor program.

Jogging and training and fitness

In recent years, jogging, which is basically a combination of walking and running, has become popular as an aid to keeping physically fit. It has received wide approval from many groups because it is a sustained type of exercise that is noncompetitive. An individual does not have to possess any particular skill to jog, and the majority of joggers range in age from 35 to 65 years. Advocates of jogging think that men and women up to the age of 65 years can learn to jog at a good pace. It is extremely important for individuals to have a medical examination and/or a stress test and to discover the limits of their heart's endurance, however, before beginning to jog. Jogging has been found beneficial to some heart-attack victims because it increases the flow of blood to the damaged heart,

---

*Olympic planners discount fear of Mexican altitudes, Medicine in Sports, **8,** Jan., 1968.
†Neuberger, Tom: What the *Research Quarterly* says about warm-up, Journal of Health, Physical Education, and Recreation **40:**75, Oct., 1969.

and it may also help some heart-attack victims to rebuild the endurance in their heart and lungs. Cooper,* author of the much publicized book entitled *Aerobics,* has stated that exercises such as jogging force the body to become conditioned to an increased need for oxygen. When the body reaches the level of fitness that meets this need, the cardiopulmonary and oxygen transport systems become more efficient. Among other benefits, jogging also helps the healthy individual who wants to lose weight.

Initiating a training and fitness program

To obtain the greatest health benefits from physical activity, certain guidelines should be followed:

1. *Assess present state of fitness.* A person who has not been exercising regularly, is obese, has a history of heart disease, or has high blood pressure should have the approval of his or her physician before engaging in any strenuous activity. Furthermore, a person who experiences while exercising symptoms such as pains in the chest, dizziness or faintness, nausea, or breathing difficulty should stop exercising immediately and see a physician.

2. *Determine exercise tolerance.* Persons starting a training program should determine their exercise tolerance (the manner in which they react to exercise). In this way it can be determined where they should start, what types of exercise they should engage in, and for how long they should exercise.

3. *Plan the fitness program.* A person should plan to get into physical condition gradually—not in just a few days. An individual who has not exercised for a long period of time will need an extended period of activity to get into proper physical condition.

4. *Engage in warm-up exercises.* Warm-up is essential prior to strenuous exercise, and the older a person is the longer is the warm-up that will be needed. Light conditioning and stretching exercises will help in preparing the body for more strenuous exercise.

5. *Recognize that an adapted program is essential.* An exercise program should be adapted to a person's needs. The same type of exercise will not be healthful and beneficial for everyone. Factors such as one's present state of fitness, medical fitness, and age are important considerations.

*Cooper, Kenneth H.: The role of exercise in our contemporary society, Journal of Health, Physical Education and Recreation **40:**22, May, 1969.

DETERRENTS TO FITNESS

There are several deterrents to a high state of fitness. Some of the more important of these are life-style, tobacco, alcohol, and drugs.

Life-style and fitness

One of the greatest deterrents to physical fitness is the general life-style of our modern age. Many people are eating the wrong foods and drinking and smoking excessively. In many cases excessive affluence is detrimental to physical fitness in that affluence directly affects diet and promotes a sedentary life in which driving is favored over walking and watching television is given priority over physical exercise.

The results of our life-styles may be seen in increased coronary heart disease at younger ages. It is no longer unusual to see coronary patients in their midtwenties or younger! Obesity has become a great problem, and persons who are overweight tend to have a poor self-image, are disinterested in physical activity, and, most importantly, have a greater risk of heart disease and other malfunctions.

Positive changes in life-style can best occur through education. This education for fitness needs to start with young children to make them aware of their bodies and the value of physical fitness to their emotional and physical well-being. In addition, public communication through literature, television, and radio should endeavor to educate adults so that they may take positive steps in improving their physical fitness.

Tobacco and fitness

Smoking speeds up the pulse rate, raises the blood pressure, constricts the blood vessels, and may cause other physical damage. There has been some evidence that cigarette smoking interferes with the ability of red blood cells to release oxygen to body tissue. Although the evidence is not fully conclusive, there is some indication that blood from heavy smokers should be rejected for donation purposes because of this deficiency. Smoking has also been linked to many diseases. For example, the correlation between cancer and smoking has been established. There is considerable evidence to indicate that smoking is detrimental to the maintenance of physical fitness. There is no

Fitness is developed in the physical education programs of the Colorado Springs Public Schools, Colorado Springs, Colorado.

evidence to indicate that it contributes to a higher level of physical performance.

Studies have been conducted in respect to smoking and physical performance. One study of 2,000 runners was conducted over several track seasons. It showed that the nonsmokers took more first places in competition than did those runners who smoked. Another study showed that students who do not smoke grow more in height, weight, and lung capacity than do those who smoke. The increase in the chest development among the nonsmokers was also greater. Tests of physical steadiness have shown that nonsmokers are steadier than smokers.

Coaches and physical educators are almost unanimous in thinking that athletic performance and muscular power are lessened by smoking. They believe that fatigue begins earlier among the smokers. Few coaches of high school and college teams knowingly permit their athletes to smoke.

Alcohol and fitness

Alcohol depresses the central nervous system. It acts on the higher brain centers that affect decisions, judgment, and memory. The control of the lower brain centers is lost, reaction time is slowed, and physical and emotional pain are reacted to more slowly.

Coaches, almost universally, will not permit their athletes to drink during the seasons of play or at any time during the school year. As in smoking, although there is considerable evidence to show that alcohol hinders physical performance, there is no evidence to show that it improves performance in any way. A great number of automobile accidents can be attributed to loss of control as a result of drinking.

Although drinking has become a popular social custom in society, the young man or woman who is striving to achieve or maintain a high level of fitness should objectively examine the evidence that shows the result of such a habit.

Drugs and fitness

Marijuana, heroin, LSD (lysergic acid diethylamide), and similar drugs detach persons from reality. They make them oblivious to danger, induce a sense of well-being by postponing feelings of fatigue, and start a habit of use that is difficult to stop.

The use of drugs such as amphetamine (found in pep pills), marijuana, cocaine, heroin, and LSD has become popular among some young people. Amphetamines have been found to produce toxic side effects and cause dependency. Research has indicated that amphetamines do not improve an individual's performance, but, rather, they give the individual an illusory feeling of an improved performance.

Some drugs have also been used in sports for which a high level of energy is required, as in long-distance cycling races. Such a practice is denounced by physical educators, coaches, and sports medicine associations. Athletes at the present time are utilizing drugs known as anabolic steroids. Many athletes, such as weight lifters, have been known to receive large doses of the male sex hormone known as testosterone. Such drugs can have serious side effects on the user. Large doses can cause atrophy of the tubules and also interfere with the functioning of the prostate gland.

The use of drugs such as marijuana, heroin, and LSD is against the law. The continued use of drugs brings about a permanent physical deterioration.

Caffeine, which can be found in coffee, tea, and cola, is a stimulant. Moderate doses of caffeine can increase motor activity. Large doses, however, can decrease the pulse rate, blood pressure, and respiratory rate and produce nervousness. Caffeine has also been found to interfere with carbohydrate and protein metabolism, which is necessary for the production of energy. Most researchers agree that large amounts of caffeine should not be a part of the athlete's daily diet.

WEIGHT CONTROL

There is no easy path to weight reduction. There are no reliable gimmicks or shortcuts,

and too many persons are overweight. Weight control involves watching one's diet and following a healthful regimen, including regular amounts of physical activity. If a person is careful about caloric intake and engages regularly in physical activity, there will be a gradual weight reduction. However, in some cases, persons step up their exercise and similarly step up their appetite, resulting in an excessive food intake.

Some research has indicated that exercise does not necessarily increase appetite and thereby make it more difficult to lose weight. The research by Mayer* and his colleagues has shown that, contrary to popular belief, exercise does not necessarily result in greater food intake. An important factor is whether the individual was active to start with. If one's pursuits are sedentary, there can be a step-up of activity without increase in appetite. Conversely, if activity is decreased below a certain point, depending on the individual, appetite does not decrease correspondingly. In some cases it may, in fact, increase. It also has been shown that an obese person does not react in the same way to exercise as a thin person. Obese persons have stores of fat that are utilized in response to needed calories. Studies of obese adults have shown that their weight gain began when their activity decreased but not their appetite. Eating is not stimulated by exercise; it is stimulated by habit.

In a few cases, obesity may be the result of disease. If a person suspects some disturbance, the first step should be to go to a physician for advice. There is great danger in following any highly commercialized solution involving gadgets and appetite depressant pills. To follow the advice of any person other than a qualified physician is risky and not only may result in a loss of hundreds of dollars but be harmful to one's health.

As far as "spot reducing" goes, medical opinion says "No."† This is an erroneous be-

*Mayer, J.: Exercise and weight control. In Exercise and fitness, Chicago, 1960, The Athletic Institute.
Mayer, J.: Exercise and weight control. In Johnson, Warren, editor: Science and medicine of exercise and sport, New York, 1960, Harper & Row, Publishers, Chapter 16.
†Journal of the American Medical Association, May 14, 1955.

lief. Weight reduction in special areas of the body such as the hips, thighs, and buttocks is not possible. There is no physiological basis for such claims. Only through a general weight reduction program can a person hope to affect the areas mentioned.

Claims made for massage and shaking devices are also ineffective, according to authoritative opinion. One noted physiologist stated that the claims of self-massage and shaking devices for loss or redistribution of fat deposits are based on misrepresentation of facts. They are useless as a means of weight loss.

STRESS

Stress, according to Selye,* is essentially the rate of all the wear and tear caused by life. Each person experiences some degree of stress during each moment of existence. Stress can be caused by an injury, but it can also be caused by a happy occasion. Stress can be good, and it can also be bad for a person.

There is mounting evidence that many chronic ailments that affect persons, especially those in middle age, are directly related to stress. The hard-driving, competitive corporation man may be recognized as a likely candidate for a heart attack at an early age. Conditions such as ulcerative colitis, asthma, migraine headaches, and ulcers are directly related to stress, as are many psychosomatic disorders.

It is interesting to note that in a study of persons designated Type A (competitive) and Type B (more relaxed), a greater incidence of heart disease was noted in Type A individuals, even when the risk factors indicated more possible B cases.

The important thing is that the body must be prepared to meet stress. The formula for enjoying life is learning how to make adjustments in a world that is constantly changing and in which events do not always run smoothly. These adjustments can more readily be made by the person who understands the body and ways of meeting stress. It is thought that, to some extent, disorders involving nervous disturbances, high blood pressure, and ulcers are caused by

lack of understanding in knowing how to adapt.

Selye points out that stress has three phases. The first is the alarm that is sounded by the endocrine, circulatory, or nervous systems. If the stressor persists, the body offers a resistance in an attempt to combat the stressor agents. Finally, if the battle is not waged successfully, the body enters a stage of exhaustion that can have severe consequences.

Michael,* in reviewing several research studies concerned with the endocrine and autonomic nervous systems, has indicated that regular exercises may increase the sensitivity of the adrenal glands. Such an increase in sensitivity may result in a greater response to stress. The important thing for the physical educator to recognize is that physical activity, it is believed, can help to break the chain of harmful stress and thus have a beneficial impact on the body. Therefore activity is essential to maintain a proper body balance and should be encouraged as an antidote to those harmful, stressful experiences that appear in every person's life.

FATIGUE

Fatigue is a phenomenon that all individuals experience. It is a temporary inability of the muscular system to perform efficiently. It is felt at the end of a hard day's work, after strong muscular effort, when one has time on one's hands with nothing to do, after one has passed through an exciting experience, and after periods of intense emotional strain. It results in a decrease in the ability to do work and a feeling of uneasiness. It is a phenomenon that may be aided by sleep, recreation, and physical activity.

There are different types of fatigue. First, there is a *physical* fatigue that a person experiences after a hard day's work, after extreme muscular work, after playing tennis all day, or after pitching hay for 8 hours. The cure for physical fatigue is a good sleep. Second, there is *mental* fatigue, which a person experiences after cramming 5 hours for an examination, after working on one's income tax for a whole evening, or after finishing the monthly report to

*Selye, Hans: The stress of life, New York, 1956, McGraw-Hill Book Co.

*Michael, Ernest D.: Stress adaption through exercise, Research Quarterly **28:**50, 1957.

the boss. Mental fatigue may also result from having nothing to do or boredom. When a person sits around without anything to occupy the mind, yawns start to appear, and a state of mental fatigue ensues. Finally, mental fatigue may be the result of a trying emotional experience, such as attending the funeral of a close friend, getting angry at a next-door neighbor, or worrying about financial problems. In many cases the cure for mental fatigue is participation in some form of recreational activity. When one is engaged in painting a beautiful picture, weaving a rug, trying to catch a bass, or getting par on the golf course, one forgets about mental problems, boredom, and emotional upsets and enjoys living. Fatigue disappears, and the individual is ready to conquer new worlds.

Karpovich lists six places where fatigue may be located, three of which may occur apart from the central nervous system. These are in the fiber of the muscle, at the points of union between the muscle fiber and its nerve or motor end plate, and in the motor nerve fiber. The other three possible seats of fatigue are located within the central nervous system. These are at the synapse, where impulses pass from one neuron to another and where fatigue causes the transmitting of impulses to be slowed, in the nerve cell body, and in the secondary end organs.

RELAXATION AND RECREATION

Relaxation contributes to one's health and may actually be in the form of physical activity. Relaxation is essentially a mental phenomenon concerned with the reduction of tensions that could originate from muscular activity but that are more likely to result from pressures of contemporary living.

A technique for achieving relaxation or nervous reeducation has been developed by Jacobson.* It has two basic steps.

In the first step the individual learns to recognize muscle tension in subtle as well as in gross terms. Gross tension is easily identified. With fists tightly clenched, one holds the arms outstretched to the side at shoulder height for 1

minute. The individual observes the feeling of exertion and discomfort in the forearms and shoulders. The arms are dropped to the side and the muscles of the arms and hands relaxed completely. The effortless relaxation, which Jacobson calls the "negative of exertion," can be noted. Subtle tension, involving less muscle effort than that just illustrated, is sometimes difficult to detect. It takes concentration and practice to learn to recognize minor tension in the trunk, neck, face, throat, and other body parts.

In the second step the individual learns to relax completely. First, the large muscle groups—arms, legs, trunk, and neck—are relaxed. Then the forehead, eyes, face, and even the throat have tension eased through a program of passive relaxation. Carried out in the proper fashion, the program teaches the subject to relax the whole body to the point of negative exertion. The result is a release of tension, an antidote to fatigue, and also an inducement to sleep.

Leisure-time activities such as games and sports, hobbies and avocations, and intellectual and artistic endeavors like painting and sculpturing are considered to be excellent means for eliminating boredom and tension. These recreational activities provide a means of relaxation. Long abused as simply childish diversion or amusement, recreation is being suggested as an antidote for some of the tensions each person experiences in daily life.

PRESIDENT'S COUNCIL ON PHYSICAL FITNESS AND SPORTS

As a result of the Kraus-Weber studies of the physical fitness status of American and European youth, President Eisenhower created the President's Council on Youth Fitness, the name being changed to the President's Council on Physical Fitness by President Kennedy. During President Johnson's administration the name was changed to the President's Council on Physical Fitness and Sports (PCPFS).

The President's Council on Physical Fitness and Sports has devoted much time to promoting a school-centered program for physical fitness. In addition, it has accomplished special working relationships with institutions of higher learning, community groups, voluntary agen-

---

*Jacobson, Edmund: Anxiety and tension control, a physiological approach, Philadelphia, 1964, J. B. Lippincott Co.

cies, and other key organizations. It has mobilized mass media to communicate to the general public the need to be fit. It has utilized television, movies, radio, and articles in national magazines effectively in this promotional campaign.

The President's Council on Physical Fitness and Sports in recent years has been responsible for the conduct of various regional physical fitness clinics that have featured some of the nation's physical fitness leaders and also the council staff. Statewide councils or commissions have been established in many states by either the governor of the state or other agency or organization. State superintendents of education have indicated their active support of the physical fitness movement in approximately one half of the states. Statewide conferences on fitness have been held in a majority of the states in the country. Several fitness films have been produced. Publications have been printed for all segments of the population, including boys, girls, and adults. Materials have been prepared for release to television stations, radio stations, and other communication media. Millions of dollars worth of free advertising has been made available to the council. Presidental Fitness Awards have been established, and demonstration centers have been developed. The PCPFS has also been active in promoting industrial fitness programs and fitness for elderly persons.

The U.S. Office of Education surveyed the nation's schools to find the impact on physical education of the President's council and found that 56% of the 108,000 public schools improved their programs during one school year. Improvement meant that they added a screening test to identify physically underdeveloped pupils, and/or a comprehensive test of physical achievement, and/or more vigorous physical activity during the class period.

PHYSICAL FITNESS OF THE NATION'S CHILDREN AND YOUTH

Studies of the physical fitness status of American boys and girls have indicated little improvement in recent years. A study was conducted by the University of Michigan for the U.S. Office of Education to determine the physical charac-

teristics of children and youth from 1965 to 1975, utilizing the AAHPER Youth Fitness Test and a national sample of 7,800 boys and girls 10 to 17 years of age. These test results were compared with a similar study for the period between 1958 and 1965. The test included these items: pull-ups for boys and flexed arm hang for girls (arm and shoulder strength), sit-ups (abdominal strength), standing long jump (leg power), 50-yard dash (speed), shuttle run (agility), and 600-yard run-walk (endurance). The fitness test scores for the 1965 to 1975 period were very similar to the 1958 to 1965 results. Girls made some minor gains in components such as muscular power and endurance.

Suggested reasons for the lack of improvement during the more recent 10-year period included the introduction into school systems across the country of voluntary rather than required physical education programs and also the use of alternative types of programs to meet school requirements in this area.

The physical fitness of American boys and girls still leaves much to be desired. Some leading physical educators believe that to achieve this objective, physical education programs should meet on a regular and, if possible, daily basis in every school and college in the nation.

Still room for improvement

There is still much progress to be made in improving the nation's level of physical fitness for children and youth. For example, an estimated 14% of the children in school today do not participate in any physical activity program, and an additional 27% participate only 1 or 2 days a week; and fewer and fewer schools provide physical education programs 5 days a week. Tests also show that boys and girls in their physical development are weak in areas such as the shoulder girdle. They are also lacking in endurance and flexibility.

STATUS OF ADULT FITNESS

In an adult physical fitness survey conducted in 1972 for the President's Council on Physical Fitness by the Opinion Research Corporation, it was discovered that 45% of all adult Americans (approximately 49 million persons) do not engage in any physical activity for the purpose of

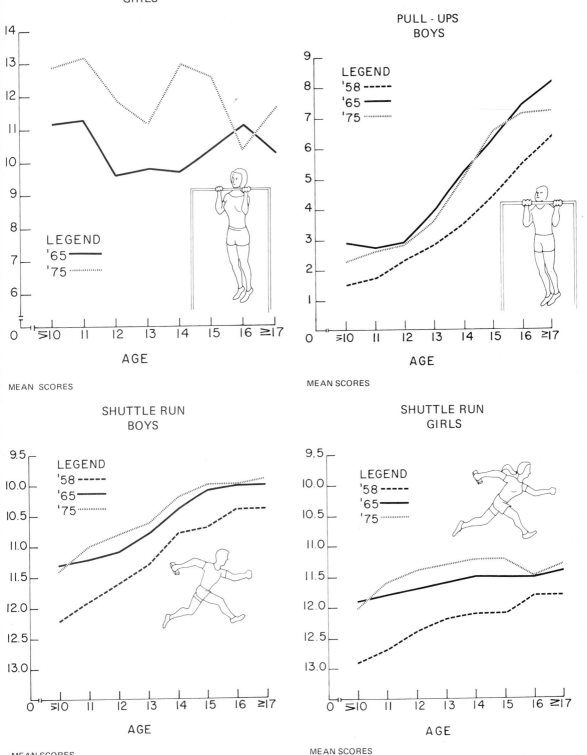

Results of physical fitness status of American boys and girls in flexed-arm hang, pull-ups, and shuttle run.

exercise. The sedentary population tends to be older, less well educated, and less affluent than those who do exercise. Walking was found to be the most popular form of exercise, and bowling was found to be the most popular sport. The great majority of adults were found to be strangers to competitive sports.

The need for adult physical fitness is a result of several conditions. Some of the more pertinent factors are the increased leisure, the changing nature of individuals' work involving less and less activity, the pressures and speed of modern existence, the prevalence of heart disease and other ailments for which exercise is thought to be a preventive factor, and the desire for greater productivity.

Industrial fitness

The adult physical fitness survey cited in this chapter is a definite indictment of the exercise habits of adults. One of the chief areas of incentive *could* and *should* be United States industry. If industrial employees could be motivated toward physical activity on a regular basis, adult exercise patterns would definitely improve. To achieve this goal, industrial officers must make a commitment to their employees, their health, and their fitness. Such a commitment will represent a sound investment in the organization.

The hidden costs to industry resulting from the physical degeneration of its employees is staggering. For example, loss of production in the United States due to premature death caused by chronic cardiovascular disease alone, according to Dr. Roy J. Shephard of the University of Toronto's Department of Physiological Hygiene, is $19.4 billion a year. In addition, there are other losses: in terms of illness, $5 billion; disruption of homelife, $5 billion; hospital and other services, $3 billion. Heart attacks alone cost industry about 132 million workdays yearly, or approximately 4% of the gross national product. Backaches, which many physicians think are caused by physical degeneration, cost American industry $1 billion each year in lost goods and services and another $225 million in workmen's compensation, according to the National Safety Council. Such statistics do not take into consideration other important factors such as shortened workdays as a result of workers' fatigue and minor aches and pains or absenteeism for several days due to illness caused by lowered physical resistance to disease.

The values, on the other hand, that would accrue to the nation's industry by instituting fitness programs in their establishments will pay huge dividends not only for the nation but also for themselves. Research studies have shown that companies with fit employees have higher performance, greater production, improved morale among their workers, reduced absenteeism, more creative ideas, and better cooperation between labor and management.

Executives, in particular, should recognize the value of being physically fit, since it may provide them with a larger salary check. A survey conducted among 50,000 executives by the Robert Half Personnel Agencies and reported in the *Wall Street Journal,* found that fitness and company position were related. About one out of three of those persons in the $10,000 to $20,000 salary bracket were overweight by more than ten pounds, whereas in the $25,000 to $50,000 bracket, only one out of ten were overweight by the same amount.

Many leading American corporations, recognizing the importance of fitness, have developed programs and provided facilities and other incentives for their employees. For example, the North American Rockwell Corporation has one of the best industrial fitness programs in the country at El Segundo, California. Begun in 1960, its goal is to have each employee and family member participate daily in the many physical activities that are provided. This program requires each participant to have a medical examination first and then be tested for components of fitness such as cardiovascular efficiency and lung capacity. The test results determine the person's level of fitness, and accordingly he or she is placed in one of five color squads: *green* (novice), *red* (average), *blue* (better), *gold* (good), and *purple,* (outstanding). Employees are encouraged to try and progress from one color squad to a higher level of fitness.

The Metropolitan Life Insurance Company has developed an effective physical fitness program in their home office in New York City for men aged 20 to 40 years. The medical director believes that these people are at a vulnerable age, since it is a time when men increase their caloric input and cut down on their physical activity. He developed a program that includes a physical fitness test involving jogging, rowing, bicycling, and sit-ups. The test determines how the subject's pulse rate responds to exercise. The yardstick is the length of time it takes the pulse to return to normal after exercise—the longer it takes the poorer physical condition the person is in. After the testing is over, subjects are informed of their physical status, provided with literature on the importance of keeping fit, and encouraged to exercise regularly.

The Xerox Corporation has invested large sums of money in its fitness program at Webster, New York, where its superb facilities include an executive fitness laboratory, putting green, skating rink, and jogging paths. The company also has an executive fitness program in downtown Rochester. Clubs are organized for the employees in sports such as sailing, skiing, scuba diving, horseback riding, judo, and square dancing. Men's and women's physical fitness classes are also offered at various times of the day throughout the year.

Any company desiring to develop a physical fitness program for its employees should strive to meet the following criteria developed by the President's Council on Physical Fitness and Sports:

The program should be an adjunct of the company's health program.

It should include a medically oriented screening test as a criterion for participation.

A person skilled in prescribing exercise should direct it.

Exercise should be tailored to the individual participant and should be progressively more strenuous for the participant to benefit from it.

Activities should be noncompetitive, that is, individuals should compete only against other participants in the program.

A system of periodic evaluation should be included to measure progress and to aid in program design.

PHYSICAL FITNESS FOR THE HANDICAPPED INDIVIDUAL

In recent years it has been recognized that physical fitness programs can benefit those in-

An instructor at the South Carolina School for the Deaf and the Blind in Spartanburg, South Carolina, helps a girl with the game of golf.

Group games help handicapped youngsters respond better to others, improve their physical fitness, and have fun.

dividuals who suffer from mental and emotional problems. In the United States it is estimated that there are over 6 million emotionally disturbed children between the age of 5 to 17 years and over 3 million mentally retarded persons under the age of 21 years. Professionals who work with delinquent youngsters point out that many are not physically fit and suffer from severe emotional and physical problems. The Physical Education Department at the Youth Development Center in New Castle, Pennsylvania,* has stated that most delinquents are healthy and physically able; however, their physical ability has not been properly developed. Authorities at the center point out that delinquent youths have not received the proper education about how to use their physical abilities for something other than self-protection and violence. Their program stresses physical fitness and swimming activities. Their officers indicate that students become motivated to participate in the program when they realize that

they can develop more self-respect by becoming physically fit.

It has also been found that physical activities can be beneficial in aiding the psychiatric patient. Marusak* studied the effects of exercise on the psychiatric patient, and on the basis of his observations it was found that physical exercises were of value in channeling aggression, increasing socialization, and improving the fitness level of these people.

All children need the opportunity to achieve success. The educable mentally retarded boy, for example, has improved his physical fitness through participation in planned physical education experiences. Amiel Solomon and Roy Pangle,† in a study of educable mentally retarded boys, administered the AAHPER Youth Physical Fitness Test to a group of forty-two youngsters. After an 8-week period of planned activities, the group that received the training

*Libicer, Stephen J., Jr.: The name of the game is fitness, Outlook **1**(2):1, 4, 1969.

*Marusak, F. M.: The use of corrective therapy in a psychiatric treatment program, Journal of the Association of Physical and Mental Rehabilitation **5**:9, 1952.
†Solomon, Amiel, and Pangle, Roy: Demonstrating physical fitness improvement in the EMR, Exceptional Children, pp. 177-181, Nov., 1967.

increased their level of fitness. For more information on physical education for the handicapped see Chapter 10.

SELF-ASSESSMENT TESTS

These tests are to assist students in determining if material and competencies presented in this chapter have been mastered.

1. Define the terms *fitness* and *physical fitness* and document with pertinent facts the statement, ''There is a fitness explosion in the United States today.''

2. Prepare a position paper on the subject that ''Physical Activity is a Key Essential for Optimum Health.''

3. Draw a line down through the middle of a sheet of paper. On the left side list the following organic systems of the human body: circulatory system, respiratory system, muscular system, digestive and excretory systems, nervous system, endocrine system. Opposite each of these body systems and on the right side of the paper, list the effects that physical activity has on each system.

4. Describe four types of persons: (1) a person who is sedentary and eats a nonnutritious diet, (2) a person who smokes two packs of cigarettes a day, (3) a person who habitually consumes large quantities of alcohol, (4) a person who takes harmful drugs. Indicate how these life-styles and habits are deterrents to a state of physical fitness.

5. Prepare a rationale to show that physical activity can contribute to weight control, the alleviation of stress, and serve as an antidote to some types of fatigue.

6. Prepare an essay in which you assess the physical fitness status of the nation's children, youth, industrial executives, adults in general, and the handicapped. Conclude your essay with recommendations for improving the physical fitness status of each group.

READING ASSIGNMENT

Bucher, Charles A.: Dimensions of physical education, ed. 2, St. Louis, 1974, The C. V. Mosby Co., Reading selections 34 to 40.

SELECTED REFERENCES

Boyer, J. L.: Changing personal health goals in the seventies, Physical Fitness News Letter, no. 8, April, 1972.

Bucher, Charles A.: Fitness and health (editorial), Educational Leadership **20**:356, 1963.

Bucher, Charles A.: How long will you live? Syndicated newspaper column, April, 1972, President's Council on Physical Fitness and Sports.

Bucher, Charles A.: Don't try to gimmick away those extra pounds. Syndicated newspaper column, Sept., 1972, President's Council on Physical Fitness and Sports.

Bucher, Charles A.: Fitness is good business. Syndicated newspaper column, Oct., 1972, President's Council on Physical Fitness and Sports.

Bucher, Charles A.: We are not as fit as our forefathers. Syndicated newspaper column, Nov., 1972, President's Council on Physical Fitness and Sports.

Bucher, Charles A.: National Adult Physical Fitness Survey: some implications, Journal of Health, Physical Education, and Recreation **45**:25, Jan., 1974.

Bucher, Charles A.: Administration of health and physical education programs, including athletics, ed. 6, St. Louis, 1975, The C. V. Mosby Co.

Bucher, Charles A.: Exercise—its plain good business, Reader's Digest, Feb., 1976.

Bucher, Charles A., and Koenig, Constance: Methods and materials for secondary school physical education, ed. 5, St. Louis, 1978, The C. V. Mosby Co.

Bucher, Charles A., Olsen, Einar A., and Willgoose, Carl E.: The foundations of health, New York, 1976, Prentice-Hall, Inc.

College Physical Education Association: Fit for college, Washington, D.C., 1959, American Association for Health, Physical Education, and Recreation.

Cooper, Kenneth H.: The role of exercise in our contemporary society, Journal of Health, Physical Education, and Recreation **40**:22, May, 1969.

de Vries, Herbert A.: Physiology of exercise for physical education and athletics, Dubuque, Iowa, 1974, William C. Brown Co., Publishers.

Duggar, Benjamin C., and Swengros, Glenn V.: The design of physical activity programs for industry, Journal of Occupational Medicine **11**(6):322, 1969.

Essentials of life and health, New York, 1977, Random House, Inc.

Falls, H. B., and others: Foundations of conditioning, New York, 1970, Academic Press, Inc.

Gendel, Evelyn S.: Women and the medical aspects of sports, Journal of Sport Health **37**:427, 1967.

Getchell, Bud: Physical fitness—a way of life, New York, 1976, John Wiley & Sons, Inc.

Hunsicker, Paul, and Reiff, Guy: Youth fitness report 1958-1965, Journal of Physical Education and Recreation **48**:31, Jan., 1977.

Johnson, Warren R.: Health in action, New York, 1977, Holt, Rinehart & Winston, Inc.

Journal of Sports Medicine and Physical Fitness, Official journal of the Fédération Internationale de Medicine Sportive, published by Edizioni Minerva Medica (Torino, Italy). See all issues.

Karpovich, P. V., and Sinning, Wayne E.: Physiology of muscular activity, ed. 7, Philadelphia, 1971, W. B. Saunders Co.

Klaus, E. J.: The athletic status of women. In Jokl, E., and Simon, E., editors: International research and sport and physical education, Springfield, Ill., 1964, Charles C Thomas, Publisher.

Mathews, D., and Fox, E. L.: The physiological basis of physical education and athletics, Philadelphia, 1971, W. B. Saunders Co.

McQuade, Walter: What stress can do to you, Fortune, p. 102, Jan., 1972.

Morehouse, Laurence E., and Miller, Augustus T.: Physiology of exercise, ed. 7, St. Louis, 1976, The C. V. Mosby Co.

National Adult Physical fitness survey: Newsletter: President's Council on Physical Fitness and Sports, May, 1973.

Neuberger, Tom: What the *Research Quarterly* says about warm-ups, Journal of Health, Physical Education, and Recreation **40:**75, Oct., 1969.

Olympic planners discount fear of Mexican altitudes, Medicine and Science in Sports **8:**1, Jan., 1968.

Physical activity and coronary heart disease, Physical Research Digest, Series 2, No. 2, April, 1972.

Ricci, Benjamin: Experiments in the physiology of human performance, Philadelphia, 1970, Lea & Febiger.

Selye, Hans: The stress of life, New York, 1956, McGraw-Hill Book Co.

Thompson, Clem W.: Some physiological effects of isometric and isotonic work in man, Research Quarterly **25:** 476, Dec., 1954.

Tips on Athletic Training XII, American Medical Association, Committee on the Medical Aspects of Sports, 1970, p. 8.

YMCA, Journal of Physical Education **64:** Nov.-Dec., 1966, Special Fitness Issue.

Additional materials on the subject of fitness may be secured from the President's Council on Physical Fitness and Sports, Washington, D.C., and the American Alliance for Health, Physical Education and Recreation, 1201 16th St., N.W., Washington, D.C. 20036.

13

Psychological foundations of physical education

INSTRUCTIONAL OBJECTIVES AND COMPETENCIES TO BE ACHIEVED

After reading this chapter the student should be able to—

1. Identify and give illustrations of cognitive, affective, and psychomotor types of learning.
2. Describe what is meant by perceptual-motor learning and how physical education can contribute to this phase of education.
3. Understand the role of motivation, maturation, individual differences, reinforcement, and intelligence in promoting and influencing learning.
4. Understand certain basic theories of learning and be able to draw implications for the teaching of physical education from these theories.
5. Show how certain factors and conditions such as perception and feedback promote the learning of motor skills.
6. Apply to the teaching of physical education such basic concepts of motor learning theory as mental practice, feedback, and mass and distributed practice.
7. Interpret what implications physical education and sport have for personality development.

The study of psychology has implications for physical educators in areas such as learning theory, motor learning, personality development, and attitudes concerning self.

The word *psychology* comes from the Greek words *psyche,* meaning mind or soul, and *logos,* meaning science. Therefore from these Greek words it can be seen that psychology is the science of the mind and the soul. Psychologists study human nature scientifically, and rather than formulate conclusions from casual observations, they sort out and check and recheck human characteristics under reliable conditions. In this manner and through the use of acceptable scientific evaluation, it is possible for psychologists to determine the condition under which certain human characteristics will operate. These data should theoretically be objective and free from prejudice and bias and focus attention on an impartial and realistic examination of all the evidence.

TYPES OF LEARNING

Bloom,* in discussing educational objectives, lists the following three educational domains: (1) cognitive, (2) affective, and (3) psychomotor. These domains represent three types of learning.

In teaching for cognitive learning, the physical educator is concerned with increasing the student's knowledge, improving problem-solving abilities, clarifying understandings, and developing and identifying concepts. The development of cognitive learning makes use of the mental process as a primary form of activity.

---

*Bloom, Benjamin S., and others: Taxonomy of educational objectives. Handbook I. Cognitive domain, New York, 1956, David McKay Co., Inc., p. 7.

Psychomotor learning includes the teaching of physical skills, such as the teaching of swimming at Cumberland Valley School District at Mechanicsburg, Pennsylvania.

The degree to which time is spent teaching for cognitive development depends on factors such as the complexity of the information to be imparted and the abilities of the students to understand the material being presented.

In teaching for affective learning, the teacher is concerned with attitudes, appreciations, and values. A primary goal of such teaching is that of developing proper and positive attitudes and appreciations toward physical education and physical activity; qualities such as good sportsmanship, respect for leadership and followership, teamwork, respect for other students and people in general; and the need to play according to the rules and regulations that structure the various physical education activities.

In teaching for psychomotor learning, the teacher of physical education is concerned with the development and/or improvement of motor skill. This type of learning is the heart of the physical education experience and should result in the achievement of general motor ability as well as selective skills in various physical education activities geared to the age, maturation level, and physical condition of each student. Since motor skill learning is such an important part of the psychological foundations of physical education, it will be emphasized in this chapter. Affective learning will be described in Chapter 14.

PERCEPTUAL-MOTOR LEARNING

Research has shown that, to some extent, a relationship exists between the development of perceptual motor skills and classroom learning. For example, the slow learner frequently performs poorly in motor skills. Also, characteristics such as hand-eye coordination, spatial awareness, and laterality are perceptual motor skills that are pertinent to scholastic achievement. Many children have learning difficulties, and in some cases it has been found that by prescribing activities to increase perception and activity in movement, beneficial results occur.

Motor activities that seem to be most closely related to perceptual-motor problems involve coordination, balance, agility, sense of direction, and awareness of space. It is believed that through early motor learnings in such areas a better base is established whereby other learnings are gained and conceptualized. Further re-

Activity designed to work on small muscle control in perceptual-motor class at the Oak View Elementary School in Fairfax, Virginia.

search, however, is needed before too many claims can be made.

The perceptual-motor process is defined as the management of information coming to the individual through the senses, the processing of this information, and then reacting in terms of overt motor behavior. In reality the perceptual-motor process is extremely complex, requiring many interrelationships of abilities on the part of the processor.

Sensory information is first recognized, discriminated, and selectively carried through nerve pathways to various levels of the brain. The initial reception of information is conducted through the primary channels of sight, hearing, feeling, and proprioception. After this, sensory information must be processed for current or future use. All information is compared, integrated, and stored within the brain on the basis of previous experiences of the individual. Information is expressed as a constant source of covert feedback impulse, which then provides a continual means for adjusting to current or future motor behavior.

Perception cannot be separated from cognition. Both must be considered as inseparable, dependent, and reciprocal. To have a thought, a person must receive and perceive hundreds of thousands of impulses from external and/or internal stimuli. From the time of conception the individual is perceiving and reacting to his or her environment.

A breakdown at any point along the perceptual chain of events can lead to dysfunction of any one or all of the processes. For example, problems can result from a difficulty in formation retrieval, from an inability to differentiate stimuli, or from faulty movement behavior. In physical education the performing child with perceptual-motor dysfunction may be considered awkward or clumsy while enjoying physical activity. The same child may or may not be able to cope with the many discrete symbols or fine motor coordinations required in the classroom.

It is believed that opportunities to use motor movements in a series of purposeful movement patterns increases the level of functioning of perception, and thus learning in individuals. Some problems of learning are thought to arise from a deprivation of sensory and motor stimulation during childhood. Many children with average and above average intelligence often have difficulty with classroom tasks such as reading, writing, and concept formation.

Specifically, some individuals have problems with balance, basic locomotor skills, hand-eye and foot-eye coordination, laterality, directionality, and body awareness. These are some of the perceptual-motor aspects of learning, and they have been shown to affect scholastic learning. It is further maintained that activities will foster good perceptual-motor development. However, at the same time it should be recognized that some of the perceptual-motor problems are too complex for the average teacher and should be referred to personnel especially trained in learning disabilities.

Teachers of physical education in the elementary school should be aware of the many ways in which problems concerned with perceptual-motor development may be displayed. These might include characteristics such as a short attention span, difficulty in reading, rigid and inflexible posture, clumsiness, poor self-concept, and a poor relationship with peers.

Physical education programs that are oriented toward movement education provide many of the experiences that contribute to the development of a child's perceptual-motor abilities.

ELEMENTS OF LEARNING

Learning implies a change in a person—a change in one's method of both practicing and performing a skill or a change in an attitude toward a particular thing. Learning implies a progressive change of behavior in an individual, although some changes are rapid, such as when insight into a problem is perceived. It implies a change that occurs as a result of experience or practice. It results in the modification of behavior as a result of training or environment. It involves aspects such as obtaining knowledge, improving one's skill in an activity, solving a problem, or making an adjustment to a new situation. It implies that knowledge or skill has been acquired as a result of instruction received in school or some other setting or as a result of a person's own initiative in personal study. Learning goes on all through life. It starts as a result of a need. When old forms of

behavior are no longer capable of meeting new situations, a need results. When individuals find that their present resources or methods of response are inadequate to satisfy a need, they may become aware that some change is necessary either in the environment, themselves, or both. For example, when a skill is not performed proficiently enough to receive commendation and approval from others, there may be a felt need to improve this skill, or one may have internalized one's own standards and not need the group as a judge.

To have an effective learning situation, education must be cognizant of certain basic forces, which serve as the frame of reference for the conduct of learning and teaching in the school environment. Some of the most important forces influencing learning are motivation, maturation, individual differences, reinforcement, and intelligence. The role of maturation is also considered.

Motivation and learning

Motivation is a basic factor to effective learning. The term *motive* refers to a condition within the individual that initiates activity directed toward a goal. Needs and drives form the basic framework for motivation. When individuals sense an unfulfilled need, they are moved to do something about it. This desire prompts people to seek a solution to the recognized need through an appropriate line of action. From the phenomenological point of view, certain needs can arise from the environment. These forces are from the outside. A comprehensive theory of motivation should take these forces into account.

This line of action may require practice, effort, mastery of knowledge, or other behavior to be successful. For example, an individual who is hungry becomes motivated to seek food, whereas at a higher level the individual who desires to pass an examination so that he or she will be permitted to practice law is desirous of acquiring the necessary knowledge.

Maslow* has developed a theory of motivation arranged in order from the most immature to the most mature needs as follows:

---

*Maslow, A. H.: A theory of human motivation, Psychological Review **50:**370, 1943.

1. *Physiological needs.* At the lowest level are the physiological needs. Here the individual is concerned with survival, and the need for food is seen as basic to the protection of the physiological being.
2. *Safety needs.* At this level the individual seeks to discover ways of avoiding danger. The individual prefers the known to the unknown and finds that he or she must establish feelings of security before he or she is free to do other things.
3. *Love and belonging needs.* The need for affection, love, and friendship fall in this group. The individual desires to be accepted by others, and having their approval enhances his or her feeling of adequacy and worth.
4. *Esteem needs.* The need to be respected by others appears at this level. The desire to be recognized as important is dominant, and the individual engages in activities that he or she hopes will lead to situations where he or she can win the respect of peers.
5. *Self-actualization.* This is the highest level of maturity. Here the individual is truly himself or herself. At this level the individual develops to full potential and becomes all that he or she is capable of becoming.

Maslow's theory of motivation is important to educators. All individuals in our school system need the opportunity to develop to their full potential. In a classroom situation, to a large extent the child's needs for affection, belonging, approval, esteem, and self-actualization are dependent on the teacher. If the child is given the opportunity to participate in activities that are personally important and is given the chance to succeed, his or her needs are satisfied. Accordingly, teachers should organize their programs so that all individuals are given the opportunity to satisfy their needs. Physical education teachers are in an excellent position to provide individual students with the opportunity to participate in activities that will lead to the satisfaction of their basic needs. In physical education the student can satisfy the need for belonging, for example, by being given the opportunity to play on a team. Here the individual gains the affection, friendship, approval, and respect of classmates.

It is important also to recognize that the child's parents or parent substitutes play a vital role in the development and satisfaction of these needs.

Maturation and learning

Maturation is concerned with determining whether or not individuals have reached a certain stage in their development that will enable them to perform a desired task. Psychologists have long advocated the principle that learning should be adjusted to the level of maturation of the individual and have viewed learning as an adjustment to the environment. At the same time, it should be understood that the learner is not always merely adjusting to the environment. One has to restructure it to meet the requirements of the task or situation. Sometimes this restructuring takes place within the individual and sometimes within the environment. Sometimes both the individual and the environment are in dynamic interaction. Psychologist Jean Piaget* has been chiefly concerned with the individual child's adjustment to the environment in which he or she lives and has attempted to determine the optimum time for presenting learning experiences to the individual. Piaget sees four major stages of the individual's growth.

1. *Sensory-motor stage.* This stage lasts from birth to about 2 years of age. At this stage the child becomes aware of the muscles and various senses and discovers mechanisms for dealing with objects and events. The beginning of language development also takes place during this stage of development.
2. *Preoperational stage.* This stage begins about 2 years of age and continues to about 6 years. Language development is the dominating factor during this stage. Through the new-found use of words, children express their feelings about the environment they inhabit. The child at this stage depends on trial and error and intuition to solve the various problems with which he or she is presented. It should be noted that the trial and error is not one that is blindly done. Insight is involved at this stage. Motor skill development begins to take form during this stage.
3. *Concrete operation stage.* This stage begins at 7 years of age and lasts until the child is 11 years. At this stage the child understands the relationships among various concrete operational groupings. The child develops the ability to solve physical problems and becomes aware

*Jennings, Frank G.: Jean Piaget: notes on learning, Saturday Review, pp. 81-83, May 20, 1967.

Movement exploration with discarded bicycle tires at the Oak View Elementary School at Fairfax, Virginia.

of the concept of reversibility (that for any operation there is an opposite operation that cancels it). Improved motor skill development also takes place at this stage, with the child developing greater movement patterns.

4. *Formal operations stage.* This stage begins at about 11 years of age and sets the foundation for the individual's adult thinking. At this stage the individual acquires the capacity for abstract thought. Logical reasoning and problem solving are dominant during this stage.

In his four developmental stages, Piaget has described the physical and intellectual growth of an individual. His greatest contribution to psychology lies in his finding that learning proceeds most rapidly when experiences presented to individuals are geared to their physical and intellectual ability. For example, according to Piaget, children should not be presented with problems to solve that require abstract thought until they reach the formal operations stage of their development.

All teachers must have a clear understanding of the concept of maturation. A program of research is necessary to help determine the intricate relationship between maturation and learning. When physical education teachers present motor skills to their students, it is essential that

they discover whether the child has reached a certain level of development that will enable successful performance. For example, if a boy is to learn a skill such as the shot put, he must be physically mature to make such an activity possible. If a teacher attempts to develop this skill before the student reaches the level of maturity necessary, the teacher will waste time and may decrease the student's motivation for learning the skill. The student may also harm himself.

Individual differences and learning

In any classroom situation the teacher must provide for the individual differences found among students. In a typical physical education class, for example, the teacher is faced with a group of boys or girls who differ in physical qualities; some are bigger than others, and some possess greater motor ability than others. There are social and economic differences; some students come from middle-class families, whereas others are disadvantaged or from broken homes. There are personality differences among students; some students are outgoing, whereas others are shy and withdrawn. Teachers must be aware of the differences among their students. The teacher who is in-

Recreation Department, City of Oakland, Calif.

Modern dancers in outdoor concert.

structing a class of inner-city youths, for example, must be aware that he or she must provide a strong model for these students. Students who come from broken homes need the guidance and support of the teacher if they are to develop to their full potential. The teacher who recognizes the need to give some students, such as a shy and withdrawn girl, a little more motivation than others will influence the child's development.

Reinforcement and learning

Reinforcement involves the condition where the relationship, or connection, between the stimulus and the response brings satisfaction to the learner, and the response is repeated when a certain stimulus is provided. In other words, it is the learning situation which increases the likelihood that a certain response will be repeated when a certain stimulus is provided. The research suggests that when there is immediate reinforcement, it is more effective than when it comes at a later time. Also, random reinforcement would appear to be more effective than continual reinforcement of the same stimulus-response situation.

Physical educators should be alert to the need

to reinforce the learning of skills and other behaviors of those under their supervision by commendation, praise, and feedback when the desired performance takes place.

Intelligence and learning

In addition to physical, social, economic, and personality differences, there are also differences in intelligence that must be recognized. In consulting the literature, one becomes aware that many different theories exist as to what constitutes intelligence. The question of whether human beings have one intelligence or several different intelligences has been well documented. Spearman* espoused the theory of general and specific intelligence, emphasizing that all mental activities have in common a general factor of intelligence, designated g, and a specific factor of intelligence, designated s, that are related only to particular activities.

Thurstone† believed general intelligence is made up of several "primary mental abilities."

---

*Spearman, Charles: The abilities of man, New York, 1927, The Macmillan Co.
†Thurstone, L. L.: Primary mental abilities, Psychometric Monograph No. I, Chicago University Press, 1938, p. 9.

primary mental abilities named were numbers (such as the ability to do arithmetic problems), verbal meaning, spatial perception, word fluency, reasoning, memory, and perceptual speed. Thurstone attempted to prove that these primary mental abilities are independent of one another. However, in testing, those who scored high on one ability such as reasoning also scored high on other abilities, thus indicating that these primary abilities may really be an expression of one general ability.

Attempts to define intelligence have estimated that there may be well over a hundred individual components of intelligence.

It is apparent that teachers must have an understanding of the principle of intelligence and some means of measuring the intelligence level of their students* if they are to present meaningful learning experiences. Both the general factor and multifactor theories of intelligence have produced a great number of tests to measure intelligence. Tests such as the Stanford-Binet and the Wechsler Intelligence Scale for Children are individual tests of intelligence based on a general theory of intelligence and concentrate heavily on measuring verbal and numerical abilities. Differential aptitude tests are tests that measure the multifactor theory of intelligence. They measure verbal reasoning, numerical abilities, mechanical reasoning clerical speed, spelling, language usage, and accuracy. The scores that an individual receives on an intelligence test such as the Stanford-Binet are known as *IQ*. IQ refers to intelligence quotient and is a ratio of the student's mental age to chronological age multiplied by 100 $\left(\frac{\text{ma}}{\text{ca}} \times 100\right)$. An IQ in the low 70s indicates an intellectual deficiency, whereas a score over 130 indicates a high intelligence level. Within a class, scores on an intelligence test may range from the low 80s and even lower to well over 130.

Educators must be cognizant of these scores. For those children who score above 130, the question may be asked: Does the class atmo-

*In some schools, it should be noted, group IQ tests are not given. Reading scores may be used by grade advisers to aid in teaching students.

sphere satisfy the intellectual needs of these students? The physical educator must be aware of those students in class who may think the activities in which they are participating are not stimulating enough. On the other hand, those children who are identified as academically weak may need extra help in discovering the solution to various problems they are required to solve. Physical educators must have a good assessment of their students, which means that individual differences are discovered so that students can be provided with the activities that will meet their needs.

THEORIES OF LEARNING

Psychologists have attempted to explain the phenomenon of learning and to answer questions such as how it best takes place and what are the laws under which it operates. The basic theories of learning, for purposes of discussion, may be divided into two broad categories. The first category may be called the connectionist theories, which state that learning consists of a bond, or connection, between a stimulus and a response or responses. The second category may be called cognitive theories. Those psychologists who support these theories believe that a human being's various perceptions, beliefs, or attitudes (cognitions or mental images) which concern the environment determine human behavior. The manner in which these "cognitions" are modified by the human being's experience indicates the learning that takes place. The basic principles underlying the cognitive theories were developed by the Gestalt psychologists.

Thorndike's laws of learning

E. L. Thorndike, a psychologist whose theories of learning have had a great impact on educators and education, believed in a stimulus–response theory, or S–R bond theory. His laws of readiness, exercise, and effect have influenced educational programs.

Thorndike developed these laws that set forth the conditions under which learning best takes place. Because psychology is a relatively new science and because there are many contradictory views as to various psychological principles, laws of learning should not be regarded as the final word. However, they are working principles and, as such, deserve the attention of all physical educators who desire to seek the most efficient and effective ways of teaching.

Law of readiness. The law of readiness means that individuals will learn much more effectively and rapidly if they are "ready"—if they have matured to that point and if there is a felt need. Learning will be satisfying if materials are presented when an individual meets these standards. This law also works in reverse. It will be annoying and dissatisfying to do something when the individual is not ready. The closer an individual is to reaching the point of readiness the more satisfying the act will be.

In physical education activities the teacher should determine whether the child is ready in respect to various sensory and kinesthetic mechanisms and in respect to strength in some cases. The teacher should ask questions such as the following: Does the child have the capacity, at this time, for certain skills? Does he or she have the proper background of experience? Is the material timely that is being presented? Should it be postponed until some future time? Most physical educators agree, for example, that athletic competition on an interscholastic basis should not be part of the program for elementary schoolchildren. The child is not mentally, emotionally, and physically ready for such an experience. There is also considerable agreement that fine-muscle activity should not play too pronounced a part in the program for young children. Instead, their program should mainly consist of activities that involve the large muscles.

Law of exercise. The law of exercise, in respect to the development of skills in physical education, means that practice makes for better coordination, more rhythmical movement, less expenditure of energy, more skill, and better performance. As a result of practice, the pathway between stimulus and response becomes more pronounced and permanent.

In many ways this law of learning is similar to the law of use and disuse. As a result of continual practice, strength is gained, but as a result of disuse, weakness ensues.

Learning in education is acquired by doing. To master the skills of bowling, swimming, or handball a person must practice. However, it should be restated that practice does not necessarily ensure perfection of the skill. Mere repetition does not mean greater skill. Practice must be meaningful, with proper attention being given to all phases of the learning process. The learner, through repetition and a clear conception of what is to be done, steadily makes progress toward the desired goal. Repetition, however, should not be blind. It is during the process of "repetition" that learning takes place.

Law of effect. The law of effect maintains that an individual will be more likely to repeat experiences which are satisfying than those which are annoying. If experiences are annoying, the learner will shift to other, satisfying responses.

This law of learning as applied to physical education means that every attempt should be made to provide situations in which individuals experience success and have a satisfying and enjoyable experience. Leadership is an important factor. Under certain types of leadership, undesirable experiences would be satisfying. One coach might approve of hitting an opponent, making this an enjoyable experience. Under other coaches such an act would be an annoying experience because it would be condemned and would not be tolerated. Leadership is the key to good teaching.

Guthrie's contiguity theory

Edwin R. Guthrie* developed the contiguity theory of learning, which emphasizes the stimulus–response association. Contiguity means that a response which is evoked by a stimulus will be repeated whenever that same stimulus recurs. The strengthening of the connection between the stimulus and the response takes place in a single trial. Guthrie believed that since associations can occur with one trial and last forever, there is no need for anything like rewards or motivation to explain learning. However, although Guthrie holds that the full connection is established in one trial, it usually appears to take place gradually. This means that all stimuli cues are not always presented in the same manner, and for this reason many stimulus–re-

*Guthrie, E. P.: The psychology of learning, revised ed., New York, 1952, Harper & Row, Publishers.

Courtesy D. M. Massé.

Wand relay in physical education class at the Waddell Elementary School in Manchester, Connecticut.

Youth Services Branch, Los Angeles City Schools, Los Angeles, Calif.

Physical education skills should be taught in the most effective way possible. Tennis instruction using stroke developer.

sponse associations must be made. In every learning situation, for example, various combinations of stimuli are presented, and correct responses need to be established for each situation. Guthrie holds that repetition and practice are essential in learning for the individual to become aware of the stimuli that will evoke the correct response.

In physical education Guthrie's theory can be applied to the learning of a skill such as the high jump. For proficiency in this skill, the student must make sure that bodily movements are always the same each time the bar is approached and be aware of all the surrounding stimuli such as the runway and position of the bar. The proficient high jumper will be one who has established a successful pattern of movements and does not deviate from it. Even the slightest change in stimuli can evoke an incorrect response. The youngster who becomes distracted by the noise of the spectators finds it difficult to clear the bar if he or she has practiced in complete silence. According to Guthrie's theory, this youngster should practice under conditions that are present during actual competition, since to achieve one's best performance the person must be aware of all the stimuli that are present at the time of competition.

Hull's reinforcement theory

Clark L. Hull* sees learning as a direct influence of reinforcement. He has established his theory on the influence of need and its reduction as the prime elements in learning. Hull emphasizes that learning occurs when the individual adapts himself or herself to the environment and that such adaptation is necessary for survival. When needs arise, the individual's survival is threatened, and the individual must act in a certain manner to reduce the need. The responses that the individual makes that lead to the reduction of the need are reinforced, resulting in habits or learning. According to Hull's theory, a stimulus causes a response that results in a need. The need evokes a response on the part of the individual, which reduces the need. The response that resulted in the reduction of the need

is then reinforced, which develops habits or learning. Hull employed drive and primary reinforcement in his early work. Later he used ideas such as drive stimulus reduction and secondary reinforcement.

Hull's theory emphasizes that habits or learning result from reactions set into motion by needs. In physical education the teacher plays an important part in satisfying the needs of the student. Teachers who explain the psychological and sociological bases for participating in an activity may stimulate students more than those who present the activity without any rationale. To elicit correct responses from students, the teacher presents material that is meaningful, and therefore lesson plans consist of material important to the learner.

One of the major implications of Hull's theory to physical education is his finding that practice periods which are extremely long or lacking in reinforcement inhibit learning. An example of this is the pole vaulter who practices hour after hour. After a long period of practice without any reinforcement, the pole vaulter finds it difficult to clear his or her usual height. However, Hull states that the inhibitions decrease after rest periods, and the next day the vaulter can again clear the accustomed height. Thus practice periods play an important role in determining the performance of an individual.

Skinner's operant conditioning theory

The main feature of B. F. Skinner's* operant conditioning theory is the fact that the stimulus which reinforces the responses does not precede it but rather follows it. In operant conditioning, behavior is elicited by the individual rather than the stimuli. In this theory of learning the individual organism first makes the desired response and then is rewarded. Reinforcement is contingent on the desired response. Skinner's main emphasis is that the individual repeats at a future time the behavior that has been previously reinforced. Behaviors that are not reinforced are seldom repeated. When the individual is rewarded, that behavior is elicited again. Extinction occurs when the behavior is no longer reinforced.

*Hull, Clark L.: Principles of behavior, New York, 1943, Appleton-Century-Crofts.

*Skinner, B. F.: The behavior of organisms, New York, 1938, Appleton-Century-Crofts.

Skinner makes the point that since teachers cannot always wait for behavior to manifest itself, they must sometimes shape the behavior of the individual. In teaching any physical skill, it is recognized that reinforcement is extremely valuable. For example, if the teacher desires a student to learn how to take the jump shot, he or she encourages the student to learn the proper form. When the student is shooting at the peak of the jump in the correct manner, the teacher indicates approval to the student. The student becomes aware of the proper form and continues to use it because the student knows the skill is being properly performed according to the teacher's standard.

Skinner has placed great emphasis on the use of audiovisual aids and teaching machines because of their reinforcement value. Since the teacher may find it difficult to reinforce the behavior of all children in a class, such machines may be useful, although some psychologists believe that they may interfere with the organization of materials into structural wholes. By means of innovations such as the videotape replay, students see themselves in action and discover their deficiencies. Such devices prove beneficial in reinforcing learning in large classes, in which the teacher cannot cope with all the individual problems that arise.

Gestalt theory

The Gestalt psychologists such as Max Wertheimer, Kurt Koffka, Wolfgang Kohler, and Kurt Lewin are greatly concerned with form and shapes. Gestalt theory is more concerned with perception than learning. One of the most important Gestalt principles having implications for physical education is the whole method theory. This theory is based on the premise that a person reacts as a whole to any situation. The whole individual attempts to achieve a goal. Furthermore, the greater the insight or understanding individuals have concerning the goal they wish to attain, such as paddling a canoe or guiding a bowling ball to a strike, the greater will be their degree of skill in that activity. Individuals react differently each time they perform a physical act. Therefore it is not just a question of practice, as it would be if individuals performed the act the same way

each time. Instead, the more insight people have of the complete act the greater their skill will be. Individuals perform the whole act and do it until an insight is gained into the situation or until they get the "feel" or the "hang" of it. Since insight is so important, dependent conditions such as a person's capacity, previous experience, and experimental setup are necessary considerations.

Information, cybernetics, or feedback theories

These theories are based on the nature of the makeup of the nervous system, particularly as the system corresponds to a modern electronic computer. Like the computer, and the process that takes place in this machine, these theories hypothesize that the human nervous system is involved with elements such as input, transmission, processing, output, and feedback. The theories maintain that learning, such as motor learning, is not a result of strengthening the stimulus–response process, as described in some of the learning theories already discussed. Instead, they believe that learning results from such things as the input, better processing of the information that comes from input, and feedback. Through such a process the results will be identified more clearly, whether positively or negatively, errors will be more readily known and corrected, and more effective learning will take place.

These theories have implications for the teaching and learning of motor skills and other behaviors desired by physical educators. The type of input that is provided, for example, the methods, materials, and procedures the instructor utilizes in teaching the skills, will be transmitted to the central nervous system. Then, within the central nervous system the processing of the input takes place; that is, it is sifted, evaluated, and interpreted. The resulting output or response will reflect the results or feedback of such input and processing, and hopefully, errors will be identified. The feedback is an extremely important part of the total process, since it will indicate whether the learning goal, in this case learning a particular motor skill or part thereof, has been achieved. If the feedback indicates that the goal has not been achieved, there is new input to correct any errors and achieve the desired goal. When the desired goal is reached, a state of equilibrium exists.

Psychoanalytic theory of learning

Psychoanalysis is a genetic as well as a dynamic theory. Learning is related to the psychosocial stages of development and must take into account the possible effect of unconscious forces, in certain cases leading to repression, fixation, and regression. All these unconscious forces are involved in the psychoanalytic theory of learning. Freud's theory stressed the importance of cognitive control in the development of a rational ego.

MOTOR LEARNING

Learning has previously been described as a progressive change in behavior resulting from experience or practice. As we have seen, many theories have attempted to explain how such a process occurs. Physical educators are primarily concerned with the learning of motor skills. Basically, motor learning is learning involving the neuromuscular system of the body. As with learning theories in general, attempts have been made to explain how the process of learning a motor skill occurs.

Factors and conditions that promote the learning of motor skills

At this point it will be helpful to consider some major factors and conditions that promote the learning of motor skills.

1. *Perception is one of the most important concepts in motor learning.* (See also the discussion of perceptual-motor learning earlier in this chapter.) Perception refers to the process of receiving and distinguishing among the available stimuli presented in any situation. It is apparent that organizing information about one's environment and interpreting it correctly are important to learning. One prime determinant in a student's attempt to acquire a motor skill is his or her ability to perceive speed, distances, and shapes of objects. Deficiencies in any of these areas make the learning of motor skills more difficult. For example, the student who has visual perception problems finds it difficult to

play baseball because of the inability to follow the flight of the ball.

A major attempt at explaining the relationship of perception and motor learning has been made by Bryant J. Cratty.* Cratty established a "three level theory of perceptual-motor behavior," which makes the assumption that the factors involved in the three levels influence the individual's learning and performance. *At the first level* are general factors in performance, including aspiration level, arousal, and task analysis. The attributes at this level influence cognition, verbalization, and several perceptual-motor abilities, such as figure-ground perception and perception of muscular tensions. *At the second level* are the main perceptual motor ability traits such as arm-leg speed, finger-wrist speed, ballistic strength, static strength, trunk strength, and wrist-arm accuracy. *At the third and highest level* are factors specific to the task and situation, such as motivation, past experiences, practice conditions, the characteristics of the situation in which the task is performed, and the movement patterns involved.

Cratty advises the physical educator and coach to become familiar with all three levels of influence on perceptual-motor performance. He emphasizes the point that attention should be focused toward their mutual influence in the learning process because both general and specific factors are involved in the learning of motor skills. For example, the lower level of the theory is associated with the alertness and arousal of the performer, which in turn is influenced by the higher level, since at this level the individual is given an assessment of his or her performance that will determine further alertness and arousal. Poor visual feedback, for example, will interfere with one's alertness and decrease the level of performance.

Cratty's theory and others that have attempted to explain the relationship between perception and motor learning have been instrumental in providing the direction needed in this important area. However, more research is necessary before conclusions can be reached as to

---

*Cratty, Bryant J.: A three level theory of perceptual-motor behavior, Quest (Monograph 6), pp. 3-10, May, 1966.

Courtesy National Broadcasting Co.

As a general rule, learning is more effective when skills are taught as whole skills and not in parts. The "whole" golf swing is demonstrated here.

the influence of perception in the learning of motor skills.

2. *The student should have an understanding of the nervous system because of its possible assistance in the development of a motor skill.* The complicated mechanism of the nervous system controls and regulates an individual's behavior and is the key to the development of neuromuscular skill. The process by which this is performed is discussed in Chapter 11.

3. *Effective motor learning is based on certain prerequisite factors.* According to Mc-Cloy,* there are prerequisites to effective motor learning, which include muscular strength, dynamic energy, ability to change direction, flexibility, agility, peripheral vision, visual acuity, concentration, an understanding of the mechanics of the activity, and an absence of inhibitory factors.

4. *Skills should not be offered to students unless they have reached a level of development commensurate with the degree of difficulty of the skill.* This principle refers to the concept of maturation previously discussed. Maturation is growth that takes place without any special training, stimulus, or practice—it just happens. It is closely associated with the physiological development of all individuals. Therefore the material must be adapted to individual maturation levels. Tennis should not be part of the primary grade physical education curriculum because the student is not ready for the activity at this time. Teachers of motor skills must determine the optimum time at which the individual is ready to learn a skill and should provide the atmosphere most beneficial for its learning. Muscular development, strength, endurance, emotional stability, and other factors are criteria that should be taken into consideration in determining the maturation levels for various physical education activities.

5. *Each individual is different from every other individual.* Teachers must be aware of the fact that individuals are different from one another and that these differences must be recognized if learning is to occur.

6. *The physical educator should be familiar*

Bowling class at the Regis High School in New York City.

with the learning curve as it applies to individuals. Learning curves are not always constant, and they are different for each individual. The learning curve depends on the person, the material being learned, and the condition surrounding the learning. Learning may start out with an initial spurt and then be followed by a period in which progress is not so rapid, or there may be no progress at all.

The initial spurt in learning may have been caused as a result of factors such as the enthusiasm for a new activity, mastering the easier parts of the task first, or the utilization of old habits in the first stages of practicing the new activity. All these factors may be present from time to time in the teaching of soccer, badminton, handball, and other physical education activities.

Many learning curves also show that progress slows down as practice continues. This would seem to be true of many physical education activities wherein the easier acts are acquired first; as the activity becomes increasingly diffi-

---

*McCloy, Charles H.: Research Quarterly **17:**28, May, 1946.

cult, the learning rate is not so rapid as during the early stages.

A period in which there is a leveling off of learning is known as a plateau. It may result from a variety of reasons, such as loss of interest, failure to grasp a clear concept of the goal to be attained, preparation for a shift from a lower to a higher level in the learning process, or poor learning conditions. Physical educators should be cognizant of plateaus and the conditions causing little or no apparent progress in the activity. They should be especially careful not to introduce certain concepts or skills too rapidly, without allowing sufficient time for their mastery. They should also watch for certain physical handicaps to learning progress, such as fatigue, eye trouble, or lack of strength. Some individuals cannot go beyond a given point because of physiological limits in respect to speed, endurance, or other physical characteristic. Physiological limits are absolute and cannot be surmounted and should be so recognized by physical education instructors. However, problems caused by physiological limits are rare, and in most cases it is the psychological limit that has to be overcome. By utilizing techniques to motivate the interest and enthusiasm of the learner, psychological limits can be overcome.

7. *Learning takes place most effectively when the student has a motive for wanting to learn.* Motivation is an inducement to action. Usually, the greater the motivation the more rapid is the learning. Motives should be intrinsic rather than extrinsic. Rewards, awards, and marks should not be a means of motivating activity. The worth of the activity in itself should be the motive. In physical education activities, motives such as the desire to develop one's body, the desire to develop skill in an activity so that leisure hours may be spent in an enjoyable manner, the desire to become a member of a group, and the desire to maintain one's health are worthwhile motives. When these are present, the stage is set for learning to take place.

8. *Learning takes place much more effectively when the student intends to learn.* If the student decides to learn a certain skill or arrives at the point where he or she sees a need for the skill, the learning situation is much more wholesome. Meaningful learning experiences presented by the teacher influence the student's intent to learn. Physical educators should stress the need of physical activity for enriched living. As the need is recognized, the intent to learn becomes greater, and learning takes place more effectively.

9. *Education is a doing phenomenon—a person learns by doing.* A person learns through his or her own responses, meaning practice or a repetition of the act. During this repetition or practice, errors should be avoided as much as possible, and the ones that are made should be corrected.

10. *The student should know the objectives toward which he or she is working.* Learning progresses much faster when objectives are clear. Thinking through the movement desired should be utilized more extensively in skill learning than it is. The student should have a clear picture of what constitutes a successful performance. For example, if high jumping is being taught, the proper form and technique should be clearly demonstrated and discussed. This can be done by the instructor discussing, demonstrating, and/or utilizing the many filmstrips and other visual aids that are available to show what is involved in the execution of the skill. In this way, after practicing for a time, students can compare their performance with the successful performance and can change their responses accordingly. As they approach the standard that has been set, the objective toward which they are working becomes increasingly clear. The physical education teacher must also make sure that the objective is within the reach of the students. When students realize that they cannot reach the goals which have been set for them, tensions arise and frustrations result, decreasing the motivation for learning.

11. *The student should receive feedback that indicates the progress that is being made.* There are basically two kinds of feedback available to the student during the performance of a motor skill. Internal feedback is related to the concept of *kinesthesis,* and external feedback is related to the concept known as *knowledge of results.* Kinesthesis is associated with the feeling of the movement and is recognized as being a con-

scious muscle sense. This conscious muscle sense is extremely important to the student during the performance of a motor skill. For example, during the shot put the teacher may tell the student to feel the movement of the body as the metal ball is released. The feel of the movement during and after completion of this skill gives an indication to the student of the performance. If one feels an awkward rather than a smooth fluid motion, it indicates that he or she is not performing correctly. Students need to develop a feeling for the correct way to run, jump, or throw. Physical education teachers should help their students to improve their "kinesthetic sense." When teachers discover their students performing the correct movements in a particular skill, they might inform the student of their findings and ask the student questions about the movement. For example, after a student successfully throws a curve ball, the teacher might ask the student: "Did you feel the ball break off your fingers?" In such a manner the teacher alerts the student to the feel of the movement and if performed correctly, hopefully it will be repeated.

External feedback or knowledge of results is also extremely valuable to the student during and after the completion of a motor skill. Knowledge that one is progressing toward a set objective is encouraging and promotes a better learning situation. Research shows that when students are aware of the progress they are making (through charts or other media), the learning process is stepped up, and the learner enjoys the work to a much greater degree. Knowledge of results should include an analytical self-evaluation to be important to the student during the learning of a motor skill. Although students view themselves on videotape replay, for example, if they have been inadequately prepared to analyze movements, viewing will be ineffective. Physical education

Youth Services Branch, Los Angeles City Schools, Los Angeles, Calif.

Cartridge loop projector used in high school golf instruction program.

teachers should make students aware of the elements that constitute a correct as opposed to an incorrect movement.

12. *Progress will be much more rapid when the learner gains satisfaction from the learning situation.* Satisfaction is associated with success. As the learner is successful in mastering a particular physical skill, the desire to learn increases so that additional success can be experienced. On the contrary, if the learner does not experience satisfaction, the situation often becomes distasteful, and the learner turns to areas in which this satisfaction may be experienced. The instructor should attempt to make sure that all members of a physical education class gain satisfaction from the activities in which they engage. Praise or other forms of rewards, to be most effective, should follow as soon as possible after the desired behavior is attained, and the best type of reward is that which gives a person a sense of achievement.

13. *The length and distribution of practice periods are important considerations for effective learning. Massed practice* refers to long and continuous practice periods, whereas *distributed practice* refers to practice periods interrupted by rest intervals. Questions of whether to emphasize massed or distributed practice in the learning of motor skills have perplexed physical educators for many years. There is a lack of solid research as to which method more easily facilitates the learning of motor skills. However, there is some agreement that practice periods are most profitable when they are short and spaced over a period of time. The number of repetitions, such as shots at the basket or serves in tennis, should be considered as the unit of practice rather than the total number of minutes spent in the practice session. Forgetting proceeds rapidly at first and then more and more slowly in the learning situation. Furthermore, fatigue works adversely on the rate of learning and also on the accuracy of learning.

14. *As a general rule, learning is more effective when skills are taught as whole skills and not in parts.* In physical education, it seems that the whole method should be followed when the material to be taught is a functional and integrated whole. This means that in swimming, which is a functional whole, the total act of

swimming is taught. You learn to swim by using your arms and legs, and this can be taught as a whole. However, the research indicates that complex skills should be broken down into their basic parts. In a complex sport such as football the game consists of blocking, broken-field running, tackling, passing, punting, and the like. Each of these skills represents a part of the whole that is football. However, they represent a functional and integrated whole by themselves and, as such, should be taught separately.

15. *Overlearning has value in the acquisition of motor skills.* The initial practice in the learning of a motor skill is important in determining how long the skill remains in possession of the learner. A partially learned skill does not remain in possession of the learner as long as one that is overlearned, that is, practiced until it establishes a pattern in the nervous system. If a skill is mastered and there is continual practice of the accomplishment, considerable time elapses before such a skill is lost to the learner.

An example of overlearning is the ability to swim. Once the skill has been mastered, an individual can still swim even after long lapses without practice in this activity. This applies to many other physical education activities. If a student wants to remember a skill, he or she should overlearn it through continued practice. However, it should be pointed out that overlearning when overdone results in diminishing returns.

Skills will usually be retained longer when the following three conditions are met: (1) when the greatest skill proficiency is gained during the early stages of learning, (2) when skills have been learned under a distributed rather than a massed practice schedule, and (3) when the performer is highly motivated in respect to the mastery and use of the skill.

16. *Speed should be emphasized in the initial stages of motor skill learning.* Physical educators are often required to make a judgment as to whether speed or accuracy should be emphasized in the initial stages of skill learning. Although some psychologists maintain that speed may lead in some cases to blindness in thinking, other researchers emphasize the speed factor. It would be desirable to be able to emphasize

both speed and accuracy; however, this is not always possible. In physical education, many skills are carried on primarily by momentum, and according to some research, speed should be emphasized in the initial stages of such learning. At this stage an emphasis on accuracy interferes with the development of momentum needed to carry on the movement. In teaching golf and tennis skills, which require momentum to be performed successfully, it is important to emphasize speed in the early stages of learning. For example, if the student attempts to develop accuracy while learning to drive the golf ball, he or she is forced to use a less desirous level of speed. Research indicates that under such circumstances a student does not develop the level of speed needed to perform the skill successfully. Physical education teachers should help students to realize that when practicing the skill at speeds they will utilize when actually performing the skill, accuracy will also tend to improve.

17. *Transfer of training can facilitate the learning of motor skills.* Transfer of training is based on the premise that a skill learned in one situation can be used in another situation. For example, the student who knows how to play tennis takes readily to badminton because both skills require similar strokes and the use of a racquet. Most psychologists agree that positive transfer most likely occurs when two tasks have similar part-whole relations involved. Again, to use the example of racquet games, since many racquet games such as platform tennis, squash, tennis, and badminton have similar part-wholes involved, it is believed that some transfer takes place. Transfer, however, is not automatic. The more meaningful and purposeful an experience the greater is the likelihood of transfer. Transfer of training occurs to a greater degree with more intelligent participants, in situations that are similar, when there is an attitude and an effort on the part of the learner to effect transfer, when there is an understanding of the principles or procedures that are foundational to the initial task, and in situations where one teaches for transfer.

Physical educators must also be aware of the concept known as *negative transfer,* which occurs when one task interferes with the learning of a second task. For example, a person being introduced to the game of golf for the first time experiences difficulty in swinging the club because of previous experience in another skill such as softball. In such cases the expression has been made: "You're swinging the golf club like a baseball bat."

Physical educators and coaches have become interested in transferring skills learned in practice sessions to gamelike situations and have attempted to make their drills as gamelike as possible. For example, during practice sessions before a basketball game, coaches have their substitutes initiate the actions of their next opponents so that when the varsity takes the floor on the night of the game, they are familiar with the opponents' style of play.

18. *Mental practice can enhance the learning of motor skills.* Mental practice is the symbolic rehearsal of a skill with the absence of gross muscular movements. The physical educator should be concerned with the role of mental practice in skill learning. Research seems to indicate that although physical practice is superior to mental practice, mental practice is better than no practice at all. A combination of physical and mental practice is best. For example, since all students cannot practice a physical skill at the same time, they can practice mentally while waiting their turn to perform. While one student is performing on the high bar, for example, another student can mentally review the essential elements that must be mastered. Of course, mental practice can also take place at other times.

19. *A knowledge of mechanical principles increases the student's total understanding of the activity in which he or she is participating.* A knowledge of mechanical principles that involve levers, laws of motion, gravity, and other factors are closely related to skill performance. Physical educators should be able to give their students sound rationale for the skills they are performing based on a knowledge of basic mechanical principles.

20. *Implementation of the principle of reinforcement will enhance learning.* One of the most fundamental laws of learning is reinforcement. In essence it means that the behavior most likely to emerge in any given situation is

The physical education program uses cable reel as an obstacle for some activities in the program at the Oak View Elementary School in Fairfax, Virginia.

one that is reinforced or found successful in a previous similar situation. Therefore the best planned learning situation will provide for an accumulation of successes. The reinforcement (reward) should follow the desired behavior almost immediately and should be associated with the behavior to be most effective. (See p. 283 for more complete discussion of reinforcement.)

21. *Errors should be eliminated early in the learning period.* As one popular magazine states: "It's easier to start a habit than to stop one." When instructing in such skills as field hockey and softball, the physical education teacher should attempt to eliminate incorrect performance as early as possible so that errors do not become a fixed part of the participant's performance. Inefficient methods, once learned, are difficult to correct.

22. *The learning situation should be such that optimum conditions are present for efficient learning.* This means that distracting elements have been eliminated from the setting, the proper mental set has been established in the mind of the student, the proper equipment and facilities are available, the learner has the proper background to understand and appreciate the material that is to be presented, and the conditions are such that a challenging teaching situation is present.

23. *A learning situation is greatly improved if the student diagnoses his or her own movements and arrives at definite conclusions as to what errors are being committed.* Self-criticism is much more conducive to good learning than teacher criticism. If one discovers one's own mistakes, they are corrected much more readily than if discovered by someone else. A masterful teacher will develop teaching situations in which the student is led to self-criticism. This is a sign of good teaching. In physical education activities, self-analysis should be encouraged so that the student may determine where improvement can be made. This, in turn, will result in a more meaningful experience.

24. *The leadership provided determines to a great degree how much learning will take place.* As far as a child is concerned, a leader does not usually have to motivate the desire to engage in physical activity. It is a part of the child's makeup. However, the leader should set up certain situations to achieve other values. The physical educator should make sure that the student has a clear picture of the objective to be accomplished and be continually alert to detect correct and incorrect responses and encourage correct performance. The physical educator should present material on the pupil's level of understanding, recognize individual differences, and utilize his or her personality to further the teaching situation.

25. *The student should become less and less dependent on the physical education instructor for help and guidance.* During the early periods of instruction when the basic techniques of the skill are being learned, instruction and help are needed frequently. However, as the fundamentals are mastered, the student should rely less on the teacher's help and more upon his or her own resources. Excessive direction by the teacher may result in apathy, defiance, escape, or scapegoating.

26. *Physical education teachers must be concerned with more than just the teaching of motor skills.* When individuals are engaged in a skill or activity, they learn more than just the details of that one skill or activity. In tennis, for example, they learn about tennis racquets and how they are constructed, tennis shoes, the various types of composition for surfaces of tennis courts, and the construction of tennis balls. They also learn about the other participants with whom they are associating, their instructor, rules of sportsmanship, tolerance, respect for the individual, competition, and respect for opponents. These concomitants in a learning situation should be recognized as being just as important as the technical aspects of the skill that the teacher is attempting to present. A principal difference between an excellent and a mediocre teacher is that the mediocre teacher is concerned only with the teaching of the mechanical aspects of a certain skill to the students, whereas the excellent teacher is concerned with the entire learning situation.

OTHER PSYCHOLOGICAL BASES FOR PHYSICAL EDUCATION

In addition to helping physical educators teach their subject matter in a more meaningful manner, psychology is related in other ways to their field of endeavor.

Physical education and psychological development

Psychology is concerned with human behavior, and physical activity can affect behavior in many ways. Scott* lists seven ways in which physical activity contributes to psychological development.

1. *Attitudes are changed.* Physical education can contribute to the development of wholesome attitudes toward factors such as exercise, learning of motor skills, fitness, and use of leisure hours. The desire for and interest in physical activity will play an important role in determining the support the profession of physical education obtains in trying to achieve its goals of a fit population.

2. *Social efficiency is improved.* Physical education has the potential, it is believed, to contribute to proper group adjustments, to the development of desirable social traits such as honesty, sportsmanship, and reliability, and to the development of a socially desirable personality. Social efficiency is discussed in Chapter 14.

3. *Improved sensory perception and responses accrue.* Although the research is inconclusive, there is some evidence that physical education can help to make a person more sensitive and responsive to the environment by the development of characteristics such as speed, visual perception, reaction time, depth perception, and kinesthetic awareness.

4. *Improved sense of well-being exists.* Physical education, it is believed, contributes to good mental health. By means of play and various forms of physical activity, an opportunity is afforded for emotional release and having fun, and it provides a supplement for daily work. Being physically active contributes to the development of a healthy personality. As William Menninger, a famous psychiatrist, stated in a speech: "Good mental health is directly related to the capacity and willingness of an individual to play. Regardless of his objections, resistances, or past practice, any individual will make a wise investment for himself if he does plan time for his play and takes it seriously."

5. *Better relaxation is promoted.* Physical education has some support to show it can help to release muscular tension, together with affording an efficient motor response. Through selected forms of physical activity, there is some evidence that some forms of stress can be alleviated and thereby relaxation promoted in the individual.

6. *Relief is provided on psychosomatic problems.* More research should be conducted to determine the contributions of physical education to certain physical states such as chronic fatigue, dysmenorrhea, and phobias. Scott points out that there is more objective evidence on the effects of exercise on dysmenorrhea than on the other aspects.

7. *Skills are acquired.* One of physical education's greatest contributions is through the development of physical skills in its programs.

Motives for participation in physical education activities

Physical educators must have an understanding of the behavioral characteristics of the persons under their supervision. In physical education it is necessary for the instructor to be aware of the reasons why people participate in physi-

*Scott, M. Gladys: The contributions of physical activity to psychological development, Research Quarterly **31**:307, May, 1960.

cal activities. Cogan* lists several motives as follows:

1. *Health and fitness*. This is an extremely important motive for participation in physical education. Associated with this motive is the student's desire to develop physical endurance and strength. Because society has placed a high value on the need for a good physique, students participate in physical education to improve their general appearance and thus win the admiration of members of the opposite sex and their peers.

2. *Social approval*. Students participate in physical education because of their desire to win social approval. Youth from the inner city often participate

---

*Cogan, Max: Motives for participation in physical education, National College Physical Education Association for Men, Proceedings of Annual Meetings, Jan. 10-13, 1968, pp. 56-63.

Courtesy of Nautilus Sports/Medical Industries, DeLand, Fla.

One motive for participation in physical education activities by many people is that of health and fitness. This Nautilus piece of equipment is used in many physical education programs.

in physical activities because this is one area where they can succeed. Students who cannot obtain academic recognition may look to physical activities as a vehicle to win the respect and admiration of others. Students who are shy and withdrawn may participate in physical education to develop the relationship with others that they need. Cogan also indicates that students participate in physical education because of a desire to gain understanding of other people that leads to the development of more positive relationships. Dancing, as an example given by Cogan, gives the student the opportunity for socially accepted body contact with members of the opposite sex.

3. *Competition, self-evaluation, and social control*. Through physical education activities, students can compete with others and assess their own liabilities and limitations. Students have a desire to compete in physical education activities because through them they can develop self-control and learn ethical qualities such as honesty and good sportsmanship.

4. *Self-esteem*. Students participate in physical education because of the desire to master particular skills and thus improve self-esteem. The boy or girl who achieves success and gains skill in such sports as tennis or bowling feels a sense of accomplishment, which in turn raises self-esteem.

5. *Creative experience*. Students participate in physical education because they desire a creative experience. Cogan indicates that the qualities of spontaneity, imagination, love of adventure, and new situations are often associated with physical education activities and satisfy the needs of students looking for creative activities. Creativity is expressed in many activities such as athletic contests, where teams develop new plays to out-think opponents, and through dance, in which students express feelings and emotions without using spoken language.

6. *Integration of personality*. Students participate in physical education activities to relieve their tensions and frustrations. Physical education is an important outlet for aggressive behavior because it provides a setting where the student can reduce tensions and frustrations in a socially accepted manner. Students realize that psychological problems can result if too much time is spent working with no time for relaxation; thus they participate in physical education activities as an escape from daily work routine.

7. *Development of specific skills*. Students are motivated to participate in physical education activities to improve their performance in a particular sport or activity in which they have particular interest.

The psychologist is interested in people's attitudes toward physical activity and also the various phenomena associated with skill learning. Cratty* lists some reasons why physical educators as well as psychologists should be interested in such relationships.

1. The social psychologist is interested in determining the attitude of young people and adults toward physical activity.
2. The physiological psychologist is interested in the relationship of such things as stress and tension to vigorous physical activity.
3. The clinical psychologist and psychiatrist are interested in such things as body image and self-concepts in the formation of a healthy personality. Some of them have also advanced the thesis that to improve cognition, visual perception, speech, and hearing, perceptual-motor characteristics must be taken into consideration.
4. Many psychological variables relate to physical activity directly involving the teaching-learning situation, the way human beings behave, and the impact of physical practice in behavioral change.
5. Many psychological parameters relate to sports that concern themselves with factors such as mental preparation of the athlete, problems of motivation, nature of movement perception, personality development of athletes, and the therapeutic values of competition.
6. Professional preparation institutions have introduced courses in recent years concerned with motor learning and psychology of motor activity.
7. Many questions need to be answered by our profession such as: What is the nature of kinesthesis? How often should physical education be taught each week? What are the causes of muscular tension? What are the conditions for the retention of a skill? The answers to these and other questions involving psychological factors will result in a superior program of physical education.

Personality development and athletics

The role of athletics in personality development is extremely important to the physical educator. Although an individual's personality is formed early in life, it can be modified by later experiences. Although still largely undetermined, some psychologists have shown through their research that individuals with certain personality traits participate in athletics, which runs counter to the notion that these traits develop as a result of an individual's athletic experience. At the same time many psychologists recognize that participation in athletics can contribute to personality development. In some cases, competitive athletics satisfy basic needs such as recognition, belonging, self-respect, and feelings of achievement, as well as provide a wholesome outlet for the drive for physical activity and creativity. These are desirable psychological effects that aid in molding socially acceptable personalities. At the same time, however, competitive athletics can produce harmful effects. If they are conducted in light of an adult's rather than a youngster's interests, community pressures, and as ends in themselves rather than as a means of fuller psychological development of students, such competition can result in undesirable social and emotional effects.

Since participation in athletics may affect an individual's personality in either a positive or negative manner, it is important for physical educators to understand why students prefer to participate in one sport or activity rather than another. Students select a particular activity because of their personality. Thune* in a comparison of weight lifters and non–weight lifters, found weight lifters to be shy, withdrawn, and often lacking confidence, and he concluded that people with this type of personality prefer this sport as opposed to others. Many students who are introverted and shy prefer the individual sports such as golf or tennis, whereas the extroverted student prefers the team sports such as baseball or football.

Singer,† in collecting data on student preferences in physical education, found that college students selected bowling as their first choice as opposed to the team sports. Singer concluded that the choice was made because students at this age want to demonstrate personal skill in activities satisfying to them. Recreation and co-educational activities were popular among col-

---

*Cratty, Bryant J.: Psychological bases of physical activity, Journal of Health, Physical Education, and Recreation **36**:71, Sept., 1965.

*Thune, John B.: Personality of weightlifters, Research Quarterly **20**:296, 1949.

†Singer, Robert N.: Motor learning and human performance, New York, 1968, The Macmillan Co., p. 319.

lege students because they are associated with adulthood.

Much research has been done in the area of personality and athletics. Studies have attempted mainly to determine the personality characteristics of the performer. In a study on the personality of the male athlete, Ogilvie* found that those athletes who achieved a high degree of success in sports were mainly extroverted. Top athletes were found to have a need to achieve success, had a need for an outlet for aggression, had the desire to dominate others, were confident, and were found to be extremely independent.

What are some of the personality traits that make an athlete a winner? In attempting to answer this question, the Institute for the Study of Athletic Motivation investigated the psychological makeup of athletes. The following four factors comprising nine traits were found dominant in outstanding athletes. These factors were de-

sire, dedication, confidence, and loyalty. Discussed separately, the factors and their traits may be seen more clearly.

1. *Desire*. Defined as the enjoyment of competition and ability to be assertive and comprising two traits: drive and assertion
2. *Dedication*. Defined as willingness to work toward goals and comprising the trait of determination
3. *Confidence*. Defined as belief in one's ability and willingness to accept responsibility and composed of three traits: self-confidence, leadership, and emotional maturity
4. *Loyalty*. Defined as commitment and composed of three traits: coachability, conscience development, and mental toughness

All these factors and associated traits vary in degree. However, they may be tested by an *Athletic Motivation Inventory* developed by the Institute for Study of Athletic Motivation.

Much of the research in this area is inconclusive. Hopefully there will be improved techniques in the future that will provide valid information about the personality of the athlete.

---

*Ogilvie, Bruce C.: The personality of the male athelte, The American Academy of Physical Education **1:**45, 1968.

Courtesy National Collegiate Athletic Association.

NCAA Championship competition in soccer. Winning an NCAA championship requires qualities such as desire, dedication, confidence, and loyalty on the part of the players.

This will help physical educators and coaches to create programs that best meet the needs of their students.

Self-attitudes and body image

Physical education teachers must be concerned with improving self-attitudes of their students. Research indicates that physical education can be an important vehicle in the improvement of one's self-image. Investigations disclose that athletic success is associated with personal and social adjustments that improve the student's feeling of worth and esteem. Physical fitness development improves an individual's mental health, and motor skill learning improves an individual's inner feelings of worth.

Operation Self-Image was conducted in the Schenectady, New York, public schools. This program consisted of early morning physical education programs combined with a nutritious breakfast and lunch. Thirty socially disadvantaged students were a part of the original program, in which the primary objective was to help these students adequately adjust to successful school and community life. Improvement in their attitudes toward themselves and the school were also desired objectives. In general, self-image did improve, and overall social attitudes improved. It was interesting to note that after the program, attitudes toward school were more negative than at the program's inception. The reasons for this were traced to the fact that prior to the program, students gave more "socially acceptable" answers, whereas after the program they were less inhibited and more responsive to the same questions.

Body image is an important concern to students. In a day and age in which society places great importance on a fit physique, individuals should develop healthy attitudes toward their bodies. The attitudes and feelings of people toward their bodies affect personality development. Sheldon and Stevens* have indicated that a person with a particular type of physique may have a definite stereotyped behavior. For example, a person may view his or her body as

something ugly, lack confidence in its performance, or believe that it is something that is well developed and can meet the challenge of any physical situation. Such feelings will affect relations with other people and also one's role in a physical education experience.

Body image is particularly important during the adolescent period. For example, some research has shown that when a boy's physique is small, not well developed, and weak over an extended period of time, his behavior is affected. He will become overly shy or assertive and will reflect internal discord. Individuals who mature late may find their relations with classmates affected when kept out of games because classmates desire to be successful in their game experience. These individuals may consequently develop an unfavorable attitude toward physical activity. On the other hand, individuals who mature early may find that although they were always the stars during early game experiences in adolescence, as their friends ma-

Courtesy Elinore Darland and the AAHPER.

Development of physical qualities affects a child's self-image and scholastic achievement. Elementary schoolchildren engaging in physical education activities.

---

*Sheldon, W. H., and Stevens, S. S.: The varieties of temperament, New York, 1942, Harper & Row, Publishers.

tured this status was lost, and the adjustment presented some difficulties. Other personality problems have been found in boys with feminine characteristics, students with narcissistic characteristics, and boys and girls who possess certain types of body mechanics and posture.

An interesting study by Jovard and Secord* discovered some significant findings concerning the relation of body attitudes to self-concept, security feelings, and body anxiety. In this study they concluded that the way one values his or her body and self are closely related, and they also found a significant correlation between negative body attitude, increased anxiety concerning pain and injury, and feelings of insecurity.

Although it may not be possible for every boy or girl to develop the type of body build they most admire, much can be done by family members, teachers, and other interested persons to help each child "be at home in his or her own body." Following are some suggestions:

1. *Understand the role of body image.* In so doing one will be better able to appreciate why some boys and girls have certain attitudes and feelings toward sports and other forms of physical activity.

2. *Use empathy in relations with those youngsters who have a poor body image.* Help them to live comfortably with their own body and physical features.

3. *Help young people to understand that it is possible in many cases to correct physical appearance.* For example, most boys and girls can improve their appearance by correcting postural faults and developing a better body build through special exercises and activities.

4. *Help each child to achieve and be successful in physical activity experiences.* Since success or failure influences self-concept and how one views new tasks and experiences, the program should be planned and organized so that each child who engages in sports and physical activities achieves success. If a youngster believes he or she is a failure, the program is also a failure. It should be noted that this means personal success rather than success based on a comparison of performance among classmates.

5. *Encourage participation in many different types of physical activities.* If properly selected and meaningfully conducted, physical activities can improve self-image, since one will develop strength, endurance, and other desirable physical qualities.

As physical educators understand the role of body image, they will be better able to understand why various students have certain attitudes and feelings toward physical activity and the contributions that physical education can make to these persons.

PHYSICAL EDUCATION AND ACADEMIC ACHIEVEMENT*

Although 9-year-old Susan had normal intelligence, she could not master the fundamentals of arithmetic, social studies, English, and writing, regardless of how hard she tried. Her academic difficulties were compounded by a partial paralysis of the right side of her body. After her parents and teachers had tried unsuccessfully to help her, she was referred to the Achievement Center for Children at Purdue University, where much research has been done on children with academic difficulties.

At the center, Susan spent 2½ years in a specially designed program of motor activity under skilled leadership. As a result, her academic and physical improvement was termed "miraculous" by her mother, the principal, and her classroom teacher. Her report card jumped two letter grades in every school subject, and for the first time she was able to participate in a full schedule of classroom activities.

Susan is just one of numerous children, most of whom do not have a physical handicap like hers, who were helped to improve academically at the center by taking part in a program of motor activities used as an integral part of a perceptual-motor training program.

More research is needed to establish and define the exact relationship of physical activity, motor skills, and health to academic achievement, but the evidence to date firmly establishes that a close affinity exists. Indeed, the kind of physical education program that leads to

---

*Secord, P., and Jovard, S.: The appraisal of body cathexis, Journal of Consulting Psychology **27**:343, 1953.

*This section is adapted from an article by Bucher, Charles A.: Health and physical education and academic achievement, National Education Association Journal **54**:38, May, 1965.

improved physical and social fitness and health are vital to the education and academic achievement of every boy and girl.

This fact has been recognized throughout history by some of the world's most profound thinkers. For example, Socrates stressed that poor health can contribute to grave mistakes in thinking. Comenius noted: "Intellectual progress is conditioned at every step by bodily vigor. To attain the best results, physical exercise must accompany and condition mental training." Rousseau observed that "an enfeebled body enervated the mind" and included a rich program of physical activities for *Emile.*

More recently, such authorities as Arnold

Gesell, Arthur T. Jersild, and the Swiss psychologist Jean Piaget found that a child's earliest learnings are motor in nature (involving neuromuscular systems and resulting in movement such as running, jumping, reaching, and the like) and form the foundation for subsequent learnings.

As D. H. Radler and Newell C. Kephart wrote in their authoritative book *Success Through Play:* "Motor activity of some kind underlies all behavior including higher thought processes. In fact behavior . . . can function no better than do the basic motor abilities upon which it is based."

Academic achievement refers to the progress

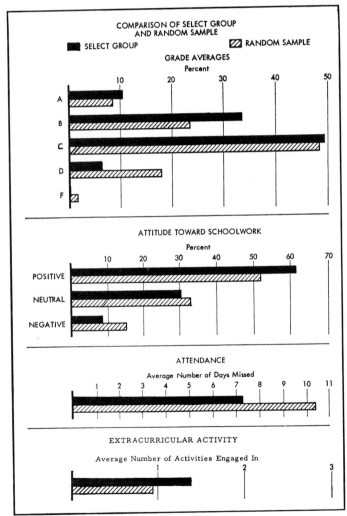

From Wilkinson, C. B.: Report to the President, Dec. 10, 1962.

Relationship of academic performance to physical fitness.

a child makes in school as measured by scores on achievement tests, grade-point averages, promotion from grade to grade, and the development of proper attitudes. As any experienced teacher knows, academic achievement requires more than intellectual capacity. Nonintellectual factors, such as the will to achieve, health, and self-concept, are almost certain to play an important part in a student's ability to achieve academically.

Motor skills and academic achievement

Physical education is related to academic achievement in at least four ways: (1) through emphasis on the development of motor skills, (2) by promoting physical fitness, (3) by imparting knowledge and modifying behavior in regard to good health practices, and (4) by aiding in the process of social and emotional development, which leads to a more positive self-concept.

Typical of the research studies confirming the relationship between motor skills and academic achievement is that of G. L. Rarick and Robert McKee, who studied twenty third graders grouped according to their motor proficiency. The study showed that the group with high motor proficiency had a greater number who achieved "excellent" or "good" ratings in reading, writing, and comprehension than the group with low motor efficiency.

In another study, Jack Keogh and David Benson experimented with the motor characteristics of forty-three underachieving boys, 10 to 14 years of age, enrolled in the Psychology Clinic School at UCLA. They found that, as individuals, one half of the boys from 10 to 12 years old exhibited poor motor performance.

Humphrey* found that motor activities are beneficial in developing skills and concepts in reading, mathematics, and science. He indicates that if an academic skill or concept is practiced during a physical education activity, that skill or concept is learned faster. For example, children can be taught the science concept of the "complete circuit" by participating in a simple activity such as the straddle ball

relay. In this activity children standing in line one behind the other, legs outstretched, roll a ball between their legs; the ball is considered the electric current, and the children are the circuit. When the ball goes outside one of the student's legs, the teacher can impress on the students the fact that the circuit is broken. Students can get an insight into the meaning of the concept being taught. Humphrey further indicates that many advanced academic skills and concepts can be introduced to children at an early age through the use of motor activities as a vehicle for learning.

A. H. Ismail, N. Kephart, and C. C. Cowell, utilizing motor aptitude tests, found that IQ and academic success could be predicted from these tests, with balance and coordination items the best predictors for estimating achievement.

Other studies indicate that the child's first learnings accrue from an interaction with the physical and social environment. Physical action provides the experience to clarify and make meaningful concepts of size, shape, direction, and other characteristics. In addition, through physical activities the child experiences sensations, has new feelings, and develops new interests as well as satisfies old curiosities.

Physical fitness and academic achievement

The importance of physical fitness was stressed by Lewis Terman more than 25 years ago. After working with gifted children, he stated: "Results of physical measurements and medical examinations provide a striking contrast to the popular stereotype of the child prodigy, so commonly depicted as a pathetic creature, an overserious, undersized, sickly, bespectacled child." He went on to say that physical weakness was found nearly 30% fewer times in children of higher intelligence than in those of lower intelligence.

Many research studies since Terman have supported the contention that physical fitness is related to academic achievement.

H. H. Clarke and Boyd O. Jarman, in a study of boys of ages 9, 12, and 15 years, found a consistent tendency for the high groups on various strength and growth measures to have higher means on both academic achievement tests and grade-point averages than low groups.

---

*Humphrey, James H.: Academic skill and concept development through motor activity, The American Academy of Physical Education 1:29, 1968.

Studies conducted at the universities of Oregon and Iowa and at Syracuse and West Point have shown a significant relationship between physical fitness and academic success and between physical fitness and leadership qualities. David Brace, F. R. Rogers, Clayton Shay, Marcia Hart, and others have done extensive research showing relationships between scholastic and academic success and physical fitness.

Health practices and academic achievement

By the development of desirable attitudes and the application of health knowledge, the student achieves maximum strength, energy, endurance, recuperative power, and sensory acuity. Furthermore, the effective physical education program helps boys and girls to understand and appreciate the value of good health as a means of achieving their greatest productivity, effectiveness, and happiness as individuals.

Social and emotional development and academic achievement

Some research has shown a relationship between scholastic success and the degree to which students are accepted by their peer group. Similarly, the boy or girl who is well grounded in motor skills usually possesses social status among his or her peers.

For example, J. B. Merriman found that poise, ascendency, and self-assurance were significantly more developed in students of high motor ability than in those with low motor ability.

Other research shows that popularity in adolescent boys is more closely associated with physical and athletic ability than with intelligence, that leadership qualities are most prevalent among school boys (and West Point cadets) who score high on physical fitness tests, and that well-adjusted students tend to participate in sports to a greater extent than poorly adjusted students.

Physical education not only affects social development but emotional development as well. Games provide release from tension after long periods of study; furthermore, achievement in physical activities gives students a sense of

pride that pays dividends in emotional satisfaction and well-being.

The value of physical education may be greater for educationally subnormal students than for average boys and girls. James N. Oliver, lecturer in education at the University of Birmingham, England, has done much research on educationally subnormal boys and has found that systematic and progressive physical conditioning yields significant mental and physical improvement. He believes such improvement resulted from the boys' feelings of achievement and of consequent improved adjustment.

GETTING AT THE "WHY" OF THE ACTIVITY

A trend in physical education is to get at the "why" of the activity as well as the activity itself. This is evidenced by the publication of high school textbooks; assignments given to students to investigate various physiological, psychological, and sociological factors related to the role of physical activity and human development; findings of some research studies which indicate that mental practice is effective in skill learning; the provision for classroom activity in state syllabuses, and the emphasis on conceptualized teaching with a realization that the most effective way to help students form general concepts is to present the concepts in many different and varied situations. Watson* supports this point of view and points out, in addition, that the formation of concepts can be furthered by providing many different experiences, some of which will be contrasting—some that include and some that do not include the desired concept—and then to encourage the formulation of the general concept and its application to specific situations that are different from those in which the concept was learned.

For many years, physical educators have been primarily activity oriented. Programs have been centered around calisthenics, games, sports, obstacle courses, dance, and other physical activities. There has been little classroom activity in which assignments are given, discussions held, laboratory experiences conducted,

---

*Watson, Goodwin: What do we know about learning? NEA Journal **52**:20, March, 1963.

questions answered, scientific principles of physical activity presented and interpreted, history of sports revealed, as well as rules, strategies, and other subject matter related to physical education presented. Some physical educators have discussed with high school students the subject of physical education to determine what knowledge, for example, they had regarding the physiological basis for physical activity. Unfortunately, most of these students did not know why physical education is important to them as individuals and the contributions it makes to their physiological, psychological, and sociological betterment. They did not know why exercise is important on a regular basis in planning their week-to-week schedules. Some students thought that physical activity is desirable to provide a break between classes and a means of having fun. Most students did not understand why physical education should be a requirement in schools and colleges. Most students have not been physically educated in this sense. It is the belief of more and more persons in the profession that all students who graduate from schools and colleges should understand and appreciate the scientific values that accrue to the person who includes physical activity as part of his or her routine throughout life. It is the belief of this group that the carryover values of school and college physcial education programs will be much greater if such subject matter is presented. These persons would hasten to explain, however, that they would continue to stress activity, but at the same time, provision would be made periodically for classroom experiences and for reading and mental problem-solving experiences.

SELECTED DEVELOPMENTS AFFECTING THE LEARNING PROCESS

There are several developments on the educational scene that portend to influence the learning process. These include performance-based learning, programmed instruction, team teaching, flexible scheduling, creativity, sensitivity training, educational television, ability grouping, and class reorganization. Because of the impact these trends may have on physical education, a short discussion is devoted to each.

Performance-based learning

Performance- or competency-based learning has evolved because of a public and professional concern for accountability. Students are taught areas of the physical education program through defined performance objectives based on psychomotor, cognitive, and affective tasks. Students are not in competition with each other but, rather, with themselves. The teacher becomes an aid to learning rather than a demonstrator, and each student proceeds at his or her own rate. In addition, resource materials are made available to students to help further their behavioral and cognitive skills.

How performance-based instruction or learning actually takes place can better be understood by reviewing the competency-based instruction (CBI) program at the University of Texas at El Paso, Texas. This program is utilized in the physical education department with prospective teachers.*

In this approach the professor explicitly outlines all factors essential for success in the program. Objectives are thoroughly defined and understood by students entering the program. This helps to focus professor-student effort toward a specific training result rather than toward nonproductive work. Students are tested prior to entering a particular program to assess those competencies already possessed by the student. Learning units are individualized to suit the needs of each student. Instruction is divided into the psychomotor, cognitive, and affective domains, and students must attain competencies in each area. Resource material is available to aid students in competency attainment. At the completion of a unit, students are tested for psychomotor, cognitive, and affective performance.

Performance-based learning is also used as a grading method. For example, in a high school in Illinois the performance objectives were written by a group of physical educators and were based on general organic, neuromuscular, emotional, social, and cognitive goals. A performance-based learning unit for freshman gymnastics, for example, was divided into a 10-day

*Freishlag, J.: Competency based instruction, Journal of Health, Physical Education, and Recreation **45:**29, Jan., 1974.

introductory unit and a 3-week advanced unit. A lecture and demonstration of the 40 selected gymnastic stunts were presented to the students, followed by the introductory unit of instruction and practice. The grading system for the introductory unit was as follows, based on satisfactory performance as predetermined by the instructor:

```
16 to 28 stunts = A
10 to 15 stunts = B
 6 to  9 stunts = C
 3 to  5 stunts = D
 0 to  2 stunts = F*
```

The advanced unit required a 3-week, instruction-demonstration period with the students, continuing from the introductory unit. A student who satisfactorily completed 29 to 40 stunts received an "A," 16 to 27 stunts a "B," and 10 to 15 stunts a "C." A performance objective unit was also prepared for sophomores required to take a 3-week unit in soccer.

The committee wrote performance objectives for all activities in the 4-year high school curriculum. The freshmen and sophomores started in the program with those teachers who desired to work with the performance objective concept. The initial evaluation was positive for both students and teachers involved in the performance-based learning units.

Programmed instruction

Programmed learning is available in many forms, but the advent of teaching machines is the best known of the various kinds of mechanical devices that utilize programmed materials. The first person believed to have experimented with teaching machines was Sidney L. Pressey at Ohio State University in the 1920s. B. F. Skinner, a psychologist at Harvard University, has given great impetus to this method of teaching, which is being used in several subject-matter areas and in some schools across the country. It has implications for physical education, especially in the area of imparting knowledge, understanding, and appreciation associated with factors such as physiological facts, rules of game, techniques, and health materials.

---

*Sherman, W.: Performance objectives, Journal of Health, Physical Education, and Recreation **42:**37, Sept., 1971.

The basic psychological principles that seem to make the teaching machine a valuable auxiliary aid to the teacher are as follows:

1. *Learning appears to progress best when acquired in small steps.* Programmed learning is based on the principle that subject matter should be broken down into small doses and that the student should be led from the simple to the complex in the learning process. However, it should be pointed out that where the steps are broken into pieces, not parts, this can interfere with the learning process.

2. *The learning process encourages students to participate actively.* Students participate by answering questions, analyzing their progress, and progressing as they achieve. They cannot be passive spectators. They become actively involved in the learning process.

3. *Rewards reinforce learning.* Students are immediately informed if the answer is correct, if they are making progress, and if they can go on to more difficult material. This reward usually proves to be a satisfying experience and enhances the learning process.

4. *Students set their own pace.* Programmed learning is tailored to either the fast or the slow learner. The individual proceeds at his or her own rate, but in either case learning is accomplished.

5. *Students learn when they are ready.* Programmed instruction is adjusted to the concept of readiness. It only presents students with learning experiences that they are capable of mastering.

6. *Students are given the opportunity to achieve success.* Because of the way teaching machines are constructed and through their technique of prompting the learner, programmed instruction helps students discover the correct answer to the problem.

The results from programmed learning have been encouraging and augur well as an effective means of instruction. In some cases a programmed text is used rather than the teaching machine. Subject matter fields such as psychology, logic, music, and foreign language utilized this medium with some degree of success. In physical education the benefits of programmed instruction have not yet been fully realized. Programmed instruction can be beneficial in teaching many basic principles, rules, and strategies of game and sports. Programmed learning will never eliminate or replace teachers, but it can free them from routine tasks so that they can devote more time to their students.

Team teaching

In its barest essentials, team teaching takes place whenever more than one teacher has responsibility for the same group of children at a given time. In its more highly organized existence, team teaching involves an instructional team of teachers who are specialists in certain areas, together with some who are nonprofessional. The team usually varies from three to six teachers responsible for 150 children or more. The students instructed by the team may all be in the same grade or in different grades and the classes in one subject or groups of subjects. The teaching team is responsible for the planning, teaching, and evaluation of the educational program for the group of children with whom they are working. One of the teachers is named the team leader and is responsible for program coordination.

Hundreds of communities throughout the United States are engaged in or planning some form of team teaching. It has been utilized in the field of physical education with success. For example, one school utilizes large-group instruction in areas such as warm-up drills, special programs and tournaments, and health instruction. These large groups are broken down into smaller groups for discussion of certain health instruction and matters that can be handled effectively in this manner. It has been found that team teaching in this community has resulted in greater flexibility. Changes can be made as the need arises; each teacher in the department plays a part in each class; outside resources, such as teachers from other departments and the community, are utilized more frequently; the needs of students are better met; the planning period provides for better teaching and evaluation; more benefits accrue for the intramural program; members of the department can better exploit their own specialties; better teacher-pupil ratio exists; and there is more effective supervision and control of classes.

In addition to team teaching, the use of teachers' aides and other paraprofessionals has come into wide use in recent years. These men and women are specifically trained to help the teacher by performing clerical duties, working with individual students who need special attention, and working with small groups. They may also perform motor coordination testing and work under supervision with children requiring improvement in this area. Teachers' aides can be a great help to the teacher if they are properly chosen, trained, and supervised.

Flexible scheduling

Flexible scheduling, sometimes called modular scheduling because of the time units involved—most frequently about 20 minutes each—is a term used to describe a school schedule in which classes do not meet for the same length of time each day. Flexible scheduling uses blocks of time to build periods of different length. For example, one module might be 20 minutes in length, a double module would be 40 minutes, a triple module would be 60 minutes, and a quadruple module would be 80 minutes. Time is left between each module for organization of classes.

One advantage of flexible scheduling over the traditional pattern of fixed scheduling, or the same allotment of time per day to a subject, is that flexible scheduling enables subjects to have varying times for instruction. For example, teachers say that usually more time is necessary in a science laboratory than for instruction in a foreign language newly introduced to students. It has been pointed out that a foreign language can be most effectively taught in shorter time periods at more frequent intervals. Flexible scheduling also provides more instructional time, more opportunity for small group instruction, and less time in study halls where learning time is not always put to the best use. With flexible scheduling, it is possible to have subject matter and courses presented under more optimum conditions, on an individual basis, and in smaller or larger groups, as best meets the needs of the subject and teacher.

With flexible scheduling it is also possible to increase the length of the school day, giving students the opportunity to do more of their school work at school, where there is greater instructional assistance available. Flexible scheduling also allows programs to be expanded not only for the academically gifted but also for the below-average student. Flexible scheduling allows the teacher more time for preparation, planning, and instruction.

Creativity

There is increased interest and stress in education on promoting creativity in the teaching process and in helping to release the creative talents of students. Creativity, as used here, is the process of giving birth to an idea. It involves thinking, exploring, and examining and a reconstruction of experiences and formation into new patterns.

Physical educators can be more creative in their own teaching by developing new ideas of presenting material, utilizing facilities, scheduling classes, and evaluating and carrying out other responsibilities. They can also open up the creative reservoirs of their students by encouraging new ideas and new movement concepts and by involving pupils more in the planning of educational experiences.

Sensitivity training or human awareness

An innovation in some educational programs, both at the school and college level, is sensitivity training, or, as it is sometimes called, human awareness. It has been the subject of sufficient discussion to warrant its inclusion in this section of the text.

In sensitivity training, participants work together in a small group situation in an attempt to better understand themselves and other people. The training group is typically called a T group. The person who leads the group is referred to as the trainer. The trainer's role is to help the group learn from its experiences.

The purpose of sensitivity training is to learn through an analysis of one's own and other people's experiences. Most groups meet for a total of 10 to 45 hours. Some of these periods are marathon sessions that go on for several hours, and during these sessions, fatigue plays a part in helping members of the group to reveal their true feelings, reactions, perceptions, and behavior. The group does not have a fixed agenda or a definite structure in its meetings. Instead, the trainer initially points out that the participants themselves will be the forces that determine how individual behavior is influenced and that the data for learning will be the behavior of the members of the group.

Assumptions underlying T group sensitivity training is that each member of the group is responsible for his or her own learning, the trainer

Courtesy Eastman Kodak Co.

Audiovisual techniques help to make subject matter more interesting for students.

facilitates the learning experience, and the experiences of the group are examined in sufficient detail so that valid generalizations may be drawn. Furthermore, assumptions include that a member of the group will be most likely to learn when honest relationships are established with other people. Sensitivity sessions, it is claimed, enable persons to be open, honest, and direct with each other. Finally, an assumption is made that human relations skills will be developed as a person examines and understands the values underlying one's own behavior and is able to practice new behavior patterns and to see the reactions achieved.

Educational instructional media

Audiovisual aids are being utilized to a greater degree in educational institutions than ever before. Educators have come to realize that the sensory experiences provided by audiovisual aids can make learning much more effective. Research in the use of audiovisual aids has found that aids contribute to a greater understanding of learning experiences. For example, the teacher may discuss the butterfly stroke in swimming; however, this concept may not be clear to the student because he or she cannot visualize the actual movements. By providing a film or picture of the stroke, the students gets a clearer picture of its component parts. Audiovisual aids also increase student interest and motivation for learning. When teachers break from their traditional verbal-centered approach and utilize such aids as television or film, students are freed from the boredom that frequently takes place in many learning experiences. The innovation of new techniques such as the videotape lets students see themselves in action, thus increasing their desire to perform.

A CONCLUDING STATEMENT

Good teachers apply psychological principles to their work. They consider several conditions in fulfilling their duties. They try first to establish rapport between themselves and their students. When this is accomplished, they will be better able to understand, accept, and help each pupil. Their objectives, expectations, and disciplinary methods are clearly stated and understood. Content of material is adjusted to each

student's level of learning and made interesting to motivate each pupil. Practice periods are adapted to the subject matter being taught and to the individual's needs and interests. Good teachers recognize and acknowledge achievements made by students and then set new objectives for them to attain. They give each child a sense of worth by letting him or her contribute and also by instilling a sense of belonging. They recognize that repetition of useful and significant information is necessary for retention of material. They know it is important to emphasize the rudiments of physical education so that students will remember and use their skills, attitudes, and knowledge in furthering learning experiences.

SELF-ASSESSMENT TESTS

These tests are to assist students in determining if material and competencies presented in this chapter have been mastered.

1. Give examples in the field of physical education of cognitive, affective, and psychomotor learning.

2. You are on the faculty of a school that is helping children with learning disabilities. Describe how perceptual-motor learning can help some of these children.

3. You are a teacher of physical education in a senior high school. You have students who need special help. Indicate what methods you would use in providing for each of the following: motivation, different maturation levels, individual physical differences, reinforcement, and individual variations in intelligence.

4. List the main concepts of and draw implications for physical education of each of the following learning theories: Thorndike's laws of learning, Guthrie's contiguity theory, Hull's reinforcement theory, Skinner's operant conditioning theory, Gestalt theory, and information, cybernetics, or feedback theories.

5. Without consulting your text, identify five factors and conditions that promote the learning of motor skills.

6. Demonstrate how you would use mental practice as one method in instructing a group of participants in learning the forehand stroke in tennis. Also, under what conditions would you use mass or distributed practice sessions in your class.

7. Assume you have been challenged to justify a claim you have made that physical education and sport can affect personality development, body image, and academic achievement. Justify your claim.

READING ASSIGNMENT

Bucher, Charles A.: Dimensions of physical education, ed. 2, St. Louis, 1974, The C. V. Mosby Co., Reading selections 41 to 48.

SELECTED REFERENCES

Bigge, Morris L.: Learning theories for teachers, New York, 1971, Harper & Row, Publishers.

Bodford, Jane: Implications of body attitudes in the teaching of physical skills, The Physical Educator **29:**85, May, 1972.

Botwin, Louis: The media approach, a happening in physical education, The Physical Educator **25:**116, Oct., 1968.

Bucher, Charles A.: Health, physical education, and academic achievement, NEA Journal **54:**38, May, 1965.

Carlson, R.: Status of research on children with perceptual-motor dysfunction, Journal of Health, Physical Education, and Recreation **43:**57, Oct., 1972.

Cogan, Max: Motives for participation in physical education, National College Physical Education Association for Men, Proceedings of Annual Meetings, Jan. 10-13, 1968, pp. 56-67.

Corbin, Charles B.: A textbook of motor development, Dubuque, Iowa, 1973, William C. Brown Co., Publishers.

Cratty, B. J.: A three level theory of perceptual-motor behavior, Quest (Monograph 6), May, 1966, pp. 3-10.

Cratty, Bryant J.: Psychological bases of physical activity, Journal of Health, Physical Education, and Recreation **36:**71, Sept., 1965.

Cratty, Bryant J.: Movement behavior and motor learning, Philadelphia, 1973, Lea & Febiger.

Cratty, Bryant J.: Teaching motor skills, Englewood Cliffs, N.J., 1973, Prentice-Hall, Inc.

Dewey, John: How we think, Boston, 1933, D. C. Heath & Co.

Drowatsky, John N.: Motor learning: principles and practices, Minneapolis, 1975, Burgess Publishing Co.

Elkind, D.: Misunderstanding about how children learn, Today's Education **61:**18, March, 1972.

Goldstein, Jacob, and Wiener, Charles: Visual movement and the bending of phenomenal space, Journal of General Psychology **80:**3, 1969.

Goodlad, John I.: Directions of curriculum change, NEA Journal **55:**33, Dec., 1966.

Guthrie, E. P.: The psychology of learning, ed. 2, New York, 1952, Harper & Row, Publishers.

Hilgard, Ernest R.: Learning theory and its application. In Schramm, W., editor: New teaching aids for the American classroom, Stanford, Calif., 1960, Institute for Communicative Research.

Hilgard, Ernest R., and Bower, Gordon H.: Theories of learning, New York, 1966, Appleton-Century-Crofts.

Hull, C. L.: Principles of behavior, New York, 1943, Appleton-Century-Crofts.

Humphrey, James H.: Academic skill and concept development through motor activity, The American Academy of Physical Education **1:**29, March, 1967.

Jennings, Frank G.: Jean Piaget; notes on learning, Saturday Review, pp. 81-83, May 20, 1967.

Klausmier, Herbert J., and Goodwin, William: Learning and human abilities: educational psychology, New York, 1975, Harper & Row, Publishers.

Koerner, J.: Educational technology, Saturday Review of Education **1:**43, 1973.

Lawther, D.: The learning of physical skills, Englewood Cliffs, N.J., 1977, Prentice-Hall, Inc.

Lockhart, Aileen S., and Johnson, Joann: Motor learning and motor performance, Dubuque, Iowa, 1971, William C. Brown Co., Publishers.

Maslow, A. H.: A theory of human motivation, Psychological Review **50:**370, 1943.

Mayer, F. C., and Grant, J. J.: Operation self-image, Journal of Health, Physical Education, and Recreation **43:**64, May, 1972.

National Association of Physical Education for College Women and National College Physical Education Association for Men: A symposium on motor learning, Quest (Monograph 6), May, 1966.

Ogilvie, Bruce C.: The personality of the male athlete, The American Academy of Physical Education **1:**45, March, 1967.

Oxendine, J. B.: Emotional arousal and motor performance, Quest (Monograph 13), p. 23, Jan., 1970.

Oxendine, Joseph B.: Psychology of motor learning, New York, 1968, Appleton-Century-Crofts.

Robb, M. D.: The dynamics of motor skill acquisition, Englewood Cliffs, N.J., 1972, Prentice-Hall, Inc.

Sage, G. H.: Introduction to motor behavior: a neuropsychological approach, Reading, Mass., 1971, Addison-Wesley.

Sheldon, W. H., and Stevens, S. S.: The varieties of temperament, New York, 1942, Harper & Row, Publishers.

Siedentop, D., and Rushall, B.: An operant model for skill acquisition, Quest (Monograph 17), p. 82, Jan., 1972.

Singer, Robert N.: Personality and sport, The Physical Educator **26:**153, Dec., 1969.

Singer, R. N.: Readings in motor learning, Philadelphia, 1972, Lea & Febiger.

Skill learning and performance, Special Issue, Research Quarterly **43:**263, 1972.

Skinner, B. F.: The behavior of organisms, New York, 1938, Appleton-Century-Crofts.

Skinner, B. F.: Reinforcement today, The American Psychologist, March, pp. 94-99, 1958.

Spearman, Charles: The abilities of man, New York, 1927, The Macmillan Co.

Thune, John B.: Personality of weightlifters, Research Quarterly **43:**263, 1972.

Thurstone, L. L.: Primary mental abilities, Psychometric Monograph No. I, Chicago, 1938, University of Chicago Press.

Totko, T. A.: The dynamics of a winner, Letterman **1:**32, 1970.

14

Sociological foundations of physical education and values and valuing

INSTRUCTIONAL OBJECTIVES AND COMPETENCIES TO BE ACHIEVED

After reading this chapter the student should be able to—

1. Explain the role of physical education in helping in the development of a sound value system.
2. Understand various theories of character and moral development and socialization and be able to draw implications for the field of physical education and sport.
3. Discuss the various sociological theories of why people play.
4. Show how sport is a socializing force in the American culture.
5. Draw implications for physical education regarding the influence of athletics on the educational process.

Physical education is an excellent vehicle for socialization. Social development is important, and physical education activities have potential for the accomplishment of this objective. Traits of leadership, moral character, and perseverance, to name only a few, are some of the social characteristics that may be positively affected in physical education programs.

Sociology is concerned with a study of people, of groups of persons, and of human activities in terms of the groups and institutions in society. It is concerned with the origin of society. It is a science interested in institutions of society such as religion, family, government, education, and recreation. It is a science in-

volved in developing a better social order characterized by good, happiness, tolerance, and racial equality.

Persons associated with educational sociology are concerned primarily with three functions: (1) the influence of education on social institutions and of group life on the individual, such as how the school affects the personality or behavior of an individual; (2) the human relations that operate in the school involving pupils, parents, and teachers and how they influence personality and behavior of an individual; and (3) the relation of the school to other institutions and elements of society, as, for example, the impact of education on the inner city.

VALUES

According to a Gallup Poll, a large majority of Americans are concerned with values and want educational institutions to do something about moral behavior in the United States. The Gallup survey found that 79% favored such instruction, whereas 15% were opposed; the remaining 6% did not commit themselves. Furthermore, the poll showed that two thirds of the persons interviewed believe that people in today's world do not live lives that are as honest and moral as those of people in years gone by.

What are values?

Various authors have set forth definitions such as the following concerning the meaning of values. "Values describe what individuals consider to be important . . . " "[They are]

Coaches are often looked up to as a source of values. Intramural activity at the University of Boulder.

centralized belief structures of the individual which deal with the ultimate goals within his life." "[They are] a motivating force, a selecting factor, an appraising concept which enable us to make choices among alternative paths of action." "[A value] is that which satisfies human desires, furthers or conserves life, and leads to the development of selves, or to self-realization." The YMCA says that values are "basic beliefs about what is good or ought to be that serve as guidelines to decision-making and actions."

Louis E. Raths and colleagues in their book, *Values and Teaching: Working With Values in the Classroom,* point out that values come from experiences and are tested. The authors compiled a list of seven stages that must be utilized to result in a value. First, for a value to result, a person must be in an atmosphere where choices can be made freely and without fear. Second, the choice must be made among several alternatives. Third, there must be thoughtful consideration of the consequences of each alternative. Fourth, there is prizing and cherishing of the value. Fifth, there is public affirmation of the choice that is made. Sixth, there is acting on the choice made. Seventh, there is

repetition with a pattern of consistency; that is, values tend to be persistent and reappear on a number of occasions in the life of a person who has such a value.

Sources of values

According to the YMCA, the sources of values include authorities like persons or institutions whose wisdom and power is generally accepted. A second source is reference groups, that is, groups of people who are looked up to by others and with whom they identify. A third source is an individual's experience or reflections on what he or she has lived through or observed.

Traditional and new approaches to values

Traditionally, methods such as the following were utilized by persons interested in instilling values in young people or other persons: setting examples or pointing to models, presenting arguments for a certain specific set of values, limiting choices to values accepted by adults or society, attempting to inspire values by emotional plea, establishing rules and regulations to contain behavior, presenting religious dogma, and making an appeal to one's conscience.

The new approach to values is entirely different. It encourages the player, student, or other individual to clarify his or her thinking, beliefs, and behavior by analyzing them and carefully thinking through the reasons for such beliefs and behavior. This procedure is known as valuing. It avoids moralizing and trying to indoctrinate the student or player with a teacher's or coach's own personal values. Instead, it tries to place the responsibility on the student to think and decide what constitutes his or her values. It is permissive. It aims at stimulating thought. It does not follow a specific formula. It tries to help persons to become aware of their own values by developing analytical skills.

Internalizing values

A hierarchy for internalizing values has been developed by David R. Krathwohl in his book, *Taxonomy of Educational Objectives, Handbook II, Affective Domain*. This taxonomy involves five stages:

1. *Receiving*—characterized by the learner becoming sensitive to the phenomena of the classroom, gymnasium, and other aspects of his or her environment. Such behavior ranges from awareness of the environment in general to attention to selective phenomena within the environment.
2. *Responding*—the learner becomes interested and responds to certain phenomena and seeks out and gains satisfaction from participating in selective activities.
3. *Valuing*—characterized by attention to the worth of a particular object, behavior, or phenomenon. This attention may range from simple acceptance to prizing and a solid commitment to a value.
4. *Organization*—different values are examined and analyzed. Conflicts are resolved and the individual begins to develop a value system.
5. *Characterization*—the learner's behavior becomes compatible with his or her value structure.

Value educator's role

The YMCA in their youth values project entitled *Valuing Youth*, identify some of the behavior that is characteristic of the value educator's role. This behavior includes helping students to (1) understand their own values, (2) see the relationships between their values and their behavior, (3) search for alternative choices and actions in achieving a value system, (4) anticipate the consequences of such actions, (5) develop skills for implementing decisions, (6) explore the ideas presented by persons of wisdom, and (7) experiment with valuing skills. The value educator also provides an environment where open and free discussions can be carried on. The value educator is nonjudgmental and respects each person's right to his or her own values. Also, a student's response is respected without unnecessary probing into the reason for such a response. Each student is encouraged to be honest in his or her discussion of values. The teacher, leader, coach, or other person, however, often raises clarifying questions that can be of both personal and social concern.

Valuing—a challenge to physical educators

As educators, all of us whether teachers or coaches, will subscribe to the belief that in our activities many opportunities occur which have implications for the development of values. These opportunities occur in our classes, when discussing such topics as alcohol or drugs, when making decisions under highly emotionalized competitive sport situations, or in many other incidents that happen in our daily involvement with students, players, and other people. It is important for physical educators to be alert to these teachable moments and to use them as a means of helping each student or player to develop a sound value system.

As one way of contributing to the development of values in each of the individuals with whom we associate it may be helpful to discuss the suggestion of former President Hester of New York University.* To make progress in this direction, he says, there is a need to return to an old-fashioned concept concerned with personal and self-respect. What persons

---

*Modified from an article by Bucher, Charles A.: Watergate fallout and health, Physical Education and Recreation, The Easterner (The Eastern District Association of the American Alliance for Health, Physical Education and Recreation), **1**, Jan., 1975.

think of themselves, to what degree they trust themselves, and how much they admire their own standards and behavior represent an important key to opening the door of a sound value system.

According to Hester, education should be concerned with helping each individual clarify his or her personal commitment to standards and values through the development of a personal code of honor. The individual is the architect of his or her own intellectual and moral development and in the final analysis makes the choices that form the foundation of personal honor.

Programs in physical education and sport that involve a cross section of American youth, have many, many opportunities to help young people develop personal codes of honor. Consequently, physical educators should exploit each opportunity that arises to accomplish this goal. Furthermore, as a result of being in our classes, playing on our teams, and associating with us, each of our students should know the importance we as teachers and leaders place on attributes such as honesty, integrity, playing according to the spirit as well as the letter of the rules, and having respect for one's opponents.

During these times through which the nation is passing, physical educators must be concerned with more than trying to develop a smooth golf swing or a championship football season. Their worth in education and their contribution to society, and especially to young people, will depend even more on how well they help each individual to develop a personal code of honor and, looking to the future, a sound value system.

CULTURAL VALUES

Social scientists have stated that in the process of evolution, human beings have had an advantage over other members of the animal kingdom because they have had the ability to transmit learned behavior from one generation to another. The learned behavior that is transmitted is recognized as human culture. It is a way of thinking, believing, and acting. Each culture has its own unique features that distinguish it from other cultures. The culture of the African Bushman is different from the culture of the American. The development of a culture will depend primarily on the various interactions that take place in one's adjustment to the social environment that has been created. As individuals recognize their role in society, they adjust and adapt to the environment.

The culture that people transmit from one generation to another consists of both material and nonmaterial developments made by human beings. The material developments are buildings and machines, to name two, and the nonmaterial developments are concerned with things such as knowledge and technology.

Moral and spiritual values are important considerations in discussing and considering the sociological interpretations of physical education. The next step is to look at human nature to discover what role these values play in people's existence and how these values can best be instilled as part of their makeup.

HUMAN NATURE

The study of sociology shows that the human being becomes a different type of individual after acquiring characteristics of human nature. The traits and characteristics that result in antisocial conduct and cause fear, hate, and worry in the world are acquired characteristics. People are not born as antisocial beings. They are not born with traits that lead to power seeking, aggrandizement, and intolerance. These traits are acquired through the environment. Through a better understanding of human nature and through a meaningful educational experience, it is possible to build a better social order for all humankind. Physical educators should understand these things so that they can utilize their work in the development of a better social order.

Original nature

Human beings are all designated as *human* at birth, but do they have those traits that comprise what is commonly referred to as *human nature?* Physical characteristics certainly do exist, but other traits identified as belonging only to the human species do not exist at birth. These traits include love, sympathy, passion, hope, jealousy, greed, and hate. The newborn infant does not have these traits but must learn them. One truly becomes "human" when one adapts oneself to the culture and learns to exist in society.

The original nature of human beings is characterized by involuntary or reflex actions, such as crying, sneezing, coughing, blinking, sucking, and wiggling. This is animal nature, which under the influence of the human environment becomes human nature.

Original nature is not predestined to take a certain shape or direction. Instead it can be molded in patterns that permit human beings to live side by side in a peaceful and happy existence. Physical education has the potentialities to contribute much to this molding process.

Human characteristics

Human nature is characterized by the acquisition of human traits that are a part of the environment in which an individual lives. It is characterized by intelligence and thinking. The human being has a thinking mechanism that enables him or her to make decisions, to control personal behavior, and to adapt to various situations.

From birth a person develops as a social being as well as an individual characterized by self-assertiveness and personal interests and desires. Immediately after birth the child shows an inclination to be a social being. Newborns, immediately after birth, have the capacity to respond to a wide variety of stimuli and especially to human facial characteristics. As the maturing process continues, the child exhibits behavior that is characterized by cooperation and a willingness to be friendly. On the other hand, the child also exhibits characteristics that display individual uniqueness, desires, and likes and dislikes. As time elapses, this person becomes more cooperative, makes friends, becomes conscious of other people's desires, and acquires to some degree a sympathetic attitude toward the desires of others. Eventually one recognizes the importance of teamwork, develops convictions and loyalties, and becomes interested in the community in which one lives and in the welfare of the nation as a whole. He or she also feels a certain responsibility for the welfare of all humankind.

At the same time, the individual has certain vested interests that he or she aims to protect. One becomes a competitor for recognition, prestige, and material possessions, and spends most of the time in furthering special and personal interests. Thus an individual develops socially. On the one hand, the individual is interested in the larger world, in other people, and in the welfare of humankind; but conversely, the individual is interested in his or her own life and personal ambitions. Physical education, through the various activities that it offers, has the potentialities for developing social traits that further personal interests and at the same time stress those characteristics that are necessary for group living.

Human nature is also characterized by a progressive advance from involuntary action to one of fixed modes of behavior. At birth the

As the maturing process continues, the child exhibits behavior that is characterized by cooperation and a willingness to be friendly.

individual possesses certain reflexes, such as crying, sneezing, and coughing. Before long set patterns of reacting to certain experiences are acquired, which soon become habits. Babies cry when they want certain things. Children acquire the habits of wearing clothes, of brushing their teeth, and of saying their prayers before bed at night. Eventually, as they grow older, they recognize that the group of people with whom they are associated in a particular environment act in certain ways and have developed certain folkways and mores.

These folkways and mores arise from the needs of the people. People discover in the course of history that certain things give them pleasure and contribute to a more enjoyable existence, whereas other things cause pain and grief. They profit from the experience of previous generations. They find some ways more expedient than others. They adopt certain methods of doing things and turn them into customs, which thus become folkways. Examples of folkways that have developed among some groups of people are the customs of a man's tipping his hat to a lady, going to town on Saturday afternoon, and eating hot dogs at the ball game.

Most groups of people attempt to improve customs or folkways as they progress. Certain ones are abandoned in light of new developments. Folkways that have been lifted to another or higher plane to better serve the needs and interests and desires of a group of people become mores. They are the folkways that through continued experience have been proved right and true and have the force of law. Examples of mores of certain countries include having one wife or husband and believing in one God.

Human needs

Another concept that needs the careful consideration of physical educators is what is called the *needs theory*. Whenever a person acts, he or she is trying to satisfy a need. Therefore physical educators should know the needs of students and of human beings in general and try to satisfy these needs in a constructive manner.

The most obvious human needs are for physical survival and well-being. Others may con-

cern themselves with the physiological, psychological, or sociological makeup of the human being. (See Maslow's statement of needs on pp. 280 and 281.)

The physiological aspects include the needs for oxygen, escape from pain-producing situations, and attention to requirements of thirst, sex, intestinal and bladder elimination, rest, sleep, and hunger. These are important to the individual as a means of survival and comfort.

The psychological needs are less obvious and concern themselves with the mind and emotions. They include love, achievement, affection, belonging, approval, recognition, acceptance, and security. A person needs acceptance, status, and achievement. These are not as easily identified by laymen, but they should be known to educators. Teachers can do much to help satisfy these basic needs of every human being.

The sociological needs are those which pertain to the pattern of how a person fits into society. These needs include cooperation, sharing, gregariousness, and love. They take into account the opinions of others, the desire to influence others, and the security one has within the group. One's self-esteem is affected by one's relations with the group.

Human needs can be realized through work, play, and recreation. If not properly nurtured, they may result in an antisocial action and personal maladjustment. Therefore the professional educator should be cognizant of these human needs and plan definite means of meeting them.

MODES OF SOCIAL LEARNING

According to Robert S. Havighurst there are three general modes of social learning by which children learn from other people, all three of which operate in a school situation.*

Reward and punishment. Children want rewards because of the joy and satisfaction they give them. On the other hand, they do not want punishment because of the pain and dissatisfaction that accrue. Rewards and punishments may be material or nonmaterial in nature. For example, a child may receive some money or a

---

*Morris, Van Cleve, and others: Becoming an educator, Boston, 1963, Houghton Mifflin Co., p. 90.

word of praise as a reward and a slap on the face or a severe scolding as a punishment.

Imitation. Imitation of other people is a common mode of learning. Such imitation may be conscious or unconscious. Children may learn early in life that rewards accrue when they do what a father or older brother, teacher, neighbor, scout leader, or other person wants them to do. Gradually, they take on patterns of behavior that imitate older persons, particularly ones with whom they feel a close emotional bond. The association results in habits of imitation that are repeated frequently and, finally, become unconscious in their application.

Didactic teaching. When a person with authority or an expert in something tells a child how to perform a particular task or what constitutes desirable behavior under specific situations, learning takes place. Teaching a boy how to bat a ball correctly is an example. This mode of social learning is effective only when accompanied by reward or punishment, or when the teacher, minister, or coach is a model person whom the child desires to imitate. Since this does not always happen, didactic teaching is sometimes a failure. Also, example may have more influence on the child than didactic teaching. For instance, if a father smokes, he may find it difficult to teach his child not to smoke.

BUILDING CHARACTER IN YOUTH

Physical education has potential for building character in children and youth. However, to realize this potential, physical educators should be familiar with the stages of character development and the best approaches to achieving this worthy goal.

Havighurst and Peck and associates,* with colleagues of the Committee on Human Development at the University of Chicago, studied boys and girls, giving them tests, talking with teachers and parents, and analyzing findings. This study suggests the existence of five stages through which the ordinary person passes in developing character.

1. *Amoral, impulsive stage.* This is a period during the first year of life or longer when the individual

follows his or her own impulses and has no moral feelings.

2. *Egocentric, expedient stage.* This period is common among children 2 to 4 years of age. It is characterized by some control over impulses in the interest of making good impressions and also self-protection from physical harm. However, there is still the "I" feeling, with focus on individual pleasures and conveniences.

3. *Conforming stage.* From 5 to 10 years of age there exists a period during which the individual attempts to conform to the demands of the social group of which he or she is a part.

4. *Irrational conscience stage.* This is the period when the example and teaching of parents are dominant, normal for children 5 to 10 years of age and older. Some adults continue in this stage. This period is characterized by a strong feeling that the parental code of morality, whether it is right or wrong, is the one that should be followed in a rigid manner.

5. *Rational conscience stage.* This is the highest level of moral conduct. The individual applies reason and experience to his or her moral code, continually trying to see the various avenues of conduct that are open and the consequences of traveling each avenue. A few adolescents get into this stage; some adults are never able to achieve it.

Some aspects of all or a few of the five stages may be noticeable in the conduct of individuals. Physical educators should recognize these various stages in the boys, girls, and adults with whom they associate and continually strive to develop higher stages of moral conduct. The more individuals can be led to foresee the moral consequences of their own behavior the higher on the scale they have risen.

In recognition of these five stages, how is character building in youth most effectively realized? John E. Grinnell* lists four approaches that have implications for the physical educator. They are as follows:

1. *Precept.* This method is based on the premise that if young people know what is right they will do it. The church, to a great extent, operates on this principle. There is general agreement that clearly understanding what is right and proper is important knowledge to communicate. However, to be most effective it must be supplemented by other approaches. In physical education it is important to

---

*Peck, Robert F., and others: Psychology of character development, New York, 1960, John Wiley & Sons, Inc.

*Grinnell, John E.: Character building in youth, Phi Delta Kappan **40:**212, 1959.

have children and youth understand clearly what is considered good moral conduct in a class, in a game, away from parents, and in many other situations. No doubt should be left in their minds as to what is the best conduct under many and varied situations.

2. *Study of lives of men and women.* Young people are impressed with great leaders. The lives of John F. Kennedy and Martin Luther King, for example, have provided the inspiration for others to achieve high moral goals. This approach can be effective if there is reading and dramatization of important moments of decision that are recaptured from the lives of great people. Such experiences will have an impact on the conduct of young people. There are many men and women in the history of sport and physical education whose moral conduct and social dedication offer shining examples of the worth of good social conduct and strong character. Branch Rickey of baseball fame, with his belief in and respect for the worth of each individual and the many trying situations he experienced in attempting to achieve what he knew to be right, will always be a cherished part of American sports history and bring inspiration to many boys and girls.

3. *Teacher's example.* The teacher leaves an imprint on students, whether it is through a sense of fairness, ability to be a regular person, generosity, or unfailing belief in the truth. Many United States'

presidents have pointed to a teacher as having helped mold their lives. The coach and physical education teacher, because of their close relationship to their pupils, play a unique role in helping to mold good behavior and strong character. By their examples, much good can be done to realize this objective.

4. *Learning to do by doing.* Grinnell points out that the most effective approach is to influence boys and girls in their moral behavior while they are participating in their school activities. They should be shown what is right and what is wrong and what is just and unjust. Many teachable moments occur each day in student government activities, sports, and physical education classes in which elements of character can be strengthened. Whether or not proper moral outcomes accrue will depend largely on the teacher. Constant supervision, high standards of conduct, strong moral values, and ethical principles will help to make this phase of the educational process a successful venture.

Kohlberg and moral development

Lawrence Kohlberg* sets forth what he considers to be a framework of moral developmen-

---

*Kohlberg, Lawrence: The claim to moral adequacy of a highest state of moral judgement, The Journal of Philosophy **70**:32, Oct. 25, 1973.

The teacher's example, according to Grinnell, can affect a person's character development. Here a teacher at the Hudson Falls Central School in Hudson Falls, New York, instructs children in ball handling.

tal stages. There are three levels and six stages.

At the *preconventional level* there are two stages. The *first stage* of moral development is "the punishment-and-obedience orientation," which Kohlberg says is where the consequences of behavior determine whether it has been good or bad, that is, if one is punished then the behavior is wrong. The *second stage* is "the instrument-relativist orientation," during which the individual believes that the right behavior is the one which results in satisfying mainly his or her own needs—only occasionally the needs of other persons.

At the *conventional level* stages three and four occur. *Stage three* is "the interpersonal concordance of 'good boy–nice girl' orientation." In other words, this is the stage where behavior that pleases and is approved by other people is the right thing to do. *Stage four* is "the law and order orientation" stage, where the individual believes in and follows respect for authority and rules as a way of maintaining the social order.

At the *postconventional, autonomous, or principled level*, stages five and six occur.

Stage five is "the social contract, legalistic orientation," which stresses the rights of each individual as defined by society. There are legalistic overtones to these rights that have implications for changes in the law for rational social consideration. *Stage six* is "the universal-ethical-principle orientation," which stresses the role of conscience based on sound ethical principles chosen by the individual, such as human rights and respect for the dignity of human beings.

Piaget's approach to socialization—rules

Piaget's assumption in regard to the socialization process implies rules and the individual's living in accordance with these rules. Such socialization or learning to live within the framework of rules is a developmental process—it occurs at various stages during the early years of life.

The *first stage* that takes place from birth to about the age of 2 years is that there is neuromuscular development with some instinctive awareness of rules. The *second stage* occurs from about 3 to 6 years of age, when there is a greater realization of rules but still the indi-

Piaget's thesis regarding socialization implies rules and the individual's living in accordance with these rules. A first-grade physical education class in swimming at the Cumberland Valley School District in Mechanicsburg, Pennsylvania.

vidual is "I" centered and as a result largely pursues his or her own rules. The *third stage,* which takes place at about 7 to 10 years of age, is what might be called the "cooperation" stage, where the individual is more concerned for rules—rules that he or she believes are absolute and unchangeable. At the same time the individual does not understand the rules completely and still utilizes them for personal purposes. The *fourth stage* is where a codification of rules takes place with an understanding on the part of the individual that they are in the best interests of society and he or she should abide by them, since they have been arrived at by mutual consent. However, they can also be changed by mutual consent. In other words, at this stage rules are internalized and become part of the behavior of the individual.

ROLE OF PLAY AS A SOCIALIZING FORCE

Play has the potential for helping human beings to have better relations with each other and to be a dynamic social force in society. To better understand the social role of play, it is necessary to examine the theories of play and the role of play in human life.

Theories of play

Sociologists have advanced many theories as to why people play. Some of the more popular of these theories are the surplus-energy or

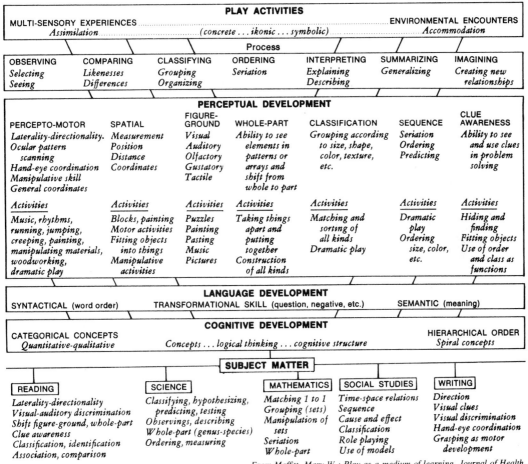

From Moffitt, Mary W.: *Play as a medium of learning, Journal of Health, Physical Education, and Recreation* **43:**45, June, 1972.

Some contributions of play activities to human development.

Spencer-Schiller theory, the recreation theory, the relaxation theory, the inheritance or recapitulation theory, the instinct or Groos theory, the social-contact theory, the self-expression theory, the wish-fulfillment theory, the domination theory, and Caillois' theory.

SURPLUS-ENERGY, OR SPENCER-SCHILLER, THEORY

Friedrich Schiller, a German poet and philosopher (1759-1805), expressed the idea of play as "the aimless expenditure of exuberant energy." This theory points out that human beings have developed many powers that cannot all act at once. As a result of this phenomenon, there is an overabundance of time and vigor not utilized in providing for immediate needs. Therefore many powers are inactive for considerable periods of time. Active, healthy nerve centers accumulate more and more energy during these inactive periods and in time are brought to a point at which there must be a letting off of the pressure. Play is an excellent medium of letting off this steam that has developed as a result of the continual bombardment of the organism by a multitude of stimuli. Schiller has also expounded what others have called the "esthetic theory," which endorses the concept that human beings play as an outlet for their creative imagination and to create beauty.

RECREATION THEORY

Guts Muths, the father of physical training in Germany, emphasized the recreative value of play in his book *Games for the Exercise and Recreation of Body and Mind*. This theory has as its premise the idea that the human body needs some form of play as a means of revitalization. Play is a medium of refreshing the body after long hours of work. It aids in the recovery of exhausted energies and is an antidote for tense nerves, mental fatigue, and emotional unrest.

RELAXATION THEORY

In many ways the relaxation theory is similar to the recreation theory. It holds that today's mode of work, which utilizes the small muscles of the eyes and the hands, is hard, tedious, and fatiguing. This type of work might lead to nervous disorders if the organism does not have some means whereby it can relax from such an ordeal. Play offers this medium. It helps a person to get out-of-doors and follow activities such as hunting, fishing, hiking, swimming, and camping. These activities are relaxing and restful and leave an individual refreshed and ready to follow another session of work.

INHERITANCE OR RECAPITULATION THEORY

G. Stanley Hall developed the recapitulation theory, which maintains that the past is the key to play. Play has been passed down from generation to generation from earliest times. Play and games are a part of each individual's inheritance. Society repeats the fundamental activities of play that were utilized by earliest humans. Activities such as running, throwing, striking, climbing, leaping, carrying, and jumping have been part of daily life for generations. The sports and games that are played today are just variations of these activities.

INSTINCT OR GROOS THEORY

The instinct theory declares that human beings have an instinctive tendency to be active at various stages of their lifetime. Children breathe, laugh, cry, creep, pull themselves up, stand, walk, run, and throw at various periods of their development. These are instinctive and appear naturally during the course of development. Therefore play is something that just naturally happens as a matter of growth and development. It is not something that is planned or purposely injected as a means of utilizing time. Instead, it is something that is natural and part of one's makeup.

SOCIAL-CONTACT THEORY

Human beings are born of parents. The parents are members of a certain group, culture, and society. Consequently, to a great extent human beings take on activities from their surroundings. Individuals will adopt the games of the group of which they are a part. In the United States this might be baseball; in England, cricket; in Spain, bullfighting; and in Norway, skiing.

SELF-EXPRESSION THEORY

Bernard S. Mason expresses a modern theory of play. He points out that people are active creatures, that their physiological and anatomical structure places limits on activity, that the degree of physical fitness at any time affects the kind of activity in which they engage, and that psychological inclinations which are the result of physiological needs and learned responses, habits, or attitudes propel them into certain types of play activities.

WISH-FULFILLMENT THEORY

People wish and dream for many things during their lifetime that can never come true. The young man who wants to be a major league baseball player or football player can, for example, turn to play activities as a means of satisfying these desires. These dreams help in achieving a sense of fulfillment that people might not otherwise be able to get.

DOMINATION THEORY

Associated with human aggressive behavior is the desire to dominate others. In many aspects of life people want to outdo others. Play activities provide people with the opportunity to satisfy this desire. By playing on a team, an individual is given the opportunity to rise to a position where he or she is recognized as the best player. An activity such as track and field provides one with an opportunity to defeat an opponent.

CAILLOIS' THEORIES OF PLAY AND CLASSIFICATION OF GAMES

In his book entitled *Man, Play, and Games,** Roger Caillois, a French sociologist, describes four types of play. He uses the term *agon, alea, mimicry,* and *ilinx* as the titles of these groups, which may be translated into the categories of *competition, chance, simulation,* and *vertigo.*

Competition. This type of play may be illustrated by sports and games of individual skill such as tennis, basketball, or chess. The competition may be simple, such as when children try to see who can hold their arms out to the side the longest.

---

*Caillois, Roger: Man, play, and games, New York, 1961, Free Press.

Chance. This type of play bases the outcome on a decision that is independent of the players such as in dice, lotto, or bingo.

Simulation. This type of play involves simulation, or imitation, when players assume roles other than their own such as playing cops and robbers or "farmer in the dell."

Vertigo. This type of play results in the deliberate production of dizziness or confusion or an attempt to destroy stability and bring about momentary disorientation. Examples of this would be children whirling around and falling down or an adult engaging in tightrope walking.

The first two types of play are more common among older youth, whereas the last two are more common among preschool children. The activities in the four types of play range, on one hand, between the extreme of uncontrolled fantasy involving an imaginative gaiety and, on the other hand, with activity that is planned and purposefully aimed at a specific result through the application of skill and effort. Caillois states that all four forms of play are universal and necessary to human development. Persons engaging in them find contributions basic to physical growth and personality development.

Table 14-1 outlines Caillois' classifications of games.

COMPETENCE MOTIVATION AND AROUSAL THEORIES OF PLAY

Two modern theories of play are play as competence motivation and play as arousal seeking, both operating on the premise that behavior exists which is not necessarily tied to the need for play as a mechanism of survival.

Play as competence motivation is demonstrated as a need of the individual to show competence to enjoy the pleasant feelings of effectance. In other words, one plays to produce environmental changes that will result in one's demonstration of competence.

Play as arousal seeking is caused by the need to generate interactions with the environment or self that elevates optimal arousal which is gratifying to the individual.

Role of play in life and education

People in all periods of history have participated in various activities to satisfy basic needs.

Table 14-1. Caillois' classification of games*

Agon (competition)	Alea (chance)	Mimicry (simulation)	Ilinx (vertigo)
Racing, wrestling, etc., athletics } Not regulated	Counting-out rhymes, heads or tails	Children's imitations, games of illusion, tag, arms, masks, disguises	Children "whirling," horseback riding, swinging, waltzing
Boxing, billiards, fencing, checkers, football, chess	Betting, roulette		Valador, traveling carnivals, skiing, mountain climbing, tightrope walking
Contests, sports in general	Simple, complex, and continuing lotteries	Theater, spectacles in general	

*Caillois, Roger: Man, play, and games, New York, 1961, Free Press, p. 36.

The need for food resulted in man becoming a hunter. The need to transmit social environment from one generation to another resulted in the formation of the family as a means for people to perpetuate themselves. The need for order and unity in society resulted in the formation of political organizations. The need for people to worship resulted in the formation of religious institutions. When humans have satisfied their basic needs, they need opportunities to engage in play activities that are an escape from daily routines. Play is an important part of a culture and reflects the behavior of the individuals and groups in society. Sociologists who desire an understanding of individual and group relationships study the play activities of the people in a society.

A society's play activities are determined by several factors. *Geographical location* is a consideration. People who live in California participate in more play activities out-of-doors than people from North Dakota because of their climate. The *natural resources* that characterize an area are a determinant. The snow-capped mountains of Colorado have helped to popularize the sport of skiing. The youngster in the inner city will engage in many activities that differ from the youngster on the farm. The type of *industrial and technological development* will determine the play activities that people engage in. The rice farmer in China who works a 14- to 16-hour day in the fields is limited in the activities in which he can participate. *Religion* also influences play. The early Puritans of New England with their strict religious beliefs thought play was a sin and a waste of time.

The development of play as an important part of society in the United States can be attributed in large measure to the rise in industrialization. Industrialization resulted in a shorter work week and increased the number of leisure hours of workers. With this increased time on their hands, more citizens turned to sports and play activities during their free time. The congestion that has resulted in the nation's cities has led to the creation of playgrounds as a means for inhabitants to satisfy their need for play. Also, the great industrial growth of this country with attendant problems such as urban growth, leisure hours, and sedentary work has accented the need for play as an essential to human health and welfare.

All men and women need the opportunity to participate in play activities. This is especially true of children and youth because of the educational value of play. Play activities give students the opportunity to imitate real-life situations, to be creative, and to express themselves. Cognitive development theorists such as Jerome Bruner have stated that children should be involved in many activities to develop a sensitivity to the world around them. Educators have indicated that games should become more and more a part of the educational curriculum in the schools. Educational developments include the "game theory," which stresses that teaching with games is an important educational asset. Giving children the opportunity to participate in situations they will face outside the classroom provides them with a picture of the

All persons need the opportunity to participate in play activities. Fourth-grade children participating in volleyball using a beach ball at the Hudson Falls Central School in Hudson Falls, New York.

various consequences of their actions. In our complex society it is important for students to become aware of the "real world" while they are still in a setting that will hopefully equip them with the tools needed to solve the problems they will face in the future.

By giving the student the opportunity to participate in many play activities, physical education plays an important role in the social development of that person. The social development objective of physical education represents a worthy goal to which all professionals in this field should contribute.

SPORT AS A SOCIALIZING FORCE*

Sport is a dynamic social force in our culture. As such, it is important to examine this phenomenon more closely.

Sociology of sport

Sport has become an important part of this nation's culture, as well as of other cultures throughout the world. It captures newspaper

---

*See Chapter 6 for a further discussion of the field of sport.

headlines, usurps television screens, produces billions of dollars a year for entrepreneurs, is a consideration in international affairs, and has social, political, legal, and educational overtones.

The big business of sport has influenced the nature of college and even secondary school sport. The best teams get the opportunity to appear on television. To field the best team, a school will attempt to attract top athletes to their institutions, ignoring at times their academic ability. Colleges have come to realize the important drawing power a star athlete can have. A college that can convince an outstanding high school player to attend and play on its team will stand a chance of getting on national television and reaping financial and other rewards. Colleges that have excellent academic programs often become better known because of their athletic endeavors.

Sport is important in society and to physical education. As a medium that permeates nearly every important aspect of life, sport has led some physical educators to believe that it should receive intensive study, particularly as it

Professional sports have gone "big time."

affects the behavior of human beings and institutions as they form the total social and cultural complex of society. They support their premise by pointing out that, according to some anthropologists and psychologists, games affect social processes and human values. However, these advocates hasten to add that sport sociology should be value free, since such a science would not be used to influence society or individual behavior for or against sport. Instead, the sport sociologist would look at sport in society in an objective manner and report the findings.

The sociology of sport is now a well-established field of study under the auspices of physical education departments in many major universities. Whereas it was once only a topic of graduate course work, it is now studied in undergraduate courses and is essential for those who are planning to go on with graduate work.

The advocates of a sociology of sport believe that sport sociologists should have a background of psychology, sociology, anthropology, and other behavioral and social sciences. Another requirement would be a background in mathematics and statistics so that one may understand the data analysis and other information that form a background for such a science.

Sport can be looked at as a social institution and can be studied in relation to its impact on other social institutions, including the military, the economy, the church, and the schools. Different aspects of sport affect other institutions dramatically, as shown by the effect of leisure on the economy. Sport as a social institution is a new concept, and much research is needed to place this area of study in its proper perspective. Topics such as the history of sport, international recognition of sport, and the true social significance of sport must be researched and accepted by the academic community.

Nature and scope of sport

Sport is a highly ambiguous term having many different meanings. Some persons refer to sport when they are speaking of athletic competition, whereas others refer to sport when they are discussing the organizational and financial status of a team. John W. Loy, Jr.* has

---

*Loy, John W., Jr.: The nature of sport: a definitional effort, Quest (Monograph 10), pp. 1-15, May, 1968.

Courtesy Cincinnati Reds, Inc.

Professional sports cater to large crowds.

stated that sport should be considered on different planes of discourse to understand its nature. He discusses sport as a *game occurrence,* as an *institutionalized game,* as a *social institution,* and as a *social situation.*

SPORT AS A GAME OCCURRENCE

In describing sport as a game. Loy maintains that sport is *playful,* is *competition,* is *physical skill, strategy,* and *chance,* and is *physical prowess.*

Sport as *play* is characterized as being free, separate, uncertain, unproductive, governed by rules, and make-believe. Sport is *free* in the sense that it is voluntary. One chooses the sport in which he or she wants to participate. The term *separate* means that sport is spatially and temporally limited. The football field, for example, is located within the confines of a stadium and is regulated by rules that control the activities of the players on the field. Sport is *uncertain.* On a third-down situation no one knows for sure what play the quarterback will call. This brings excitement and tension to the event. Sport is *unproductive* in the sense that the only thing produced during any competitive

event is the game, and the production of the game is carried out in a fixed setting according to certain rules. Sport is *governed by rules.* The basketball player who receives a fifth personal foul in a college basketball game is automatically disqualified from further play. Sport is *make-believe* in the sense that in a game situation, for example, obstacles are artificially created to be overcome.

Sport as a game occurrence means *competition.* Competition can be between one individual and another, between teams, and between an individual or team and an animate object of nature, such as a bullfight. It can be between an individual or team and an inanimate object of nature, such as in mountain climbing, and between an individual or team and an "ideal" standard, such as when a team attempts to set a new record.

Sport as a game occurrence means *physical skill, strategy,* and *chance.* Games of physical skill, such as wrestling, are determined by the player's physical ability. Games of strategy, such as checkers, are determined by the player's rational choice among several various possible solutions. Games of chance, such as roulette or a dice game, are determined by guesses.

Sport as a game occurrence means *physical prowess*. The major attribute that distinguishes sport from games is physical prowess, which refers to the practice and learning of a skill that must be developed if one is to succeed in sport competition. The physical abilities relevant to success in competition are qualities such as strength, speed, and endurance.

SPORT AS AN INSTITUTIONALIZED GAME

The institutionalization of a game refers to the fact that a game has a past tradition and definite guidelines for future goals. Baseball and football have past traditions and are highly organized, with many plans already in progress for determining the future goals of these sports. Baseball, for example, is in the process of determining what cities are to be given franchises when the next expansion develops. Sport as an institutionalized game is discussed in its *organizational, technological, symbolic,* and *educational* spheres.

The *organizational* aspect of sport is discussed in terms of teams, sponsorship, and government. In a game, team members are usually selected spontaneously, whereas in sport, teams are generally selected with care. Once a game is over, the team usually disbands, whereas in sport, once a team is created, membership is established, and a stable social organization is maintained. In sport there are sponsoring bodies such as those that sponsor the Little Leagues. On a higher level there are business corporations, which sponsor AAU teams. Sport is also governed. There are organizations that control the activities taking place, such as the NCAA at the college level and the AAU at the amateur level.

Sport *technology* denotes the material equipment, physical skills, and body of knowledge

Courtesy Sport Magazine.

Sports are a social institution.

necessary for competition. The technological aspects of a sport can be either intrinsic or extrinsic. Intrinsic technological aspects of a sport, like basketball, are the physical skills necessary to play the game effectively. The extrinsic technological aspects are the physical equipment such as the basketball court, the physical skills possessed by the coach, and the knowledge possessed by the coach and spectators.

The *symbolic* aspects of a sport are concerned with the elements of secrecy, display, and ritual. Secrecy occurs when teams hold training sites that are closed to all outsiders. Sport is display in the sense that an athlete dresses in a uniform. Sport is ritual, such as the shaking of hands between basketball players before the opening jump and the flip of the coin at the 50-yard line prior to the opening kickoff in a football game.

The *educational* sphere of sport is concerned with the transmission of skills and knowledge that is necessary if one is to succeed in sport competition. In sport one needs much skill, knowledge, and expert instruction by coaches to be successful.

SPORT AS A SOCIAL INSTITUTION

When speaking of sport as a social institution, Loy refers to the sport order. This is composed of all social organizations in society that are responsible for organizing, facilitating, and regulating the human actions in sport situations. Four levels of social organizations within the sport order are distinguished: the primary, technical, managerial, and corporate levels. A social organization at the primary level is an informally organized sport team, such as a sandlot baseball team, in which there are face-to-face relationships among all members of the team and there is no formal administrative leadership. At the technical level, organizations officially designate administrative leadership positions. The college athletic program with its athletic directors and coaches is an example. At the managerial level, organizations are too large for each member to know every other member, but they are small enough so that members know the administrative leadership. The professional sport team is an example of the manage-

rial level. Organizations at the corporate level are bureaucratic in nature, with centralized authority, protocol, and interpersonal relationships. The major governing bodies of professional sport are characteristic of a corporate organization.

SPORT AS A SOCIAL SITUATION

Sport as a social situation or social system, as it is sometimes called, is an important concern for the sport sociologist. The sport sociologist is interested in why people get involved in sport and what effect their involvement has on other aspects of their lives. Involvement in a social system is analyzed in terms of degree and kinds of involvement. Degree of involvement refers to the frequency, duration, and intensity of involvement. Kinds of involvement are expressed in terms of an individual's relationship to the "means of production" of a game. There are producers who are characterized as primary, secondary, and tertiary. The primary producers are the athletes who play the game. The secondary producers do not play the game but have direct technological consequences for the outcome of the game. Secondary producers include club owners, officials, and team physicians. The tertiary producers do not actively engage in the sport and have no direct technological consequences for the outcome of the game. Cheerleaders and bandleaders are examples.

Consumers, like producers, are designated as being primary, secondary, or tertiary. Primary consumers are those who make up the "live" attendance at a sport contest. Secondary customers are those who become involved in sporting events by viewing them on television or listening to them on the radio. Tertiary consumers become involved in sport through conversations with others and through reading about sport in a newspaper.

Sport is an important part of American culture

Sport is not just concerned with two teams meeting each other on the playing field. Sport activities are an important part of this nation's culture, and sport sociologists face a challenge in interpreting the role of sport in our way of life. Sport activities in the United States have been found by sociologists to be related to religion, economics, education, and government, to name a few.

Throughout the nation's history, sport has been influenced by religious beliefs and economic conditions. During the nation's early developmental years, sport activities, especially in New England, were severely hampered because of the religious attitude of the Puritan settlers. Religious attitudes have changed, and some religious institutions are now extremely active in sport. Throughout the nation, organizations such as the Catholic Youth Organization and B'nai B'rith provide activities that give youth the opportunity to participate in sport. Schools and colleges under religious control sponsor sport programs.

Sport and the economic conditions of the nation are closely aligned. When the nation was developing, there was little opportunity to participate in sport. However, the rise in industrialization and the resultant increased leisure time has led to an increased awareness of sport. Sport activities have become an important part of the American way of life. Americans by the millions not only take part in sporting events, through active participation, but also spend millions of dollars on sport equipment. They also enjoy sporting events solely as spectators and fans.

In the area of education, sport has become a part of schools and colleges in the nation. Physical education, intramurals, and athletic programs have been created by educational institutions to give young people the opportunity to play in these activities. Sport programs in schools in recent years have been associated with improving the fitness of our youth. The national government under the leadership of President Eisenhower and, later, Presidents Ken-

Courtesy University of Chicago.

One hundred years of football. Artist Arnold Friberg's painting of the first football game, Princeton at Rutgers, 1869. Bewildered spectators, all 200 to 300 of them, sat on fence rails or in buckboards and watched twenty-five–man teams play soccer-style game. After much "headlong running, wild shouting and frantic kicking," Rutgers won, 6 goals to 4.

nedy, Johnson, Nixon, Ford, and Carter initiated and is supporting the President's Council on Physical Fitness and Sports, which has been concerned with improving the fitness of the nation's youth.

SOME SOCIOLOGICAL IMPLICATIONS OF EDUCATIONAL ATHLETICS

Since athletics play such an important role in American culture and in physical education programs, it is interesting to examine some of the sociological implications of sports.

Influence of society on interscholastic athletics

The contemporary public likes athletic competition. This has been evident at the professional level, the college level, the senior high school level, and, in recent years, the junior high school level. Sport has become a part of the nation's culture. The interest and popularity of athletics have affected educational programs of schools and colleges.

1. *The place of sport in education has been largely determined by society rather than by educators.* Whether a sport is popular in schools and colleges depends to a great extent on the amount of public interest, spectator approval, and newspaper space it generates. Basketball, track, football, and baseball have traditionally rated higher with the public than other activities.

It would appear that what the public supports, educators tend to adopt. Young people grow up in this type of environment and many times are interested in a sport because society has accented its importance rather than because of the contributions the sport makes to them as individuals.

2. *Athletics frequently have become a medium of entertainment rather than serving to fulfill educational objectives.* The popularity of sports in the United States is frequently related to their value as entertainment rather than their value as education. Thomas Woody, former Professor of Education at the University of Pennsylvania, made direct reference to this development when he stated: "Scholastic contests, despite their best efforts to the contrary,

are often spectacles to entertain idle multitudes, rather than to serve educational ends."*

3. *Parental and community interest in schools may increase as a result of athletics.* Athletics may result in an increased interest by the parents in the schools. As a result, better communication may occur between the school and the community.

Many parents desire their children to participate in a successful athletic program. What parents consider a successful program and what educators consider a successful athletic program may be diametrically opposed. Since athletics often place reflected glory on the parents and relatives of the youngsters, parents frequently want their children to participate and to win.

4. *Pressures on girls' athletics are not as severe, but this is changing.* For many years, society maintained a greater degree of athletic competition for boys than for girls. In recent years, there have been many changes in women's athletics as a result of the women's movement and Title IX. Eleanor Metheny,† Professor Emeritus of Education and Physical Education at the University of Southern California, published a provocative article concerning the effect of cultural mores rather than physical consideration on participation in athletics for girls. She tells of how the women in Russia put the shot and hurl the javelin with a great degree of skill and no evidence of physical damage. "Since there seems to be no differences in physical structure between European and American women, the differences must stem solely from the different concepts of roles appropriate for women in the countries in which they live."* She states further that "the resolution of any specific issue relating to girls and athletics is inextricably bound up in these unresolved larger social issues."

5. *The need: proper educational perspective.* Research reveals a need for greater understanding concerning the role of athletics in the school program. Educators, as well as the entire com-

---

*Woody, Thomas: School athletics and social good, Journal of Educational Sociology **28:**246, 1955.

†Metheny, Eleanor: Relative values in athletics for girls, Journal of Educational Sociology **28:**268, 1955.

munity, need to reevaluate the relation of society to education as it concerns athletics. The manner in which this phase of the school program can best meet the needs of youth should be considered at each educational level.

Some benefits claimed for athletics

Good sportsmanship. Although disputed by some researchers, competitive athletics, according to some educators and sports leaders, can teach the art of winning and losing gracefully, the spirit of being fair to others, observance of the spirit as well as the letter of the rules, and the maintenance of a friendly attitude toward all individuals involved in the game situation.

Walter E. Damon* made a statement several years ago that many people believe is as true today, which is that competition contributes to team spirit and to motivation and meets the interests of people. In a study about delinquent boys, Damon found that a boy has the chance to be more than an individual. He can become a part of something. Damon believes that the strain of tough competition, together with the push to win, is not detrimental but is actually good for all boys and for delinquent or potentially delinquent boys.

Cooperation. Competitive athletics, some educators also think, provide a social laboratory for the student to learn how to work with others in a cooperative manner, to contribute toward the common purposes of the group, to promote a feeling of social consciousness, and to develop an understanding of the rights and feelings of others.

James B. Nolan, former Deputy Commissioner of the Police Department in the City of New York, reported that play becomes a way of learning about life—that respect for the rights of others is impressed on children through the rules that they are expected to obey and expect their playmates to obey in turn. He believes that they must get along with their own side and guard the rights of the other side, learn about the importance of individual merit, gain a

knowledge of fair play and a knowledge of social behavior, the "shall" and the "shall not," and that, in short, there is no better arena for democracy.

Acceptance of all persons regardless of race, creed, or origin. Competitive athletics may teach the appreciation and acceptance of all persons in terms of their ability, performance, and worth, according to some educators. Individual attitudes are applauded for their achievements, regardless of background and team affiliation. Opportunities are afforded for every person to achieve and to be recognized, regardless of economic or social class.

Traits of good citizenship. It is believed by some educators (although disputed by some researchers) that competitive athletics help in developing those traits of good citizenship essential to democratic living. This include qualities such as initiative, trustworthiness, dependability, social consciousness, loyalty, and respect for the individual. Jordan L. Larson,* former president of the American Association of School Administrators, expressed views that still exist today when he discussed the contributions of athletics to good citizenship. He pointed out that the ideals of fair play, sportsmanship, and clean living are all part of athletics and are attributes capable of being carried on into adult life. In describing his team in a small school in Iowa many years ago, Larson stated that a great respect was gained for their metropolitan neighbors and that their city neighbors in return began to better understand the boys from the country. From his observations as a coach, athletic official, and school administrator, it was his contention that athletics tended to foster respect for the work of the individual regardless of race, creed, or economic background and that good citizenship qualities could definitely result from competitive play.

Leadership. Competitive athletics, according to some educators, contribute to qualities of leadership. Hale† reviewed a study by Jeanne

---

*Damon, Walter E.: Competitive athletics helps delinquent boys, Journal of Health, Physical Education, and Recreation **29**:14, Jan., 1958.

*Larson, Jordan L.: Athletics and good citizenship, Journal of Educational Sociology **28**:258, 1955.
†Hale, Creighton J.: What research says about athletics for pre-high school age children, Journal of Health, Physical Education, and Recreation **30**:19, Dec., 1959.

Doyl Lareau of the University of California. It was reported that girls in grades eight and nine were given the UC Interest Inventory tests to determine the relationship between athletic competition and personal and social adjustment. The results revealed that girls with experience in athletic competition showed better personal and social adjustment, were more popular, and exhibited higher leadership qualities. Thus it may be that through athletics, opportunities are provided for accepting responsibility, making decisions, influencing others, and developing other qualities important to leadership.

Followership. Studies by Lareau* and Salz† tend to indicate that competitive athletics develop traits of a successful followership, including such qualities as respect for authority and outstanding leadership, abiding by the rules, cooperation with those in command, a recognition of the rights of others, and a sense of fairness. The student may also learn to take criticism without a feeling of hostility or resentment.

Self-discipline. Athletic competition develops abilities of self-discipline and determination. The rigorous training involved in many athletic events forces individuals to push themselves to achieve maximum effort. Athletes must be disciplined to make sacrifices and have the determination to achieve success. Winning is not only based on physical skill but also on the will and desire to achieve success.

Additional avenues for social acquaintances. Competitive athletics according to some educators, pave the way to new acquaintances, since the athletic individual appears to be more socially mobile and extroverted than the nonathletic individual. He or she has broadened interests, belongs to more organizations, and has many opportunities to meet students from other schools.

*Lareau, Jeanne Doyle: The relationship between athletic competition and personal and social adjustment on junior high school girls, unpublished master's dissertation, University of California, 1950.
†Salz, Art: Comparative study of personalities of Little League champions, other players in Little League, and nonplaying peers, unpublished master's thesis, Pennsylvania State University, 1957.

Social poise and understanding of self. Competitive athletics contribute to social poise, self-composure, and confidence, according to some educators. They also provide people with a socially acceptable outlet for their aggression. Human beings have had to repress their basic aggressive tendencies to exist peacefully in society. However, at times, because of the pressure of life, there is need for people to "let off steam." The football game or wrestling match is an excellent safety valve for a person's aggressive behavior.

Biddulph,* attempted to determine the personal and social adjustment of secondary school boys with high athletic achievement. The results indicated that the superior athlete at the secondary school level had a higher mean self-adjustment score on the California Test of Personality than other boys. The superior athletes had a significantly higher mean score on the teachers' ratings and sociograms. The athlete also rated considerably higher on the adjustment items as rated by their teachers. The superior athletic group listed more personal friends and were chosen more frequently by others. It was concluded as a result of this study that students ranking high on athletic achievement tests demonstrate significantly a greater degree of personal and social adjustment than those of low athletic achievement.

The athlete may learn to appreciate the uniqueness of each person and more about himself or herself and is in a position to develop responsibility for personal actions and to acquire a willingness to accept the results of these actions.

Social consciousness with an accompanying sense of values. According to some physical educators, the athlete develops a concern for teammates and opponents. The athlete takes increased interest in the school and community and learns firsthand the importance of sharing with others, adhering to the rules, and promoting a way of life that fosters morality, ethical behavior, and the concern for individual dignity and worth. Values concerning what is right and what is wrong become familiar, and

*Biddulph, Lowell G.: Athletic achievement and the personal and social adjustment of high school boys, Research Quarterly **25:**1, March, 1954.

an adherence to democratic principles and a respect for others is developed.

Suggested harm caused by athletics

Ego-centered athletes. There is a great glorification of the star athlete by both the school and the community. These few select youngsters are frequently singled out from the team to receive special publicity and attention. There is a concentration on the few superior players instead of the many. An overemphasis on publicity often results. Consequently, these youngsters may develop inflated ideas about themselves. They begin to assume that they are "special" and should receive extra favors because of their reputations.

False values. False values may likely be developed because of the emphasis placed on the star athlete or even athletics in general. The team practice session or the actual game may become more important to the youngster than any other out-of-class activity; a boy may begin to acquire the attitude that he is destined to be-

come an "All-American" and therefore must give his full time to this endeavor. And, as the community becomes more interested in the program, the youngster may become more concerned that the spectator be pleased and less concerned about personal needs.

Harmful pressures. When parents and members of the community develop the kind of interest in interscholastic sports that has as its main objective "winning," pressures that affect the players are likely to result. A boy or girl may feel the need to win to please the public and gain acceptance. Thus a constant overstimulation of the student progresses as he or she strives to reach adult goals.

Loss of identity. Athletics can lead to a loss of identity on the part of the individual. At a symposium* on problems of the black athlete, one of the major problems discussed was the

---

*Ruffer, William A.: Symposium on problems of the black athlete, Journal of Health, Physical Education, and Recreation **42:**17, Feb., 1971.

Courtesy Don Canham.

Varsity athletics have great potential for good, but they also may cause harm among athletes. Varsity football at the University of Michigan.

dehumanizing factor of athletics that affects both black and white individuals. Symposium chairman, William Ruffer, emphasized the point that the athlete is not a college student in the generally accepted definition of the term. College athletes sometimes have a special dining arrangement, live in a separate dormitory, and may take a reduced academic course load. They have a controlled life guided by athletic directors and coaches, who are not always sensitive to their needs. College athletes have a socially regulated life. Although many colleges are reforming their athletic policies, some are still pursuing strict authoritarian procedures that prevent athletes from making their own decisions and living their own lives.

Inequitable use of facilities, leadership, and money. Athletics are only one phase of the total physical education program. Yet the amount of facilities, the number of personnel, and the proportion of money to be spent are often distributed in an inequitable proportion to the interscholastic program.

Distortion of the educational program leading to overspecialization. At times, so great an emphasis is placed on producing successful athletic teams that the educational program may suffer. The academic achievement of both the participants and the nonparticipants may begin to diminish as student interests are captured by the constant excitement and tension of their team and their heroes. The young competitive player may become one sided in his or her own interests, with athletics becoming much too large and important in his or her thinking and purposes.

Aggression and violence. There are two theories of aggression that have been proposed that directly involve athletics. One theory states that aggression is instinctive, and because society is aggressive by nature, athletics serve to channel these tendencies. The other theory asserts that aggression is learned behavior, and athletics aid in teaching aggression. Therefore one might deduce that athletics contribute to a violent society. Although these two theories appear to be incompatible, they hold a valuable lesson for physical educators. Rather than accepting or rejecting either theory, one must reconsider sport curriculums and evaluate the degree of aggres-

siveness produced by an activity in terms of its value and harmfulness to the participants.

Conditions under which athletics become sociologically valuable

All participants—the focus of attention. There must be equal opportunity for all students to participate in the competitive athletic program, with activities included that are individually adapted to the student. Athletics can be valuable when all students are given the opportunity to learn, to practice, and to play and when playing facilities and the coach's time are allocated among all students.

Results in the study by Biddulph* concerning the relation between personal and social adjustment of secondary school boys of high athletic achievement and the personal and social adjustment of secondary school boys of low athletic achievement led him to conclude that athletics should be provided for all boys and not the special few. Since students ranking high in athletic achievement demonstrated a significantly greater degree of personal and social adjustment than those boys with low athletic achievement, Biddulph concluded that it is important for all boys to develop motor ability, with a greater emphasis on intramural athletic activities rather than on interscholastic activities, which tend to neglect the majority of boys.

Focus on the individual student. Athletics must be molded and shaped for the student—not the student for athletics. In the report by the Joint Committee on Athletic Competition,† the substance of which is as true today as when it was written, the following conditions were revealed as necessary for beneficial effects pertaining to the individual student through participation in competitive athletics: Instruction must be fitted to meet the needs of the players; sports should be included that are appropriate for the age, maturity, skill, stage of growth, and physi-

---

*Biddulph, Lowell G.: Athletic achievement and the personal and social adjustment of high school boys, Research Quarterly **25**:1, March, 1954.

†Joint Committee on Athletic Competition for Children of Elementary and Junior High School Age: Desirable athletic competition for children, Washington, D.C., 1952, American Association for Health, Physical Education, and Recreation, pp. 4, 13-24.

cal makeup of the players; safeguards should be provided for the health and well-being of the participants; the program should be free of undesirable publicity and promotion; and opportunities should be given for a balance of interest and activities on the part of all participants.

Outgrowth of intramurals and extramurals. The athletic program should represent a natural outgrowth of the intramural and extramural program. The class instructional program and the intramural and extramural programs should be functioning effectively for all students before interschool athletics are considered. Strong physical education classes and intramural programs should form the base of athletic competition in the schools—a base that builds and is finally capped with more highly organized, competitive games of the interscholastic type.

Leadership. Sound and qualified leadership is essential to the properly functioning athletic program. Leadership plays an important role in setting qualities of fairness, self-control, and honesty. Good coaching, then, together with adequate supervision, must serve to prevent undesirable practices and to eliminate pressures. Leaders must see that the program is always conducted with regard to the best interests of the students.

Implications for the physical education program

The impact that society has had on athletics in education presents a challenge to educators to (1) properly interpret to the community the role of athletics in education and (2) prevent undesirable pressures and practices that are not educationally sound. When conducted in accordance with desirable standards such as those of leadership and program content, athletics have the potential for accomplishing beneficial effects. However, when not conducted in accordance with desirable standards, athletics can be detrimental and harmful to the student.

SELF-ASSESSMENT TESTS

These tests are to assist students in determining if material and competencies presented in this chapter have been mastered.

1. You are aware that a large majority of people would like something done about improving moral behavior in the United States. Assume that you are a coach of a basketball team. As the coach, what could you do, and how would you do it, to contribute a sound value system in the players?

2. Compare Kohlberg's framework of moral developmental stages with Piaget's approach to socialization that involves living in accordance with certain rules.

3. Prepare a paper that summarizes the various theories of play discussed in this chapter.

4. Define a socializing force and describe some of its dimensions. Analyze sport as a socializing force in light of your definition and dimensions.

5. Prepare a set of guidelines that, if utilized, would ensure that athletics would contribute to sound educational objectives.

READING ASSIGNMENT

Bucher, Charles A., and Goldman, Myra: Dimensions of physical education, St. Louis, 1969, The C. V. Mosby Co., Reading selections 51 to 56.

SELECTED REFERENCES

Amir, Y.: Contact hypothesis in ethnic relations, Psychological Bulletin **71:**310, 1969.

Berryman, Jack W.: Sport history as social history, Quest (Monograph 20), p. 65, June, 1973.

Bucher, Charles A.: Interscholastic athletics at the junior high school level, Albany, New York, 1965, The University of the State of New York, State Education Department.

Bucher, Charles A.: Administrative dimensions of health and physical education programs, including athletics, St. Louis, 1971, The C. V. Mosby Co.

Bucher, Charles, and Bucher, Richard: Recreation for today's society, Englewood Cliffs, N.J., 1974, Prentice-Hall, Inc.

Bucher, Charles A., and Koenig, Constance: Methods and materials of secondary school physical education, ed. 5, St. Louis, 1978, The C. V. Mosby Co.

Cratty, Bryant J.: Social dimensions of physical activity, Englewood Cliffs, N.J., 1967, Prentice-Hall, Inc.

Editors of Winston Press: Viewpoints: red and yellow, black and brown, Minneapolis, 1972, Winston Press.

Ellis, M. S.: Play and its theories re-examined, Parks and Recreation **4:**51, Aug., 1971.

Frederickson, Florence S.: Sports and the cultures of man. In Loy, John W., and Kenyon, Gerald S., editors: Sport, culture and society: a reader on the sociology of sport, London, 1969, The Macmillan Co.

Gibson, Dorothy W.: Social perspectives on education, New York, 1965, John Wiley & Sons, Inc.

Havighurst, Robert J., and Newgarten, Bernice L.: Society on education, Boston, 1957, Allyn & Bacon, Inc.

Hellison, Donald R.: Humanistic physical education,

Englewood Cliffs, N.J., 1973, Prentice-Hall, Inc.

Hollander, E. P.: Principles and methods of social psychology, New York, 1971, Oxford University Press.

Jones, Frank B.: Intercollegiate and interscholastic athletic program in the 1970's: a report to the Athletic Institute Board of Directors, Sportscope 15(2):16, 1970.

Kenyon, Gerald S., and Loy, John W.: Toward a sociology of sport, Journal of Health, Physical Education, and Recreation 36:24, May, 1965.

Kohlberg, Lawrence: Moral education for a society in moral transition, Educational Leadership, p. 46, Oct., 1975.

Kohlberg, Lawrence: The cognitive-developmental approach to moral education, Phi Delta Kappan 56:670, June, 1975.

Loy, John W.: The nature of sport: a definitional effort, Quest (Monograph 10), pp. 1-15, May, 1969.

Loy, John W., and Kenyon, Gerald S.: Sport, culture and society: a reader on the sociology of sport, London, 1969, The Macmillan Co.

Oxendine, Joseph B.: Social development—the forgotten objective? Journal of Health, Physical Education, and Recreation 37:23, May, 1966.

Parker, Franklin: Sport, play, and physical education in cultural perspective, Journal of Health, Physical Education, and Recreation 36:29, April, 1965.

Peatling, John H.: Signs of structure and signs of dissonance: adult responses to a piagerian, Union College Character Research Project, Schenectady, N.Y., 1976.

Perry, John, and Perry, Erna: The social web, San Francisco, 1973, Canfield Press.

Piaget, Jean: The moral judgment of the child, Glencoe, Ill., 1948, The Free Press.

Pickard, J. P.: Problems of the cities, The Journal Boys' Clubs of America 7:3, Winter, 1971-1972.

Raths, L. E., and others: Values and teaching, Columbus, 1966, Charles E. Merrill Publishing Co.

Ruffer, William A.: Symposium on problems of the black athlete, Journal of Health, Physical Education, and Recreation 42:11, Feb., 1971.

Rushall, Brent S., and Siedentop, Daryl: The development and control of behavior in sport and physical education, Philadelphia, 1972, Lea & Febiger.

Shane, H. G.: The future mandates new moral directions, emerging moral dimensions in society: implications for schooling, Washington, D.C., 1975, Association for Supervision and Curriculum Development.

Singer, Robert, and others: Physical education—an interdisciplinary approach, New York, 1972, The Macmillan Co.

Talamini, John T., and Page, Charles H.: Sport & Society—an anthology, Boston, 1973, Little, Brown & Company.

Tandy, R., and Laflin, J.: Aggression and sport: two theories, Journal of Health, Physical Education, and Recreation 44:19, Feb., 1973.

Ulrich, Celeste: The social matrix of physical education, Englewood Cliffs, N.J., 1968, Prentice-Hall, Inc.

Weiss, Paul: Sport—a philosophic inquiry, Carbondale, Ill., 1969, Southern Illinois University Press.

Woodward, Kenneth L.: Moral education, Newsweek, p. 74, March 1, 1976.

PART FOUR

SETTINGS FOR PHYSICAL EDUCATION PROGRAMS

15 ■ Settings for physical education activities and programs

The Branch Rickey Gymnasium and Field House at Ohio Wesleyan University, Delaware, Ohio.

15

Settings for physical education activities and programs

INSTRUCTIONAL OBJECTIVES AND COMPETENCIES TO BE ACHIEVED

After reading this chapter the student should be able to—

1. Describe and identify key characteristics of the various developing settings for physical education programs.
2. Describe and identify key characteristics of various established settings for physical education programs.
3. Discuss how the public's interest in physical fitness is resulting in more physical education programs.
4. Show how elementary school physical education has and is changing.
5. Identify new developments in physical education programs at the elementary, middle school, junior high school, senior high school, and college educational levels.
6. Conduct a self-evaluation to determine the setting in which to work.

Physical education activities are conducted in many and varied settings, some of which are comparatively new with developing physical education programs, such as can be found in the corporate sector. Other settings are well established, such as schools, colleges, and youth-serving organizations.

DEVELOPING SETTINGS FOR PHYSICAL EDUCATION PROGRAMS

Developing settings for physical education activities and programs are becoming increas-ingly evident, particularly in respect to industrial fitness, health spas, and centers for the elderly.

Industry turns to fitness

An estimated 50,000 business concerns in the United States spend approximately $5 billion annually on their physical fitness and recreational programs.

Hard-headed business people rarely spend huge sums of company money on programs that do not promise their investors some return. In this case the payoff from fitness, according to these business people, can be summed up with one phrase—increased productivity. Some government agencies and major corporations indicate that physically fit employees turn out more and better work than their sedentary colleagues. They also maintain that fit employees stay on the job longer, rise faster and higher in the firm, seem to think more clearly, and generally get more out of their job—and out of life.

The business firms endorsing and providing fitness programs range from major corporations to small repair shops. The facilities run the gamut from a completely equipped, multi-million dollar gymnasium, including swimming pool, to a handball court painted on the brick wall of an adjacent tenement building.

Unfortunately, not every program contributes in a major way to employee fitness. Some are nothing more than a sauna and a massage table, where top executives of a firm can unwind after a tough day; others are just occasional inter-departmental softball, bowling, or golf matches

Many businessmen engage in various forms of physical activity at the Aerobics Activity Center, Dallas, Texas.

where exercise is minimal and there is little oxygen-increasing benefit; and still others pay only lip service to the idea of fitness rather than promote actual participation.

Nevertheless, there are many well-founded company fitness programs in the United States, and the number is increasing day by day. Clearly, industry's growing interest in employee fitness is not a matter of sheer altruism. "It's good business to keep our personnel healthy," says the President of Life of Georgia, "because it means less lost time. I'm also convinced that if we can add a few years to our employees' lives, it will means a tremendous financial savings for the company."

Forbes magazine is a business firm that believes in employee fitness. Its philosophy is stated as follows, "If you take care of your employees, your employees will take care of their work." This organization provides every employee the opportunity to engage in exercise and physical activity, and up to 3 hours a week

of activity can be done on company time. A Fitness Center Director, trained in physical education, is in charge of the program and facilities. The program includes regular fitness classes plus opportunities to engage in competitive sports. Equipment includes a gymnasium equipped with various types of exercise equipment and roof facilities for activities such as racquet ball and handball. Locker rooms are available for both men and women. There are approximately 170 employees in the organization with fitness records kept on their activities and progress.

Both labor and management recognize the importance of physical education activities as part of the industrial recreational program that pays mental and physical dividends to all participants. It further results in better health, more efficiency, greater production, and more happiness for employer and employee. Recreational programs in which physical activities play an important part have been organized in industrial plants and in various commercial agencies, such as insurance companies, banks, and department stores. These programs are financed in various ways: by the company, by the employees, or jointly by management and labor. Skating rinks, dance halls, swimming pools, gymnasiums, bowling alleys, and outdoor areas are some of the facilities provided. Activities include bowling, tennis, horseshoes, volleyball, basketball, softball, golf, fishing, outings, table tennis, and baseball. Some companies have developed playgrounds in those sections of a community where their employees live, whereas others have leased large buildings where sports can be held and camps where men and women employees, as well as children of employees, have an opportunity to relax and enjoy the out-of-doors.

A typical company recreation program frequently offers more than one half of its activities in athletic or sports activities. The popularity of these activities among the workers is usually the factor that creates this situation. These activities are offered on an individual participation basis; in family groups; in the form of intramural-type leagues, interdepartmental teams and leagues, varsity teams, club groups; and on a class instruction basis.

Courtesy The Forbes Magazine Fitness Center.

Health spas

According to a Federal Trade Commission survey, there are 2,000 health spas in the United States. The Yellow Pages in telephone directories throughout the nation indicate that there are 4,000 health spas.

The health spa industry in this country is an estimated multi-billion dollar industry that is growing rapidly because of the current national emphasis on physical fitness and exercise. Many of these health spas are reputable and provide their customers with worthwhile programs of activity and fitness advice. At the same time, there are some that charge high rates, have a poorly trained staff, offer inadequate facilities, and engage in misleading advertising.

Bills and regulations have been introduced in the legislatures of several states and municipalities to protect the consumer. However, these bills are difficult to pass, with the result that many abuses still exist since the potential consumer does not have sufficient information to make a sound decision on what constitutes a proper health spa.

The National Association of Physical Fitness Centers, which was recently established, is trying to bring credibility to the health spa industry, but because of the lucrative nature of this type of business the progress is slow.

Since there are many health spas, they represent a setting where physical education should establish its expertise on a much wider scale than exists at present.

One example of a health spa or club is the New York Health and Racquet Club, which provides fitness facilities at three different locations in Manhattan. It is available 7 days a week for both men and women members.

This club points out that a special program is planned for each individual member. Classes are approximately 30 to 35 minutes in length, providing activities such as the following: calisthenics, yoga, belly dancing, karate, and dance. The organization also features Nautilus machines. To instruct classes, the club points out, the instructor must have a college background in physical education or dance and go through an orientation program. Membership fees are approximately $300 a year with a $100 initiation fee. Such fees enable a member to use any of the three clubs in Manhattan. Facilities include, in addition to the Nautilus machines, swimming pool, whirlpool, bicycle-riding machines, massage and sun rooms, health food and drink garden, and exercise rooms. The club has also announced the opening of a new Stress Physiology Center at one of their locations.

Glen Swengros, former Vice-President of Health Industries, Inc., and now with the President's Council on Physical Fitness and Sports, points out that the health spa idea will expand in the years ahead for the following reasons:

1. The high cost of other types of recreation
2. The accessibility of health spas to the general population
3. The gasoline problem—the public will use leisure time close to home
4. The high divorce rate with the desire for improved body cosmetics by newly divorced or separated persons
5. The great amount of leisure time that the American public possesses
6. The fact that heavily populated areas have few natural outlets for physical activity
7. The exposure provided by national advertising programs relating to the values of physical fitness

Centers for the elderly

In recent years the elderly have received considerable attention on the part of the United States government and other agencies. Much of this attention is focused on the elderly because of inflation and their economic plight, as well as the many other problems that their forced retirement in many cases brings. The elderly constitute about 11% of the population at the present time, and this percentage is increasing year by year.

There is also concern for the physical fitness of the elderly and their need to be physically active to maintain a state of optimum health. For example, the National Association for Human Development, in cooperation with the President's Council on Physical Fitness and Sports, is conducting a national program to develop model exercise and fitness activities for people over 60 years of age. This is being done in association with the Administration on Aging of the U.S. Department of Health, Education, and Welfare.

As a result of this national program, there is a nationwide expansion of programs for the elderly by recreation agencies and centers in the states, counties, and villages. Also, other adult

programs and physical activities and physical fitness for the elderly are becoming concerns and settings for physical education programs.

Since they are comparatively new, many centers for the elderly have not established high-quality physical education programs to date. However, these programs are growing in number and centers for the elderly represent a setting for developing physical education programs.

A visit to one center produced these observations. The program consisted mainly of folk dancing and square dancing twice a week, Monday afternoons from 2:00 to 4:00 P.M. and Thursday nights from 7:30 to 9:30 P.M. The program was held in a gymnasium, and the instructor was a person about 60 years of age who was graceful, enthusiastic, and very friendly. The music was supplied by a sound system set up in the gymnasium.

Various dances were performed by everyone with great enthusiasm. The atmosphere was relaxed, and the participants had an excellent sense of timing, rhythm, and coordination. They danced for 2 hours with only short breaks between dances. Everyone present participated.

One woman said that she did not know how to dance until she came to the program a year earlier, and now she loves the activity. Another woman said that she could not play football or basketball, but she loved dancing and it provided her with a great amount of healthful physical exercise.

The instructor's philosophy concerning the program was that it was excellent for socialization purposes, and in addition, the dances provided for a full range of movements for coordination and balance. The program, he felt, also enhanced the self-esteem of the participants and helped to give them confidence.

Programs of physical education for the elderly are not confined to dance. Many centers have a wide range of physical activities to offer their members.

ESTABLISHED SETTINGS FOR PHYSICAL EDUCATION PROGRAMS

There are many established settings for physical education programs. Those described here include public and private schools and colleges, service organizations, youth organizations, recreational areas, athletic clubs and other sport organizations, professional and commercial areas, camps, governmental and welfare agencies, churches, hospitals, penal institutions, and other countries.

Public and private schools and colleges

Physical education activities play an important part in the nation's schools and colleges, which may be categorized as nursery schools, kindergartens, primary grades, upper elementary grades, middle schools, junior high schools, senior high schools, junior colleges, colleges, and universities.

The nation's schools and colleges in the future will continue to be the settings where most physical educators will find work because of the continued demand for teachers in these institutions.

Nearly 65 million people in the United States—students, teachers, and administrators—are participating full time in the nation's educational enterprise. The vast educational establishment consists of more than 16,000 school districts, nearly 90,000 elementary and secondary schools, and about 3,000 universities, colleges, and junior colleges. An estimated more than 100,000 physical educators are employed in the secondary schools and colleges. The nation is committing between $80 and $100 billion each year to education, public and nonpublic, at all levels.

The public and private school enrollment in all institutions from kindergarten to graduate school is more than 60 million, with approximately 10 million persons in higher education alone.

More men are entering the teaching profession. Fifteen years ago the men made up approximately 26% of the nation's teaching staff. Today the figure is approximately 34% (men make up about 25% of the elementary school faculty and 42% of secondary school faculties). Some facts about teachers in the schools follow:

Average age. The average is 35 years of age; women teachers average almost 4 years older than men teachers.

Marital status. About 72% of public school teachers are or have been married.

Experience. The median teacher has 8 years of teaching experience.

Degrees. Over 97% of all public school teachers have a bachelor's degree and over 61% have a master's or higher degree.

ELEMENTARY SCHOOL

The objectives of elementary school education include the following:

1. The child should be viewed as an individual with differing physical, mental, emotional, and social needs.
2. Cognitive and movement skills should be stressed.
3. Children should be encouraged to develop attitudes, habits, values, and understandings.
4. Children should improve in muscular strength, endurance, flexibility, ability, and coordination and should learn how these factors play a part in physical fitness.
5. Social growth in sports should be an important part of all programs.

Some reasons given by physical educators about why they like teaching in the elementary schools include the following:

1. It offers a combination of opportunity, reward, challenge, and deep gratification for services performed.
2. Pupils are motivated, eager, and enthusiastic and take pride in their progress.
3. The child has a natural craving for activity that makes work a pleasure.
4. At the elementary level, it is possible to witness rapid, visible advancement of pupils.
5. It is a joy to work with happy youngsters.
6. There is a great challenge in working with children during their most impressionable and formative years.
7. There are more job openings at the elementary level.
8. The personal satisfaction is great when a small hand slips into yours and a voice says, "I like you."

New look in elementary school physical education. Elementary school physical education has changed. Physical activities were conducted formerly during the recess period, but today they are a regular part of the school day. Traditionally, the classroom teacher was responsible for physical education, but today increasing

Parachute activity as part of the physical education program at Public School No. 15 in Brooklyn, New York.

emphasis is placed on providing resource help for the teacher, and in many instances a physical education specialist conducts the program. Years ago there was little appreciation fo physical education as a contributing factor to scholastic achievement, but today it is considered an integral part of the total education program. Years ago physical education was considered to be a subject that had no relationship to other subjects in the curriculum, but today there is an interdisciplinary emphasis that includes subjects such as art, music, and mathematics. Formerly, little attention was given to the slow learner and the child with learning disabilities, but today perceptual-motor training is being emphasized. And most important, in the past the emphasis in elementary school physical education was on free play and an assortment of meaningless physical activity, but today it is on movement education. Finally, the person who desires to teach elementary school physical education now specializes in this field of endeavor.

Teaching in the elementary school today represents a challenge and an opportunity for the physical educator who is interested in and loves children. This is the time when a solid foundation of movement experiences can be provided children as the base for future development and accomplishment in various forms of

physical activity, including sports. A new physical education is being stressed. It is also a time when the open school, nongraded school, team teaching, and other new and exciting developments are a part of the educational picture.

Physical education in the elementary school is emerging as the art and science of human movement. It instils in the child the "why" of movement, the "how" of movement, and the physiological, sociological, and psychological results of movement. In addition, there is concern for movement skills and motor patterns that comprise the movement repertoire of human beings. As a result, teachers are being hired to implement the new look in elementary school physical education. The outstanding teacher is one who nurtures students in the development of body awareness and movement skills.

Movement experiences are being recognized as educationally desirable in the early life of the child. In addition to helping children scholastically, movement experiences have many social benefits, such as interpersonal relations and a recognition of individual differences. Furthermore, it is through movement that the children express themselves, are creative, develop a positive self-image, and gain a better understanding of their physical selves. Children at this age

Physical education in the elementary school is emerging as the art and science of human movement. Part of the movement education program at the Hudson Falls Central School at Hudson Falls, New York, is swinging on the ropes.

need numerous physical experiences, using basic skills involved with crawling, running, jumping, skipping, hopping, dodging, bending, twisting, rolling, hanging, climbing, kicking, carrying, pulling, and balancing. It is through such movement experiences that young children explore, develop, and grow in a meaningful manner.

New developments. Curriculum changes are obvious on the elementary school level, with great stress being placed on interdisciplinary emphasis, movement education, and perceptual-motor learning. The curriculum also continues to stress the individual child, how the child feels about himself or herself, and the child's social relationships with adults and other children. Individualized learning, in which students progress at their own rate, is compatible with problem solving, inquiring, discovery, and a creative approach to learning.

Every child a winner. Health and optimum physical education for elementary schoolchildren was a 4-year funded project in Ocilla, Georgia. It is based on the concept that every child is a winner when he or she functions up to capacity. It shows the value of individualized

movement experiences and the benefits that accrue to young children. The program establishes and supports the principle that human values such as moving, learning, joy, and accomplishment can be part and parcel of a well-designed physical education program. The program shows that selected movement activities can lead to creativity, intellectual involvement, and self-direction. Movement education, including problem-solving experiences, form the foundation of the program. It stresses space awareness, body awareness, quality of movement, and relationships. A film has been prepared and many publications are available to persons who are interested in knowing more about this innovative program that has received such wide acclaim throughout the nation.*

MIDDLE SCHOOL

The middle school, a comparatively new movement in American education, is designed to provide an educational program for preadolescents and early adolescents that begins where

---

*If interested, write: Every Child A Winner, Box 141, Ocilla, Ga. 31774.

Guidelines for elementary school physical education program*

The instructional program for elementary students should have the following guidelines:

1. Program excellence should contribute to self-reliance and complete functioning of students.
2. A comprehensive physical education program must meet the needs of all children: gifted, slow-learning, handicapped, culturally deprived, and the average child.
3. Maximum involvement of each student in mental, motor, and emotional responses will result in positive changes in behavior.
4. A variety of learning experiences should result in the development of concepts, values, and behavior of a physically educated person.
5. Curriculum content should be organized so that attitudes, learning, and skills take place in a sequential and developmental manner.
6. Teaching must be both teacher directed and self directed, and the instructional program should be designed to (a) teach the whole child, (b) encourage development of physical fitness, (c) develop motor skills, (d) encourage creativity, (e) emphasize elements of safety, (f) motivate self-expression and realization of self-concept, and (g) stimulate social development.
7. Instruction should include use of audiovisual materials, small groups and individualized instruction, as well as intramural and extramural activities.

*The Elementary School Physical Education Commission of the AAHPER Physical Education Division and the Physical Education Division Committees of AAHPER (secondary and college levels) met separately to outline appropriate guidelines for physical education programs at each level. These committees prepared three position papers: "Essentials of a Quality Elementary School Physical Education Program," "Guidelines for Secondary School Physical Education," and "Guide to Excellence for Physical Education in Colleges and Universities." These papers have as their prime objective the delineation of essential elements for excellence in physical education programs. The basic instructional guidelines are set forth in adapted form for each educational level.

the school for earlier childhood ends and continues to the school for adolescents. There are more than 2,600 middle schools in the United States. Children in the middle school generally range in age from 9 to 14 years, with 10 to 13 years being most common. Middle schools usually house grades five through eight, although several other administrative patterns exist. Some characteristics of the middle school are that it tries to combine the best features of the self-contained classroom of the elementary school with the departmentalized pattern of the secondary school, it emphasizes self-understanding with programs that aim at the problems of young adolescents, and it stresses self-direction for learning.

The physical education program in the middle school is part of a developmental program that builds on the movement experiences of earlier grades. Such a program is based on children's growth and development characteristics and the physical activities that meet their needs at these particular stages of development.

Some educators indicate that research shows that the physical growth which takes place in children during this period of transition represents a most vital educational concern and cannot be ignored. The curriculum should provide for an interrelationship in the areas of the fine arts, physical education, social studies, and practical arts.

Supporters of the middle school concept see this organizational pattern as an opportunity for physical educators to develop an entirely new curriculum—one that is not patterned after junior or senior high school programs. Many new concepts and activities are becoming a part of the middle school approach to learning, including individualized instruction, coeducational programs, minicourses, resource centers, and laboratory experiences.

To find out more about what is happening at the middle school and junior high school levels, the Middle School Physical Education Committee developed a survey to elicit information concerning specific programs.* Schools se-

*Stafford, E.: Middle schools: status of physical education programs, Journal of Health, Physical Education, and Recreation **45:**25, Feb., 1974.

lected to participate in the survey were suggested by the state supervisors, who were asked to recommend junior high schools and middle schools that were considered to have outstanding physical education programs. Usable questionnaires were received from 281 schools representing forty-nine of the fifty states.

The questionnaires revealed to a great extent the current status of physical education programs in middle schools. Class sizes were smaller than those of the junior high schools or intermediate schools. The middle schools, however, reported offering a daily period of physical education in only 31% of schools polled as opposed to a daily period of physical education in 49% of intermediate schools and 45% of junior high schools. Required physical education is a generally accepted fact in the majority of schools. Only nine schools reported some form of elective program.

The study further revealed that the most popular activities being taught in the physical education classes were volleyball, soccer, wrestling, gymnastics, bowling, golf, swimming, tennis, badminton, field hockey, folk and square dance, track and field, and rhythms.

New developments in middle school physical education. Creative programming is appearing with greater frequency in middle schools. Some programs of instruction follow.

A middle school in Ohio encourages a philosophy of freedom through its facilities and curriculum design. There are no formal classrooms, hallways, bells, or closed offices. A hundred students occupy a large octagonally shaped area called a *learning pod.* An interdisciplinary team of four teachers and several students design and implement each learning experience. What are the implications of such an educational philosophy for physical education programming? The physical education program has evolved from the overall learning approach, and its goals include the following:

1. Instilling an appreciation for enjoyment of physical activity
2. Developing motor patterns that will complement a student's self-concept
3. Helping students accept their limitations and expand to their greatest potentialities
4. Encouraging creativity and providing social experiences

A middle school in Rhode Island employs team teaching in its curriculum pattern, which provides for coeducational teaching. For example, in the seventh-grade basketball unit, boys and girls meet together to review the rules and practice the basic skills of dribbling, passing, foul shooting, and lay-ups.

A middle school in Wisconsin participates in coordinated program planning in which physical educators combine their expertise with teachers in other areas to develop meaningful educational experiences for students. For example, a unit on bicycling is taught from the mechanical, safety, exercise, and distance aspects of the activity.

SECONDARY SCHOOL

The secondary school level refers to grades that follow elementary school, starting with grade seven and continuing to the college years. Secondary schools are organized according to various administrative patterns. Some of the more prevalent patterns are the traditional high school or 8-4 system, the combined junior and senior high school or 6-6 or 7-5 plan, the 6-3-3 system in which the junior high school is grouped separately, the 4-4-4 plan with the middle school, and the 6-2-4 system with the 4-year high school.

The primary functions allocated to the secondary school include promoting the student's total development, including intellectual powers, a basic knowledge of major fields of study, and his or her unique talents, whatever they may be. A second purpose is to help the student achieve a better understanding of personal abilities, interests, and potentialities. A third purpose is to orient the student in various fields of work so that he or she may learn how personal abilities and interests relate to these areas of endeavor. A fourth purpose is to help each student develop a sound system of values. A fifth purpose is to help the student develop a philosophy of life together with the skills, health, interests, appreciations, and social attributes essential to a good life. A sixth purpose is to develop an understanding of the democratic process and the role of the student in furthering this way of life.

Some reasons given by physical educators as

to why they like teaching at the secondary school level include the following:

1. Love of team sports
2. Excitement of and interest in coaching sports
3. The compartmentalization of subject matter
4. An interesting group of students with whom to work
5. Satisfaction derived in seeing students transfer skills from physical education class to after-school intramurals and recreation
6. The challenge of guiding students through the awkward, transitional period of unrest and uncertainty of the junior high school years
7. The inspiration derived in working on a staff with other professional colleagues
8. Love of more highly organized games and activities

Junior high school. In junior high schools the physical education program includes aquatics, posture work, dual and individual sports, self-testing activities, formal activities, games and relays, sports of higher organization, rhythmics and dancing, contests, apparatus, and tumbling and stunts.

The activities must be selected with care because of the anatomical and physiological nature of this age group. Pupils at this level are susceptible to fatigue, are in a period of rapid growth, and find it difficult to coordinate their actions, which results in awkwardness. There must be careful supervision by qualified personnel of all physical education activities so that the student may experience optimum development. In some school systems the physical education programs in the junior high school grades (seventh, eighth, and ninth) are administered in much the same way as the first six grades. The classroom teachers handle the physical education programs for their respective grades. In other school systems the junior high school is separate from the elementary and senior high schools. In this particular type of setup, it is common to find trained physical education men and women handling the classes in physical education. In still other school systems one or more grades of the junior high school are included in the senior high school building, where trained physical education personnel usually handle the classes. The teachers on the junior

Guidelines for secondary school physical education program

Many of the guidelines proposed by the elementary committee are also valid for secondary and college instructional programs. The conclusions of the secondary school position paper are given here in adapted format.

1. The instructional program must meet the differing needs of all students and be geared to the developmental needs of each pupil.
2. The program should be balanced between team and individual sports, aquatics, gymnastics, self-testing activities, dance, and rhythms.
3. Progression should be sequential in specific skills and movement patterns.
4. Elective learning opportunities should be offered.
5. Knowledge of the human body and the principles of human movement is essential.
6. Creativity, self-direction, and vigorous activity, in addition to safety principles, should be encouraged.
7. Physical fitness and skills that can be employed in a comprehensive intramural, interscholastic, and recreational program for all pupils should be emphasized.
8. The development of human relationships and the encouragement of pupils who have difficulty because of physical, social, and emotional problems is essential to an excellent program.

high school level should be specialists in physical education. They should be sympathetic to the problems of boys and girls and should be able to guide children successfully during this formative period. They should understand the needs of children and their interests and capacities and should realize that they may be of exceptional service to students during this time when they are planning for the future.

New developments in junior high school physical education. A variety of new approaches to physical education is taking place at the junior high school level. Some innovative programming is noted in the following examples.

The parallel bars provide a medium for movement experiences at Junior High School No. 51 in Brooklyn, New York.

A junior high school in Minnesota has its required programs organized on competency levels and scheduled on a modular system. The modular schedule places students in physical activity for three double periods a week. The program is conducted on a coeducational, team teaching, and differentiated staffing basis and includes team sports, lifetime activities, dance, and physical conditioning programs.

A junior high school in Ohio offers minicourses on an all-school basis. The school schedule is modified during a 4-week period to allow for a period during the school day for minicourses. In a recent year the students could select from thirty-two minicourses. Activities such as roller skating, baton twirling, fencing, bowling, table tennis, and archery were offered.

A junior high school in Illinois has an enrollment of about 500 students in grades six through eight. The intramural sports program supplements the basic instructional program and is offered Tuesday through Thursday. Approximately 80% of the boys and 65% of the girls participate in the program.

Senior high school. The senior high school physical education program should be the responsibility of specialized persons. During high school more stress is placed on team games of higher organization and on dual and individual games. It is also during this period that students should develop sufficient skill so that when they leave school they will have the necessary fundamental skill, the desire, and the knowledge to participate successfully and enjoyably. Because many students do not go to college, it is essential that they acquire this skill, knowledge, and interest before they leave school. The competitive element is prominent in high school students, and the more highly organized games, intramural and interscholastic sports, and field and play days offer an opportunity for students to give vent to this instinct. However, the physical education teacher, through careful supervision and guidance, must ensure that the activity is not too strenuous and that excessive demands are not placed on the participant.

The program of activities in high school includes a core and an elective program, including such activities as basketball, formal activities, field hockey, advanced rhythms, volleyball, tumbling, track and field, touch football, swimming, softball, soccer, archery, badminton, bowling, tennis, dance, winter activities,

Courtesy Gwen R. Waters.

High school physical education class in archery at Hughes Junior High School, Los Angeles City Schools, Los Angeles City Unified School District, Los Angeles, California.

handball, golf, camping, and corrective activities.

The preparatory school and private school have much the same type of program as is found in the senior high school. In many of these schools, however, the advantages for a well-rounded and successful physical education program are much greater. Because of small enrollments, beautiful athletic fields, spacious gymnasia, and swimming pools, these schools may offer a program that is in many ways superior to those found in many public schools, colleges, and universities.

New developments in high school physical education programs. High schools have also introduced many new programs that include independent study, curriculum planning by students, minicourse offerings, and the elimination of grades. Some of these programs are discussed here.

A high school in Massachusetts has a program in which students take an active role in curriculum planning. For example, students plan what and how they are going to learn the gymnastics unit of the physical education class. Days are set aside for students to determine objectives and steps needed to reach a specific goal and to make a commitment to learning and improvement. Students put their objectives in writing and then set about achieving them. Instruction is provided, and grading is a cooperative venture between students and teachers. An evaluation sheet completed near the end of the program indicated that students had positive feelings about gymnastics and the concept of goal-centered learning.

A high school in Indiana has introduced the idea of minicourses into the activity program. Twice a month during the spring semester, students attend sixty different special interest activities selected from 170 offerings. Time for these activities is gained by shortening each regular period by 5 minutes. Activities include guidance and instruction, and recreation areas and community resource people are utilized whenever possible. Table tennis, yoga, golf, riflery, sport fishing, and hunting are only a few of the recreational activities offered.

A high school in New York is an experimental school that divides its 8-hour day into twenty-two computer scheduled modules. Classes may last for two or three modules (called *mods*) and vary in length on different days. Also, blocks of independent study time are included in the daily schedule. Evaluation of progress is in terms of achievement of designated behavioral objectives rather than by better grades. Each department maintains a resource center staffed by teachers and paraprofessionals. Available at the resource centers are Dewey Independent Study Kits (DISKs), which are prepared courses offered by each department for full credit. The physical education resource center is held in the gymnasium when regular classes are not scheduled. Activities offered at the resource center are the same as those taught in regular classes or are purely recreational in nature. Students may work independently in physical education with DISKs.

COLLEGE AND UNIVERSITY

There are many types of colleges, including public and private; large and small, resident and nonresident; urban and rural; secular or sectarian; liberal, technical, or professional; 2-year or 4-year; coeducational; or a combination of these.

Colleges and universities take their goals and direction from many sources. The founders, faculty, trustees, donors, alumni, or administration of a college or university might indicate that it is to devote its endeavors to agriculture or to the liberal arts, or training teachers or to preparing architects, to ensuring social competence or to promoting intellectual growth, to preparing for a profession or to getting a general education, or to a combination of these purposes.

In other words, the purposes of colleges are varied—all do not have the same goals.

Some reasons given by physical educators as to why they like teaching at the college level include the following:

1. Students are more mature.
2. The instructor and professor have more freedom.
3. Professional preparation programs offer opportunities to train future professional leaders.
4. Campus living is satisfying, as is college life in general.
5. There is more prestige in teaching at the college level.
6. There are more opportunities to participate in work of professional associations.
7. Opportunities to improve one's own educational background by taking graduate work are greater.

The status of general instructional physical education programs in colleges and universities throughout the United States does not show continued growth at the present time. Although a large majority of higher education institutions still offer physical education programs for the general college student, some are cutting back on these programs or making them voluntary. In recent years there has also been a shift from a 2-year requirement to a 1-year requirement. On the other hand, there is an increased tendency to offer physical education as a credit course. In regard to activities the lifetime sports and recreational activities are being stressed, and the majority of courses are coeducational in nature.

New developments in college physical education programs. Some of the new developments in college physical education include independent study in physical education where, with faculty guidance, students pursue a special project as opposed to attending and participating in the conventional physical education class. Examples of projects are competing in a bowling tournament, attending a conference on sports, or participating in a dance program. Another new development worthy of mention is the foundation or theory course in which students get at the "why" of physical education. Foundation courses cover topics and items such as an evaluation of a person's health and fitness, body mechanics, health concepts, cardiovascular fitness, values of physical education, principles of exercise, training techniques, and kinesiological principles. Another new development is the addition of many new activities to the college curriculum such as scuba diving, judo, cross-country skiing, jogging, rock climbing, and sport parachuting. These activities may be offered in the required physical education program or on a club basis.

Sport clubs provide interested participants an opportunity for social group experiences and the enjoyment of a particular sports activity. Clubs have many different interests, including water ballet, table tennis, boating, and ice skating. Most sports clubs provide for student administration and financing. Financing may be derived from the student body through student fees, dances, exhibition games, and the like. The club should provide for some relationship to the athletic administration of the institution. Procedures and policies clarifying this relationship should be a part of the club's bylaws. Such a relationship is necessary in matters of equipment and facility use, eligibility insurance, travel, injuries, and program assistance.

The 2-year college. There are more than 1,100 2-year colleges in the United States. Ap-

proximately one third of these colleges are private, with two thirds being public. Enrollment in 2-year colleges is more than 3 million, with more male than female students. The average enrollment for a junior college is approximately 1,600 to 2,000 students. Most of the 2-year colleges require physical education for approximately 2 hours a week for each of the 2 years. In a few colleges, physical education is required the first year and is made elective the second year. The activities offered in the first year are predominantly team sports. Activities offered in the second year include individual, dual, and carry-over sports, along with team sports. The most common activities offered in the 2-year colleges include basketball, gymnastics, track and field, volleyball, tennis, touch football, soccer, golf, archery, bowling, weight lifting, wrestling, swimming, field hockey, badminton, and dancing.

Some colleges require a textbook as part of the physical education experience. Many 2-year colleges require health courses for their students, and these are frequently taught by physical education professors. A majority of the 2-year colleges have a director of physical education who frequently is also the athletic director.

Soccer is part of the physical education program at New York University, New York.

In the future it would appear that physical education programs would become more purposive and provide initial preparation for those students desiring to make physical education a career, offer 2 years of basic instruction in physical education activities, meet the needs of the atypical student, provide college credit for courses taken, develop a broad intramural and intercollegiate program, engage in research activities, and help college students in the development of lifetime skills and understanding and appreciation of the importance of physical activity throughout life for their physical, mental, and social betterment.

The extent of the athletic program in 2-year colleges appears to be directly related to the size of the school and the method of financing. Community colleges and branches of state universities exhibit the most athletic teams and have the largest student bodies. Private junior colleges have smaller enrollments and fewer athletic teams. Eligibility requirements are usually based on certain academic standards, class attendance, amateur status, and health status. The majority of junior colleges belong to the National Junior College Athletic Association (NJCAA) and accept their rules of eligibility.

Most 2-year colleges prefer professionally trained coaches, who are usually drawn from the physical education staff and other faculty members. Compensation is given for coaching in the form of extra pay, by including coaching in the base salary, and by reduced teaching loads.

Physical education is an integral part of the 2-year college curriculum, with more than 80% of the schools requiring physical education. In addition, most colleges have intramural programs that are usually financed by student activity fees.

California and New York are two of many states that have instituted extensive systems of junior and community colleges, which have been developed so that students may live at home or do not have to travel far and still continue their education beyond high school. For some students these colleges may provide terminal formal education, and for others they may provide the first 2 years of a 4-year college course. These schools recognize the value of regular physical education classes, as well as a broad athletic program for their students.

The 4-year college and university. The college and university physical education program is designed to provide opportunities for physical conditioning, developing skills in recreational and leisure-time activities, and participating in intramural and intercollegiate athletic competition. In the basic instructional or service physical education programs, college students usually participate for 2 years in various team sports, dual and individual activities, rhythmical activities, and recreational sports for the purpose of maintaining good physical condition. Probably the most beneficial result from participation is the development of physical skills, making it possible for students to continue physical activity after leaving college.

Guidelines for college and university physical education program

The college position paper concluded that colleges and universities should provide instruction in physical education as a part of the general education program. The guidelines for the instructional program include the following:

1. All students should have an opportunity to participate in physical education programs of their choice, and professional counsel should be made available to aid students in their choice of courses.
2. Programs should be innovative in meeting the needs of all students and should include independent and tutorial study.
3. Policies that pertain to advanced placement, credit by examination, requirements, and grading should reflect the institutional philosophy.
4. Participation in intramurals, extramurals, and intercollegiate athletics should not substitute for instructional classes in physical education.
5. Non–physical education activities should also not substitute for physical education requirements.
6. Research should be conducted to improve the quality of the physical education program.

Most college programs offer some freedom in the choice of activities so that students may further develop their skills in a sport in which they have particular interest. The intramural and intercollegiate sports program plays an important part in college and university physical education programs as well as in 2-year colleges. Intramural athletics offer an opportunity for all students, regardless of degree of skill, to participate. Leagues are usually formed according to some method of homogeneous grouping and in such a manner as to add flavor and interest to the competition. In many colleges, fraternities, sororities, and other organizations enter teams, providing additional vigor and interest to the rivalry. Participants in intercollegiate sports are for the more skilled players in various sports such as basketball, football, baseball, track, swimming, soccer, and tennis. Teams in these various sports vie with teams from other schools. The Association of Intercollegiate Women's Athletics, the National Collegiate Athletic Association, and the National Association for Intercollegiate Athletics are set up to govern, regulate, and establish standards for this competition.

In addition to the teaching of service courses for college students, there is also a need for physical education instructors in the many teacher-education institutions throughout the country. As the demand for more physical education personnel grows, there will be an equal demand for teachers to train this personnel. Those who work in teacher-training institutions teach courses such as anatomy, physiology, methods and materials, tests and measurements, remedial physical education, principles of physical education, and organization and administration of the physical education program. They also teach various skill courses in the activities and provide other necessary experiences such as camping and outdoor education.

SPECIAL SCHOOLS

In addition to the public and private schools that serve many of the nation's children and youth, there are also special schools in which other pupils are enrolled. These include trade and vocational schools, schools for intellectually and physically handicapped persons, and schools for men and women who are primarily interested in adult education.

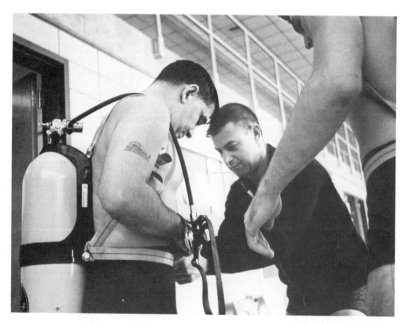

Photo by LeMoyne Coates.

A physical education class at St. Louis Community College at Florissant Valley in Missouri.

Trade and vocational schools. Many schools exist to prepare for careers in certain trades, crafts, and other vocations. The privately operated schools of commerce, technical institutes, and schools for dental assistants are a mere sampling of the types of schools one sees constantly advertised in newspapers, magazines, subways, or buses. Most of these schools offer some type of physical education program for their students that is usually similar to those discussed under secondary education and exist in the junior and senior high schools of the nation.

Schools for handicapped individuals. Opportunities exist for teaching individuals who have special physical afflictions such as blindness, deafness, or hearing difficulties, who are crippled, or who find they can obtain greater benefits by pursuing an education with individuals who have similar handicaps. Directors of special education have been appointed in state departments of education, and colleges and universities have introduced courses for the professional preparation of teachers specializing in the education of exceptional children. School, college, and university programs in which the handicapped are taught have been established. Foundations and agencies, such as the American Foundation for the Blind, Inc., have been established. In addition to teachers and counselors being needed to work with handicapped children, they are also needed to work with handicapped adults.

Wherever possible, the handicapped are taught in regular school and college classes. Nevertheless, in many instances in which the affliction warrants, education has proved more satisfactory in schools and colleges especially adapted for such purposes.

Schools for adults. Adult education is thriving throughout the country. Programs are being established in most communities that provide experiences for men and women who desire to enrich their lives. These experiences cover the gamut of educational activities including English, music, Spanish, art, and typewriting.

A class of major students at Hampton Institute, Hampton, Virginia.

They also provide opportunities to develop physical fitness, skill in some sport or dance, or other area of competency associated with physical education.

Service organizations

Many service organizations such as the YMCA, American Red Cross, settlement houses, and the armed forces provide employment for physical educators.

YOUNG MEN'S CHRISTIAN ASSOCIATION, YOUNG WOMEN'S CHRISTIAN ASSOCIATION, YOUNG MEN'S HEBREW ASSOCIATION, AND YOUNG WOMEN'S HEBREW ASSOCIATION

The YMCA, YWCA, YMHA, YWHA, and similar service organizations serve the people of various communities where they have been established, both the young and adult population. Religious training was the main purpose in forming many of these organizations. However, physical activities are now an important part of their programs. Classes in various physical activities; athletic leagues and contests for industries, churches, young people's groups, and boys' and girls' groups; and camping programs are a few of the activities organized and administered by these voluntary agencies. The cost of financing such organizations is usually met through membership dues, community chest drives, and contributions of private individuals.

These organizations are designed to improve society physically, morally, mentally, and spiritually through their programs of physical activity. An example of the extent to which these organizations render services in this country and throughout the world can be seen in the Young Men's Christian Association. There are more than 1,800 YMCAs in the United States and 120 in Canada, and the YMCA operates in more than seventy countries. There are more than 7.5 million members in the YMCA and over 2 million members in the YWCA. Approximately 1,500 physical educators are employed by YMCAs in the United States.

Usually these agencies have directors for the physical activities who have received specialized training in their field. Many organizations have complete staffs of trained physical education personnel who aid in the organization and administration of the programs.

A typical physical activity schedule of a YMCA is shown in Table 15-1.

AMERICAN RED CROSS

The American Red Cross in its various program offerings provides a setting for physical education activities, especially along institutional lines. These activities are mainly concerned with some phase of aquatics, water safety, first aid, and hospital recreation. Through this organization, many qualified persons in physical education help to demonstrate proper techniques and procedures in these activities to interested persons throughout the country and help to provide for the needs of individuals who have been hospitalized.

SETTLEMENT AND NEIGHBORHOOD HOUSES

Settlement and neighborhood houses are largely confined to cities. In many communities they are also known as community centers or community houses. They are usually organized and administered by a religious or social welfare group in the low-income or ethnic neighborhoods of cities. Their aim is to establish a higher standard of living by improving the spiritual, mental, and cultural welfare of the people. They work with all people, regardless of age, sex, and national or racial origin. They give special attention to children. They offer varied programs of activities, which include arts and crafts, athletics, games, singing, dancing, photography, music, dramatics, and discussion forums. Physical education activities play an important role in many of these centers where they have gymnasia, playgrounds, summer camps, swimming pools, and game rooms. Physical directors and staff occupy prominent positions in many of these social enterprises. Physical activity offers participants the opportunity for self-expression and helps them gain a better outlook on life in the midst of poverty and poor living conditions.

ARMED FORCES AND UNITED SERVICE ORGANIZATIONS

The Army, Navy, Marine, Coast Guard, National Guard, and Air Force have extensive physical activity programs that aid in keeping service personnel in good mental and physical

Table 15-1. YMCA physical activity schedule

Activities	Mon.	Tues.	Wed.	Thurs.	Fri.	Sat.
Basketball	4:15-5:30 6:00-7:30	4:15-8:00	4:15-5:30 6:00-8:00	4:15-8:00	4:15-5:30 6:00-7:30	3:30-9:00
Boxing (furnish own speed bag)	10:00-10:00	10:00-10:00	10:00-10:00	10:00-10:00	10:00-10:00	9:00-9:00
Boy's swimming class						9:00-1:00
Calisthenics	12:15-12:45 5:30-6:00	12:15-12:45 6:00-6:30	12:15-12:45 5:30-6:00	12:15-12:45 6:00-6:30	12:15-12:45 5:30-6:00	
Father and son swim					7:00-10:00	1:00-9:00
Fencing	8:00-10:00				8:00-10:00	
Gymnastics		8:00-10:00		8:00-10:00		
Handball (reservation required)	10:00-10:00	10:00-10:00	10:00-10:00	10:00-10:00	10:00-10:00	9:00-9:00
Lifesaving (as scheduled)		8:00-10:00		8:00-10:00		
Swimming—beginners (1st Mon. each month)	7:00-7:45		7:00-7:45			
Swimming—intermediate and advanced (1st Mon. each month)	7:45-8:30		7:45-8:30			
Scuba (as scheduled)			Pool 8:00-10:00	Classroom 8:00-10:00		
Special programs—gym			8:00-10:00			
Squash (reservation required)	10:00-10:00	10:00-10:00	10:00-10:00	10:00-10:00	10:00-10:00	9:00-9:00
Track	9:00-10:00	9:00-10:00	9:00-10:00	9:00-10:00	9:00-10:00	9:00-9:00
Volleyball	12:45-2:00 6:00-8:00		Advanced 12:45-2:00 6:00-8:00		12:45-2:00 6:00-8:00	
Weight lifting and body building	9:00-10:00	9:00-10:00	9:00-10:00	9:00-10:00	9:00-10:00	9:00-9:00
Wrestling	8:00-10:00				8:00-10:00	

condition. Furthermore, the United Service Organizations (USO), an appendage to these various branches of the armed forces, also utilize such programs of activity. The United Service Organizations consist of agencies such as the Young Men's Christian Association, Young Women's Christian Association, Travelers' Aid, Salvation Army, Catholic Charities Organization, Jewish Welfare Board, and Camp Shows, Incorporated.

The armed forces utilize thousands of acres of land, hundreds of gymnasia and other buildings, hundreds of swimming pools, and thousands of qualified persons in physical education to organize and administer a physical training program. These programs are designed to keep military and naval forces in good physical and mental condition at all times, to develop skills so that officers and men will have the foundational equipment to spend leisure hours in a worthwhile manner, and to help build morale through a broad sports program. The armed

Table 15-2. Sports participation at one army installation*

Sport	No. of participants	Sport	No. of participants
Boxing	244,517	Fencing	1,830
Bowling	17,282,040	Skeet	210,858
	(Frames bowled)	Horseshoes	326,958
Swimming	489,036	Gymnastics	89,603
Tennis	172,982	Roller skating	44,840
Badminton	243,589	Judo	19,380
Track	85,594	Archery	12,440
Golf	602,902	Wrestling	41,987
Equestrian	4,200	Curling	120
Basketball	20,168	Trampoline	8,355
Fishing	143,833	Shuffleboard	260
Handball	183,622	Skiing	11,580
Weight lifting	269,463	Soccer	16,030
Volleyball	12,544	Boating	1,623
Table tennis	1,690,014	Hunting	400
Squash	15,239	Surfing	117,280

*Personal communication

forces have long known that a strong United States means a healthy and physically fit United States.

Youth organizations

There are many clubs and organizations for boys and girls that provide a setting for physical education activities. Some organizations that fall in this group are the Boy Scouts of America, Boys' Brigades of America, Girl Scouts, Camp Fire Girls, Big Brother and Big Sister Foundation, 4-H Clubs, Boys' Clubs of America, Girls' Clubs of America, Boy Rangers of America, Hi-Y, Y-Teens, Red Shield Clubs, Future Farmers of America, and Pioneer Youth of America. Some of these organizations are international as well as national in scope. The extent of their membership is great. For example, the Boys' Clubs of America have about 1,000 clubs, with over 1 million boys as members. Girls' Clubs of America have more than 200,000 members. The Girl Scouts of the United States have about 536,000 adult members and nearly 3 million girl members. In addition, girl scouting in the United States is affiliated with the World Association of Girl Guides and Girl Scouts. The association links together more than 5.5 million members in over sixty-five countries. The Boy Scouts of America have over 4 million registered scouts and more

than 1.5 million volunteer adult leaders. Big Brothers of America have more than 60,000 members and 200 member agencies. There are 600,000 members of Campfire Girls, Inc. The 4-H Program includes over 5 million members.

The American Youth Hostels, Inc., with an estimated 80,000 members is an agency that provides overnight housing facilities for individuals who are anxious to travel, see, and study conditions in various parts of the United States and other countries. There are youth hostels in many different countries. The mode of transportation in most cases is either hiking or bicycling. Every year many groups of young people, under trained leaders, set out for some distant point. The educational benefits derived from such an experience have proved valuable. Personnel are needed to provide the necessary leadership, and physical educators are qualified, by reason of their training, to play an important part in this movement.

The purpose of these organizations is to serve youth in a manner that will prepare them for adulthood and make them better citizens. They are interested in developing in each boy and girl characteristics such as self-reliance, courage, and patriotism. They encourage the development of skills for the worthy use of leisure time. They promote projects that result in better physical and mental health, stronger character, and a sounder physical condition. For example, the four ''Hs'' of the 4-H Club stand for ''Head, Heart, Hand, and Health'' development.

Physical education activities play a major part in the program of activities for these various clubs and organizations. Out-of-door activities on the playground and in the camp are as important as indoor activities in the gymnasium and in the swimming pool. Sports and other physical education activities strongly appeal to boys and girls, and as long as this interest exists, physical activity will be an essential phase of the total program.

Recreational areas

Most communities have playgrounds. In small towns the playground functions during the summer months; in larger towns they function in the spring, summer, and fall; and in many large cities they are organized and administered on a year-round basis. Playgrounds are established mainly for children and young people, although adults frequently participate in many of the activities offered. The playground is a place where children may develop skills,

enjoy themselves in wholesome physical activity, develop healthy bodies, and develop good citizenship traits under competent leadership. The type of facilities and equipment varies from playground to playground, depending on the amount of money available for such a purpose and the value placed on such an enterprise by the community concerned. On well-equipped playgrounds, facilities and equipment may be found for all types of games, athletics, dancing, swimming, self-testing activities, and arts and crafts. The number of staff members varies with the size of the playground. Both men and women may be found supervising and directing playgrounds and the special activities within a single playground.

In addition to playgrounds, communities and apartment dwellings are including recreation areas where swimming pools, paddle tennis courts, and other activity areas exist. This is particularly true where new housing developments are coming into being, and developers are making it a practice to include facilities for physical activities for the occupants.

Many parks and green spaces have also been

Children are taken to the farm as part of the recreation program in the Division of Municipal Recreation and Adult Education, Milwaukee Public Schools.

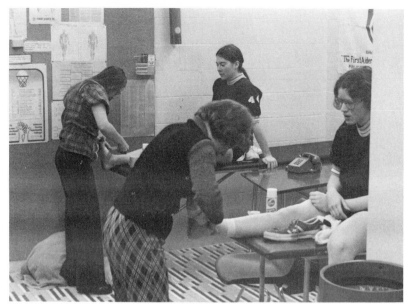

Courtesy Cramer Products, Inc., Gardner, Kansas.

Women athletic trainers at work in a sport organization.

From Michaelson, Mike: Judo, now it's a safe family sport,
Today's Health, Feb., 1969.

Judo as a recreational activity.

developed, and they utilize the services of physical educators. These may be located in a community, city, county, park, or other place where recreational facilities have been created for the use of the populace.

Athletic clubs and other sport organizations

Because of the increased popularity of sports and physical activity in the United States during the late 1800s and early 1900s, many athletic clubs were organized. The membership at that time was usually composed of young adults who wanted a place where they might engage in some form of wholesome physical activity. The idea has gradually grown, until today numerous athletic clubs and other sports organizations are mushrooming all over the nation. The membership in these organizations is great. Some clubs cater to the wealthy, whereas others serve persons in various income brackets. At first these athletic clubs offered many sports, but today many clubs also cater to individuals who are interested mainly in one sport or, at the most, a very few. Thus can be found organizations such as archery clubs, fencing clubs, golf clubs, tennis clubs, fishing clubs, rod and gun clubs, bowling clubs, yachting clubs, and polo clubs. Also, many country clubs stress social life, as

well as sports such as golf, tennis, and swimming. Many of these clubs are staffed with professionals who are experts in some particular sport, as well as other individuals trained in various physical education activities.

In addition to the organizations that have been mentioned, there are Turnvereins and Sokol organizations that are designed to provide a place for physical activities primarily of a gymnastic variety and also a place for social activities.

Professional and commercial areas

The area of professional sports and other physical education activities offers a setting for many highly skilled individuals. Professional football, basketball, baseball, hockey, golf, soccer, and tennis are a few of these areas, and in addition, there are other physical education activities that have professional possibilities, such as gymnastic acts, aquatics, and dancing. In the commerical area can be found dance studios, theaters, radio and television programs, roller rinks, golf courses, swimming pools, bowling alleys, sports equipment stores, resort areas, reducing and exercise clubs, and many places of amusement that utilize physical education activities as a means of entertainment. As a rule, the public wants to be entertained,

Courtesy American Broadcasting Co.

Baseball as a professional sport.

and physical educators have capitalized on this desire.

Camps

Camping has grown in popularity until today there are numerous camps located in nearly every section of the country. There are over 20,000 camps throughout the nation. These are operated by cities, counties, and states; by social agencies such as churches, schools, and settlements; by youth-serving agencies like YMCA, YWCA, YMHA, YWHA, Boy Scouts, Girl Scouts, Camp Fire Girls, 4-H Clubs, and Boys' Clubs Federations; by employer and labor organizations; and by private individuals and corporations. Some camps are operated for profit, whereas others work on a nonprofit basis. Some are open only during the summer months, others during the spring, summer, and fall, and others all year round. Some are for children, others for adults, and still others for adults and children. Some are day camps, whereas others operate on a seasonal basis. Some are for just one sex, and others operate on a corecreational basis. Tennis, football, basketball, baseball, horseback riding, and other activity camps have been opened to provide a place for the young person interested in developing further skill in a particular sports activity.

Regardless of the type of camp, most utilize physical education activities as one of the main features in their program. They stress outdoor living and offer such activities as sailing, swimming, canoeing, all types of athletics, horseback riding, archery, and dancing.

Government and welfare agencies

Several governmental agencies such as state departments of education, city boards of education, U.S. Office of Education, President's Council on Physical Fitness and Sports, and other agencies utilize physical education personnel to direct, administer, and supervise programs. In addition, they act in a consulting capacity to the schools, industry, and other groups that have need for their services.

Village, county, city, state, and national governmental units have provided settings for physical education activities as well as privately supported welfare agencies. Some of these settings are orphanages, homes for the aged, and

wildlife preserves. Two federally supported programs, the Teacher Corps and VISTA, will be discussed.

TEACHER CORPS

The Teacher Corps is involved in projects to develop innovative methods of teaching children from low-income areas. The Teacher Corps was created by federal legislation in 1965, and members are currently serving in more than 160 school districts. Programs exist in the Appalachian and Ozark areas, migrant communities, Mexican-American barrios, and correctional institutions. The major priority of the Teacher Corps is the upgrading of education in poverty areas. Most applicants are recent college graduates; however, a program does exist for undergraduates that helps them to complete their education and work in the Corps at the same time.

VISTA—VOLUNTEERS IN SERVICE TO AMERICA

The VISTA volunteer program of the Office of Economic Opportunity represents a people-to-people program, whereby federal, state, and local governments and various organizations can participate in projects to help relieve poverty. VISTA volunteers come from all races and backgrounds. Some are recruited from poverty areas and are called community volunteers.

There are various projects in the VISTA program, but the alleviation of poverty is the prime concern. For example, one VISTA volunteer acts as legal counsel for the Lower Eastside Action Project (LEAP) in New York. LEAP students are dropouts from school with learning problems. The LEAP school allows students to study in the areas they choose and has met with great success. Other projects include work with migrant farm workers, Appalachia residents, and Indian groups. A program called Minority Mobilization is a Mexican-American project that has about 110 Chicano VISTA volunteers providing health and legal services to Mexican-American communities.

Churches

Protestant, Catholic, Jewish, and other religious leaders recognize that the religious life of human beings is closely tied in with their physical, mental, and social life. They are beginning to see that all are essential to living a "good" life. Furthermore, the old Puritan idea that play is sinful and something that should not be associated with the church is rapidly becoming a thing of the past. The church is concerned with how it can help people to spend their leisure hours in a more profitable manner and how it can further promote fellowship and social and physical well-being among its members. There are over 325,000 churches in this country, with a membership of more than 130 million people.

Many churches are providing leadership and facilities so that physical education activities may become a vital part of their programs. Frequently, gymnasia, bowling alleys, tennis courts, and various items of apparatus are part of a church's physical plant. Churches are organizing programs of physical activity around various age groups. They are finding that it aids considerably in helping to attract youth to the church.

The Catholic Youth Organization, for example, sponsors a vigorous and interesting sports program. This organization serves not only boys and girls of high school age but also youth not attending school.

Hospitals

The utilization of physical education activities in hospitals is rather new. Federal hospitals utilize various physical education activities to some extent, as do the Veterans Administration Hospitals. In federal hospitals the American Red Cross is largely responsible for such a program, whereas the Veterans Administration has its own specialized staff located in central and regional offices and in each hospital. The entire program of physical activity in these hospitals is under the close supervision of the medical staff. The activities offered vary according to the condition of the patient and the facilities available. It is individual work to a great degree, and the activity must be adapted to the needs of the patient. A person suffering from a cardiac ailment might need restricted exercise, whereas, according to many physicians, a neuropsychiatric patient would need to engage

Physical education and recreational activities are a part of the program at The Children's Orthopedic Hospital and Medical Center, Seattle, Washington.

in active sports to alleviate the mental condition. Therefore it can be seen that sports and other types of physical activity are a form of therapy for individuals who are hospitalized and as such are becoming recognized as a part of the total hospital program.

Penal institutions

The method of treating criminals, delinquents, and individuals who have displayed antisocial conduct has changed greatly during recent years. The repercussions of some prison riots are promoting more change. Formerly, it was thought that inmates of a penal institution should be regimented, disciplined, and forced to pay for their crimes or misdoings by suffering the rigid routine of prison life. It was believed that they should not enjoy their existence, or should they be allowed to participate in any activities from which they might receive some satisfaction. Today, however, prison and reform-school authorities realize that inmates may be rehabilitated. Through a planned program of reeducation, criminals or delinquents may learn to develop social responsibility to the extent that when they are freed, they may become useful and responsible citizens.

Jackson Prison in Jackson, Michigan, is an example of a penal institution where athletics are used as a medium to help in the rehabilitation of inmates. The program includes weight lifting, baseball, tennis, volleyball, touch football, handball, basketball, and miniature golf. Nearly all the prisoners participate in some activity and part of the program, which includes intramurals and varsity competition.

In any program of rehabilitation and reeducation, sports can play and are playing a valuable and important part. They contribute to the physical and mental health of the participants and also aid in demonstrating the need for cooperation, fair play, and other desirable traits.

There are over a million people in the United States in institutions for the delinquent, defective, and dependent. With such a large group of the population in these institutions, physical education activities have much to offer in helping to rehabilitate individuals so that they may serve society in a constructive manner. The inmates in institutions such as reformatories, prisons, workhouses, penitentiaries, jails, prison farms, and detention homes in particular should have the benefits of what a physical education program under qualified leadership has to offer.

Other countries

For a discussion of physical education activities in other countries, see Chapter 7.

CONSIDERATIONS FOR PHYSICAL EDUCATORS IN SELECTING A SETTING IN WHICH TO WORK

There are many settings in which physical education activities are administered, supervised, taught, coached, performed, and carried out as parts of school and other organizational programs. Physical educators will be interested in seeking job opportunities and in performing services in one of these settings, depending on pertinent factors relating to their qualifications for the job and their ability to perform effectively. Some considerations in selecting a setting include professional preparation, abilities, interests, and job availability.

Professional preparation

The preparation an individual has had will play a part in the selection of a setting. A person who has prepared for elementary school teaching will obviously be interested in teaching at that educational level, just as the person who has prepared for college teaching wants to be situated in an institution of higher learning. Such preparation has oriented the individual to a particular setting and provided knowledge, understanding, and skill to do an effective job in that location. Therefore professional preparation plays an important part in determining the setting in which the individual will work.

Abilities

It is important to match personal abilities with the job and setting. At an early age Einstein showed an uncanny aptitude with figures, and Henry Ford showed superior ability working with machines and gadgets. These great leaders had abilities that helped them to be successful in their work. Some people have greater ability than others in the area of research, which might better qualify them for college work. Others may demonstrate ability in working with children, which might better qualify them for elementary school work, or exceptional skill in golf, which might better qualify them as a professional in a country club. Each person should match his or her abilities against several settings as a means of arriving at the right decision for a successful career. Strong preference should be given to those settings for which there is tangible evidence that the individual possesses outstanding ability for success in those areas.

Interests

Other things being equal, the setting where there is greatest interest should offer a better chance for success because the person will be doing what he or she wants to do. However, if other factors such as abilities are not taken into consideration, it may mean that the job will not be done well. There are people with exceptional interest in engineering who are poor in mathematics, which would jeopardize their chances for success.

Since interests may change, it is also important to evaluate them carefully to cement realistic desires and rule out passing fancies.

Job availability

Professional preparation, abilities, and interests are important, but at the same time there is a practical consideration—job availability. A person who spends 4 or 5 years preparing for a career naturally wants to find a job in his or her field. It may be that chances of obtaining employment in one setting may be brighter than in another. Therefore availability of work is a consideration that cannot be overlooked.

SELF-ASSESSMENT TESTS

These tests are to assist students in determining if material and competencies presented in this chapter have been mastered.

1. Assume you are an exercise physiologist employed in an executive fitness program in industry. Describe the physical education program in which you work. Why is such a program of importance to industry?

2. Prepare a chart listing all the established settings for physical education programs described in

this chapter. Utilize and complete the format shown below:

Established setting	Population served	Objectives	Number and extent of physical education programs in each setting

3. You are a newspaper reporter and have been assigned the task of reporting on the extent of the public's interest in physical fitness. Prepare a story for your newspaper providing supportive evidence to show the extent of such interest.

4. Assume that you are an elementary school physical education teacher. Compare the physical education program you offer your children with that offered 15 or 20 years ago.

5. How is physical education changing at all educational levels? Describe some of the new developments that are taking place at each educational level.

6. Prepare a list of settings where physical education programs are conducted. Opposite each setting describe the personal qualifications that you believe would be essential to being a success as a physical educator working in that setting. Rate your own qualifications in regard to each setting.

READING ASSIGNMENT

Bucher, Charles A.: Dimensions of physical education, ed. 2, St. Louis, 1974, The C. V. Mosby Co., Reading selections 12, 17, 19, and 20.

SELECTED REFERENCES

Bird, J.: Physical education and the middle school student, Journal of Health, Physical Education, and Recreation **44:**25, March, 1973.

Boojarma, L. M., and Messing, A.: A survey of women's intercollegiate athletic programs at junior colleges in the United States, Juco Review **25:**37, 1973.

Bucher, Charles A.: Physical education for life, New York, 1969, McGraw-Hill Book Co.

Bucher, Charles A.: Administration of health and physical education programs, including athletics, ed. 6, St. Louis, 1975, The C. V. Mosby Co.

Bucher, Charles A.: Exercise—it's plain good business, Reader's Digest, Feb., 1976.

Bucher, Charles A., and Bucher, Richard: Recreation for today's society, Englewood Cliffs, N.J., 1974, Prentice-Hall, Inc.

Bucher, Charles A., and Koenig, Constance: Methods and materials for secondary school physical education, ed. 5, St. Louis, 1978, The C. V. Mosby Co.

Bucher, Charles A., and Reade, Evelyn M.: Physical education and health in the elementary school, New York, 1971, The Macmillan Co.

Burton, Elsie C.: The new physical education for elementary school children, Boston, 1977, Houghton Mifflin Co.

Clayton, Robert D., and Clayton, Joyce A.: Concepts and careers in physical education, Minneapolis, 1977, Burgess Publishing Co.

Eichhorn, Donald H.: The middle school, New York, 1966, The Library of Education, The Center for Applied Research in Education, Inc.

Elementary School Physical Education Commission of the American Association for Health, Physical Education, and Recreation Physical Education Division (1968-1969): Essentials of a quality elementary school physical education program, Journal of Health, Physical Education, and Recreation **42**:42, April, 1971.

Insley, Gerald S.: Practical guidelines for the teaching of physical education, Reading, Mass., 1973, Addison-Wesley Publishing Co., Inc.

Miller, Arthur G., and others: Physical education—teaching human movement in the elementary schools, Englewood Cliffs, N.J., 1974, Prentice-Hall, Inc.

Munson, C., and Stafford, E.: Middle schools: a variety of approaches to physical education, Journal of Health, Physical Education, and Recreation **45**:29, 1974.

Physical Education Division Committee: Guidelines for secondary school physical education, Journal of Health, Physical Education, and Recreation **42**:47, April, 1971.

Physical Education Division Committee: Guide to excellence for physical education in colleges and universities, Journal of Health, Physical Education, and Recreation **42**:51, April, 1971.

Physical education in the junior college, Journal of Health, Physical Education, and Recreation **36**:33, April 1965.

Rosewarren, Leonard: The YMCA physical directorship, Journal of Physical Education **63**:70, Jan.-Feb., 1966.

Rosenberg, S.: Meet the Teacher Corps, Parents, p. 50, April, 1972.

Schurr, Evelyn L.: Movement experiences for children, Englewood Cliffs, N.J., 1975, Prentice-Hall, Inc.

Seefeldt, V.: Middle schools: issues and future directions in physical education, Journal of Health, Physical Education, and Recreation **45**:29, Feb., 1974.

Shriver, Sargent: Five years with the Peace Corps, Saturday Review, p. 14, April, 1966.

Stafford, E.: Middle schools: status of physical education programs, Journal of Health, Physical Education, and Recreation **45**:25, Feb., 1974.

The now physical education, Journal of Health, Physical Education, and Recreation **44**:23, Sept., 1973.

PART FIVE

RELATION OF PHYSICAL EDUCATION TO HEALTH EDUCATION, RECREATION, LEISURE SERVICES, CAMPING, AND OUTDOOR EDUCATION

16 ■ Physical education and the school health program

17 ■ Recreation, leisure services, camping, and outdoor education

Courtesy the Division of Municipal Recreation and Adult Education, Milwaukee Public Schools.

16

Physical education and the school health program

INSTRUCTIONAL OBJECTIVES AND COMPETENCIES TO BE ACHIEVED

After reading this chapter the student should be able to—

1. Trace the history of health education programs in American schools and colleges and discuss the reasons why they are an important part of educational curricula.
2. Explain the relationship of the physical education program to the school health program.
3. Describe the characteristics of each of the following areas of the school health program: teaching for health, living healthfully at school, services for health improvement, and what the physical educator's responsibilities are in each area.
4. Be familiar with the outcomes expected from the school health program.
5. Outline the professional preparation needed to be a health educator.

Health-related problems such as drug and alcohol abuse, poor physical fitness, inadequate nutrition, venereal disease, and pollution play an important role in people's lives. Therefore health education is needed to cope with these and other problems. If young people are provided with the scientific facts, they will be able to make informed choices regarding matters that relate to their health. Health education can play an important role in eliminating many problems that adversely affect young people, adults, and society in general.

Public health officials, physicians, dentists, and other representatives of professional services are taking more interest in school health programs. Furthermore, research in the health area is providing new and better direction to help schools and colleges in changing the health behavior of young people.

DEFINITION OF HEALTH

Health has been defined in many ways. Jesse F. Williams,* more than 50 years ago, proposed the definition that health is "the quality of life that renders the individual fit to live most and to serve best." Oberteuffer,† defines health as "the condition of the organism which measures the degree to which its aggregate powers are able to function."

Authorities in the field of health stress concepts such as the three-dimensional makeup of health—physical, mental, and social—and not merely the absence of disease or infirmity; the homeostatic balance that enables human beings to function harmoniously; the adaptability of the individual to various environmental factors affecting his or her well-being; and the readiness of the individual to meet present and future needs.

All these concepts reflect what is meant by health. Each of the concepts reflects a state of being essential to a full and productive life. Furthermore, to have this state of being, certain health practices are essential, otherwise the

---

*Williams, Jesse F.: Personal hygiene applied, Philadelphia, 1925, W. B. Saunders Co.
†Oberteuffer, Delbert, and others: School health education, New York, 1972, Harper & Row, Publishers.

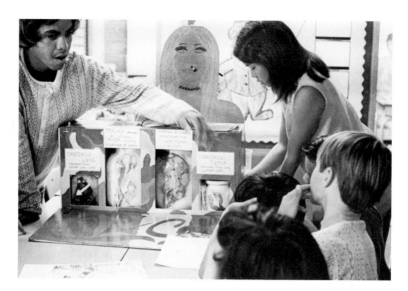

Health class at Henry J. Kaiser High School, Honolulu, Hawaii, examining cancerous lungs related to smoking.

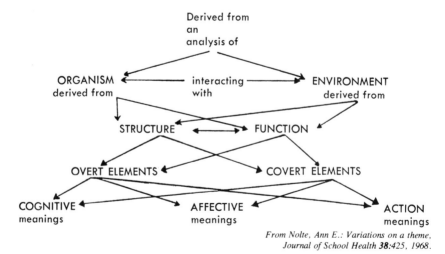

From Nolte, Ann E.: Variations on a theme,
Journal of School Health **38**:425, 1968.

Discipline of health.

homeostatic balance or the steady state may be disrupted and ill health result. Consequently, health education is essential to better assure that proper health habits are established early in life.

Nolte* has graphically portrayed what she believes constitutes the discipline of health. This diagram, shown on p. 372, gives greater meaning to the nature and definition of health by showing how it is affected by the interaction of the organism with the environment and how the discipline of health must be concerned with the cognitive, affective, and action domains.

HISTORY OF THE SCHOOL HEALTH PROGRAM

The health program in the schools is a phase of the educational process that attempts to build in the student a sound foundation of scientific health knowledge, health attitudes, and health habits.

Health science, a comparatively new subject in the school program, derives its foundations from the biological, behavioral, and health sciences. It is an academic field and subject. It helps human beings to apply scientific health discoveries to their daily lives.

The earliest forms of health programs in the schools were evidenced in the latter part of the nineteenth century and were concerned primarily with the temperance movement. A large amount of time was devoted to discussing the ill effects of alcohol on the human body. A state program of health instruction was introduced in Ohio in 1872 as a result of pressure from the Women's Christian Temperance Union. Early instruction in health, other than that of temperance, emphasized a knowledge of the structure and function of the human body.

During the early part of the twentieth century a movement started that emphasized the formation of healthful attitudes and habits. Instead of stressing the names of the various anatomical parts of the human body or the harmful effects of alcohol, the emphasis was along the lines of better living.

On June 28, 1937, the Department of School Health and Physical Education of the National Education Association and the American Physical Education Association were combined to form the American Association for Health and Physical Education. This was in keeping with the rise of health to a place of importance in the educational system. In 1974 health became a separate association within the American Alliance for Health, Physical Education, and Recreation.

The results of the medical examinations reported to Selective Service officials during World War II, which pointed out the incidence of dental caries, postural abnormalities, and other defects, gave impetus to an increased emphasis on health in the schools. These statistics also did much to stimulate thinking toward better preparation of health teachers. Teacher-training institutions were called on to make provision in their programs for such preparation.

Currently health programs in schools and colleges are gaining increasing stature as educators recognize the importance of instilling in young and old alike a body of health knowledge based on scientific fact, wholesome health attitudes, and desirable health practices. Health education is not unique to the United States. It is included in many educative programs throughout the world.

Concept approach to health education

The last decade has witnessed considerable progress in the utilization of the concept approach to the teaching of health. The concepts and conceptual frameworks that have been identified represent the key or central ideals that should be emphasized in health education curriculums at various educational levels. These concepts, which are essential to good health practices, are designed to make students aware of the many health choices they must make, the responsibility they have for making wise choices, and the results of the decisions that they do make.

School Health Education Study

A significant study in the area of health education that utilized the conceptual approach was the School Health Education Study, which conducted a nationwide survey of health education

*Nolte, Ann E.: Variations on a theme, Journal of School Health **38**:425, 1968.

in the public schools, including the testing of students at all grade levels.

Concepts that evolved from their research, the School Health Education Study concluded, can have an impact on the cognitive (knowledge, intellectual abilities, and skills) and affective (values, attitudes, and appreciations) domains.

The concept approach outlined by the School Health Education Study recognized the three closely interwoven dimensions of health: mental, physical, and social. Furthermore, it stressed the triad of health education—the unity of human beings in respect to their physical, mental, and social aspects; the knowledges, attitudes, and practices important to influencing health behavior; and the focus of health education on the individual, family, and community. All these components of the triad are interdependent and constantly interacting.

The study identified three key concepts, ten conceptual statements, and thirty-one substantive elements that represent the conceptual framework for health. The three key concepts are growing and developing, interacting, and decision making, all of which are closely interrelated. Ten additional concepts were identified as follows*:

1. Growth and development influences and is influenced by the structure and functioning of the individual.
2. Growing and developing follows a predictable sequence yet is unique for each individual.
3. Protection and promotion of health is an individual, community, and international responsibility.
4. The potential for hazards and accidents exists, whatever the environment.
5. There are reciprocal relationships involving man, disease, and environment.
6. The family serves to perpetuate humankind and to fulfill certain health needs.
7. Personal health practices are affected by a complexity of forces, often conflicting.
8. Utilization of health information, products,

*Payne, Arlene (reviewer): Health education: a conceptual approach to curriculum, The National Elementary Principal **48:**70, 1968. Copyright 1968, National Association of Elementary School Principals, NEA. All rights reserved.

and services is guided by values and perceptions.
9. Use of substances that modify mood and behavior arises from a variety of motivations.
10. Food selection and eating patterns are determined by physical, mental, economic, and cultural factors.

A UNIFIED APPROACH TO HEALTH TEACHING

The AAHPER prepared a position statement concerning a unified approach to health teaching.* It found, in many cases, that current health topics (drugs, venereal disease, sexuality) were hastily treated to "solve" a specific problem, and frequently these topics would be forgotten the next year.

The recommendations of the AAHPER position statement included the following points:

1. There should be scope and sequence from kin-

*AAHPER: A unified approach to health teaching, The Journal of School Health **41:**171, 1971.

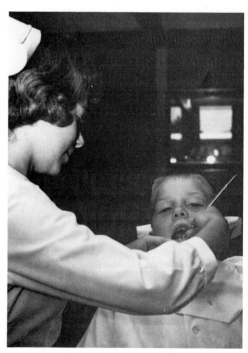

Courtesy Indiana State Board of Health Bulletin.

A dental inspection of a student.

dergarten through grade twelve in a unified approach to health instruction.

2. Curriculum development should include the identification of specific courses including conduct, learning activities, and evaluation techniques.
3. Curriculum content in health courses should be correlated and integrated with other subject areas.
4. The health curriculum should represent the thinking of school personnel, curriculum directors, state and federal consultants, and voluntary and official health agencies.
5. Teachers of health should be specifically prepared and have a genuine interest in health education.

RELATIONSHIP OF PHYSICAL EDUCATION TO THE SCHOOL HEALTH PROGRAM

Health and physical education are not synonymous and their activities are different. At the same time, they have common goals and are closely related, and physical education personnel can play an important part in school health programs. Although concentrated or direct health instruction is needed, health education should take place not only in the classroom but on the athletic field, playground, swimming pool, and gymnasium and in every other room and part of the school plant. The health program utilizes the services of the physician, nurse, dentist, physical educator, home economics teacher, and other specialized personnel in furthering its program of health instruction, health services, and healthful school living.

Many schools find it economically impossible to have both a health educator and a physical educator on the staff. In such cases the physical educator who has adequate training in health can do much in the way of organizing and coordinating a working health program. In larger communities, where sufficient funds make it possible to have personnel with broader training and experience in the health education area, the physical educator can still play a prominent part in helping in various health activities. Through the program of physical activities, the physical educator can play a major role in contributing to the health of every student with whom he or she works.

Physical educators interested in contributing most to the health of the student should, in addition to having a working knowledge of many health areas, know the health aspects of physical activity and the outcomes of sports and activity programs that have implications for the individual's physical, emotional, and social welfare. There is also a need for physical educators to know what constitutes desirable activities, the special problems of physical education relating to girls and women, and the need for a knowledge of things such as first aid, body mechanics, and adapted physical education.

It is essential that coaches be familiar with the (1) growth, development, and psychology of adolescent boys and girls; (2) health needs of adolescents; (3) health practices and injury prevention relating to athletics; (4) first-aid principles; (5) physiology of exercise and knowledge of physical fitness; and (6) conduct of athletic programs that contribute to the physical, mental, emotional, and social development of the participants.

Health and physical education teachers must work closely together, since in many cases they use the same facilities, perform duties in each other's area, work on committees together, and have professional books and magazines that cover the literature of both fields. Both are concerned with the total health of the individual. Both are concerned with the physical as well as the social, mental, emotional, and spiritual aspects of health. Both should help one another and follow practices that will provide the most benefits for the greatest number of people.

Physical educators teach health

A survey conducted several years ago showed that in approximately one third of the states, 75% or more of the health education in junior and senior high schools was being taught by physical educators. In twenty-one states, 70% or less of the health education was being taught by physical educators. More recent surveys show that there is a trend toward more trained health educators assuming the responsibility for teaching health classes. However, many physical educators still continue to teach health classes in the nation's schools.

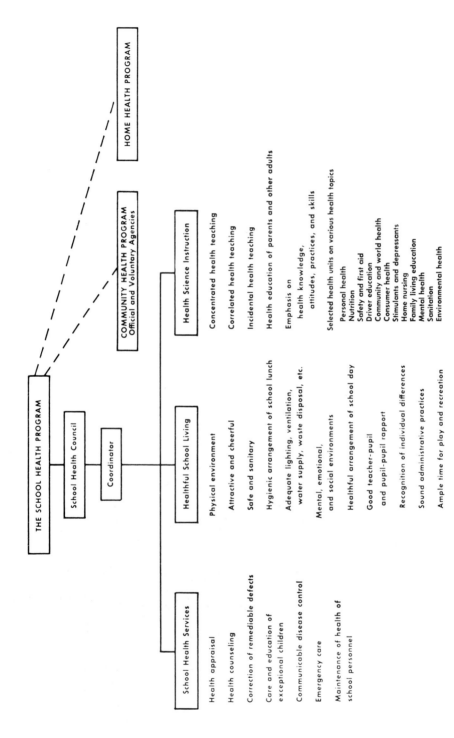

Suggested health education for schools of the United States.

Health class at the Henry J. Kaiser High School, Honolulu, Hawaii, collecting a distillation of tars from various brands of cigarettes.

According to the most recent survey of State School Health Programs,* ten out of thirty states that certify teachers of health education include dual certification in health and physical education. Two states and the District of Columbia only offer dual certification in health and physical education. One state provides for certification only in physical education. Most of the remaining states have no requirements for teaching health other than general teacher certification credentials.

AREAS OF SCHOOL AND COLLEGE HEALTH PROGRAMS

The school health program is divided into three parts: teaching for health, living healthfully at school, and services for health improvement.

Teaching for health

The school has a major responsibility in the area of health instruction. It instructs children and youths in subjects such as the structure and functioning of their bodies, the causes and

methods of preventing certain diseases, the factors contributing to and maintaining good health, and the role of the community in the health program. Such an instructional program, if planned wisely and taught intelligently, will contribute to sound health habits and attitudes on the part of the student.

Health instruction avoids too much stress on the field of disease and medicine. Teachers primarily teach health, how to live correctly, and how to protect one's body against infection rather than teaching disease and medicine. Proper health instruction impresses on each individual the responsibility for his or her own health and, as a member of a community, for the health of others.

Teaching for health takes place in many ways in the school. There is provision for concentrated health teaching in courses specifically set up for this purpose. Health teaching also takes place in other subjects in which aspects of health pertinent to these subjects are covered. An example would be the subject of nutrition in a home economics course. In addition, such instruction takes place incidentally when a "teachable moment" occurs. An example would be when some young person has become addicted to drugs and is hospitalized. Further-

---

*American School Health Association: School health in America—a survey of state health programs, Kent, Ohio, 1976, The Association.

more, through many school experiences such as the school lunch and the medical examination, opportunities arise for teaching health.

The personnel chiefly involved in instructing and in transmitting health knowledge to students include the health educator, elementary school teacher, physical education teacher, biology teacher, general science teacher, home economics teacher, social studies teacher, school nurse, dental hygienist, school lunch manager, and parents.

The physical educator who is teaching health should do the following:

1. Discover the health needs and interests of students.
2. Organize meaningful health units in terms of health needs and interests of students.
3. Know thoroughly the subject matter that is imparted to students.
4. Possess an understanding of what constitutes a well-rounded school health program and the teacher's part in it.
5. Utilize problem solving and other recommended methods in teaching for health.
6. Possess an enthusiasm for the teaching of health.
7. Take time to prepare thoroughly for classes.
8. Make classes interesting and exciting experiences for the students.
9. Provide students with opportunities to participate and exercise their initiative.
10. Use up-to-date textbooks that have been carefully evaluated as to their worth for classes.
11. Provide an attractive setting for classes.
12. Tap the many resources in the school and community that are available and that will make health teaching more dynamic.
13. Assist students in solving their own health problems.

STATUS OF HEALTH INSTRUCTION AT
THE SECONDARY LEVEL

A survey conducted a few years ago by Leigh* provides a profile of the emphasis on health instruction at the secondary level. From the information received, data were extracted that related to (1) subject matter content, (2) teaching approaches, and (3) regulations in re-

*Leigh, Terrence: Nationwide profile of health instruction, School Health Review **4:**35, May-June, 1973.

gard to instruction. Information derived from this survey is discussed here.

Curriculum guidelines. Thirty-two of the forty-four states responding indicated that they had a curriculum guide to assist teachers with their health instruction programs. Five states indicated that they had no guide at present, but guides were in the process of development. States where there were no guidelines indicated that budget cutbacks and other problems had curtailed the development of guidelines, although the states had a high interest in health instruction.

The health topics most frequently mentioned for instruction at this level were family living, nutrition, mental- emotional health, disease, safety, consumer health, and drugs and narcotics.

According to the 1976 report of the American School Health Association entitled *School Health in America,* drugs, tobacco, and alcohol are the most frequently required health topics by state legislation (thirty-five states).

Additional materials. Thirty-two of the forty-four responding states have materials other than the curriculum guide. These materials usually pertained to topics such as programs evaluating drugs, family living or sex education, alcohol, venereal disease, and tobacco. Supplementary materials often include position papers and appraisals of state laws governing health instruction.

Teaching strategies. Teaching strategies were a part of many curriculum guidelines or accessory guides. Some of these strategies in order of their mention are class discussion, guest speakers, experimentation or demonstration, individual reports, audiovisual aids, role playing, field trips, bulletin boards, and community or school surveys.

Required health instruction. Most states require health education in one form or another. Eleven states indicated that general instruction in health is required some time during the secondary school years. Four states require that only certain topics be taught, and sixteen additional states require both specific and general health instruction. Time and grade requirements varied widely from 150 minutes a week each year in grades seven to twelve and 20 minutes

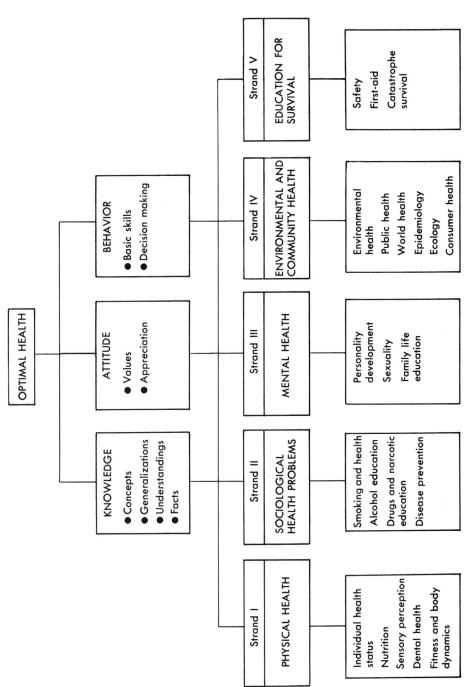

Content and basic aims of New York Health Education Program.

a day in grades nine to twelve to no requirement at all in reference to time and year level.

STATUS OF HEALTH INSTRUCTION IN 2-YEAR COLLEGES

Results of one survey indicated that about one half of the institutions responded positively to offering a basic health course for their students. The survey also indicated that the basic course was required during the first or second year. The credit hours given varied between one and three. A few institutions offered health courses beyond the basic health course.

It is interesting to note that a definite shortage of qualified, certified health education instructors was cited. Only five schools responded that their health instructors were health education teachers certified by the state to teach health courses. Fifteen instructors had health and physical education backgrounds, and most had only physical education backgrounds. Others reportedly teaching health courses included the college nurse, registered nurse, home economics instructor, a physician, and science and biology instructors.

STATUS OF HEALTH INSTRUCTION IN 4-YEAR COLLEGES

A recent survey concerning the status of required health education courses in colleges and universities reveals a trend toward eliminating the requirement for health courses in many such institutions. Those which offer a health course included topics such as alcohol, drugs, tobacco, sex education, the environment, mental health, and preparation for marriage.

CRITICAL HEALTH AREAS

Certain health areas are receiving increased attention from educators because of the acute problems associated with them. For this reason they have been called "critical health problems." Six of the most pressing of these problems are concerned with family life education, venereal disease, tobacco smoking, drug abuse, alcohol abuse, and the environment. Teachers have a responsibility for developing key concepts in each of these health areas.

Family life education. Family life education, which includes sex education, plays a prominent role in some schools and colleges.

Health education class at Henry J. Kaiser High School, Honolulu, Hawaii, discussing tobacco smoking.

With adequate planning, effective community interaction, outstanding teaching, and appropriate subject matter, much good is done. The emphasis throughout the program is on human sexuality, or how boys and girls and men and women fulfill their roles in life. Each student is helped to identify his or her own masculine or feminine role in school, at play, at home, and at work. The core of one's identity is one's sexual role.

Family life education is designed to help young people grow and develop in a way that will be meaningful and lead to the achievement of maturity, emotional independence, and a responsible relationship with the opposite sex. To achieve these goals, boys and girls and young people need a knowledge of their physical, mental, social, and emotional selves and an understanding of their role in the family and the means of achieving good human relationships. Teachers should know their subject matter, be comfortable in using the language of sex, and be aware of the great social changes in progress in our society. Audiovisual aids, books, and other materials should be up to date and appropriate for students. Resource people, such as nurses, clergymen, physicians, psychologists, and social workers, can make a valuable contribution to the program.

In general, a family life education program concerns itself in early childhood with such matters as an understanding of sex differences, developing a wholesome attitude toward sex, helping boys and girls to relate emotionally to their peers, showing them to be good family members, and providing an understanding of such physiological facts as how a baby grows in the body of the mother. In middle childhood an attempt is made to help boys and girls develop wholesome attitudes toward themselves, respecting their right to have opinions, and helping them to experience success and to develop confidence. Furthermore, there is a need to help boys and girls to understand the growth process and the role of inheritance in this process, to develop respect for social customs, and to respect life itself. Later childhood finds the student recognizing his or her appropriate sex role and developing a sound standard of values in human relations. Early and later adolescence finds boys

and girls accepting masculine or feminine roles through appropriate behavior in boy-girl relations and developing an understanding of the physical change they experience as adolescents.

Venereal disease. Recent surveys indicate that venereal disease is spreading at alarming rates. The age group most often infected is young people between the ages of 15 and 24 years. A recent study indicated that one of every 250 teenagers was infected with some form of venereal disease. These statistics only tell part of the story, since most cases of venereal disease, especially those among young people, go unreported. The incidence of venereal disease is really much greater than the statistics indicate. Health education classes openly discuss the facts of venereal disease and educate students concerning symptoms and treatment of these infections.

Tobacco smoking. Poisons present in tobacco smoke taken into the body can cause damage to the smoker. The physiological effects of smoking are not compatible with a healthy, efficient body. Cigarette smoking is damaging to the cilia of the lungs, affects heart and respiration rate, and affects blood pressure. It is linked with cancer of the lung, chronic bronchitis, and heart disease. Cigarette smokers have a higher death rate from certain diseases than nonsmokers. Smoking sometimes interferes with physical activities. In addition, smoking is the greatest single cause of fires.

Perhaps the most significant change in smoking in recent years is the increase in the number of smokers at an early age. One frequently sees students in the elementary and middle schools puffing on cigarettes. Partly as a result of intensive advertising that glamorizes the habit and partly because parental influences have relaxed, young people now smoke in public and sometimes at home with little adult disapproval. Slightly less than one out of every three American teenagers smokes, and an estimated 2 million new smokers between the ages of 12 and 17 years are added each year, many of them acquiring the habit early in life. According to the U.S. Public Health Service, if present lung cancer rates continue, an estimated 1 million of today's schoolchildren will develop lung cancer during their lifetime. Nearly 10% of habitual

SMOKING AND LIFE EXPECTANCY

PRESENT AGE	PACK-A-DAY SMOKERS can expect to live to age	2-PACK-A-DAY SMOKERS can expect to live to age	NON-SMOKERS can expect to live to age
25	68.1	65.3	73.6
30	68.4	65.8	73.9
35	68.8	66.3	74.2
40	69.3	66.9	74.5
45	70.0	68.0	75.0
50	71.0	69.3	75.6
55	72.4	71.0	76.4
60	74.1	73.2	77.6
65	76.2	75.7	79.1

DATA:
American Cancer Society

From Today's Health **46**:*72, 1968.*

smoking starts at the seventh-grade level, with youngsters experimenting at earlier ages. It is important therefore to start adequate instruction in the intermediate grades concerning the use of tobacco and continue on into high school and college years.

The school period is an excellent time to provide the beginning of instruction on tobacco and smoking. It provides an opportunity to acquaint boys and girls with an understanding of what tobacco is, the health hazards associated with smoking, and the economics of smoking. With meaningful instruction, proper understanding and attitudes can be developed that can result in intelligent decisions by the students as to whether or not they will use tobacco.

Drugs and drug abuse. Americans spend more than $5 billion each year on medical drugs. Drugs used to treat disease have proved

an extremely worthwhile contribution to humanity. New discoveries by scientists are constantly producing new drugs that assist in fighting disease, alleviating pain, and providing treatment for various human ailments.

So that drugs may be used properly and constructively by human beings, an educational program is needed to help adults and especially youths understand their use, the contributions they make, and the dangers involved when they are misused.

There is increasing concern among many health authorities and interested citizens regarding not only the indiscriminate use of drugs by adults but, even more important, drug experimentation among youth. Narcotic, or habit-forming, drugs detach a person from reality. They make him or her unaware of danger. Some drugs induce a sense of well-being by postponing feelings of fatigue. Some drugs have been used by participants in sports in which a high level of energy is required, but such practice is denounced by physical educators, coaches, and sports medicine associations.

Marijuana is a drug that young people sometimes experiment with, thinking it will not be harmful. Others turn to stronger drugs such as morphine, heroin, and lysergic acid diethylamide (LSD). These stronger drugs are usually peddled by some law-breaking individual. The constant search by the "pusher" for new victims and new markets for illegal wares has caused much crime and the practice of preying on young and innocent youth. The typical drug addict needs from $10 to $50 a day to maintain the habit. Thus, as the illegal sellers push their drugs on the market, the drug user often turns to petty thefts, shoplifting, burglary, and other crimes to secure the price of a fix.

Plastic cement, model airplane glue, gasoline, and other chemical substances have been used in recent years by unsuspecting youths who sniff these materials to acquire sensations that resemble acute alcoholic intoxication. The results of such sniffing can be extremely harmful. Continuous inhaling can produce double vision, hallucinations, stupor, amnesia, and unconsciousness. The fumes can seriously damage the liver, the kidneys, the brain, and other parts of the body. Moreover, the use of such chemicals may also lead to using stronger drugs and ultimately to addiction with its dreaded withdrawal sickness.

The time to help youth with respect to drugs and drug addiction is before they are tempted to experiment with dangerous drugs. This, of course, means a drug educational program starting in the early school years. If youngsters are well informed regarding drugs—their nature, use, and abuse—when they encounter this problem and are tempted, they will have a resource of information that will enable them to make an intelligent choice about whether they want to experiment, with all the harmful impact on their health, success, and future that drug use implies. Without such information they may readily fall prey to addicts and other uninformed youth who are seeking some form of a "kick" of which they do not know the consequences.

Alcohol. In recent years many young people have turned to alcohol, and excessive drinking among high school and college students has become a major problem. Many become disenchanted with drugs and their harmful effects and start drinking alcohol, which is now legal for those over the age of 18 years. Seven out of ten Americans use alcoholic beverages at the cost of more than $12 billion a year. Drinking enjoys a place in the social scheme that is accorded few other practices. Millions of dollars are spent on advertising by alcohol producers to promote the sale of alcoholic beverages. Tax revenues from the sale of alcoholic beverages help fill local, state, and federal treasuries in the amount of approximately $4 billion annually.

Despite the large role that alcohol and drinking play in the economy, their use presents serious personal and social consequences that cannot be ignored. Drinking may well lead to absenteeism from work, crime, and automobile accidents; an increased work load and cost are placed on hospitals, jails, and welfare agencies; innumerable problems accrue to the alcoholics' children and families.

Although some persons drink to relax and to socialize, others use alcohol as a means to escape from their problems or for other deep-seated psychological reasons. Young people sometimes start drinking as a result of giving in to social pressures or because of a desire to go along with the group. What these people want is the approval of their friends; they fear that if they do not drink, they will not be accepted. Some young people drink because they think it is adult to do so. Others say they drink to have fun or excitement.

Persons vary in the way they behave under the influence of alcohol. The only general statement that can be made is that they will not display their normal personality but, instead, one which has been altered by the depression of the mental processes by intoxication or the accumulation of the toxic effects of alcohol. Some persons will be happy or silly, whereas others become belligerent, noisy, vulgar, or morose.

One of the truly serious problems concerned with alcohol is alcoholism. One of every fifteen drinkers will fall victim to that sickness. Unfortunately, there is no way to predict who that one will be.

In making the choice whether or not to drink, the important thing for young people is to make a decision based on the facts. Most young people know the arguments in favor of social drinking in moderation. But it is also important for them to know about drinking in our society as it involves lawbreaking, automobile deaths, wrecked lives, and broken homes. If they choose to drink, young people should look at the health risks they run and, most importantly, at their responsibility for their actions. If young people choose not to drink they will have decided that the liabilities of alcohol far outweigh its benefits and that good health habits suggest they abstain. Whatever their choice, it should be their own, made freely, based on the facts as to what is best for them.

The early school years are not too early to develop concepts that will help children to better understand the role of alcohol in our culture and whether they should drink when they are older.

The environment. In recent years the subject of environment and its pollution has become a critical health area. The study of the environment and its relation to the living creatures in it—including their relations to one another—is called *ecology*. Understanding of ecology and research in it are becoming more and more important, since people have been placing ever larger demands on the environment and, in the process, bringing about ever more severe

Courtesy Bureau of Land Management, U.S. Department of Interior.

The subject of the environment and its pollution has become a critical health area. Discouragement of littering is necessary for the preservation of environmental beauty.

changes in it. The result has been serious damage to some parts of the environment to the point that scientists are wondering how much longer the environment will be able to meet the demands that humankind places on it.

Ecology, among other things, studies the resources of the environment or of a particular portion of it together with the demands placed on those resources by the creatures that live in it. For example, the ecology of a pond is studied by determining what resources the pond has—how much oxygen in the water, how much mineral nutrients that living organisms require. It is also important to know what creatures live in the pond, how they live, how fast they reproduce, which of them eat the others, and so on. If a pond is studied over many years, certain changes in the ecology will probably be noted. For example, as vegetation and vegetable debris build up at the bottom of the pond, these may absorb oxygen, reducing the oxygen content of the pond's water. If there is a natural flow of water into or out of the pond, changes in this flow will change the ecology of the pond as well. And if life forms in the pond change—perhaps as a result of people fishing in it or polluting it—the pond itself will change because different life forms produce different conditions in the environment. The ecology of a small pond is of no great concern to humankind, with one important exception: The things that are learned from a limited, small environment such as the pond often have implications for a much larger environment—the nation and the world. The study of ponds, among many other things, shows that natural forces and living creatures other than human beings do not change the environment rapidly or in a large way. Human beings, by contrast, affect their environment in enormous ways and in short periods of time.

In recent years it has been increasingly recognized that we are polluting the air we breathe, the waters where we swim or fish, the food we eat, and many other things. There are also problems such as noise pollution, which is affecting our hearing. The car that we drive, the detergents that wash our dishes, and the chemicals that are used to kill insects are affecting our way of life and, particularly important to health educators, they are affecting human health.

The energy crisis is another critically important environmental problem. Depletion of energy resources has resulted in a shortage of available energy supplies. The crisis is not short term, and further depletion of resources only adds to an already serious problem. Conservation of energy supplies and intensive research projects are essential if catastrophic effects to society are to be avoided.

Schools and colleges have a responsibility to bring to the attention of young people and the public in general the consequences of such pollution and, particularly, the implications it has for our health and well-being. Since environmental pollution has become so deadly in its impact and so critical to our way of life, it is a subject that is taught in many health education programs.

Living healthfully at school

The second area into which the school health program may be divided is that of healthful school living. This implies that the time children spend in school should be spent in an environment and atmosphere conducive to physical, social, mental, and emotional health. The environment will be sanitary and cheerful, the teacher will have a pleasing personality, the school program will be well balanced, and educational methods will be in accordance with good health standards. According to the 1976 survey of the American School Health Association, entitled *School Health in America*, thirty-two states have established standards for the environmental quality of schools.

A sanitary and cheerful school environment has implications for healthful school living. Factors such as proper lighting, ventilation, facilities, play areas, and seating should be taken into consideration. The teacher, administrator, and custodian all play an important part in accomplishing this objective. The teacher must assume responsibility for the classroom. Among other things, he or she should see that the classroom is at an optimum temperature, is clean, has adequate lighting, and is equipped with seats that fit the children. The administrator and custodian should see that the school in general meets proper healthful living standards

Courtesy Gwen R. Waters.

A class on safety in bicycling at University High School, Los Angeles City Schools, Los Angeles City Unified School District, Los Angeles, California.

and that the teacher is given help and support in attempts to accomplish this objective.

The teacher's personality has a strong bearing on the health of children. The teacher should have a sense of humor, ready smile, sympathetic attitude, and good health. This will help children to adjust satisfactorily to school living, to enjoy their time in school, to have a successful experience, and to feel that they belong.

A well-balanced school program is a necessity for healthful school living. There must be adequate time for rest, relaxation, play, and study. Close work with books and writing materials should not be of such length as to cause undue fatigue. Play periods should be of adequate length to enable the child to have sufficient exercise. Lunch periods should be long enough to allow for leisurely eating.

Educational methods should be in accordance with good health practices. Class size should be such as to allow the teacher to give personal attention to each student and at the same time

allow for group experiences. The teaching load should not be too demanding of the teacher's time and efforts. Promotion policies should conform to what is in the best interests of the child's health. Home-school relationships should allow for adequately knowing the child's background and permitting parents to be informed as to the child's progress in school. Homework should contribute to the development of the whole child, which takes into consideration the so-called academic needs and also needs in respect to essentials such as recreation, leisure, and play.

Personnel involved in providing a healthful school environment are the school administrator, classroom teacher, custodian, city health department, sanitarian, school physician, school nurse, health educator, physical educator, school bus driver, and school lunch director.

The physical educator interested in students living healthfully at school should do the following:

1. Meet with the school physician, nurse, and others to determine how best to contribute to a healthful environment.
2. Participate in the work of the school health council; if none exists, interpret the need for one.
3. Provide experiences for living healthfully at school.
4. Help students assume an increasing responsibility for a clean and sanitary environment.
5. Try in every way possible to obtain good mental health to be a living example for the students.
6. Set an example for the child in healthful living.
7. Motivate the child to be well and happy.
8. Help supervise various activities that directly affect health, such as school lunch, rest periods, and the like.
9. Be aware of individual differences of students.
10. Keep emotions under control at all times.
11. Provide in every way possible for the safety of students so that accidents may be kept to a minimum.
12. Check regularly the temperature, ventilation, lighting, water supply, waste disposal, and other physical features to see that they provide for the health of students.

Services for health improvement

Health services are an important part of any school health program and should include health appraisal and counseling, correction of remediable defects, emergency care of sickness and injury, communicable disease control and prevention, and education of the exceptional child.

Health appraisal and counseling are achieved in the schools as a result of medical, dental, and psychological examinations; teachers' observations; screening tests for vision and hearing; and records of growth and height statistics. The best results in these various phases of health appraisal are obtained when medical examinations are given to children before entering school and each year that the child is in school, when vision and hearing tests are given annually, and when there is continual teacher observation. As a result of the findings of the various examinations and observations, health counseling with both pupils and parents should take place as conditions warrant.

Although it is usually recognized by authorities in the field of health that it is desirable to have complete medical examinations every year, this is not regarded as being practical by many school administrators. In such cases a *minimum* program would provide for medical examinations before entering school and approximately every third year the child is in school.

Health appraisal and counseling will be of little value unless there is a "follow-through" to see that remediable health defects are corrected. This is an important health service. There should be periodical checks to see that such things as dental caries are remedied, eyeglasses are provided, and other defects attended to. School health programs can render a valuable service if they follow through to see that the remediable defects they discover are corrected.

Emergency care of sickness and injury is needed for the great number of children who are regularly injured as a result of accidents or who become unexpectedly sick when at school. The teacher, as well as the nurse, school physician, and administrator, has responsibilities in this emergency program. Through proper first-aid procedures, safety education, and regard for the health of children, the injured or sick child will be properly and quickly cared for and accidents reduced.

Communicable disease prevention and control should be included in school health services. In carrying out this function, schools should coordinate their program and work with the local department of health. Measures such as isolating the child suspected of having a contagious disease, educating the parents to take advantage of immunization and other preventive measures, informing the health department of suspected cases of communicable disease, encouraging sick children and teachers to stay home, and teaching the causes of the development and spread of diseases are a few services that may be rendered in this phase of school health.

Another health service that should be included in the school health program is the provision of an adequate educational program for the exceptional child. This includes children handicapped by physical or mental disabilities;

those with speech, vision, hearing, and nutritional deficiencies; and those with emotional disorders needing special attention. It also refers to the gifted child who needs special attention. Special provisions for these children guarantee a better educational experience, with a greater saving of human resources. For example, sight-saving classes may be held for the children with vision defects, lip-reading instruction for some of those with hearing defects, and a restricted program for children with a history of rheumatic heart disease and those convalescing from serious illness.

Other school health services that should not be overlooked include protecting the health of school personnel, providing a healthful environment, and providing learning opportunities that promote health.

The personnel involved in the school health services program include school and family physicians, school and public health nurses, school and family dentists and dental hygienists, school dietitian, health educator, physical educator, classroom teacher, school administrator, guidance counselor, psychologist, and parents.

The physical educator interested in health services for students should do the following:

1. Meet with the school physician and nurse to determine how to contribute most to the health services program.
2. Become acquainted with the parents and homes of students.
3. See that children needing special care are referred to proper places for help.
4. Be versed in first-aid procedures.
5. Continually be on the alert for children with deviations from normal behavior and signs of communicable diseases.
6. If feasible, be present at health examinations of students.
7. Follow through in cooperation with the nurse to see that remediable health defects are corrected.
8. Prescribe a physical education program to meet the physical needs of each student.

The nurse is a key person in school and college health programs. A nurse counseling a student at Staten Island Community College, Staten Island, New York.

9. Utilize their position to provide wise health counseling to both students and parents.

10. See that athletes are given a medical examination and provided with other health services as needed.

KEY PERSONNEL IN HEALTH PROGRAMS

The key personnel in school and college health programs are as follows:

Teacher of health. Is the most important person for an effective school health program.

Health coordinator. Has the job of developing effective working relationships with school, college, and community health programs and coordinating the total school or college health program with the general education program.

School administrator. Can provide leadership that ensures a sound health program, qualified personnel, adequate budget, proper facilities, and the sympathy and support of faculty and parents.

Physician. Plays a key role in the conduct of medical examinations, correction of remediable defects, and support to the total school health program.

Nurse. Provides liaison with medical personnel on the one hand and with students, teachers, and parents on the other; can stimulate support for and give direction to all phases of the school health program.

Physical educator. Can contribute much to the school health program; is in a position to impress on students the importance of gaining desirable health knowledge, developing desirable health attitudes, and forming desirable health practices, since many teachable moments occur in a physical education program to teach about health opportunities closely related to the health and fitness of students.

Dentist. Conducts dental examinations, gives or supervises oral prophylaxis, and advises on curriculum material in dental hygiene.

Dental hygienist. Usually assists dentists and does oral prophylaxis; has the opportunity to relate work to educational outcomes.

Speech therapist. Helps to correct speech defects by meeting with students individually and in groups, giving them exercises and drills for their individual problems.

Nutritionist. Plans student meals and can also be of help with nutritional problems of students and as a consultant on subject matter for health education.

Guidance counselor. Concerned with area of health as it relates to student effectiveness and productivity and has the opportunity to impress on students the role of health in scholastic and vocational success.

Custodian. Helps to ensure healthful school living by providing a sanitary school environment.

OUTCOMES OF SCHOOL HEALTH PROGRAMS

The long-term, overall outcome to be expected from the school health program is improved human health. This refers to all aspects of health, including physical, mental, emotional, and social aspects. It applies to all individuals, regardless of race, color, economic status, creed, or national origin. The school has the responsibility to do everything within its power to see that all students achieve and maintain optimum health. This applies not only from a legal point of view but also from the standpoint that the educational experience will be much more meaningful if optimum health exists. A child learns more easily and better when in a state of good health.

The commonly mentioned educational outcomes to be expected from the school health program are concerned with the development of health knowledge, desirable health attitudes, desirable health practices, and health skills.

Development of health knowledge

To develop health knowledge, health education must present and interpret scientific health data that will then be used for personal guidance. Such information will help individuals to recognize health problems and to solve them by utilizing valid and helpful information. It will also serve as a basis for the formulation of desirable health attitudes. In the complex society that exists today, many choices confront individuals with regard to factors that affect their health. For this reason a reliable store of knowledge is essential.

Knowledge of health will vary with different ages. For younger children there should be an attempt to provide experiences that will show the importance of living healthfully. Such settings as the cafeteria, lavatory, and medical examination room offer these opportunities. As the individual grows older, the scientific knowledge for following certain health practices and ways of living can be presented. Some areas of health knowledge that should be understood by students and adults include nutrition, the need for rest, sleep, and exercise, protection of the body against changing temperature conditions, contagious disease control, the dangers of self-medication, and community resources for health.

If students are properly health educated, for example, they should understand the germ theory of disease and also have a desire to prevent disease whenever possible by means of desirable health practices. Boys and girls should understand where to find the health services necessary to cope with various types of health problems. Young people should know the effects of using tobacco, narcotic drugs, alcohol, and other depressants and stimulants. In addition, they should appreciate the fact that health is everybody's business—each person has a responsibility for the health of others in the family, community, nation, and world. This is especially important in today's world if environmental pollution is to be stopped. There should be a recognition of the part played by nutrition, physical activity, rest, and sleep in physical fitness; the part played by safety in accident prevention; and the importance of good mental health. If such topics are brought to the

attention of persons everywhere and if the proper health attitudes and practices are developed, better health will result.

Development of desirable health attitudes

Health attitudes refer to the health interests of the individual or the motives that impel a person to act in a certain way. Health knowledge will have little worth unless the person is interested and motivated to the point that he or she wants to apply this knowledge to everyday living. Attitudes, motives, drives, or impulses, if properly established, will result in the person's seeking scientific knowledge and utilizing it as a guide to living. This interest, drive, or motivation must be dynamic to the point at which it results in behavior changes.

The school health program must be directed at developing those attitudes which will result in optimum health. Students should have an interest in and be motivated toward possessing a state of buoyant health, feeling "fit as a fiddle," being well rested and well fed, having wholesome thoughts free from anger, jealousy, hate, and worry, being strong, and possessing

Courtesy Mrs. Seymour Manheimer, Bowie, Md., and the School Health Review.

Health instruction taking place in a school in Maryland.

enough physical power to perform life's routine tasks. They should have the right attitudes toward health knowledge, healthful school living, and health services. If such interests exist within the individual, proper health practices will follow. Health should not be an end in itself except in cases of severe illness. Health is a means to an end, a medium that aids in achieving noble purposes and contributes to enriched living.

Another factor that motivates people to good health is the desire to avoid the pain and disturbances that accompany ill health. They do not like toothaches, headaches, or indigestion because of the pain or distraction involved. However, developing health attitudes in a negative manner through fear of pain or other disagreeable conditions does not seem to be a sound approach.

A strong argument for developing proper attitudes or interests centers around the goals a person is trying to achieve in life and how optimum health can help to achieve such goals. This is the strongest incentive or interest that can be developed in a person. If a person wants to become a successful artist, businessman, dancer, homemaker, or parent, it is beneficial to possess good health so that the study, training, hard work, trials, and obstacles that one encounters can be met successfully. Optimum health will aid in the accomplishment of such goals. As the biologist Jennings has pointed out, the body can attend to only one thing at a time. If its attention is focused on a backache or an ulcer, it cannot be focused satisfactorily on essential work that must be done. Centering health attitudes or interests on life goals is dynamic because it represents an aid to accomplishment, achievement, and enjoyable living.

Development of desirable health practices

Desirable health practices represent the application of scientific health knowledge to one's living routine. The health practices that a person adopts will determine in great measure the health of that person. Practices or habits harmful to optimum health, such as failure to obtain proper rest or exercise, overeating, drug addiction, overdrinking, and smoking or failure to observe certain precautions against contract-

ing diseases, will usually result in poor health.

Knowledge does not necessarily ensure good health practices. An individual may have all the statistics as to the results of speeding at 70 miles an hour, but unless this information is applied, it is useless. The health of an individual can be affected only by applying that which is known. At the same time, knowledge will seldom be applied unless an incentive, interest, or attitude exists that impels its application. Therefore it can be seen that to have a good school health program, it is important to recognize the close relationship which exists among health knowledge, health attitudes, and health practices. Each contributes to the other.

Development of health and safety skills

Certain skills should be learned in the health and safety education program in the schools. These include neuromuscular skills in first aid, home nursing, and safety and driver education. It takes skill to put splints on a broken leg or to administer artificial respiration. It takes skill to read a thermometer or to care for a sick person. It takes skill to put out a fire effectively or help in the case of an accident. And it takes skill to drive in city traffic or to park on a steep hill. These skills are taught in various aspects of the school health and safety program and are outcomes that are expected from students who participate in these educational experiences. It should be remembered, however, that skill requires refresher training periodically so that a person is always ready in the event of an emergency.

QUALIFICATIONS AND PROFESSIONAL PREPARATION OF HEALTH EDUCATORS

Health educators have the task of improving health practices, attitudes, and knowledge of children and adults. They should be interested in community as well as personal health problems and be devoted to encouraging and stimulating people to recognize the importance of good health for themselves and others. The health educator may act in the capacity of a teacher of concentrated courses in health education, a coordinator of a school or public health program, or a staff member of some voluntary health association such as the American Red Cross.

The personality of health educators is of particular concern. These individuals should be well adjusted and well integrated emotionally, mentally, and physically if they are to be successful in developing these characteristics in others. Such persons must also be interested in human beings and possess skill and understanding in human relations so that health objectives may be realized.

It is important that health educators have a mastery of certain specialized health knowledge and skills and have proper attitudes. Such knowledge, skills, and attitudes will help health educators to identify the health needs and interests of individuals with whom they come in contact, provide a health program that will meet these needs and interests, and promote the profession so that human lives may be enriched. This means that many experiences should be included in the training of persons entering this specialized field. These experiences may be divided into general education, professional education, and specialized education.

General education experiences will constitute about one half the total professional preparation curriculum and include knowledge and skill in the communicative arts; an understanding of sociological principles; an appreciation of history of different peoples, with their various social, racial, and cultural characteristics; and the fine and practical arts that afford a medium of expression, of releasing emotions, for richer understanding of life, and for promoting mental health. The science area is important to the health educator and should include anatomy and kinesiology, physiology, bacteriology, biology, zoology, chemistry, physics, child and adolescent psychology, human growth and development, general psychology, and mental health.

In professional education it is important for the health educator to have a mastery of the philosophies, techniques, principles, and evaluative procedures characteristic of the most advanced and best thinking in education. Professional courses in educational philosophy, methods of teaching, and practice teaching would come in this area.

The specialized health education area should include personal and community health, nutrition, family and child health, first aid and safety, methods and materials, organization and administration of school health programs, public health (including the basic principles of environmental sanitation and communicable disease control), and health counseling.

Teacher certification in health education

In recent years there has been a trend among many school systems to employ full-time health instructors. Schools have come to recognize the specialized nature of health instruction and are seeking teachers who have special college preparation in health education.

Many health teachers are prepared to teach both health and physical education. This "two-field" preparation has made the teacher marketable, but what about his or her accountability in regard to health teaching? Certification to teach health education is recommended as a prerequisite for being employed as a health teacher. The scope of health education continues to expand, and the most qualified persons are needed to teach in this area.

CAREERS IN HEALTH EDUCATION

A physical educator with interest, training, and qualifications for health work may be interested in exploring the possibilities of a career in this field. The increased emphasis given to health education augurs well for job opportunities in community and educational programs throughout the United States. Furthermore, some insurance companies, youth agencies, and organizations concerned with various diseases and health problems employ people trained in health education. The attention being given to safety education means more positions for people with special training in this field in industry and government, as well as in the schools and other settings.

For those persons interested in specializing in safety education, several job opportunities are available in schools, colleges, industry, transportation agencies, and other organizations and agencies. Safety educators devote their time to promoting safety considerations and reducing accidents. Jobs are available as supervisors of safety education and teachers of driver education in schools, as safety supervisors or safety directors in industry and government, as supervisors or consultants in community safety, or as teachers of safety and/or driver education in colleges and universities. According to the American School Health Association's 1976 survey, entitled *School Health in America,* safety education is mandated in sixteen states.

SELF-ASSESSMENT TESTS

These tests are to assist students in determining if material and competencies presented in this chapter have been mastered.

1. Identify what you consider to be the key reasons why health education has become a part of the curriculum in many schools and colleges in the United States. Justify your answer.

2. Analyze the field of health education and also that of physical education in respect to each of the following:

Objectives	Program content	Qualifications of teachers	Professional organizations to which members belong

Compare your findings for each field and list the similarities and the differences between each.

3. Construct and complete a chart according to the following format:

Physical educator's responsibilities in the school health program

Teaching for health	Living healthfully at school	Health careers

4. Assume you are a physical educator who has been assigned to teach health education in a high school. Describe some of the outcomes you would expect to achieve as a result of your teaching.

5. You have been thinking about changing your major from physical education to health education. Outline the professional preparation program you would need to follow to become a health educator.

READING SELECTION

Bucher, Charles A.: Dimensions of physical education, ed. 2, St. Louis, 1974, The C. V. Mosby Co., Reading selections 17 and 18.

SELECTED REFERENCES

AAHPER: A unified approach to health teaching, The Journal of School Health **41:**171, 1971.

Bucher, C. A., Olsen, E., and Willgoose, C.: The foundation of health, Englewood Cliffs, N.J., 1976, Prentice-Hall, Inc.

Curriculum Commission of the School Health Division, AAHPER: A guide for development of a health education curriculum, School Health Review **2:**35, Sept., 1971.

Elson, Lawrence M.: It's your body, New York, 1975, McGraw-Hill Book Co.

Greenberg, J. S.: Emerging educational concepts and health instruction, The Journal of School Health **42:**356, 1972.

Hafen, Brent Q.: Man, health and environment, Minneapolis, 1972, Burgess Publishing Co.

Hicks, D. A.: Professional preparation of health education in the 70's, The Journal of School Health **42:**243, 1972.

Johnson, Warren R.: Health in action, New York, 1977, Holt, Rinehart & Winston, Inc.

Johnson, Warren R., and Belzer, Edwin G.: Human sexual behavior and sex education, Philadelphia, 1973, Lea & Febiger.

Joint Committee on Health Education Terminology: Health education definitions, School Health Review **4:**25, Nov.-Dec., 1973.

Jones, Kenneth L., and others: Dimensions—a changing concept of health, San Francisco, 1974, Canfield Press.

Jones, Kenneth L., and others: Principles of health science, New York, 1975, Harper & Row, Publishers.

Jourard, Sidney M.: Healthy personality, New York, 1974, Macmillan Publishing Co.

Leigh, T.: Nationwide profile of health instruction, School Health Review **4:**35, May-June, 1973.

Levy, M., Greene, W., and Jenne, F.: Competency based professional preparation, School Health Review **3:**26, July-Aug., 1972.

Oberteuffer, Delbert, and others: School health education, New York, 1972, Harper & Row, Publishers.

Projections of the joint committee on health problems in education of the NEA and AMA: School health—1985, School Health Review **3:**2, May-June, 1972.

Randall, H. B.: School health in the 70's, The Journal of School Health **41:**125, 1971.

Read, Donald H., and Greene, Walter H.: Health and modern man, New York, 1973, Macmillan Publishing Co.

Schiller, Patricia: Creative approach to sex education and counselling, New York, 1973, Association Press.

Sinacore, John S.: Health—a quality of life, New York, 1974, Macmillan Publishing Co.

Sinacore, John S., and Sinacore, Angela C.: Introductory health—a vital issue, New York, 1975, Macmillan Publishing Co.

Slocum, H. M.: Teacher preparation in health education, School Health Review **2:**8, Feb., 1971.

Willgoose, Carl: Health education for secondary schools, Philadelphia, 1977, W. B. Saunders Co.

Willgoose, C. E.: Health education in the elementary school, ed. 3, Philadelphia, 1974, W. B. Saunders Co.

17

Recreation, leisure services, camping, and outdoor education

After reading this chapter the student should be able to—

1. Understand the objectives, needs, and trends for recreation and leisure programs.
2. Identify the various settings for recreation and leisure services and the types of programs and positions that are offered and available in these settings.
3. Describe the qualifications and professional preparation needed by recreators and the role that physical educators can play in recreation and leisure programs.
4. Define camping and outdoor education and list the needs, objectives, and settings for each.
5. Outline the types of programs that exist in camping and outdoor education, the worth of each program to students, and the role that physical educators can play in each program.

Recreation, leisure services, camping, and outdoor education represent areas closely allied to physical education and fields in which many physical educators work.

RECREATION AND LEISURE SERVICES

Recreation and leisure services are concerned with those activities in which a person partici-
pates during hours other than work. They imply that the individual has chosen certain activities in which to engage voluntarily because of an inner, self-motivating desire. Such participation gives him or her a satisfying experience and develops physical, social, mental, and/or esthetic qualities contributing to a better existence.

It has been estimated that the American worker has an average of 675 hours of free time annually, not including vacation time. When this time is added, the amount of free time is close to 800 hours annually or roughly 1 out of every 12 months.* With this much free time it is essential that recreation and leisure services programs be developed to help people fully enjoy these hours in a constructive manner.

The kind of recreation and leisure that education is advocating can be characterized by five descriptive terms as follows:

1. *Leisure time.* To be recreation the activity must be engaged in during one's free time. From this point of view, work cannot be one's recreation.
2. *Enjoyable.* The activity engaged in must be satisfying and enjoyable to the participant.
3. *Voluntary.* The individual must have chosen, of his or her own volition, to engage in this pursuit; there must have been no coercion.
4. *Constructive.* The activity is constructive. It is

---

*Hodgson, J. D.: Leisure and the American worker, Journal of Health, Physical Education, and Recreation **43**:38, March, 1972.

Camping out in winter is part of the program in the Division of Municipal Recreation and Adult Education, Milwaukee Public Schools.

not harmful to the person physically, socially, or in any other way. It helps one to become a better integrated individual.

5. *Nonsurvival.* Eating and sleeping are not recreational activities in themselves. One may engage in a picnic in which a dinner is involved, but other facets of the affair, such as the social games and fellowship, are important parts of the recreational activity.

Objectives of recreation and leisure services

The field of recreation and leisure services has many worthwhile objectives. The American Alliance for Health, Physical Education, and Recreation states that this special field contributes to the satisfaction of basic human needs for creative self-expression; helps to promote total health—physical, emotional, mental, and social; provides an antidote to the strains and tensions of life; provides an avenue to abundant personal and family living; and develops effective citizenship and vitalizes democracy.

One of the best statements of objectives was discussed by The Commission on Goals for American Recreation.* The objectives are as follows.

1. *Personal fulfillment.* Recreation recognizes the need for people to become all that they are capable of becoming and the contribution that recreation can make to this goal.
2. *Democratic human relations.* Recreation recognizes that it has goals that contribute to individuals as well as to the democratic society of which they are a part.
3. *Leisure skills and interests.* Recreation has the goal of meeting the interests of people and developing skills that will provide the incentive, motivation, and medium for spending free time in a constructive and worthwhile manner.
4. *Health and fitness.* Recreation recognizes the importance of contributing to the alleviation of conditions such as mental illness, stress, and physical inactivity that prevail in many segments of the American society.
5. *Creative expression and esthetic appreciation.*

---

*The Commission on Goals for American Recreation: Goals for American recreation, Washington, D.C., 1964, American Association for Health, Physical Education, and Recreation.

Recreation attempts to provide the environment, leadership, materials, and motivation where creativity, personal expression, and esthetic appreciation on the part of the participant exist.

6. *Environment for living in a leisure society.* Recreation plays an important role in encouraging such things as preservation of natural resources, construction of playgrounds and recreation centers, and awakening the population to an appreciation of esthetic and cultural values.

History of recreation and leisure services

Recreation and leisure, to some extent, have always been a part of the lives of all people, of every race, nation, and creed. In many cases,

people have spent their leisure hours in a constructive and worthwhile manner by participating in activities such as music, dances, games, sports, painting, and other arts. In early history the Chinese, Hindu, Persian, Egyptian, Babylonian, and Greek peoples left evidence of these pursuits.

In the United States there have been many milestones in the progress of recreation to a place of national importance. The land that is now Central Park in New York City was purchased in 1853, and the Boston Sand Gardens for children were opened by the Massachusetts Emergency and Hygiene Association in 1885. In 1889 playgrounds were opened in New York and in 1892 at Hull House in Chicago. The

AVERAGE LENGTH OF LIFE (ACTUAL YEARS)		40	70	75
DIFFERENT ERAS		1885	1950	2000
PERCENTAGE OF TOTAL LIFETIME SPENT IN ACTIVITIES SHOWN	SCHOOL	5.6	4.0	4.8
	WORK	26	15.3	7.9
	LEISURE	7.8	20.7	27.1
	EAT & SLEEP	60.5	59.9	60.2

From Still, Joseph W.: Geriatrics 12:577, 1957.

The use of time in three generations.

"Playground" idea spread to other cities, which included Brookline, Massachusetts, Louisville, Kentucky, and Los Angeles, California. The Playground Association of America was founded in 1906, with Dr. Luther H. Gulick as president. This same association became known as the National Recreation Association, and today it is part of the National Recreation and Park Association.

In 1938 the word *recreation* was officially made a part of the title of the American Association for Health, Physical Education, and Recreation. In 1952 the First National Recreation Workshop was held at Jackson's Mill, West Virginia. In 1954 the Council for the Advancement of Hospital Recreation was or-

ganized. In 1956 the International Recreation Association was established. In 1962 the Bureau of Outdoor Recreation was established in the U.S. Department of Interior. In 1965 five of the leading organizations that were most directly concerned with the profession of recreation merged and formed the National Recreation and Park Association.

Since the turn of the century, recreation has been considered more and more to be a fundamental human need. Social factors such as modern science and technology with their added leisure; urbanization with its need for publicly sponsored recreation; the changing impersonal and mechanized nature of work with its need for activities of a more personal nature;

Courtesy South Carolina Department of Parks, Recreation and Tourism, Columbia, S.C.

Beautiful scenery surrounds Table Rock State Park in South Carolina's Blue Ridge Mountains. The park, located at the foot of Table Rock Mountain near Pickens, South Carolina, has a nature trail and a variety of recreational activities.

the growth of transportation with its implications for greater travel during leisure hours; and the school's interest in recreation and its sponsorship of programs have been responsible for a great growth in recreation and leisure services in recent years.

More than 3,000 communities in this country are sponsoring public recreation programs under school or local government auspices. In addition, volunteer and private organizations have recreational programs.

The American people are becoming recreation conscious, with nine out of ten Americans taking part in some form of outdoor recreation; nearly one out of two participates in some form of water recreation, one out of three works around the yard and in the garden, one out of ten has special hobbies such as woodworking, one out of about twenty sings or plays a musical instrument, and approximately one out of twenty participates in the nation's camp grounds.

Need for recreation and leisure services with implications for physical education

All individuals should experience the joy that comes from engaging in recreation activities that fit their needs, interests, and desires. The Constitution of the United States sets forth a fundamental belief that each individual is endowed with certain inalienable rights; among these are life, liberty, and the pursuit of happiness. Recreation can contribute to the attainment of such vital concepts.

A survey conducted at New York University included many thousands of people, covering a wide range of occupations and including an age range of 4 to 80 years. This study indicated that the leading characteristics of happy people were (1) interest in work, (2) interest in hobbies, (3) interest in others, (4) lack of interest in material things, and (5) rendering a service to individuals and groups.

Dr. William Menninger, noted physician and psychologist, pointed out in a speech before the National Recreation Association that the happy and healthy person is the one who has recreational pursuits. This person participates in some recreational activity to supplement routine daily work. He further states: "Good mental health is directly related to the capacity and willingness of an individual to play. Regardless of his objectives, resistances or past practice, any individual will make a wise investment if he plans time for his play and takes it seriously."

A survey of student opinion regarding extracurricular activities, which has implications for school recreation and physical education programs, was made at a high school in Texas. The survey revealed that more than half the students questioned indicated that their involvement in such activities was based on enjoyment of the activities themselves. Approximately 68% of the students considered extracurricular activities as important as their classwork. Most students engaged in one or two activities.

A doctoral study by Norvel Clark, which was done at New York University, investigated the needs and interests of junior high school students in the Bedford-Stuyvesant area of Brooklyn, New York. The study was done with the intent of developing an activity program based on the identified needs and interests.

The study revealed the rank order of needs of children as evaluated by experts in the field of education, social group work, recreation, and community education. The needs were as follows: (1) the need to achieve, (2) the need for economic security, (3) the need to belong, (4) the need for love and affection, (5) the need for self-respect through participation, (6) the need for variety as relief from boredom and ignorance, (7) the need to feel free from intense feelings of guilt, and (8) the need to be free from fear.

The study also revealed that more than 85% of students were interested in team and individual sports, which the panel of experts rated high as to the contribution they made to the objectives of the organization.

Recreation and physical education programs in communities from coast to coast are being challenged to provide all types of activities that cut across the needs, interests, and desires of human beings. Such activities must include arts and crafts, boating, nature study, gardening, all sorts of games and sports, literary activities, music, dramatics, nature study, camping, parties, and many others. In addition to offering a broad and varied program, it is a further essential that all the resources of a community be

Stanley Park Pitch and Putt provides a beautiful setting for a relaxing recreational game of golf.

mobilized and coordinated so that the best possible program can be offered.

Leisure

There have been several definitions and interpretations of *leisure*. The word comes from the Greek *scole,* and this means that there is a relationship between leisure and education. The English word *leisure* is more closely related to the Latin *licere,* which means "to be free."

The classical interpretation of leisure, according to Sebastian de Grazia in his book *Of Time, Work and Leisure,* was that free time cannot be identified directly with leisure, since leisure implies such things as a state of being, a mental attitude involving contemplation and serenity. Thus, according to de Grazia, anyone can have free time, but not every person can have leisure.

Aristotle thought of leisure as a state of existence or being in which one engages in activity for its own sake. Furthermore, leisure was in contrast to work in the formal sense. Instead it involved such activities as art and philosophical discussion.

The most common definition and interpretation of leisure is that it represents the free time that one has after necessities have been taken care of and work has been performed. It represents the time when the person has a choice of what to do: travel, study, play a musical instrument, or play a sport.

One important implication for the physical educator regarding leisure is that it represents a time when many individuals engage in sports or other forms of physical education activity. In a sense they utilize their leisure to play. The word *play* comes from the Anglo-Saxon word *plega,* which means a game or sport. The Latin word *plaga* refers to a blow, stroke, or thrust. Thus one plays a game by striking a ball, stroking a racquet, or thrusting as in fencing. Leisure, then, is a time when one can play and enables one to express and enjoy oneself.

The amount of leisure available to most persons is increasing as a result of our automated existence and common belief that people should enjoy the fruits of their labors. At the same time, educators recognize that to have a strong society, leisure hours must be spent in a constructive manner and utilized to help individuals develop those areas of self where shortages exist in their personal development. For example, one may wish to know more about and appreciate the fine arts, and thus leisure time represents an opportunity to achieve this goal. Another example would be the opportunity that leisure provides the person who spends long hours every day at a desk doing mental work to spend time engaging in some physical activity.

Education, including physical education, can do much to provide the skills, understanding, appreciations, attitudes, and values that will motivate human beings to spend their leisure hours in a profitable manner.

Settings for recreation and leisure services

Recreation and leisure service activities are conducted in a variety of settings that afford many job opportunities for persons trained in recreation.

Government. Recreation and leisure services programs are carried on at all government levels: federal, state, county, township, municipal, and school district. For example, approximately fifty federal agencies and 230 state agencies play important roles in respect to recreation and park development. The National Park Service, National Forest Service, U.S. Army Corp of Engineers, the Bureau of Land Management, the Bureau of Indian Affairs, the Bureau of Reclamation, the Tennessee Valley Authority, the Fish and Wildlife Service, and the Bureau of Outdoor Recreation are a few of the federal agencies that participate or are involved in recreational services. State park departments, state conservation departments, and state education departments are involved in recreational services at the state level of government. Community recreation is provided by the local government. It is controlled, financed, and administered by the community. Community recreation departments and park departments, for example, sponsor recreation programs.

Industries. The nation's great industrial concerns, such as Lockheed Aircraft, North Ameri-

can Rockwell, Xerox, and Eastman Kodak Company, sponsor recreation programs for their employees.

Hospitals. Recreation programs are provided in many veterans, municipal, county, and other hospitals for the benefit of patients. The therapeutic values have been well established for the ill and handicapped.

Schools and colleges. Elementary and secondary schools and colleges and universities in some sections of the country provide recreation programs. School recreation is frequently provided by a board of education for students and in some cases for the adult population.

Home. The family unit is becoming a center for much recreation.

Commercial establishments. Amusement parks, movie houses, bowling alleys, and many other forms of recreation abound from coast to coast.

Service clubs for the armed forces. The United Service Organization is an example of a recreation program provided for individuals who serve in the armed forces.

Churches and religious organizations. Many churches and religious organizations, especially in large metropolitan areas, have extensive recreation programs for their parishioners.

Voluntary youth-serving agencies. Many agencies for young people such as the Boy Scouts and the Girl Scouts are interested in how these boys and girls spend their free time, and therefore they sponsor recreation programs. Other voluntary agencies offering recreational services are museums, libraries, and granges. Also, private voluntary agencies organized around special interests of certain groups, such as music specialties and photographic specialties, offer recreation programs.

Clubs. Boating, tennis, golf, and other clubs represent private recreation agencies that operate their own facilities for the benefit of the membership of the club.

Trends and challenges in recreation and leisure services

Innovations in recreation and leisure services are being introduced all around the nation. The area of recreation is still in its early stages, and there are many concepts that must be tried and evaluated. Some trends in this field are considered in the following discussion.

URBAN RECREATION

Urban recreation has a great challenge to meet. Inner-city areas are rapidly decaying, and there is a desperate need for excellence in recreation programs. In many inner-city areas the community has responded to its recreational needs with such diverse programs as mobile recreation units and local recreation centers.

A survey taken by Kraus of Temple University, Philadelphia, of recreation and park administrators in eight major cities (Atlanta, Boston, Chicago, Detroit, Los Angeles, Philadelphia, San Francisco, and Washington, D.C.) and in forty-five other cities with populations of over 150,000 determined how these cities are responding to the urban crisis in recreation.

The results of this survey indicate that these urban areas had suffered from budget cutbacks. There was a significant decrease in new recreational facilities, and in many cases there were freezes on hiring additional personnel. Other problems cited included crime, vandalism, racial misconduct, and poverty.

Among the cities surveyed, some noted that additional financial aid was obtained through federal grants, special funding, and industrial sources. Programs had been introduced to develop ethnic or racial interests. Mobile recreation vans could easily move a swimming pool or small gymnasium into a given area. These vans also brought cultural programs such as drama, dance, and puppet shows. Youth programs attacking such problems as drug abuse and crime also become a part of the recreation program.

It was found that many cities were making an effort to hire more minority group workers in their programs and to have greater community involvement. Neighborhood centers were preferred to develop greater local participation, but city facilities were also used in certain phases of the program.

COMMUNITY RECREATION PROGRAMS

Community recreation programs are growing. Many communities have year-round pro-

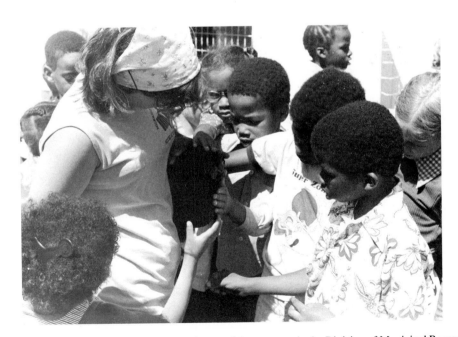

Getting acquainted with nature's animals is part of the program in the Division of Municipal Recreation and Adult Education, Milwaukee Public Schools.

grams for persons of all ages that include adult education classes, fitness programs, swimming pool–tennis court complexes, camp programs for children, and summer recreation programs for all residents.

An interesting 8-week summer program was conducted in a city in New York State. This city has a population of 8,000 people. Some events in the program were a trip to the Cooperstown Baseball Hall of Fame: a trip to Yankee Stadium; a trip to MacArthur Stadium in Syracuse, New York; carnivals; gymnasium activity days; and full day programs that included an art festival, a bike races, a field day, citywide picnic, and an all-city swimming meet.

Colleges also participate in community recreation as exhibited by the physical education department of a community college in New Jersey. This college sponsored adult fitness programs, community athletic programs, and walk-in recreation activities in which an individual could utilize certain facilities on a drop-in basis during the day. The implementation of such programs is invaluable to the community and enhances community-college relations.

THERAPEUTIC RECREATION

Therapeutic recreation programs are rapidly gaining in popularity and numbers. They are located in settings such as hospitals and nursing homes and play an important role in rehabilitating the residents. This phase of recreation service is concerned with programs for the ill, disabled, handicapped, and aged persons who, because of their condition, are unable to participate in programs for the healthy, physically active person.

COMMERCIAL RECREATION PROGRAMS

Commercial recreation has grown rapidly in recent years. Such recreation attractions as Disneyland, Disney World, Sea World, and Cypress Gardens attract millions of visitors each year. Advantages of these attractions include factors such as numerous recreational activities located in one central area, good weather and excellent locations, and an increase of tourism within the state where the complex is operated. However, there are certain disadvantages. Because of the energy crisis, many people have been unable to drive their cars to these recrea-

Courtesy Big Surf.

Big Surf is a commercial recreation venture in Tempe, Arizona.

tion areas, inflation and high prices in some cases have reduced attendance, and the local ecology has been disrupted.

THERE IS A NATIONAL AWARENESS OF THE NEED TO PROTECT THE ENVIRONMENT

Americans are increasingly beginning to realize the degree to which healthy land, air, and water are essential to the nation's and world's well-being. The quality of the environment is a major consideration of the government and people. Park and recreational professionals, for example, have an opportunity to participate and play a major role in making communities, cities, and suburbs healthy environments. This can be done by developing education programs that stress proper use and enjoyment of the environment, increasing recreation opportunities for all persons, making parks more active centers of city life, and building recreation and natural beauty into housing programs.

INNER-CITY PROBLEMS REQUIRE MORE ATTENTION TO RECREATIONAL POSSIBILITIES

The problems of our growing cities, with their increased crime rates, higher costs of living, growing welfare rolls, transportation difficulties, and lack of proper recreation facilities, provide fertile ground for major contributions by the recreation profession. Among innovations being suggested and tried are new concepts regarding park-school development to further recreational opportunities for all city inhabitants, recreation-education parks with transportation being provided for city youth, and recreation plazas that might involve closing off streets, putting in swimming pools, and providing indoor spaces for youth activities.

STATES ARE JOINING FORCES TO MEET RECREATIONAL NEEDS OF THEIR CITIZENS AND VISITORS

The states of Vermont and New Hampshire, have signed a Plan of Cooperation whereby the recreational services of each state work cooperatively together. This was the first such formal agreement between the recreation services in two states, and it is expected to develop into a trend throughout the country as the demand for recreation services increase. The Vermont–New Hampshire plan calls for an interchange of publications, discussions of state directors of recreation, and leadership training programs in recreation.

A visit to the farm is part of the program in the Division of Municipal Recreation and Adult Education, Milwaukee Public Schools.

THERE IS FEDERAL GOVERNMENT INVOLVEMENT IN ATTEMPTING TO PRESERVE AND IMPROVE THE BEAUTY OF THE UNITED STATES

The national government recognizes that the growing population is swallowing up areas of natural beauty, and therefore it is taking measures to provide for a beautiful country, such as making the capitol the nation's showcase, beautifying locations throughout the United States, planning land acquisition for conservation purposes, conducting research, preserving wildlife, retaining and improving scenic and historical sites, offering improved outdoor recreation to more people, improving water and waterways, and controlling pollution of streams and rivers.

AMERICAN COMMUNITIES ARE BECOMING RECREATION MINDED

Many villages, cities, and communities from coast to coast are acquiring and developing their green spaces, restoring national shrines, rehabilitating depressed and inner-city neighborhoods, providing programs for the elderly, setting aside acreage for recreation, advocating "See America First," establishing neighborhood playgrounds, making provision for the physically and mentally handicapped to share in the benefits of recreational programs, stressing the performing arts, and developing sports programs.

THERE IS COMMUNITY-SCHOOL COOPERATION IN RECREATION PROGRAMS

Community-school cooperation in recreation is illustrated by the following two examples. In Flint, Michigan, as a result of the impetus provided by Charles Stewart Mott and the Mott Foundation, recreation programs exist in the schools, bringing people of all nationalities, economic status, and other types of backgrounds together on commonly owned property—the public schools. The program includes all types of recreational activities, ranging from roller skating to an international program that involves approximately 1,000 athletes and their families in Flint, Michigan, and Hamilton, Canada.

Another example of community-school rec-

reation is in Los Angeles, where the city school district, through its Youth Services Section, sponsors a program in which millions participate over the course of any one year. More than 550 recreation sites are utilized, and more than 4,000 full-time and part-time personnel are involved in the leadership phase of the program. A year-round, 107-acre camp is utilized where outdoor education is carried on. A day camp is also in operation. The program utilizes the recreational experiences in the Youth Services Program as a laboratory experience for skills learned in the classroom.

RELIGION RECOGNIZES THE VALUE OF RECREATION

Many churches throughout the United States have gymnasiums and recreation centers as part of their facility complex. The Southern Baptists, for example, in one year spent approximately $150 million on facilities used primarily for recreation.

THE CULTURAL EXPLOSION HAS AN IMPACT ON RECREATION

The increased national interest in music, art, concerts, exhibitions, and other cultural interests is affecting recreation. Recreation programs are expanding their offerings to include specialists in the various arts. The public is encouraged to participate more.

The recreation and leisure services program

The primary purpose of a recreation and leisure services program is to provide a wide variety of activities so that the needs and interests of the entire population are met as far as practical and possible.

Activities that comprise the offerings for recreation programs may be classified into several groups. Some of the more common activities are as follows:

Musical activities
1. Instrumental
2. Orchestral
3. Community sings
4. Choral groups
5. Barber shop quartets

Dance
1. Folk
2. Square
3. Social
4. Modern

Arts and crafts
1. Plastics
2. Leathercraft
3. Graphic arts
4. Ceramics
5. Metalcraft

6. Photography
7. Stenciling and block printing
8. Sewing

Sports and games
1. Archery
2. Badminton
3. Bowling

4. Fencing
5. Golf
6. Hopscotch

Dramatics
1. Plays
2. Festivals

3. Clubs

Outdoor activities
1. Campfires
2. Outdoor cooking
3. Woodcraft
4. Camping

5. Canoeing
6. Conservation
7. Fishing
8. Orienteering

Miscellaneous
1. Horticulture
2. Forums

3. Cards
4. Hobby clubs

Schools and recreation and leisure services

The school has a definite relationship to recreation and leisure services. It has the responsibility of utilizing resources such as students, facilities, personnel, and programs to help in the attainment of recreation objectives, and it also has the responsibility of providing experiences within the framework of the educational program. The cardinal principle of "worthy use of leisure time" can be fulfilled to a considerable extent if school authorities accept their responsibilities in achieving recreational objectives.

The Second National Conference on School Recreation* made the following recommendations, which included setting forth a series of principles and statements regarding school-centered recreation and municipal-school recreation. These principles and statements are presented in adapted form.

---

*Report of the Second National Conference on School Recreation: Twentieth century recreation: reengagement of school and community, November 7-9, 1962, Washington, D.C., 1963, American Association for Health, Physical Education and Recreation.

School-centered recreation

1. Schools should accept, as a major responsibility, education for leisure.
2. Schools and colleges should provide their students with opportunities for participation in wholesome, creative activities.
3. The facilities and resources of a school should be made available for recreation purposes when needed.
4. Where community recreation programs are missing or inadequate, the school should take the initiative and provide recreation programs for young and old alike.
5. The school should cooperate with community organizations and agencies interested in or already sponsoring recreation programs.
6. The school should appoint a person to act as a community school director who would be responsible for the recreation-education program in the school.
7. Recreation and education are not identical, but each has its own uniqueness and distinctive features.
8. The community school director should provide in-service recreation education for the staff.
9. The federal level of government has a responsibility to stimulate recreation programs.
10. Recreation depends on public understanding and support for its existence.
11. Recreation should be concerned with exploiting the interests of people.
12. The recreation program should consist of many varied activities.
13. Recreation should be concerned with contributing to the mental health of the individual.

Municipal-school recreation

1. The school should accept the responsibility to educate for the worthy use of leisure, contribute to recreation in the instructional program, mobilize community resources, and cooperatively plan facilities for recreation. The college and university should promote research in recreation and provide professional preparation programs in this specialized area.
2. There should be joint planning of municipal school recreation based on stated principles and brought about by state departments of education and local boards of education.
3. School facilities should be available for recreational use.

WAYS IN WHICH
THE SCHOOL PROGRAM CAN
DEVELOP RESOURCES FOR LEISURE

Although there is controversy over who should be responsible for leisure education, the schools seem best equipped to play a major role. Essentials such as leadership, facilities, and equipment are readily available. In addition, it is the center of community life and represents a common meeting ground for the entire population, as well as the children who attend school. Furthermore, because many students do not go on to college, the major part of this work must be done in the elementary and secondary schools.

All subjects in the educational program have a contribution to make in developing resources for leisure. The science subjects, for example, should emphasize to a greater degree than they do at present a study of ecology, the environment, birds, trees, rocks, and flowers as an incentive to forming hobbies. The art department should be concerned with making jewelry and artificial flowers, decorating furniture, painting designs on materials, and painting as a hobby instead of turning out highly skilled work. English could do a better job with informal dramatics, storytelling, and creative writing. The social sciences could create a greater desire to participate in community activity and develop a better environment in which to live. They could also study the furniture of various periods of history as an incentive to antique collecting. Why not include more costume designing in home economics and stimulate to a greater degree the creative joy of cooking? Geography classes, when studying the various countries of the world, could obtain stamps from each as an incentive to stamp collecting.

Physical education could emphasize to a greater degree the individual activities such as fishing and tieing trout flies, bait casting, swimming, bowling, golf, tennis, canoeing, horse riding, camping, and hiking.

The school with its wide and varied educational offering has infinite opportunities to develop resources for leisure. During this day and age of mass production, application of atomic energy to industry, and increasing amounts of leisure, schools are being challenged to accept this responsibility.

Types of positions in recreation and leisure services

The number of recreation workers and professionals has grown as the field has received greater acceptance as a profession. A survey conducted by the NRPA in cooperation with the Bureau of Outdoor Recreation and the Office of Open Space and Urban Beautification showed more than 250,500 full- and part-time recreation personnel and approximately 88,000 full- and part-time recreation professionals.

The field of recreation has developed to the point where it offers a promising arena of employment for individuals trained in this specialized work. In recent years, training institutions have developed curriculums to provide the necessary leadership for the field of recreation. Many positions are open for the qualified person, including the following: superintendents, general supervisors, directors, play leaders, and supervisors of special activities in recreation departments; directors' assistants and area specialists in youth-serving organizations; consultants, executive officers, research workers, and assistants in government agencies; teachers in colleges, universities, and professional schools; administrative positions in commercial recreation; directors and area specialists for hospital recreation programs; positions with organizations such as 4-H clubs; and directors of church recreation programs.

Various types of recreation positions for which the aspiring student can prepare are as follows:

1. Superintendent of recreation
2. Assistant superintendent of recreation
3. Recreation director
4. Recreation supervisor
5. Recreation center director
6. Consultant in recreation
7. Field representative
8. Executive director
9. Hospital recreation supervisor
10. Camp recreation coordinator
11. Extension specialist
12. Service club director
13. Girls' worker or boys' worker
14. District recreation supervisor
15. Recreation leader
16. Supervisor of special activities
17. Recreation therapist
18. Recreation educator

Positions are also available in therapeutic recreation programs for the mentally and physically handicapped. This phase of recreation service is concerned with programs for the ill, disabled, handicapped, and aged persons who, because of their condition, are not able to participate in community recreation programs for the normal, physically active person. In addition to rendering direct services to such people, there are also opportunities to supervise and administer programs in a variety of medical settings and other places that support such programs. Persons working with ill or handicapped persons should take courses such as survey of physical defects, group dynamics and human relations, psychology of the physically handicapped, abnormal psychology, recreational crafts, social recreation, and physical rehabilitation.

Qualifications for the recreation and leisure services specialist

The person who works in the field of recreation and leisure services, whether full time or as a physical educator or other specialist, needs particular qualifications including an interest in and liking for people, emotional maturity, enthusiasm and skill, desire to render a service, professional preparation, and professional mindedness.

INTEREST IN AND LIKING FOR PEOPLE

The person who works in recreation must have faith in people and recognize the worth of each individual. The recreation leader should have qualifications that permit easy access to people of all races and creeds and should be sympathetic and understanding in the many human associations related to work in the recrea-

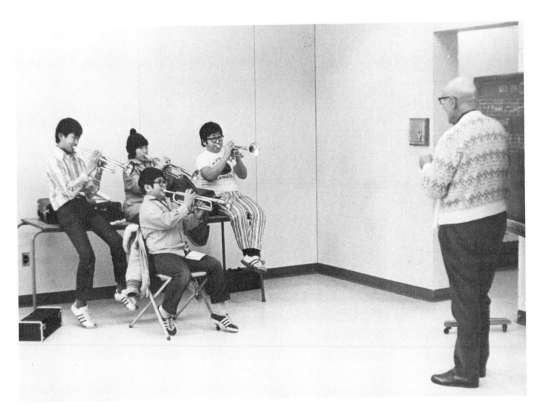

Courtesy Board of Parks and Public Recreation, Vancouver, British Columbia.

One qualification for a recreator is an interest in and liking for people. This recreation leader is conducting a music class.

tion program. People participate in the recreation program on a voluntary basis. They come of their own choice, and they can also leave of their own free will. Therefore it is important to provide all individuals with experiences that will satisfy the needs for which they attend.

EMOTIONAL MATURITY

The person who works in recreation must have an adult outlook on life, good mental and physical health, the ability to accept others' opinions and personalities for what they are, and a pleasing, friendly personality.

ENTHUSIASM AND SKILL

The person who works in recreation should be enthusiastic about recreation and the contribution such programs can make to human welfare. He or she should have skill in the organization and administration of particular activities or the program as a whole. The recreation leader should possess productive energy that can be channeled in the right directions.

DESIRE TO RENDER A SERVICE

The person who works in recreation should be interested in rendering a service to humankind. The recreator must like work and count rewards not in terms of material things but in terms of what he or she does for people.

EDUCATION

The person who works in recreation must be educated in the true sense of the word. The recreation leader should have a broad background of general education and, in addition, be well prepared in the activities taught and the particular specialized tasks performed.

INTEREST IN PROFESSION

The person who works in recreation should be interested in building the profession. The recreator should maintain a high code of professional ethics, join professional associations and be active in them, conduct himself or herself in a manner that will bring credit to the profession, and continually try to work toward a better profession that renders greater services to humanity.

Professional preparation of the recreation and leisure services specialist

The preparation of the recreation and leisure services leader should be thorough and complete. The biological sciences, general education, social sciences, arts, humanities, and professional recreation courses are required over a 4-year period. Important areas where competencies are needed include the principles involved in the organization and administration of recreation agencies, philosophy of recreation and leisure, laws and governmental organization that affect recreation programs, and skills and technical knowledge relating to such areas as music, arts and crafts, athletics, and social activities.

According to one survey, most undergraduate curriculums in recreation and/or park administration in colleges and universities are located in a department or a division of health, physical education, and recreation, and the college in which these special areas are located is usually the college of education. The types of degrees offered include the B.S., B.A., and A.A.

Performance of recreation and leisure services work by physical educators

Physical education and recreation are not synonymous, but they are closely related, and physical education personnel can play a prominent role in recreation programs. The field of recreation and leisure services utilizes not only physical education activities but also many other activities in which individuals desire to participate during their leisure hours. This means that, although games and sports play a prominent part, many other activities less physically active in nature are utilized. However, physical education activities have implications for recreation. The skills that are developed and instruction that takes place in physical education classes have a definite carry-over value.

A person trained in physical education has a contribution to make to recreation, and many are playing prominent roles in this field today. When recreation was in its embryo state, the physical educator was usually the logical person to assume leadership for such a program. Today, however, in many large municipal recrea-

Choose a Career in RECREATION

Choosing a career in Recreation, Parks, and Conservation is choosing a life of Leadership.

Few fields of endeavor offer the variety of experience and responsibilities as does the recreation, park, and conservation field. Administration, finance, public relations, planning, community action, group leadership, and personnel direction are all part of the daily life of the recreation leader. And, when the day is done, the personal satisfaction which results from the contributions you have made to the better life of the community and the enrichment of our nation is proof of the wise selection in choosing recreation as a career.

PUBLIC

Public recreation includes administration, supervision and leadership in:

Community Sponsored Programs
School Sponsored Programs
County Sponsored Programs
State Sponsored Programs
Federal Recreation Agencies

(All public recreation is paid for by taxes through city, county, state or national government, depending upon the position described.)

INDUSTRIAL

Industrial Recreation includes administration, supervision and leadership in:

Management Sponsored Programs.
Employee Sponsored Programs.
Cooperative Programs financed by Management:
and (A) Operated by Employees or
(B) Operated by Both Management and Employees.
Association or Institution Type Programs.

ILL and HANDICAPPED

Recreation for the Ill and Handicapped includes administration, supervision and leadership in medically approved recreation programs for hospitalized patients and for ill and handicapped persons in special schools and institutions. Recreation activities are used as a means of stimulating healthy response in patients, enriching their lives and in helping them achieve a better social adjustment.

ARMED FORCES

Civilian positions with the Armed Forces include direction of clubs, libraries, hobby shops and entertainment (sports, drama and music) for active duty military personnel and their dependents.

RECREATION EDUCATION

Recreation education is a basic responsibility of the home and school for preparing the individual for worthy use of leisure Professionally it includes the continual responsibility on the part of the recreationist, as well as the teaching of recreation professional courses in a junior college, college or university.

VOLUNTARY

Voluntary and youth serving programs include scouts, boy's and girl's clubs, Y's, and other agencies which derive support from public and private subscription.

COMMERCIAL

Commercial recreation includes the operation and management of privately owned enterprises offering recreation and entertainment to the public for a set individual charge.

PARKS

Parks management is closely allied with recreation as a result of a growing trend in government to join park management agencies with recreation agencies to better serve the total recreational needs of the people. Because recreationists are trained to plan for the effective use of facilities, as well as their care and upkeep, the recreation professional with the proper combination of training and experience will be the logical person to guide the total development and management of park and recreation facilities and programs for the public benefit.

Printed by
The Middle-Atlantic District Advisory Committee
of the
National Recreation and Park Association

Courtesy National Recreation and Park Association.

tion programs and in other areas, those with specialized training in recreation are providing much of the leadership. Physical educators, however, still play a prominent part in this work. Because of the nature of their training, physical educators direct many recreation programs in communities where insufficient funds make it impossible to hire a full-time recreational leader; they act as specialists in the area of athletics and other physical education activities in large city, industrial, and other recreational programs; and they play an important part in communities that utilize school facilities for the community recreation program. Physical educators are also called on to serve in many other recreational capacities such as playground directors, supervisors, and camp directors.

Opportunities for placement

The continued and expanded interest in recreation means many job openings in the years to come. There are more than 3,000 publicly sponsored local and county agencies engaged in recreation. Many more will be needed in the future. More than 30,000 companies now have recreation programs, and this number will expand considerably in the next decade. As people get more leisure time, there will be a greater need for professional people to help them spend this leisure in as constructive a way as possible.

The growth in recreation is assured because of such factors as the recognized contribution that recreation activities can make to optimum health, the growth in disposable income, and the increase in the amount of leisure time.

The demands for qualified recreators has been estimated at about 3,000 new people a year. One estimate suggests that in the 1980s 220,000 recreation specialists in the area of recreation and parks will be needed.

During the 1980s employment in the administration and management of public recreation facilities and tourist and private recreation services is expected to be approximately 1.4 million.

The growth of recreational services does not stop here, however. In rural areas it is expected an estimated 350,000 full-time positions will be available in farm and other rural recreational enterprises during the 1980s.

New careers and areas of specialization are available as a result of the expansion and growth of recreational services. These include rural recreation, industrial recreation, therapeutic recreation, forest recreation, recreation planning, recreation and/or park administration, and public or community recreation.

The rewards for those young people who go into recreation as a career will include the satisfaction of improving the social well-being of human beings, contributing to community development and a better environment, providing the resources for the worthy use of leisure time, and a financial return that compares favorably with many other professions.

An interesting approach to career recruitment in recreation was conducted by the Evanston, Illinois, Recreation Department as part of their "Careers in Recreation" training program. Its major purpose was to educate high school age youth about opportunities in recreation so that they could intelligently consider the field for advanced study and eventually a professional career.

The initial group of fifteen students were selected for an "in-service" training program for high school students. It was conducted by the supervisor of community centers and summer playgrounds. From the initial group, nine subsequently passed a written examination, served a practical 5-week apprenticeship, and then accepted regular employment in the summer recreation program of the department. Six of the original nine returned for two more summers of recreational service. The positions held were salaried, and students received a certificate for completing the course. These students and subsequent ones who qualified received preferential consideration for part-time work during the school year. The program also introduced a scholarship competition for students wishing to major in recreation. It is interesting to note that the first scholarship winner was a 4-year veteran of the program and had been on the recreation staff throughout his high school career.

The Evanston Department of Recreation did not limit its program to high school students but also endeavored to attract college students to the field of recreation. The department has cooperated with surrounding universities by offering an internship program for undergraduate credit.

Programs such as the ones offered by the Evanston department are essential in filling the gap of career education for those interested in recreation. Results like those in Evanston are extremely gratifying, and program support is strengthened year after year.

CAMPING AND OUTDOOR EDUCATION

Throughout the country, educators and students are "turning-on" to outdoor education and camping. Outdoor learning laboratories take studying out of the books and the classroom and into the out-of-doors, where observations and experiments are equal to thousands of written words. When students of the Hillsborough County School System, Tampa, Florida, enter their 365-acre outdoor learning laboratory, they have a chance to truly experience what they have been taught. The learning laboratory teaches ecology, conservation, zoology, mammalogy, and entomology, as well as mathematics, language arts, and the social sciences.

Outdoor education is not just nature study, it represents a vital part of the educational program at all educational levels and in all subjects including art, social studies, mathematics, physical education, and industrial arts.

School camping and outdoor education are not synonymous. Outdoor education is education in and also about the out-of-doors. It includes school camping. The camp provides a laboratory by which many facets of the out-of-doors can be studied firsthand, and the camp experience helps to develop qualities important to preparing young people for the lives they will live.

The worth of camping and outdoor education in the school program has been well established. The teacher of physical education, as well as all teachers at the elementary, secondary, and college levels, can benefit from studying the objectives, contributions, program, administration, and other aspects of these important fields. In the future, education will utilize these programs more and more, and individuals trained in these areas will find many opportunities to apply their knowledge and experience.

The public concern about the environment, energy, and ecology accents the importance of students knowing more about the out-of-doors and how they can help in preventing it from becoming polluted and misused.

Camping and outdoor education and today's environmental concerns

Former United States Education Commissioner James E. Allen recommended that every school should have an opportunity for environmental study so that students would grow up with the realization that the environment represents everything that makes up the world and that all its numberless elements are interdependent.

In a natural undisturbed situation, life of all kinds tends to assemble, to live, to reproduce, and to furnish food for each other. Basically this ecological system (relationship between organisms and their environment) consists of the predator living off the prey. However, many factors can enter into this picture of undisturbed natural situation and bring about change.

As a result of a rapidly increasing population and the demand for a higher and higher standard of living, people have succeeded in destroying many valuable insects, fish, and animal life by polluting the air and water, by producing excessive amounts of radiation, by carelessly using insecticides, and by constantly increasing the nuisance of noise. As a consequence, human kind is threatening to destroy itself as well as other living things.

Human beings, since their advent on the earth, have been adjusting to their environment to improve their security and comfort. At the same time, however, urbanization—with its increased congestion and noise, the development of chemicals for a myriad of uses, the multitude of waste products cast off by industrial plants, and the intensified use of streams and lakes for purposes of refuse disposal—has contributed to the artificial contamination of the environment.

As a result of all this, people have multiplied their traditional problem of water pollution, have initiated a new set of problems in the protection of the food supply, and have succeeded in thoroughly contaminating the most abundant natural resource—the atmosphere.

As indicated by Allen, the schools must do something about environmental problems facing our nation and the world. A logical school experience in which some of this education can take place is the camping and outdoor education program. Of course, this in turn has implications for physical education, since the environment represents an important setting for various sports and other physical activities.

Objectives of camping and outdoor education

Many objectives have been listed for camping and outdoor education programs. Some of the more important objectives that have been enumerated over the years as being the reasons why such programs should exist in our schools are as follows:

1. Students learn to live democratically with other children and adults.
2. Students learn more about the physical environment and the importance and preservation of our vast wealth of natural resources. They also learn about the ecological aspects of the environment.
3. An appreciation for the out-of-doors and the contributions it can make to enriched living is developed.
4. Those qualities that make for good citizenship such as responsibility, leadership, teamwork, and honesty are developed.
5. The contribution that the out-of-doors can make to good health is more appreciated.
6. The love of adventure, which is part of the makeup of children and youth, is satisfied.
7. Students are stimulated to learn about native materials and to see their relationship to the learning that takes place in the classroom.
8. Worthwhile skills in recreation such as map reading, fishing, and canoeing are developed.
9. Benefits are derived from wholesome work experiences.
10. Students learn to depend on personal resources in practicing the rules of healthful living.
11. Students learn some of the basic rules of safety.

The Cleveland Heights, Ohio, public schools list as objectives for outdoor education the following:

1. To teach citizenship
2. To teach principles of natural science

San Diego City Schools,
San Diego, Calif.

Camping and outdoor education program.

3. To teach principles of conservation
4. To teach health and physical education
5. To teach other subject-matter aspects related to the camping situation

These objectives are worthy goals and tie in closely with the social, intellectual, and health aims of general education. Children develop socially by learning to live democratically. Responsibilities for maintaining a camp are assumed by all. All children, regardless of national origin, color, or other difference, are respected as individuals who can contribute to the group enterprise. They also develop intellectually as they satisfy their lust for adventure. Children see the wonders of nature firsthand. They learn about conservation, soil, water, and animal and bird life. A camping experience also promotes good health. The out-of-doors, together with healthful activity, interesting projects, and congenial classmates, improves the general fitness of children. They usually leave camp with a ruddy glow of the cheeks and sparkling eyes that reflect the new things they have seen and learned.

Some settings for outdoor education

School and community gardens and farms. Experiences can be provided relating to agriculture, bird and animal study, conservation, gardening, and milk production.

School areas in general. Experiences can be provided for studying such products of nature as plants, shrubs, birds, trees, and fish.

School forests. Where large wooded areas exist, experiences can be provided in reforestation, conservation, and the growth and wise use of forests.

Museums. Many different types of museums offer opportunities for experiences in areas such as archeological exploration, art appreciation, historical milestones, scientific accomplishments, and bird and animal life.

Zoos. Zoos provide opportunities for experiences in the study of animals, birds, and other wildlife.

Camps. Camps offer opportunities for such things as group living, work experience, and development of outdoor skills.

Opportunities for outdoor education are available everywhere in the country. In addition

Camping and outdoor education, Florida A. & M. University, Tallahassee, Florida.

to the fields, woods, and lakes, many private or public sanctuaries, museums, parks, camps, and zoos can be used for such purposes.

Programs for camping and outdoor education

Camp Quest is the setting for the camping and outdoor education program for the LeMars Community School District of LeMars, Iowa. The program, for students enrolled in grades seven and eight, includes such recreation and physical education activities as archery, croquet, softball, volleyball, soccer, horseshoes, and basketball, and such projects as astronomy, rocks and minerals, fossils, entomology, agronomy, forestry, aquatic life, and ornithology. Six 1-week camps are held, Monday through Friday, during the months of June and July.

Environmental encounters are growing in popularity. These are experiences that focus the attention of young people on the relationship of economic, ecological, political, and social dimensions of living. A suburban neighborhood in Detroit investigates how the athletic field is watered, and the students also studied well drilling, water runoff, the costs of water, and watershed problems. In Washington, D.C., the students in a lot adjacent to Madison Elementary School helped to develop an outdoor environmental laboratory. In the greater Milwaukee area the public schools utilize several community resources as sites for their outdoor education program. In Philadelphia, the Parkway School uses over seventy facilities for their outdoor education program.

The San Diego city schools utilize the school camp experience to make studies in science and conservation more interesting and meaningful. Some of the learning experiences they describe are as follows:

Astronomy. Studying about stars and planets by looking at them through telescopes; visiting the Palomar Observatory and Museum
Geology. Digging into the earth to find rocks and minerals for study; reading the story of the soil profiles; studying soil and earth features
Meteorology. Observing and identifying weather; measuring weather phenomena at camp with accurate instruments; maintaining a weather station at camp
Ecology. Hiking to see and study the relationship of living things to their environment

Conservation. Learning about the problems of the land and working to help the land through soil erosion control, beetle control, tree planting, reduction of fire hazards, and forest improvement
Botany and biology. Studying birds, insects, animals, and plants in the field and pond; collecting specimens
Forestry. Learning woodmanship and the safe use of forestry tools and equipment
Survival skills. Using map and compass on hikes; considering problems of food, shelter, and safety on a "survival hike"

Many other communities and school systems provide interesting and varied outdoor education and camping experiences. Some of these programs are discussed here.

Jefferson County, Colorado. In the sixth-grade school all students spend a week of the school year studying microecology. This is the study of living things and their relationship to the environment in a limited area approximately 3 feet square by 6 feet high. The plot is studied for specimens, heat and cold, wind, mapping, animal and plant life, soil, rocks, and other related factors.

Chesterfield, New Jersey. An area of the Chesterfield Elementary School grounds was set aside and transformed into facsimiles of three types of New Jersey environmental areas: the lowland pine barrens, the highlands, and the central woodland. Students learn about these areas by thorough investigation of the plants, animals, and insects common to each region.

Green-Castle-Antrim, Pennsylvania School District. A 60-acre site that included a pond that had become a trash-filled mudhole was cleaned up, and the pond now serves as a laboratory and a place where wild birds rest. A farmhouse with a converted barn that houses laboratory facilities and learning centers, 30 acres of farmland, and a nature trail comprise this outstanding education site.

Environmental resource center. Hempstead, New York, devised plans for the construction of an Environmental Resource Center located on the Atlantic Ocean. This center provides year-round recreational opportunities for physically and mentally handicapped, emotionally disturbed, and nonhandicapped participants.

Hempstead began the ANCHOR (Answering the Needs of Children with Handicaps through Organized Recreation) Program in 1968. One

Courtesy John Goss.

Camping and outdoor education at Westchester County Recreation Camp, Croton, New York.

hundred fifty children were in the initial program, and this number has more than tripled since that time. The resource center includes facilities for games, open space, playgrounds, camping, crafts, nature walks, and gardens. In addition, beach activities are available, and indoor activities are held in the center building complex, which includes a combination auditorium and cafeteria.*

Worth of camping and outdoor education

The values of school camping and outdoor education are very much in evidence as a result of the many experiments that have been conducted throughout the United States. For purposes of discussion it might be said that the values of such experiences are threefold: (1) they meet the social needs of the child, (2) they meet

the intellectual needs of the child, and (3) they meet the health needs of the child.

A camping and outdoor education experience is an essential part of every child's school experience because it helps to develop the child socially. In a camp setting, children learn to live democratically. They mix with children of various creeds, national origins, races, economic status, and abilities. They aid in planning the program that will be followed during their camp stay; they assume part of the responsibility for the upkeep of the camp, such as making their own beds, helping in the kitchen, sweeping their cabins, and fixing the tennis courts; and they experience cooperative living. The children get away from home and from their parents. They lose their feeling of dependency on others and learn to do things for themselves and rely on their own resources. This is especially important in our society because of the increase in divorce and separations, in single parent families, and in families where both parents work.

---

*McGrath, R.: Environmental resource centers, Journal of Health, Physical Education, and Recreation **44**:46, Jan., 1973.

The camp experience also provides an enjoyable experience for the child. A child is naturally active and seeks adventure. This experience provides the opportunity to release some of this adventure and satisfy the "wanderlust" urge.

A camping and outdoor education experience is an essential part of every child's school experience because it helps to develop the child intellectually. While living in a camp or in another outdoor education setting, the child learns about the soil, forests, water, and animal and bird life. The child learns about the value of the nation's natural resources and how they should be conserved. Learning is accomplished by doing rather than through the medium of textbooks. Instead of looking at the picture of a bird in a book, the child actually sees the bird chirping on the branch of a tree. Instead of reading about soil erosion in a textbook, the child sees how it really occurs. Instead of being told about the four basic groups of food, the child has the opportunity to plan a diet that meets good nutritional standards. Instead of reading about the values of democratic living, the child actually experiences it. Many new things are experienced that are not possible at home or within the four walls of a school building. Camping is also of special value to children who do not learn easily from books. In many cases the knowledge accumulated through actual experience is much more enlightening and beneficial.

Camping and outdoor education are an essential part of every child's school experience because they help to meet the health needs of the child. Camps are located away from the turmoil, confusion, noise, and rush of urban life. Children have their meals at a regular time, obtain sufficient sleep, and participate in wholesome activity in the out-of-doors. They wear clothing that does not restrict movement, that permits the absorption of healthful sun rays, and that they are not afraid to get dirty. The food is good. They are doing things that are natural for them to do. It is an outlet for their dynamic personalities. It is much more healthful, both physically and mentally, than living in a "push-button" existence with its lack of recreation, relaxation, and opportunity for enjoyable experiences. It is like living in another world, and children come away refreshed.

Future of outdoor education

The variety of outdoor education programs and the geographical involvement throughout the United States enhances the already promising future of outdoor education programs in the years ahead. Some factors that contribute to their success are discussed here.

1. *Outdoor education experiences are becoming available to a greater number of individuals.* Outdoor education programs were once limited to specific elementary school grades. However, the trend toward providing more outdoor experiences has now reached junior and senior high school students, college students, and adult education groups as well.

2. *A diversity of environments is being utilized.* School site learning has increased with new school development, putting acreage aside for outdoor education purposes. Schools with limited space are seeking community and privately held acres where outdoor education can best take place. Farms, zoos, and botanical gar-

Outdoor education is an important part of the students' program at Uni High, Los Angeles City Schools, Los Angeles City Unified School District, Los Angeles, California.

dens are becoming adventurous areas for learning about the environment.

3. *The community is becoming increasingly involved in outdoor education.* This is just another aspect of the community and school sharing their resources to promote education. Community-owned outdoor facilities, personnel, instructional material, and funds can be used cooperatively for the benefit of all.

4. *Outdoor education as an integral part of the curriculum.* Every learning experience should be examined in terms of how its teaching can be enhanced through outdoor education. Teachers and other staff members should become cognizant of this approach to learning.

5. *Outdoor education seeks an equalization among the cognitive, affective, and psychomotor objectives.* All three types of learning objectives take place in an outdoor educational experience. Students learn about a particular situation (cognitive objective), the appreciation of a learning experience (affective objective), and the emotional and skill aspects derived from participating in an outdoor experience (psychomotor objective).

6. *Outdoor education contributes positively to an understanding of environmental problems.* We live in an age of acute concern with the environment, energy, and ecology. Reading about pollution is not nearly as impressive as going down to a local polluted stream and cleaning it up. What the students do and learn will play an important role in their environmental activism as adults.

Implications for the physical education teacher

If camping and outdoor education are to render their greatest service to the student, effective leadership must be present. Regardless of how elaborate the camping facilities, the size of the budget, and the number of opportunities available for educational trips, true education will not take place unless the teachers, counselors, and leaders can interpret, discuss, guide, and educate the student. Physical education teachers can provide much of this leadership. The close alliance that exists between their field and that of camping as a result of a common in-

Courtesy County of Westchester Department of Parks, Recreation and Conservation, N.Y.

Day campers using the facilities of Mountain Lakes Camps at North Salem, New York, identify flora on the nature trail hike. The camps are operated by the County of Westchester Department of Parks, Recreation and Conservation.

terest in the out-of-doors, sports, and other activities, makes it possible for them to take a leading role in this movement.

Physical educators are proficient in the teaching of many activities being stressed by outdoor education specialists. These include casting and fishing; shooting and hunting; boating, sailing, canoeing, and other water activities; and winter sports such as skiing and skating. Persons must be trained as camp administrators, camp counselors, and instructors. Classroom teachers must receive special instruction to orient them to the camping program. School administrators must be informed and their cooperation and support enlisted. These are only a few of the opportunities and challenges facing leaders in camping and outdoor education. Physical education personnel should play a major role in meeting these opportunities and challenges.

Those interested in becoming active in the camping and outdoor education movement should have special preparation in this area. Courses such as camp counseling, camp administration, crafts, guidance, and psychology, together with an actual camp experience, will prove helpful. In addition, a person should have (1) an understanding of human beings, (2) an understanding of the outdoors and its relationship to humans, and (3) the skills and knowledge essential to teaching about the out-of-doors.

SELF-ASSESSMENT TESTS

These tests are to assist students in determining if material and competencies presented in this chapter have been mastered.

1. Without consulting your text, outline the objectives, need, and trends for recreation and leisure programs.

2. Assume the role of a recreator in three different settings where recreation and leisure programs exist. Describe the type of program that exists in each setting and what duties recreators perform in each setting.

3. As a physical educator, you have been offered a job in a recreation program. The employer asks you to describe what role you can play in the program. What do you say? How does this role differ from that of a person who has been professionally trained in the field of recreation and leisure studies.

4. One child whom you know goes to camp. Describe the program she is exposed to. Another child is

involved in an outdoor education program in a neighborhood school. Describe the program he is exposed to.

5. Prepare a report on camping and outdoor education, providing facts about why both are important for students and the role that physical educators can play in such programs.

READING ASSIGNMENT

Bucher, Charles A.: Dimensions of physical education, ed. 2, St. Louis, 1974, The C. V. Mosby Co., Reading selection 17, 19-21.

SELECTED REFERENCES

A guide to planning and conducting environmental study area workshops, Washington, D.C., 1972, National Education Association.

Bannon, Joseph H.: Problem solving in recreation and parks, Englewood Cliffs, N.J., 1972, Prentice-Hall, Inc.

Bucher, Charles A., and Bucher, Richard: Recreation for today's society, Englewood Cliffs, N.J., 1974, Prentice-Hall, Inc.

Bureau of Outdoor Recreation, U.S. Department of the Interior: Outdoor recreation action, published periodically by the Department of the Interior, Washington, D.C.

Donaldson, G. W.: Journal of Outdoor Education, Northern Illinois University, DeKalb, Ill. (back and current issues).

Donaldson, G. W., and Donaldson, A.: Outdoor education: its promising future, Journal of Health, Physical Education, and Recreation **43**:23, April, 1972.

Hodgson, J. D.: Leisure and the American worker, Journal of Health, Physical Education, and Recreation **43**:38, March, 1972.

Kraus, Richard: Recreation and leisure in modern society, New York, 1971, Appleton-Century-Crofts.

Kraus, Richard: Today's crisis in urban recreation, Journal of Health, Physical Education, and Recreation **44**:29, June, 1973.

Kraus, Richard: Recreation today—program planning and leadership, Santa Monica, Calif., 1977, Goodyear Publishing Co., Inc.

McGrath, R.: Environmental Resource Center, Journal of Health, Physical Education, and Recreation **44**:46, Jan., 1973.

McKinney, W., and Ford, P.: What is the profession doing about education for leisure? Journal of Health, Physical Education, and Recreation **43**:49, May, 1972.

Nanus, B., and Adelman, H.: Forecast for leisure, Journal of Health, Physical Education, and Recreation **44**:61, Jan., 1973.

Staffo, D.: A community recreation program, Journal of Health, Physical Education, and Recreation **44**:47, May, 1973.

Staley, Edwin: Leisure and the quality of life, Washington, D.C., 1972, American Association for Health, Physical Education, and Recreation.

Strobbe, J.: The year-round school and recreation, Journal of Health, Physical Education, and Recreation **43**:51, March, 1972.

PART SIX

LEADERSHIP IN PHYSICAL EDUCATION

Courtesy Cumberland Valley School District, Mechanicsburg, Pa.

18

Teaching physical education—professional considerations

After reading this chapter the student should
be able to—
1. Assess whether or not a student has the
   qualifications to teach and to be a professional physical educator.
2. Understand the progress that has been
   made over the years in the professional
   preparation of physical educators and
   some important factors to consider when
   selecting a professional preparation program in which to train.
3. Identify various areas in which a student
   may specialize within physical education.
4. Appreciate many of the problems faced
   by a beginning teacher of physical education and how to resolve some of these
   problems.
5. Before graduation and becoming a
   teacher, think through such important
   considerations as teaching style, code of
   ethics, accountability, and how teachers
   are evaluated.

The teaching profession has more than 2 million men and women employed at the various
educational levels. In the elementary and secondary schools combined, about one third of
these teachers are men, and two thirds are wom-
en. Contrary to what exists in many fields of endeavor, teachers as a group like their work, as
evidenced in a survey conducted by the Na-

tional Education Association that showed that
three fourths of teachers would choose teaching
again if they were starting over in a career.

Teaching is one of the favorite choices of a
profession for high school and college students
today. Surveys consistently show that teaching
has great appeal for young people who are trying to decide on a career that holds challenge
and satisfaction for the future.

THE TEACHING PROFESSION—
WHAT IT OFFERS

Teaching offers many rewards. Probably
most important of all is that it offers an opportunity to help shape young people's lives. Other
rewards include the privilege of being a member of a profession that is growing in respect
and importance in the world as well as in the
United States. It offers an opportunity to mingle
with some of the great thinkers and leaders of
the academic community. It offers opportunities to travel and to better understand the world.
It motivates self-improvement and intellectual
growth. It provides increasingly better economic benefits in the form of salaries, retirement
benefits, sick leaves, insurance, medical help,
and sabbatical leaves. It provides security under
the tenure laws that exist in most states.

The rewards that accrue from teaching depend to a large degree on the individual and
what each person makes of his or her opportunities. The inner rewards, plus the financial and
other benefits, can be great for the person who

421

applies himself or herself diligently and sincerely to assigned tasks.

QUALIFICATIONS FOR TEACHING

Many studies have been made of characteristics of a good teacher and the abilities most useful for a teaching career. Six personal traits are listed by the Future Teachers of America based on the studies that have been conducted.*

1. *Do you like to be with people?* If you like group activities, belong to clubs, enjoy serving on committees, know all types of people and are sympathetic to their peculiarities, have a wide circle of friends, and are always seeking more, you probably meet this criterion essential to success in teaching.

2. *Are you a scholar? Do you often lose yourself in a book?* Do you enjoy mastering a subject and read because you want to? Are you in the top one third of your class, and do you belong to honor societies? Do you recognize that you must learn before you can teach?

3. *Do you have a sense of humor?* Can you laugh at yourself, not take yourself too seriously, apply a light approach to ease a tense situation, take a happy view of life, shake off the blues quickly, and see the funny side of a situation?

4. *Are you in good physical and mental health?* Since the hours of teaching are long and the work demanding, do you have plenty of pep, energy, and stamina, are you usually poised and emotionally well balanced, do you take criticism without becoming angry or depressed, and do you keep your voice pleasant and calm even when upset?

5. *Do you like to help others?* Do you have the urge to serve others; enjoy working with youngsters; volunteer to help out in church, schools, hospitals, or nursing homes; and offer your services to local charity drives?

6. *Are you often the leader in group activities?* Since a teacher must have leadership qualities, do you ever organize activities in your circle of friends, have you been elected to office in a club or class, and have you demonstrated leadership ability?

*Future Teachers of America: How's your T.Q.—a checklist to explore your aptitude for teaching, Washington, D.C., National Education Association.

QUALIFICATIONS FOR TEACHERS OF PHYSICAL EDUCATION

A young person considering physical education as a career should carefully evaluate his or her qualifications for this field of work.

Need for well-trained teachers in physical education

The physical education profession needs teachers who possess the enthusiasm, culture, and other qualities listed in the accompanying

---

Letter describing type of physical education teacher an employer desires on his staff

Waterloo Public Schools
Waterloo, Iowa

Dear Sir:

Here are some traits that I look for in hiring a teacher of physical education:

I prefer a neat, cultured, enthusiastic person in excellent health with poise and emotional stability.

In checking educational qualifications, I particularly look for the ratings in health, scholarship, discipline, and cooperation. It is important that the person is able to cooperate and get along with co-workers. Thus the individual should be well-adjusted, possess the ability to think practically, and be able to adjust to new situations.

I am interested in a teacher who will be able to have good discipline and at the same time is interested in the welfare of his or her students. It is also important that this person be interested in growing on the job and able to take constructive criticism.

A person with creative ideas who has a wholesome influence on the students as well as his or her fellow teachers is an asset to any faculty.

Once the person is hired and we like his or her work, and he or she is happy in the work, we prefer to have this person stay on the job for a number of years.

Sincerely yours,
Finn B. Ericksen, Director
Health and Physical Education

employer's letter and who know subject matter, possess skills, are articulate, and have the respect of their students.

Specific qualifications for physical educators

The individual desiring to become a member of the physical education profession should be able to meet various requirements, including the following.

HIGH SCHOOL AND COLLEGE

The candidate should be a graduate of an approved high school and an approved college or university preparing teachers for physical education.

INTELLIGENCE AND FOUNDATIONAL SCIENCES

The candidate should possess that degree of intelligence needed to qualify for successful teaching. Furthermore, since the physical education profession is based on the foundational sciences of anatomy, physiology, biology, kinesiology, sociology, and psychology, the prospective candidate should have some aptitude for these sciences.

ORAL AND WRITTEN ENGLISH

The candidate should meet acceptable standards in oral and written English. The candidate should be able to write in an acceptable manner, with special attention to punctuation, choice of words, sentence structure, and logical organization. The speech of physical educators is under continuous scrutiny, and they are frequently called on to speak in public. The nature of their positions makes it imperative that they use acceptable English in their speaking and writing.

HEALTH

The candidate should be able to pass health examinations satisfactorily, including an examination of the skin, teeth, eyes, ears, chest, heart, feet, and posture, and show good personal health history, mental health, and emotional stability. The candidate must be free from any physical or mental defects that would prevent successful teaching in physical education.

Physical education is a strenuous type of work and therefore demands that members of the profession be in a state of buoyant, robust health so that they may carry out their duties with efficiency and regularity. They should also remember that they are building healthy bodies; therefore they should be a good testimonial for what they teach.

PERSONALITY

The candidate should possess a personality suitable for teaching. Enthusiasm, friendliness, cheerfulness, industry, cooperation, firmness and forcefulness in supporting one's convictions, dependability, self-control, integrity, social adaptability, and likeableness are factors that can determine in great measure whether an individual will be a success or a failure as a teacher. Whether the right social traits are developed in children will depend largely on the personality of the leader. Therefore it is essential that the teacher of physical education be able to enlist the respect, cooperation, and admiration of the students through his or her personality, magnetism, and leadership.

INTEREST IN TEACHING

Candidates should have a sincere interest in the teaching of physical education as a profession. Unless individuals have a firm belief in the value of physical education and a desire to help extend the benefits of such an endeavor to others, they should not enter this work. Persons sincerely interested in physical education enjoy teaching individuals to participate in the gamut of activities incorporated in such programs, helping others to realize the happiness and thrilling experiences of participation that they enjoy, and helping to develop citizenship traits conducive to democratic living.

MOTOR ABILITY

The candidate should possess an acceptable standard of motor ability. Physical skills are the basis of the physical education profession. If the physical educator is to teach various games and activities to others, it is necessary to have skill in some of them. Otherwise, it would be similar to an individual who does not know how to use a saw planning to be a carpenter, a per-

A person desiring to become a member of the physical education profession has to meet certain qualifications. A teacher of physical education in the Oak View Elementary School in Fairfax, Virginia, teaching children tumbling, utilizing an old aircraft inner tube.

Courtesy ACTION/Peace Corps.

An important qualification for a teacher is an interest in teaching and some degree of motor ability. A Peace Corps volunteer in Bangkok, Thailand.

son who cannot drive, a bus driver, or a person who does not know what a spark plug is, an auto mechanic. Physical skills are basic to the physical education profession.

WORKING WITH PEOPLE

The candidate should enjoy working with people. Therefore a member of the physical education profession should get along well with other persons, be interested in people, be able to adapt to various social settings, be able to attain respect, and should enjoy working with children and young people. The effectiveness of the work performed rests on human relations. If positive relations do not prevail, the objectives for which the profession strives will not be realized.

SENSE OF HUMOR

The candidate should have a sense of humor. The teacher who can see the humor in numerous classroom incidents, a joke told by a colleague, or a remark made by a student possesses a trait that helps him or her to get along better with others, makes life more interesting for students, and aids in the dispelling of gloom.

• • •

The qualifications listed are necessary for all who desire to enter the physical education profession. In establishing such standards, it is understood that all individuals are not qualified to be physical educators any more than all are qualified for careers in medicine, law, or social work. A person's future happiness depends on making the right decision. A poet said it this way:

> Each is given a bag of tools . . .
> A carving block and a book of rules.
> Each must make ere life be done
> A stumbling block or a steppingstone.*

DECIDING WHETHER TO BECOME A TEACHER

Some guidelines that may help the college student or other person in deciding whether to

---

*Quoted from Committee on Vocational Guidance, American Association for Health, Physical Education, and Recreation: Research Quarterly **13:**145, May, 1942.

become a member of the teaching profession include the following.

An individual's interests and aptitudes should be carefully tested. The person considering teaching should know that he or she likes to work with children and young people by actually seeking out experiences in a camp or other situation where this quality can be tested. Also, there are many tests and other instruments that can be used to analyze a person's aptitude for teaching objectively.

The person should make the decision and not permit parents, neighbors, or close friends to influence the decision. The guidance and advice of others is important and valuable, but the final decision should be made by the individual.

An analysis of personality is an important consideration. How well a person can interact with young people, with colleagues on the job, and with the community and other groups of persons should be considered. Furthermore, other aspects of one's personality such as mental and emotional health, physical health, and prejudices are important considerations.

The decision should not be rushed. A person should be sure that this is the type of work he or she wants and is best equipped to do. Also, it is wise to determine if this is the type of work where one can make the greatest contribution to society. Such a decision may take time.

PREPARATION OF THE PHYSICAL EDUCATOR

The professional preparation of physical educators has changed dramatically in recent years. For example, students are now more involved in their own education, there is more emphasis on motor learning, more undergraduate time is spent with elementary and secondary school boys and girls, and students are learning more about the problems of handicapped children.

The student of physical education, as well as physical education personnel in the field, should be familiar with the role of professional preparation in physical education. Such information will help interested persons to realize what constitutes adequate training for physical education leaders. In turn, they can bring their

Courtesy President's Council on Physical Fitness and Sports.

The professional preparation of the physical education teacher has received much more attention in recent years. A physical educator demonstrates the correct way to conduct a class.

influence to bear on teacher-training institutions so that proper preparation will be provided.

Objectives of professional preparation

The goals of professional preparation have been set forth by many professional organizations. These goals include the need to graduate educated men and women who are prepared and committed to teaching, to influence not only the intellectual life of students but also the emotional and ethical aspects of their professional careers, and to acquaint prospective teachers with the rights and responsibilities of professional service.

History of professional preparation

The history of professional preparation programs in physical education dates back more than a hundred years. During this time there has been a steady growth in their number and quality.

BEGINNINGS

Since the first class of teachers was graduated from the Normal Institute of Physical Education in Boston in 1861, the preparation of teachers in physical education has progressed rapidly. The 10 weeks' course at this institution, founded by Dio Lewis, had regular instruction in hygiene, physiology, anatomy, and gymnastics, in addition to an interpretation of and practical work in the "Swedish Movement Cure."

The North American Turnerbund, the second normal school for the training of teachers in physical education, opened its doors in 1866 in New York City, offering a 1-year course.

Dr. Dudley Allen Sargent, an early leader in physical education in the United States, brought his influence to bear on teacher preparation starting in 1881. The Sargent School, as it was called, trained almost exclusively women who planned to teach physical education.

The Brooklyn Normal School for Physical

Education, under the directorship of Dr. William C. Anderson, came into existence in 1886. This school placed principal emphasis on training the student in the theory and practice of gymnastics.

In 1886 the International Young Men's Christian Association College at Springfield, Massachusetts, was established. This college, better known as Springfield College, offered a professional course for young men who expected to teach physical education in the YMCA.

In 1889 Mrs. Mary Hemenway established and later endowed the Boston Normal School of Gymnastics, which in 1909 became the Department of Hygiene and Physical Education of Wellesley. Baron Posse, a teacher in this Normal School, organized his own gymnasium in 1890, calling it the Posse Normal School of Gymnastics.

Prior to World War I, physical educators received their professional preparation primarily in normal schools. A study made by Ruth Elliot in 1927 lists the private normal schools of physical education engaged in training physical education personnel, the date of their establishment, and the length of curriculums. This list, shown in Table 18-1, is significant, since it indicates the gradual lengthening of curriculums in the training of prospective physical education teachers.

GROWTH OF TEACHER EDUCATION
PROGRAMS

Colleges and universities soon followed the normal schools in the preparation of teachers in physical education. The University of Washington, with a professional course in physical education organized in 1896, is usually thought to be the first state university to offer work in this area. However, in 1894 Bowen, at the State Normal School at Ypsilanti, Michigan, was responsible for the first attempt to train teachers in physical education in a state-controlled institution.

The University of California, Indiana University, and the University of Nebraska initiated courses in this area from 1897 to 1898, placing particular emphasis on the areas of anthropometry, physical examinations, anatomy, physiology of exercise, hygienic gymnastics, and the history of physical culture.

In the early 1900s privately endowed colleges and universities began to consider training for leadership in physical education. Oberlin College in 1900, Teachers College, Columbia University, in 1903, and Wellesley College in 1909 were among the first of these institutions.

Shortly after World War I, approximately thirty-five states passed legislation requiring the teaching of health and physical education in the public schools. Such legislation was a stimulant to teacher preparation in the field of physical education.

A few outstanding leaders in the field of education began to look beyond the mere teaching of gymnastics and subjects related to it and emphasize subjects rich in cultural background, foundation sciences, and courses in the general field of education. In the early 1920s courses in education began to be introduced, as well as courses concerned with psychology, fundamental sciences, and methodology.

With the advent of courses in physical education in some of the larger universities leading to a bachelor's degree with a major in physical education, more and more graduates found their way into elementary schools and subsequently into the secondary field.

One by one the various states began to require 4 years of training with a degree, and it was not unusual to find minimum requirements in courses in education, psychology, and foundation sciences, as well as courses in physical education. The period from 1920 to 1930, when institutions such as New York University, Teachers College, Columbia University, and Springfield College began to offer courses beyond the first 4 years of college, was a milestone in the advancement of the professional preparation of teachers of physical education.

Important in professional preparation programs after 1920 until the present was the initiation of more stringent admission requirements by teacher-training institutions.

A series of professional preparation conferences were held, starting with the Jackson's Mill Conference in 1948.

One conference held on professional prepara-

Table 18-1. Normal schools of physical education*

Name of school	Date established	Length of present curriculums in years	Degrees granted	Affiliation with college or university
Normal College of the American Gymnastic Union, Indianapolis, Ind.	1866	1,2,3,4	BPE, MPE	
Sargent School of Physical Education, Cambridge, Mass.	1881	3		
Arnold College of Hygiene and Physical Education (New Haven Normal School of Gymnastics)	1886	2,3	BPE	
International YMCA College, Springfield, Mass.	1886	2, 4	BPE, MPE	
Chautauqua School of Physical Education, Chautauqua, N.Y.	1888	1, 3	BS, M Ed	New York University
Formerly Boston Normal School of Gymnastics, Boston, Mass.	1889	2, 5†	MS, AB	1909 became Department of Hygiene and Physical Education, Wellesley College
School of Physical Education, YMCA College, Chicago, Ill.	1890	4	BPE	
Posse-Nissen School of Physical Education, Boston, Mass.	1890	1, 3		
Savage School of Physical Education, New York, N.Y.	1898	3		
Chicago Normal School of Physical Education, Chicago, Ill.	1903	1,2,3		
American College of Physical Education, Chicago, Ill.	1908	2,3,4	BPE	
Battle Creek College, School of Physical Education, Battle Creek, Mich.	1909	3,4	BS in PE	
Boston School of Physical Education, Boston, Mass.	1913	3		Boston University
Columbia Normal School of Physical Education, Chicago, Ill.	1913	(3 mo., 2-6 mo., 9 mo.)		
Newark School of Hygiene and Physical Education, Newark, N.J.	1917	2,3		
Central School of Hygiene and Physical Education, New York, N.Y.	1919	3		New York University
Marjorie Webster School Expression Physical Education, Washington, D.C.	1920	1,2	BPE	
Ithaca School of Physical Education, Ithaca, N.Y.	1923	3,4	BPE	
Bouve School of Physical Education, Boston, Mass.	1925	3		

*Elliot, Ruth: The organization of professional training in physical education in state universities, New York, 1927, Teachers College Contributions to Education, No. 268, Columbia University, p. 9.
†For college graduates only.

tion took place in New Orleans, Louisiana, in 1973. The conference developed standards and guidelines for curriculum building and program planning for training professionals in dance, physical education, recreation education, safety education, and school health education. It stressed new ideas, competencies, and experiences for the various specialties and gave particular attention to accountability, evaluation, accreditation, certification, and differentiated staffing.

Teacher education in physical education has continued to expand. After World War I and again after World War II, great eras of expanding teacher education programs developed in various colleges and universities. In 1918 there were twenty institutions preparing teachers of physical education; in 1929, 139; in 1944, 295; in 1946, approximately 361; and today, nearly 700.

The Professional Preparation Panel of the AAHPER has compiled a listing of colleges and universities offering major preparation programs in health, physical education, and recreation.* The information indicates programs provided at the undergraduate and graduate levels in the three areas and combinations thereof. A list of institutions accredited by the National Council of Accreditation of Teacher Education (NACTE) may be obtained directly from NACTE, 1950 Pennsylvania Ave., N.W., Washington, D.C. 20036.

Two-year colleges and professional preparation

With more and more students taking their higher education in 2-year colleges and with many students interested in sports and physical education, the 2-year college has become involved with the professional preparation of teachers of physical education. A National Conference on Professional Preparation in Health Education, Physical Education, and Recreation, held by the AAHPER, stressed that the freshman and sophomore years should be viewed primarily as general education. How-

ever, several leaders in physical education have pointed out that the student who has made a vocational choice by the time he or she enters college should be offered some professional education during the first 2 years and that it is not realistic to insist that this vocational interest be delayed until the junior year in college. These leaders agree that a major share of the program should be devoted to general education, but at the same time, they point out, it is possible to orient the student to the field of specialization by providing experiences such as an introductory course in a professional field and, in addition, to strengthen the basic skill background of the student. These leaders, however, point out that a prerequisite to such experience should be a qualified staff and adequate facilities to do the job properly.

Competency-based teacher education

Competency-based teacher education may be defined as a program of teacher education in which the competencies to be acquired by the student and the criteria to be applied in assessing the desired competencies are clearly designated. Prospective teachers are held accountable for meeting the specified criteria, which include attitudes, skills, understandings, and behaviors.

Generally, three basic criteria are used in assessing a prospective teacher's competencies. They include (1) cognitive, (2) performance, and (3) product assessment. Cognitive or knowledge criteria assess a student's understanding of what he or she has learned. Performance criteria assess teaching-learning behavior, and product criteria assess the effectiveness of teaching on the student.

The Teacher Education and Certification Section of the New York State Regents Plan for the Development of Post-secondary Education identifies a specific goal and several convictions regarding the future of certification of professional personnel.* The goal is to establish a system of certification by which the state can assure the public that professional personnel in

---

*American Alliance for Health, Physical Education, and Recreation: HPER directory of professional preparation institutions, Journal of Health, Physical Education, and Recreation 45:35, Sept., 1974.

*The University of the State of New York: Format for submission of teacher education program proposals, Albany, The State Education Department, Division of Teacher Education and Certification.

the schools possess and maintain demonstrated competence to enable students to learn. The underlying convictions of Regents Plan are as follows: (1) the basis for certification should be teacher competence rather than total reliance on college courses, and (2) the preparation of teachers should involve a number of pertinent agencies and individuals, including schools, higher institutions of learning, professional staffs, and other relevant agencies.

As in other competency-based programs, many challenges still exist, and total execution of such a program (acceptable to all involved) is not yet employed in many teacher-training institutions. But the trend is definitely beginning to take hold, and in the future, competency-based teacher education should be a reality in a majority of colleges and universities.

Specialization within physical education

There are areas of concentration at both the undergraduate and graduate levels within physical education where specialization can take place. Those areas commonly include athletic training, athletic coaching, and athletic administration; elementary and/or secondary school physical education; physical education for the handicapped; dance; exercise physiology; ergonomics and biomechanics; and the behavioral aspects of sport.

ATHLETIC TRAINING

Athletic trainer professional preparation and certification comprise a relatively new concept in physical education programs. Athletic trainers usually complete a 4-year college curriculum that emphasizes the biological and physical sciences, psychology, coaching techniques, first aid and safety, nutrition, and other related areas. The National Athletic Trainers Association (NATA) highly recommends a certification program that provides for a major area of study in physical education and health and/or another secondary education field with the necessary courses required for state licensure. To become an NATA certified athletic trainer, the

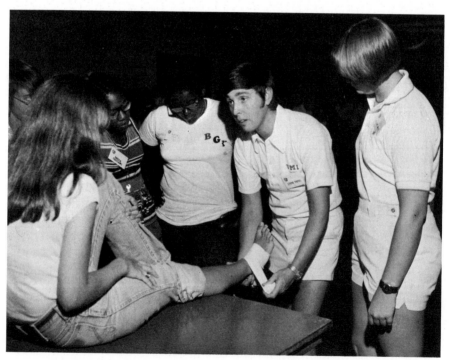

Courtesy Cramer Products, Inc., Gardner, Kan.

Athletic trainers need professional preparation for their duties. An athletic trainer at work.

student must complete the recommended course of study, present proof of 1-year active membership in the NATA, and pass practical and written examinations.

ATHLETIC COACHING AND ADMINISTRATION

Those persons who are particularly interested in coaching various sports and/or the administration of athletic programs will find that some institutions of higher learning offer these as areas of specialization. Usually there is a core of general education and physical education requirements and then an in-depth offering of experiences concerned with courses such as methods and materials for coaching various sports, officiating, first aid and care of injuries, administration of athletic programs, financial management, public relations, and the legal aspects of athletic programs.

ELEMENTARY AND/OR SECONDARY SCHOOL PHYSICAL EDUCATION

The latest surveys show that most professional preparation institutions still offer a combined specialization in both elementary and secondary school physical education. However, more and more professional preparing institutions are offering their students an opportunity to specialize in elementary school physical education. With the current emphasis on movement education, perceptual-motor learning, and interdisciplinary analysis, there is a need to provide experiences that will prepare the physical educator so that he or she will have the expertise to work with children in an effective and meaningful manner. (For further information on elementary school physical education see Chapter 15.)

PHYSICAL EDUCATION FOR THE HANDICAPPED

Teaching handicapped persons is becoming a rewarding area for specialization among physical educators who are interested in working with the mentally and physically handicapped and other types of atypical individuals. Such specialization is becoming increasingly evident since the passage of Public Law 94-142, which provides for the education of the handicapped at

Courtesy Cramer Products, Inc., Gardner, Kan.

The athletic coach needs to be familiar with the care and prevention of injuries on the athletic field.

public expense. (For more information on this area of specialization see Chapter 10.)

DANCE

Dance is becoming a popular and rewarding area of specialization for physical educators who wish to render a service by helping young persons to better understand their bodies and to express themselves through rhythmical activity. Although many opportunities present themselves in elementary and secondary schools and also in dance studios and community agencies and recreation programs, the college and university levels (where more often than not dance

teachers work in departments, divisions, or schools of physical education) also offer many opportunities to serve. There has been considerable expansion of dance programs in recent years in institutions of higher learning. Liberal arts colleges are offering expanded programs of dance experiences for their students, professional preparation programs are training teachers of physical education with an emphasis in the area of the dance, and other institutions are providing instruction in modern, ballroom, and folk dancing for the general student body.

As the dancing program in schools and col-

Dancers at Florida A. & M. University, Tallahassee, Florida.

leges becomes increasingly popular, there is a demand for teachers of physical education who are specialists in the various phases of dance. Prospective teachers interested in dance will find more positions available if they prepare themselves to teach the other activities in the physical education program as well. Opportunities for teaching dance alone are limited.

In addition to schools and colleges, dance personnel are needed in other places such as the theater, private studios, recreation centers, armed forces, summer camps, and hospital therapy. Roles that dance personnel play include that of teacher, performer, choreographer, notator, and director in a concert group and in television, movie, and theater productions. To render the service of teaching dance effectively requires a study of the scientific principles of body movement; an understanding of dance forms, dance composition, and technique; skills of notation; theories relating to costuming, staging, and lighting; and also a good grounding in the scientific foundations of physical education and a sound general education.

EXERCISE PHYSIOLOGY

In recent years there has been much interest in exercise physiology. The fitness explosion has given even further impetus to specialization in this area. Also, industrial fitness programs are seeking exercise physiologists. Furthermore, the involvement of increasing numbers of girls and women in athletic programs has provided a challenge to specialists and researchers in this area to determine the physiological characteristics and the potentialities of the female athlete.

ERGONOMICS AND BIOMECHANICS

The desire to know more about the anatomical and physiological bases of human performance is causing more physical educators to seek expertise in these areas of specialization.

BEHAVIORAL FOUNDATIONS OF SPORT

The psychology of sport and the sociology of sport continue to gain emphasis in physical education. As a result, some physical educators are

specializing in these areas, although the number of professional preparing institutions that provide appropriate in-depth concentration is limited.

Considerations in selecting a professional preparation program

Many factors should be taken into consideration when selecting a teacher-training institution to prepare for work in physical education. The institution of higher learning should meet desirable standards as established by the profession. The physical educator's chances for employment and for success on the job will depend to a great extent on the experiences and opportunities that are provided during this training period. To make an informed decision, the prospective physical educator should consider such factors as the following when evaluating the training institution.

SELECTING TEACHER-TRAINING INSTITUTION

There are many teacher-training institutions throughout the United States that prepare students for the profession of physical education. However, all the institutions that prepare teachers for this specialized work do not adhere to the highest standards of the profession. A careful analysis of various institutions will acquaint the prospective physical educator with their qualifications for preparing teachers of physical education. Such items as faculty, library facilities, purposes, quality and length of curriculums, accreditation, reputation, and placement are a few of the factors that should be taken into consideration.

REVIEWING COLLEGE ENTRANCE REQUIREMENTS

As a general rule, a person desiring to prepare for the teaching of physical education is required to meet college entrance requirements. The standard college preparatory course should be taken by all high school students who want to prepare for this work. Entrance requirements vary from state to state, and interested individuals should consult the institution or institutions in which they are interested.

ANALYZING THE COST

The cost of preparing for the teaching of physical education varies with the institution. Usually the cost is lower in tax-supported institutions such as state colleges and state universities. Students with limited financial resources may supplement their income through scholarships, fellowships, loan funds, and part-time employment. To obtain further information on financial aid, interested persons should contact the college or university of their choice, the U.S. Office of Education, the State Department of Education where the person is a resident, and the AAHPER.

RECOGNIZING THE NEED FOR COLLEGE PREPARATION

A college degree should be held by all who plan to make a career of physical education. Without this minimum preparation there will be few opportunities for employment. Furthermore, the trend is more and more in the direction of an extended period of training. The degree usually granted at the end of the 4-year period is that of Bachelor of Science, Bachelor of Science in Education, or Bachelor of Arts. The Master of Education or Master of Arts degree is frequently granted at the end of the fifth year of training.

ACCREDITATION

Accreditation in the area of professional preparation is a system or evaluation procedure which certifies that certain colleges and universities have approved programs for training physical education teachers. Three ways in which accreditation can take place is by governmental agencies such as state departments of education, regional accrediting agencies such as the Northcentral Association for Colleges and Secondary Schools, and professional associations such as the AAHPER.

What does NCATE accreditation mean to the graduate of an accredited school? This is a question that every student should ask. First, school and college administrators will be hesitant to hire any person who has not graduated from an accredited school. Second, it helps in moving from one state to another and taking a position in another section of the country. In fact, some states do not require the applicant to meet all the detailed state certification regulations if he or she has graduated from a college that has NCATE endorsement. Third, NCATE–endorsed programs are better planned, have higher standards of admission and retention, better staff, higher professional requirements in general, and render more outstanding professional services to their students and graduates. These are a few reasons why each student and teacher has a personal stake in and responsibility for the accreditation of teacher education programs.

Graduate work

Graduate work in all areas of education is receiving increased emphasis. Some of the developments in this area stress that graduate students should be carefully selected on the basis of their educational backgrounds, degree of motivation, intellectual competence, and maturity. In most cases, the student should be prepared for advanced study by having a sound grounding in his or her specialty. A feature that should be common to all graduate courses is the emphasis on mature thinking, extensive reading, and original work. Also, graduate courses are research oriented. They examine the research in various fields of study and critically evaluate its worth to the program.

Advanced study includes the master's degree, sixth-year or professional certificate, and doctoral degree. The master's degree usually requires the equivalent of 1 full year's work beyond the bachelor's degree; the sixth-year or professional certificate requires 1 full year beyond the master's; and the doctoral degree varies from 2 to 3 years beyond the sixth-year or professional certificate. Frequently, physical educators omit the sixth-year or professional certificate and work directly on the doctoral degree after the conferring of the master's degree.

In addition to the educational improvement that accrues to the graduate student, there are also material benefits. Some states grant provisional certificates after graduation from undergraduate programs and then permanent certification after a certain number of graduate credit hours have been taken. Most school systems recognize graduate work in their salary schedules so that, with additional professional preparation, there is increased income.

The student who finds that additional financial aid is needed to pursue graduate work should investigate the following four kinds of financial aid:

Fellowships and graduate assistantships. Many graduate schools in physical education offer grants of money for further study. This grant may include teaching some activity in a college service physical education program or doing some form of work as a means of obtaining aid.

Scholarships. An outright grant of money for graduate work not requiring service or repayment is termed a *scholarship*. These are awarded to outstanding physical educators who have demonstrated merit and leadership qualities and who require financial assistance to pursue graduate study.

Grant-in-aid. A grant-in-aid is usually thought of as an outright grant of money for a specialized purpose. For example, it could be given to a graduate student to work on a specific research project in physical education.

Loans. Colleges, universities, state governments, banks, and the national government offer loans to students at moderately low interest rates to pay for educational needs.

Individuals going into physical education work and desiring to have a successful career should take some graduate work in their special fields. It will assist them in their personal growth and in rendering a greater service.

THE BEGINNING TEACHER

There is a high turnover rate of first-year teachers. Although some teachers change positions after the first year to improve their status, others leave the profession because of dissatisfaction and discouragement and because they have found the job of adjusting to the hard realities of teaching too difficult for them to master. Several research studies have been conducted to determine the reasons teachers give for job satisfaction or dissatisfaction. These include teacher-administrative factors, physical conditions, teacher-community factors, teacher-faculty factors, teacher-student and teacher-parent factors, and salary and security factors.

A survey of fifty teachers indicated the fol-

The teacher of physical education needs to take work beyond the bachelor's degree to keep up with the trends in the field. A physical educator at Hudson Falls Central School, Hudson Falls, New York, teaches gymnastics to students.

lowing as some problems that beginning teachers face:

1. Difficulties arising as a result of the lack of facilities
2. Large size of classes, making it difficult to teach effectively
3. Teaching assignments in addition to the primary responsibility of teaching physical education
4. Discipline problems with students
5. Conflicting methodology between what beginning teachers were taught in professional preparation institutions and established patterns of experienced teachers
6. Clerical work—difficulty in keeping records up to date
7. Problems encountered in obtaining books and supplies
8. Problems encountered in obtaining cooperative attitude from other teachers
9. Lack of departmental meetings to discuss common problems
10. Failure to find time for personal recreation

Directors of physical education look at problems of beginning teachers

Several directors of physical education in school systems across the nation were contacted to determine what they think are the most difficult problems faced by beginning teachers. Since these administrators had an opportunity to observe beginning teachers as they embarked on their professional careers, their experiences should be of value in helping new teachers make a good start. The thinking of these administrators may be summarized under the following headings.

ORGANIZATION

Many problems of beginning teachers, the directors believe, are caused by poor organization that can easily be corrected. Some of the beginning teachers are not accustomed to moving large groups of students from one place to another and from one formation to another. They are not thoroughly familiar with the various methods of class organization for various activities. Sometimes they do not have proper organization in respect to caring for uniforms, lockers, towel fees, and many routine duties important in the efficient running of a physical education program.

These problems concerned with organization can be easily remedied if the beginning teacher will study the problems concerned, become familiar with various types of organization, and ask questions and help of experienced teachers.

TEACHING

The beginning teacher is sometimes an excellent performer in various physical education activities, and it is difficult for the teacher to realize that some students do not know how to throw or jump or perform other basic skills. Also, much time is frequently spent on implementing games rather than in teaching basic fundamentals and skills. Sometimes there is a tendency to teach the units the teacher is interested and does well in and minimize those in which he or she is weak.

The beginning teacher needs to put into effect the tools learned during undergraduate training. This includes presenting skills within the ability of the pupil, utilizing appropriate teaching techniques, planning lessons, and finally recognizing one's shortcomings in physical education and trying hard to correct the deficiencies through in-service training. Planning is necessary—even the teacher of long experience needs at least a brief written plan. Teaching means to teach an activity or skill and not to "tell" pupils to do something or merely supervise activities in a gymnasium. Finally, the teacher should do self-evaluation each day and faithfully try to eliminate weaknesses and expand strengths.

TEACHER-STUDENT RELATIONSHIPS

Students will frequently test the authority of the new teacher, and sometimes the teacher does not meet the test. Discipline problems may arise, and the teacher, instead of facing them directly, refers students to the principal's office. The beginning teacher should recognize that sometimes disciplinary problems are a result of the teacher's lack of planning and class organization. The teacher may expect too much from students. Students may not be adequately motivated. The teacher may show favoritism to certain students, especially athletes.

The beginning teacher needs to establish rapport with students, being firm, pleasant, and consistent. It is necessary that the teacher learn to know boys and girls as human beings and not just "numbers" and establish a friendship with them without becoming one of them.

TEACHER-TEACHER RELATIONSHIPS

Physical education, including sports, tends to isolate teachers of physical education from the rest of the building and often from colleagues in other subject-matter areas. As a result, some beginning teachers fail to realize the importance of participating in general building activities with all teachers, attending faculty meetings regularly, and becoming an integral part of the staff.

From the beginning the new teacher should become acquainted with other members of the faculty, work cooperatively with them, share committee responsibilities, and try to be respected by all.

MAKING ADJUSTMENTS

The beginning teacher often finds facilities, staff, equipment, and other conditions on the

The teacher of physical education needs to have rapport with students. A physical educator at Oak View Elementary School in Fairfax, Virginia, gives instruction about how to use gym scooters.

job far below expectations and far from ideal. The new teacher should realize that teachers do not always have ideal situations; in fact, very few do. Many of them are faced with poor equipment, limited facilities, changing weather conditions, and other substandard situations.

The new teacher should adjust to the position, the school, other teachers, school policies, procedures, and routines. Regardless of the situation, the conditions that prevail should be accepted as a challenge to see how excellent a teaching job can be accomplished in spite of the limiting factors that exist.

Teachers can eliminate some problems before assuming the position

The teacher should carefully evaluate the position before accepting its responsibilities. Unfortunately some teachers accept positions in schools and communities in which they do not fit or belong, and consequently problems arise. Many complex factors related to proper adjustment on the job are usually associated with the nature of the person, the nature of the environment, and the interaction of the two. It is therefore important that the applicant carefully weigh the position that is available and his or her abilities and personal characteristics for handling this position effectively. If this is done, many problems will be foreseen, and the qualities and preparation needed to handle them successfully will be evaluated realistically.

Two advance considerations important to the beginning teacher are knowledge of the conditions of employment and pertinent factors about the school and community. Some considerations regarding the conditions of employment include knowledge of classes to be handled, sports to be coached, clubs to be sponsored, homeroom assignments, length of the school day, school obligations, compensation to be received, sick leave, tenure, sabbaticals, health insurance, and other pertinent facts. Only as the beginning teacher has a complete understanding of such responsibilities will he or she be able to prepare sufficiently, both mentally and physically, for the position. Pertinent factors about the school and community that should be known by the teacher before accepting a position include such items as community traditions, economic status, philosophy of education, political philosophy, projected future growth, and a history of the school and community. These factors will have implications for the type of students to be taught, the parents with whom the teacher will work, the community of which the teacher is to be a part, and the social, political, and educational climate within which the teacher must work.

TEACHING STYLE

Teaching style is an expression of the educator's individuality in relation to stated philosophy and program objectives and is being given much attention in today's educational programs. Additionally, an educator's teaching style is reflected in one's methodology of teaching and in class organization and management.

There are two basic kinds of teaching style— teacher centered and student centered, but there are many variations and overlappings of these styles. This discussion will apply to the teaching style utilized by physical educators.

The teacher-centered physical educator is often described as being autocratic. This educator's philosophy of physical education is stated in terms of a personal relationship to the profession and a personal conception of the goals of the profession in relation to teaching. He or she will evaluate the basketball unit as a success if the dribble, the hook shot, and foul shooting have been taught to the class so that the students can perform to a common standard. Satisfaction to the autocratic physical educator is based not so much on student success but on teacher accomplishment in terms of teacher-centered objectives. The teacher-centered physical educator is somewhat of a perfectionist and expects that all the students will be able to perform a

Courtesy Gwen R. Waters.

Each teacher has his or her own particular teaching style. A teacher of modern dance at Hughes Junior High School of the Los Angeles City Schools, Los Angeles City Unified School District, Los Angeles, California.

certain skill in the same way. He or she does not seem to realize that all students do not have the ability to meet a single standard of performance. This style of teaching is frequently geared to those students who can measure up to the teacher's criteria for success. He or she is also a rather rigid individual, and the students are motivated more by fear of failure than by an inner desire to succeed. Furthermore, instruction is likely to follow tried-and-tested methodology.

The student-centered physical educator is sometimes thought of as a democratic teacher. This educator's philosophy is stated in terms of the relationship of physical education to general education. The program objectives are stated in terms of student needs and interests, and evaluation is based on how well the program has succeeded in meeting these needs and interests. This teacher is especially cognizant of differences in student ability and avoids setting common criteria for skill performance. The student-centered physical educator is usually flexible and will adapt a lesson if it is not accomplishing its purpose. This teacher welcomes innovations because of the belief that the latest techniques and methodology will better contribute to students. He or she also attempts to teach students to think for themselves, to be creative, to express themselves, and to ask questions.

A teaching style develops gradually and is unique to each educator because of the myriad individual variations and shadings that may be applied to a style. There are various influences that affect the development of an individual's style. Two of the most important are the undergraduate professional preparing program and the student teaching experience. A third influence is the philosophy of the school system.

CODE OF ETHICS

The representative assembly of the National Education Association adopted a Code of Ethics of the Education Profession. The Board of Directors of the AAHPER formally endorsed the code.

The code consists of four principles. *Principle One* outlines the commitment to the *student* and indicates the cooperative, helpful, and professional relationship that exists between the student and teacher. *Principle Two* outlines the commitment to the *public* and spells out the important role of educators in the development of educational programs and policies and their interpretation for the public. *Principle Three* outlines the commitment to the *profession* and indicates the need to raise educational standards, improve the service to people, and develop a worthwhile and respected profession. *Principle Four* outlines the commitment to *professional employment practices* and explains the importance of acting in accordance with high ideals of professional service that embody personal integrity, dignity, and mutual respect.

The code is designed to show the magnitude of the education profession and to judge ourselves and colleagues in accordance with the provisions of this code.

TEACHER ACCOUNTABILITY

There is increasing stress among educational systems across the country to develop a system of professional accountability for teachers. The aim of such a movement is to develop objective standards as a means of improving school effectiveness. Among other things it is designed to show which teaching and school methods have proved most effective in achieving specific educational goals. It will protect successful teachers against unfair criticisms by providing proof of their effectiveness; for those teachers who are not effective, it will indicate the additional training and help they need to become effective teachers.

Some educators and lay people believe that teachers in the past have not been accountable to a great degree for helping their students achieve a certain standard of performance and certain changes in behavior. Although some teachers have been dedicated and successful in helping their students to achieve goals far beyond what many students in other school systems achieve, others have been apathetic in regard to their students' achievement records.

There is a need to define the performance objectives for students and staff members in every school, assess the school and nonschool factors that influence student performance, and develop an administrative structure that can operate effectively on an accountability basis.

Model of the accountability system.

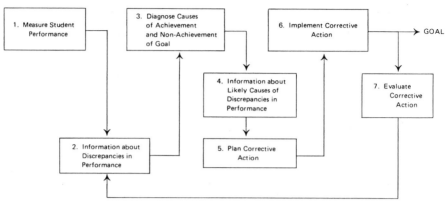

From McDonald, Frederick J., and Forehand, Garlie A.: A design for accountability
in education, New York University Education Quarterly 4:7, Winter, 1973.

At the present time there is considerable discussion concerning how teachers should be evaluated. Questions have been raised as to whether teachers should be rated on the basis of their own performance in the classroom or gymnasium or on the basis of the performance of their students and whether their personality should be taken into consideration in the evaluation process.

TEACHER EVALUATION

Teacher evaluation has become an important consideration in determining promotions, in-service education, tenure, merit salary raises, and, most important, the improvement of teaching. Some general guidelines that are being used for the evaluation of teachers include the following:

Appraisal involves the teachers themselves. Evaluation is a cooperative venture, and teachers are involved in the development of the criteria for evaluation.

Evaluation is centered on performance. The job that is to be accomplished is the point of focus, with other extraneous factors omitted.

Evaluation is concerned with helping the teacher to grow on the job. The purpose of evaluation is to help teachers to evaluate their strengths and weaknesses and to maintain those strengths and reduce the weaknesses.

Evaluation looks to the future. It is concerned with developing a better program and a better school system.

Evaluation of teachers is well organized and administered. It is clearly outlined, and every teacher knows the step-by-step approach to be followed.

Some of the methods of evaluation of teachers include the following:

Observation of teachers in the classroom or in the gymnasium. The National Education Association Research Division, in studying this method, reported that the median length of time for the most recent observation was 22 minutes; about 25% of teachers were notified 1 day in advance that the observation would take place; and about 50% of teachers reported that a conference followed the observation period with the teacher's performance being discussed and evaluated. Nearly one half of the teachers reported that the observation was helpful to them.

Videotaping. With this method a videotape is made of the teacher's performance, after which an evaluation takes place.

Student progress. With this method standardized tests are used to determine what progress the student has made as a result of exposure to the teacher. The AAHPER Cooperative Physical Education Tests distributed by the Educational Testing Service in Princeton, New Jersey, are excellent for this purpose.

Teacher evaluation

TEACHER: Socrates

A. Personal qualifications

	Rating (high to low)					Comments
	1	2	3	4	5	
1. Personal appearance	☐	☐	☐	☐	☑	Dresses in an old sheet draped about his body
2. Self-confidence	☐	☐	☐	☐	☑	Not sure of himself—always asking questions
3. Use of English	☐	☐	☐	☑	☐	Speaks with a heavy Greek accent
4. Adaptability	☐	☐	☐	☐	☑	Prone to suicide by poison when under duress

B. Class management

	1	2	3	4	5	Comments
1. Organization	☐	☐	☐	☐	☑	Does not keep a seating chart
2. Room appearance	☐	☐	☐	☑	☐	Does not have eye-catching bulletin boards
3. Utilization of supplies	☑	☐	☐	☐	☐	Does not use supplies

C. Teacher-Pupil relationships

	1	2	3	4	5	Comments
1. Tact and consideration	☐	☐	☐	☐	☑	Places student in embarrassing situation by asking questions
2. Attitude of class	☐	☑	☐	☐	☐	Class is friendly

D. Techniques of teaching

	1	2	3	4	5	Comments
1. Daily preparation	☐	☐	☐	☐	☑	Does not keep daily lesson plans
2. Attention to course of study	☐	☐	☑	☐	☐	Quite flexible—allows students to wander to different topics
3. Knowledge of subject matter	☐	☐	☐	☐	☑	Does not know material—has to question pupils to gain knowledge

E. Professional attitude

	1	2	3	4	5	Comments
1. Professional ethics	☐	☐	☐	☐	☑	Does not belong to professional association or PTA
2. In-service training	☐	☐	☐	☐	☑	Complete failure here—has not even bothered to attend college
3. Parent relationships	☐	☐	☐	☐	☑	Needs to improve in this area—parents are trying to get rid of him

RECOMMENDATION: Does not have a place in Education. Should not be rehired.

From Saturday Review, July 21, 1962.

Performance objectives. Some schools have adopted a "management by objectives" approach to teacher evaluation. Goals are determined and are usually in terms of long- and short-range objectives.

Multiple evaluators. The use of many evaluators in the evaluation of teachers avoids the one-sided factor inherent in a single evaluator. Multiple evaluations are elicited from students, parents, peers, supervisors, subordinates, and outside professional evaluators.

Multiple-based evaluation technique. This method combines evaluation according to a listing of predetermined characteristics of an effective teacher, as well as a performance-based evaluation.

Data bank evaluation. In this method, pertinent data concerning teacher performance are kept on file. Items such as parent or student written complaints, positive comments, notations by supervisors, classroom observations, and other data that would be helpful in evaluating performance are kept for review.

Student performance as an indicator. Student achievement based on predetermined performance objectives is used as a basis for teacher evaluation.

Ratings. Ratings vary and may consist of an overall estimate of a teacher's effectiveness or consist of separate evaluations of specific teacher behavior and traits. Self-ratings may also be used. Ratings may be conducted by the teacher's peers, by students, or by administrative personnel and may include judgments based on observation of student progress. Rating scales, to be effective, must be based on criteria such as objectivity, reliability, sensitivity, validity, and utility.

As part of a self-evaluation process, some teachers ask the student to respond to certain multiple choice questions that indicate (1) interest level in activity; (2) skills learned; (3) time spent outside of class on activity; (4) knowledge gained; and (5) rating of instructor as to understanding his or her instructions, organization of presentation, enthusiasm, knowledge, skill, and interest in students. There is often space left for the student to express opinions, in paragraph form, about changes in curriculum or teaching methods.

At college and university levels the evaluation of teacher performance is sometimes more difficult than at precollege levels because of the unwillingness of the faculty to permit members of the administration or other persons to observe them in the classroom or some other place for this purpose. Various methods have been devised in institutions of higher learning to rate faculty members, including statements from department heads, ratings by colleagues, ratings by students, and ratings by deans and other administrative personnel.

A question frequently arises in the development of any system of teacher evaluation: What constitutes effectiveness as it relates to a teacher in a particular school or college situation? Several studies have been conducted with some interesting findings. For example, there is only a slight correlation between intelligence and the rated success of an instructor. The relationship of knowledge of subject matter to teaching effectiveness appears to be a pertinent factor in particular teaching situations. A teacher's demonstration of good scholarship while a student in college appears to have little positive relationship to good teaching. There is some evidence to show that teachers who have demonstrated high levels of professional knowledge on national teachers' examinations are more effective teachers. However, the evidence here is rather sparse. The relationship of long-term experience to effectiveness also seems to have questionable value. The first 5 years of teaching seems to enhance teacher effectiveness the most. Cultural background, socioeconomic status, sex, and marital status have little value in predicting teacher effectiveness. Finally, there is little evidence to show that any specified aptitude for teaching exists. The studies indicate that more research needs to be done to establish what constitutes teacher effectiveness on the job.

Teacher evaluation is a difficult and sensitive area. A combination of evaluative procedures may be the best answer, but, as of this writing, much research still has to be done in this area. Most administrators, teachers, and students do agree on the necessity of accountability; now the best possible methods of evaluation must be attained to produce the highest caliber of education.

SELF-ASSESSMENT TESTS

These tests are to assist students in determining if material and competencies presented in this chapter have been mastered.

1. In light of the qualifications for teachers in general and for physical educators in particular, assess your own qualifications for this field of endeavor.

2. Trace the history of professional preparation in the field of physical education from 1861 to the present. What are some important items to consider today in selecting a professional preparing institution for the study of physical education.

3. Prepare a chart that includes the various areas of specialization within physical education and the qualifications needed for each area of specialization.

4. Assume you have accepted a position teaching physical education in a high school. How would you deal with the following problems:

A small gymnasium, 50 by 60 feet, and six classes of fifty students each

Loud and rude students

Lack of help from other teachers

No department meetings

A 12-hour day

5. Describe what teaching style and code of ethics you plan to follow as a physical educator on the job. Describe the advantages and disadvantages of each of various methods of evaluating teachers and what method you believe is best.

READING ASSIGNMENT

Bucher, Charles A.: Dimensions of physical education, ed. 2, St. Louis, 1974, The C. V. Mosby Co., Reading selections 56 to 61.

SELECTED REFERENCES

Annand, V.: PELT—Physical education leadership training, Journal of Health, Physical Education, and Recreation **44:**50, Oct., 1973.

Bucher, Charles A., and Koenig, Constance: Methods and materials of secondary school physical education, ed. 5, St. Louis, 1978, The C. V. Mosby Co.

Clayton, Robert D., and Clayton, Joyce: Concepts and careers in physical education, Minneapolis, 1977, Burgess Publishing Co.

Elam, Stanley: Performance based teacher education: what is the state of the art? Quest (Monograph 18), June, 1972, p. 14.

Field, D.: Accountability for the physical educator, Journal of Health, Physical Education, and Recreation **44:** 37, Feb., 1973.

Fisher, M.: Assessing the competence of prospective physical education teachers, The Physical Educator **29:**93, May, 1972.

Jornat, L.: Self-appraisal checklist for physical education teachers in high school, The Physical Educator **27:** 160, Dec., 1970.

Le Grand, L.: Better teaching through student evaluation, The Physical Educator **28:**201, Dec., 1971.

National Education Association: Problems of teachers, NEA Research Bulletin **49:**103, Dec., 1971.

National Education Association: New approaches in the evaluation of school personnel, NEA Research Bulletin **50:**40, May, 1972.

Office of Education, U.S. Department of Health, Education, and Welfare: How teachers make a difference, Washington, D.C., 1971, Government Printing Office.

Yee, Albert H.: Becoming a teacher in America, Quest (Monograph 18), June, 1972, p. 67.

19

Duties and services performed by physical educators

After reading this chapter the student should be able to—

1. Be familiar in general with the many duties and services performed by physical educators in a variety of settings.
2. Identify the special duties involved in teaching various activities and subjects and different types of students in schools and colleges.
3. Know the special duties involved with such responsibilities as athletic training, coaching, conducting exercise programs, counseling, measurement and evaluation, and administration.
4. Understand the capacities in which physical educators serve and the teaching loads they assume.
5. Appreciate the many duties and services that will need to be performed by a physical educator in his or her first position.

The concept of a physical educator who performs duties and providing services only for schoolchildren is outmoded. Physical educators have been involved in providing many other services, including those rendered in community recreation programs, coaching, programs for the handicapped, and therapeutic work in hospitals and mental institutions. In addition, physical educators are now also employed by industrial plants, health spas, clubs, camps, penal institutions, and other establishments. The training of a physical educator prepares him or her for providing services and performing duties in many different areas and for many different types of people.

Physical education is a rapidly expanding field of endeavor. It has been estimated that there are over 200,000 men and women in the United States who perform physical education duties related to the field of education alone. There are more than 40,000 members in the American Alliance for Health, Physical Education, and Recreation, an organization that is active in furthering physical education. The emphasis on physical fitness and the popularity of exercise and other physical activity programs has given physical education an added importance in the American society. The different games and sports played in this country are innumerable. These and other physical education activities are conducted in the smallest town and in the largest city; in backyards and in public sports stadia; in public school classrooms, gymnasia, and swimming pools; in the YMCA, YWCA, YMHA, and YWHA; in industrial plants and in athletic clubs; in settlement houses and in public playgrounds; in boys' and girls' clubs; in adult and senior recreation centers; in hospitals; and in correctional institutions.

The duties performed and services rendered by physical education personnel for purposes of convenience may be organized as follows:

Teaching
    Movement experiences including games and other selected activities
    Dance
    Handicapped persons

Teachers (professional preparation programs)

Health education, safety, and driver education

Recreation, camping and outdoor education

Other teaching responsibilities

Coaching and athletic training

Conducting exercise programs in health spas, industrial fitness centers, and other organizations

Conducting research

Performing administrative functions

Counseling

Interpreting the worth of physical education

Measurement and evaluation duties

Community responsibilities

TEACHING
Movement experiences including games and other selected activities

Physical educators are called on to teach many and varied forms of physical activity. These include movement education, team games, dual and individual sports, rhythms and dancing, formal activities, aquatic activities, outdoor winter sports, gymnastics, and other activities.

Movement education, including movement exploration experiences, are utilized throughout the educational program. Rhythms and dancing are offered in most programs. Although movement education is most popular at the elementary school level, social dancing, folk dancing, rhythms, gymnastic dancing, square dancing, tap dancing, and modern dancing have an important place in elementary, junior high, and senior high schools and colleges.

The most popular team games on all levels of instruction in the schools are baseball, softball, basketball, touch football, volleyball, soccer, and field hockey. The most popular on the elementary level are softball, basketball, and volleyball; on the junior high school level, baseball, softball, basketball, soccer, touch football, and volleyball; on the senior high school level, volleyball, basketball, baseball, softball, football, touch football, soccer, and field hockey; on the college level, volleyball, baseball, basketball, softball, touch football, and field hockey.

A variety of dual and individual sports are offered. Among the ones most frequently included in physical education programs are track, badminton, table tennis, deck tennis,

Students engage in parachute activities at Public School No. 15 in Brooklyn, New York.

handball, horseshoes, tennis, archery, golf, and shuffleboard.

Formal activities are extensively utilized in programs of physical education. Of these activities, calisthenics is the most frequently mentioned, with marching second. Although it is evident that the games-type program is popular, many physical educators also utilize some of the more formal activities in their classes.

When facilities make it possible, aquatic activities are a phase of many physical education programs. However, in the public schools the lack of swimming pools makes such an activity impossible for many boys and girls. Other agencies, such as the YMCA, frequently have pools as part of their physical plant. When aquatic activities are a part of the program, swimming, diving, lifesaving, water games, scuba diving, and sometimes canoeing, sailing, and rowing are offered.

Outdoor winter sports form a group of activities that are included in most programs. Climatic conditions in certain parts of the country and the desire to stay indoors during inclement weather cause some physical educators to omit these sports. When such activities are a part of the program, skating, snow games, ice hockey, skiing, and tobogganing are the most popular.

Gymnastics are included in the majority of physical education programs. Such activities as tumbling, pyramid building, apparatus, rope climbing, and acrobatics are popular.

Some of the other activities offered, which do not seem to fit logically into the previous groupings, are self-testing activities, relays, games of low organization, activities adapted to the handicapped, and camping. Each of these is popular throughout the public schools and other agencies of the country that utilize physical education activities in their program.

Games are a popular pastime for the young and the old, for boys and girls, and for men and women. They offer an opportunity for all to obtain exercise, fun, and relaxation. They can play an important part in developing physical fitness and developing skills for use in leisure time, now and, perhaps more important, in later years. Older people who believe in the value of exercising to keep active and healthy participate in some activity—tennis, skating, swimming—that they learned at an early age.

The teaching of games represents one of the main components of any physical education program; therefore physical educators must be familiar with many of them. They should know the essential features of the various games, rules, methods of organization, values received from participation, equipment and facilities needed, and ways of motivating the participants. They should also possess motor skill in as many of these activities as possible. The ability to demonstrate a particular skill aids greatly in the teaching process and also increases the prestige of the teacher in the eyes of students.

Dance

Dancing is one of the oldest arts and is an important part of many physical education programs from the primary grades through college. As far back as one can go into history, popular dancing was a pastime in the lives of all peoples. The members of early tribal groups danced as part of their religious festivals, in preparing for combat, and for entertainment. Dance has come down through the ages, bringing with it an account of the way people lived in other lands and other times. It is a means of communication. Through dance one may creatively express feelings about people, forces of nature, and other phases of our culture. It provides enjoyment, a means of emotional release, and expression of desires in action. It results in beneficial physiological effects by stimulating the various organic systems of the body. It helps to develop balance, control, and poise and provides the opportunity to respond to music through movement.

The dance program consists of *fundamental rhythms,* such as running, walking, skipping, jumping, hopping, and the imitation of real and imaginary characters through rhythmic activities; *folk dances* and *singing games,* such as "Farmer in the Dell," "Csebogar," "Pop Goes the Weasel," "Norweigian Mountain March," and "Schottische"; *athletic* or *gymnastic dancing,* which is dancing done with vigor and which includes such acts as cart-

A dance class at Hampton Institute, Hampton, Virginia.

A physical educator teaches golf at the South Carolina School for the Deaf and the Blind at Spartanburg, South Carolina.

Job analysis for an elementary school physical education teacher

A teacher in the Lafayette Elementary School in Waterloo, Iowa, lists the following as some of her duties:

I teach physical education grades four, five, and six. Many activities are included in the program: games, sports, tumbling, rhythms, rope jumping, ball bouncing, track and field, posture improvement, marching, and exercises for physical fitness. The sports include modified football (football-kickball), soccer (kickball), modified volleyball, modified basketball (captain ball), and softball.

The sixth grade plays several games with other schools each year. An arrangement is made to have members from both schools on the same team. The sixth graders do not compete on a school-against-school basis.

We try to check for physical fitness once a week, that is, chinning, sit-ups, squat thrusts. The children help check each other in their squads.

After playing a game or after any physical activity, we usually discuss what we've done. Suggestions are given for improving our next activity. We discuss what we thought we did well. I stress good sportsmanship and we comment on that. Sometimes I make and give tests over such sports as softball and basketball.

I teach art, literature, and music to grades four, five, and six; and also, fourth-grade spelling and social studies.

Some of the things I specifically try to do in my physical education classes are:

1. Offer proper incentives and ideals.
2. Help build better citizens—physically, mentally, and morally.
3. Develop health habits—posture and exercise.
4. Help each child to feel he or she is needed and has a very important part in everything we do.
5. Help each child to work for improvement.
6. Help to organize and direct big-muscle activity.

Job analysis for a senior high school physical education teacher

A teacher at Dickinson Senior High School, Jersey City, New Jersey, discusses a typical day at work, which includes the following:

1. The school day consists of seven periods of 45 minutes each. This teacher teaches six periods of physical education and has one free period.
2. During three of the class periods, he is head teacher; during the remaining three, he assists.
3. The head teacher is responsible for knowing each boy by name and determining achievement levels.
4. As assistant teacher, he is responsible for attendance or dressing room supervision.
5. This teacher also coaches during football season and takes the football team to training camp for 5 days at the start of the season.

wheels, rolls, running, and skipping; *social or ballroom dancing,* which is rapidly being included in many physical education programs for its social value; *modern dancing,* which is a medium of expressing oneself creatively and esthetically through movement; and *tap dancing.*

The elementary school program in rhythms and dance includes fundamental rhythms, pantomimic and dramatic dances, dramatic and signing games, folk dances, and character dances. Dance may constitute as much as 20% to 40% of the entire physical education program.

In junior and senior high school the more popular phases of the dance program include social, folk, square, and modern dancing.

At the college and university level, folk, square, ballroom, and modern dancing are frequently included in the curriculum. In addition, courses such as the history and philosophy of dance, methods of teaching various forms of dance, dance production, and cultural concepts of dance are offered.

Handicapped persons

Physical educators render services and perform duties for handicapped students. Their duties in this area include (1) counseling students so that they have a meaningful physical education experience, (2) helping students to correct atypical conditions that can be improved, (3) assisting each student to achieve the highest level of physical fitness with his or her limitations, (4) providing safety measures to protect students from participating in activities that would aggravate their condition, (5) assisting students to understand the value of body mechanics and to understand their particular limitations, and (6) developing a feeling of self-worth and a positive self-concept in each student (For further information about programs for the handicapped, see Chapter 10.)

Teachers (professional preparation programs)

For those physical educators who aspire to the college and university level and who are interested in helping to shape the future of their field of endeavor by contributing to the preparation of future leaders of their field, there are many opportunities to render this valuable service in the more than 600 institutions that have such programs.

The qualifications for teaching in professional preparation programs include advanced degrees, a good academic record, an interest in and understanding of college students, a broad view of educational problems, and, many times, previous experience at elementary or secondary school levels. The college teacher must be particularly well versed and competent in the field and have desirable personality and nonacademic traits, such as good character. The sought-after teacher is one who can be characterized as truth seeking, humble, steadfast, and possessing a sympathetic understanding for human beings.

A professor in a professional preparation program might render a variety of services, including teaching such courses as history and philosophy of physical education, tests and measurements, motor learning, methods, skills, organization and administration, programs for the atypical individual, and health observation. In addition, there might be research activities, committee service, advice and counsel of students, writing, community service, consulting, and participating in the work of professional associations.

A college or university staff usually includes various instructional ranks, including that of instructor, assistant professor, associate professor, and professor. In some cases there are distinguished professors. Furthermore, there is usually a head or chairperson of the department, division, and, in some cases, a dean of a school or college of physical education, health, and recreation.

The services rendered by physical educators in professional preparation programs can be rewarding. By providing experiences that will help to develop those qualities, competencies, and attributes in students preparing to become leaders in the field and by doing an outstanding job in this training experience, a teacher's work will live on forever in the lives of students and other leaders of future generations.

Health education, safety, and driver education

Physical educators may have physical education duties only, or they may, in addition, have health education responsibilities. Although health education is making great strides toward having specialized personnel handling the health duties, there is still a lack of adequately trained personnel to take over all of the health education duties in the country. Furthermore, many communities are too poor financially to assume the responsibility of having both physical educators and health educators. It is in cases such as these that physical educators are assuming health education responsibilities.

The health education subjects and activities that physical educators are asked to teach and conduct are similar for both men and women. (See Chapter 16 for a fuller discussion of the health education program.)

Besides the teaching of health subjects, the responsibility for holding guidance conferences, administering vision and hearing tests,

giving home-bound instruction, and teaching crippled children play an important part in many programs.

Safety education has become an important part of the programs of school systems, and in many cases, physical educators are asked to assume duties in this field of endeavor. Duties include organizing safety patrols, instructing a unit of safety in the health curriculum, cooperating with community agencies interested in promoting a safe community, supervising playgrounds and athletic facilities in a manner that will promote safety, and other responsibilities involving the promotion of safe living in the educational program. In some school systems, safety education supervisors are appointed to coordinate the entire safety program.

Driver education is a common responsibility of teachers of physical education. The great expansion of this type of education is readily apparent. Studies have shown the effectiveness of driver education in reducing automobile accidents. Other studies have shown that programs are more effective when offered as a separate course and when the teacher has had special preparation in teaching driver education and traffic safety.

Recreation and leisure services, camping, and outdoor education

Recreation and leisure services programs in schools, communities, youth-serving agencies, industry, hospitals, and other organizations are growing rapidly. These programs are designed to provide young and old with profitable activities in which they can engage during their leisure hours. Special skills are needed for physical educators working in such programs. Games, sports, dance, and rhythms play an important role in many communities. It is a common practice for school physical educators to find supplementary work in the recreation programs of their communities.

Various personal attributes are important for the physical educator desiring to perform services in recreation programs. These characteristics include integrity, friendly personality, enthusiasm, initiative, organizing ability, and other qualifications that will aid in the achievement of recreation objectives. It is especially

Camping and outdoor education at Florida A. & M. University, Tallahassee, Florida.

important that the person working in recreation understand and appreciate human beings. He or she must have respect for the human personality; a broad social viewpoint; the desire to inculcate a high standard of moral and spiritual values; a recognition of the needs, interests, and desires of individuals; an appreciation of the part that recreation can play in meeting these needs and interests; and a desire to serve humanity. There is also a special need for recreators to have an understanding and appreciation of community structure and the place of recreation at the "grass roots" level of this structure.

Many physical educators also render services in camping and outdoor education programs, which are recognized as having an educational value that should be experienced by every boy and girl. Some camps throughout the United States are associated with school systems, and camping is a part of the educational experience. Outdoor education programs in camps and other settings are also becoming popular.

Outside the field of education, camps are sponsored by state, county, and municipal government and by organizations such as churches, Boy Scouts and Girl Scouts, YMCA,

YWCA, YMHA, and YWHA groups, 4-H clubs, and private corporations.

Any individual trained in physical education may play a major part in the organization and administration of any school camp. Because of his or her training in education, specialized skills that make up a great part of the program of any camp, and experiences in working with others in a camp situation, this individual is in a most important position to play a major role in this trend back to nature.

Other teaching responsibilities

In smaller schools especially, administrators frequently hire physical educators who can also teach some other subject. This procedure is followed because of financial limitations, small staffs, and low enrollments.

In determining the duties of physical educators, a national survey found that general science and biology are the subjects most often assigned to physical educators. The second most frequently assigned area is social studies, with subjects such as American history, civics, ancient history, problems of American democracy, and geography on the list. English also ranks high. Mathematics, drawing, design, representation, speech correction, industrial arts, lip reading, chemistry, physics, home economics, arts and crafts, agriculture, commercial subjects, and music are also assigned as part of a physical educator's duties in some schools.

COACHING AND ATHLETIC TRAINING

Both men and women are called on to coach intramural, interscholastic, and intercollegiate sports. Such duties are common in public schools, increasing progressively from the elementary to the college levels, and are also functions of the individual who works for other agencies.

A study of one state showed that 87.3% of the physical education instructors in the junior high schools and 97.4% of those in the senior high schools of the state had coaching duties. A survey of intramural or interscholastic activities that physical educators are called on to coach showed that an individual preparing to follow this profession should be familiar with many activities. The activities that are most commonly assigned to physical educators as coaching responsibilities are basketball, softball, volleyball, baseball, track, touch football, swimming, tennis, soccer, field hockey, football, speedball, cross country, golf, bowling.

A position statement concerning the professional status of collegiate coaches was prepared by the Joint Committee on Physical Education and Athletics of the AAHPER, the National College Physical Education Association for Men, and the National Collegiate Athletic Association. According to this position statement, coaches who are employed in intercollegiate athletic programs generally have the following responsibilities:

1. Responsibilities that fall entirely within the intercollegiate athletic program
2. A combination of coaching of intercollegiate athletics and teaching general skill courses within the basic physical education program
3. A combination of coaching intercollegiate athletics and teaching in the professional preparation program for physical educators and athletic coaches

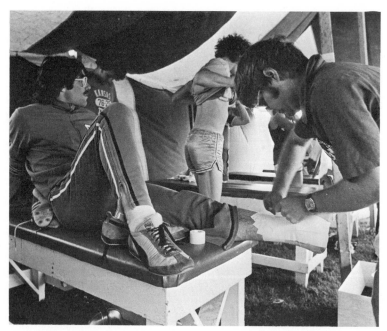

Courtesy Cramer Products, Inc., Gardner, Kan.

The athletic trainer has several specific duties in the conduct of a physical education and sport program.

The athletic trainer also has specific duties in the conduct of a physical education program, which include (1) performing preventive measures such as taping ankles; (2) referring injured athletes and students to appropriate medical personnel for treatment; (3) counseling teachers, athletes, and students in prevention of accidents and care of athletic injuries; and (4) providing various therapeutic measures authorized by medical personnel such as application of heat, massage, and exercise.

CONDUCTING EXERCISE PROGRAMS IN HEALTH SPAS, INDUSTRIAL FITNESS CENTERS, AND OTHER ORGANIZATIONS

Many physical educators are finding employment in health spas, industrial fitness programs, centers for the elderly, and other places where there is a desire to improve the fitness of the members of the organization. The number of these programs has mushroomed in recent years with the extensive publicity that fitness has received on television and in books, magazines, and newspapers. As a result of this extensive exposure, much of the population is becoming fitness conscious, and there is a need for trained personnel to conduct these programs.

Duties performed in these centers vary from organization to organization. If it is a large industrial corporation program for executives, for example, the physical educator will probably be responsible to medical personnel and will help in the conduct of exercise programs for management personnel under the watchful eyes of the physician. In many cases the physical educator in these programs is trained in the field of exercises physiology. If duties are performed in a health spa, on the other hand, the physical educator is likely to have much more freedom in prescribing exercise programs for the membership. However, in the majority of establishments that sponsor exercise programs, physical education personnel will have such duties and perform such services as (1) helping to assess the physical fitness status of the members, (2) prescribing physical activity regimens for the members, (3) supervising the prescribed exercise programs, (4) determining progress made and keeping records of such progress, and (5) maintaining equipment that is utilized in the exercise programs.

In some cases, physical educators will be in complete charge of the business operation, with

Courtesy the Forbes Magazine fitness center.

Employees engaging in exercise activities at the Forbes Magazine fitness center.

the result that duties will also include items such as keeping the books, budgeting funds, purchasing supplies and equipment, and conducting a public relations program.

CONDUCTING RESEARCH

The purpose of research in any field is to push back the frontiers of knowledge. Physical education has lagged behind other fields in both its production and its use of research, and it has tended to rely heavily on research done in related fields.

The major physical education research publication, *Research Quarterly,* has made a concerted effort in recent years to improve and stimulate the quality of research. Considerable physical education research is being done by graduate students who publish their theses and dissertations in the *Research Quarterly.*

Many leading colleges and universities have built or are building research laboratories. Most graduate programs on the master's and doctoral level require the completion of a course in research design and also a research project.

The tools of research in physical education include both the tried and tested and the newer, more sophisticated devices. Dynamometers, ergometers, treadmills, tensiometers, goniometers, fleximeters, silhouettographs, reaction timers, and the techniques of slow- and stop-motion cameras, special projection devices, and other means are used to measure the range of the body's abilities and reactions.

Considerable physical education research has been conducted in the area of physical fitness, although the mechanics of movement in various sports skills have also been intensively scrutinized. In spite of the recent advances, much research remains to be done in the areas of motor learning, biomechanics, movement education, skill testing, physical fitness and physical ability, teaching methods, and curriculum.

Any occupation that desires to achieve the status of a profession must continually be pioneering and be on the cutting edge of new developments, uncovering new knowledge, supporting hypotheses that have been formulated, and determining new truths pertinent to its field. Therefore physical educators recognize the importance of conducting research to achieve this status and accomplish these objectives. Some of the research that has been conducted by physical educators in the past has been neither significant nor conducted according to sound scientific procedures. However, with the renewed emphasis on this service and duty and the increased recognition of its significance and value in advancing physical education, more scholarly research is gradually being accomplished.

Physical educators who desire to render a service in the field of research should become well grounded in the sciences, research methodology, quantitative methods of treating data, understanding of laboratory testing, and organization and conduct of research studies. These competencies take considerable time to develop and usually require many years of graduate work, including pursuing programs leading to masters' and doctoral degrees. For those persons who have the interest and develop the competencies, however, there are many opportunities for rendering a valuable professional service. More than thirty colleges and universities engaged in physical education work now have research laboratories where research experimentation is carried on. There are job opportunities open to qualified physical educators for conducting research on a full-time basis, carrying on research in addition to their teaching responsibilitities, and serving as laboratory and research assistants. In addition, research opportunities are available in voluntary agencies, industry, and other settings.

There is a trend today toward interdisciplinary research, with a team approach being utilized. In such cases the physical educator–researcher and a psychologist or sociologist, for example, work together, combining their knowledge and skills on problems that cut across both their fields of endeavor.

Although research is stressed in most graduate programs, the undergraduate should also become familiar with the research experience. This can be accomplished by becoming familiar with the various sources of research findings, achieving competence in the ability to interpret findings of studies, developing skill in the formulation of a research study, and actually working on a research project. In the more sophisticated professional preparation institutions, the research process is integrated into many courses.

Every physical educator should be acquainted with the Educational Research Information Center, commonly called ERIC. This is a nationwide service designed to provide the results of new educational research to teachers, administrators, researchers, and others who need it. ERIC consists of a headquarters office in Washington, D.C., and a network of clearinghouses in universities and other institutions throughout the United States. Each of the designated clearinghouses is responsible for information in a particular area of education. The staff of each clearinghouse selects and abstracts all relevant documents on the particular subject to which they have been assigned. Central ERIC then coordinates the efforts of all clearinghouses, records the research on microfilm and in pamphlet form, and makes it available to educators at a nominal cost. Therefore if an educator desires to have information on the disadvantaged, motor learning, personnel services, junior colleges, or reading, the researched information available on these subjects can be secured.

A federal agency, The National Institute of Education, has educational research as one of its prime objectives. In the spring of 1974, for example, between 7 and 10 million dollars was awarded for field-initiated educational research. Further information may be obtained from the U.S. Department of Health, Education, and Welfare, National Institute of Education, Washington, D.C. 20202.

PERFORMING ADMINISTRATIVE FUNCTIONS

A valuable service is rendered by those physical educators who administer programs in schools, colleges, governmental agencies, and other agencies, wherever they exist. Such work requires special qualifications if one is to perform the service well. Such qualifications would include a knowledge of the theory of administration, integrity, administrative mind, ability to instill good human relations, ability to make decisions, health and fitness for the job, willingness to accept responsibility, under-standing of work, command of administrative technique, and intellectual capacity.

It is being recognized increasingly that administration is not a matter of hit or miss, trial and error, or expediency. Instead, a theory of administration is emerging. It is further recognized that from a study of this administrative theory one will gain insights into how to administer and how human beings work most effectively. Administrative theory will also help in the identification of problems that need to be solved if an effective working organization is to exist. Although some educators oppose the idea that a framework of theory can be established, it seems assured that administration is rapidly becoming a science and is thereby characterized by more objectivity, reliability, and a systematic structure of substance. Such theory explains what administration is and provides guides to administrative action.

Those students who aspire to administrative positions in physical education, in addition to mastering the theory of administration, should also recognize that one of the most important services they render is to human beings. Although some functions and areas can be somewhat mechanical—such as office management, budget making and financial accounting, purchase and care of supplies and equipment, legal liability, insurance management, curriculum planning, public relations, teacher and program evaluation, and facility management—relations with staff, colleagues, and the public in general can never become mechanical and routine. The administrator must always be sympathetic and understanding, friendly and considerate, honest and fair. In other words, the administrator must be an expert in the area of human relations.

One further point should be mentioned. There is a trend for both men and women to be hired as administrators. In the past, when an administrative opportunity opened, the man was always the first to be considered. Although the odds in some situations are still in favor of the man, they have been reduced considerably. Sex is no longer the important factor it was years ago in the selection of an administrator. Today the phrase "equal opportunity employer" is a sign of the times.

Several types of administrative positions exist for the physical educator who desires to render this type of service.

Most schools and colleges have physical education, including athletic programs. In addition, many youth-serving and other types of agencies also have these programs for their members. As a result, physical educators are frequently hired to administer these specialized offerings. In some cases one person is designated to administer the physical education instructional program, the intramural and extramural, the adapted and the interscholastic or intercollegiate athletic program. In other situations these programs are separated, with personnel in charge of administering each of the programs. In some states a director's certificate is issued after specialized training has been pursued. It certifies those persons who are qualified to direct programs in these specialized areas.

In addition to interscholastic, intercollegiate, and intramural athletics and other programs, clubs, varsity clubs, and physical fitness clubs, sometimes need special administrative services for which the physical educator qualifies. In the administration of such programs, duties must be performed that relate to fiscal management, public relations, personnel management, facility management, insurance management, curriculum planning, and other responsibilities that go with such a position.

Effective management of the administrative service requires an individual with good human relations, personal qualities that relate to the group that composes the organization one is administering, a reasonable degree of intelligence, initiative, persistence, creativity, and an understanding of the job that needs to be done. Following are some of the administrative duties:

Supervision of plant equipment
General maintenace and repair of equipment and facilities
Establishing office regulations and procedures and carrying out departmental policies
Formulating and administering budget
Conducting inventories
Preparing reports on various phases of work

Maintaining records
Administering intramural program
Making arrangements for athletic events
Securing officials
Organizing and administering field and play days
Organizing and administering interschool athletic program
Preparing attendance reports
Procuring supplies
Planning in-service education programs
Preparing notices and announcements
Coordinating program with other departments
Interviewing sales persons
Developing curriculum materials
Preparing schedule for classes
Developing plan for determining student marks
Developing program for evaluation

COUNSELING

Physical educators play a unique role in the life of each person with whom they come in contact. One of the greatest services that can be rendered is that of counseling boys and girls as well as adults, about matters that affect their physical selves and the development of their personalities. Most people are concerned with their body image, how to build physical fitness, the way to gain strength, how to become skilled in their favorite physical activities, suggestions for developing poise, how to maintain weight control, finding the path to a beautiful body, and a host of other desires and interests. They want to sit down and discuss face to face some of the physical changes that are taking place in their bodies, what they mean, and what they should do about them. They want to know what it means if they smoke, drink, or use drugs. They want to have information on why they are required to attend physical education class, learn skills, and know certain physiological facts.

To be an effective counselor, physical educators must have a sincere desire to help people. They must recognize that this is an important service, and they must want and be prepared to render it most effectively.

To be an effective counselor, physical educators must be acquainted with how human beings grow and develop, their developmental tasks, and the problems they experience. Physical educators must be able to clarify their prob-

Student counseling taking place in a conference/lecture room in the gymnasium at Washington State University, Pullman, Washington.

lems, give encouragement, offer friendship, and provide a feeling of belonging.

Effective counselors will get as much information as possible about the person needing advice. In so doing, they will talk with parents, use school records, and know other sources of help when referral becomes necessary. They will work closely in a school situation with the guidance officer and the personnel in this area.

The physical educator can render a valuable counseling service to all persons who are interested in and have problems that relate to his or her specialty. This service can go beyond students in the school to men and women in the community who want accurate information that will help them solve some of their physical problems.

Cassidy,* in discussing counseling, points out that counselors should function in six areas: (1) set climate, (2) locate needs, (3) provide goal-centered instruction, (4) change the situa-

tion by changing relationships, (5) make referrals to other school or community personnel, and (6) keep records.

INTERPRETING THE WORTH OF PHYSICAL EDUCATION

Physical educators can and should render the service of interpreting the values of physical activity to human welfare. When the scientific values to each individual become known by students, educators, parents, and the public in general, they will be more likely to make physical activity a regular part of their personal regimen and thereby contribute to their health and well-being. Unfortunately too many people do not recognize the need for making physical activity a regular part of their routines. Consequently, they may be less productive, healthy, and active and unable to obtain the most that life has to offer. A service can be rendered to humanity by interpreting physical education in lay terms—terms that each boy and girl, man and woman, businessman and others will understand and be able to identify with. Interpretation must be relevant to human beings,

*Cassidy, Rosalind: Counseling in the physical education program, New York, 1959, Appleton-Century-Crofts, pp. 5-6.

their needs, their health, their welfare, their future, and their well-being. Accurate and significant facts need to be presented regarding the biological, psychological, and sociological advantages of physical education. Physical educators who are well trained themselves in the scientific foundations of their field will render the greatest service in interpreting the program to others. They will provide scientific, accurate information that can be supported through research as to the worth of their field. They will have outstanding programs in their school, agency, or college, knowing that this is a strong medium of interpreting the worth of their field. They will symbolize through their appearance and health habits the values that physical education provides. They will exploit every opportunity to speak to their academic colleagues, the community, and civic and other groups about their field of endeavor.

MEASUREMENT AND EVALUATION DUTIES

The more popular measurement and evaluation techniques used by physical educators are those which measure the health, physical fitness, knowledge, skill, and adaptability of their subjects.

The medical examination continues to be the most common procedure for checking on an individual's health status. This is utilized by schools as a routine procedure in examining students periodically and for participation in interscholastic sports and by various agencies and institutions for checking on the advisability of an individual's participating in physical activity. It is conducted by physicians.

Other techniques also utilized extensively for determining various physical traits and characteristics are organic, stress, skill, knowledge, and adaptation tests. Organic tests are designed to measure such things as the efficiency and quality of an individual's cardiovascular system, nutritional status, strength, and physical fitness. Skill tests measure such things as an individual's general motor ability, general motor capacity, motor educability, and skill in specific activities. Physical education and health education knowledge tests include such areas as rules, strategies, techniques, health

knowledge, and attitudes. Adaptation tests are concerned with measuring certain character and personality traits.

In some schools, self-evaluation on the part of the student is utilized. The student in cooperation with the teacher sets certain performance goals that he or she wishes to accomplish. The student is then evaluated in respect to these objectives.

Another evaluation technique that is utilized to some extent has to do with program evaluation. This is concerned with administrative items in the conduct of a program, including leadership, time element, facilities, and participation.

COMMUNITY RESPONSIBILITIES

Most physical educators throughout the country have community responsibilities. These are usually engaged in voluntarily. However, the special qualifications and skills of physical education persons make them a likely target for requests from community groups to assist with youth and other programs. Some of the more common agencies in which physical educators are affiliated are church activities, social or recreational clubs, fraternal or lodge activities, service clubs, civic welfare organizations, and political clubs.

Physical educators should be interested in providing leadership for their communities in programs involving sports, athletics, and recreational activities. By exercising a leadership role, they can help to ensure that such programs are organized and administered in the best interests of youths and adults. It also offers an opportunity to interpret physical education to the public in general. In so doing, physical educators become respected and important leaders in the community and gain greater support for their school program.

CAPACITIES IN WHICH PHYSICAL EDUCATORS SERVE

The findings of a national survey show that physical educators perform in several capacities.

Teachers of physical education throughout the United States serve in an administrative and/or teaching capacity. The distribution of administrative and teaching positions showed that approximately one half of both men and women physical educators have a combination of administrative and teaching positions. Many physical educators work in small towns where it is common to find in the public schools one man and one woman, who perform administrative and teaching duties.

Although many physical educators have a combination of administrative and teaching positions, others have teaching positions or administrative positions only. The larger the physical education program the greater the need for personnel whose sole function is teaching and for personnel whose primary responsibility is administration.

Some of the capacities in which physical education teachers served, as revealed by this nationwide survey, include the following positions throughout the country, which are concerned solely with physical education activities:

Teacher of physical education
Teacher of physical education for the handicapped
Supervisor and teacher of physical education
Director and teacher of physical education
Supervisor, director, and teacher of physical education
Coach of varsity sports
Director of athletics
Physical educator in the YMCA, YWCA, YMHA, YWHA
Resource physical educator on the elementary level
County supervisor of physical education
Research worker
Supervisor of physical education on the elementary level
Supervisor of physical education on the secondary level
Director of intramurals
Chairperson of the department of physical education

Positions throughout the United States concerned with physical education and health duties include the following:

Supervisor of health and physical education
Director of physical education and health
Supervisor and teacher of health and physical education
Director and teacher of health and physical education

Supervisor, director, and teacher of physical education, and coordinator and teacher of health
Director and teacher of physical education and coordinator and teacher of health
Director and teacher of physical education and teacher of health
Teacher of health and physical education
Director of physical education, health, and recreation

TEACHING LOADS

Teaching load varies considerably from school district to school district and from college to college. There is little uniformity, although the National Education Association has suggested that every teacher should have at least two free periods a day.

Teaching loads should be arranged so that the preparation and planning needed are taken into consideration, as well as the physical and nervous energy expended by a teacher in a class situation. The number of different classes taught daily is a better yardstick in most cases than the number of hours taught daily because of the planning required for each class presentation. The physical educator needs time to consult with teachers, give students additional help, plan the program, and perform the many duties connected with the teaching process.

College and university teaching loads are usually computed on a different basis than at the elementary and secondary school levels. The normal college load is 12 hours of teaching. However, in some cases the physical education class is not considered on a one-to-one basis. For example, it might take 2 hours in the gymnasium to equal 1 hour in a classroom subject. Of course, the best arrangement is to have teaching in the gymnasium carry the same weight as teaching in the classroom. Also, at the college and university level, other responsibilities such as advisement, research, administration, and some committee assignments may be taken into consideration in figuring load.

SELECTED GENERAL RESPONSIBILITIES OF THE PHYSICAL EDUCATOR REGARDLESS OF SETTING

There are certain responsibilities that each physical educator must assume on accepting a position. These responsibilities are as follows:

Knowing the objectives of the profession of physical education

Planning and administering a physical education program in the light of these objectives

Providing effective leadership to achieve these objectives

Scientifically measuring and evaluating the physical education program to determine if the objectives are being accomplished

Reevaluating the program of physical education in the light of results obtained through measurement and evaluation techniques

Knowing objectives of profession

In the first place, the physical education person must know and fully understand the objectives of the physical education profession. The more immediate or specific objectives, together with the long-term goals, should be present in the physical educator's mind, whether he

or she is teaching a class in the public schools or working in a YMCA, health spa, industry, camp, or settlement house. They will serve as guides for what the physical educator is striving to accomplish today, tomorrow, next year, and ultimately. As a result of a knowledge and understanding of the objectives of physical education, the program will be better planned, the leadership will be better, and the results obtained will be much more fruitful.

Planning a physical education program

The physical educator has the responsibility for planning and administering a program in the light of its objectives. This means that interests and needs of individuals whom it will serve, as well as other considerations such as the prevailing philosophy, will be taken into consideration. It means that a varied program of activities will be selected. Furthermore, factors such as facilities, personnel, equipment, state legislation, size of class, time allotment, and

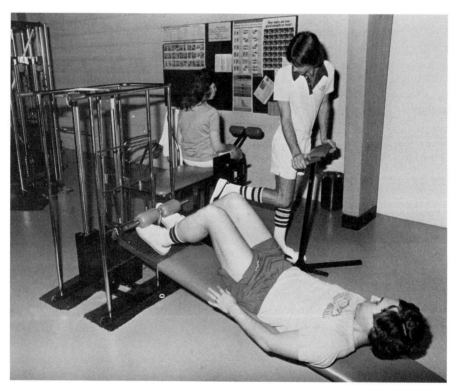

Courtesy Fitness Director B. Arnold, Fitness and Recreation Center,
Xerox Corporation, Leesburg, Va.

Physical educators perform duties in industrial fitness programs.

climatic conditions will be taken into consideration. Provisions will also be made for the physical, social, skill, and intellectual development of the participant.

In planning a physical education program, an effort should also be made to utilize the latest research and scientific findings in the methods that are used.

Providing leadership

The physical educator has the responsibility for providing effective leadership to achieve the objectives of physical education. Outstanding leadership will be concerned with helping each person develop to his or her greatest possible capacity—physically, neuromuscularly, intellectually, and socially.

Physical educators should also realize that their responsibility extends beyond the immediate group of persons with whom they are working to the rest of the school, institution, or agency with which they are associated. All physical educators should believe that the wider their associations the greater personal enjoyment and happiness and the greater the extension of the benefits of physical education.

The informal and play type of physical education program that sometimes exists offers an opportunity for indolent physical educators to conduct a program without providing effective leadership. They can throw out a ball or pass out the equipment and then loaf. To provide effective leadership, physical educators must be alert to every opportunity that arises so that they may aid in developing the individual to optimum capacity.

Effective leadership also will not be provided by the coach if winning is stressed as the main objective instead of such outcomes as courtesy, sympathy, respect for authority, fairness, and abiding by the rules. Effective leadership will not be provided if physical education classes are neglected and the teacher's entire efforts are put into coaching.

The physical educator's example plays a major role in providing leadership. One's effectiveness will depend to a great degree on what example is set in respect to such things as health habits, sportsmanship qualities, and relationships with people.

Determining whether objectives are being accomplished

The physical educator has the responsibility for utilizing scientifically valid measurement and evaluation techniques to determine whether the objectives of physical education are being accomplished.

If the physical educator is to evaluate the various types of programs and instruction and if he or she is to know what is being achieved through these programs and instruction and if the objectives that have been set are being met, it is imperative that acceptable measurement and evaluation techniques are used. These will enable individual and program weaknesses, quality of instruction, and progress achieved to be determined.

Some current measurement and evaluation techniques have failed to be scientifically evaluated or else have fallen below acceptable standards. In view of these conditions, it is necessary to ensure that only materials which meet acceptable scientific criteria are used. There are several excellent measurement and evaluation books in physical education that list and discuss scientific instruments and tests that will yield valid results.

Measurement and evaluation techniques enable one to determine an individual's physical condition, traits, or characteristics in respect to physical, motor, intellectual, and social development. Furthermore, they enable the physical educator to evaluate practices concerned with program administration, leadership, facilities, and activities. They may be utilized for purposes of guidance, motivation, diagnosis, ability grouping, prognosis, research, grading, and determining achievement. They should, however, be considered as tools and not as ends in themselves.

Reevaluating program

The physical educator has the responsibility for reevaluating the program in the light of measurement and evaluation results. The results that are compiled, tabulated, and analyzed should aid in determining whether the program being followed and the techniques being used are satisfactory and accomplishing the objectives of physical education. If, through a careful analysis, it appears that progress is not being made, the program and instructional techniques should be reevaluated in light of the findings and the necessary changes made. Such a procedure places physical education on a more scientific basis and enables it to render a greater service to participants in the program. Tests should not be given just for the sake of testing and the results placed in a file and allowed to gather dust. Instead they should be utilized to further the program and to help the individuals who are participating. Furthermore, they should not take up too much of the time allotted to the program.

GROUPS TO WHOM PHYSICAL EDUCATORS IN SCHOOLS AND COLLEGES ARE ACCOUNTABLE

The physical educator performs duties for the student, the department, the faculty and school, the community, and the profession.

The student

The teacher's first accountability is to the student. The teacher should know the student physically, mentally, emotionally, and socially, as well as his or her background, needs, and characteristics. The teacher should view the student as a growing and maturing human being who can be guided by the teacher and helped to progress toward worthwhile educational goals. The teacher has the responsibility to help the student develop skills, master the knowledge, and acquire attitudes and social qualities that will help this person fulfill his or her potential.

The department

The teacher is usually one member of a team—the faculty and staff of the department of physical education. The duties that befall the department, such as program planning, grading, testing, counseling, caring for equipment and facilities, and keeping records, must be shared by members of the department. Ethical standards of conduct should prevail, and there should be mutual support of colleagues. Each member of the staff should strive to be a valuable and important member of the team.

The faculty and school

The teacher must also recognize that he or she is a member of a school faculty. This position carries with it many responsibilities that are a part of administering a program for students. All teachers must share in this endeavor, which includes obligations in regard to upholding school policies, sharing mutual responsibilities such as supervising student activities, and respecting the total curriculum. Teachers of physical education must see the total educational plan and how all parts of it contribute to the education of young people. Physical education is an important part of the total plan, but at the same time it is only one part. Furthermore, since school faculty meetings represent an important medium for school planning, discussion of problems, and interpreting to colleagues each area of the curriculum, physical educators have a responsibility to be in attendance at these meetings.

The community

The physical educator is accountable to the community. The support gained for the program of which he or she is a part depends largely on the program itself and the way in which the citizens of the community view it. The responsibilities of the physical education staff in developing a close community relationship include presenting a sound program, giving leadership to community-sponsored activities in their field of endeavor, and supporting worthwhile community endeavors.

The profession

All physical educators owe some time and effort to the profession of which they are a part. This obligation can be carried out by joining professional organizations, serving on committees and as officers of the associations, and supporting professional endeavors. Physical educators should also be in attendance at professional meetings and be familiar with the literature and developments related to the profession.

WHAT THE BEGINNING PHYSICAL EDUCATOR SHOULD EXPECT

The beginning physical educator is not going to find an ideal situation when he or she assumes the first job. Many times the theory learned in college is not applicable in a practical situation. The facilities may be limited, the community uninformed, the people disinterested, and administrators and colleagues uncooperative. These and other obstacles must be hurdled one at a time. However, physical educators should never lose the enthusiasm that prompted them to go into this chosen field of work. In time, with hard work and a wholesome attitude, changes will occur, and a more desirable situation will develop.

A few factors the beginning physical educator should recognize in taking the first job are as follows.

The workday and workweek will be long. The physical educator can expect to work 50, 60, or 70 hours weekly. The many duties to perform, persons to see, and obligations to render all make for a long day and week. One should expect long hours, but if a good job is done, the rewards will be great.

The daily schedule will be strenuous. The new physical educator may find that he or she has to work through an entire day with the exception of a small break for lunch. Some organizations require physical educators to supervise the parking lot, watch the lunchroom at the noon hour, see students who need to be disciplined after school, monitor detention halls, and perform 101 tasks. The new physical educator should take these extra responsibilities as part of the routine. However, after a period of time has been spent on the job, there should be an attempt to eliminate some of these undesirable tasks so that more time can be given to physical education responsibilities.

The clerical work will be heavy. The beginning physical educator will be involved in completing monthly attendance forms, requisitions for equipment, and many other records requiring clerical work. All these take time away from physical education duties and, as such, cannot be fully justified. However, the physical educator should recognize this as part of the job and undertake the responsibility.

The materials and facilities may be inadequate. Certain materials, in the form of equipment and supplies, as well as adequate facilities for physical education classes, are essential. However, because of the cost, in many communities they are not provided. The beginning physical educator should be sympathetic and understanding but, nevertheless, should strive to interpret the need for new materials and facilities so that a better job can be accomplished.

SELF-ASSESSMENT TESTS

These tests are to assist students in determining if material and competencies presented in this chapter have been mastered.

1. Outline the nature and scope of duties and services that physical educators perform.

2. List all the areas where physical educators teach, such as teaching movement experiences and handicapped persons, and then indicate some of the duties and services rendered by the physical educator assigned to each responsibility.

3. Describe the special duties performed by physical educators who have the following positions: coach, athletic trainer, researcher, exercise physiologist in industry, health spa director, and administrator.

4. You are a senior in college. A freshman major in physical education asks you a question about the various capacities in which physical educators perform their duties and what constitutes a normal teaching load. Give your answer.

5. You are student teaching. What duties do you perform in this capacity? What duties and services should you expect to perform as a full-time beginning physical education teacher?

READING ASSIGNMENT

Bucher, Charles A.: Dimensions of physical education, ed. 2, St. Louis, 1974, The C. V. Mosby Co., Reading selections 7, 9, 10, 17, 31, 41, 47, 49, 55, 56, and 60.

SELECTED REFERENCES

American Association for Health, Physical Education, and Recreation: Promising practices in elementary school physical education, Washington, D.C., 1969, The Association.

Arnheim, Daniel D., Auxter, David, and Crowe, Walter C.: Principles and methods of adapted physical education, ed. 2, St. Louis, 1973, The C. V. Mosby Co.

A Symposium by Selected Physical Educators: Dance as an art form in physical education, Journal of Health, Physical Education, and Recreation **35**:19, Jan., 1964.

Bucher, Charles A.: Health, physical education, and academic achievement, NEA Journal **54**:5, May, 1965.

Bucher, Charles A.: Administrative dimensions of health and physical education, including athletics, St. Louis, 1971, The C. V. Mosby Co.

Bucher, Charles A.: Administration of health and physical education programs including athletics, ed. 6, St. Louis, 1975, The C. V. Mosby Co.

Bucher, Charles A., and Bucher, Richard: Recreation for today's society, Englewood Cliffs, N.J., 1974, Prentice-Hall, Inc.

Bucher, Charles A., and Koenig, Constance: Methods and materials for secondary school physical education, ed. 5, St. Louis, 1978, The C. V. Mosby Co.

Bucher, Charles A., and Reade, Evelyn M.: Physical education and health in the elementary school, New York, 1971, Macmillan Publishing Co.

Carlton, Lessie, and Moore, Robert H.: Culturally disadvantaged children can be helped, NEA Journal **55**:13, Sept., 1966.

Cassidy, Rosalind: Counseling in the physical education program, New York, 1959, Appleton-Century-Crofts.

Christensen, Dagney: Creativity in teaching physical education to the physically handicapped child, Journal of Health, Physical Education, and Recreation **41**:73, March, 1970.

Clayton, Robert D., and Clayton, Joyce: Concepts and careers in physical education, Minneapolis, 1977, Burgess Publishing Co.

Fait, Hollis F.: Special physical education: adaptive, corrective, developmental, Philadelphia, 1972, W. B. Saunders Co.

Fantini, Mario D., and Weinstein, Gerald: The disadvantaged, New York, 1968, Harper & Row, Publishers.

Hammerman, Donald R., and Hammerman, William M.: Teaching in the outdoors, Minneapolis, 1972, Burgess Publishing Co.

Hanson, Carl H.: Teaching the handicapped child, Today's Education **58**:46, Dec. 1969.

Hellison, Donald R.: Humanistic physical education: a behavioral perspective, Englewood Cliffs, N.J., 1973, Prentice-Hall, Inc.

Jensen, Clayne R.: Outdoor recreation in America: trends, problems, and opportunities, Minneapolis, 1973, Burgess Publishing Co.

Kleinman, Seymour: What future for dance in physical education? Journal of Health, Physical Education, and Recreation **40**:101, Nov.-Dec., 1969.

Mayshark, Cyrus, and Foster, Roy A.: Health education in secondary schools: integrating the critical incident technique, ed. 3, St. Louis, 1972, The C. V. Mosby Co.

Mudra, Darrell: The coach and the learning process, Journal of Health, Physical Education, and Recreation **41**:26, May, 1970.

Oliver, James N.: Physical education for the visually handicapped, Journal of Health, Physical Education, and Recreation **41**:37, June, 1970.

Riessman, Frank: The culturally deprived child, New York, 1962, Harper & Row, Publishers.

Shriver, Eunice Kennedy: A new day for the mentally retarded, The Physical Educator **25**:99, Oct., 1968.

Willgoose, Carl E.: Health teaching in secondary schools, Philadelphia, 1977, W. B. Saunders Co.

PART SEVEN

THE PROFESSION

Courtesy D. M. Massé.

Wand relay at Waddell Elementary School, Manchester, Connecticut.

20

Professional organizations

INSTRUCTIONAL OBJECTIVES AND COMPETENCIES TO BE ACHIEVED

After reading this chapter the student should be able to—

1. Appreciate why professional organizations exist and why it is important for physical educators to be active members of these organizations.
2. Identify the major professional organizations associated with the field of physical education, including their purpose, nature of their membership, and relationship to the field of physical education.
3. Describe in detail the nature, purpose, and scope of the activities of the American Alliance for Health, Physical Education, and Recreation.

Professional organizations* are the heartbeat of the profession. The greatest changes in the profession have their beginnings in organization meetings and conferences. Curriculum development, teacher certification requirements, scholarly research, and hundreds of other topics are discussed in detail at conferences. The physical education profession has an imposing list of associations concerned with every aspect of the field.

All physical educators should belong to their state and national associations and to others, as far as it is practical and possible. The fact that many physical educators do not belong to their national association, for example, is indicated by statistics which show there are probably

---

*International professional organizations are discussed in Chapter 7.

more than 200,000 persons in the field today and approximately 40,000 members of the national association. Yet the thousands who are not members accept, experience, and participate in the advances, better working conditions, and benefits that the association has accomplished. This should not be the case. If all physical educators belonged to and worked for their professional organizations, the concerted effort of such a large professional group would result in greater benefits and more prestige for the profession.

WHY BELONG TO A PROFESSIONAL ASSOCIATION?

There are many advantages in belonging to a professional organization. Factors that every physical educator should recognize about such membership include the following:

1. *They provide opportunities for service.* With the many offices, committee responsibilities, and program functions that professional associations provide, the individual has an opportunity to render a service for the betterment of this field of work.

2. *They provide a channel of communication.* Communication in a profession is essential so that members may know about what is going on, the latest developments in teaching techniques, new emphases in program content, and many other trends that are happening continuously in a growing profession. Through associations, an effective channel of communications exists by way of the publications, meetings, and announcements that are periodically made.

3. *They provide a means for interpreting the profession.* There is a need to interpret one's

profession to the public on national, state, and local levels. This interpretation is essential if public support is to be achieved for the services rendered by the professional practitioner. The professional association provides an opportunity for the best thinking and ideas to be articulately interpreted far and wide. As a result of such endeavors, recognition, respect, prestige, and cooperation with other areas of education, professions, and the public in general can be achieved.

4. *They provide a source of help in solving one's professional and personal problems.* Each physical educator has problems, both professional and personal. Through their officers, members, conferences, and other media, professional associations can play an important role in solving these problems. If a person is a member of an association, he or she does not "go it alone" but, instead, is surrounded by professional help on all sides. Associations are interested in helping and rendering a service. The associations can be of assistance, for example, in solving a professional problem involving the administration of an adapted program or a personal problem of life insurance.

5. *They provide an opportunity for fellowship.* Through association conferences and meetings the physical educator gets to know others doing similar work, and this common denominator results in friendships and many enjoyable professional and social occasions. A person literally gets a "shot in the arm" by associating with other persons dedicated to the same field of endeavor.

6. *They provide an organ for research.* Professions must continually conduct research to determine how effective their programs are, how many contributions they are rendering to human beings, how valid their techniques are, and the answers to many other questions that must be known if the profession is to move ahead and render an increasingly larger service.

7. *They yield a feeling of belonging.* A basic psychological need is to have a feeling of being part of a group and accomplishing work that is recognized and important. A professional association can contribute much in meeting this human need.

8. *They provide a means for distributing costs.* The work accomplished by a professional

association is designed to help the members who belong to the association. The work accomplished requires financial means. By joining a professional association, physical educators help to share the expenses that they rightfully have the responsibility to share. If one participates in the benefits, one should also share in the costs of achieving these benefits.

PROFESSIONAL ORGANIZATIONS

It would be difficult to discuss all the organizations that pertain to the physical education profession. However, some of these organizations with which the physical educator should be familiar are discussed.

Amateur Athletic Union*

The Amateur Athletic Union (AAU) was founded in 1888. Its principal aim at that time was to protect amateur sports from being corrupted by unscrupulous athletes who, by such means as "fixed" games, side betting, and competing for money, were using amateur sports as a medium of profit. The leaders of the newly founded AAU proceeded to set down a clear definition of amateurism and established clear-cut standards that outlawed unscrupulous practices. Today the AAU is the largest and most influential organization governing amateur sports in the world. It serves as the governing body in the United States for such amateur sports as the following: basketball, baton twirling, bobsledding, boxing, gymnastics, handball, horseshoe pitching, judo, luge, skibobbing, swimming and diving, synchronized swimming, trampoline, water polo, weight lifting, and wrestling.

The objectives of the AAU include the following:

1. The encouragement and development of amateur sport and physical fitness
2. Maintaining integrity in competition
3. Making facilities and opportunities available to all
4. Providing the best possible contestants to represent the United States in international competition

*Some of the following information is taken from *You and the AAU*, a leaflet published by the Amateur Athletic Union, Indianapolis, Indiana.

The activities of the AAU are many and varied. It sponsors many adult programs, including fitness development programs. The AAU conducts pre-Olympic trials to aid with the selection of competitors, and today, as in the past, is involved in raising funds for the participation of American athletes in the Olympics. The AAU is the official representative of the United States in many international sports federations. Since 1949 it has sponsored an annual Junior Olympics for boys and girls between the ages of 9 and 17 years.

The AAU is directed by a Board of Governors, who serve without compensation. The paid employees of the AAU are the Executive Director and a staff of administrators, clerks, and secretaries.

The list of AAU publications includes *Amateur Athlete Yearbook,* a monthly magazine; AAU *News,* published monthly; *Directory of the* AAU, published annually; *Official* AAU *Handbook;* various sports guides and records; as well as rule books for the sports it governs.

Headquarters are at 3400 West 86th St., Indianapolis, Ind. 46268.

American Academy of Physical Education

The American Academy of Physical Education was established "to advance knowledge, raise standards, and bestow honors in the field of physical education, health education, and recreation." This academy was founded in 1926. Clark W. Hetherington, R. Tait McKenzie, Thomas Storey, William Burdick, and Jay B. Nash were the first members. It presently has about 100 members.

Individuals are elected to membership in this academy as a result of qualifications that include making significant contributions to these specialized fields through research, writing, or exceptional service. The principal types of fellows or memberships are designated active and associate fellows, fellows in memoriam, associate fellows (in the United States), and corresponding fellows (from other countries).

The academy is committed to the function of furthering scholarship and excellence in the field of physical education. It confers awards for excellent literary, administrative, and research contributions to individuals and citations to organizations or institutions.

In a publication entitled *The Academy Papers,* the academy publishes, from time to time, papers presented by fellows, position statements, studies developed for and by the academy, and the R. Tait McKenzie Memorial Lecture presented at its annual meeting.

American Alliance for Health, Physical Education, and Recreation

The American Alliance for Health, Physical Education, and Recreation (AAHPER) was established in 1885 under the title of American Association for Advancement of Physical Education. The leaders in this initial organization were some thirty-five physicians, educators, and other individuals. They were called together by Dr. William G. Anderson, then on the staff of Adelphi Academy. Other physical education leaders who were prominent in the early history of the association were Dr. Hitchcock of Amherst, Dr. Sargent of Harvard, Dr. Gulick of the Young Men's Christian Association, Dr. Arnold of Arnold College, and Dr. Savage of Oberlin College. In 1903 the name of the association was changed to American Physical Education Association. In 1937 the Departments of School Health and Physical Education of the National Education Association were combined to form the American Association for Health and Physical Education, a department of the National Education Association. In 1938 the term *recreation* was added to the title.

In 1974 the AAHPER was officially reorganized to give more visibility and autonomy to the various specialties and fields of endeavor of which the organization is composed. Each of the major areas of endeavor became an association with its own offices, budget, etc., and the AAHPER in its totality became an alliance.

Under the reorganization plan, the AAHPER is now the American Alliance for Health, Physical Education, and Recreation. Following are the seven associations that comprise this alliance:

American Association for Leisure and Recreation Services (AALRS)
American School and Community Safety Association (ASCSA)
Association for the Advancement of Health Education (AAHE)
Association for Research, Administration, and Professional Councils (ARAPC)

National Association for Girls and Women in Sport (NAGWS)
National Association for Sports and Physical Education (NASPE)
National Dance Association (NDA)

Since the National Association for Girls and Women in Sport (NAGWS) has taken on new dimensions since the passage of Title IX and with a membership of approximately 13,000, its various substructures are listed here:

Affiliated Boards of Officials
Association for Intercollegiate Athletics for Women
Organization of Athletic Administrators
National Intramural Sports Council
National Coaches Council
Organization of GWS State Chairpersons
Athletic Training Council

The national office of the American Alliance for Health, Physical Education, and Recreation is located at 1201 16th St. N.W., Washington, D.C. 20036.

The publications of the alliance are many and varied. Starting in 1896, the *American Physical Education Review* was the official publication.

This was discontinued in 1929 when it was combined with the *Pentathlon,* the publication of the Middle West Society of Physical Education. Then the new publication of the association became known as the *Journal of Health and Physical Education.* This periodical is known at the present time as the *Journal of Physical Education and Recreation.* The AAHPER also publishes the *Research Quarterly, Update,* and *School Health Review.* In addition, it publishes many other pamphlets, books, and materials pertinent to the work of the alliance.

The services performed by the alliance include the following:

1. Holding state, district, and national conventions periodically
2. Acting as a clearinghouse for information concerning positions in health, physical education, and recreation
3. Publishing pamphlets, brochures, and other pertinent information
4. Influencing public opinion
5. Providing consultant services in related areas
6. Acting as a consultant to the President's Council on Physical Fitness and Sports
7. Working with legislatures concerning education and research programs

Exhibit hall at an AAHPER convention.

Members of the AAHPER are designated as professional members, associate members, fellows, life members, life fellows, student members, honorary members, emeritus members, and contributing members.

The AAHPER Student Action Council (SAC) is an organization of students that works for the benefit of its members through student involvement. The group's objectives include (1) greater student involvement in AAHPER, (2) promotion of professionalism among majors, and (3) the promotion of professional interest groups. The alliance in cooperation with SAC has made available special membership plans for students.

American College of Sports Medicine

On April 23, 1954, a few outstanding leaders in the fields of medicine, physiology, and physical education met in New York City and founded the American College of Sports Medicine (ACSM). The purposes this group set forth for the association include the following:

1. To promote and advance scientific studies concerning sports and other motor activities
2. To cooperate with other organizations concerned with sports medicine and related areas
3. To encourage research and postgraduate work in related areas
4. To publish a journal and maintain a library concerned with sports medicine and related areas

Current membership in the organization consists of representatives of nearly every state in the Union, as well as of many foreign countries. Of the three membership categories (medicine, physiology, physical education), the most numerous is physical education, with medicine being a close second.

The college is affiliated with the International Federation of Sportive Medicine, an organization that has played an important role for many years in Europe and South America. The official publication of the International Federation of Sports Medicine is the *Journal of Sports Medicine and Physical Fitness.* In 1969 the college began publication of a periodical entitled *Medicine and Science in Sports.*

The activities of the college and the research papers cover topics such as the treatment and prevention of athletic injuries, the effects of physical activity on health, and the scientific aspects of training.

The constitution of the American College of Sports Medicine provides for various types of membership. They are fellows, members, student members, fellows emeriti, and honorary fellows.*

The American College of Sports Medicine has its national office at the University of Wisconsin, 1440 Monroe St., Madison, Wis. 53706.

American Corrective Therapy Association

The American Corrective Therapy Association (ACTA), formerly the Association for Physical and Mental Rehabilitation, is a nationwide professional organization operated for educational and scientific purposes.

It was formally organized in October, 1946, by a group of corrective therapists attending a special course of instruction at the Veterans Administration Hospital, Topeka, Kansas.

In 1969 the name of the organization was changed to the American Corrective Therapy Association.†

The objectives of the association include the following:

1. Promotion of medically prescribed therapy
2. Advancement of education and training in related areas
3. Encouragement of research and publication of related articles
4. Engagement in and encouragement of activities that would be advantageous to medical rehabilitation

Membership in the American Corrective Therapy Association is divided into four categories:

1. *Active:* for those actively engaged in corrective or exercise therapy under the supervision of a licensed physician
2. *Professional:* for those working in allied fields

---

*Constitution and By-Laws.
†Information taken from a letter from the Executive Director.

3. *Associate:* for those interested in the field and wishing to receive the *Journal*
4. *Student:* for students enrolled in accredited school of health and physical education

Through its recruitment and placement committee, the association has much to offer its membership in the following areas of rehabilitation employment:

1. Special schools and camps for handicapped and atypical children
2. Government, public, and private rehabilitation clinics and hospitals: general medical and surgical, neuropsychiatric, and domiciliary
3. Armed services hospitals
4. Nursing homes
5. Recreational programs for the handicapped
6. Research

The association publishes the *Journal of American Corrective Therapy,* formerly the *Journal of the Association for Physical and Mental Rehabilitation,* which is a bimonthly magazine that contains information on education and scientific research; an *Information Bulletin;* and the yearly *Association Brochure.*

For more information contact the American Corrective Therapy Association, located at V.A. Hospital, 1030 Jefferson Ave., Memphis, Tenn. 38104.

American School Health Association

The American School Health Association (ASHA) is interested in improving health services, health instruction, and healthful living in the nation's schools. It was organized October 13, 1926,* as the American Association of School Physicians, and for some time only physicians were eligible to become members. The number of persons who belonged to the organization in its early years was small, but the association grew rapidly.

In 1927 the name was changed to the School Physicians Association, and a journal was published called the *School Physicians' Bulletin.* In 1937 the name of the organization was changed again to the American School Health Association. The membership requirements were broadened to include not only physicians but

also dentists, nurses, nutritionists, public health workers, and others whose professional training included the premedical sciences and who were engaged in school health work. During this transition period, the name of the official publication was changed from the *School Physicians' Bulletin* to the *Journal of School Health.*

The American School Health Association works closely with the American Public Health Association. Annual meetings are held jointly, and ideas are exchanged. Much of the work performed by the association is done through committees.

Membership in the association, in addition to providing a subscription to the *Journal of School Health,* offers other advantages, including informational service and the opportunity to help in promoting higher standards for the profession and to participate in other work to advance the profession. The address of the American School Health Association is ASHA Building, P.O. Box 416, Kent, Ohio 44240.

Association for Intercollegiate Athletics for Women (AIAW)

The Association for Intercollegiate Athletics for Women was established in 1971 by the Division of Girls' and Women's Sports (DGWS) of the AAHPER. The purpose for founding this association was to provide an autonomous organization to lead and govern women's intercollegiate sports programs. All colleges and universities were invited to become active or associate institutional members in 1971-1972. Seventy-three colleges and universities became associate members and 205 charter members. The first officers of the newly formed association took over in July, 1972. By the time the first Delegate Assembly was held in Kansas City, November 4-6, 1973, there were 405 institutional members; today there are approximately 800 members.

The DGWS, Commissioners of intercollegiate athletics for women, and the executive board of the AIAW worked for many years carefully planning the new organization prior to the first delegate assembly. At this initial assembly meeting a constitution and bylaws were developed.

The association aims at encouraging equality

---

*Information taken from Program, Nov. 13, 1968.

of opportunity for girls and women, as well as excellence of performance that is consistent with sound higher educational goals.* For more information contact the AAHPER at 1201 16th St., N.W., Washington, D.C. 20036.

Canadian Association for Health, Physical Education, and Recreation

The Canadian Association for Health, Physical Education, and Recreation (CAHPER) was organized originally as the Canadian Physical Education Association in 1933 through the joint efforts of the Quebec Physical Education Association and the Toronto Physical Education Association. The "father" of physical education in Canada was the late Dr. Arthur S. Lamb of McGill University, which was the alma mater of Dr. James Naismith and Dr. R. Tait McKenzie.

In 1948 the association changed its name to the Canadian Association for Health, Physical Education, and Recreation. In 1951 it became an incorporated body, the original signing officers being John Lang, Iveagh Munro, and Gordon Wright, three outstanding Canadian physical educators.

The aims of the association are as follows:

1. To encourage the improvement of the standards of those engaged in the furtherance of health education, physical education, and recreation
2. To provide such means of promotion as will serve the establishment of adequate programs under the direction of approved leadership
3. To stimulate a wide, intelligent, and active interest in health education, physical education, and recreation
4. To acquire and disseminate accurate information concerning it
5. To cooperate with kindred interests and organizations in the furtherance of these aims

The various types of memberships in the CAHPER are a fellow membership, a professional membership, an associate membership, and a student membership. The address of CAHPER is 333 River Rd., Vanier City, Ontario, Canada.

---

*Girls' and Women's Sports: First AIAW Delegate Assembly, Journal of Health, Physical Education, and Recreation **45:**79, March, 1974.

The publication of the CAHPER is the *Journal of the Canadian Association for Health, Physical Education, and Recreation.* It is published six times a year. The membership of the association provides each province of Canada having representation.

College Sports Information Directors of America

The College Sports Information Directors of America (SIDS) was formed in 1957 after separating from the American College Public Relations Association. The primary objectives of the organization include standardizing sport statistics, press box procedures and routines, and score books. The organization is composed of individuals in college and university sports information departments, public relations departments, and news bureaus. The association has active, associate, and student memberships.

Some of the activities sponsored by SIDS include the sponsorship of university and college division and academic all-American football, basketball, and baseball teams. The SIDS gives the Jake Wade Award annually to a person associated with the communication media for outstanding work in covering or working with colleges. SIDS also supports the Helms Hall Foundation and Hall of Fame and annually makes awards to individuals named to the Helms Hall of Fame by SIDS. The organization also publishes a monthly *News-Digest.*

For more information write the Secretary-Treasurer, Princeton University, c/o Jadwin Gymnasium, Princeton, N.J. 08540.

Delta Psi Kappa

Delta Psi Kappa is a professional organization for women majors or minors in health, physical education, and recreation. The purpose of this organization is to stimulate fellowship among women in these specialized fields, to promote high educational standards, and to promote opportunities and mutual service among the women in these professions.

Delta Psi Kappa was founded in 1916 with thirteen members and was incorporated by the state of Indiana. Chapters have gradually been established in various colleges and universities throughout the United States, and alumnae organizations have been set up in some cities. Delta Psi Kappa recently absorbed Phi Delta Pi, a national professional education fraternity for women.

Through various funds and wards, Delta Psi Kappa helps to stimulate high educational standards and worthwhile projects. It supports an Educational Loan Fund for promising members who wish to use it for study. It also has a biennial Research Fellowship Fund that is used to make an award to a woman doing some outstanding research in health, physical education, and recreation.

The official publication of Delta Psi Kappa is *The Foil,* which is published semiannually. The fraternity also publishes a newsletter semiannually entitled *The Psi Kap Shield.*

A minimum of ten women must constitute a group petitioning the national organization for membership. There are six kinds of membership: active, alumnae, inactive, honorary, alumnae associate, and active associate.

The address of Delta Psi Kappa is Route 1, Box 125, Winnecone, Wis. 54986.

National Association of Intercollegiate Athletics

The National Association of Intercollegiate Athletics (NAIA) is a group of colleges and universities organized for the purpose of attacking cooperatively the problems that face them in the administration of a sound, challenging intercollegiate athletic program.

The association is recognized as a "small college" organization. The enrollment of the institutions in it ranges from a few colleges, with under 200 students, to many institutions, with enrollment between 3,000 and 6,500 students. The average enrollment of the institutions with the NAIA, however, is approximately 1,172 students.

Within the membership are all types of institutions, from the private college and university, of which many are controlled and financed by religious denominations, to the state college and university.

Publications include the *NAIA News, NAIA Coach, NAIA Official Records Book,* and the *NAIA Handbook.*

Membership in the NAIA is based on the size of the undergraduate male enrollment of the member college and is on a sliding scale.

The objectives of this association as stated in its constitution include the following:

1. To establish an acceptance code of ethics
2. To establish uniform officiating and interpretation of rules
3. To establish uniformity of equipment
4. To cooperate with other organizations
5. To establish an acceptable eligibility code
6. To cooperate in the solution of related problems
7. To publicize the national association
8. To conduct research projects in related areas
9. To improve public relations
10. To establish a financially sound association

The NAIA has a national office at 1205 Baltimore, Kansas City, Mo. 64105.

National Association of Physical Education for College Women—now part of National Association for Physical Education in Higher Education (NAPEHE)

The National Association of Physical Education for College Women, although formally organized in 1924, had its beginning before this time. In 1909 Miss Amy Morris Homans issued an invitation to directors of physical education to meet at Wellesley College. This group continued to meet annually after this first meeting with Miss Homans and gradually grew into the Eastern Society, which was organized in 1915. Later, in 1917 and 1921 the Midwest and Western Societies, respectively, were organized. Then, in 1924 these three societies united and formed a national association at a meeting in Kansas City. The national association represents five district regional groups.

The purpose of the National Association of Physical Education for College Women is to investigate and study problems that characterize departments of physical education for women in the various colleges and universities. Since its inception, this organization has concerned itself with such problems as establishing standards for policies, equipment, and programs; promoting research studies and making findings available to all; promoting sane athletic policies in institutions of higher learning; and developing an interest in women's health, skill development, and proper emotional adjustment.

Membership is open to all women teachers of

physical education in colleges and universities. To be a member of the national organization, one must be a member of the district organization. Honorary members of the National Association of Physical Education for College Women pay no dues. Active and associate members pay a small fee yearly. The national association holds meetings biennially, whereas the districts hold their meetings annually.

In June, 1978, the National Association for College Women joined forces with the National College of Physical Education Association for Men to form one association, the *National Association for Physical Education in Higher Education* (NAPEHE). An interim board of directors composed of officers of both associations will hold office for a period of a year.

National Collegiate Athletic Association

The history of the National Collegiate Athletic Association (NCAA) began in the early 1900s. Because of the alarming number of football injuries and the fact that there was no uniform or national control of the game of football, a conference of representatives of universities and colleges, primarily from the eastern section of the United States, was held on December 12, 1905. Preliminary plans were made for a national body to assist in the formulation of sound requirements for intercollegiate athletics, particularly football, and the name Intercollegiate Athletic Association was suggested. At a meeting March 31, 1906, a constitution and by-laws were adopted and issued. The first annual convention of the Intercollegiate Athletic Association was held at the Murray Hill Hotel, New York City, on December 29, 1906. On December 29, 1910, the name of the association was changed to the National Collegiate Athletic Association.

The purposes of the NCAA are designed to uphold the principles of institutional control of all collegiate sports; to maintain a uniform code of amateurism in conjunction with sound eligibility rules, scholarship requirements, and good sportsmanship; to promote and assist in the expansion of intercollegiate and intramural sports; to formulate, copyright, and publish the official rules of play; to sponsor and supervise regional and national meets and tournaments for member institutions (presently the NCAA conducts national meets and tournaments in many sports); to preserve collegiate athletic records; and to serve as headquarters for collegiate athletic matters of national import.

To achieve membership in the NCAA, a college must be accredited and compete in a minimum of four sports each year on an intercollegiate level. At least one sport must be engaged in during the normal three major sport seasons. Dues are scaled according to the enrollment of the college.

The NCAA is a voluntary association of member* institutions and affiliated associations. Its services include the following:

1. Serving as a discussion, legislative, and administrative body for college athletics
2. Maintaining a national headquarters staff
3. Publishing official guides in nine sports
4. Conducting national championship events in many sports
5. Participating in United States Olympic and Pan-American athletic events
6. Maintaining a central clearing and counseling agency in the field of college athletic administration
7. Providing a film library covering play in national meets and tournaments
8. Administering group travel and medical insurance programs for its member institutions

The NCAA has an office at U.S. Highway 50 and Nall Ave., P.O. Box 1906, Shawnee Mission, Kan. 66222.

National College Physical Education Association for Men—now part of National Association for Physical Education in Higher Education (NAPEHE)

In 1897 the National College Physical Education Association for Men (NCPEAM) was founded under the name of the Society of College Gymnasium Directors. In 1909 it became known as the Society of College Directors of Physical Education and in 1933 as the College Physical Education Association.

The men present at the organization in 1897 included Dr. Anderson of Yale, Dr. Sargent of Harvard, Dr. Seaver of Yale, Dr. Linhart of Ohio State, Dr. Savage of Columbia, Professor Goldie of Princeton, Mr. Marvel of Wes-

---

*Encyclopedia of associations, ed. 8, Detroit, 1973, Gale Research Co., Booktower.

leyan, Mr. F. H. Cann of New York University, and Mr. Sharp of Yale.

The association was formed for men performing health and physical education work in colleges. The purpose of the organization is the advancement of college health, physical education, and recreation in institutions of higher learning. The association meets annually.

The National College Physical Education Association for Men has three types of members. First, there are active members, or those who are directly engaged in some phase of college health, physical education, or recreation; second, associate members, or those to whom the association has extended membership by reason of work related to the fields of health, physical education, and recreation but who are not teaching in a college; and, third, honorary members, or those who have been selected by the association and who may be active or former active members. Represented in the association are more than 300 different colleges in five countries.

The official publication of the NCPEAM is *The Proceedings of the College Physical Education Association*. The NCPEAM also publishes the monograph *Quest* in conjunction with the National Association for Physical Education of College Women.

In June, 1978, the NCPEAM joined with the National Association for Physical Education of College Women to form one association. The new association is called the *National Association for Physical Education in Higher Education* (NAPEHE).

National Education Association

Every physical educator associated with the schools in the United States should be familiar with the National Education Association (NEA). Its central offices are located at 1201 16th St. N.W., Washington, D.C. 20036.

T. W. Valentine and D. B. Hager were the two educators who were largely responsible for calling the first meeting of the National Teachers Association in 1857. This was the organization that later became known as the National Education Association. The first meeting of the National Teachers Association was on August 26, 1857, in Philadelphia. Forty-three

educators representing twelve states were in attendance.

The purposes and services of the National Education Association are concerned with promoting education in this country. In doing so, it works toward the advancement of the interests of those in the teaching profession, helps to better care for the welfare of all American youth, and is interested in and strives to provide for the education of all individuals.

Any student enrolled in a teacher education program in a college or university may become a student NEA member at a reduced rate by joining a chapter of the student National Education Association. The membership year is from September 1 to August 31.

The publications of the National Education Association are too numerous to list in this chapter. However, the one that has the widest circulation and that is representative of the association is *Today's Education*.

National Federation of State High School Associations (Athletic)

The National Federation of State High School Associations (Athletic) (NFSHSA) was founded in 1920. It consists of a federation of the fifty state high school athletic associations in the United States; in addition, there are nine Canadian affiliates. The total membership in the association consists of more than 20,000 high schools. The purposes of the NFSHSA are to protect the interests of high school athletics as they occur on an interstate basis and to coordinate the activities of the various state high school athletic associations. The federation publishes various materials relating to high school athletics, and it also is involved in testing equipment used in athletic programs. For more information write to the NFSHSA, 400 Leslie St., P.O. Box 98, Elgin, Ill. 60120

National Intramural Association*

In the school year 1948-1949 William Wasson, an instructor at Dillard University in New Orleans, received a Carnegie grant-in-aid to study intramural programs in twenty-five col-

---

*The information on the National Intramural Association was contributed by Ellis J. Mendelsohn.

leges and universities. It was from this study that he conceived the idea of having the intramural directors meet annually and of developing a medium through which an exchange of information and ideas could take place.

The first meeting was held at Dillard University on February 22 and 23, 1950. At this meeting the National Intramural Association was formed.

The National Intramural Association is an affiliate member of the AAHPER. Its objectives are as follows:

1. To provide a common meeting ground for intramural directors and members of their staff to discuss current problems and policies
2. To provide an opportunity to exchange ideas and thoughts for improvement in the operation of the intramural program
3. To determine policy, principles, and procedures to guide intramural directors in performance of their duties
4. To promote and encourage intramural and recreational programs
5. To serve as a medium for the publication of research papers on intramurals of both members and nonmembers
6. To work in close cooperation with the AAHPER, the National Recreation and Park Association, and the Educational Policy Committee of our respective institutions

The official publication of the National Intramural Association is *The Proceedings of the Annual Intramural Conference.*

Membership in the association, in addition to providing a subscription for a copy of the annual conference proceedings, offers other advantages, including information service and an opportunity to help in promoting higher standards for the profession.

National Junior College Athletic Association

The National Junior College Athletic Association (NJCAA) is an organization composed of the majority of junior colleges in the United States that sponsor intercollegiate athletic programs. The NJCAA was conceived in 1937 and became a functioning organization on May 14, 1938. The primary purpose of this organization is to promote and supervise a national program of junior college sports and activities that would achieve the educational objectives of athletics.*

The association is organized into nineteen regions. The member colleges elect a regional director in each of the nineteen regions and conduct their regional affairs within the framework of NJCAA constitution and by-laws. The regional directors hold their annual legislative assembly meeting at Hutchinson, Kansas, to determine the policies, procedures, and programs of the NJCAA.

The NJCAA conducts national championship events in football, cross-country, basketball, wrestling, golf, and tennis. In addition, the association sponsors national invitational events in rifle, soccer, swimming, gymnastics, lacrosse, and skiing.†

The NJCAA has several official publications. The *JUCO Review* presents and interprets the program of the NJCAA to its members. The *NJCAA Handbook* is a compilation of the constitution, by-laws, policies, procedures, programs, eligibility, rules, and history of the organization. In addition to these publications, the organization publishes numerous materials that keep its members informed of the latest developments within the organization.†

The National Junior College Athletic Association is a nonprofit organization. The income received from its programs is turned back toward broadening the scope of the organization and bettering the program for the member colleges.†

The address of the NJCAA is Box 1586, Hutchinson, Kan. 67501.

National Recreation and Park Association

The National Recreation and Park Association (NRPA) is an organization dedicated to the conservation and beautification of the environment and the development, improvement, and expansion of park and recreation programs, facilities, leadership, and services. It is an independent, nonprofit organization whose primary goal is to continue the advance of environmental quality and an improved quality of life.‡

The National Recreation and Park Associa-

---

*National Junior College Athletic Association Handbook.
† National Junior College Athletic Association Brochure.
‡ PROFILE of National Recreation and Park Association.

Photo by LeMoyne Coates.

Colleges like St. Louis Community College at Florissant Valley, Missouri, benefit from the National Junior College Athletic Association.

tion had at least part of its beginnings in 1906 when the Playground Association of America was organized. At the time of the founding of this association, only forty-one cities reportedly had playgrounds with qualified leadership. One of the association's main objectives was to achieve the goal of having adequately trained men and women conducting play and recreation programs on a community basis. It also furthered the cause of spending leisure in a wholesome, profitable manner.

In 1965 the American Association of Zoological Parks and Aquariums, the American Institute of Park Executives, the American Recreation Society, the National Conference on State Parks, and the National Recreation Association united to form the National Recreation and Park Association. (In 1971 the American Association of Zoological Parks and Aquariums again became an independent organization.)

The objectives of the NRPA are public policy formation, education, community service, citizen development service, and professional development services.

The national headquarters of the NRPA is at 1601 N. Kent St., Arlington, Va. 22209, where a professional staff of specialists in parks, recreation, conservation, and associated fields is carrying on the work of the association.*

North American Society for the Psychology of Sport and Physical Activity

The North American Society for the Psychology of Sport and Physical Activity (NASPSPA) was founded in 1965 and became incorporated as a nonprofit corporation in 1967. NASPSPA is affiliated with the International Society for the Psychology of Sports (ISPS).†

The society is composed of professional people (psychologists, psychiatrists, and physical educators) whose primary purpose is to promote scientific research and relations within the framework of sport psychology and physical activity by means of meetings, investigations, publications, and other activities. Membership in NASPSPA is open to all people interested in the psychology of sports and physical activity.

The society publishes the *Sport Psychology Bulletin,* a quarterly bulletin, which keeps its members informed about affairs of the society,

---

*NRPA Fact Sheet.
†Encyclopedia of associations, ed. 8, Detroit, 1973, Gale Research Co., Booktower.

as well as the field of sports psychology in general. The society also publishes newsletters detailing the activities of the annual convention, which is usually held in the spring. For further information concerning the NASPSPA write to the society at 91 Children's Research Center, University of Illinois, Champaign, Ill. 61820.

The Philosophic Society for the Study of Sport

The Philosophic Society for the Study of Sport is a new organization founded in 1972 at the annual meeting of the American Philosophical Association, Eastern Division. The initial membership includes persons with varied backgrounds and skills, all having a widespread interest in the philosophy of sport. The central thrust of the organization is the scholarly investigation of sport, including implications for practical pursuit. There are four types of membership: sustaining, active, constituent, and student. There is no headquarters office.

Phi Epsilon Kappa Fraternity*

Phi Epsilon Kappa Fraternity was founded on April 12, 1912, at the Normal College, American Gymnastics Union, Indianapolis, Indiana. In 1920, with the establishment of the Beta chapter at the American College of Physical Education, it became a national organization.

The objectives of the Phi Epsilon Kappa Fraternity are as follows:

1. To further the individual welfare of its members
2. To foster scientific research in the fields of health education, physical education, recreation education, and safety education
3. To facilitate the exchange of information and experience gained in the various countries of the world concerning matters relating to the interdependent areas of health education, physical education, recreation education, and safety education, including programs, methods, techniques, material, training, and research
4. To promote sound community understanding leading to adequate support of these educational programs
5. To raise professional standards and ethics

---

*All information taken from a letter from the Executive Secretary.

Collegiate chapters must limit themselves to students and teachers of health education, physical education, recreation education, or safety education. Alumni chapters may propose and accept men professionally engaged in health education, physical education, recreation education, or safety education within the territory of their jurisdiction.

There are four types of membership in the fraternity. The active membership in collegiate chapters is for students and teachers in colleges and universities where a chartered chapter has been installed and in alumni chapters for men in physical education work. The honorary membership is for prominent persons in physical education work who have received the approval of the Grand Chapter. The extraordinary membership is for individuals who have retired from active physical education work and have been approved by an alumni chapter. Life membership is for alumni members who pay a prescribed fee.

The Phi Epsilon Kappa Fraternity publishes a professional magazine, *The Physical Educator,* which is available to nonmembers on a subscription basis. There are also other publications.

The central office of the Phi Epsilon Kappa Fraternity is at 619 E. 10th St., Indianapolis, Ind. 46219.

Physical Education Society of the Young Men's Christian Association of North America

The Physical Education Society of the Young Men's Christian Association of North America was founded in 1903. The purposes of this organization, as originally established, are as follows:

1. To unite in one body those professional workers in the Young Men's Christian Association who are related to physical education
2. To promote a fraternal spirit and fellowship among the members
3. To engage in original research
4. To study technical and professional problems
5. To cooperate with constituent or related bodies

The society includes over 900 persons in the YMCAS of North America. There are seven chapters in the society, divided geographically throughout the nation, such as Southern Area and New England.

The society, through its program, attempts to help in the realization of the objectives of the Young Men's Christian Association. When the YMCA was founded in London in 1844, physical as well as spiritual, educational, and social needs were recognized as being an essential for youth.

The first meeting of physical directors was held in Jamestown, New York, in 1902. In this same year the periodical *Physical Training* was published. This was later changed to the *Journal of Physical Education* and is published bimonthly.

For information about this association write to the National YMCA Headquarters, 291 Broadway, New York, N.Y. 10007.

Society of State Directors of Health, Physical Education, and Recreation

The idea and the initial impetus for the Society of State Directors of Health, Physical Education, and Recreation may be credited to James E. Rogers. The first meeting of the association was held in 1926, with Dr. Carl L. Schrader, State Director of Massachusetts, as the first president. James Rogers was elected secretary and served in this capacity for 15 years. The constitution for this organization was adopted in 1944.

The "basic beliefs"* of the society are concerned with the (1) comprehensive school health program; (2) physical education in preprimary, elementary, and secondary school programs, including instruction, extraclass activities and interscholastic athletics; and (3) school and community recreation. The "basic beliefs" call for a broad, constructive, continuing series of educational experiences in health, physical education, and recreation for every boy and girl every day throughout the entire school year. These "beliefs" also emphasize the school's responsibilities regarding the health, fitness, recreation, and self-improvement of adult members in the community.

The society has passed many resolutions during its history that have been pertinent to programs of health, physical education, and recreation. The society has also assisted in planning new facilities, written professional articles, and cooperated with various official and nonofficial agencies. The main publication of the society is *A Statement of Basic Beliefs.*

The society may be reached at the Office of Education, U.S. Department of Health, Education and Welfare, 400 Maryland Ave. S.W., Washington, D.C. 20202.

U.S. Collegiate Sports Council*

The U.S. Collegiate Sports Council (USCSC), an affiliate of the International University Sports Federation (FISU), was founded in 1968. The council has five members. They are the National Collegiate Athletic Association, National Intercollegiate Athletic Association, National Junior College Athletic Association, U.S. National Association, and American Alliance for Health, Physical Education, and Recreation.

The general purpose of the USCSC is to promote international understanding through collegiate athletics and physical education. The specific purpose of the association is to encourage increased United States' participation in the activities sponsored by the International University Sports Federation.

The USCSC organizes the U.S. teams for competition in aquatics, basketball, fencing, figure skating, gymnastics, ice hockey, judo, skiing, tennis, track and field, volleyball, and water polo. Competition in these activities is sponsored by the International University Sports Federation. The address of the USCSC is 1201 16th St. N.W., Washington, D.C. 20006.

Young Women's Christian Association of the U.S. of America

The Young Women's Christian Association (YWCA) was one of the first organizations for women to be founded in this country. It dates back to 1855, and since that time it has spread rapidly. Today there are YWCAS in seventy-eight countries. In the United States alone there

---

*The Society of State Directors of Health, Physical Education, and Recreation: A statement of basic beliefs, 1972.

*Data taken from Encyclopedia of associations, ed. 8, Detroit, 1973, Gale Research Co., Booktower.

are more than 8,100 locations where over 2.4 million persons participate as members of the YWCA. These locations include building-centered operations, decentralized units, residences, camps, colleges and university associations, and YWCA–USO Clubs.*

The Young Women's Christian Association has as its objectives the furtherance of democratic living and promoting educational and recreational programs to enrich the lives of girls and women.

The YWCA works for community health by means of a program that improves the health and welfare of girls and women. Members may participate in activities designed to improve one's knowledge of body mechanics, sex education, nutrition, family life, various diseases, and other areas necessary for healthful living. Through health education committees it has done research in respect to girls and women. It furthers coeducational activities.

Regular publications are *YWCA Magazine* (nine issues a year); *Y-Teen Scene* (four issues); *Interact* (student, five issues); *Staff-to-Staff Newsletter* (four issues); and *Public Affairs Newsletter* (six issues).

National headquarters of the YWCA is at 600 Lexington Ave., New York, N.Y. 10022.

SELF-ASSESSMENT TESTS

These tests are to assist students in determining if material and competencies presented in this chapter have been mastered.

1. You are president of the major club at your college. Your faculty advisor has asked you to make a

*The story of the YWCA (leaflet) and interview with Association and News Director.

presentation to the members of the major club on the topic: "Why Every Physical Educator Should Belong to Professional Physical Education Organizations." Write out your presentation. When you have finished, have a contest and see how many professional organizations each member of the club can list. Award a prize to the student who names the greatest number of professional organizations.

2. Identify each of the following professional organizations in a brief paragraph. Assume that you are preparing this report for a person who has never heard of these organizations before:

> Amateur Athletic Union
> American Academy of Physical Education
> AAHPER
> American College of Sports Medicine
> Association of Intercollegiate Athletics for Women
> Canadian Association for HPER
> Delta Psi Kappa
> National Association for Physical Education for College Women
> National College Physical Education Association for Men
> National Intramural Association
> National Junior College Athletic Association
> Phi Epsilon Kappa

3. Describe the AAHPER in detail, citing its purpose, types of membership, publications, and various associations that make up the alliance. Cite ten reasons why a student should be a member of the AAHPER and also be active in the Student Action Corps.

SELECTED REFERENCES

Material and information for each association should be obtained by writing directly to the association or organization in question.

21

Certification requirements and employment opportunities in physical education

INSTRUCTIONAL OBJECTIVES AND COMPETENCIES TO BE ACHIEVED

After reading this chapter the student should be able to—

1. Recognize the value of going to college and preparing for work in the field of physical education.
2. Ascertain what certification requirements should be met to teach physical education, coach, and be an athletic trainer in schools throughout the United States and to know the trends in certification requirements in today's changing educational scene.
3. Determine what employment opportunities exist today in teaching physical education in schools and colleges.
4. Determine what employment opportunities exist today in alternate physical education careers and allied areas, such as in health spas, industrial recreation and fitness programs, programs for the elderly, athletic and sport administration, correctional institutions, tourism, and health and recreation programs.
5. Formulate a plan for securing a position on graduation from college.

Certification requirements and employment opportunities for physical educators are in a period of transition. One important development is the trend to change certification requirements in the form of course credits to specific skill, knowledge, and other competencies. In the area of employment an important change is that physical educators are seeking alternate careers to teaching in schools and colleges. These and other developments make it especially important for the prospective physical educator to plan carefully for the future.

CONTINUED VALUE OF A COLLEGE DEGREE

Despite the opinion of some economists, other persons, and a few research studies, indicating that the noncollege graduate is just as well off economically and in other ways as the college degree recipient, there is new evidence to show that this is not true. According to recent research by the nonprofit Conference Board (a well-respected New York research organization) that conducts research in the areas of economics and management, a college degree represents an excellent investment from an economic point of view as well as in other ways.

Leonard A. Lecht, director of special projects research for the Conference Board, points out that in recent years the economic differential for college graduates has diminished.* For example, men 25 years of age and over with a college education received on an average 46% more income than high school graduates in 1969, but by 1974 this differential had dropped

---

*A college degree still maintains its aura, New York Times, July 20, 1977.

to 36%. However, Lecht adds, the average male college graduate still had a differential in his favor of $4,500.

To emphasize the importance of a college degree, Lecht points out that research indicates the decline of the last few years definitely should not be projected into the future. Some of the reasons why he is optimistic is that the research conducted by the Conference Board shows that the job squeeze is likely to ease in the coming years, making the college degree even more attractive to employers for the following reasons:

> Fewer people will be entering the labor market because of declining birth rates.
>
> Between 1974 and 1985 about 2.1 million jobs will have opened up for college graduates because of more stringent educational requirements (males)
>
> The growth in college enrollment is declining, with fewer persons competing for positions.
>
> Professional and technical employment is expected to continue to grow more rapidly than overall total employment.
>
> College graduates are three times less likely to become unemployed as noncollege graduates.
>
> Income progression is greater for college graduates.

The Conference Board's research stresses the economic value of a college degree for men. In light of equal opportunity employment for women, Title IX, and other developments, employment opportunities for women should be even brighter than for men in the future.

This research further stresses the economic value of a college education, but the physical educator after reading this chapter will find that there are many other benefits which will accrue as a result of a college degree. For example, the American Association of State Colleges and Universities cites that their research conducted by the Carnegie Commission on Higher Education, as well as that of other organizations, shows that "On the whole, college graduates are more satisfied with their work and their lives than noncollege graduates."

Physical educators, in most cases, must be certified before they can search for employment. Therefore certification is discussed in the first part of this chapter, followed by an exami-

nation of employment opportunities for physical educators, both within the teaching ranks and in alternate careers.

CERTIFICATION REQUIREMENTS

Years ago physical educators received little training and were required to meet few standards for teaching and in other fields of work. Gradually, however, as various states passed legislation incorporating physical education as part of school programs, as the length of preparatory period for physical educators increased, and as the work of physical education became recognized as a vital experience in education, more stress was placed on the importance of employing adequately trained people for physical education positions.

Although physical educators may find employment in some positions without meeting formal certification requirements, the trend is more and more in the direction of such requirements. Since teaching is one area of employment where considerable emphasis is placed on certification, this field of work will be stressed in this discussion.

Certification requirements represent a first step in any system that attempts to fill positions on the basis of merit. The minimum requirements for teaching, which comprise the rules and regulations concerning state teachers' certificates, are designed primarily to secure personnel who are professionally and personally well equipped. They are designed to protect children from poorly prepared and inefficient teachers, to protect the teaching profession from unqualified teachers whose standards are so low that instruction suffers, and finally, to protect administrators from local pressures urging the appointment of teachers who are not qualified for teaching positions.

A survey of the teacher certification requirements indicates a lack of uniformity for the certification of teachers in general and physical education teachers in particular. At the same time there are some conclusions and trends that may be drawn.

The certification requirements that prevail for the teaching of physical education have a considerable difference in nomenclature and qualifications listed. The physical educator who de-

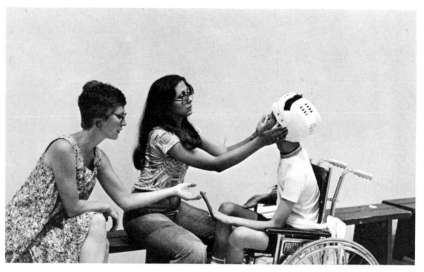

Courtesy Project Active.

Physical educators work with the handicapped at Monmouth College in New Jersey.

sires to teach in a particular state selects courses and develops competencies that will qualify him or her for teaching there. It is almost an impossibility to prepare for the teaching of physical education in all fifty states. However, if a physical educator's work is planned with care, the certification requirements for many states may be met with only an additional summer session's training or less.

The specialization requirements for certification in physical education, according to my survey, range from 47 semester hours to a low of 21 semester hours. However, where competency-based certification is in existence, the emphasis is on competencies acquired rather than courses and semester hour credits. Specific physical education courses and competencies that are required for certification vary from state to state. One survey identified some of the courses and competencies that are required in the various states: zoology, biology, anatomy, physiology, physiology of exercise, kinesiology, adapted physical education, first aid and safety, physical education activities, history and philosophy of physical education, administration of physical education, tests and measurements, health, and recreation.

General areas for certification requirements

There are ten general areas in which states have governing regulations for teacher certification. Since states differ in their requirements, however, the prospective teacher should inquire directly from the state education department, division of teacher certification, for exact requirements. To summarize these ten areas and the requirements presently established in the fifty states, the District of Columbia, and Puerto Rico, the following information is presented.

1. *Citizenship.* The District of Columbia, and Puerto Rico require United States citizenship or a declaration of intention clause. The teacher must be a citizen of the United States to qualify.

2. *Oath of allegiance of loyalty.* Approximately one half of the states, and the District of Columbia, and Puerto Rico require a loyalty oath for teacher certification. The others usually have a written statement that must be signed.

3. *Age.* The age requirement varies among states. The lowest age limit is 17 years. In general, 18 or 19 years of age is acceptable in states specifying a particular age. Some states have no stipulation in this regard.

4. *Professional preparation.* It is in this area that the greatest differences in state requirements may be

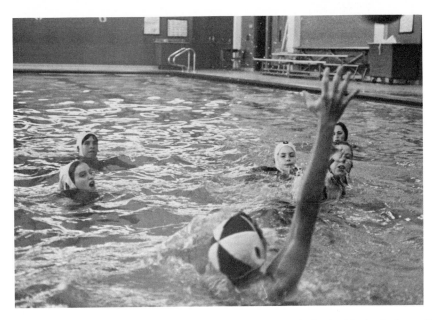

Coeducational water polo at the Cumberland Valley School District in Mechanicsburg, Pennsylvania.

found. Several states have specific courses that must be taken by candidates for certification. For example, American government and/or history, school health education, and the United States Constitution. Some of these special state requirements must be met before the first year of teaching, whereas others may be fulfilled within a certain period of time.

5. *Recommendation.* A large majority of states require a teaching candidate to have a recommendation from college or from the last place of employment.

6. *Fee.* A fee for certification, ranging from $1 to $20, is required in a majority of the states.

7. *Health certificate.* Approximately one half of the states, the District of Columbia, and Puerto Rico require a general health certificate; several states, the District of Columbia, and Puerto Rico require a chest x-ray examination.

8. *Employment.* Candidates from other states may need to have secured employment to become certified within some states.

9. *Course of study.* Beside these general areas of state requirements, basic and minimum regulations regarding the course of study must be followed for a candidate to qualify for specific certification in physical education. Again, the states differ in the number of credit hours necessary within the subject of physical education.

10. *Degrees.* In most states and the District of Co-

lumbia the bachelor's degree is required for regular certification of beginning school teachers. Five years of preparation are required for the regular certification of beginning school teachers.

Because of differences among states in regard to the ten general areas of certification that have been outlined, a certificate to teach in one state does not necessarily permit a teacher to teach in a different state. Reciprocity among states in the same region of the country is a growing reality but uncommon at the present time.

A further problem in certification presents itself where localities within a state have specific regulations governing selection of teachers. These are often more rigid than standards established by the state itself and usually involve factors such as teacher preparation or experience. An applicant may also have to pass a written and oral examination for local licensing. Information regarding local teaching requirements generally can be secured by writing to the board of education of the city in question.

Applicants for teaching positions should try to determine state and local regulations far in advance, if possible. In so doing they may select courses of study in college to meet the requirements. They should submit their applications ahead of time to become certified before accepting a position.

Types of certification

The type and value of certificates issued by the states vary nearly as much as do their regulations. In one state, for example, there may be two categories of certification, permanent and probationary, whereas in another state there may be many variations of certificates. The certificate to teach physical education is generally limited to this special field of work, but its validity may be for 1 year (probationary) or for life (permanent).

The value of the certificate again depends on state regulations. It may enable the holder to teach in any public school system within that state, except those where local standards require further qualifications. It may qualify the teacher to teach in neighboring states, depending on reciprocity agreements. It may also permit teaching in private schools within the state.

The prospective teacher or the experienced teacher seeking employment in a different state should not let these differences in state requirements and qualifications become a hindrance. An inquiry sent to the state or local department of education will provide the necessary information regarding certification.

Certification trends

Trends are clearly noticeable throughout the country in the certification of teachers. One thing that is obvious in studying certification requirements in the various states is that changes are taking place, five of the most significant of which are competency-based certification, approval of professional preparation programs by state departments of education, certification of coaches, separate certification of health and physical education teachers, and separate certification of elementary and secondary school teachers of physical education.

COMPETENCY-BASED CERTIFICATION

Support continues for an acceptable format of competency-based certification that focuses on the relevance of teacher preparation and compe-tence to state certification. It will take a number of years before certification laws based on competency are utilized in many states. The planning period is here now, and new approaches to competency-based certification are being tried and evaluated. Only through this process will a plan emerge that is acceptable to teachers, administrators, employers, and students. Many states have already gone on record in support of competency-based certification, and several states are already using this method of certification.

APPROVAL OF PROFESSIONAL PREPARATION PROGRAMS BY STATE DEPARTMENTS OF EDUCATION

There is a trend toward placing the responsibility for certification on the college or university where the prospective teacher receives his or her training. Several states have initiated such a certification program. In such cases the state department of education approves an institution's teacher-training program, and then the institution of higher learning recommends to the state department of education the students who have successfully completed the training program and who should be certified.

CERTIFICATION OF COACHES

There appears to be a trend toward the certification of coaches of athletic teams at the secondary school level throughout the United States. At the present time all states require that coaching personnel be certified to teach. Many states have no specific certification requirements for coaching but stress that coaching personnel should, if possible, be prepared in physical education. Several states are considering the certification of coaches, and a few states have some type of requirement for coaching.

An estimated one fourth of all head coaches in secondary schools throughout the United States have no professional preparation for this particular function. Many coaches obviously are not trained in the field of physical education. In view of the important responsibility that coaches have for the sound physical education and safety of their players, this represents a critical problem. Some coaches, for example, know nothing about first aid and thus when injuries occur, are at a loss to know what should be done to ensure the health of the injured player.

The lack of preparation of coaching personnel has resulted in a determined effort on the part of many educators, including physical education personnel, certification officials, the American Alliance for Health, Physical Education, and Recreation, Association of Men's Athletics, and others, to require coaches to have at least minimum preparation in this field. The AAHPER points out that such preparation should include medical aspects of athletic coaching, which includes a knowledge of medical examinations, protective equipment and facilities, training, injuries, and safety problems; princi-

ples and problems of coaching, including such areas as personal qualities of the coach, organization for athletics, training rules, and coaching ethics; theory and techniques of coaching, including educational implications of athletics, scouting, and rules and regulations; kinesiological foundations of coaching, including knowledge of the human anatomy and mechanics of movement; and physiological foundations of coaching, including exercise physiology factors, nutrition, drugs, and conditioning. As a result of this national effort, a few states have instituted some requirements to ensure better qualified coaches.

Standards for coaching certification were identified by the AAHPER through their Task Force on Certification of high school coaches.

Coaches need special preparation for their duties.

Following are the essential areas identified by the task force:

1. Medical aspects of athletic coaching
2. Sociological and psychological aspects of coaching
3. Theory and techniques of coaching
4. Kinesiological foundations of coaching
5. Physiological foundations of coaching

The Illinois Association for Professional Preparation in Health, Physical Education, and Recreation believed that the state should establish certification standards for academic teachers who desire to coach and recommended the following:

1. Coaches should have a major or minor in physical education or a major or minor in coaching.
2. Fifteen semester hours should be taken in the following areas:
   a. Medical aspects of athletic training
   b. Principles and problems of coaching
   c. Theory and techniques of coaching
   d. Kinesiological foundations of coaching
   e. Physiological foundations of coaching

Some of the states that provide some type of certification requirements for coaching personnel and the nature of the requirements follow.

Minnesota. Head coach of football, basketball, track, hockey, wrestling, or baseball in a secondary or elementary school must be certified either in physical education or a special coaching requirement in physical education.

Iowa. Coaching personnel must be certified to teach and must have completed an approved program of professional preparation either in physical education or in the coaching of athletics.

South Dakota. At least 18 semester hours in the fields of health and physical education must be taken by coaching personnel.

Oklahoma. Coaching as a major assignment (3 hours a day) requires a physical education certificate.

Indiana. Varsity head football and basketball coaches in senior high school are required to be licensed in the field of physical education. All other coaches in grades seven to twelve must be licensed as a teacher and have a minimum of 8 semester hours of work in first aid and other courses related to the area of physical growth and development.

Wyoming. A coaching endorsement is entered on the teaching certificate after the applicant has taken one course in coaching that sport in which he or she is involved and also a course in first aid.

CERTIFICATION OF ATHLETIC TRAINERS

The certified athletic trainer is a relatively new concept in high school and college physical education programs. The certified trainer completes a 4-year program that stresses the biological and physical sciences, psychology, coaching techniques, first aid and safety, nutrition, and other courses in physical and health education. He or she should be prepared to take the national certification examination in athletic training and receive subsequent approval of the National Association of Athletic Trainers (NATA) as certified athletic trainers.

The role of the athletic trainer in athletic injury prevention and treatment is essential. It is unfortunate that athletic trainers are poorly represented at the high school level, with only about a hundred schools having a full-time, teacher-athletic trainer. Compounding this situation is the inadequate medical and injury prevention training of most coaches. Even if the coach has been well prepared in these areas, there is not sufficient time to carry out coaching duties and also responsibilities of the athletic trainer.

The duties of the athletic trainer include the following:

1. Prevention and care of injuries associated with competitive athletics
2. Preparation and utilization of an athletic conditioning program
3. Administration of first aid as needed
4. Application of devices such as strapping or bandaging to prevent injury
5. Administration of therapeutic techniques under the direction of a physician
6. Development and supervision of a rehabilitation program for injured athletes under supervision of the team physician
7. Selection, care, and fitting of equipment
8. Supervision of training menus and diets
9. Supervision of safety factors involved in facilities and use of equipment

The professional preparation of athletic trainers consists of required courses in the sciences, psychology, coaching techniques, first aid and safety, nutrition, exercise, and other related subjects. The National Association of Athletic Trainers has an approved educational program for athletic trainers that stipulates se-

a respected and growing profession, to further one's self-development and personal growth, to travel, and to participate in unlimited exciting experiences with children, youth, and adults. Furthermore, in many school systems it offers tenure, sabbatical leaves, sick leaves, retirement benefits, and a strongly organized profession.

Tenure. Many school systems provide tenure for teachers who serve successful probationary periods of 3 to 5 years. This means that the teacher who has tenure cannot be dismissed, demoted, or suspended, except as prescribed by law and according to prescribed procedures.

Sabbatical leaves. Many school systems have sabbatical leave schedules. Teachers, after a period of satisfactory service, 7 years, for example, may take 1 year or a semester with pay or partial pay to improve themselves professionally, such as by pursuing graduate work, traveling, or performing research.

Sick leaves. Many school systems across the country are instituting sick leave provisions for the teacher and family. Teachers are permitted to take time from their jobs when ill and still draw full salary. School systems usually designate the amount of time that may be used for such a purpose, frequently 5 to 10 days.

Retirement benefits. Most states have some provision for retirement benefits for teachers. After a stipulated period of service, usually from 25 to 35 years, and a minimum age, perhaps 55 to 65 years, the teacher may retire and draw a regular retirement benefit, which is generally computed on the amount of salary one earned. There is a trend toward using a fixed formula, such as 2% times a final average salary times the number of years a teacher has served, as a basis for determining a person's retirement benefits. In addition, most states are now covered by Social Security, which gives teachers additional benefits on retirement.

Strongly organized profession. Teachers now have a voice in their own affairs. Teacher militancy, in combination with a recognition by parents that education should have a high priority in the United States, has had its impact on teachers as well as on the public in general. The teaching profession has gained a new respect and, as a result, it is a more attractive field in which to work.

Water polo, grades 6 to 8 in Cumberland Valley School District, Mechanicsburg, Pennsylvania.

TEACHER SUPPLY AND DEMAND

Thousands of qualified teachers are unable to find positions in the nation's schools and colleges. Taxpayer revolts against rising educational costs, with some school districts reducing the size of their staffs, a levelling off of student enrollments, and an oversupply of teachers are some of the reasons for this dilemma.

The reasons for the oversupply are many and varied, but the main one seems to be that the number of teachers has grown while the number of student enrollments have declined.

With regard to student enrollments and number of teachers, the population trend changed greatly from the early 1950s through the middle 1960s, when the schools had large enrollments that began with the post-World War II baby boom. At the same time these large enrollments were dependent on a low supply of teachers who were born during the low-birthrate depression years. The situation has now reversed itself. A further answer to the increased number of teachers is that many disadvantaged minorities, such as blacks and Puerto Ricans, are now entering teaching at a much larger rate than before. Another consideration is the nation's birthrate, which has declined from 4.1 million in 1963 to approximately 3 million annually at present.

There are many bright spots to the current situation, however. The oversupply of teachers makes it possible for the selection, training, and appointment process to stress quality more than it has in past years. It has made it possible to eliminate the unsuitable and incompetent teacher. Furthermore, it has enabled school districts to replace substandard teachers, many of whom held emergency certificates. Finally, it has made it possible to have a lower student-teacher ratio, thus improving the learning climate of the classroom and gymnasium.

Those states which have reported an increased need for teachers list as the reasons factors such as added curricular offerings, reduction in class size, and new positions resulting from federal legislation.

Beginning teachers should not look on the present teacher employment situation as unpromising because many vacancies still exist for the well-qualified person. Teachers who are planning to teach at the elementary school level will find many vacancies. Teachers will be needed to replace those who retire, die, or leave the profession for other reasons. New teachers will be needed to reduce the student-teacher ratio. In addition, it is expected that teachers will be needed to replace persons with substandard teaching certificates. Furthermore, increased emphasis on the education of young children, children in low-income areas, and the handicapped means that more teachers will be needed.

There will be a need for new secondary school teachers for the next few years to reflect some improvement in the student-teacher ratio, to replace teachers who retire, die, or leave the field for other reasons, and to replace persons who do not meet certification requirements. Most job openings will come from the need to replace teachers who for various reasons may leave the field. Also, considerable additional demand for teachers may be generated by federal legislation that provides for supplementary educational centers and a national Teachers Corps (federally recruited teachers and teacher-interns for low-income areas). Furthermore, many teachers trained for secondary schools may qualify for junior college positions, where demand for teachers is expected to increase.

Daniel E. Griffiths, Dean of the School of Education at New York University, has indicated that a teacher shortage may occur again in the future because of the present oversupply and scare talk and their psychological effect in keeping students from majoring in education. The regional director of the Federal Bureau of Labor Statistics indicated that no other profession will provide more job opportunities in the future than teaching.

College teaching opportunities in the years ahead will provide employment for many persons. More teachers will be needed annually to replace those who retire, die, or leave the profession for other reasons. Furthermore, the fact that new degree recipients may be drained from the college teaching ranks by better paying opportunities in industry, government, and nonprofit organizations may increase the critical need to meet the demand in many fields.

EMPLOYMENT OF TEACHERS IN PHYSICAL EDUCATION

The supply and demand situation in physical education is excellent in certain areas of concentration within the field, but the supply exceeds the demand in some large cities and other locations. Furthermore, the demand for women and other minority physical educators appears to be greater than that for men.

The equal opportunity movement. Qualified women and other minority physical educators are in greater demand, it appears, than the rank and file of other members of the profession. Women and blacks in the past, for example, have seldom had equal employment opportunities with other physical educators. However, the statement on announcements of various position openings, ''We are an Equal Opportunity Employer,'' has changed this situation significantly. Leaders in the profession, school and college administrators, teacher-training institutions, and business and other organizations have stepped up their recruitment programs for members of minority groups. Furthermore, the emphasis on girls' and women's sports as well as the growth of sports in general in the American culture have resulted in more employment opportunities for women. In addition, the great number of blacks in the sports world along with the equal opportunity movement has increased the opportunities for this segment of the American population.

Encouraging employment developments. Physical education is playing an increasing role in the total educational endeavor of the United States. The President's Council on Physical Fitness and Sports is one agency that has done much to encourage the promotion of physical education, not only among the youth but also among the adult population. Furthermore, the increased recognition of the contribution that physical activity can make to physical, mental, and social health is a factor. Of course, the recent improvement in the nation's economy is a positive factor in the employment picture. There are many other encouraging employment developments that augur well for the future of physical education.

Elementary school physical education programs. The elementary school offers an opportunity to specialize in physical education. The elementary school physical education specialist is being hired in more and more elementary schools across the country. The surge in movement education is taking hold, with the need for more physical education personnel trained in this area. Specialists are particularly needed in grades four to six. These physical educators may work with classroom teachers or teach the physical education classes themselves. If this practice becomes nationwide, many more physical education teachers will be needed—a premise supported by the fact that there are about 84,000 public elementary schools as contrasted with about 26,000 high schools.

Higher education programs. Higher education programs are continuing to employ many physical educators, particularly in professional preparation programs. However, in most cases advanced degrees and specialization in certain areas of physical education are prerequisites. Many notices from colleges and universities across the nation are sent out concerning position openings in the service courses of physical education as well as in coaching and other fields. However, many of the colleges and universities also are looking for people with advanced degrees in biomechanics, motor development, motor performance and learning, exercise physiology, sports sociology, sports history, sports administration, elementary school physical education, physical education for the handicapped, sports medicine, sports psychology, and research.

Stress on the handicapped. The emphasis on the handicapped student, including the mentally retarded and physically handicapped, together with mainstreaming and the research that shows the contribution physical education can make to these students, has opened up an entirely new area for employment.

Inner-city programs. The problems encountered by large cities with their ghettos and poverty pockets, together with the appeal of physical education and sports for inner-city children and youth, augurs well for the contribution that professionals can make to such important areas of the nation.

Coaches trained in physical education. It is common practice for states to permit anyone to

Physical educators coach all types of sports. This cross-country team has been coached by a physical educator at Regis High School, New York City.

coach who has a teaching certificate. As a result, a large percentage of coaches are teachers of subjects other than physical education. However, the new trend across the country to hire coaches who have been trained in physical education should result in many new employment opportunities as more and more states adopt such a practice, since more physical educators will be needed to work in school athletic programs.

Athletic trainers. The trend toward hiring both men and women certified athletic trainers is growing. Athletic training is a unique and stimulating profession for those who are interested in athletics, injury prevention, rehabilitation, and counseling.

Pre-school children. There is a trend to provide education for children at an earlier age; for example, many children are starting at 3 years of age. These programs include physical education and therefore provide an opportunity for employment in nursery schools and other agencies that provide programs for pre-school children.

Dance. Dance is an area of physical education that has grown considerably in recent years. Physical educators are specializing in dance at the graduate level and developing expertise in this area as a means of finding employment in many schools, agencies, and college where dance programs exist.

Lower ratio of teachers to students. Pressures are being exerted in some sections of the country to have smaller classes for each teacher. Physical educators can do a better job with fewer students, as the English teacher does, and the goal of achieving a lower student-teacher ratio must be accomplished. This will mean that more teachers of physical education will be needed.

Expansion of sports. Sports are playing a more prominent role in the American culture. As a result, more leaders will be needed to teach and guide programs involved with various sports. (See Chapter 6.)

Summer school programs. Some states have experimented with summer school programs at the precollege level. The results have been highly satisfactory and should create a need for more teachers.

Teaching opportunities abroad. There are many opportunities for physical educators to teach in other countries. (See Chapter 7.)

Federal legislation. Governmental legislation and innovations such as the Elementary and Secondary Education Act, the Higher Education Act, and the Teachers Corps will increase the need for teachers. These programs place special emphasis on children and adults who need greater educational opportunities. Such innovations will mean greater attention to all individuals in society, regardless of intellect, physical condition, economic status, race, and other characteristics that differentiate human beings. Consequently, there will be a demand for more teachers of varying specialties to provide such programs.

EMPLOYMENT OPPORTUNITIES IN ALTERNATE CAREERS

Physical educators seeking employment should consider the many alternate careers to teaching. The interest in health and fitness in sports, physical fitness and recreation programs, and industrial and other organizations has created new opportunities for employment.

Emphasis on physical fitness and sports

With federal backing the United States is becoming fitness conscious. On all sides there is evidence of increased emphasis on physical education to enhance the well-being of youth and adults. This emphasis has also carried over into industrial fitness. Many corporations are establishing physical fitness centers for their executives and other employees. Health spas are also multiplying by leaps and bounds. In addition to the emphasis on physical fitness, there is a great interest in sports on the part of Americans. These developments mean the need for more physical educators.

Health spas

Health spas have mushroomed in numbers in recent years. One person has indicated that there are 4,000 health spas listed in the yellow pages of telephone directories in this country. Many commercial enterprises have been established to capitalize on the desire to be physically fit, to have a slim figure, and to look one's best. It is a multi-billion dollar industry. As a result, some health spas are only seeking the public's dollar rather than trying to be of service to the many individuals who visit their establishments. However, at the same time there are many health spas that are reputable, are hiring trained personnel, and have excellent programs. Physical educators not only will find a setting for employment in health spas but they also can contribute to upgrading the standards of operation of these businesses.

To enhance employment opportunities for physical educators, the University of Utah has developed a health spa area of specialization within their professional preparation curriculum.* The curriculum is a combination of a 4-year commercial physical education track that is interdisciplinary in nature, offers a business minor, and provides for on-site experiences in the health club industry. Courses required include psychology, leisure studies, health science, diet and nutrition, physical therapy, accounting, marketing, weight training, posture and conditioning, first aid, training room procedures, adult fitness, motor learning, and water safety.

The program at Utah, it would appear, is on the cutting edge of the profession, pioneering in an area that vitally needs trained physical educators. It is a program of the future.

Industrial recreation and fitness

Pepsi Co., to motivate employees to be physically fit, requires its top executives to run regularly, to engage in outdoor exercise, and during inclement weather to exercise in the company's superbly equipped gymnasium. Rockwell International in Los Angeles gives their employees medical screening and then places them in one of five color squads, depending on their level of fitness. A typical novice squad meets three times a week for a 10-minute discussion on matters such as why oxygen-increasing exercises are so important, 40 minutes of gradually more strenuous exercises, followed by a 10-minute cool-down period. The newcomers are warned that the 16-week session may involve the hardest physical work they have ever done.

---

*Henschen, Keith: Health spa certification, Careers in Physical Education, The National Association for Physical Education for College Women and the National College Physical Education Association for Men, 1975.

Businessmen engage in a game of touch football at the Aerobics Activity Center, Dallas, Texas.

At the same time they are told that each week will bring significant fitness improvements, as shown by tape, scale, pulse, blood pressure, and stress-test readings.

Corporate America's increased interest in physical fitness may be best symbolized by a unique event held yearly in Dallas. Called the Tyler Cup in honor of the Dallas-based corporation that sponsors it, the event in a recent year attracted more than 130 leaders in business from eleven states and the District of Columbia, including thirteen company presidents, seven board chairmen, six chief executive officers, one chief operating officer, eight executive vice presidents, and twelve senior vice presidents. These men, confirmed runners all, entered as four-man teams in several 2-mile heats. Why do they come so far just to run around a track? "The main idea is to promote fitness among business leaders, their employees and families," says Tyler Corporation President, Joseph McKinsey. "These men have gotten the message of fitness. They will take it back to the 500,000 employees they represent."

These examples represent only a few of the 50,000 industrial concerns who provide recreation and fitness programs for their employees.

The corporate setting is a place where many physical educators are and can be employed.

Programs for the elderly

There are an increasing number of employment opportunities for physical educators in programs for the elderly, which are offered in YMCAS and YWCAS, nursing homes, centers for the elderly, retirement homes, recreation departments, and other special agencies for the elderly. These programs need physical educators trained in special types of exercise, activity, and recreational activities and programs for the elderly. In a few states legislation has been passed requiring an activities director to be employed by nursing homes.

There has been considerable research in recent years which shows that elderly persons are not engaging sufficiently in physical activities, and as a result their health is impaired.

Leslie* has written a highly interesting and informative article on "Fitness Programs for the Aging" and career opportunities in this

---

*Leslie, David K.: Fitness programs for the aging, Careers in Physical Education, The National Association for Physical Education of College Women and the National College Physical Education Association for Men, 1975.

Employment opportunities are increasing in industrial fitness and recreation programs. Fitness participants jog at the Fitness and Recreation Center, Xerox Corporation, Leesburg, Virginia.

field. Leslie cites the need for fitness programs for the elderly, pointing out that today there is a lack of an adequate physical education experience for the elderly, labor-saving devices have encouraged a more sedentary existence, and the stereotypes of the elderly suggest loss of physical abilities. He then goes on to cite research evidence to show that in many cases physical and mental deterioration can be slowed. He also stresses the need for trained leaders in physical education to conduct programs for this age group. In respect to the training needed by such leaders, in addition to the general education and physical education courses, it would be helpful if courses could be taken such as biology of aging, sociology of aging, health and aging, fitness and therapeutic programs for the elderly, recreation programs for the elderly, and field experience in working with the elderly.

Athletic and sport administration

With the great growth of sports in the United States there are many employment opportunities for physical educators, some of which exist in educational institutions as a director of ath-

letics, coach, business manager, or in some other capacity. However, there are also many athletic and sport administration opportunities outside the educational domain, associated with business management, publicity and promotion, marketing, supervisor of sport facilities, trainers, coaches, and athletic directors. These positions occur in professional sports, country clubs, tennis and other sport facilities, and sport associations. Women as well as men are needed in these positions.

Vanderzwaag* has explored sport administration and has developed a tentative 4-year model curriculum that can be utilized for preparing for a career in sport administration. This model includes University Core Requirements in the humanities and other general requirement of 36 credits; Basic Sport Studies Courses, including psychology and psychology of sport of 12 credits; Sport Studies Seminars, covering special sport studies of 3 points; Business Ad-

---

*Vanderzwaag, Harold J.: Sport administration, Careers in Physical Education, The National Association for Physical Education of College Women and the National College Physical Education Association for Men, 1975.

ministration Courses, relating to areas such as finance, accounting, and management of 30 credit hours; Electives in Economics of 12 points; and an Internship for an entire semester of 15 points. Vanderzwaag has also outlined a three-semester program for institutions that cannot offer the 4-year program.

The internship experience should be carefully organized and planned so that students will be assigned to some sport organization where they will obtain the necessary experience and training.

Correctional institutions

Correctional institutions offer a setting where well-planned physical education programs are needed. The new concept of trying to rehabilitate persons who have come in conflict with law and order implies the need for experiences that include physical as well as mental activity.

Johnson,* in his article, "Preparing Physical Educators for Employment in Correctional Institutions," cites considerable research to show that present correctional institution programs can be improved considerably and that recreational physical activity programs are needed to satisfy basic human needs, to provide outlets for inner aggressions, and as a medium of rehabilitation.

Johnson suggests that any professional preparing program in this area should have cognate courses in departments such as social work, psychology, sociology, and political science. Also, a meaningful field experience for students is important so that they become familiar with correctional institutions and sensitive to the needs of inmates.

Tourism

Donald E. Hawkins† cites tourism as an alternate career for physical educators. He indi-

*Johnson, Theodore W. H.: Preparing physical educators for employment in correctional institutions, Careers in Physical Education, The National Association for Physical Education for College Women and The National College Physical Education Association for Men, 1975.
†Hawkins, Donald E.: Touring, Careers in Physical Education, The National Association for Physical Education of College Women and The National College Physical Education Association for Men, 1975.

cates that there is a lack of professionalism in the tourism industry at the present time and that there is a great need for professionals to conduct many of the activities that are a part of this field of work. He cites how tourism contributes in the neighborhood of $50 billion to the country's economy each year, that it supports more than 2.3 million persons, and that the demand for tourism is very great.

Hawkins suggests that a professional preparing curriculum in this area should include experiences such as an understanding of the dimensions of tourism, management skills that include financial analysis, policy and legal review, and management science; a knowledge and skill in integrating functions of government with private industry at various governmental levels; and tourism operations, administration of tourism services, field work, and research.

EMPLOYMENT OF PHYSICAL EDUCATORS IN ALLIED AREAS

A significant development during recent years has been the increased emphasis on allied areas such as recreation, health education, camping, leisure studies, and physical therapy. Although these are fields of endeavor distinct and separate from physical education, nevertheless some aspects of these specialties offer opportunities for physical educators. Furthermore, in some areas of the country, shortages of trained personnel force these responsibilities on physical educators.

According to the U.S. Department of Labor, at the present time a serious need exists for persons in the field of recreation and leisure studies, and these opportunities are expected to increase. Shortages presently exist for trained recreation workers, particularly in local governments, hospitals, and youth-serving agencies. As a result of this shortage and the great demand for qualified persons, many physical educators will be able to obtain full- or part-time employment in these programs.

The Boys' Clubs of America are a rapidly growing national movement, with a new club being started somewhere in the nation on the average of one every 8 days. The Boys' Clubs of America point out that they have a great need for more people.

The American National Red Cross points out that college graduates with majors in health, physical education and recreation can find employment with them if they are interested, motivated, have the right type of personality, and possess leadership potential. For example, they state that they are seeking recreation aides and physical educators for their programs of service in military hospitals and clubmobile programs overseas. They also point out that graduates with a physical education major who have had teaching experience and possess knowledge of community organization may be employed as safety service representatives on the staff of American National Red Cross and as directors of safety services in many larger chapters.

The preceding description represents only a sampling of employment opportunities for physical educators in allied fields. Others that might be explored, depending on a person's qualifications and interests, are work in voluntary youth agencies such as the YWCA, YMCA, and Young Men's and Young Women's Hebrew Associations, camping and outdoor education, churches, resort areas, and the armed forces. Many opportunities are available if one will take time to investigate them thoroughly.

SUGGESTIONS FOR QUALIFIED PHYSICAL EDUCATORS TO FOLLOW DURING COLLEGE YEARS IN SECURING A POSITION

The prospective physical educator should start to plan not later than early in the college years for obtaining a position after graduation. It may be too late to wait until the senior year has arrived. Some suggestions follow that have proved worth while for prospective physical educators who make plans while in college.

Plan your career well in advance

It is important to start career planning as early as possible. As part of this procedure it is wise to investigate carefully one's abilities and interests as well as the employment outlook in the career in which one is interested. This means reading the professional literature in regard to careers to see if one has the qualifications necessary for success in a particular specialty. It means arranging counseling sessions with faculty members, professionals in the field engaged in physical education and fitness endeavors and related careers, and asking them many questions about careers in physical education. It means getting accurate facts in regard to various career options to determine realistically the chances of obtaining employment on graduation. It means attending professional meetings and getting the latest information on job prospects as well as finding out about new trends and developments in the field in which one desires to become acquainted. It means talking with prospective employers to find out about grass-root operations in the career in which one is interested.

Specialize

The day of the general practitioner is disappearing. This is the day of specialization. In physical education one should decide as early as possible concerning a career in health spa management, athletic administration, working with handicapped persons, motor learning, exercise physiology, or other specialization and where the best prospects for employment and success exist.

Know more about your field than anyone else

After deciding on the career option you will pursue, read, study, investigate, get experience, and prepare thoroughly for this career so that you possess an expertise that will be recognized by any prospective employer. Also, take the necessary courses and develop the necessary skills and other competencies. Such preparation will help you to be respected for your expertise. Do not be content with only a superficial knowledge of the field—know more about the specialty than anyone else.

Acquire professional experience

Try to obtain as much practical experience as possible in the area of specialization you have selected. Plan for an internship in the field as part of your undergraduate experience. Visit as many existing programs as possible. For example, if you are interested in industrial fitness, make arrangements to see many different industrial fitness programs. If health spas are your interest, see as many of these establishments as possible. Ask questions during these visits and know what the programs are like in actual practice. Talk with the people in charge and particularly those individuals who have positions similar to the one to which you aspire. A good time to obtain field experience is during summer vacations. Try to get a position in the type of program in which you are interested. Pay more attention to the type of experience that you will receive than to the salary check that goes with it. In the long run the experience will pay better dividends, both professionally and economically.

LANDING THE JOB

During your senior year in college it is important to find employment in the position for which you have prepared. Some advice that should be of assistance if you have prepared yourself during the undergraduate years is incorporated in the following suggestions.

Start early

Start looking well in advance of the time you want to begin to work. Administrators and employers plan far ahead of their needs. Know what you want and start early to achieve your goal.

Know where the jobs are

Do considerable research to find out what positions are available. Talk with friends, faculty, and alumni and register with your college placement bureau. Write to school systems, health clubs, industrial companies, and other agencies where you would like to work and inquire if they anticipate any vacancies in your specialty.

Keep your credentials up to date

Be sure that your credentials include the type of information which employers need and want. There should be references from people who know you and your abilities, interests, and other qualifications. Ask these people in advance if they would be willing to write a reference for your credential file. Ask if you can use their names. Prepare a list of your qualifications: personal, preparation, experience, and

any other information in which a prospective employer might be interested. Register with a commercial agency if you think it will help, but be selective and use an agency that is particular about its candidates.

Many state education associations and state departments of education also provide placement services for a small fee. Some education associations place nonmembers as well as members. The American Alliance for Health, Physical Education, and Recreation maintains a placement service for its members. It sends personal data forms of qualified applicants to employers, and then employers make all further contacts directly with applicants. Members of the alliance who desire to enroll with this placement service should request personal data forms from the National Office, AAHPER Placement Service. An AAHPER placement booth is also maintained each year at the national convention to assist members who desire to seek new positions.

Other key sources of information include the following:

1. *The superintendent of schools or director of personnel in a particular school district.* Names and addresses of these officers are listed in the U.S. Office of Education's annual *Education Directory,* Part 2, Public School Systems (available from the Superintendent of Documents, U.S. Government Printing Office, Washington, D.C. 20401).
2. *U.S. Employment Service.* Offices throughout the country list vacancies and help place educators without charge.
3. *NEA Search.* This is a computerized education locator service providing a nationwide clearinghouse to inform prospective employers and employees of available applicants and positions. The address is 1201 16th St. N.W., Washington, D.C. 20036.
4. *Association for School, College, and University Staffing.* This is a placement service located at the National Communication and Service Center, Inc., Box 166, Hershey, Pa. 17033.

Write an application letter that will land the job

On writing a letter of application, use good form, be sincere, appeal to the interest of the employer, offer a service rather than apply for a job, and be specific as to your qualifications.

Leave a favorable impression during the interview

The interview is the culmination of the search. Dress conservatively, put on a smile, use a firm handshake, be on time, answer questions directly, speak so that you can be heard, volunteer any information you think is important, and listen to what the employer says.

Good luck!

A CONCLUDING STATEMENT

The old adage that there is always a job for a well-qualified person is usually true in the field of physical education. Students who have the essential qualifications for this work and who conscientiously apply themselves should not have any difficulty in finding employment in a setting that will utilize their training and fulfill their ambitions.

The value of physical education to enriched living and potentialities for building a better society are being increasingly recognized by the public. There is ample room for many qualified young men and women in this growing profession. There is no room for those who cannot meet the professional standards that have been established. Therefore the best advice that can be offered to students who desire to find employment in physical education is, first, to make sure that they are equipped to do the job. If a student is not equipped, other fields of endeavor should be sought for which one's talents can be more effectively utilized. If a person is qualified, he or she should feel confident of the future because this individual is a member of a profession that is just beginning to realize its potentialities.

SELF-ASSESSMENT TESTS

These tests are to assist students in determining if material and competencies presented in this chapter have been mastered.

1. Estimate the monetary value to you of a college degree and of preparing for the field of physical education over an extended 40-year period. What does it come to? More importantly, identify the other values of being a physical educator on which a dollar sign cannot be placed.

2. Discuss the range of certification requirements for teaching, including items such as citizenship, oath of allegiance, age, professional preparation, recommendations, health, employment, course of study, and degrees. What are the trends regarding the certification of teachers?

3. Analyze teacher supply and demand and factors that affect physical education positions in schools and colleges and project teaching employment opportunities for the next decade.

4. List all the various settings and types of positions open to physical educators today. Have each member of your class, after he or she has read this chapter, rate each position on its opportunities for employment on graduation from college. The positions with the best employment potential should be rated number 1, those with average employment potential should be rated number 2, and those with poor employment potential should be rated number 3. Add up the class ratings and see what they indicate.

5. Develop a step-by-step realistic plan that you will follow to secure a physical education position upon graduation from college.

SELECTED REFERENCES

Calandra, Gerald N.: Job hunting for fun and profit, Journal of Physical Education and Recreation **46**:19, Nov.-Dec., 1975.

Clayton, Robert D., and Clayton, Joyce: Concepts and careers in physical education, Minneapolis, 1977, Burgess Publishing Co.

Finn, Peter: Career education and physical education, Journal of Physical Education and Recreation **47**:29, Jan., 1976.

Grebe, Keith R., and Leslie, David K.: Coaching salaries: approaching equality, The Physical Educator **33**:126, Oct., 1976.

Groves, Richard: Helping students find positions in a tight job market, Journal of Physical Education and Recreation **47**:43, May, 1976.

Lepley, Paul M., and others: Alternative careers for physical educators, Journal of Physical Education and Recreation **48**:29, Jan., 1977.

Moore, Clarence A.: Practical hints for seeking employment, Journal of Physical Education and Recreation **46**: 18, May, 1975.

Note: For certification requirements for teaching, write directly to State Certification Bureau, State Department of Education or Public Instruction at the state capitol of the state in which you are interested. For certification for other fields, write directly to the agency's headquarters.

22

Challenges facing physical education

INSTRUCTIONAL OBJECTIVES AND COMPETENCIES TO BE ACHIEVED

After reading this chapter the student should be able to—

1. Identify some of the challenges facing the physical education profession.
2. Evaluate why the tightening job market, need for young scholarly leaders, fragmentation of physical education, closing the gap between research and practice, need to be creative, and the need to provide more opportunities for women and minority groups are challenges facing the physical education profession.
3. Think about the challenges facing physical education and propose well thought-through solutions that will assist physical education in meeting these challenges.

This text has attempted to show what a challenging field of endeavor physical education is for the student who has a sincere interest in this work. It has attempted to point out an interpretation of the true meaning of physical education, the diversified types of work and settings where it takes place, its need in present-day living, its scientific bases, and the duties and requirements of its leadership. This text has attempted to impress on the student's mind his or her part in raising the profession to lofty heights.

The closing chapter of this text discusses briefly a few of the challenges facing the physical education profession today. It is hoped that students will keep these in mind, discuss them

in their classes, and attempt to meet them whenever they may appear in their work. In so doing, physical education can be aided in realizing its potentialities.

TIGHTENING JOB MARKET

Physical education is in a buyer's market. In other words, there are more physical educators being prepared than there are jobs available. Such a situation represents a challenge. Although there is no ready answer, a possible solution has several dimensions that might be considered:

Professional preparing institutions could be more selective in whom they permit to prepare for the field of physical education, thus helping to reduce the supply of physical educators. At the same time those persons who graduate, as a result of the selective process, will be more attractive to prospective employers.

Professional preparing institutions could stress quality programs more than they do at the present time so that their graduates are assets rather than liabilities to the profession. Physical educators who graduate from quality programs will help to enhance the worth of physical education to the consumer, and as a result there will be an increased demand for such specialists.

More professional preparing institutions could provide training in and encourage major students to consider careers other than teaching physical education in schools and colleges. In other words, areas of concentration such as athletic training, exercise physiology, and biomechanics should be considered as alternate careers.

Professional preparing institutions could adopt a

Students engage in a rope-climbing exercise at Hudson Falls Central School, Hudson Falls, New York.

policy whereby they will not prepare a greater number of students than they can place in positions on graduation. The institution of higher education that admits students into the major physical education program not only has the responsibility for providing an excellent training program but also has the responsibility for finding employment for these students on graduation.

NEED FOR YOUNG SCHOLARLY LEADERS AT A TIME WHEN FACULTIES ARE BECOMING MORE STABLE

Schools and colleges are being affected by the economic conditions of the times, and one major result of a shortage of funds is a more stable faculty. Teachers and professors are staying in their positions longer, and fewer new faculty are being hired. There are inadequate funds to serve all educational needs, such as hiring new faculty, building new facilities, and purchasing necessary supplies and equipment.

In addition, enrollments have peaked in elementary and secondary schools and will soon crest in institutions of higher education. As a result, the numbers of students in educational institutions are already declining or will do so in the near future, and this means that fewer teachers will be needed. The increased number of girls and women participating in sports has taxed facilities as well as physical education and athletic budgets, placing further strain on funds that normally might be utilized for new faculty. Furthermore, according to some educators, faculties are getting older rather than younger.

What is the solution to such a dilemma? Finding the answer represents a real challenge to the physical education profession, which desperately needs an influx of new, scholarly, energetic, and well-trained future leaders. Although there is no ready answer to such a problem, some solutions that might be explored and investigated are discussed.

Since there will always be teacher attrition because of retirement, death, and personnel leaving the field, physical education should develop a rationale for obtaining a high priority rating when authorizations for new personnel are issued. This rationale should show that physical education requires new faculty for the following reasons:

Reducing class size to make physical education classes more comparable with other classes, such as English and science, so that a greater service may be rendered to the student

Developing more dynamic programs, particularly of an interdisciplinary nature, that will enhance the worth of physical education in the educational process

Providing for handicapped students as required under Public Law 94-142

Having on the faculty physical educators who have expertise in movement education, exercise physiology, athletic training, biomechanics, and physical education for the handicapped

Providing for a physical education specialist in each elementary school

Providing for an enriched athletic program for girls and women in light of Title IX regulations

Requiring all athletic coaches of interscholastic sports at the precollege level to be trained in physical education

There is a need for scholarly young leaders in physical education. The first grade at Cumberland Valley School District, Mechanicsburg, Pennsylvania, gets the attention of a physical educator.

FRAGMENTATION OF PHYSICAL EDUCATION

Physical education is experiencing an era of specialization. Some physical educators are specializing in health club operation, physical education for the handicapped, athletic administration, and other areas where their services are needed. Such specialization can mean fragmentation and lack of cohesiveness among members of the profession if a warm and strong family relationship is not established. One strength of the medical profession, for example, rests on the fact that regardless of whether physicians are internists, orthopedists, or other specialists, they are loyal to the medical profession and a majority are members of the American Medical Association.

The old adage that "United we stand and divided we fall" should be recognized by all persons who engage in work associated with physical education. Although specialization is desirable and necessary, physical educators should recognize that a common bond should hold all the various specialties together in the physical education profession.

Physical education and athletics may be used as an example where some fragmentation exists. Over the course of history some persons who have concentrated on teaching physical education and some who have specialized in coaching and athletes have at times disassociated themselves from each other in many professional ways. Many college coaches, for example, give their allegiance to professional organizations other than the AAHPER, which is commonly regarded as the mother organization of physical education. Some coaches rarely attend and participate in the AAHPER or other meetings where physical educators congregate. Instead, they may associate more with athletic associations and other coaches who frequently are not trained in the field of physical education.

Something needs to be done, not only to bring all coaches into the fold and under the professional umbrella of physical education but also to see that specialties other than coaching retain their loyalty to physical education.

Physical education is being challenged to provide the glue that will hold all specialties together in a strong, united, professional relationship. Although one specialist in physical education may work in the gymnasium and another in the laboratory or one in industry and another in a health club, this should not mean a loss of professional togetherness. A close working relationship is needed to upgrade the profession and provide quality leadership and programs for all areas of concentration within the field of physical education.

CLOSING THE GAP BETWEEN RESEARCH AND PRACTICE

Basically, there are three aspects of closing the gap between research and practice in physical education that constitute a challenge to all professionals.

The first part of this challenge is that physical education has available valid research findings that are not being applied in programs across the country. For example, much is known about learning theory in general and about motor learning in particular—but it is not applied. There are even some excellent articles in the professional literature and one or two books that have summarized the pertinent research findings in motor learning. However, some of the skill teaching that goes on today is a hit-and-miss procedure based on traditional ways of doing things or on an individual teacher's own unscientific opinion. In addition to learning theory, much is known but not applied in human behavior, physical fitness, activity and weight control, body image, and other important considerations in physical education. This gap between what is known to be right and what is practiced must be closed. This is indeed a major challenge, which requires the proper dissemination of research information and the desire and interest on the part of physical educators to see that it becomes part of their programs.

A second phase of the problem is that more scholarly research is needed on many of the problems with which physical educators are faced today. For example, the profession needs to know such things as the value of selected physical education activities and programs for inner-city youth, the relation of coaching styles to the development of certain character traits in youth, the most desirable length and frequency of practice periods for teaching badminton and other activities and skills, the kind of physical education program most beneficial for emotionally disturbed children, and the value of movement education compared with traditional physical education in the development of skill in various team sports. These represent only a few examples of problems that, if the answers were known and applied, would produce physical education programs more scientifically based, as well as contribute significantly more to the consumers of their services.

The third phase of this problem is that of interpreting the research findings. Many physical educators do not understand research terminology and how to interpret research findings. It is a language far beyond their grasp. As a result, research fails to be used in many cases. One answer to this problem is to have significant research studies interpreted in "lay" language that is meaningful to the physical educator on the job. It might be helpful for physical educators to read reports of technical subjects in magazines such as *Reader's Digest* and *Newsweek*. Even the most technical details are spelled out so that the material and information is intelligible to a person with only a grade school education. Consequently, the material is read by great numbers of people, and the circulation of these magazines runs into millions of copies. Similarly, the physical education profession must also have someone perform this task who has communication skills for these classical studies that have implications for physical education programs. If this can be done, programs of physical education will be upgraded considerably.

The challenge of closing the gap between research and practice represents one that must be met if physical education is to become a respected, established profession.

NEED TO BE CREATIVE

Of all the challenges facing physical education today, the need for creativity is extremely important. Creativity, as used here, refers to the discovery of something in physical education that is truly new and that will be an achievement in its own right. Examples of creativity in the history of the world were the development of the theory of relativity and the invention of the telephone. In education it was such things as the nongraded school and the teaching machine. An example in physical education might be the development of the game of basketball by Naismith. Each of these examples of creativity resulted in a novel work that was accepted as useful and satisfying to society.

Physical education has had few exciting and dynamic creative ideas in its history. It desperately needs some at the present time to pull it out of its doldrums and help it to play a more dynamic role in education. More creative ideas are needed like Wood's "new physical education," Laban's "movement education," and Hetherington's "fundamental education."

Physical educators need to think more about the present status of their field of endeavor, including the problems they face and the goals they wish to achieve, and then come up with some creative ideas that will help to solve these problems and achieve these goals.

A review of the literature reveals some characteristics of the creative person. The creative individual will possess imagination, inner maturity, the ability to think and to analyze, a rich background of knowledge in his or her field, and flexibility in approaching problems. This person will be skeptical of accepted ideas and less suspicious of new ones, persistent, sensitive to the environment, fluent in the production of ideas, and self-confident.

Charles Patrick, in his book entitled *What is Creative Thinking?*, points out that creative thinking proceeds through several distinct stages. For example, there is the *preparation stage,* in which individuals become familiar with their field and the situation where it is desired to produce creative ideas. Intuition will not come without hard work, prior education, and a thorough understanding of the field. A second stage is *incubation,* in which the problem is defined, various suggestions and solutions are considered, and much thought takes place. A third stage is *illumination,* in which a specific idea is envisioned and the individual begins to explore and work toward a solution. Finally, there is the *verification stage,* in which the idea is tested, altered, and eventually completed and utilized. These steps to creativity indicate that to be productive of new ideas requires much study, thought, and critical evaluation. It does not occur automatically.

Each physical educator should strive to be more creative. As a result, new ideas will be born, and better physical education programs will develop. Major students in professional preparation institutions and young leaders in the field represent persons who have the potential for giving birth to new ideas that will make physical education more relevant to the rapidly changing world in which we live.

NEED TO PROVIDE MORE OPPORTUNITIES FOR WOMEN AND MINORITY GROUPS

Although physical education is not the only profession that has failed to provide sufficient opportunities for women and minority group members, it can move at a faster rate to meet the challenge of accepting these individuals on an equal basis.

Dancers perform at Florida A. & M. University in Tallahassee, Florida.

Women, in spite of Title IX, are being neglected in some school and college athletic programs. Some have had limited access to athletic activities, have experienced difficulty in obtaining equipment and facilities, and have generally taken a backseat to men's athletic programs. Budgets are frequently inadequate and many times are much less than the boys' or men's athletic programs at the same school or college. For example, a recent survey cited that an optimal budget for a women's intercollegiate program is more than $21,000 as compared to the actual average budget of under $10,000. The average budget is therefore approximately 40% to 45% of what is considered essential to meet the needs of a women's program.

Blacks and other minority group members have also suffered from discrimination, both professionally and as students. Some black students are encouraged in athletics because of a particular skill, but there is a lack of human interest shown to these individuals. Some attend college on athletic scholarships but are not encouraged to excel academically and may not receive their degrees. Some are "used" for their skills and forgotten after the game. Black physical educators are sometimes given less responsible positions than their white counterparts and find it difficult to advance in the school or college hierarchy.

The challenge is there for the profession to meet. Discrimination will not end through the passage of legislation alone; action is needed on the part of everyone involved in the profession. Some recommendations for action include the following:

1. Female, black, and minority group applicants must be actively sought for professional positions.
2. All discriminatory personnel practices must be eliminated.
3. Promising female, black, and minority group students should be encouraged to become professionals and seek training as physical educators.

NEED TO PROVIDE PHYSICAL EDUCATION OPPORTUNITIES TO THE INNER CITY

The challenge of inner-city and disadvantaged students weighs heavily as a professional responsibility. The physical educator can have a dramatic impact on the disadvantaged child. This child is often haunted by a fear of failure, and physical education can help to overcome that fear and instill a positive self-concept. In inner-city areas, physical education programs should serve as the keystone of the educational curriculum. If motivated by understanding teachers, these youngsters can develop an interest in learning through innovations in physical education programs. For example, dance may be used as a medium to teach the child about different cultures. Physical educators should also work closely with other teachers to provide a well-integrated curriculum.

The challenge of meeting the needs of the disadvantaged should be a major priority among physical educators. It is a challenge that can be met by each individual on a daily person-to-person basis.

NEED FOR ACCOUNTABILITY

The need for accountability is essential for physical educators. They must be accountable to students, the profession, society, and themselves. Only through accountability can physical educators render a unique and worthwhile service to society in general and to their profession in particular.

A CONCLUDING STATEMENT

Physical education has been effectively contributing to the betterment of society for many years. However, it can do a more effective job; it can be a greater profession; it can contribute more to enriched living for the total population. These achievements will be possible if the professional students of physical education take up the many challenges that confront their field of endeavor and, after careful thought and deliberation, devise plans that will result in physical education achieving its true potentialities.

Physical education is proud of those qualified students now training for this specialized work. It has faith in them to do the job and knows they will accept the challenges facing their field of endeavor. It wishes them the best of success and the most of happiness in a field of endeavor that has no equal for satisfaction derived from conscientious efforts.

SELF-ASSESSMENT TESTS

These tests are to assist students in determining if material and competencies presented in this chapter have been mastered.

1. In light of this course, what challenges do you believe the physical education profession faces today?

2. Why is each of the following challenges facing the physical education profession a critical problem for this field of endeavor:

Tightening job market
Need for young scholarly leaders
Fragmentation of physical education
Closing the gap between research and practice
Need to be creative
Need to provide more opportunities for women and minority groups

3. Propose a well thought-through solution for each of the challenges identified in this chapter and also for other challenges identified by your class.

READING ASSIGNMENT

Bucher, Charles A.: Dimensions of physical education, ed. 2, St. Louis, 1974, The C. V. Mosby Co., Reading selections 56, 62, and 63.

SELECTED REFERENCES

Review the last twelve issues of the *Journal of Physical Education and Recreation*.

Index